SELECTED LETTERS OF CICERO

SELECTED LETTERS OF CICERO

EDITED, WITH AN INTRO-
DUCTION AND NOTES, BY
FRANK FROST ABBOTT

UNIVERSITY OF OKLAHOMA PRESS : NORMAN

PA 6297
A23
1964

International Standard Book Number: 0–8061–0615–8

Library of Congress Catalog Number: 64–11337

New edition published by the University of Oklahoma Press, Publishing Division of the University, Norman, Oklahoma, from the original edition published by Ginn and Company, Boston. Manufactured in the United States of America. First printing of the new edition, 1964; second printing, 1971.

PREFACE

——•+❉+•——

Cicero's letters are of such wide range and varied interest that it is an exceptionally difficult task to edit a limited number which shall be fairly representative of the whole, and it is hoped that those readers who fail to find some of their favorite letters in this volume will bear this difficulty in mind. The editor has chosen in particular the letters which Cicero wrote to the members of his own family and to his intimate friends upon personal subjects, in the hope of throwing as much light as possible upon Cicero's private character, his tastes, his daily life, and his relations with his personal and literary friends. At the same time it is hoped that letters bearing upon political matters have been included in sufficient number to present a good outline of Cicero's public life and of his times. The letters are arranged chronologically.

The text of the *Epistulae ad familiares* is that of Mendelssohn, with slight changes in a few passages generally recognized as corrupt and not readable. C. F. W. Müller's edition is the basis for the text of the *Epistulae ad Quintum fratrem*, and Wesenberg's for that of the *Epistulae ad Atticum*, Bks. I.–XI. and XIV.–XVI., but in very many cases the reading of the Medicean MS., which Wesenberg rejects, has been restored, and in certain other cases the more probable conjectures of Lehmann and others have been substituted for the emendations accepted by Wesenberg. The text of Bks. XII. and XIII. of the *Epistulae ad Atticum* is that of O. E. Schmidt.   For further particulars the reader may consult the Introduction and the statement in the Critical Appendix.

The orthography has been, in general, conformed to the standards established by Brambach and by Georges in his *Lexikon der lateinischen Wortformen.*

In the Introduction and the Commentary attention has been directed in particular to the characteristics of epistolary and colloquial Latin.   A full discussion of these peculiarities would have far transcended the limits of this book.   The editor has therefore contented himself with a statement in the Introduction of the most important divergencies which the Letters show in lexicography, syntax, and style from the standard in those matters in formal Latin, and has supplemented this general statement by more detailed notes at the proper points in the Commentary.

The works which the editor has found most service in the preparation of the Introduction and Commentary are mentioned in the list given on a subsequent page, and although his indebtedness is usually noted specifically in the Commentary, he feels under special obligation to the editions of Tyrrell, Watson, Süpfle-Böckel, and Hofmann-Andresen, and to the writings of O. E. Schmidt and Landgraf.

But, above all, the editor would gratefully acknowledge the deep obligation which he is under to Professors C. L. Smith and Tracy Peck, the editors-in-chief of this Series, for the careful criticism which they have given to this work while it has been passing through the press.   F. F. A.

Chicago, Illinois,
        August 2, 1897.

CONTENTS

———•❧❀☙•———

Omnes autem Ciceronis epistulas legendas censeo, mea sententia vel magis quam omnes eius orationes. Epistulis Ciceronis nihil est perfectius.

FRONTO ad Antoninum, II. 5.

Abbreviations used most Frequently in the Introduction and Commentary

Att. = *Epistulae ad Atticum.*

Fam. = *Epistulae ad familiares.*

Caelius, Fam. = Letter of Caelius in the collection *ad fam.* (Letters by other writers indicated similarly.)

Intr. = General introduction.

Arch. f. lat. Lex. = *Archiv für lateinische Lexikographie.*

Becher = F. Becher, *Ueber d. Sprachgebrauch d. Caelius,* Nordhausen, 1888.

Böckel = Süpfle-Böckel (*Epistulae Selectae,* 9th ed., Karlsruhe, 1885).

C. I. L. = *Corpus inscriptionum Latinarum.*

Gurlitt = L. Gurlitt, *De M. Tulli Ciceronis epistulis earumque pristina collectione,* Göttingen, 1879.

Herzog = E. Herzog, *Geschichte u. System d. röm. Staatsverfassung,* vols. I.–II., Leipzig, 1884–91.

Hofmann (or Andresen) = *Ausgewählte Briefe,* Berlin, 1884–85. Vol I.[5] by Hofmann, vol. II.[2] by Andresen.

Hofmann krit. Apparat = F. Hofmann, *Der kritische Apparat zu Ciceros Briefen an Atticus,* Berlin, 1862.

Landgraf = G. Landgraf, *Bemerkungen zum sermo cotidianus in den Briefen Ciceros u. an Cicero,* in *Blätter f. d. bayerische Gymnasialwesen,* 1880, pp. 274–280 and 317–331.

Madvig = J. N. Madvig, *Die Verfassung u. Verwaltung d. röm. Staates,* Leipzig, 1882.

Manutius = *Paulli Manutii Commentarius,* Leipzig, 1779–80.

Mendelssohn = L. Mendelssohn, *M. Tulli Ciceronis Epistularum libri sedecim,* Leipzig, 1893.

Meyer = P. Meyer, *De Ciceronis in epistolis ad Atticum sermone,* Bayreuth, 1887.

Rauschen = G. Rauschen, *Ephemerides Tullianae,* Bonn, 1886.

Rebling = O. Rebling, *Versuch einer Charakteristik d. röm. Umgangssprache,* Kiel, 1883.

Ruete = E. Ruete, *Die Correspondenz Ciceros in den Jahren 44 u. 43*, Marburg, 1883.

Schmalz, Z. f. G. w. = J. H. Schmalz in *Zeitschrift f. d. Gymnasialwesen*.

Schmidt, Briefw. = O. E. Schmidt, *Der Briefwechsel d. M. Tullius Cicero*, Leipzig, 1893.

Schmidt, Handschr. = O. E. Schmidt, *Die handschriftliche Ueberlieferung d. Briefe Ciceros an Atticus, Q. Cicero, M. Brutus in Italien*, Leipzig, 1887.

Schmidt, Kämpfe = O. E. Schmidt, *Die letzten Kämpfe d. röm. Republik*, Leipzig, 1884.

Sternkopf = W. Sternkopf, *Quaestiones chronologicae*, Marburg, 1884, and *Zur Chronologie u. Erklärung d. Briefe Ciceros aus. d. Jahren 48 u. 47*, Dortmund, 1891.

Stinner = A. Stinner, *De eo quo Cicero in epistolis usus est sermone*, Oppeln, 1879.

Tyrrell = R. Y. Tyrrell, *The Correspondence of M. Tullius Cicero*, vols. I.-IV., Dublin, 1884–94.

Watson = A. Watson, *Cicero, Select Letters*, 3d ed., Oxford, 1881.

Willems = P. Willems, *Le Sénat de la République Romaine*, vols. I.–III., Louvain, 1883.

THE ORDER OF THE LETTERS

THIS EDITION.	ORDINARY ARRANGEMENT.	THIS EDITION.	ORDINARY ARRANGEMENT.	THIS EDITION.	ORDINARY ARRANGEMENT.
LXXXVIII	Att. 15. 11	XCIII	Fam. 16. 26	XCVII	Fam. 11. 9
LXXXIX	Fam. 7. 22	XCIV	" 9. 24	XCVIII	" 10. 15
XC	" 16. 21	XCV	" 12. 5	XCIX	" 11. 12
XCI	" 11. 27	XCVI	" 10. 12	C	" 10. 24
XCII	" 11. 28				

EPISTVLAE AD FAMILIARES.

ORDINARY ARRANGEMENT.	THIS EDITION.	ORDINARY ARRANGEMENT.	THIS EDITION.	ORDINARY ARRANGEMENT.	THIS EDITION.
Fam. 2. 8	XXXIII	Fam. 8. 1	XXXI	Fam. 13. 50	LXXXIV
" 2. 11	XXXVI	" 8. 15	XLVIII	" 13. 72	LXXI
" 2. 16	LI	" 8. 16	L	" 14. 2	XIII
" 3. 2	XXIX	" 9. 1	LX	" 14. 4	XI
" 4. 5	LXXV	" 9. 8	LXXX	" 14. 8	LVI
" 4. 6	LXXVI	" 9. 9	LII	" 14. 11	LVII
" 4. 12	LXXVIII	" 9. 11	LXXIII	" 14. 12	LIII
" 5. 7	III	" 9. 14	LXXXVII	" 14. 14	XLIII
" 5. 12	XVIII	" 9. 15	LXVII	" 14. 15	LVIII
" 5. 14	LXXVII	" 9. 16	LXI	" 14. 17	LV
" 5. 15	LXXIX	" 9. 17	LXIV	" 14. 19	LIV
" 6. 6	LXV	" 9. 18	LXII	" 14. 20	LIX
" 6. 14	LXVI	" 9. 20	LXIII	" 15. 4	XXXIV
" 6. 15	LXXXV	" 9. 24	XCIV	" 15. 5	XXXVII
" 7. 1	XIX	" 10. 12	XCVI	" 15. 6	XXXVIII
" 7. 5	XXI	" 10. 15	XCVIII	" 15. 17	LXX
" 7. 10	XXV	" 10. 24	C	" 16. 4	XXXIX
" 7. 15	XXVIII	" 11. 1	LXXXVI	" 16. 6	XL
" 7. 16	XXIV	" 11. 9	XCVII	" 16. 9	XLI
" 7. 18	XXVI	" 11. 12	XCIX	" 16. 11	XLII
" 7. 22	LXXXIX	" 11. 27	XCI	" 16. 16	XXVII
" 7. 23	IV	" 11. 28	XCII	" 16. 21	XC
" 7. 24	LXXXI	" 12. 5	XCV	" 16. 26	XCIII
" 7.25	LXXXII	" 13. 1	XXXII		

Epistvlae ad Atticvm.

Ordinary Arrangement.	This Edition.	Ordinary Arrangement.	This Edition.	Ordinary Arrangement.	This Edition.
Att. 1. 1	I	Att. 3. 22	XIV	Att. 9. 6A	XLVII
" 1. 2	II	" 4. 1	XV	" 9. 11A	XLIX
" 1. 16	V	" 4.4B	XVII	" 12. 1	LXIX
" 1. 17	VI	" 5. 1	XXX	" 12. 11	LXVIII
" 2. 19	VII	" 6. 1	XXXV	" 12. 16	LXXII
" 2. 22	VIII	" 8. 3	XLV	" 12. 32	LXXIV
" 2. 23	IX	" 8.12D	XLIV	" 13. 52	LXXXIII
" 3. 4	X	" 8. 13	XLVI	" 15. 11	LXXXVIII
" 3. 12	XII				

Epistvlae ad Qvintvm Fratrem.

Ordinary Arrangement.	This Edition.	Ordinary Arrangement.	This Edition.	Ordinary Arrangement.	This Edition.
Q. fr. 2. 3	XVI	Q. fr. 2. 15 (16)	XXII	Q. fr. 3. 5, 6	XXIII
" 2. 9 (11)	XX				

INTRODUCTION

———•◦❈◦•———

CICERO'S PUBLIC LIFE AND CONTEMPORARY POLITICS.

I. CICERO'S EARLY LIFE AND THE *CURSUS HONORUM*.

(Aet. 1–44. B.C. 106–63. Epist. I.–II.)

1. M. Tullius Cicero was born at Arpinum, Jan. 3, 106 B.C.[1] His father's family removed to Rome while Cicero was still a boy,[2] and here, like other boys of the period, Cicero pursued the study of Greek and Latin literature, rhetoric, and, somewhat later, philosophy and jurisprudence. His studies were interrupted in 89 B.C. by a year's service in the Social War,[3] but at its close they were taken up again with his old vigor. His chosen profession was that of the law, and in 81 B.C. he made his first appearance at the bar in defending P. Quinctius. A far more important event was his defense of Sex. Roscius of Ameria in the following year. Some political significance attaches to the trial, as Cicero's real antagonist, Chrysogonus,[4] was a favorite of the dictator Sulla.

2. Possibly to escape the consequent displeasure of Sulla, but more probably for the sake of his health, Cicero left Rome and spent nearly two years at Athens, Rhodes, and in Asia Minor,[5] being mainly engaged in the study of

---

[1] *Brutus*, 161 ; *Att.* 7. 5. 3.
[2] Cicero, when a boy, met Archias at Rome ; *pro Arch.* 1.
[3] *Philipp* 12. 27.
[4] *pro Sex. Rosc.* 6.
[5] *Brutus*, 314–6.

philosophy and oratory. Cicero's study of philosophy during this period determined his subsequent philosophical attitude, while his work under Molon of Rhodes enabled him to cultivate a less florid style of oratory than that which characterized his earlier orations. At Athens he also made the acquaintance of T. Pomponius Atticus.[1]

3. Cicero's marriage to Terentia, a woman of some property and of good family, must have taken place soon after his return to Rome, or just before his departure from the city.[2] Two years after his return, in 76 B.C., he was quaestor, and had charge of Western Sicily, with Lilybaeum as his headquarters. His achievements in Sicily made little impression at Rome,[3] but the intimate acquaintance which he gained with the island and its people served him in good stead when he made his first real appearance in politics six years later as the prosecutor of Verres.

Verres, who had been governor of Sicily from 73 to 71 B.C., was charged by the Sicilians with extortion and cruelty. Cicero, who conducted the prosecution, presented the facts in such a masterly way that Hortensius, the advocate of Verres, withdrew from the case, and Verres himself went into exile.[4]

4. His prosecution of Verres as well as his defense of Roscius Amerinus (80 B.C.) and of Cornelius Sulla (in 62 B.C.) have caused much discussion of Cicero's political tendencies during this early period. All three of these cases had a pronounced political character, and in all three Cicero was the advocate of democratic interests. He defended Roscius against the attacks of Sulla's favorite, during the lifetime of that champion of the aristocratic cause. He prosecuted Verres without mercy, although Verres was

[1] *de Fin.* 5. 1.

[2] Tullia was betrothed in 66 B.C. Cf. *Att.* 1. 3. 3.

[3] *pro Plancio*, 64, 65.

[4] Plutarch, *Cic.* 7, 8; *in Verr.* 2. 2. 192.

backed by the entire senatorial party, which felt that its prestige and its privileges were at stake in the trial. He defended Cornelius Sulla against the charge of having taken part in the Catilinarian conspiracy, although it is probable that Sulla at least sympathized with the purposes of the democratic leader.[1] It may be said, and perhaps with truth, that in all three cases Cicero appeared as a lawyer and not in any sense as a politician. We cannot help feeling, however, that in Cicero's day, as would be the case in our own time, in a legal contest involving political interests, the advocates on either side of the question must have belonged in most instances to the political party whose interests would be promoted by the success of that side. What could be more natural than that Cicero, belonging to the equestrian class, whose rights and privileges had been so seriously curtailed in the aristocratic reaction of Sulla, should oppose the aristocracy at some points? The aid which his action gave to the democratic cause does not, however, stamp him as a democrat.

5. As a candidate for the aedileship for 69 B.C., and for the praetorship for 66 B.C., Cicero led all of his rivals at the polls.[2] Both offices he filled with distinction, and although as praetor he showed, as in earlier years, slight democratic tendencies,[3] his personal integrity and his intimate knowledge of the law made his administration of the office wise and honorable. Throughout this period, even during his incumbency of the two offices just mentioned, Cicero followed unremittingly his profession of the law, appearing in defense, among others, of Fonteius, Caecina, and Cluentius.

6. The personal admiration which Cicero felt for Pompey, his political sympathy with that leader, and perhaps his

[1] *pro Sulla*, 7. 22 ; *de Off.* 2. 29 ; *Fam.* 15. 17. 2.

[2] *in Pison.* 2 ; *de leg. Manil.* 2.

[3] Herzog, I. p. 538.

desire to link his own fortunes with those of Pompey, led
Cicero to approve of the Gabinian law,[1] and to lend his
active support to the Manilian law in 66 B.C.   In supporting
the latter measure Cicero delivered his first political speech,
and notwithstanding the united opposition of the Optimates,
who appreciated the danger which threatened the oligarch-
ical principles and policy from placing such autocratic
power in the hands of a single man, the bill became a law.

7. At the conclusion of his praetorship Cicero declined
a province,[2] and devoted all his energy to his candidacy for
the consulship.   Cicero's political attitude underwent a
slight change in the two or three years preceding his consulship.   He had never been an out and out democrat, but
had opposed the abuses of the aristocratic system rather
than that system in its entirety.   The subsidence of that
spirit of opposition which often characterizes youth, his
political ambitions, and the growth of a radical faction in
the democratic party with anarchical tendencies, all conspired to draw him nearer to the Optimates.   Both Marcus
and his brother Quintus felt that the support of the senatorial party was essential, and that all suspicion of a democratic leaning on the part of Marcus must be removed, as is
indicated by a significant passage in a political pamphlet
which Quintus addressed to his brother at this time: *Hi
rogandi omnes sunt diligenter et ad eos adlegandum est persua-
dendumque iis nos semper cum optimatibus de re publica
sensisse, minime popularis fuisse; si quid locuti populariter
videamur, id nos eo consilio fecisse, ut nobis Cn. Pompeium
adiungeremus,*[3] etc.   The Optimates at first saw in Cicero
only the *novus homo*, the prosecutor of Verres, and the
advocate of the Manilian law[4]; but the revolutionary pur-

---

[1] *de leg. Manil.* 52.

[2] *pro Mur.* 42.

[3] *de Pet. Cons.* 5.

[4] Cf. note on *nobiles homines*, *Epist.* II.

poses of Catiline and his party drove the aristocracy to the
support of Cicero, and he was elected by a good majority
with C. Antonius as his colleague.

8. Throughout his consulship Cicero's policy was that of
a moderate member of the senatorial party. He opposed
the proposition made by the tribune, Rullus, to divide the
ager publicus in Campania; he opposed a measure to relieve
the children of those proscribed by Sulla ; he defended the
law of Otho which reserved certain seats in the theatre to
the knights ; he defended C. Rabirius on the charge of
murder brought against him by the democrats,[1] and he suppressed the Catilinarian conspiracy; but it was significant
of the future that, when Cicero retired at the end of this
year of office, the tribune Q. Metellus Nepos forbade him to
make a parting speech [2] on the ground that in punishing
the Catilinarian conspirators he had put Roman citizens to
death without a trial.

II. Cicero, Clodius, and the Triumvirs.

(Aet. 45-48. b.c. 62-59. Epist. III.-IX.)

9. The year 62 b.c. opened with a series of bitter attacks
upon the senate by Pompey's tool, the tribune Metellus
Nepos, supported by the praetor C. Julius Caesar. Against
Cicero, his consulship, and the execution of the conspirators,
Metellus made his fiercest onslaughts,[3] but the Optimates
were too strong for their opponents. Metellus fled to Pompey [4] for protection and Caesar was forbidden for a time to
administer the duties of his office.[5] It was during this
period of political uproar that Cicero delivered one of the
most charming of his orations, in defending the claim to
citizenship of his old friend and teacher, Archias.

[1] *Att.* 2. 1. 3.
[2] *Fam.* 5. 2. 7.
[3] *Fam.* 5. 2. 8 ; Dio Cassius, 37. 42.
[4] Plut. *Cat. Min.* 29.
[5] Suet. *Iul.* 16.

10. In December of this year, while Caesar was absent in Spain, a festival was held at his house in honor of the goddess Bona Dea, which it was unlawful for men to attend; but during the meeting, P. Clodius, a patrician, was found to be present in disguise (cf. *Epist.* V.). A judicial investigation of the matter was made, but Clodius secured an acquittal through the kind offices of Crassus, who bribed a majority of the jurors. Cicero does not seem to have taken an active part in the discussion of the Clodian matter in the senate,[1] but when, in the trial, Clodius attempted to establish an alibi by offering evidence to prove that he was at Interamna, ninety miles from Rome, at the time of the sacrilege, Cicero went on the witness stand and testified that he had seen Clodius in Rome within three hours of the time he claimed to have been at Interamna.[2]

The anger of Clodius was aroused still more by the humiliation which he suffered in debate at Cicero's hands,[3] so that henceforth he thought of little else than avenging himself upon Cicero. The clash between Clodius and the senate, and the desire which Clodius felt to injure Cicero, threw Clodius into the arms of the democratic party, so that the affair, which at the outset was a purely personal one, developed into a political antagonism.[4]

11. In Jan., 61 B.C., before the trial of Clodius took place, Pompey returned from the East. Both the senatorial party and the democratic party were anxious to secure his support; but, with that fatuity which characterized his conduct so often, he satisfied neither faction. The senate, however, found an opportunity to punish him for his coldness toward them by declining either to ratify his arrangements in the

---

[1] *Att.* I. 16 (*Epist.* V.).

[2] *Att.* 2. I. 5 ; *Schol. Bob.* p. 330, 15 ff. ed. Or.

[3] *Att.* I. 16. 10 (*Epist.* V.).

[4] For another view, cf. Beesly, *Catiline, Clodius, and Tiberius.*

East or to give the accustomed gratuities to his veterans ; but his hopes for the next year were raised by the election of his adherent, L. Afranius, to the consulship for 60 B.C. Clodius had been absent for a year as quaestor in Sicily, and Cicero, although not foreseeing definitely the danger which threatened him, looked forward with some anxiety to the return of Clodius.

12. A variety of causes conspired in 60 B.C. to weaken the conservative party. The knights, who farmed the provincial revenues, in a large degree, finding that they had made their bids too high, wished to cancel their contracts.[1] The senate would not give its consent. It also passed a measure to investigate the bribery of the jury in the Clodian trial, and as many of the suspected jurors were *equites*, that class regarded the measure as a political attack upon themselves.[1] The senatorial party was also weakened by the death of one of its most judicious leaders, Q. Catulus, in the spring of 60 B.C.,[2] by the indifference of others, like Lucullus, and by the ascendency of extremists like Cato and Favonius.[3]

13. It was under these circumstances that Caesar returned, fresh from his victories in Spain, to sue for the consulship. Pompey had won from the senate nothing but a triumph, and willingly made common cause with Caesar. The coalition was strengthened by the addition of Crassus, and thus, in the summer of 60 B.C., the so-called First Triumvirate was secretly formed.[4]

The triumvirs carried out the first item in their programme by the election of Caesar to the consulship for 59 B.C., but with Bibulus,[5] an extreme aristocrat, as his colleague ; and notwithstanding the violent opposition of Bibu-

[1] *Att.* 1. 17. 8–10 (*Epist.* VI.).   [3] *Att.* 2. 1. 8.
[2] *Att.* 1. 20. 3.   [4] Vell. Paterc. 2. 44.
[5] Suet. *Iul.* 19.

lus and the Optimates, Caesar secured the passage of an agrarian law [1] and bills ratifying Pompey's arrangements in the East,[2] while the people, under the leadership of the tribune P. Vatinius, approved a bill assigning to Caesar, from Mar. 1, 59 B.C., the provinces of Cisalpine Gaul and Illyricum, with an army of three legions for five years, to which the senate, apparently of its own motion, added Transalpine Gaul and a fourth legion.[3]

14. After the return of Caesar, Cicero took little part in politics. He did not sympathize with the uncompromising attitude of the senate, he was hurt by the coldness of Pompey towards himself, and disappointed by that leader's selfish aims. While appreciating the irresistible power of the Triumvirate, he saw a ray of hope in the apparent unpopularity of the triumvirs,[4] whose rule, he believed, could not last long. Clodius continued straight on toward his cherished purpose of avenging himself upon Cicero. With that end in view he caused himself to be adopted by a plebeian, Fonteius, and secured an election as tribune for the year 58.

Cicero would seem to have been blind to his own danger. He knew of the enmity of Clodius, but did not fear him, so that he made no opposition to his adoption or his election, and as late as Nov., 59 B.C., writes in a confident way of the future.[5] The conduct of Caesar, who appreciated Cicero's danger, was most generous. He offered Cicero the position of *legatus* in Gaul.[6] This offer, however, Cicero declined, as well as that of a *legatio libera*,[6] and a position on the commission to divide the public land in Campania.[7]

---

[1] *Att.* 2. 16. 1 f. ; 2. 18. 2 ; Vell. Paterc. 2. 44.

[2] Dio Cass. 38. 7.

[3] Dio Cass. 38. 8 ; Suet. *Iul.* 22.

[4] *Att.* 2. 19. 3 (*Epist.* VII.).

[5] *Q. fr.* 1. 2. 16 and concluding note to *Epist.* IX.

[6] *Att.* 2. 18. 3.

[7] *Att.* 2. 19. 4 (*Epist.* VII.).

III. CICERO'S BANISHMENT AND RECALL.

(Aet. 49–50. B.C. 58–57. Epist. X.–XIV.)

15. Clodius skilfully prepared the way for an attack upon Cicero by securing the passage of certain popular measures, and, having gained the support of the consuls A. Gabinius and L. Piso, between Mar. 20 and 25, 58 B.C.,[1] he secured the adoption of a bill enacting : *qui civem Romanum indemnatum interemisset, ei aqua et igni interdiceretur.*[2] The principle of this bill was not new, and no one was mentioned in it by name, but Cicero knew that it was directed against himself. There can be little doubt that, in view of the Porcian and Sempronian laws, the execution of Lentulus and his fellow-conspirators, who were not allowed to make an appeal to the people, was unconstitutional. Cicero's plea, that the passage of the *senatus consultum ultimum* suspended this privilege, and that Lentulus and the others, by conspiring with the Allobroges, had lost their right as citizens, is not a sufficient answer. At all events, Cicero's cause was a hopeless one. The senators and knights were powerless, the consuls would give no help, and the triumvirs were not loath to have Cicero and Cato, who was at this time sent to Cyprus on a difficult mission, removed from the city before Caesar's departure.

16. This state of things had induced Cicero to withdraw from the city before the law of Clodius was passed, and soon after his departure the latter promulgated another proposition in the following form : *velitis iubeatis ut M. Tullio aqua et igni interdictum sit.*[3] This bill, with the subsequent modification that the interdiction should hold good within a limit of 400 miles,[4] was adopted about Apr. 20.[5] Cicero's

---

[1] Upon sections 15,16, cf. *Cicero's Journey into Exile*, by C. L. Smith in *Harvard Studies*, vol. VII, pp. 65–84.

[2] Vell. Paterc. 2. 45.

[3] *De Dom.* 47.

[4] Cf. *Att.* 3. 4, notes (*Epist.* X.).

[5] Cf. Rauschen, p. 7; Smith, p. 79.

house upon the Palatine was torn down, and a portion of the site was consecrated to Liberty. His property elsewhere was despoiled, and Terentia was forced to seek protection with her half-sister Fabia.

17. After lingering for a time in Italy, Cicero went to Thessalonica, where he remained for several months as the guest of his friend, the quaestor Cn. Plancius. He was in a very despondent condition,[1] as all the efforts which his friends made to secure his recall were thwarted by Clodius. The year 57 B.C. opened under better auspices. The consuls P. Lentulus Spinther and Metellus Nepos were friendly, and the tribunes were in the main Cicero's supporters ; but all this might have accomplished little, had it not been for the fact that Pompey, who had taken offense at Clodius, actively supported the cause of Cicero. At last, Aug. 4, a law was passed in the *comitia centuriata* authorizing Cicero's return.[2] Cicero had already come to Dyrrachium in Nov., 58 B.C., in order that he might receive news more quickly, and Aug. 4, 57 B.C., he sailed for Brundisium. He was received most enthusiastically in the towns through which he passed on his way to Rome, and in Rome itself, which he reached Sept. 4,[3] after an absence of a year and a half.

IV. Under the Triumvirate.

(Aet. 51-55. B.C. 56-52. Epist. XV.-XXVIII.)

18. Circumstances at this time conspired to raise the political hopes of Cicero and the Optimates. The people in Rome and throughout Italy had shown great delight on the occasion of Cicero's return. His recall was not only a

[1] Cf. Intr. to *Att.* 3.4 (*Epist.* X.), and, in general, *Att.* Bk. 3 and *Fam.* Bk. 14.

[2] *Att.* 4. 1. 4.
[3] *Att.* 4. 1. 5.

personal victory for him, but also a political victory for the
Optimates.   Through the favorable action of the *pontifices*,
Cicero had recovered his building site on the Palatine and
damages for the loss of his house and villas.   The unani-
mous acquittal, in Mar., 56 B.C., of P. Sestius, Cicero's
foremost champion in 57 B.C., who was prosecuted on a
charge *de ambitu et de vi,* was a decided triumph for Cicero
and the *Boni.*[1]   Furthermore, there was a lack of harmony
in the party of the triumvirs.   Emboldened by this state of
things, the senate, on Apr. 5, 56 B.C., adopted Cicero's
motion *ut de agro Campano . . . Idibus Maiis referretur.*[2]
The law at which this motion to reconsider was directed
was Caesar's agrarian law of 59 B.C., assigning lands in
Campania to Pompey's veterans.   Success in repealing this
law would also undoubtedly lead to an attack upon all the
legislation of the year 59 B.C.

19. The sequel of his motion in the senate is best told
by Cicero himself (*Fam.* I. 9. 9): *Quem* (i.e. *Quintum*) *cum
in Sardinia Pompeius, paucis post diebus quam Luca* (the place
of conference with Caesar) *discesserat, convenisset, ' te,'
inquit, 'ipsum cupio; nihil opportunius potuit accidere: nisi
cum Marco fratre diligenter egeris, dependendum tibi est, quod
mihi pro illo spopondisti.'   Quid multa ? questus est graviter ;
sua merita commemoravit ; quid egisset saepissime de actis
Caesaris cum ipso meo fratre quidque sibi is de me recepisset, in
memoriam redegit seque, quae de mea salute egisset, voluntate
Caesaris egisse ipsum meum fratrem testatus est: cuius causam
dignitatemque mihi ut commendaret, rogavit, ut eam ne oppug-
narem, si nollem aut non possem tueri.*   This important
passage furnishes the explanation of that remarkable change
which Cicero's political attitude underwent in 56 B.C.
Quintus had promised Pompey that his brother, if recalled,
would not oppose the triumvirs.   As a man of honor,

---

[1] *Q. fr.* 2. 4. 1.   [2] *Fam.* I. 9. 8.

Marcus could not but recognize the binding force of this promise made in his behalf — made, though it was, in a moment of weakness and despair. To this consideration must also be added Cicero's positive gratitude for Pompey's services in securing his recall, and his recognition of the power of the triumvirs to punish him severely if he persisted in his independent course. Cicero withdrew his motion,[1] and, for the next five years, gave up all opposition to the plans of the triumvirs. Other circumstances conspired to make this the only feasible course for Cicero to pursue. The policy of the Optimates was hopelessly selfish and headstrong, while they themselves showed that petty jealousy of Cicero which had characterized their conduct on many previous occasions[2]; and finally, when Quintus Cicero took service with Caesar in 54 B.C.,[3] political opposition to Caesar might have proved the ruin of Quintus.

These circumstances may justify Cicero's failure to oppose the triumvirs, but they cannot fully excuse the subservient attitude which he assumed toward them from the summer of 56 to the close of 52 B.C., notably, in defending Vatinius at Caesar's request[4] and Gabinius at Pompey's,[5] in 54 B.C., and in heaping praises upon Caesar in his oration *de Prov. Cons.*, in 56 B.C. Cicero's own statement in *Fam.* 1. 9, of his attitude during this period should be read in this connection.

20. The compact between Caesar, Pompey, and Crassus was renewed at Luca in Apr., 56 B.C.,[6] and, in accordance with its terms, Pompey and Crassus were elected to the consulship for the following year, and, during their term of office, secured the passage of laws assigning Spain to

[1] *Q. fr.* 2. 6. 2.
[2] *Att.* 4. 2. 5.
[3] *Q. fr.* 2. 10 (12). 4.
[4] *Fam.* 1. 9. 19.
[5] *Q. fr.* 3. 1. 15; *Pro. Rab. Post.* 32.
[6] *Q. fr.* 2. 5. 3; Suet. *Iul.* 24.

Pompey[1] and Syria to Crassus[2] for five years, and prolonging Caesar's proconsulship for the same period.

Cicero took little part in politics during the years 55 and 54 B.C., and his letters exhibit his discouragement in regard to them.[3] They indicate, however, the growth of a cordial feeling between him and Caesar.[4] Much of Cicero's attention was given to literature. To this period belong the *De Oratore*, the *De Re Publica*,[5] and several speeches ; among them, one in defense of Cn. Plancius, who received Cicero so generously at Thessalonica during the latter's exile.

21. The violence and disorder, with their accompaniment of bribery and political intrigue,[6] which had prevailed almost uninterruptedly from midsummer of the year 54 B.C., reached its climax in Jan., 52 B.C., in a riotous contest between the followers of Clodius and Milo, which resulted in the death of the former,[7] and, as a last resort, Pompey was elected sole consul on the 24th of the intercalary month of this year.[8] This sudden elevation to extraordinary power completed the separation of Pompey from Caesar.

Several circumstances which occurred during the previous two years had paved the way for this result. First of all the death of Julia, Caesar's daughter and Pompey's wife, in 54 B.C.,[9] and the subsequent refusal of Pompey to enter into another family alliance with Caesar, severed a link which had bound the two men together ; but a still more important factor was the defeat and death of Crassus in the East in 53 B.C.[10] The indefinite continuance of a triumvirate was possible, but the existence of a duumvirate was impossible,

---

[1] Plut. *Cat. Min.* 43 ; *Pomp.* 52.

[2] Plut.*Cat.Min.*43; Liv.*Epit.*105.

[3] E.g. *Q. fr.* 3. 9. 1 f.

[4] *Q. fr.* 2. 13 (15a). 1 ; 3. 5 (and 6). 3.

[5] *Att.* 4. 13. 2 ; *Q. fr.* 3. 5. 1.

[6] *Q.fr.* 3. 3. 2.

[7] Ascon. *in Milon.* p. 32 ; Dio Cass. 40. 48–50.

[8] Ascon. *in Milon.* p. 37 ; Liv. *Epit.* 107.

[9] Liv. *Epit.* 106 ; Dio Cass. 39. 64.

[10] Liv. *Epit.* 106.

and the time seemed to Pompey ripe for strengthening himself and humbling his rival. He was practically dictator in Rome, and still retained his governorship of Spain, while his rival, Caesar, was far away in Gaul, engaged with Vercingetorix, his bravest and ablest enemy, in a life and death struggle,[1] which might end with him as the Parthian campaign had ended with Crassus.

After assuming office Pompey secured the passage of laws imposing heavier penalties for bribery and violence,[2] prolonging his proconsulship of Spain for five years,[3] and a law *de iure magistratuum*,[4] providing that candidates for office must appear in person a certain number of days before the election, and that those who had held office in Rome must wait five years before assuming the government of a province. Caesar was, however, exempted from the operation of the first clause of this law by a special measure,[5] and also by a provision unconstitutionally appended to the law itself as an afterthought by Pompey.[6] The second provision in the law was, however, intended to bring Caesar low. Even if he should succeed in securing an election to the consulship, it would be easy, after his term of office had expired, to prosecute him and to convict him of using violence in his candidacy for the consulship in 60 B.C., under the new law *de vi*, which was retroactive.

V. THE PROCONSULSHIP.

(Aet. 56–57. B.C. 51–50. Epist. XXIX.–XLI.)

22. The law *de iure magistratuum*, which made it incumbent upon those who had held office at Rome to wait five years before assuming the government of a province, forced

---

[1] Caes. *B. G.* 7. 63–89.
[2] Ascon. *in Milon.* p. 37.
[3] Plut. *Pomp.* 55.
[4] Dio Cass. 40. 56.
[5] *Att.* 8. 3. 3.
[6] Suet. *Iul.* 28.

the senate to assign provinces to ex-officials who had not yet held governorships abroad. Cicero was one of the number, and to him the province of Cilicia was assigned in Mar., 51 B.C., much against his will.[1] He left Rome in the early part of May,[2] and, traveling by the way of Brundisium, Athens, and Ephesus, reached Laodicea, the first city of his province, July 31.[3]

23. He found affairs in his province, which included Cilicia, Pamphylia, Pisidia, Isauria, Lycaonia, and Cyprus, in a most unpromising condition. From without, a descent of the Parthians was threatened,[4] which he must resist with a most inadequate force of only two legions, which were scattered throughout the province and demoralized by mutiny and the inefficiency of their officers.[5] The condition of the provincials was still more disheartening. Appius Claudius, Cicero's predecessor, had practically turned over the provinces to Roman *publicani* and usurers,[6] among the latter of whom M. Brutus figured conspicuously. From the outset Cicero set himself to work to remedy this state of things.[7] He fixed the normal rate of interest at 12%, although Brutus had required in one instance 48%[8]; he prevented all extortion, he removed the money lenders' agents from official positions, and administered the law with justice and regularity.

24. In military matters he showed almost as much wisdom and efficiency. The mutinous troops were brought under discipline,[9] while the justice of his government enabled him to augment his own troops with those of his allies. With this combined force he took the field in September. The victory

---

[1] *Fam.* 3. 2. 1.

[2] *Att.* 5. 1.

[3] *Att.* 5. 16. 2.

[4] *Fam.* 15. 4. 7 (*Epist.* XXXIV.).

[5] *Fam.* 15. 4. 2 (*Epist.* XXXIV.).

[6] *Att.* 5. 16. 2 ; 6. 2. 7–9.

[7] *Att.* 5. 16. 3.

[8] *Att.* 6. 2. 7.

[9] *Fam.* 15. 4. 2 (*Epist.* XXXIV.).

which Cassius won over the Parthians near Antioch averted the threatened invasion of Cilicia, and Cicero directed his forces against the independent people near Mt. Amanus,[1] where, after a complete victory, he had the satisfaction of hearing himself saluted '*imperator*' by his troops.[2]

25. Toward the end of Dec., 51 B.C., Cicero was in Tarsus and sent thence official letters to the consuls asking for a *supplicatio*,[3] accompanied by a letter of similar purport to Cato, the senatorial leader.[4] The senate voted the *supplicatio*,[5] and, turning over his province to the quaestor Caelius Caldus, on July 30, Cicero set out on his homeward journey in high hopes of a triumph. There is no more honorable period in Cicero's life than that of his proconsulship in Cilicia ; and with the difficulties which he had to face, and the poor means at his disposal, his success as an administrator was highly creditable. The fact that he did not reorganize his province on a permanent basis, as Caesar reorganized Gaul, is to be attributed to the shortness of his tenure of office and the wretchedness of the aristocratic system of government, and not to Cicero's own inability or unwillingness. Cicero traveled slowly homeward by the way of Rhodes[6] and Athens, accompanied by his brother, his son, his nephew, and his freedman Tiro, who was obliged to remain at Patrae on account of illness.[7] On Nov. 24, 50 B.C., he reached Brundisium, where he was met by his wife Terentia.[8] After a delay of several weeks at his villas near Naples, Cicero at last reached Rome, Jan. 4, 49 B.C.,[9] after an absence from the city of a year and eight months.

[1] *Fam.* 15. 4. 8 (*Epist.* XXXIV.).
[2] *Att.* 5. 20. 3.
[3] *Fam.* 15. 10 and 13.
[4] *Fam.* 15. 4 (*Epist.* XXXIV.).
[5] *Fam.* 8. 11. 2.
[6] *Fam.* 2. 17. 1 ; 14. 5. 1.
[7] *Fam.* 16. 1. 2.
[8] *Fam.* 16. 9. 2.
[9] *Fam.* 16. 11. 2.

VI. Caesar or Pompey ? [1]

(Aet. 58–59. B.C. 49–48. Epist. XLII.–LIII.)

26. Cicero, upon his arrival, found political affairs in a turmoil. The *lex Vatinia* of 59 B.C. (§ 13) had assigned Gallia Cisalpina and Illyricum to Caesar for a period of five years, dating from Mar. 1, 59 B.C.[2] By the *lex Pompeia Licinia*, passed in 55 B.C. (§ 20), Caesar's term of office was extended for a period of five years, — probably, therefore, to Mar. 1, 49 B.C.[3] Special legislation of the year 52 B.C. had allowed Caesar to sue, in 49 B.C., for the consulship, without personally attending the canvass (§ 21). His successor in the provinces would not naturally begin his term of office until Jan. 1, 48 B.C., and in accordance with the regular practice in such cases, Caesar might count upon holding his provinces until that time, when he would pass from the provincial government to the consulship at Rome, and thus avoid the snares which his enemies at Rome would otherwise have set for him. But to frustrate this plan, M. Marcellus, the consul, a bitter opponent of Caesar, attempted on Dec. 10, 50 B.C. to induce the senate to pass the *senatus consultum ultimum*. Failing in this, he proceeded to Naples, and on his own motion requested Pompey to take charge of the legions near Luceria[4] and defend the state. Pompey accepted the command of the legions.

27. This overt act hastened the course of events. On Dec. 21 Curio, Caesar's agent, left Rome to go to Caesar,[5] and returned in time to present a formal ultimatum (cf.

---

[1] For a good statement of the events of this period, cf. *Der Ausbruch des Bürgerkriegs, 49 v. Chr.*, by H. Nissen, in von Sybel's *Historische Zeitschrift* for 1881, pp. 48–105 and 409–445.

[2] Herzog, I. p. 552. n. 2. [4] Orosius, 6. 15 ; Cic. *Att.* 7.
[3] Watson, pp. 287–290. 5. 4.
[5] Schmidt, *Briefw.* p. 99.

Epist. XLII., intr.) to the senate Jan. 1, 49 B.C., when the consuls L. Lentulus Crus and C. Claudius Marcellus assumed
office. Caesar's proposals were not accepted, and a resolution was passed declaring that he would be acting *adversus
rem publicam* if he did not give up his army by July 1, 49 B.C.[1];
and on Jan. 7 the *senatus consultum ultimum*[2] was passed, upon
which the tribunes Antonius and Cassius,[3] as well as Curio
and Caelius, set out for Caesar's camp.

28. Cicero's position made him an eminently fit person
to effect a compromise.[4] He proposed that Pompey should
go to Spain, and that Caesar should not be compelled to
attend his canvass in person[5]; but his efforts were fruitless.
On Jan. 10 Caesar crossed the Rubicon[6] with five cohorts
and marched toward Rome, taking Pisaurum, Fanum, and
Ancona on his way. On Jan. 14 the senate passed the
decretum tumultus,[7] but the news of Caesar's rapid advance
forced Pompey, the consuls, and senators to leave Rome,[8]
Jan. 17, and hurry southward.

29. Cicero left the city the same day. The senate had
assigned the Campanian district to him, but he saw that
little could be done,[9] because the inhabitants of Campania
had many of them received their lands through Caesar's
law (§ 13). Furthermore he hoped for peace, and thought
that neutrality on his part would best fit him to act as
mediator between the opposing forces; and to maintain his
neutral position, he gave up his appointment in Campania
just before leaving the city, and took charge, in a civil capa-
city, of the Roman Campagna and the coast of Latium.[10]

[1] Cf. Caes. *B. C.* 1. 2. 6; 1. 9. 2.
[2] Caes. *B. C.* 1. 5.
[3] Cf. *nulla vi expulsi, Epist.*
XLII. 2 n.
[4] *Epist.* XLII. intr.
[5] *Fam.* 6. 6. 5, 6.

[6] Schmidt, *Briefw.* p. 104. n. 2.
[7] Schmidt, *Briefw.* p. 113.
[8] *Att.* 9. 10. 4; *Fam.* 16. 12. 2.
[9] *Att.* 8. 3. 4.
[10] *Att.* 7. 11. 5; 8. 11d. 5;
Schmidt, *Briefw.* pp. 116–120.

The Pompeians, after planning a rendezvous at Luceria,[1] hurried toward Brundisium, whither Pompey peremptorily summoned Cicero.[2] Nevertheless he remained in Formiae, hoping still to effect a reconciliation between Caesar and Pompey,[3] and, with this hope in mind, he had an interview with Caesar at Formiae,[4] Mar. 28. In this interview Caesar requested him to go to Rome and use his best efforts to secure peace, but when Cicero mentioned the terms which he should propose, Caesar refused to accept them.

30. This meeting put an end to his hesitation. He felt sure that all hope of a reconciliation was gone, as neither party would submit terms which the other could accept. Cicero has been often accused of indecision during this period, but unjustly so. In his opinion there was right and wrong with each party, and civil war was an evil to be avoided at all hazards. He used every possible means, therefore, to avert the catastrophe, but without success. Recognizing the inevitable, he cast in his lot with the man to whom he personally owed most ; for the choice lay, not between Caesar and the Republic, but between Caesar and Pompey ; *nec mehercule hoc facio rei publicae causa, quam funditus deletam puto, sed ne quis me putet ingratum in eum qui me levavit iis incommodis* (i.e. of exile) *quibus idem adfecerat (Att.* 9. 19. 2).

31. On June 7, 49 B.C., Cicero, accompanied by his brother, his son, and his nephew, sailed from Formiae to join Pompey near Dyrrachium,[5] which place he reached, after stopping for several months on the estate of Atticus in Epirus, toward the close of the year 49 B.C., some eight

---

[1] *Att.* 8. 1. 1.
[2] *Att.* 8. 11c.
[3] *Att.* 9. 6a (*Epist.* XLVII.), and
[4] *Att.* 9. 18. 1.

Att. 9. 11a (*Epist.* XLIX.), are of special interest in this connection.

[5] *Fam.* 14. 7. 2.

or nine months after the arrival of the Pompeian forces.[1] In the meantime Caesar, displaying extraordinary energy,[2] tact, and consideration,[3] had made himself master of Italy, where he found the people kindly disposed toward him[3], had restored order at Rome, had defeated the Pompeian lieutenants, Afranius, Petreius, and Varro, in Spain ; and in Jan., 48 B.C., he crossed the Adriatic and began the offensive operations against Pompey which ended in the victory near Pharsalus, Aug. 9, 48 B.C. Pompey fled, but was murdered about three weeks later, while landing at Pelusium in Egypt.[4]

Cicero had been coldly received by the Pompeians at Dyrrachium,[5] and had little to do with the preparation for the struggle.[6] A serious indisposition also kept him at Dyrrachium, so that he was not present at the battle of Pharsalus.[7]

VII. UNDER CAESAR'S GOVERNMENT.

(Aet. 60–62. B.C. 47–45. Epist. LIV.–LXXXIV.)

32. After the battle of Pharsalus Cicero remained for a time at Corcyra [8] and Patrae,[9] and then decided to return to Italy. He reached Brundisium [10] in Oct., 48 B.C., and stayed there until Sept., 47 B.C., passing one of the most miserable years of his life. He was distressed by both political and domestic anxieties. He had returned contrary to the express orders of Caesar, who had forbidden the Pompeians to enter Italy.[11] He was therefore a political fugitive in a city filled

[1] Schmidt, *Briefw.* pp. 183–4.
[2] *Att.* 8. 9. 4.
[3] *Att.* 8. 13.
[4] Caes. *B. C.* 3. 104.
[5] *Att.* 11. 6. 6.
[6] *Att.* 11. 4. 1.
[7] *Att.* 11. 4. 2 ; *Fam.* 9. 18. 2 ; Plut. *Cic.* 39.
[8] *Att.* 11. 5. 4.
[9] *Fam.* 13. 17. 1.
[10] *Fam.* 14. 12.
[11] *Att.* 11. 7. 2.

with hostile soldiers. At the same time Caesar's critical position in Egypt[1] made it quite possible that the Pompeian cause might succeed after all, in which case Cicero's standing would be still more precarious. His family affairs were equally distressing: Tullia, his daughter, was most unhappy with her husband Dolabella; Terentia's management of his property[2] during his absence had caused him a deal of vexation ; an unfortunate misunderstanding had sprung up with his brother Quintus.[3]

33. Cicero's anxiety in regard to his own position was somewhat relieved in Sept., 47 B.C., by the arrival of Caesar, who generously gave him permission to remain in Italy.[4] He went almost directly to Rome, and his letters in the main, up to the close of 46 B.C., were written either in that city or at his villas at Tusculum and Cumae. The battle of Thapsus was fought Apr. 6, 46 B.C., and by it Caesar's supremacy in Africa was established; but the tidings of this important battle and even of the violent deaths[5] of the Pompeian leaders, Scipio, Petreius, Afranius, and Juba,[6] do not seem to have stirred Rome so deeply as the news that Cato had taken his own life at Utica,[7] feeling that the cause of the Republic was beyond hope. The little memoir which Cicero wrote of his personal and political friend[8] called forth opposition pamphlets from the Caesarians, Hirtius[9] and Brutus,[10] and even Caesar found time on the eve of the battle of Munda to write an '*Anticato*.'[11]

34. Cicero gave much of his time to literature during this period. The *Orator* was written and the *Brutus* finished in

---

[1] *Bell. Alex.* 21, 22.

[2] *Att.* 11. 24. 3, etc.

[3] *Att.* 11. 9. 3.

[4] Plut. *Cic.* 39; Dio Cass. 46. 22.

[5] Cf. *Epist.* LXII. 2 n.

[6] *Bell. Afr.* 94–6.

[7] *Bell. Afr.* 88.

[8] *Att.* 12. 4. 2 ; 12. 5. 2.

[9] *Att.* 12. 40. 1.

[10] *Att.* 12. 21. 1.

[11] Suet. *Iul.* 56.

46 B.C.[1] Although he attended the meetings of the senate, he took little active part in politics, save in working to secure the recall of some Pompeians who were still in exile. At one time Cicero hoped that Caesar would follow a conservative course and would at least restore the senate to its old position and influence, and it was with this hope in his mind that he spoke so warmly of him in his oration *pro Marcello;* but he soon saw clearly that it was Caesar's purpose to retain the supreme power in his own hands, especially when, at the close of the year 46, Caesar, on departing for Spain, left the city in charge of eight *praefecti*, who were directly responsible to his personal representatives, Cornelius Balbus and C. Oppius.[2]

35. Caesar defeated the last of the Pompeians, who had rallied under the leadership of Labienus and the two sons of Pompey, at Munda,[3] Mar. 17, 45 B.C., and returned to Rome in September to continue the reforms which he had already begun, and to make preparations for his great campaign against the Parthians in the following year. In the meantime a conspiracy was forming against him, led by a few disappointed office-seekers and fanatics, and fostered by the traditional Roman prejudice against the title of *rex* and the regal insignia. The indiscreet act of Antony and of some other personal friend (or enemy?), in offering a diadem to Caesar,[4] and in crowning his statue with a laurel wreath,[5] strengthened the conspiracy, while Caesar's own course in openly assuming supreme power, a course far removed from the more diplomatic policy of his successor Augustus, must have offended the more conservative element. The meeting of the senate on Mar. 15, 44 B.C., furnished a suitable occasion, the presentation of a petition by L. Tillius

---

[1] *Att.* 12. 6. 3.
[2] Suet. *Iul.* 76; Dio Cass. 43. 28; Cic. *Fam.* 6. 8. 1; Tac. *Ann.* 12. 60.
[3] *Bell. Hisp.* 31.
[4] *Philipp.* 2. 85.
[5] Plut. *Caes.* 61.

Cimber a convenient opportunity, and the conspirators accomplished their purpose of assassinating Caesar.[1]

VIII. Cicero and the *LIBERATORES*.

(Aet. 63–64. B.C. 44–43. Epist. LXXXV.–C.)

36. Soon after the murder of Caesar, the assassins, or the *liberatores*, as they were termed by Cicero, distrusting the temper of the people, withdrew to the Capitol,[2] which was guarded by the gladiators of D. Brutus. Here they were visited in the evening by a number of prominent men, among them being Cicero. He himself had had no part in the formation of the plot which led to Caesar's assassination or in its execution,[3] but his satisfaction at the removal of Caesar is plainly shown in a jubilant letter[4] written to L. Basilus, one of the conspirators, probably on the day of the assassination.

37. M. Antonius, who was Caesar's colleague in the consulship, gained possession of all his private treasure and political papers,[5] but thought it wise to leave the adjustment of affairs to the senate.[6] The senate met Mar. 17, and adopted Cicero's proposal to ratify Caesar's acts and to grant amnesty to the conspirators.[7] At the same time arrangements were made for the burial of Caesar at the public expense and for the publication of his will. The funeral took place between Mar. 20 and 23,[8] and the people, whose sympathy for Caesar was increased on hearing his generous bequests to them, were inflamed to such a degree

---

[1] Suet. *Iul.* 81, 82.
[2] Appian, *B. C.* 2. 120.
[3] *Fam.* 12. 2. 1; *Philipp.* 2. 25.
[4] *Fam.* 6. 15.
[5] Appian, *B. C.* 2. 125.
[6] *Philipp.* 1. 1, 2.

[7] Appian, *B. C.* 2. 135; Cic. *Philipp.* 1. 16 ff.; *Fam.* 12. 1; cf. also Schmidt, *Kämpfe*, pp. 687-700.
[8] Ruete, *Die Correspondenz Ciceros in den Jahren 44 und 43*, p. 16.

by the funeral oration of Antony[1] that the conspirators were obliged to withdraw from the city.

38. With the help of Caesar's confidential secretary Faberius, Antony proceeded to strengthen himself by altering Caesar's papers and even by forging new documents.[2] To all this the senate could offer no resistance, but the further development of Antony's plans was interrupted by the arrival in April of C. Octavius,[3] Caesar's adopted son and heir. The position of this young man, as Caesar's adopted son, and his manly spirit won him a hearty welcome from the Gallic veterans, and by his generous and tactful treatment of them he succeeded in drawing large numbers from Antony's support to his own side. At the same time his deference to Cicero,[4] and his apparently unselfish desire to serve the state, excited for a time the liveliest hopes in the breasts of the republicans.

39. Cicero took little part in politics for some time after the important meeting of the senate, Mar. 17. He feared that by the death of Caesar Rome had merely exchanged one tyrant for another,[5] and as early as May he writes prophetically to Atticus, *mihi autem non est dubium quin res spectet ad castra.*[6] His discouragement was almost converted into despair when, on meeting M. Brutus and C. Cassius at Antium, June 8, he found that they were absolutely without purpose or plan. *Prorsus dissolutum offendi navigium* (i.e. the ship of state) *vel potius dissipatum; nihil consilio, nihil ratione, nihil ordine.*[7] He decided to leave Italy for a time and was actually at Leucopetra on his way to Greece when he heard that a reconciliation between Antony and the *liberatores* was probable.[8] On hearing this news, he returned

---

[1] *Philipp.* 2. 91 ; *Att.* 14. 10. 1;
Suet. *Iul.* 84, 85.
[2] *Philipp.* 3. 30, 31; 5. 10–12.
[3] *Att.* 14. 10. 3.
[4] *Att.* 14. 11. 2.
[5] *Att.* 14. 12. 1.
[6] *Att.* 14. 21. 3.
[7] *Att.* 15. 11. 3 ; cf. also 14. 6. 2.
[8] *Philipp.* 1. 7, 8 ; *Att.* 16. 7. 1.

to Rome to take part in the meeting of the senate which was called for Sept. 1.

40. He found matters however in a far less favorable condition than he had hoped to find them, and absented himself from the meeting of the senate, Sept. 1, on the plea of illness. Antony was angry at Cicero's absence and threatened to tear his house down.[1] On the following day Cicero appeared in the senate and delivered his first Philippic.[2] It was an outspoken criticism of Antony's action, but was free from personality. On Sept. 19 Antony made a violent reply to Cicero's criticism.[3]

The province of Macedonia had at first been assigned to Antony for the year 43,[4] but in June, in spite of the opposition of the senate, he secured the passage of a bill in the *comitia* assigning to him Gallia Cisalpina, with Gallia Transalpina perhaps, in place of Macedonia.[5] He doubtless preferred Gallia Cisalpina, as it would enable him to remain nearer Rome and because it was the key to Italy.[6] He left the city Nov. 28, hastening toward the north with three legions and his body-guard to dispossess D. Brutus,[7] to whom Gallia Cisalpina had fallen under the arrangements of Caesar.

41. At this point Cicero's active participation in the struggle with Antony begins. He saw the weak and the strong points of the senatorial cause. His judgment was unerring and his courage unfaltering. He saw that Octavius must be attached to the senatorial party, and Octavius was invested with the *imperium* and authorized, in coöperation with the consuls of 43 B.C., to conduct the war against Antony.[8] He appreciated that at all hazards

---

[1] *Philipp.* 5. 19.
[2] *Philipp.* 1. 16; *ad Brut.* 2. 3. 4.
[3] *Fam.* 12. 2. 1.
[4] Schmidt, *Kämpfe*, pp. 701–6.
[5] Appian, *B. C.* 3. 30; Schmidt, *Kämpfe*, p. 714.
[6] Schmidt, *Kämpfe*, p. 713.
[7] Appian, *B. C.* 3. 45.
[8] *Mon. Ancyran.* 1; Appian, *B. C.* 3. 51.

D. Brutus must make a determined stand in Gallia Cisalpina, and that the governors of the neighboring provinces must be induced to rally to his support. He wrote therefore urgent letters to D. Brutus, to Plancus in northern Gaul, to Lepidus in southern Gaul, and to Pollio in Spain.[1] Brutus and Cassius in the East were apprised of the course of events in Italy,[2] and the senate was urged to take bold action.

42. His efforts were at the outset crowned with success, for on Dec. 20, 44 B.C.,[3] the senate repealed the law which assigned Gallia Cisalpina and Transalpina to Antony, lengthened the terms of office of D. Brutus and Plancus, and directed the other provincial governors to remain at their posts until the senate should send out their successors. Octavius and Hirtius, one of the consuls, left Rome in the early part of 43 B.C. to relieve D. Brutus,[4] who was besieged by Antony in Mutina, and Pansa, the other consul, followed in March with four more legions of recruits.[5] After some preliminary skirmishing in which Antony gained the advantage,[6] a decisive battle was fought near Mutina, Apr. 21,[7] in which his army was completely defeated. But the victory was dearly bought. Hirtius fell upon the field of battle, and Pansa was mortally wounded[8] and died two days later. The command of the forces acting against Antony was assigned to D. Brutus. Octavius, who had good reason to feel aggrieved at this slight,[9] withdrew from further participation in the struggle, and marched to Rome at the head of eight legions, demanding the consulship.[9] There was no means at hand to withstand him, and Aug. 19 he was elected consul, although but nineteen years of age.[9]

[1] Cf. *Fam.* Bk. 10.

[2] Cf. *Fam.* Bk. 12, and *Epist. ad Brut.*

[3] Cf. *Philipp.* 3 ; *Fam.* 12. 22. 3.

[4] *Fam.* 12. 5. 2.

[5] *Fam.* 10. 30. 1.

[6] *Fam.* 10. 30.

[7] Cf. Mendelssohn, p. 458, n. 3.

[8] Liv. *Epit.* 119.

[9] Liv. *Epit.* 119; Appian, *B. C.* 3. 80–94 ; Suet. *Aug.* 26.

Meanwhile, in the north, Antony was strengthened by the accession of Lepidus,[1] Plancus, and Pollio.[2] D. Brutus was deserted by his troops, and while seeking to escape was murdered at Aquileia.[3]

43. In the East the cause of the *liberatores* had been more successful. In the early part of 43 B.C. M. Brutus reached the province of Macedonia, which had been assigned to him by Caesar, and was recognized as the legal governor by his predecessor Q. Hortensius.[4] Cassius also took possession of his province, Syria. Both of them succeeded in levying large bodies of troops and in defeating C. Antonius,[5] the brother of Marcus, and Dolabella,[6] who had come out to take possession of Macedonia and Syria respectively, by virtue of measures whose passage Antony had secured. The senatorial party was in the meantime urging Brutus and Cassius to return and protect Italy from the troops of Antony.[7] Cicero also wrote to both leaders, asking them to adopt this course,[8] but their entreaties were without effect.

44. In Italy matters were rapidly advancing to a crisis. Octavius, soon after his elevation to the consulship, marched northward, met Antony near Bononia in Oct., 43 B.C., and with M. Lepidus formed a compact for the adjustment of affairs in Italy and for the prosecution of the war in the East against the *liberatores*[9]; and in November, by a vote of the *comitia*, Antony, Lepidus, and Octavius were appointed commissioners 'for the reorganization of the state' for a period of five years.[10]

---

[1] *Fam.* 10. 23. 2.

[2] Vell. Paterc. 2. 63.

[3] Appian, *B. C.* 3. 97, 98.

[4] *Philipp.* 10. 13.

[5] Plut. *Brut.* 26 and 28.

[6] Vell. Paterc. 2. 69.

[7] Appian, *B. C.* 3. 85.

[8] *ad Brut.* 1. 14. 2; 1. 18. 1; *Fam.* 12. 10. 3.

[9] Dio Cass. 46. 55, 56; Appian, *B. C.* 3. 97; Liv. *Epit.* 120.

[10] *Mon. Ancyran.* 1; Liv. *Epit.* 120; Dio Cass. 46. 56.

The first step of the triumvirs was to remove their enemies at Rome, and Cicero's name was included in the list of the proscribed, notwithstanding the protest of Octavius. Cicero at first thought of seeking refuge in the East, and actually set sail from Astura for that purpose, but the unfavorable weather and his own unwillingness to leave his native land held him back, and the emissaries of Antony found him still in his Formian villa when they reached that place, Dec. 7. His faithful slaves attempted to save him even at the last moment by hurrying him on board a ship which lay in the harbor, but he was overtaken by his pursuers, and, forbidding his followers to make resistance, gave himself up to death at the hands of his assassins.[1]

THE PRIVATE LIFE OF CICERO.

45. Cicero's father was in moderate circumstances, and from him Cicero inherited the family estate at Arpinum and a house in the Carinae. The dower of his wife Terentia amounted to 480,000 sesterces,[2] but the larger part of his income was derived from legacies left to him by admirers or by men to whom he had rendered professional service. In 44 B.C. Cicero boasted[3] that he had received more than 20,000,000 sesterces from this source. And one of his legacies, from the philosopher Diodotus,[4] is said to have amounted to 10,000,000 sesterces. Possibly Cicero received also a share of the profits which C. Antonius, his colleague in the consulship, made in his province.[5]

---

[1] Plut. *Cic.* 47–9.
[2] Plut. *Cic.* 8.
[3] *Philipp.* 2. 40.
[4] *Att.* 2. 20. 6. The correctness

of the text is, however, questioned by Tyrrell, vol. I². p. 35.
[5] *Att.* 1. 12. 2; 1. 13. 6; 1. 14. 7; *Fam.* 5. 5.

Cicero did not apparently increase his property to any great extent by productive investments. A large part of it in fact was invested in houses and villas in Rome and in the country districts of Italy. Besides his town house upon the Palatine, which he bought of M. Crassus in 62 B.C. for 3,500,000 sesterces,[1] Cicero owned villas at Arpinum, Tusculum, Antium, Astura, Formiae, Cumae, Puteoli, and Pompeii, and lodges along some of the more frequented Italian roads. Large sums of money were spent in decorating and furnishing these different residences[2] and upon their proper maintenance. When, in addition to these heavy expenses, we bear in mind his great fondness for works of art and literature,[3] his generous mode of living, his openhandedness to friends and clients, and his social ambition for his son and daughter,[4] it is evident that even the enormous sums stated would be scarcely sufficient to meet his needs.

46. In fact Cicero was frequently in great financial difficulty, and was relieved only by loans made to him by his friend Atticus, or by P. Sulla,[5] or still worse by his political enemy Caesar[6] or by the money-lenders at Rome. With skilful management probably his fortune would have been sufficient to meet the demands made upon it, but he was so much engrossed in politics, literature, and the practice of his profession that he had little time or inclination for business affairs. Then, too, during his exile and during his absence at the outbreak of the civil war, his finances were wretchedly muddled by Terentia and her untrustworthy steward Philotimus.[7]

---

[1] *Fam.* 5. 6. 2.

[2] *Att.* 2. 1. 11; 4. 2. 7.

[3] *Fam.* 7. 23; *Att.* 1. 9. 2; 1. 4. 3; 1. 7; 1. 10. 4.

[4] *Att.* 12. 32. 2 ; 11. 25. 3; 11. 23. 3.

[5] Gellius, 12. 12. 2.

[6] *Att.* 5. 10. 4; 7. 8. 5.

[7] *Fam.* 4. 14. 3; *Att.* 11. 2. 2, etc.

47. In his financial dealings Cicero was honorable and high-minded. He declined to make money, as even his friends Atticus and M. Brutus did, by loaning money at usurious rates. His upright management of Cilicia was in marked contrast to the almost universal practices of his contemporaries. He paid his debts conscientiously, although not always with promptness, because of his frequent financial embarrassment. In some other points Cicero does not show as strict a sense of honor : he did not scruple to open certain letters from his brother Quintus to a third person, which fell into his hands, and which, as he suspected, contained slanderous statements in regard to himself[1]; he dictated to the secretary of Atticus a letter in praise of Caelius and then read it to Caelius as an authentic epistle from Atticus[2]; in another letter he even speculates upon the feasibility of disavowing an oration which had offended Curio.[3] The question of ethics involved in the defense of Catiline scarcely belongs here and has been discussed elsewhere.[4] It should be remembered in partial extenuation of these facts that the code of honor in such matters was not so strict in Cicero's day as it is in our own, and that his lot was cast in times when life and fortune hung by a slender thread.

48. Cicero's enthusiastic study of Greek and Latin literature at Rome, and later at Athens and Rhodes, has already been noted (§§ 1, 2). These habits of study continued throughout his life, and gave him such a fund of general information as few of his contemporaries possessed. Still he was not a man of profound learning, even in his chosen profession. He was rather a man of cultivated tastes and broad sympathies. Of his knowledge of the literature, history, and antiquities of Greece and Rome, his letters,

---

[1] *Att.* 11. 9. 2.
[2] *Att.* 6. 6. 4.
[3] *Att.* 3. 12. 2.
[4] Cf. *Epist.* II. notes.

especially those to Atticus, offer constant illustration. He prided himself upon the fluency with which he could use Greek in speaking and writing. He was an insatiable book-buyer and a connoisseur in art (§ 45 n. 3). The circle of his friends included every one worth knowing at Rome, — politicians, whether of the aristocratic or democratic factions, literary men, business men, and men of leisure.

No better proof could be desired of Cicero's sympathetic nature and manysidedness than the fact that he drew to himself persons of all tastes, beliefs, and ages. He was a friend not only of the eminent jurist Servius Sulpicius Rufus, and the learned antiquary Varro, but also of Caesar's witty *aide-de-camp* Trebatius, of the clever young politician Caelius, and the accomplished Caerellia.

49. In his family relations Cicero was a true and court-eous husband, a father indulgent to his children, but wisely thoughtful for their interests. In his relations with his wife Terentia he stands in honorable contrast to many prominent men of his time, and his divorce from her, which took place after a married life of thirty years, was the almost inevitable result of the lack of sympathy existing between two such opposite natures; and a knowledge of the great frequency of divorce in his day may properly modify the severity of our judgment upon him in this matter.

His second wife Publilia, who was much younger than himself, he probably married for her money,[1] and the union proved utterly disagreeable to him. All the wealth of his affection was bestowed upon his daughter Tullia. Her nature was impressionable like his own, so that she under-stood her father and sympathized with him in his periods of exaltation and depression, while the unhappiness which followed her through life only served to bring out her father's tenderness.

[1] *Fam.* 4. 14. 3.

No one could have been more unlike Cicero than his only son Marcus, and it would be humorous, if it were not pathetic, to see the orator hopefully instructing the would-be soldier in the mysteries of philosophy and law. But when the boy had taken up the profession of arms under Brutus, and thus brought to naught the father's hope that his son would succeed him at the bar and in the senate, Cicero gracefully accepted the inevitable. He followed his son's movements with the liveliest interest, and heard with paternal pride the reports of his prowess.

To his brother Quintus, Cicero was always loyal and devoted. Their friendly relations were broken but once,[1] and then only for a brief period. They were men of very different temperaments. Marcus acted in general with deliberation; sometimes, in fact, he hesitated too long. Quintus was nervous and impulsive.

One dwells, however, with most pleasure upon Cicero's treatment of his personal dependents. Not only his favorite freedman Tiro, but the very slaves of his household enjoyed his kindness and generosity.

50. This sympathetic sensitiveness in Cicero's nature gives to his character its special charm, and constitutes at the same time its principal weakness. Those moments of exaltation and of depression, those periods when he help-lessly fluctuates between different courses of action,[2] find their explanation in this quality. His humor is determined by the circumstances of the moment. He lacks, therefore, the calm poise of the less impressionable nature. He fails to give things their proper proportions, and consequently his forecasts of the future are generally either too sanguine or too gloomy. It was this quality, of course, which made him an opportunist in politics.

---

[1] *Att.* 11. 5. 4; 11. 12. 1.

[2] E.g. in 58 and 49 B.C. Cf. introductory note to *Epist.* X.

A man so constituted could find real pleasure only in
Rome.   He was charmed for a time with the new sensations
which country life gave him, but it soon became irksome.
Of all his villas, the Tusculanum, perched upon one of the
hills which overlook Rome, and within easy reach of all the
political and social news of the city, was his favorite, and
we are not surprised when he writes from Cilicia: *urbem,
urbem, mi Rufe, cole et in ista luce vive: omnis peregrinatio —
quod ego ab adulescentia iudicavi — obscura et sordidast.*[1]

51. No sketch, however brief, of Cicero's private life
would he complete without some reference to the connection
between it and his philosophical work.   In the early part
of the year 46 B.C. he was divorced from Terentia,[2] in
November his son Marcus left Rome to pursue his studies
in Athens,[3] and, hardest of all to bear, in Feb., 45 B.C., his
beloved daughter Tullia died.[4]   Cicero was overwhelmed
with grief, and at his lonely villa upon a little island in the
river Astura, gave himself up to the perusal of such books
as he thought would help him to bear his loss[5]; and as he
gradually gained some control over his feelings, he began
the composition of works in a similar vein.   His purpose
gradually widened until it included the development of a
complete philosophical system, and for twelve months he
wrote and published philosophical works with incredible
rapidity; but the impulse to the work is to be found in the
domestic misfortunes which befell him in the autumn and
winter of 46–45 B.C., and the personal element is noticeable
in all of his philosophical work, especially in the Tusculan
Disputations.   We find also in studying his domestic life
the main factor which determined his philosophical attitude.
He could not accept the doctrines of either of the two

[1] *Fam.* 2. 12. 2.
[2] Plut. *Cic.* 41.
[4] Schmidt, *Briefw.* p. 271.
[3] *Att.* 12. 8 (written Nov. 11, 46 B.C.).
[5] *Att.* 12. 15.

most influential schools in his day, — the Epicurean and the Stoic, — because his tender recollections of Tullia made him recoil from the materialism of the one and the coldness of the other. He became, therefore, an eclectic.

CICERO'S FAMILY AND FRIENDS.

TERENTIA AND PUBLILIA.

52. A fair knowledge of the relations existing between Cicero and his wife Terentia may be gained from the letters of Bk. 14, *ad Fam.*, all of which are addressed to her. In the early letters of this correspondence written in 58 B.C., after twenty years of married life, Cicero expresses himself in most affectionate terms. After this date, with the exception of one letter in 50 B.C., which is mainly upon business matters, there are no letters to Terentia up to 49 B.C., although this interval includes the period of his proconsulship, when he wrote so many letters to his personal and political friends. Even the letters of the year 49, when Cicero was in so much anxiety, are very infrequent. The rest of the letters of Bk. 14, belonging to the next two years, are brief and formal. It appears that an estrangement gradually grew up between them which culminated in their divorce in the early part of 46 B.C. In December of the same year he married his rich ward Publilia[1]; but Publilia could not conceal her chagrin at finding herself second to Tullia in his affection, and when she evinced joy a few months later at Tullia's death, Cicero sent her to her mother and could not be induced to receive her back into his favor.[2]

---

[1] Plut. *Cic.* 41 ; Cic. *Fam.* 4. 14. 1 and 3. Cf. also Schmidt, *Briefw.* p. 268. [2] *Att.* 12. 32. 1.

TULLIA.

53. Tullia, Cicero's only daughter, was probably born in 79 or 78 B.C. In 66 B.C. she was betrothed to C. Calpurnius Piso Frugi,[1] and married him sometime within the next three years. He died during the year of Cicero's exile.[2] In 56 B.C. Tullia married Furius Crassipes.[3] The match was regarded as a good one, but for reasons unknown to us Crassipes and Tullia were soon divorced. Her next matrimonial venture was with P. Cornelius Dolabella,[4] the Caesarian politician. Their married life proved to be a most unhappy one, and they were probably divorced towards the close of the year 46 B.C.[5] Tullia herself died in Feb., 45 B.C.,[6] and her father was plunged in the deepest grief, in which his friends Caesar, Lucceius, Sulpicius, and others sought to comfort him by letters of condolence.[7]

MARCUS TULLIUS CICERO *FILIUS*.

54. Cicero's only son Marcus was born in 65 B.C. The father gave his personal attention for some time to the young man's education, and sent him later to Athens to pursue his studies, in the hope that he would take up the legal profession; but the young man's tastes were averse to study, and the appearance of Brutus at Athens, in 44 B.C., was enough to cause his enlistment in the army of the *liberatores*, in which he served with distinction.[8] He espoused the cause of Octavius against Antony, was made consul by the former in 30 B.C.,[9] and is last heard of as proconsul of Asia.

[1] *Att.* 1. 3. 3.
[2] *pro Sest.* 68.
[3] *Q. fr.* 2. 4. 2.
[4] *Att.* 6. 6. 1 ; *Fam.* 8. 6. 1.
[5] *Fam.* 6. 18. 5.

[6] Schmidt, *Briefw.* p. 271.
[7] *Att.* 13. 20. 1; *Fam.* 4. 5; 5. 13; 5. 14; *Att.* 12. 13. 1.
[8] *ad Brut.* 2. 3.
[9] Plut. *Cic.* 49.

Quintus Tullius Cicero.

55. Quintus Cicero was a man of considerable ability; and, although he never reached the consulship, he was aedile in 65 and praetor in 62 B.C. At first he was inclined to attach himself to Pompey, and in 57 B.C. served as the latter's *legatus* in Sardinia,[1] but three years later he joined Caesar in Gaul and took part in the invasion of Britain. In the civil war, after some hesitation, he espoused the cause of Pompey, but after the battle of Pharsalus he sought and obtained pardon from Caesar. In 43 B.C. he was proscribed with Marcus and put to death. Four of his letters are extant,[2] as well as a long document addressed to Marcus when the latter was a candidate for the consulship.

Publius Cornelius Dolabella.

56. Cicero was somewhat disturbed[3] upon hearing, while in Cilicia, that his daughter Tullia was betrothed to Dolabella, for the young man's career was notorious, and Cicero himself had twice defended him against serious charges. These fears were well grounded, for Dolabella neglected Tullia, and in 46 B.C. they were divorced. Probably in the hope that Caesar's programme included cancellation of debts,[4] Dolabella joined his party in the civil war and was designated as Caesar's successor in the consulship for 44 B.C., during the projected Parthian war. In this office he at first showed some sympathy for the party of Brutus and Cassius, but later the promise of the province of Syria induced him to side with Antony. He met his death[5] while attempting to take this province from one of the conspirators (§ 43).

[1] *Q fr.* 2. 2. 1.
[2] *Fam.* 16. 8; 16; 26; 27.
[3] *Fam.* 2. 15. 2; *Att.* 6. 6. 1.
[4] *Fam.* 2. 16. 5.
[5] Vell. Paterc. 2. 69.

Marcus Tullius Tiro.

57. Tiro, the slave and freedman, deserves a place among the members of Cicero's family because of the intimate terms upon which he lived with all the members of it. He was his master's secretary and accompanied him wherever he went. Cicero's affection for him is evident from the letters of Bk. 16, *ad Fam.*, most of which are letters written to Tiro by Cicero. He was a man of cultivation, and his criticism was of great service to Cicero, who writes to him: *tu, qui* κανὼν *esse meorum scriptorum soles*.[1] He did some independent literary work in writing a life of his patron,[2] in making a collection of his witticisms,[3] and in editing a collection of stenographical abbreviations. He apparently wrote some tragedies also.[4]

Titus Pomponius Atticus.

58. Atticus was born in 109 B.C.,[5] and spent his early life at Rome; but the dreadful events which attended the war between Marius and Sulla led him to withdraw from Rome in 86 B.C. and take up his residence at Athens,[6] where Cicero made his acquaintance about 79 B.C. His father left him 2,000,000 sesterces, and his uncle Q. Caecilius 10,000,000[7] more. This property he found means of increasing by judicious investments, as he managed the business affairs of Cato, Hortensius, Cicero, and others,[8] made loans to individuals and towns,[9] carried on the business of a publisher,[10] and even kept trained bands of

---

[1] *Fam.* 16. 17. 1.
[2] Plut. *Cic.* 49.
[3] Quint. 6. 3. 5.
[4] *Fam.* 16. 18. 3.
[5] Nep. *Att.* 21, 22.
[6] Nep. *Att.* 2.
[7] Nep. *Att.* 5.
[8] Nep. *Att.* 15.
[9] Nep. *Att.* 8; Cic. *Att.* 1. 13. 1; 16. 16 a. 4, 5.
[10] *Att.* 2. 1. 2; 12. 40. 1; 12. 45. 3.

gladiators.[1] He abstained carefully from all participation in politics, and yet was on intimate terms with members of all political parties. His philosophical views were in harmony with his political attitude, as he was an Epicurean. His sister Pomponia married Q. Cicero.

The intimate friendship which existed between Atticus and Cicero had a practical as well as a sentimental basis. Atticus found it profitable to act as Cicero's financial agent, and he found the letters of recommendation, which his friend wrote for him to the governors of provinces, of great service, while Cicero derived great profit from the advice and help which Atticus rendered him in domestic, political, literary, and financial matters. Atticus died in 32 B.C.[2]

LETTER WRITING.

59. In Cicero's time letters were commonly written either upon waxen tablets or papyrus. Reference is made in Cic. *in Cat.* 3. 5 to a letter upon waxen tablets, and they were not infrequently used as late as the fifth century A.D.[3]; but the introduction into Italy of papyrus, which is mentioned as early as the time of Ennius,[4] gradually restricted the use of waxen tablets, so that, in so far as letters were concerned, they were in general used only in writing to a correspondent near at hand, especially when one hoped for an immediate answer upon the tablets sent. Thus Cicero writes to Lepta : *simul atque accepi a Seleuco tuo litteras, statim quaesivi e Balbo per codicillos quid esset in lege.*[5] Such occasional notes were called *codicilli*,[6] as indicated in the extract, or sometimes

---

[1] *Att.* 4. 4 b. 2 ; 4. 8 a. 2.
[2] Nep. *Att.* 22.
[3] Thompson, *Greek and Latin Palaeography*, p. 22.

[4] Marquardt, *Handbuch*, vol. VII. p. 808, n. 1.
[5] *Fam.* 6. 18. 1.
[6] Cf. also Seneca, *Ep.* 55. 11.

pugillares. For letters, however, sent to a distance, as most of Cicero's were, papyrus was a much more convenient substance, and probably the great majority of his letters were written upon it.[1] Parchment had not yet come into use for letter writing.[2]

60. The papyrus plant was grown principally in Egypt. It grows in water two or three feet deep, and the plant reaches a height of five or six feet. The method of manufacturing writing material from it is described by Pliny.[3] The stem of the plant was cut into thin strips, and these strips were laid parallel to one another upon a smooth surface; another set of strips was laid upon these at right angles, and the two layers were glued together by the gum which exuded from the strips when they were moistened with water. The layers were then hammered together into a single sheet, called a *plagula,* which was exposed to the sun to dry. The sheets were from 5 to 10 inches long, and probably one sufficed for an ordinary letter. If more space was needed, several sheets were pasted together. The center of the papyrus industry was Alexandria.

61. Ink (*atramentum,* or *atramentum librarium*) was ordinarily made from the liquid of the cuttle fish,[4] or from a composition of soot and gum.[5] The inkstand (*atramentarium*) was commonly cylindrical and often had two compartments, one for black and one for red ink. Pens (*calami*) were made of reeds grown chiefly in Egypt,[6] and were kept in a case (*calamarium* or *theca calamaria*) made usually of leather. The other articles which completed a writing outfit were a piece of lead (*plumbum*) and a ruler (*regula*) for

---

[1] Cf., however, *exaravi, Epist.* LXIX. 1 n.

[2] Birt, *Das antike Buchwesen,* p. 61.

[3] *N. H.* 13. 74–83; cf. also Birt, pp. 227–247.

[4] Persius, 3. 13.

[5] Plin. *N. H.* 35. 6. 25.

[6] Martial, 14. 38.

ruling lines, a pen-knife (*scalprum librarium*) for sharpening the pens, and a sponge for erasing ink.

62. The letter regularly opened and closed with certain formulae which varied according to the relations in which the writer and recipient stood. Thus, in writing to an intimate friend like Paetus, Cicero might open his letter thus: *Cicero Paeto*,[1] or *Cicero Paeto S.*[2] (i.e. *salutem*), or *Cicero Paeto S. D.*[3] (i.e. *salutem dicit*); or in a little more formal letter the praenomen or cognomen of one or of both might be added, e.g. *M. Cicero S. D. A. Caecinae*[4] or *Cicero S. D. M. Fadio Gallo.*[5] In formal letters, if either the writer or the recipient held an office, his title was added, e.g. *M. Cicero Imp. S. D. L. Paulo Cos.*[6]; still more formally, *M. Tullius M. F. Cicero Procos. S. D. Cos. Pr. Tr. Pl. Senatui*[7] (i.e. *M. Tullius Marci filius Cicero pro consule salutem dicit consulibus praetoribus tribunis plebis senatui*).

In addressing the members of one's own family it was customary to add *Suo* (or *Suae*), e.g. *Tullius Terentiae Suae S. P.*[8] (i.e. *salutem plurimam*). After this address there often appeared some formula like *si vales, bene est*, either written out in full or in the abbreviation *s. v. b. e.* or *s. v. b.* (i.e. *benest*).[9] Cicero himself rarely used this formula.[10]

In writing to the members of one's own household, apparently some closing formula was ordinarily used. Such formulae are found at the end of all the letters to Terentia and to Tiro. Among those used are the following: *vale, etiam atque etiam vale, vale salve, fac valeas meque diligas, cura ut valeas, ama nos et vale.*[11] In writing to others than

---

[1] *Fam.* 9. 20.
[2] *Fam.* 9. 21.
[3] *Fam.* 9. 24.
[4] *Fam.* 6. 5.
[5] *Fam.* 7. 23.
[6] *Fam.* 15. 13.

[7] *Fam.* 15. 2.
[8] *Fam.* 14. 7; cf. sect. 69.
[9] *Fam.* 11. 3; cf. also *Epist.* LII. 1 n. See Sen. *Ep.* 15. 1 ; Pliny, *Ep.* 1. 11.
[10] Cf. *Epist.* LVI. n.
[11] Cf. *nos diliges, Epist.* XVIII. (end) n.

the members of one's household, closing formulae were less frequently used. For instance, all of the seventeen letters from Caelius [1] close abruptly. The date and place of writing, if indicated at all, are usually given at the end of the letter, the name of the place being in the ablative (sometimes with a preposition) or the locative, e.g. *d.* (i.e. *data, datae* or *datum*) *a. d. III. Non. Oct. Thessalonica, XVII. K. Apr. Corduba, K. Oct. de Venusino, ex Arpinati VI. Non., data XVI. Kal. Sextiles Thessalonicae.*

63. When a letter was ready to be sent, it was rolled up; a thread was wound about the middle of it and sometimes passed through the papyrus itself, and a seal was attached to the ends of the string. [2] The seal was the guarantee of genuineness; so, for instance, upon one occasion, when Cicero had opened some letters from Quintus to certain friends, on the suspicion that they contained slanderous remarks about himself, he was not afraid of the consequences, because Pomponia, the wife of Quintus, who was not on good terms with her husband, had her husband's seal and would not object to sealing the letters again. [3] The seal often had for its design the likeness of the owner [4] or of one of his ancestors. [5] Wax was commonly used to receive the impression, but sometimes Asiatic chalk. [6] Upon the outside of the roll the name of the person addressed was written in the dative, sometimes with his title and the place where he could be found, e.g. *M. Lucretio flamini Martis decurioni Pompeiis.* [7]

---

[1] *Fam.* Bk. 8.

[2] Fronto ad M. Caesar. 1. 8, p. 24 Naber : *Versus, quos mihi miseras, remisi tibi per Victorinum nostrum, atque ita remisi; chartam diligenter lino transui et ita linum obsignavi, ne musculus iste aliquid aliqua rimari possit.*

[3] *Att.* 11. 9. 2.

[4] Plaut. *Pseud.* 56 and 988.

[5] *in Cat.* 3. 10.

[6] *pro Flacco*, 37.

[7] From a Pompeian wall-painting preserved in the Museum at Naples.

64. Letters were often written by secretaries from dictation, but most of Cicero's letters to Atticus and Quintus at least were written with his own hand; for in 59 B.C. he writes to Atticus: *numquam ante arbitror te epistulam meam legisse, nisi mea manu scriptam*[1]*;* and in 49 B.C.: *lippitudinis meae signum tibi sit librarii manus*[2]*;* and in 54 B.C. to Quintus: *scribis enim te meas litteras superiores vix legere potuisse, in quo nihil eorum, mi frater, fuit quae putas; neque enim occupatus eram neque perturbatus nec iratus alicui, sed hoc facio semper ut, quicunque calamus in manus meas venerit, eo sic utar tamquam bono.*[3] During the latter part of his life, however, especially during the years 44 and 43 B.C., even the letters to Atticus were written by a secretary.[4] Cicero's principal secretary was Tiro. Mention is also made of another, Spintharus by name.[5]

As there was no postal system at that time, letters had to be sent by one's own messengers (*tabellarii*) or the messengers of one's friends. This made the composition of a letter a more serious matter in Cicero's day than it is in ours. But his letters were not always studied productions: some of them were written while he was traveling; others between the courses at dinner[6]; and he writes to Cassius[7]: *praeposteros habes tabellarios . . . cum a me discedunt, flagitant litteras . . . atque id ipsum facerent commodius, si mihi aliquid spatii ad scribendum darent, sed petasati veniunt, comites ad portam exspectare dicunt.*

Some idea of the speed with which letters were carried may be gathered from the following instances: letters arrived at Rome from Brundisium on the sixth day, from Sicily on

[1] *Att.* 2. 23. 1.
[2] *Att.* 8. 13. 1.
[3] *Q. fr.* 2. 14 (15b). 1; cf. also 2. 15 (16). 1.
[4] *Att.* 15. 20. 4; 12. 32. 1.
[5] *Att.* 13. 25. 3.
[6] *Att.* 14. 6. 2; 14. 12. 3; cf. *dictavi ambulans, Epist.* IX. 1 n.
[7] *Fam.* 15. 17. 1.

the seventh day, from Britain on the thirty-third day, from Africa and also from Athens on the twenty-first day, from Syria on the fiftieth day.[1]   A messenger in Cicero's time traveled from 40 to 50 (Roman) miles per day.[2]

CICERO'S CORRESPONDENCE AND ITS FIRST PUBLICATION.

65. The earliest letter (*Att.* 1. 5) in the correspondence was written in 68 B.C.; the latest (*Fam.* 10. 24), a letter from Plancus to Cicero, bears the date of July 28, 43 B.C.   Cicero's last extant letter (*Fam.* 10. 29) was written July 6, 43 B.C. The correspondence with Atticus closes with *Att.* 16. 15 in Dec. 44 B.C.   The fact that the extant correspondence stops several months before his death is probably due to the circumstance that the attitude of Octavius changed in the summer of 43 B.C., and Cicero's letters after that date were not published because of the strictures they contained upon the conduct of Octavius.   The following tables indicate the extant and lost collections of letters :

EXTANT COLLECTIONS.

Ad Familiares . . .	16 bks.
Ad Atticum . . .	16 "
Ad Quintum fratrem .	3 "
Ad M. Brutum . .	2 "
Total	37 bks.

LOST COLLECTIONS.

Ad Axium	2 bks.
Ad M. Brutum . . .	7 "
Ad Caesarem . . .	3 bks.
Ad Calvum	2 "
Ad filium	2 "
Ad Hirtium	9 "
Ad Nepotem	2 "
Ad Octavium . . .	3 "
Ad Pansam	3 "
Ad Pompeium . . .	4 "
Total	37 bks.

[1] C. Bardt, *Quaestiones Tullianae.*

[2] E. Ruete, *Die Correspondenz Ciceros,* p. 121.

The extant collections contain about 870 letters, of which 423 are included in the Bks. *ad Fam.*, 394 in the Bks. *ad Att.*, and the remainder is divided almost equally between the other two collections. The correspondence contains 98 letters from 31 other persons than Cicero. Seventy-three of these letters are found in the Bks. *ad Fam.*

66. The collection of letters *ad Fam.* seems to be made up of three parts[1]: (i) Bk. 13, (ii) Bks. 1–9 and 14–16, (iii) Bks. 10–12. The letters of Bk. 13 are all letters of recommendation, and were probably collected and perhaps published in the summer of 44 B.C. Of the other books, 1–9 and 14–16 contain epistles, other than letters of recommendation, written before the summer of 44 B.C.; and Bks. 10–12 contain letters written later than that date. The date of publication of parts ii and iii is not known. In view of the criticisms made upon Antony in some of these letters, perhaps they were not published until after the battle of Actium, or still later.[2] The title *Epistulae ad Familiares* is modern.

Tiro, Cicero's secretary, was making a collection of Cicero's letters in 44 B.C.[3] The collection of letters *ad Fam.* contains no letters from Tiro, but many addressed to him, even by other people than Cicero. He is therefore almost certainly the editor of this collection.

67. The collection *ad Atticum* contains no letter from Atticus. This state of things, together with the well-known fact that Atticus was a publisher, and that Cornelius Nepos says[4] that such a collection of Cicero's letters, not yet published, was in the possession of Atticus, makes it almost certain that these letters were arranged for publication by him. It is probable that they were not published until

---

[1] Cf. in general L. Gurlitt, *De M. Tulli Ciceronis epistulis earumque pristina collectione.*

[2] Cf. Mendelssohn, *M. Tulli*

Ciceronis Epistularum Libri Sedecim, p. iii. n.

[3] *Att.* 16. 5. 5.

[4] Nep. *Att.* 16.

after his death (32 B.C.).[1] Some of the men of note upon whom Cicero had expressed unfavorable opinions were still living in 32 B.C., and the publication of these letters would therefore have been indiscreet. The books in the collection *ad Att.* stand in chronological order, and the letters within the books are arranged chronologically, but not with accuracy.

With the *Epistulae ad Quintum fratrem* may be mentioned the *Commentariolum Petitionis*,[2] a document which Quintus sent to his brother when the latter was a candidate for the consulship. The letters proper, as well as the *Epistulae ad M. Brutum*, were edited by Tiro.[3] There were originally nine books of the letters to Brutus, but seven of them have been lost. Those which remain are probably Bks. 9 and 8 of the original collection. The authenticity of the *Epist. ad M. Brut.* has been seriously doubted, but, with the exception perhaps of 1. 16 and 17,[4] they are now commonly regarded as authentic.

68. A few references to Cicero's letters during the Middle Ages are found,[5] but they do not seem to have been as well known as his philosophical writings. In the year 1389, however, Coluccio Salutato, the Florentine chancellor, obtained from Vercelli a copy of a Ciceronian manuscript, which was found to contain the *Epist. ad Fam.*[6] This manuscript and the copy secured by Coluccio are now in the Laurentian Library at Florence. The former belongs to the

---

[1] Bücheler (*Rhein. Mus.* 1879, p. 352) believes that they were published between 60 and 65 A.D., but his argument is not convincing.

[2] Upon the authenticity of the *Commentariolum Petitionis*, cf. Tyrrell, vol. I.[2] pp. 110–121; Hen-

drickson, *Amer. Jour. of Philol.* vol. XIII. no. 2.

[3] Gurlitt, p. 17.

[4] K. Schirmer, *Ueber die Sprache des M. Brutus in den bei Cicero überlieferten Briefen*, pp. 25–6.

[5] Mendelssohn, pp. iv–x.

[6] Mendelssohn, pp. xi – xii. ; Schmidt, *Briefw.* pp. 449–451.

ninth or tenth century and contains all of the *Epist. ad Fam.* This manuscript, in the opinion of most editors, is of paramount authority for the text. Bks. 1–8 of this collection are also found in two manuscripts of the twelfth century, one in the library of the British Museum and the other in the National Library at Paris. Another manuscript of the eleventh century in the British Museum and one of the fifteenth or sixteenth century at Rome contain Bks. 9–16.

In 1345 Petrarch discovered at Verona a manuscript containing the *Epist. ad Att.*, *ad Q. fr.*, and *ad M. Brut.*, and, although the original and Petrarch's copy are both lost, another copy, made for Coluccio Salutato, survived and is preserved in the Laurentian Library at Florence. The only other independent sources for the text of these letters are a few leaves at Würzburg and Munich, and a manuscript known to us only through the marginal readings in one of the early editions, that of Cratander, published in Basel in 1528.

LANGUAGE AND STYLE.

69. For a complete and scientific study of the language and style of Cicero's correspondence an examination of the Latinity of the thirty-one writers from whom letters are preserved would be necessary. Some of these writers, e.g. Caelius (Bk. 8, *ad Fam.*), have left us sufficient material upon which to base a fair estimate of their individual characteristics ; but such a discussion would be too extended for our purposes. An examination, however, of the letters reveals certain elements common to the correspondence as a whole which differentiate epistolary Latin from the language used in more formal writing. Epistolary Latin is one of the forms of the *sermo cotidianus*, the speech used in the familiar intercourse of everyday life, as opposed to the more formal diction adopted in literary compositions intended for a more general audience or body of readers.

70. Formal and informal Latin, if they may be so designated, are in their origin independent of one another. At the moment when Latin literature began, inasmuch as differences in culture did not exist, there was but one Latin spoken by patrician and plebeian alike. With the appearance of literature, Latin developed along two different lines. The poets, especially Ennius, in adapting Latin to literary purposes, adopted certain words and forms of expression and rejected others. On the other hand, the people, in their daily life, were more conservative, retaining much of that which literature rejected,[1] while at the same time they adopted many new forms of expression which formal literature either did not employ at all or accepted at a later date. In particular these literary pioneers, being steeped in Greek literature, unconsciously sought to develop literary Latin in accordance with the genius of the Greek language. This latter influence acted only indirectly upon colloquial speech.

71. The cleft thus resulting continued to widen, until, in course of time, certain distinct and interesting differences are noticeable between formal and informal Latin. Of course important differences are found only between the extremes of these two forms of speech. Cicero himself intimates that we may expect to find in his letters evidences of colloquialism, for he writes to his friend Paetus (*Fam.* 9. 21. 1) : *Quid tibi ego videor in epistulis ? nonne plebeio sermone agere tecum ?* . . . *epistulas vero cotidianis verbis texere solemus.*[2]

72. A number of factors tend to vary the character of this *sermo cotidianus* as it is used in letter writing. Some

[1] Cf. note to *mi, Epist.* XCIII. 2.
[2] Cf. also note to *levia nostratia, Epist.* XXXVI. 1.

of these are the character of the person addressed and his relations to the writer, the subject or subjects discussed, the occupation and culture of the writer, the time and place in which the letter is written, and the other circumstances attending the composition.

With local differences in familiar speech and with those which time effects, the student who confines his attention to Cicero's correspondence is not concerned, as the letters fall within a period of twenty-five years, and were written by men who spoke Latin as it was spoken in the city of Rome. The other factors are of interest. One cannot fail to notice the freedom and informality with which Cicero writes to his friend Atticus or his brother Quintus, as compared with the tone which he adopts to those less intimately related to him. It is in the letters addressed to these two persons that we find the greatest divergence from formal standards. The subject and purpose of a letter exert a potent influence upon its character. The 'open letter' to Lentulus (*Fam.* I. 9), for example, which was to serve as a political pamphlet, takes a tone entirely different from that of the gossipy letters to Trebatius and Paetus. Most of Cicero's correspondents were men of some culture, and there is consequently a uniformity of style and a nearer approximation to formal Latin than we should find in the letters of uncultivated men, but in Pompey and Curius, for instance, we find little suggestion of literary training, but rather the flavor of the camp and of mercantile life. The circumstances under which a letter is written influence perceptibly the character of its language and style. This is especially true of Cicero's own letters, because his nature was peculiarly sensitive to the circumstances surrounding him at the moment; and the letters which he wrote while in exile (e.g. *Att.* Bk. 3.), offer, in their laxity of style, striking illustrations of the way in which the intensity of his feeling was reflected, not merely in the thought expressed, but in the form in which it found expression. Cf., for instance, note to *ante oculos, Epist.* XIII. 3, and note to *cuicuimodi, Epist.* XIV.

73. The student of Plautus, of Terence, of Horace in his Satires, and of Petronius, will find, as might be expected, many points of contact between the language of these writers and the language of the Letters, with such differences in general as result from the influences just noted. It is interesting also to observe that many stylistic peculiarities which we ordinarily recognize as the distinguishing characteristics of Silver Latin, first come to the surface in Cicero's correspondence. A full discussion of the Latinity of the correspondence is impossible here, but a few epistolary peculiarities of more or less frequency are noted in the following paragraphs. Further remarks upon these points and upon similar ones will be found in the commentary.

A. LEXICOGRAPHY AND ORTHOGRAPHY.

74. *New Formations.* In general a fairly large number of words are found in the Letters which do not occur elsewhere in Latin, but the majority of them were probably not new. Still, such formations as *facteon, Sullaturit, tocullio, Lentulitas, susurrator,* and *subrostrani,* which have a genuine Plautine ring, must have resulted from the inspiration of the moment. Cf. note to *facteon, Epist.* V. 13.

75. *Verbal Substantives.* Of especial frequency are verbal substantives in *-tio,* etc., such as *denuntiatio* (Plancus, *Fam.* 10. 8. 4), and *praevaricator* (Caelius, *Fam.* 8. 11. 1). These substantives condense an idea into a single word and thus secure the brevity at which a letter-writer often aims.

76. *Diminutives.* Perhaps the most characteristic form in the Letters is the diminutive. The diminutive ending is added to substantives, to adjectives, to adverbs, and even to the comparative form of the adjective and adverb, and suggests often some emotion on the part of the writer. Cf. note to *pulchellus, Epist.* V. 10.

77. *Words compounded with* per- *and* sub-. Equally common is the use with adjectives, adverbs, and verbs of the prefixes *per-* and *sub-*, which respectively strengthen and weaken the force of the words to which they are attached; e.g. *perbenivolus* (*Fam.* 14. 4. 6), *subirascor*, 'I am a trifle provoked' (*Att.* 9. 7. 7). The use of these prefixes is not by any means unknown in formal literature, but in epistolary Latin it gives rise to many new and strange compounds, e.g. *pervesperi* (*Fam.* 9. 2. 1), *subinanis* (*Att.* 2. 17. 2), and *subturpiculus* (*Att.* 4. 5. 1). It is in the freedom with which such compounds were formed, and the frequency with which they were used, that colloquial Latin was distinguished from formal Latin. These compounds had gone so far toward supplanting the simple words in familiar speech that in some cases they differed in no wise from them, as is shown in the phrase *quae parcius frater perscripserat* (Q. Cic., *Fam.* 16. 27. 1). Cf. also note to *pertumultuose, Epist.* XXXIV. 3.

78. *Verbs compounded with* ad-, con-, *etc.* In this connection mention may be made of verbs compounded with *ad-, con-, de-,* and *dis-,* which are used in the Letters not only with great frequency, but often when they do not apparently differ in meaning from the simple verbs. Compounds with *dis-* are especially noteworthy. Cf. note to *discupio, Epist.* XLVIII. 2.

79. *Frequentatives.* Frequentatives are used with such freedom, and so often in the double form (e.g. *ventito,* Matius, *Fam.* 11. 28. 7), or with the addition of such words as *saepe* or *crebro,* as, for instance, *ostentare crebro solebat* (Dolabella, *Fam.* 9. 9. 2), that one is at first inclined to think that the frequentative has lost its characteristic force in such cases; but it is more probable that in the double frequentative, and in the expressions just noted we have an illustration of the colloquial fondness for unduly emphasizing a fact.

80. *Hybrids.* A few hybrids are found in the Letters, but apparently only in the more familiar letters to Atticus, e.g. *Pseudocato, Att.* 1. 14. 6; *tocullio, Att.* 2. 1. 12; *facteon, Att.* 1. 16. 13.

81. *Archaism.* As was remarked above, colloquial Latin was conservative in retaining certain forms and expressions which became obsolete in formal Latin. Instances in point are *dicier*, an obsolete infinitive form (Vatin., *Fam.* 5. 9. 1), *isto = istuc* (Cael., *Fam.* 8. 15. 2 *et passim*), *illi = illic* (Cael., *Fam.* 8. 15. 2), *qui* (abl.) (*Fam.* 2. 16. 2), *ast = at* (*Att.* 1. 16. 17; 3. 15. 6), and *absque = sine* (*Att.* 1. 19. 1). These forms, as might be expected, are more frequent in the letters of the less cultivated or more colloquial of Cicero's correspondents. They are very rarely found in Cicero's own letters. Cf. note to *isto, Epist.* XLVIII. 2, and especially to *mi, Epist.* XCIII. 2.

82. *Contracted Forms.* Of most interest in this connection is the occurrence in the tenses of the perfect system of syncopated forms, which are used far more freely in epistolary than in formal Latin. In fact, the comparative frequency of such forms in a letter seems to depend upon its informality. In the seventeen letters from Caelius (Bk. 8, *ad Fam.*), which are very familiar in their tone, syncopation takes place in the perfect tenses fifty-five times, while full forms occur but four times. Typical examples from the Letters are *consuesti* (Caecina, *Fam.* 6. 7. 6), *pugnarunt* (Cael., *Fam.* 8. 11. 2), *peccasse* (Q. Cic., *Fam.* 16. 26. 1), and *decreram* (Plancus, *Fam.* 10. 21. 2). About half of the 140 syncopated verb forms which occur in the letters addressed to Cicero belong to the first conjugation. Cf. also notes to *decesse, Epist.* XIX. 2, *commorit, Epist.* XLVIII. 1, and *Ravennaest, Epist.* XXXI. 4.

B. Syntax.

The Substantive.

83. (*a*) The *accusative* is used a little more freely in the Letters than in formal literature. It occurs after verbs of thought and the expression of thought, and after verbs signifying *to strive, to laugh, to hope,* etc.; e.g. *hoc a te praesens contendissem* (Cael., *Fam.* 8. 16. 4); *Catulum mihi narras* (*Fam.* 9. 15. 3); *iurare Iovem Lapidem* (*Fam.* 7. 12. 2); *quam primum haec risum veni* (Cael., *Fam.* 8. 14. 4). Two accusatives occur in a few instances after verbs signifying *to seek, to warn,* etc. ; e.g. *illud autem te peto* (Dolabella, *Fam.* 9. 9. 2); *quod et res publica me et nostra amicitia hortatur* (Cato, *Fam.* 15. 5. 1); and an adverbial accusative made up of *partem* and the adjective *magnam* or *maiorem* or *minimam* is found several times ; e.g. *curare soles libenter, ut ego maiorem partem nihil curare* (Cael., *Fam.* 8. 9. 3). Cf. note to *illud te peto, Epist.* LII. 2.

(*b*) With the exception of a few Grecisms, e.g. *cogitatio dignissima tuae virtutis* (Balbus, *Att.* 8. 15a. 1), the only thing noteworthy with respect to the *genitive* consists in the rather free use of the genitive of quality and the partitive genitive. Cf. *aliquo terrarum, Epist.* LXXXVI. 3 n.

(*c*) The *dative of reference* and the *ethical dative* are great favorites in the Letters, the latter especially with *at, ecce,* and *hic.* Perhaps in their use of the ethical dative Cicero and his correspondents have been surpassed only by the writers of comedy. Cf. *ecce tibi et Bruti et tuae litterae* (*Att.* 14. 19. 1) ; *at ille tibi . . . pergit Brundisium* (*Att.* 8. 8. 2). Cf. also notes to *minori curae, Epist.* XXV. 2, and to *ecce, Epist.* XXXV. 23.

(*d*) Certain public events, recurring at regular or irregular intervals, were of such importance in the eyes of the people that they were used in marking the date of an event.

This practice gives rise to such colloquial *ablatives of time* as *novis magistratibus* (Cael., *Fam.* 8. 10. 3), *gladiatoribus* (Pollio, *Fam.* 10. 32. 3), *summis Circensibus* (Cael., *Fam.* 8. 12. 3). The preposition *in* with the ablative is several times used instead of a conditional or temporal phrase. Cf. *in victoria hominis necessarii = cum vicisset homo necessarius* (Matius, *Fam.* 11. 28. 2).

The Verb.

84. (*a*) Passing over certain isolated cases which remind one of the Plautine usage, where the indicative occurs instead of the classical subjunctive, the use of the *indicative in subordinate clauses in the indirect discourse* and in *questions of deliberation* deserves special notice. Cf. *scito Balbum tum fuisse Aquini, cum tibi est dictum* (*Fam.* 16. 24. 2); *nolito commoveri, si audieris me regredi, si forte Caesar ad me veniet* (Pompeius, *Att.* 8. 12c. 2); *quid mi auctor es? advolone an maneo?* (*Att.* 13. 40. 2); cf. also notes to *quam sollicitus sum, Epist.* XLVIII. 1, and *quam conversa res est, Epist.* XLVI. 2.

(*b*) The present *subjunctive* of the definite second person singular in positive commands is of rather frequent occurrence, especially in closing formulae, e.g. *ei dicas plurimam salutem et suavissimae Atticae* (*Att.* 16. 7. 8); *cautus sis, mi Tiro* (*Fam.* 16. 9. 4). The future indicative and *vis* (second person singular of *volo*) with the infinitive are often used as polite substitutes for the imperative, e.g. *tu interea non cessabis et ea quae habes instituta perpolies nosque diliges* (*Fam.* 5. 12. 10); *visne tu te, Servi, cohibere?* (Sulpicius, *Fam.* 4. 5. 4).

The fact has been recently demonstrated[1] that, 'in the whole field of classical prose from the beginning of the Ciceronian period to the end of the Augustan period, there

[1] Elmer, *The Latin Prohibitive.*

is but a single example of *ne* with the indefinite second person present subjunctive in a prohibition'[1]; and that, furthermore, prohibitions expressed by *ne* with the present or the perfect subjunctive, lack the dignity of the *noli*-construction, and are consequently confined to informal Latin.[2] Quite naturally, therefore, many of these prohibitions expressed by *ne* with the present subjunctive, and the majority of those expressed by *ne* with the perfect subjunctive, to be found in classical prose, are in the correspondence of Cicero,[3] and twelve of the fourteen cases of the last-mentioned construction, which is the more colloquial of the two, occur in letters to Cicero's most familiar correspondents, e.g. '*tu, malum,*' *inquies,* '*actum ne agas*' (*Att.* 9. 18. 3); *iocum autem illius de sua egestate ne sis aspernatus* (*Q. fr.* 2. 10 (12). 5).

(*c*) The so-called *epistolary use of the tenses* is the commonest peculiarity in the use of tenses to be found in the Letters. The writer of the letter imagines himself in the place of the recipient, and therefore uses a tense of past time in speaking of an event which was exactly or approximately contemporaneous with the writing of the letter. This usage is most frequent with verbs indicating the writing of a letter, or the sending of a letter or messenger,[4] as *ego tibi aliquid de meis scriptis mittam: nihil erat absoluti* (*Att.* 1. 16. 18); *quae mihi veniebant in mentem, quae ad te pertinere arbitrabar, quod in Ciliciam proficiscebar, existimavi me ad te oportere scribere* (*Fam.* 2. 18. 3). Cf. also note to *profecti sumus, Epist.* XI. 3.

(*d*) Many interesting instances occur of the use of *habere* with the *perfect participle passive*, but if a few cases

1 Elmer, p. 5.

2 Elmer, pp. 17, 19.

3 Elmer, pp. 4, 17, 18.

4 For a more detailed statement of the principle, cf. Zimmermann's *De epistulari temporum usu Ciceroniano.*

be excepted, as, perhaps, *si . . . quae Lepido digna sunt, perspecta habes* (Lepidus, *Fam.* 10. 34. 4), this combination is not strictly synonymous with the perfect. Cf. note to *sollicitum habent, Epist.* LI. 1. For the use of the future perfect instead of the future, cf. note to *dimisero, Epist.* XV. 2.

The Adverb.

85. (*a*) One of the most noticeable characteristics in the syntax of the Letters consists in the use of the adverb with *esse*. This usage is frequent in colloquial Latin of all periods. It is commonly found with adverbs of place (*prope, praesto, procul,* etc.), and the general and particular adverbs of manner (*ita, contra, aliter, bene, recte, tuto,* etc.) ; e.g., *sit modo recte in Hispaniis* (*Att.* 10. 12a. 2) ; *sed quidvis est melius quam sic esse ut sumus* (*Fam.* 16. 12. 4). In this construction *esse* is something more than a simple copula.

(*b*) More rarely, but in a few clear cases, the adverb is used in place of an attributive adjective ; e.g. *meae ullae privatim iniuriae* (Lentulus, *Fam.* 12. 14. 3). Cf. also note to *circumcirca, Epist.* LXXV. 4, and to *sic, Epist.* V. 3.

Parataxis.

86. The Letters, in common with other literary compositions which affect the *sermo cotidianus*, admit the paratactical arrangement more freely than formal Latin does. This fact is evident (1) in the use of coördination rather than subordination ; e.g. *hanc ergo plagam effugi per duos superiores Marcellorum consulatus, cum est actum de provincia Caesaris, nunc incido in discrimen ipsum* (*Att.* 7. 1. 5), for *cum effugissem,* etc. ; (2) in the paratactical use of the subjunctive in certain common formulae, e.g. *fac diligas* (*Att.* 3. 13. 2) ; (3) in the parenthetical use of certain verbs of thinking, e.g. *sed, opinor, quiescamus* (*Att.* 9. 6. 2) ;

cuiusmodi velim, puto, quaeris (Cael., *Fam.* 8. 3. 3). Cf. also notes to *ut facta est, Epist.* V. 3, and *opinor, Epist.* XXXI. 4.

C. STYLE.

I. SINGLE WORDS.

87. *The Substantive.* (*a*) *Abstract Nouns* are used freely in the plural, not only in accordance with the principles stated by Draeger (*Hist. Synt.*[2] vol. I. pp. 18–21), but also to indicate persons, e.g. *dignitates hominum*, 'persons of distinction.'

(*b*) *Personal Pronouns*, especially those of the first and second person singular, are used lavishly in many epistles, when neither contrast nor proper emphasis makes them necessary. Good illustrations of this pleonastic use are found in *Fam.* 4. 5. In this connection may be mentioned the occasional use of *tute* (Sulpicius, *Fam.* 4. 5. 5), and *meme* (Vatinius, *Fam.* 5. 9. 1).

88. *The Adjective.* (*a*) As elsewhere in colloquial Latin, adjectives, especially those expressing affection and admiration, are frequently joined to proper nouns, e.g. *mi iucundissime Cicero* (Dolabella, *Fam.* 9. 9. 3).

(*b*) *Possessive Pronouns* of the first or second person are applied in the Letters (1) to members of the writer's family; (2) to members of the recipient's family; (3) to those who are closely related to the writer or recipient; (4) to a person through the mention of whom a disagreeable subject is to be introduced, e.g. cf. *Furnium nostrum* (Caesar, *Att.* 9. 6a); and (5) to personal enemies or those held in contempt, e.g. *Pompeius tuus* (Cael., *Fam.* 8. 9. 5).

89. *The Verb.* Periphrastic expressions made up of *facere* and an object are often used instead of a simple verb, e.g. *convicium facere* (*Att.* 1. 14. 5). Items of news are frequently introduced by *scito*, e.g. *scito C. Sempronium Rufum, mel ac delicias tuas, calumniam maximo plausu tulisse* (Cael., *Fam.* 8. 8. 1); or by *habeto* and *sic habeto*, e.g. *sic habeto, mi Tiro, neminem esse qui me amet*, etc. (*Fam.* 16. 4. 4). Cf. notes to *Epist.* XXVI. 1, to *testificor*, *Epist.* L. 1, and to *invidiam facere*, *Epist.* LXXXVI. 6.

90. *The Adverb.* The colloquial use of *intensive adverbs* is one of the most striking stylistic peculiarities of the Letters. In this respect the language of Cicero's correspondence is even more remarkable than that of Roman comedy or satire. The adverbs which are used most frequently with an intensive force are *bene, male, misere, nimio, perquam, pulchre, quam, sane, sane quam, satis, valde, valde quam*, and *vehementer;* e.g. *bene magna* (C. Cassius, *Fam.* 12. 13. 4), *misere nolle* (C. Cassius, *Fam.* 12. 12. 3), *pulchre intellegere* (Brutus and Cassius, *Fam.* 11. 3. 3), *sane quam sum gavisus* (D. Brutus, *Fam.* 11. 13. 4), and *vehementer* four times (Cicero *filius, Fam.* 16. 21). Cf. also Index to the Notes under *male, sane*, etc.

91. *The Preposition. De* is used very frequently to introduce a new topic, e.g. *de mandatis quod tibi curae fuit, est mihi gratum* (Cicero *filius, Fam.* 16. 21. 8). Its place is sometimes taken by a clause with *quod*, e.g. *quod ad rem publicam attinet, in unam causam omnis contentio conlecta est* (Cael., *Fam.* 8. 11. 3); *quod de agraria lege quaeris, sane iam videtur refrixisse; quod me de Pompeii familiaritate obiurgas, nolim ita existimes*, etc. (*Att.* 2. 1. 6).

92. *The Interjection.* A conversational tone is given to many of the familiar letters by the frequent use of interjections, e.g. *ecce, heus*, etc., some of which, as, for instance, *hui* (*Epist.* XLVIII. 2) and *apage* (Vatin., *Fam.* 5. 10a. 1), belong exclusively to vulgar Latin. Cf. also § 98.

II. Phraseology.

93. *Alliteration.* While alliteration is found in the prose
and poetry of all periods, it is especially common in ancient
legal and religious formulae and in popular sayings. As
the latter appear in large numbers in the more familiar
letters, alliteration becomes one of the stylistic characteristics of Cicero's correspondence. Cf. *cura, cogitatio, . . .
commentatio causarum* (*Fam.* 9. 20. 1) ; *opera et oleum* (*Att.*
2. 17. 1).

94. *Asyndeton.* In addition to asyndeton for emphasis
and between clauses in lively narration, which is found
in contemporaneous formal literature, Böckel [1] calls attention
to two classes of cases in which asyndeton occurs in the
Letters, as it does in other colloquial literature, with great
frequency : (1) between two expressions of opposite meaning, e.g. *palam secreto* (Cael., *Fam.* 8. 1. 4), *velit nolit* (*Q.
fr.* 3. 8. 4) ; (2) between two expressions of similar meaning,
e.g. *intercedendi impediendi* (*Fam.* 8. 8. 6), *certa clara* (*Att.* 16.
13c. 2). Many of these expressions, like those discussed
under *Alliteration*, are stereotyped popular phrases.

95. *Brevity.* Brevity is secured in many cases by the use
of pregnant expressions, and by the omission of words and
phrases not absolutely necessary to the sense. The words
most commonly omitted are *esse, dicere* (many forms of both
words are omitted), *fieri, aedes,* and the pronoun as an
object or as the subject of an infinitive.

In some instances more uncommon ellipses occur, e.g.
ex Gallia [*provincia*] *Lepidi* (Pollio, *Fam.* 10. 33. 4); *hoc
magis animadversum est, quod intactus ab sibilo pervenerat
Hortensius ad senectutem ; sed tum tam bene* (*sibilatus est*) *ut
in totam vitam quoivis satis esset* (Cael., *Fam.* 8. 2. 1). Cf.
also § 75, and note to *a Vestae, Epist.* XIII. 2.

[1] *Att.* 8. 3. 3.

96. *Extravagance in Expression.* Formal literary compositions which are intended for publication, and which must therefore submit to the criticism of the general public, are more reserved in their expression than is the familiar intercourse between friends, whether carried on by conversation or correspondence. Abundant illustration of this fact is offered in the letters which passed between Cicero and his intimate friends, both in the use of single words and complete statements, e.g. *immortalis* = *magnas* (Plancus, *Fam.* 10. 11. 1): *immortalis ago tibi gratias; infinitis* = *multis* (Pollio, *Fam.* 10. 32. 4): *infinitis pollicitationibus.* Cf. also *nam, cum maximam cepissem laetitiam ex humanissimi et carissimi patris epistula, tum vero iucundissimae tuae litterae cumulum mihi gaudii attulerunt* (Cicero *filius, Fam.* 16. 21. 1). Cf. note to *demiror, Epist.* XXVI. 4.

97. *Greek Words and Phrases.* As Tyrrell remarks,[1] Greek words and phrases generally appear in the Correspondence as technical terms in philosophy, rhetoric, politics, medicine, and as slang phrases. Doubtless, also, as Cicero himself intimates, Greek was occasionally used as a possible protection if a letter should fall into the hands of an enemy. The Greek technical terms played the same part with reference to Latin that many of the corresponding technical terms borrowed from Latin play in modern composition, while the Greek popular expressions in the Letters may be compared with current French phrases. Cf. also note to παρρησίαν, *Epist.* V. 8.

98. *Exclamatory Questions.* These questions belong to the language of everyday life, and almost every one of the familiar letters offers illustrations of the use of such exclamatory phrases as *quid iam ? cur hoc ?* etc. Cf. also § 92 and note to *quid quaeris, Epist.* V. 4.

99. *Figurative Language.* One of the most pronounced

[1] Vol. I.² pp. 66–7.

characteristics of colloquial language is its fondness for the picturesque. This is secured mainly by the use of metaphors. One of the commonest figures employed in the Letters is that drawn from heat and cold, — the former indicating activity, the latter inertia: e.g. *illi rumores de comitiis Transpadanorum Cumarum tenus caluerunt* (Cael., *Fam.* 8. 1. 2); *cum Romae a iudiciis forum refrixerit* (*Att.* 1. 1. 2); *scripsi Curionem valde frigere, iam calet* (Cael., *Fam.* 8. 6. 5). Commercial, legal, and popular expressions, in a figurative sense, also occur in great variety. Cf. also notes to *quas ego pugnas et quantas strages edidi*, *Epist.* V. 1, and *medicinam*, *Epist.* IX. 2.

100. *Polite Phrases.* Such polite phrases as *si me amas* (e.g. Vatin., *Fam.*, 5. 9. 1), *amabo te* (e.g. Cael., *Fam.* 8. 6. 5), and such terms of endearment as *mel ac deliciae tuae* (Cael., *Fam.* 8. 8. 1), are naturally of frequent occurrence. Apparently the Plautine *sis* (*si vis*) and *sodes* are not used. Cf. also notes to *nostri amores*, *Epist.* VII. 2, *si me amas*, *Epist.* XIII. 3, and *molestum*, *Epist.* XVIII. 10.

101. *Pleonasm.* While aiming at brevity in some cases, in others familiar speech indulges itself in duplicative or pleonastic expressions for the sake of emphasis or distinctness, in much the same way as it employs extravagant language. Instances from the Letters are *rursus reducere* (Balbus, *Att.* 8. 15a. 1); *malle potius* (Cato, *Fam.* 15. 5. 2); *nostro iudicio . . . existimamus* (Balbus and Oppius, *Att.* 9. 7a. 1), *ostentare crebro* (Dolabella, *Fam.* 9. 9. 2). On 'double expressions,' cf. note to *oro obsecro*, *Epist.* L. 1. See also § 79.

102. *Popular and Proverbial Expressions.* The informal character of the Letters is shown, not so much by the frequent use of these expressions, although their number in the aggregate is large, as by the fact that they are unaccompanied by any such apologetic phrase as *ut aiunt*, by which Cicero commonly introduces proverbial expressions and popular sayings in formal composition. Instances of popular expressions are *duo parietes de eadem fidelia dealbare* (Curius, *Fam.* 7. 29. 2) ; *sus Minervam* [*docet*] (*Fam.* 9. 18. 3) ; *pictus et politus* (*Att.* 2. 21. 4); *sciens prudensque* (Cael., *Fam.* 8. 16. 5).

103. *Play upon Words, etc.* In the same connection mention may be made of the fondness which Cicero and some of his correspondents show for playing upon words in their familiar letters. Illustrations are *tu istic te Hateriano iure* [jurisprudence] *delectas, ego me hic Hirtiano* [*iure*, 'sauce'] (*Fam.* 9. 18. 3) ; *tu, qui ceteris cavere didicisti, in Britannia ne ab essedariis decipiaris caveto*, 'you who have learned how to draw up securities for others, look out for your own security — and don't be taken in by the essedarii' (*Fam.* 7. 6. 2). Cicero's letters to his legal friend Trebatius (*Fam.* Bk. 7) are full of legal puns. Other good instances of similar witticisms are to be found in *Att.* 1. 16. 10 and in the letters to Paetus (*Fam.* Bk. 9). Cf. also notes to *honoris causa*, *Epist.* XIX. 2, and *occidione occisum*, XXXIV. 7. Cicero had a great reputation for wit of this sort (cf. *Fam.* 9. 16. 4), and after his death his secretary Tiro edited his witty sayings. Cf. Quint. 6. 3. 5 ; Macrob. *Sat.* 2. 1. 12.

104. In conclusion it may be noted that in his discussion of public and private affairs of a delicate character, Cicero often considered it discreet to express himself in language which would be unintelligible to every one save the person for whom the letter in question was intended. As he himself puts it in one case : *sed haec scripsi properans et mehercule timide; posthac ad te aut, si perfidelem habebo cui dem, scribam plane omnia aut, si obscure scribam, tu tamen intelleges; in iis epistulis me Laelium, te Furium faciam* ; *cetera erunt* ἐν αἰνιγμοῖς (*Att.* 2. 19. 5). As a result of this policy there are some puzzling passages in the Letters which still frustrate the efforts of commentators to explain them. The difficulty of such passages is often increased by the ill-founded conjectures of early editors, or by the mistakes of copyists who were puzzled by obscure phrases or by unfamiliar Greek words. To these difficulties must be added the fact that in general only one side of the correspondence is preserved to us, and that brief reference is often made to persons and events about whose character our information can only be conjectural. In view of these facts, the success which has attended the interpretation of the Letters is remarkable.

CICERO'S LETTERS

—••✦❈✦••—

I. (*Att.* 1. 1.)

CICERO ATTICO SAL.

Petitionis nostrae, quam tibi summae curae esse 1
scio, huiusmodi ratio est, quod adhuc coniectura pro-
videri possit. Prensat unus P. Galba: sine fuco ac
fallaciis more maiorum negatur. Vt opinio est hominum, non aliena rationi nostrae fuit illius haec praepropera prensatio; nam illi ita negant vulgo ut mihi
se debere dicant: ita quiddam spero nobis profici, cum

I. Rome, July, 65 B.C. The
tenth letter of the extant correspondence ; the earlier letters being
Att. I. 5, 6, 7 (68 B.C.) ; 9, 8, 10,
11 (67 B.C.); 3, 4 (66 B.C.). The
letter is interesting for the light
which it throws in general upon
methods of electioneering at
Rome, and in particular upon
Cicero's political plans and prospects a year before the elections
at which he intended to be a candidate for the consulship. On the
elections, cf. also Herzog, I. pp.
654–661.

Cicero Attico sal.: cf. Intr. 62.
This form of greeting, which precedes all the extant letters to Atticus, is probably not authentic.

1. **petitionis** : technical expression for a political canvass. Its
position indicates that it is the
subject of the letter. — **summae**

curae: cf. *minori curae*, Ep. XXV.
2 n. — **prensat**, etc.: *i.e.* 'Galba
alone is making an open canvass';
probably with reference to the
practice of personally seeking
votes or winning friends by shak-
ing hands with, and talking with,
voters in the Forum and other
public places. — **unus**: Antonius
and Cornificius have not yet begun
an active canvass, although their
intentions are known. On P. Sulpicius Galba, cf. *Verr.* i. 30. —
fuco ac fallaciis: see Intr. 93;
cf. below, *more maiorum, praepropera prensatio, frontem ferias.*
— **more maiorum**: to be joined
closely with **negatur**; cf. similar
expressions, *Fam.* 7. 18. 3 *ego te
Balbo . . . more Romano commendabo*, and *Fam.* 7. 5. 3.— **praepropera**: Galba is canvassing in
July, 65 B.C., although the election

hoc percrebrescit, plurimos nostros amicos inveniri. Nos autem initium prensandi facere cogitaramus eo ipso tempore quo tuum puerum cum his litteris proficisci Cincius dicebat, in campo comitiis tribuniciis a. d. xvi Kalend. Sextiles. Competitores, qui certi esse videantur, Galba et Antonius et Q. Cornificius — puto te in hoc aut risisse aut ingemuisse; ut frontem ferias, sunt qui etiam Caesonium putent. Aquilium non arbitramur, qui denegat et iuravit morbum et illud suum regnum iudiciale opposuit; Catilina, si iudicatum erit meridie non lucere, certus erit competitor; de Aufidio et de Palicano non puto te exspectare dum

will not take place before July, 64 B.C. — **cogitaramus** and **dicebat**: epistolary tenses, representing respectively the perfect and present; cf. Intr. 84 *c*. The statement is put in the form in which the facts would present themselves to Atticus when the letter should be received. — **puerum**, *servant;* referring to the *tabellarius* (see Intr. 64). — **Cincius**: one of the agents (*procuratores*) of Atticus. — **a.d. xvi Kalend. Sextiles**: this was not the formal announcement (*professio*) on Cicero's part of his intention of standing for the consulship, as the latter would be made on the day on which notice of the election was given, *i.e.* three *nunainae,* or 17 days, before the day of the election. Cf. Herzog, I. p. 656, 1092, n. 2. — **Antonius**: Cicero's colleague in 63 B.C. — **Q. Cornificius**: the father of the orator and politician Q. Cornificius, to whom *Fam.* 12. 17–30 are addressed. — **risisse aut ingemuisse**: on hearing that such nobodies aspire to the consulship. The situation, while humorous, is also one to excite the indignation of a patriot. — **frontem ferias**: cf. *Brut.* 278 *nulla perturbatio animi, nulla corporis, frons non percussa, non femur.* Cicero speaks of Caesonius in a very different way in *Verr.* i. 29 *homo in rebus iudicandis spectatus et cognitus.* — **Aquilium**: *sc. competitorem fore.* C. Aquilius Gallus was praetor with Cicero in 66 B.C. — **iuravit morbum**: the simple acc. after *iurare* is rare. The phrase is probably a legal one ; cf. *Fam.* 8. 3 *cum calumniam iurasset. Iurare morbum* means 'to take an oath that one is ill' as an excuse for the nonperformance of some duty. — **regnum iudiciale**: Aquilius was a well-known jurist (*pro Caec.* 77), too much occupied with legal business to engage in politics. Cf. *regno forensi,* Ep. LXII. 1. — **iudicatum erit**: in the approaching trial of Catiline for misappropriation of public funds. The accuser was Cicero's subsequent enemy Clodius. — **Aufidio**: a former praetor in Asia (cf. *pro Flacco,* 45). — **Palicano**: a tribune in 71 B.C. Cicero's actual opponents at the polls were Galba and Catiline, patri-

scribam. De iis qui nunc petunt, Caesar certus puta- 2
tur; Thermus cum Silano contendere existimatur, qui
sic inopes et ab amicis et existimatione sunt ut mihi
videatur non esse ἀδύνατον Curium obducere, sed hoc
praeter me nemini videtur. Nostris rationibus maxime
conducere videtur Thermum fieri cum Caesare; nemo
est enim ex iis qui nunc petunt qui, si in nostrum
annum reciderit, firmior candidatus fore videatur, propterea quod curator est viae Flaminiae, quae tum erit absoluta sane facile; eum libenter nunc Caesari consulem

cians; C. Antonius, Q. Cornificius,
L. Cassius Longinus, and C. Licinius Sacerdos, plebeians (cf. Ascon. *argum.* to *Or. in toga cand.*).

2. **qui nunc petunt,** *who are
candidates this year.* — **Caesar:**
L. Julius Caesar, uncle of Antony the triumvir, and, by the
second marriage of his sister
Julia, brother-in-law of Lentulus,
the Catilinarian conspirator. He
tried unsuccessfully to mediate in
43 B.C. between the senate and
Antony (*Phil.* 8. 1). He was
placed by Antony upon the list of
the proscribed in return for the
consent of Octavius to the murder
of Cicero, and escaped death only
through the devotion of his sister
Julia. — **certus:** here 'sure to win.'
This expectation was realized. —
Thermus cum Silano: the consuls for 64 B.C. (cf. Ep. II.) were
L. Julius Caesar and C. Marcius
Figulus, so that either another
candidate than the three mentioned
here came to the front and was
elected, or else Thermus became
Figulus by adoption and held the
office under that name. It was
D. Junius Silanus who, as *consul
designatus*, and therefore first
speaker in the senate, proposed
that Lentulus and his fellow-con-

spirators should be put to death
(*Cat.* 4. 7). — **Thermus . . . existimatur:** *i.e.* it is expected that
there will be a hard fight between
Thermus and Silanus. — **ab amicis :** *ab* is not infrequently used to
introduce a limitation with adjectives which signify power, equip-
ment, or their opposites, *e.g. ab
equitatu firmus,* Ep. XCVIII. 2; *ab
omni re sumus paratiores, Fam.* 10.
8. 6, and elsewhere. — **Curium obducere:** *i.e.* to run Curius in opposition. Curius, evidently a man
held in light esteem, may have
been the Quintus Curius who informed Cicero of Catiline's plans.
— **Thermum fieri:** *sc. consulem.*
— **si in nostrum annum reciderit,** *if he goes over to my year,*
i.e. to the election for 63 B.C.
— **viae Flaminiae:** the great
northern thoroughfare from Rome
to the Adriatic. The completion
(**absoluta**) of this road would, as
Cicero thinks, give Thermus political prestige and influence, and
therefore make him a dangerous
opponent a year later, although at
the time of writing he has few
followers (**inopes ab amicis**).
" The great Roman roads, such as
the *via Appia, Flaminia,* etc., were
called *viae praetoriae* or *consula-*

accuderim. Petitorum haec est adhuc informata cogitatio. Nos in omni munere candidatorio fungendo
summam adhibebimus diligentiam et fortasse, quoniam
videtur in suffragiis multum posse Gallia, cum Romae
a iudiciis forum refrixerit, excurremus mense Septembri legati ad Pisonem, ut Ianuario revertamur. Cum
perspexero voluntates nobilium, scribam ad te. Cetera
spero prolixa esse, his dumtaxat urbanis competitoribus; illam manum tu mihi cura ut praestes, quoniam
propius abes, Pompei, nostri amici: nega me ei iratum

res, and were under the charge of *curatores.*" Tyrrell from Momm. *St. R.* II³. p. 454. — **accuderim** : the conjecture of Boot (see Crit. App.) ; a Plautine word. — **informata cogitatio,** *general impression.* — **Gallia** (*Cispadana*): it possessed the right of suffrage; cf. *Phil.* 2. 76 *municipia coloniasque Galliae a qua nos . . . petere consulatum solebamus.* — **cum . . . refrixerit,** *when the heat of business in the courts at Rome shall have cooled down.* On **refrixerit,** cf. Intr. 99. — **mense Septembri:** the *ludi Magni* or *Romani* began Sept. 4 and lasted 15 days, and later in the year came the *ludi Plebeii,* the *Saturnalia,* etc., so that little legal business could be done between Sept. 1 and Jan. 1.— **legati:** the reference is to a *legatio libera,* an unofficial embassy. Senators favored with such a privilege could travel for their own pleasure or profit with the title and the rights of a *legatus,* and receive supplies from government agents without performing any official duties. The provinces found this senatorial junketing such a burden that Cicero in his consulship placed certain limitations upon it. — **Pisonem :** proconsul in Gallia

Narbonensis. He was afterwards defended by Cicero against a charge of maladministration (*repetundae*) while governor of this province. — **voluntates nobilium:** the aristocracy were probably at this moment little inclined to support Cicero's candidacy, and voted for him the next year only because he was the candidate most likely to defeat Catiline and the democrats. — **his . . . competitoribus,** *provided that civilians are my only rivals ;* for if some one returns from a successful military campaign to stand for the consulship, the result will be more uncertain. — **manum:** the support of Pompey. By the provisions of the Manilian law, Pompey had the year before been given charge of the war against Mithridates. Cicero's advocacy of that bill would naturally secure for him Pompey's support in the consular election. Atticus, who was at this time in Athens, and therefore nearer than Cicero to Pompey, was asked to make sure of Pompey's assistance; or, perhaps, as Tyrrell thinks, **manum** refers to the followers of Pompey, some of whom might return to Rome in time for the election.

fore, si ad mea comitia non venerit.   Atque haec 3
huiusmodi sunt.   Sed est quod abs te mihi ignosci
pervelim.   Caecilius, avunculus tuus, a P. Vario cum
magna pecunia fraudaretur, agere coepit cum eius fratre A. Caninio Satyro de iis rebus quas eum dolo malo
mancipio accepisse de Vario diceret; una agebant
ceteri creditores, in quibus erat L. Lucullus et P. Scipio et is quem putabant magistrum fore, si bona veni-

---

3. **pervelim**: cf. Intr. 77. —
Caecilius: for the relations existing between Caecilius and Atticus
and the desire of Atticus to continue on good terms with his
uncle, cf. Nepos, *Att.* 5 *habebat
avunculum Q. Caecilium, equitem
Romanum, familiarem L. Luculli,
divitem, difficillima natura. Cuius
sic asperitatem veritus est, ut, quem
nemo ferre posset, huius sine offensi-
one ad summam senectutem retinu-
erit benevolentiam. Quo facto tulit
pietatis fructum. Caecilius enim
moriens testamento adoptavit eum
heredemque fecit ex dodrante; ex
qua hereditate accepit circiter cen-
tiens sestertium.* Cf. also Intr. 58.
Cicero's dilemma is therefore a
serious one. If he accedes to the
request of Caecilius, and appears
against Satyrus, he will antagonize
Satyrus and the latter's friend
Domitius, who are at present very
friendly to him and would be of
great service to him politically. If
he declines to accommodate Caecilius, he will offend the crabbed
old gentleman and Atticus in some
degree, and perhaps jeopardize the
chances of Atticus for his uncle's
property. Caecilius died five years
later (*Att.* 3. 20. I). — **agere . . .
cum**, *has begun a suit against.* —
fratre, *cousin;* cf. *Att.* 1. 5. 1. —
dolo malo: the formulae *de dolo
malo,* first drawn up by the juris-
consult Aquilius Gallus (§ 1), were
used in actions for damages on
the ground of fraud. *Cum ex eo
(Aquilio) quaereretur quid esset
dolus malus, respondebat, cum esset
aliud simulatum, aliud actum*
(Cic. *de Off.* 3. 60). In this case
Varius would seem to have transferred his property to Satyrus, to
save it from seizure by the creditors. — **mancipio accepisse,** *to
have purchased.* mancipio (*manus + capio*) refers to the practice
on the part of the purchaser of
laying his hand upon the article
purchased in the presence of five
witnesses, as the binding act in his
acquisition of the article. — **diceret**: 'by a carelessness of expression, the verb of saying or thinking is sometimes put in the subjunctive instead of the thing said'
(Tyrrell). — **L. Lucullus**: Pompey's predecessor in command of
the army acting against Mithridates. — **P. Scipio**: best known
as commander of the Pompeian
forces at the battle of Thapsus
in 46 B.C. Cf. *Bell. Afr.* 79–86.
— **magistrum** (*sc. auctionis*): the
bids at auctions were received and
called out by the *praeco,* but the
general management of such a sale
was in the hands of a *magister auctionis,* who kept a record of the
articles sold and in general was the
legal representative of the owner.

rent, L. Pontius.   Verum hoc ridiculum est de magis-
tro.   Nunc cognosce rem.   Rogavit me Caecilius ut
adessem contra Satyrum.   Dies fere nullus est quin
hic Satyrus domum meam ventitet; observat L. Domitium maxime, me habet proximum; fuit et mihi et Q.
4 fratri magno usui in nostris petitionibus.   Sane sum
perturbatus cum ipsius Satyri familiaritate, tum Do-
miti, in quo uno maxime ambitio nostra nititur.   De-
monstravi haec Caecilio; simul et illud ostendi, si ipse
unus cum illo uno contenderet, me ei satisfacturum
fuisse, nunc in causa universorum creditorum, hominum praesertim amplissimorum, qui sine eo quem Caecilius suo nomine perhiberet facile causam communem
sustinerent, aequum esse eum et officio meo consulere
et tempori.   Durius accipere hoc mihi visus est quam
vellem et quam homines belli solent, et postea prorsus
ab instituta nostra paucorum dierum consuetudine
longe refugit.   Abs te peto ut mihi hoc ignoscas et
me existimes humanitate esse prohibitum, ne contra
amici summam existimationem miserrimo eius tempore

— **L. Pontius** (*Aquila*) : in later
years an active opponent of Caesar
and one of the conspirators against
him. He was killed near Mutina, in
the battle against Antony, in which
Hirtius fell (*Fam.* 10. 33. 4). —
adessem: in the legal sense of
appearing as an *advocatus*. — **L.
Domitium** (*Ahenobarbum*) : best
known as the commandant of the
fortress of Corfinium in 49 B.C.
The loss of this town through the
irresolution and cowardice of Domitius removed the main obstacle
in the way of Caesar's march to
Rome. The intense interest felt
by the Pompeians at that time in
his fate is plainly indicated by *Att.*

8. 12 c; 8. 7; 8. 8.   He was killed
while fleeing from Pharsalus. —
in nostris petitionibus: Marcus
Cicero had been quaestor, aedile,
and praetor; Quintus had probably held the quaestorship and
aedileship.

4. **ambitio nostra,** *my political
hopes.* — **illo:** *i.e. Satyro.* — **officio
. . . tempori,** *my duty* (to Satyrus)
and (the exigency of) *my position*
(as a candidate). — **homines belli,**
gentlemen. — **abs te**: archaic, and
more frequent in Cicero's earlier
writings (cf. § 3).   In later years
he inclines to *a te.* — **ne . . . venirem**: a conviction for *dolus malus*
would have been followed by *in-*

venirem, cum is omnia sua studia et officia in me con-
tulisset; quod si voles in me esse durior, ambitionem
putabis mihi obstitisse; ego autem arbitror, etiamsi id
sit, mihi ignoscendum esse, ἐπεὶ οὐχ ἱερήϊον οὐδὲ βοείην ;
vides enim in quo cursu simus et quam omnes gratias
non modo retinendas, verum etiam acquirendas putemus.   Spero tibi me causam probasse, cupio quidem
certe.   Hermathena tua valde me delectat et posita 5
ita belle est ut totum gymnasium eius ἀνάθημα esse
videatur.   Multum te amamus.

II. (*Att.* I. 2.)

CICERO ATTICO SAL.

L. Iulio Caesare C. Marcio Figulo consulibus filiolo 1

famia (Tyrrell). — ἐπεὶ οὐχ ἱερήϊον
οὐδὲ βοείην: *Il.* XXII. 159. The
meaning is 'since it is no small
prize I fight for.'

5. **Hermathena**: a double-
faced statue or bust, similar to
those found in excavations to-day.
One face was that of Hermes, the
other that of Athena. — **ut totum
gymnasium . . . videatur**: this
is the MS. reading, but is scarcely
intelligible; perhaps it means, 'so
that the whole gymnasium seems
to be an offering to it' (Watson).
— **multum te amamus**: a colloquial expression of gratitude.

II. Rome, the latter part of 65
B.C. The historical value of this
letter springs from the fact that it
fixes the date of the birth of Cicero's son (65 B.C.), that it contains
the main point in the evidence with
reference to Cicero's defense of
Catiline against the charge of misappropriation of public money, and
accounts for the absence of letters
between Cicero and Atticus from

64–62 B.C. inclusive (cf. last sentence).

1. **L. Iulio Caesare C. Marcio
Figulo consulibus**: the natural
meaning would be, 'in the consulship of,' etc., and would make
64 B.C. the date of this letter, but
the reference to the approaching
trial of Catiline proves that it
must have been written in 65 B.C.,
after the election of the new consuls, as the trial was begun and finished in that year. The brevity and
apparent lack of feeling in Cicero's
announcement to his most intimate friend of the birth of his
son has called forth severe criticisms from his enemies, and apologies from his friends (cf. Abeken,
pp. 33, 34) — quite without reason.
Both parties have failed to see the
gay humor of the passage which
couples this important event in his
family life with the most important
event in the political world. For
an account of the new consuls, cf.
Ep. I. — **filiolo**: for an account

me auctum scito salva Terentia.　Abs te tamdiu nihil
litterarum!　Ego de meis ad te rationibus scripsi antea
diligenter.　Hoc tempore Catilinam, competitorem
nostrum, defendere cogitamus.　Iudices habemus quos
voluimus, summa accusatoris voluntate.　Spero, si absolutus erit, coniunctiorem illum nobis fore in ratione
2 petitionis; sin aliter acciderit, humaniter feremus.　Tuo
adventu nobis opus est maturo; nam prorsus summa
hominum est opinio tuos familiares, nobiles homines,

of him, see Intr. 54. — **scito**, *let
me inform you;* a favorite expression borrowed from colloquial
Latin, for introducing a bit of
news. Cf. the use of *habeto* and *sic
habeto*, Ep. XXVI. 1 n.—**Terentia:**
cf. Intr. 52. — **abs te . . . ego,**
not a word from YOU *in so long a
time, while* I, etc.　For **abs te**,
cf. Ep. I. 4 n.— **hoc tempore . . .
cogitamus :** it will never be certainly known whether Cicero did
defend Catiline in 65 B.C. or not,
but this passage certainly indicates
such an intention on his part, and
there is no satisfactory reason for
believing that he did not carry out
his purpose.　The fact that Cicero
believed in Catiline's guilt (cf. Ep.
I. 1) would not, perhaps, have de-
terred him, as he in later years
undertook the defense of Vatinius,
Gabinius, and C. Antonius, equally
notorious men, under still more
questionable circumstances, when
political considerations, as in this
case, made it seem advisable. For
the arguments in support of the
opposite view, cf. Tyrrell, I². pp.
8, 9. — **summa accusatoris voluntate :** the charge was brought
by P. Clodius. The accuser had
the right of challenging peremp-to-
rily a certain number of jurors,
and the phrase quoted above
would indicate that Clodius had

availed himself of this privilege in
rejecting jurors who were likely to
vote for a conviction. If this view
be correct, Clodius was really acting in the interest of Catiline in
bringing the charge, since if Catiline were acquitted, he could not
be put on trial again.　This method of protecting criminals, called
praevaricatio, became commoner
in later years (cf. Plin. *Epist.* 3.
9. 33–35).　The method to be
employed in securing an acquittal
for Catiline casts more of a shad-
ow upon Cicero's honor than the
fact that he intended to undertake
or did undertake the defense.

2. **tuos familiares :** probably
ironical, although it is true that
Atticus was intimate with many of
the prominent men in Rome (cf.
Nep. *Atticus*, 15, 16, 18). — **nobiles homines . . . fore :** referring probably to the aristocracy
as a body; cf. *voluntates nobilium*,
Ep. I. 2 n, and the following significant utterance in regard to the
attitude of the Optimates from
the *de Petitione Consulatus*, 13,
written by Quintus to his brother
a few months later, *noli putare
eos, qui sunt eo honore usi, non
videre, tu cum idem sis adeptus,
quid dignitatis habiturus sis : eos
vero, qui consularibus familiis nati
locum maiorum consecuti non sunt,*

adversarios honori nostro fore.   Ad eorum voluntatem
mihi conciliandam maximo te mihi usui fore video.
Quare Ianuario mense, ut constituisti, cura ut Romae
sis.

III. (*Fam.* 5. 7.)

M. TVLLIVS M. F. CICERO S. D. CN. POMPEIO CN. F.
MAGNO IMPERATORI.

S. t. e. q. v. b. e.   Ex litteris tuis, quas publice mi- 1
sisti, cepi una cum omnibus incredibilem voluptatem;
tantam enim spem oti ostendisti quantam ego semper
omnibus te uno fretus pollicebar.   Sed hoc scito, tuos

suspicor tibi, nisi si qui admodum te amant, invidere. Hortensius and Crassus may have been particularly in Cicero's thoughts. Besides the feeling of distrust which certain members of the aristocracy cherished toward this *novus homo,* many of them were offended by his previous democratic tendencies as shown, for instance, in the prosecution of Verres, and by his willingness to rob the oligarchy of its power for the benefit of Pompey in the case of the Manilian law. Cf. *de Pet. Cons.* 4, 5; Sall. *Cat.* 23 end, and Intr. 4. — **Ianuario . . . Romae sis**: the next letter to Atticus (*Att.* 1. 12) was written in 61 B.C. The break in the correspondence is explained by the presence of Atticus in Rome or its vicinity.

III. Rome, Apr., 62 B.C. In Dec., 63 B.C. Cicero had sent to Pompey, who was in the East, a somewhat lengthy letter (now lost), in which he had given a *résumé* of the achievements of his consulship. This letter, written proba-

bly in that egotistical vein which characterizes many of Cicero's utterances in regard to his consulship, apparently offended Pompey, who replied in a brief, unsympathetic letter. At the same time, Pompey sent a letter to the senate containing no word of commendation for Cicero. The letter before us was written upon the receipt of these two epistles. For the formula of greeting, see Intr. 62.

1. **S. t. e. q. v. b. e.** : for *si tu exercitusque valetis, bene est;* a stereotyped form of salutation which Cicero uses only in official or formal letters, or in replying to some one who has employed it in writing to him. Intr. 62. — **publice,** *officially,* to the magistrates and senate. Cf. *Fam.* 15. 1. — **tantam . . . spem oti**: along with the carrying out of other projects, Pompey had in 64 B.C. reduced Syria and Cilicia into provinces, so that his work of subjugation in the East was practically ended. — **pollicebar**: in particular in the oration for the Manilian law. —

veteres hostis, novos amicos vehementer litteris per-
2 culsos atque ex magna spe deturbatos iacere. Ad me
autem litteras quas misisti, quamquam exiguam signifi-
cationem tuae erga me voluntatis habebant, tamen mihi
scito iucundas fuisse; nulla enim re tam laetari soleo
quam meorum officiorum conscientia, quibus si quando
non mutue respondetur, apud me plus offici residere
facillime patior. Illud non dubito, quin, si te mea
summa erga te studia parum mihi adiunxerint, res p.
3 nos inter nos conciliatura coniuncturaque sit. Ac, ne
ignores quid ego in tuis litteris desiderarim, scribam
aperte, sicut et mea natura et nostra amicitia postulat.
Res eas gessi, quarum aliquam in tuis litteris et nostrae
necessitudinis et rei p. causa gratulationem exspectavi,
quam ego abs te praetermissam esse arbitror quod
verebare ne cuius animum offenderes; sed scito ea,
quae nos pro salute patriae gessimus, orbis terrae iudicio ac testimonio comprobari, quae, cum veneris, tanto
consilio tantaque animi magnitudine a me gesta esse
cognosces, ut tibi, multo maiori quam Africanus fuit,

veteres hostis, novos amicos:
the democrats, probably, to whose
support Pompey owed his present
position. Probably the friendly
tone of Pompey's letter to the
senate made them fear an alliance
between Pompey and that body.
— **iacere,** *are overwhelmed.*

2. **mea . . . studia:** Cicero's
efforts in behalf of the Manilian
law, his advocacy of a *senatus consultum* decreeing a thanksgiving
of 10 days in honor of Pompey's
victories in the East (cf. *Prov.
Cons.* 27), as well as various complimentary public utterances, *e.g.
Cat.* 4. 21.

3. **in tuis litteris:** the clause

ne . . . offenderes shows that
Cicero is referring to Pompey's letter to the senate (Böckel). — **ne
. . . offenderes:** those who sympathized with the Catilinarian conspirators, those who on constitutional grounds opposed their execution, the democrats in general,
and Cicero's enemies in particular,
would have all taken umbrage if
Pompey had approved Cicero's
course in 63 B.C. — **orbis terrae:**
the entire world, while *orbis terrarum* indicates the Roman world.
The phrase employed here is used,
therefore, to exaggerate Cicero's
fame. — **Africanus . . . Laelium:**
Böckel quotes, in explanation of

iam me, non multo minorem quam Laelium, facile et in
re p. et in amicitia adiunctum esse patiare.

IV. (*Fam.* 7. 23.)

CICERO S. D. M. FADIO GALLO.

Tantum quod ex Arpinati veneram cum mihi a te 1
litterae redditae sunt, ab eodemque accepi Aviani litteras, in quibus hoc inerat liberalissimum, nomina se
facturum, cum venisset, qua ego vellem die.   Fac,
quaeso, qui ego sum, esse te: estne aut tui pudoris aut
nostri primum rogare de die, deinde plus annua postulare ?   Sed essent, mi Galle, omnia facilia, si et ea
mercatus esses quae ego desiderabam, et ad eam summam quam volueram; ac tamen ista ipsa, quae te
emisse scribis, non solum rata mihi erunt, sed etiam
grata; plane enim intellego te non modo studio, sed

Cicero's meaning, *de Re Pub.* 1.
18 *fuit enim hoc in amicitia quasi
quoddam ius inter illos, ut militiae
propter eximiam belli gloriam Af-
ricanum ut deum coleret Laelius,
domi vicissim Laelium, quod aetate
antecedebat, observaret in parentis
loco Scipio.* — **Laelium**: attracted
into acc. by **me**.
   IV. Rome, 62 B.C. M. Fadius
Gallus was a personal friend of
Cicero, to whom he wrote *Fam.*
7. 23–27. Cf. *Fam.* 13. 59 *M.
Fadium unice diligo summaque
mihi cum eo consuetudo et fami-
liaritas est pervetus.*   He was a
man of artistic and literary tastes.
Like Cicero, he wrote a eulogy of
Cato. Cf. Ep. LXXXI. 2.
   1. **tantum quod**: equivalent to
commodum; cf. *Att.* 15. 13. 7.
This usage, perhaps a colloquial

one, became comparatively frequent in post-Augustan prose, *e.g.
navis Alexandrina, quae tantum
quod appulerat,* Suet. *Aug.* 98. —
Arpinati: Cicero inherited his
villa at Arpinum from his father
(*de Leg. Agr.* 3. 8). He had fitted
it up in imitation of the villa of
Atticus at Buthrotum. — **Aviani** :
as the sequel shows, Gallus had
made certain purchases of Avianius for Cicero, and Avianius generously offered to delay recording
them until it should suit Cicero's
convenience to pay.   *Nomina facere* is a commercial expression,
meaning to set down items of debt
in an account book. — **rogare de
die** (*sc. solutionis*): 'to ask for
credit' (Tyrrell). — **annua**: *sc. die.*
— **mi Galle**: cf. *mi Pomponi*, Ep.
X n.

etiam amore usum, quae te delectarint, hominem, ut
ego semper iudicavi, in omni iudicio elegantissimum,

2 quae me digna putaris, coemisse. Sed velim maneat
Damasippus in sententia; prorsus enim ex istis empti-
onibus nullam desidero; tu autem ignarus instituti
mei, quanti ego genus omnino signorum omnium non
aestimo, tanti ista quattuor aut quinque sumpsisti.
Bacchas istas cum Musis Metelli comparas. Quid simile? primum ipsas ego Musas numquam tanti putassem, atque id fecissem Musis omnibus approbantibus,
sed tamen erat aptum bibliothecae studiisque nostris
congruens; Bacchis vero ubi est apud me locus? ' At
pulchellae sunt.' Novi optime et saepe vidi: nominatim
tibi signa mihi nota mandassem, si probassem; ea enim
signa ego emere soleo, quae ad similitudinem gymnasi-
orum exornent mihi in palaestra locum. Martis vero
signum quo mihi, pacis auctori? Gaudeo nullum Saturni signum fuisse; haec enim duo signa putarem mihi
aes alienum attulisse. Mercuri mallem aliquod fuisset:

3 felicius, puto, cum Avianio transigere possemus. Quod

2. **Damasippus** had apparently
promised to take the statues if
they did not please Cicero. — **genus omnino signorum omnium.**
all the statues in the world. —
Musis Metelli: statues in the
possession of Metellus. — **tanti
putassem:** *sc.* as you paid for
your Bacchae. — **Musis omnibus
approbantibus:** the Muses themselves would not have been offended at being rated at a lower
price than you paid for the Bacchae. — **erat,** *would have been.* —
Martis . . . pacis auctori: the
Bacchae in Cicero's study would be
absurd enough, but the statue of
Mars would be still more ridiculous

for a man who prided himself upon
being a *dux togatus.* Cf. *Cat.* 3. 23
*togati me uno togato duce et im-
peratore vicistis.* — **aes alienum :**
the quaint comment of Manutius
is: *Martis enim et Saturni signa
nihil prosperum promittere, astrologi confirmant: stulte, qui divi-
nationem rerum futurarum, quae
soli Deo notae sunt, ad suam sci-
entiam revocent.* — **Mercuri :** the
god of good luck, especially in
money matters ; cf. Hor. *Sat.* 2. 3.
68 *reiecta praeda, quam praesens
Mercurius fert ;* Pers. 6. 62 *sum
tibi Mercurius ; venio deus huc ego
ut ille pingitur ;* and Plautus
Amph. 1–14.— **felicius . . . trans-**

tibi destinaras trapezophorum, si te delectat, habebis; sin autem sententiam mutasti, ego habebo scilicet. Ista quidem summa ne ego multo libentius emerim deversorium Tarracinae, ne semper hospiti molestus sim. Omnino liberti mei video esse culpam, cui plane res certas mandaram, itemque Iuni, quem puto tibi notum esse, Aviani familiarem. Exhedria quaedam mihi nova sunt instituta in porticula Tusculani: ea volebam tabellis ornare; etenim, si quid generis istiusmodi me delectat, pictura delectat. Sed tamen, si ista mihi sunt habenda, certiorem velim me facias, ubi sint, quando arcessantur, quo genere vecturae; si enim Damasippus in sententia non manebit, aliquem Pseudodamasippum vel cum iactura reperiemus. Quod ad me de domo scribis iterum, iam id ego proficiscens mandaram meae Tulliae; ea enim ipsa hora acceperam tuas litteras. Egeram etiam cum tuo Nicia, quod is utitur, ut scis, familiariter Cassio. Vt redii autem, prius quam tuas legi has proximas litteras, quaesivi de mea Tullia quid egisset. **4**

igere possemus : *i.e.* with the help of Mercury, the god of bargains.

3. **trapezophorum** : strictly a 'table bearer,' but here, as in a few other passages, it seems to indicate the table itself, perhaps because the support or legs were often made of marble or ivory (Juv. II. 122 ff.) cut into fantastic shapes, *e.g.* of griffins or dolphins, and thus formed the most conspicuous and ornamental part of the table. Cf. also Tyrrell, II. p. 239. — **ne ego** : cf. *ne*, Ep. XVII. 2 n. — **deversorium** : the meagre hotel accommodations in Italy (cf. Hor. *Sat.* I. 5, especially vv. 71–76) made it desirable for wealthy peo-

ple to own houses at which they could stop for a night while journeying from one place to another. Cicero had such lodges apparently at Sinuessa, Cales, and Anagnia. — **exhedria** : these were rooms in private houses set apart for lectures and discussions. Cf. also Tyrrell, II. p. 241. — **Pseudodamasippum** : some imitator of Damasippus. Damasippus (perhaps only a type) was notorious 20 years later, in Horace's time, for his crazy enthusiasm in collecting bric-a-brac and statues ; cf. Hor. *Sat.* 2. 3. 18 ff.

4. **Cassio** : Gallus had probably rented or bought a house from Cassius (Tyrrell conjectures *Crasso*, as the latter had a sister named

Per Liciniam se egisse dicebat (sed opinor Cassium
uti non ita multum sorore); eam porro negare se
audere, cum vir abesset — est enim profectus in Hispaniam Dexius —, illo et absente et insciente migrare.
Est mihi gratissimum tanti a te aestimatam consuetudinem vitae victusque nostri, primum ut eam domum
sumeres, ut non modo prope me, sed plane mecum
habitare posses, deinde ut migrare tanto opere festines.
Sed ne vivam, si tibi concedo, ut eius rei tu cupidior
sis quam ego sum: itaque omnia experiar; video enim
quid mea intersit, quid utriusque nostrum. Si quid
egero, faciam ut scias. Tu et ad omnia rescribes et
quando te exspectem facies me, si tibi videtur, certiorem.

V. (*Att.* i. 16.)

CICERO ATTICO SAL.

1   Quaeris ex me quid acciderit de iudicio, quod tam
praeter opinionem omnium factum sit, et simul vis

Licinia). Licinia, the sister of Cassius, is at present occupying the
house, and does not wish to make
a change during the absence of
her husband in Spain. — **ne vivam** : Cicero's favorite assevera-
tions in the letters are *moriar*, *si*
(*Att.* 5. 20. 6); *ne vivam*, *si* (*Att.*
4. 17. 5); and *ne sim salvus*, *si*
(*Att.* 16. 13 A. 1). His less elegant
correspondent Caelius writes *peream*, *si* (Ep. XLVIII. 2). Horace
uses the latter expression in *Sat.*
2. 1. 6 *peream male*, *si ;* cf. also
dispeream, *ni*, 1. 9. 47.

V. Rome, May, 61 B.C. This
letter tells the story of the trial
of Clodius for sacrilege. Cf.
also Intr. 10 and *Att.* 1. 13. 3.
Knowing the conclusive evidence

against Clodius, the indignation
of the *pontifices*, and the determined stand taken by the senate
in ordering an inquiry, Atticus is
surprised to hear of his acquittal,
and has asked for an explanation.
Cicero in this letter replies to that
inquiry, and explains the condition
of things in the commonwealth
and his own attitude towards Clodius. For further details of the
sacrilege of Clodius, cf. *Att.* 1. 12.
3; 1. 14. 5. On Caesar's attitude
during the trial, cf. Suet. *Iul.* 74
*testis citatus, negavit se quicquam
comperisse, quamvis et mater Aurelia et soror Iulia apud eosdem
iudices omnia ex fide rettulissent.*
On the attitude of Pompey, cf.
Att. 1. 14. 1, 2. The conduct of

scire quo modo ego minus quam soleam proeliatus sim. Respondebo tibi ὕστερον πρότερον Ὁμηρικῶς. Ego enim, quam diu senatus auctoritas mihi defendenda fuit, sic acriter et vehementer proeliatus sum ut clamor concursusque maxima cum mea laude fierent. Quod si tibi umquam sum visus in re publica fortis, certe me in illa causa admiratus esses. Cum enim ille ad contiones confugisset, in iisque meo nomine ad invidiam uteretur, di immortales! quas ego pugnas et quantas

criminal trials in a Roman court was entrusted to the *praetor*, his *consilium*, and the *iudices*. The *praetor* passed upon questions of law, in the decision of which he was assisted by the *consilium*, a body of jurists called in to give legal advice, while questions of fact were relegated to the *iudices*. A list of several hundred *iudices*, chosen under the *lex Aurelia* of 70 B.C. from the ranks of the senators, knights, and *tribuni aerarii* (fiscal officials of the tribes; cf. Momm. *St. R.* III. 189–196), was published at the beginning of each year. From this list the *iudices* for a particular trial were selected by lot. A verdict rendered by a majority of them was valid.

1. **quaeris**: Atticus in his letter had asked Cicero two questions: (1) why the trial of Clodius resulted so unexpectedly in an acquittal; (2) why Cicero proved so poor a fighter. Cicero replies to the second question first, the answer extending to the sentence, *itaque, si causam*, etc., 2, and then to the first one. He applies to this inverted order the phrase ὕστερον πρότερον Ὁμηρικῶς, because, in the first book of the Odyssey, Odysseus is introduced in the midst of his wanderings,

his previous adventures being narrated in subsequent books. — **quod . . . factum sit**: the subjunctive is used because the reason is urged by Atticus. — **senatus auctoritas**: cf. *Att.* I. 14. 5 *cum decerneretur frequenti senatu, contra pugnante Pisone, ad pedes omnium singillatim accidente Clodio, ut consules populum cohortarentur ad rogationem accipiendam.* — **ille**: Clodius. — **cum . . . uteretur**: after the passage in the senate of the resolution given above, *Clodius contiones miseras habebat, in quibus Lucullum, Hortensium, C. Pisonem, Messallam consulem contumeliose laedebat; me tantum 'comperisse' omnia criminabatur (Att. I. 14. 5).* The word '*comperi*' Cicero had unfortunately used so often with reference to the movements of the Catilinarian conspirators (cf. *in Cat.* I. 10 and 3. 4) that it had evidently become a byword with his enemies, and was used by Clodius in taunting him; cf. also *Fam.* 5. 5. 2. — **quas ego**, etc.: cf. also *proeliatus sum* above. Just such extravagant figures drawn from military life as Plautus puts into the mouth of the scheming slave or parasite who has outgeneraled his opponent; cf. *e.g. Capt.* 153, *M. G.* 815, 1156, and the striking passage

strages edidi! quos impetus in Pisonem, in Curionem,
in totam illam manum feci! quo modo sum insectatus
levitatem senum, libidinem iuventutis! Saepe, ita me
di iuvent, te non solum auctorem consiliorum meorum, verum etiam spectatorem pugnarum mirificarum
2 desideravi. Postea vero quam Hortensius excogitavit
ut legem de religione Fufius tribunus pl. ferret, in qua
nihil aliud a consulari rogatione differebat nisi iudicum
genus — in eo autem erant omnia — pugnavitque ut
ita fieret, quod et sibi et aliis persuaserat nullis illum

221–227. With such a warlike people as the Romans were, such metaphors were very natural and effective in the language of every-day life. The use of them here harmonizes with the colloquial tone of the entire letter; cf. also Intr. 99. — **Pisonem**: though consul, and ordered by the senate to further the passage of the law by the *comitia*, Piso was really acting in the interests of Clodius. Cf. note to *senatus auctoritas* above. — **Curionem**: father of the Curio who, as tribune in 50 B.C., defended Caesar so brilliantly in the senate. He led the opposition in the senate to the bill of investigation (*Att.* I. 14. 5). — **senum**: Piso and the elder Curio. — **iuventutis**: the younger Curio and young men like him.

2. **Hortensius**: consul in 69 B.C., and the most prominent leader of the Optimates at this time. He had been the leading orator in Rome until Cicero appeared; cf. *Brut.* I. I. — **de religione**: concerning the sacrilege which had been committed. — **legem ferret**: a technical expression, used of *bringing forward a bill*. A *rogatio* was a bill submitted to the people for confirmation in the *comitia*,

for which the people *were asked* to vote, and affirmative ballots were marked V · R (*uti rogas*). The *rogatio* was in this case to be submitted by a consul (*rogatio consularis*) in accordance with the resolution of the senate quoted above. Cf. note to *senatus auctoritas.* — **iudicum genus**: by the action of the senate, which was submitted to the people for confirmation, a special tribunal would have been established for the trial of Clodius, in which the presiding *praetor* would have chosen the *iudices*. Through the treachery of Piso and the use of force by Clodius this bill was not passed in the *comitia* (*Att.* I. 14. 5). About the middle of February, Fufius, acting in the interests of Clodius, and carrying out a compromise accepted by Hortensius, allowed the passage by the *comitia* of a bill which provided for a court of inquiry, but left the *iudices* to be chosen as usual by lot, since the friends of Clodius thought that in this way a venal jury could be secured more easily, as the defense would have the right under this arrangement to reject a certain number of jurors. — **nullis iudicibus**: the negation belongs logically with **posse**.

iudicibus effugere posse, contraxi vela perspiciens inopiam iudicum neque dixi quicquam pro testimonio, nisi
quod erat ita notum atque testatum ut non possem
praeterire.   Itaque, si causam quaeris absolutionis, ut
iam πρὸς τὸ πρότερον revertar, egestas iudicum fuit et
turpitudo; id autem ut accideret, commissum est Hortensi consilio, qui, dum veritus est ne Fufius ei legi
intercederet, quae ex senatus consulto ferebatur, non
vidit illud, satius esse illum in infamia relinqui ac sordibus quam infirmo iudicio committi, sed ductus odio
properavit rem deducere in iudicium, cum illum plum-
beo gladio iugulatum iri tamen diceret.   Sed iudicium 3
si quaeris quale fuerit, incredibili exitu, sic uti nunc
ex eventu ab aliis, a me tamen ex ipso initio consilium
Hortensi reprehendatur.   Nam, ut reiectio facta est

— **contraxi vela**: Cicero is fond
of figures drawn from ships or
shipwreck; cf., for instance, *Fam.*
12. 25. 5 *quam ob rem, mi Quinte,
conscende nobiscum, et quidem ad
puppim; una navis est iam bonorum omnium, quam quidem nos
damus operam ut rectam teneamus;
utinam prospero cursu! sed, quicumque venti erunt, ars nostra
certe non aberit.* Cf. also the reference to the *shipwrecked* fortunes
of Catiline's followers, and the
comparison of the conspirators to
bilge-water in the *ship of state*
(*in Cat.* 2. 7). — **inopiam**: their
poverty and probable venality. —
neque dixi . . . testatum: Clodius tried to establish an alibi
by proving that on the night in
question he was at Interamna,
90 miles from Rome, while Cicero
testified that Clodius had visited
his house that very day, within
three hours of the time in question (cf. *Att.* 2. 1. 5; Plut. *Cic.* 29).

— πρὸς τὸ πρότερον : to return to
the first question, *i.e. quid acciderit
de iudicio.* — **infamia**, *disgrace*, not
technically, 'loss of citizenship.' —
sordibus: the mourning worn by
persons accused (Watson). — **iugulatum iri** : scarcely a literary
word, but borrowed from colloquial Latin. Thus, cf. Plaut. *Stich.*
581 *ita mi auctores fuere, ut egomet me hodie iugularem fame;* cf.
also Hor. *Sat.* I. 7. 35. — **diceret** :
cf. *diceret*, Ep. I. 3 n.

3. **incredibili exitu**: *sc. fuit;*
cf. Intr. 95. — sic has here the
force of a predicate adjective
after *fuit* to be supplied: 'the
trial was of such a nature.' Cf.
Plaut. *Trin.* 46, Catull. 3. 13,
Hor. *Sat.* 2. 2. 120, Petronius 46;
and see Intr. 85. — **reiectio**: the
prosecution and the defense had,
as with us, the privilege of 'peremptorily challenging' a certain
number of *iudices,* whose places
were then filled by new men. Cf.

clamoribus maximis, cum accusator tamquam censor
bonus homines nequissimos reiceret, reus tamquam
clemens lanista frugalissimum quemque secerneret, ut
primum iudices consederunt, valde diffidere boni coeperunt. Non enim umquam turpior in ludo talario con-
sessus fuit: maculosi senatores, nudi equites, tribuni
non tam aerarii quam, ut appellantur, aerati; pauci
tamen boni inerant, quos reiectione fugare ille non

voluntate, Ep. II. 1 n. — **accusator**: L. Lentulus Crus. — **lanista**:
an owner and trainer of bands of
gladiators. As the kind-hearted
lanista avoids sending his best
gladiators into encounters where
they will be sure to lose their
lives, so the defendant avoids
sending honest men into a jury-
box where they will lose their reputation. For another explanation,
see Tyrrell. The correlation of **ut
facta est** and **ut primum . . .
consederunt** would not be found
in careful prose.— **in ludo talario**:
the *vestis talaris* reached to the
ankles, and was not worn by respectable people (cf. Gell. 6. [7.]
12), and a *ludus talarius* was
probably an entertainment of a
low class where the performers
wore this garment; cf. Fronto,
Ep. p. 160 Naber *laudo censoris
illud, qui ludos talarios (effugeret),
quod semet ipsum diceret, cum ea
praeterisset, difficile dignitati servire, quin ad modum crotali aut
cymbali pedem poneret.* — **maculosi**: perhaps in its general sense,
perhaps with special reference to
men after whose names the censors
had placed a *nota*. — **nudi**, *desti-
tute;* cf. *inopiam*, 2 n. — **tribuni
. . . aerati**: this is difficult to
understand. The common reading is, **non tam aerati . . . aerarii.** The term *aerarii* was some-

times applied to citizens of the
lowest class, outside the limits of
the centuries of the Servian constitution, the 'riffraff' of the pop-
ulation; and the phrase is understood as meaning, 'not so much
tribunes with money (**aerati**) as
tribunes without money or reputation (**aerarii**).' The objections
to this explanation are that the
point is obscure, and that in a list
of the three classes of people
composing the jury, where the
technical designations have been
used in two instances, we expect
to find the third term used, and
used in the technical sense, *i.e.* we
expect *senatores . . . equites, tribuni
non tam aerarii*. The transposi-
tion by a copyist of *aerarii* (or
aerari, as the MS. really reads)
and *aerati* would not be unnatural.
If we may adopt the reading **non
tam aerarii . . . aerati**, the expression would mean 'not so much
tribunes who *have* money (for the
tribuni aerarii had money in
their charge) as tribunes who are
to be *had* for money (**aerati**).'
This reading brings into relief the
essential point, viz. the *venality*
of the judges. This conjecture
was first put forward by Muretus.
Cicero is quoting one of those
witticisms current in Rome which
are so frequent in his letters; 'not
so much **tribuni aerarii** as, to

potuerat, qui maesti inter sui dissimiles et maerentes sedebant et contagione turpitudinis vehementer permovebantur. Hic, ut quaeque res ad consilium primis 4 postulationibus referebatur, incredibilis erat severitas nulla varietate sententiarum: nihil impetrabat reus, plus accusatori dabatur quam postulabat. Triumphabat — quid quaeris? — Hortensius se vidisse tantum; nemo erat qui illum reum ac non miliens condemnatum arbitraretur. Me vero teste producto credo te ex acclamatione Clodi advocatorum audisse quae consurrectio iudicum facta sit, ut me circumsteterint, ut aperte iugula sua pro meo capite P. Clodio ostentarint: quae mihi res multo honorificentior visa est quam aut illa,

quote the current witticism, **tribuni aerati.'** — **maesti . . . et maerentes: maesti** seems to refer rather to the sorrow shown by the looks and general aspect, **maerentes** to sorrow expressed in words (Tyrrell). Possibly for **maerentes** we should read *mirantes.*

4. **primis postulationibus**: the preliminary legal questions concerning the conduct of the trial. The term *consilium* was sometimes applied to the jury, but here and in 5 it refers to the body of jurists who were called in to give legal advice to the praetor (cf. Madvig, *Verf. u. Verw. d. röm. St.* II. 255, Momm. *St. R.* I³. 307–319). In the trial of Quinctius, the *consilium* was composed of three men (Cic. *pro Quinct.* 54). — **quid quaeris?** *in a word.* Cf. *Att.* 2. 1. 4 *praeclare Metellus impedit et impediet. Quid quaeris? Est consul* φιλόπατρις *et, ut semper iudicavi, natura bonus.* Such exclamatory questions are very frequent in Latin comedy (cf. Plaut.

M. G. 322, 472, 818, 834; also Hor. *Ep.* 1. 10. 8, etc.), and their frequency and variety in Cicero's letters is a strong indication of the colloquial tone of the letters. Some of these familiar questions which are used to give animation to the narrative are *quid est* and *quid iam* (Ep. XLVIII. 1), *quid ergo* (*Fam* 8. 12. 2), *cur hoc* (*Fam.* 8. 17. 2), and *quid dicam de,* etc. (Ep. XC. 4). Cf. also Intr. 98. — **se vidisse tantum**, *that he had shown such foresight.* — **nemo ... arbitraretur**, *there was no one who thought of him as accused but rather as convicted a thousand times over.* The use of *miliens* harmonizes with the extravagant tone of the letter. Cf. n. on *quas ego* above, and Intr. 96.— **ex acclamatione ... facta sit,** *how the* iudices *in consequence of the outcry made by the supporters of Clodius rose in a body.* The laxity of the Roman court in allowing an expression of partisan feeling in the courtroom and in maintaining no surveillance over the jury during the

cum iurare tui cives Xenocratem testimonium dicentem
prohibuerunt, aut cum tabulas Metelli Numidici, cum
eae, ut mos est, circumferrentur, nostri iudices aspicere
5 noluerunt; multo haec, inquam, nostra res maior.   Itaque iudicum vocibus, cum ego sic ab iis, ut salus patriae, defenderer, fractus reus et una patroni omnes
conciderunt, ad me autem eadem frequentia postridie
convenit, quacum abiens consulatu sum domum reductus.   Clamare praeclari Ariopagitae se non esse venturos nisi praesidio constituto.   Refertur ad consilium:
una sola sententia praesidium non desideravit.   De-
fertur res ad senatum: gravissime ornatissimeque de-
cernitur; laudantur iudices; datur negotium magistratibus;   responsurum   hominem   nemo   arbitrabatur.
Ἔσπετε νῦν μοι, Μοῦσαι, — ὅππως δὴ πρῶτον πῦρ
ἔμπεσε.   Nosti Calvum ex Nanneianis, illum laudato-

---

trial (5) is noticeable. — **Xenocratem, Metelli Numidici**: both in-
cidents are again mentioned in Cic.
pro Balb. 11, 12, though without
Xenocrates's name. Metellus was
tried for misappropriation of public
money while propraetor in Africa.
Cicero's vanity is shown by his expression of pleasure at the complimentary action of a jury whose
character he has just criticised so
severely, and whose conduct he
immediately proceeds to condemn
with equal severity. — **tui cives**:
the Athenians are called in jest
the fellow-citizens of Atticus because of the fondness which Atticus had shown for Athens, as indicated by his long stay in the city.
Perhaps Cicero has in mind also
his friend's cognomen. The Athenians wished to bestow upon Atticus Athenian citizenship (Nepos,
Att. 3. 1), but he declined it. —

tabulas, *accounts; sc.* of public
funds managed by him.
   5. **conciderunt**, *collapsed;* like
fractus,   used   colloquially. —
postridie convenit: *i.e.* in the
morning to pay their respects. —
quacum . . . reductus: at the
conclusion of his consulship, Cicero took an oath before the people
that he had saved the commonwealth, and then occurred the incident to which he refers; *quo quidem tempore is meus domum fuit
e foro reditus nemo, nisi qui
mecum esset, civium esse in numero
videretur*, Cic. *in Pis.* 7. — **Ariopagitae**: ironical. — **una sola . . .
desideravit**: there was only one
vote in the negative. — **negotium**: *sc.* of protecting the jury. —
ἔσπετε, etc.: Hom. *Il.* XVI. 112,
113. — **Calvum**: in a recent letter,
Att. 1. 14. 3, Cicero had written
to Atticus of a speech made by

rem meum, de cuius oratione erga me honorifica ad te
scripseram: biduo per unum servum, et eum ex gladi-
atorio ludo, confecit totum negotium: arcessivit ad se,
promisit, intercessit, dedit; iam vero — o di boni, rem
perditam! — etiam noctes certarum mulierum atque
adulescentulorum nobilium introductiones nonnullis
iudicibus pro mercedis cumulo fuerunt. Ita, summo
discessu bonorum, pleno foro servorum, xxv iudices
ita fortes tamen fuerunt ut summo proposito periculo
vel perire maluerint quam perdere omnia: xxxi fuerunt quos fames magis quam fama commoveret; quorum Catulus cum vidisset quendam, 'Quid vos,' inquit,
'praesidium a nobis postulabatis? An ne nummi vobis
eriperentur timebatis?' Habes, ut brevissime potui, 6
genus iudici et causam absolutionis. Quaeris dein-
ceps qui nunc sit status rerum et qui meus. Rei publicae statum illum, quem tu meo consilio, ego divino
confirmatum putabam, qui bonorum omnium coniunctione et auctoritate consulatus mei fixus et fundatus
videbatur, nisi quis nos deus respexerit, elapsum scito
esse de manibus uno hoc iudicio, si iudicium est tri-
ginta homines populi Romani levissimos ac nequissimos nummulis acceptis ius ac fas omne delere et, quod

Crassus complimentary to him ;
the clause, **de cuius oratione**,
etc., shows, therefore, that **Calvum** refers to Crassus. *Calvus*
was apparently a nickname given
to Crassus, perhaps because of
his baldness. — **ex Nanneianis**:
if the reading is correct, a thrust
at Crassus, understood by Atticus but unintelligible to us. —
arcessivit: *sc. iudices*. — **intercessit**: *i.e.* gave security for the
payment. — **summo discessu
bonorum**, *notwithstanding the*

withdrawal of all honest men. —
**quos fames magis quam fama
commoveret**, *who were influenced
more by hunger than by honor.*
Cf. Intr. 103. — **Catulus**: consul
in 78 B.C. Cf. Cic. *de lege Manil.*
51.

6. **bonorum omnium con-
iunctione**: Cicero prided himself
upon the reconciliation of the
senators and knights which his
consulship had brought about. Cf.
Cic. *in Cat.* 4. 15.—**si iudicium est**,
etc., *if it can be called a trial when*

omnes non modo homines, verum etiam pecudes factum
esse sciant, id Talnam et Plautum et Spongiam et
ceteras huiusmodi quisquilias statuere numquam esse
7 factum.   Sed tamen, ut te de re publica consoler, non
ita ut sperarunt mali, tanto imposito rei publicae vulnere, alacris exsultat improbitas in victoria.   Nam
plane ita putaverunt, cum religio, cum pudicitia, cum
iudiciorum fides, cum senatus auctoritas concidisset,
fore ut aperte victrix nequitia ac libido poenas ab
optimo quoque peteret sui doloris, quem improbissimo
8 cuique inusserat severitas consulatus mei.   Idem ego
ille — non enim mihi videor insolenter gloriari, cum de
me apud te loquor in ea praesertim epistula quam nolo
aliis legi — idem, inquam, ego recreavi adflictos animos bonorum, unumquemque confirmans, excitans; in-
sectandis vero exagitandisque nummariis iudicibus
omnem omnibus studiosis ac fautoribus illius victoriae

thirty, etc. — **non modo homines,
verum etiam pecudes**: a proverbial expression. — **Talnam,
Plautum,** and **Spongiam**: ficti-
tious names given in derision of the
low origin of the judges.— **ceteras
huiusmodi quisquilias,** *the rest
of the riffraff of that ilk.* — **quisquilias**: a colloquial word. Cf.
Novius, *Tog.* 88, Ribbeck; cf. also
Italian *quisquiglia.*
   7. **senatus auctoritas**: the senate had taken the initiative in
bringing Clodius to justice. —
poenas ab optimo quoque: the
earliest indication, perhaps, in
Cicero's letters of his conscious-
ness that the democratic party
was planning to punish those who
were responsible for the execution
of the Catilinarian conspirators.
   8. **idem ego ille**: *sc.* whose severity had made the wicked suffer. —

aliis legi, *to be read to others.*
This explanation of **legi** as equivalent to *recitari* is justified by Ep.
LX. 1 *ex iis litteris quas Atticus a
te missas mihi legit, quid ageres et
ubi esses cognovi.* The use of **epistula** (not *litterae*) harmonizes
with the expression **quam nolo
aliis legi,** and emphasizes, what is
evident in the letter itself, its confidential character; *epistula* was
usually applied to a personal letter. — **victoriae**: join with παρρησίαν. — **omnem παρρησίαν** eripui, *I took all the brag out of.*
Greek words and expressions in
the letters are often from the literary slang of the period., *e.g.*
(*Att.* 7. 1. 5) ἐπίτηκτα, ' veneering ';
(*Att.* 10. 17. 1) ἐκτένεια, ' gush,' and
in many cases play the same part
in colloquial Latin (cf. Tyrrell,
I.² p. 67) that French phrases do

παρρησίαν eripui, Pisonem consulem nulla in re consistere umquam sum passus, desponsam homini iam
Syriam ademi, senatum ad pristinam suam severitatem
revocavi atque abiectum excitavi, Clodium praesentem
fregi in senatu cum oratione perpetua plenissima gravitatis, tum altercatione huiusmodi, ex qua licet pauca
degustes — nam cetera non possunt habere neque vim
neque venustatem remoto illo studio contentionis, quem
ἀγῶνα vos appellatis.　Nam, ut Idibus Maiis in sena- 9
tum convenimus, rogatus ego sententiam multa dixi de
summa re publica, atque ille locus inductus a me est
divinitus, ne una plaga accepta patres conscripti conci-
derent, ne deficerent; vulnus esse eiusmodi, quod mihi
nec dissimulandum nec pertimescendum videretur, ne
aut ignorando stultissimi aut metuendo ignavissimi
iudicaremur.　Bis absolutum esse Lentulum, bis Catilinam: hunc tertium iam esse a iudicibus in rem publicam immissum.　'Erras, Clodi: non te iudices urbi,

with us, *e.g.* (*Att.* 12. 45. 2) ἀκηδία,
'*ennui*,' (*Att.* 7. 1. 5) ὁδοῦ πάρεργον,
'*en passant*.'　Cf. Intr. 97. — consistere, *to get a footing*. — desponsam (not *decretam*) : *i.e.*
promised to Piso by Pompey,
who had just organized Syria
into a province, but not officially
assigned to him by the senate.
— vos, *you Athenians*.　Cf. *tui
cives*, 4.

9. Idibus Maiis: this fixes the
date of the letter as later than
May 15. — rogatus sententiam:
the technical expression used of
the action of the presiding consul
in asking senators their views on
the question before the senate.
The rules of the Roman senate
allowed a senator to depart from
the special topic under consideration, and *de summa re publica dicere*.

Cf. Willems, II. 186. — ille locus, etc., *the following point was
developed by me with telling effect.*
— Lentulum : Catiline's fellow-
conspirator, who was accused *de
peculatu* in 80 B.C., and at a later
date underwent a similar experience. — Catilinam : tried on a
charge of '*repetundae*' in 65 B.C.
(cf. intr. to Ep. II.).　He was
again on trial, in 64 B.C., for
the murder of M. Marius Gra-
tidianus.　No mention is made
here of the charge of incest
brought in 73 B.C. against the
Vestal Fabia, sister of Cicero's
wife Terentia, in which Catiline
was implicated.　Cicero regarded
the charge as unfounded, and
wished, furthermore, to spare the
good name of Terentia's family.
— immissum: properly used of

sed carceri reservarunt, neque te retinere in civitate,
sed exsilio privare voluerunt. Quam ob rem, patres
conscripti, erigite animos, retinete vestram dignitatem.
Manet illa in re publica bonorum consensio; dolor
accessit bonis viris, virtus non est imminuta; nihil est
damni factum novi, sed quod erat, inventum est: in
unius hominis perditi iudicio plures similes reperti
10 sunt.' Sed quid ago? paene orationem in epistulam
inclusi. Redeo ad altercationem. Surgit pulchellus

wild beasts. Catiline is compared
to a wolf, Cic. *in Cat.* 2. 2. — **reservarunt**: Cicero addressed Catiline in 64 B.C. in almost the same
language: *O miser, qui non sentias illo iudicio te non absolutum,
verum ad aliquod severius iudicium ac maius supplicium reserva-
tum* (*Or. in tog. cand.*). — **exsilio
privare**: if Clodius had been convicted, he would have been exiled.
The *iudices*, by acquitting him,
have deprived him of the safety
which exile would give, and allowed him an open field in which
to commit a crime punishable with
death, the *carcer* being the common place of execution for citizens. The oration of which this
was a part was entitled, *Oratio in
P. Clodium et C. Curionem*, and
has been preserved in a frag-
mentary form. — **illa . . . consensio**: 'that harmony which my
consulship secured.' Cf. note on
6. — **quod erat, inventum est**:
the jurors who acquitted Clodius
were venal before; the trial had
merely brought that fact to light.

10. **pulchellus**: diminutive of
pulcher, a parody upon Clodius's
cognomen *Pulcher*, while at the
same time it contains an ironical
allusion to his lack of personal
beauty, to which Cicero refers,
Or. in P. Clod. et C. Cur.: sed

*credo postquam speculum tibi ad-
latum est longe te a pulchris
abesse sensisti.* **Pulchellus** may
also be used in derision of the
effeminacy of Clodius, for, speaking of the group of young men
to whom Clodius belonged, Cicero says, *concursabant barbatuli
iuvenes, totus ille grex Catilinae,
Att.* 1. 14. 5. Well-trimmed beards
marked the climax of dandyism.
Diminutives do not always indicate that the individual in question is smaller than others of its
kind, but that the speaker feels
affection, pity, or contempt for
it. Thus Cicero speaks of his
daughter as *Tulliola* (my darling
Tullia), *Att.* 4. 1. 4; Servius, referring to the sad death of the
same woman, speaks of her as a
muliercula, Fam. 4. 5. 4; while
the predominant feeling suggested
by *pulchellus* is one of contempt.
Such a use of the diminutive is
especially common in colloquial
language. Diminutive adjectives
and adverbs with this force are
farther removed from formal language than diminutive nouns, and
the very fact that these adjectives
and adverbs are not infrequent in
Cicero's letters is one of the
strongest indications of the familiar character of the letters. Cf.
misellus (*Att.* 3. 23. 5), *vetulus*

puer; obicit mihi me ad Baias fuisse.   Falsum, sed
tamen quid huic ?   ' Simile est,' inquam, ' quasi dicas
in operto fuisse.' — ' Quid,' inquit, ' homini Arpinati
cum aquis calidis ? '   ' Narra,' inquam, ' patrono tuo,
qui Arpinatis aquas concupivit'; nosti enim marinas.
— 'Quousque,' inquit, 'hunc regem feremus ?'   'Regem
appellas,' inquam, ' cum Rex tui mentionem nullam fecerit ? '   Ille autem Regis hereditatem spe
devorarat. — ' Domum,' inquit, ' emisti.'   ' Putes,' in-

(*Att.* 13. 29. 1), and even from
comparatives, *minusculus* (*Att.* 14.
13. 5), and *meliuscule* (*Att.* 4. 6.
2). Cf. also Intr. 76. — **ad Baias**:
Clodius twits Cicero with living
at the fashionable seaside resort
Baiae, whose reputation for strict-
ness of morals was a little questionable.   Cicero, disdaining to
defend himself, intimates that
Clodius had been found once in
far more suspicious surroundings,
i.e. at the festival of the Bona Dea.
— **falsum, sed tamen quid huic**
(*sc. falsum id esse responderem*):
addressed to Atticus, not to Clodius.   One of Cicero's houses
was at Puteoli, so that while he
could technically deny having a
villa at Baiae, he was within the
circle of its influence, as he himself felt, for he refers to the place
as *Cratera illum delicatum* ('Cra-
ter with its well-known allure-
ments '), *Att.* 2. 8. 2. — **in operto**
(*Bonae Deae*): a technical phrase,
'at the mystic rites.'— **quid homini Arpinati cum aquis calidis:**
i.e. what business has a countryman from Arpinum at a water-
ing-place?   Cicero replies, ' Make
that remark to your patron (Curio)
who was terribly anxious for the
springs of a countryman from
Arpinum.'   The *Aquae Arpinatis*
were medicinal springs upon an
estate once belonging to C. Marius.   Cicero parries the thrust
at his provincialism, therefore,
by referring to the fact that
one of Rome's most illustrious
men lived in his native town Arpinum, and hits Clodius through
Curio, for the latter had obtained
the estate during the Sullan pro-
scriptions, and therefore not in an
honorable way. — **nosti enim marinas:** addressed to Atticus. These
springs were perhaps called *mari-
nae* because they were near the
sea-coast.— **regem appellas, cum
. . . fecerit,** *do you talk of a rex,
when Rex made no mention of
you ?* Q. Marcius Rex was brother-
in-law of Clodius, and at his death
passed over the latter entirely in
his will. — **ille autem**, etc.: a parenthetical explanation to Atticus,
as the death of Rex had occurred
very recently.— **domum**: Cicero's
house was in the most fashionable
part of the city, on the Palatine,
and cost him $150,000 (*Fam.* 5. 6.
2).   Cf. Intr. 45.   Clodius wishes
to characterize Cicero as a par-
venu, and perhaps to suggest that
the money had been obtained in
a questionable way. Gell.12.12 tells
us that the money for the purchase
of the house came from P. Cornelius Sulla, who was defended
by Cicero in 62 B.C. — **putes:**

quam, 'dicere: iudices emisti.' — 'Iuranti,' inquit,
'tibi non crediderunt.' 'Mihi vero,' inquam, 'xxv
iudices crediderunt, xxxi, quoniam nummos ante acce-
perunt, tibi nihil crediderunt.'   Magnis clamoribus
11 adflictus conticuit et concidit.   Noster autem status
est hic: apud bonos iidem sumus quos reliquisti, apud
sordem urbis et faecem multo melius nunc quam reliquisti.   Nam et illud nobis non obest, videri nostrum
testimonium non valuisse: missus est sanguis invidiae
sine dolore, atque etiam hoc magis, quod omnes illi
fautores illius flagiti rem manifestam illam redemptam
esse a iudicibus confitentur.   Accedit illud, quod illa
contionalis hirudo aerari, misera ac ieiuna plebecula,
me ab hoc Magno unice diligi putat ; et hercule multa

indefinite second person, while
the subject of **dicere** is *te*, referring to Clodius. — iuranti: *i.e.*
when he gave his testimony. If
the judges had believed Cicero's
testimony, they would have convicted Clodius. — **crediderunt...
crediderunt**: the play upon words
can be reproduced in English by
the word 'trusted.' Cf. Intr. 103.
— concidit: cf. 5 n.

  11. **noster autem status**: with
these words the third topic of the
letter begins, Cicero's political and
personal fortunes. — melius: cf.
Intr. 85 *a*. — quam reliquisti: we
should expect *quam quos nos reliquisti*. — et illud non obest: this
calls for *et illud prodest*, but the
form of expression undergoes
change, and the place of the
second correlative is taken by
accedit illud. — missus est, *has
been let;* a surgical expression.
Cf. *Att.* 6. 1. 2 *sic Appius, cum
ἐξ ἀφαιρέσεως provinciam curarit,
sanguinem miserit, quicquid
potuit detraxerit, mihi tradiderit*

enectam, προσανατρεφομένην *eam a
me non libenter videt;* cf. also
Livy, 3. 54. 4. — sine dolore: *i.e.*
without weakening Cicero, for the
reason indicated in the following
passage.— **rem manifestam**, etc.:
'that the case was clear, and an
acquittal secured from the jurors
by the use of money.' — **contionalis hirudo aerari**: the populace who spent their time in the
contiones, instead of being at work,
and who lived upon largesses of
corn granted by the *leges frumentariae*. — **plebecula**: the diminutive
expresses contempt; cf. note to
pulchellus, 10. The populace was
composed largely of freedmen.
Cicero refers to them elsewhere
(*Att.* 2. 16. 1) as *pedisequi*, 'lack-
eys.' His earlier democratic tendencies would seem to have given
way already to aristocratic sympathies. — **Magno**: *i.e.* Pompey. The
force of **putat** is a common one:
'The people think that I am loved
by Pompey, but they are mistaken.'
Only four months before Cicero

et iucunda consuetudine coniuncti inter nos sumus, usque eo, ut nostri isti comissatores coniurationis, barbatuli iuvenes, illum in sermonibus Cn. Ciceronem appellent. Itaque et ludis et gladiatoribus mirandas ἐπισημασίας sine ulla pastoricia fistula auferebamus. Nunc est exspectatio comitiorum, in quae omnibus invi- 12 tis trudit noster Magnus Auli filium, atque in eo neque auctoritate neque gratia pugnat, sed quibus Philippus omnia castella expugnari posse dicebat in quae modo asellus onustus auro posset ascendere; consul autem ille deterioris histrionis similis suscepisse negotium dicitur et domi divisores habere, quod ego non credo.

had indulged in this caustic arraignment of Pompey: *nihil come, nihil simplex, nihil ἐν τοῖς πολιτικοῖς illustre, nihil honestum, nihil forte, nihil liberum (Att.* i. 13. 4). — isti comissatores coniurationis, *those who conspired only over their wine-cups* (Tyrrell). — barbatuli: Caelius, Dolabella, Curio *filius,* Clodius, etc. Cf. note to *pulchellus,* 10.— Cn. Ciceronem: the nickname given to Pompey may suggest that he was as vacillating as Cicero in his actions, as Mommsen explains it, or that the friendship between Cicero and Pompey was so close as to make them one. — ludis et gladiatoribus: colloquial ablatives of time. Cf. Intr. 83 *d.* Such colloquial ablatives Cicero has with one exception (*Philipp.* 9. 16) avoided outside the letters. The *ludi* referred to were probably the *ludi Megalenses* in April. — ἐπισημασίας: these indications of popularity were probably given when Cicero and Pompey entered while the games were being held. For a similar scene when Caesar and Curio entered the theatre, cf. Ep.

VII. 3.— pastoricia fistula: shrill whistles were used by a politician's opponents to drown the applause of his supporters. Hissing was also common (Ep. VII. 2).

12. comitiorum: the consular election. — Auli filium: *i.e.* L. Afranius. By designating him as Auli filium Cicero means perhaps that Afranius was himself a man of no worth. He was consul in 60 B.C., proconsul of Gallia Cisalpina in 59 B.C., was pardoned by Caesar for espousing the cause of Pompey in the Civil War, joined the Pompeian forces again, and was captured and put to death after the battle of Thapsus. — Philippus: the methods of Philip of Macedon had become proverbial. Cf. Hor. *Od.* 3. 16. 13-15 *diffidit urbium portas vir Macedo et subruit aemulos reges muneribus.* In Juv. 12. 47 he is *callidus emptor Olynthi.* — consul . . . ille: *i.e.* Piso. — deterioris histrionis: a δευτεραγωνιστής. Pompey takes the leading rôle in this comedy of the election of Afranius, and the consul Piso plays the second part. — divisores : men to distribute money. — quod ego

Sed senatus consulta duo iam facta sunt odiosa, quod
in consulem facta putantur, Catone et Domitio postu-
lante: unum, ut apud magistratus inquiri liceret, alterum, cuius domi divisores habitarent, adversus rem
13 publicam. Lurco autem tribunus pl., qui magistratum
insimulatum lege Aelia iniit, solutus est et Aelia et
Fufia, ut legem de ambitu ferret, quam ille bono auspicio claudus homo promulgavit. Ita comitia in a. d. VI
Kal. Sext. dilata sunt. Novi est in lege hoc, ut qui
nummos in tribubus pronuntiarit, si non dederit, im-
pune sit, sin dederit, ut, quoad vivat, singulis tribubus

non credo: the context would
indicate that Cicero did believe
the story, and this saving clause
may have been added for fear
that the letter might be inter-
cepted. — Domitio: cf. Ep. I. 3 n.
— unum . . . alterum: one, that
the houses of the magistrates
might be searched for professional
bribers or money to be used in
bribery; the other, that if bribery
agents were found at the house of
a magistrate, such a magistrate
should be considered guilty of an
offense against the public weal.
As the person of a magistrate
was inviolable during his term of
office, this was the only action
possible against him. Cf. Momm.
St. R. I. 705. — adversus rem
publicam: (*sc. eum facere*).

13. Lurco autem, etc., *furthermore Lurco the plebeian tribune, who
has taken a magistracy impugned
by the Aelian law, has been exempted from the operation of both the
Aelian and Fufian laws, in order
that he might bring forward his
bill in regard to bribery, which he
has published under good auspices,
seeing that he is a lame man.* The
leges Aelia et Fufia gave elections
precedence in point of time over

the introduction of new laws. By
the postponement of the *comitia*
in order that Lurco might bring in
his bill, this section of the law
was suspended. Cf. Mommsen,
St. R. I. 83 and 111, n. 4. — magistratum insimulatum lege Aelia: one portion of the Aelian law,
passed about 155 B.C., apparently
for the first time gave to magistrates the right to take the auspices before the meeting of the
concilium plebis, and, by announc-
ing them as unfavorable, to in-
terfere with the action of the
tribune who presided over this
assembly. Cf. Herzog, I. 419,
1163. By the Aelian law, therefore, Lurco's own office was *in-
simulatus.* — bono auspicio claudus homo: ironical. In early
days bodily infirmity debarred a
man from office altogether. The
proposal of a bill by a lame man,
therefore, scarcely augured well
for its success. — quoad vivat: *i.e.*
every year for the rest of his life.
— HS. : the usual abbreviation
for *sestertius* and *sestertium*, derived from IIS(emis), as the sestertius was worth 2½ *asses*. The
horizontal stroke indicates that
the symbols have a numerical

HS. cɔ cɔ cɔ debeat. Dixi hanc legem P. Clodium
iam ante servasse; pronuntiare enim solitum esse et
non dare. Sed, heus tu! videsne consulatum illum
nostrum, quem Curio antea ἀποθέωσιν vocabat, si hic
factus erit, Fabam Mimum futurum? Quare, ut opinor,
φιλοσοφητέον, id quod tu facis, et istos consulatus non
flocci facteon.   Quod ad me scribis te in Asiam statu- 14
isse non ire, equidem mallem ut ires, ac vereor ne
quid in ista re minus commode fiat; sed tamen non
possum reprehendere consilium tuum, praesertim cum
egomet in provinciam non sim profectus.   Epigramma- 15

value. — **HS. cɔ cɔ cɔ** : 3000
sesterces, or more than $120.00.
As there were 35 tribes, the an-
nual fine would have been over
$4200. — **heus tu !** a colloquial
exclamation, commonly followed
in Plautus by a command. Cf.
Bacch. 327 ; cf. also Intr. 92. —
hic: *i.e.* Afranius. — **factus erit:**
sc. consul. — **Fabam Mimum:** if
the reading is correct, perhaps
Böckel's explanation is the most
plausible one. The *mimus* (a kind
of farce) was a popular form of
entertainment. One of these farces
well known at Rome was called
the *Faba Mimus.*   Both here
and in the other passage (Seneca,
᾽Αποκολοκύντωσις, 9) where the expression occurs, the writer is speaking on the subject of an apotheosis. Now the Pythagoreans were
the most prominent teachers of
re-incarnation, and at the same
time laid down certain rules in regard to the use of beans as an
article of diet. The *Faba Mimus*
may therefore have been a parody
on the teachings of Pythagoras
upon these two points, and well
known for its wit or nonsense, so
that the meaning of the passage
may be, 'if Afranius is elected

consul, that consulship of mine,
which Curio used in mockery to
call an apotheosis, will be the sort
of an apotheosis that one sees in
the 'Bean Farce,' for my com-
panion in apotheosis will be this
nobody Afranius.' See Crit. Append. — **φιλοσοφητέον,** *one must
play the philosopher.* — **id quod tu
facis:** Atticus throughout his life,
except during Cicero's consulship and his candidacy for that
office, held aloof from politics,
following in this respect the teachings of his school, the Epicurean.
— **facteon:** a hybrid form, instead
of *faciendum,* suggested by **φιλοσοφητέον,** and after the analogy
of the Greek verbal in -τέον with
the accusative after it. Cf. Intr. 74.

14. te in Asiam, etc.: Quintus
Cicero, who was going out to
Asia as propraetor, had invited
his brother-in-law Atticus, to accompany him as *legatus.* Cf. Ep.
VI. 7 n. — **vereor ne quid,** etc.:
Quintus *did* take umbrage at the
refusal of Atticus.   Cicero would
also have gladly seen Atticus go, to
restrain his hot-headed brother. —
cum egomet, etc.: Cicero declined a province at the close of
his consulship.

tis tuis, quae in Amaltheo posuisti, contenti erimus,
praesertim cum et Thyillus nos reliquerit et Archias
nihil de me scripserit, ac vereor ne, Lucullis quoniam
Graecum poëma condidit, nunc ad Caecilianam fabulam
16 spectet.   Antonio tuo nomine gratias egi eamque epistulam Mallio dedi.   Ad te ideo antea rarius scripsi,
quod non habebam idoneum cui darem, nec satis scie-
17 bam quo darem.   Valde te venditavi.   Cincius si
quid ad me tui negoti detulerit, suscipiam; sed nunc
magis in suo est occupatus, in quo ego ei non desum.
Tu, si uno in loco es futurus, crebras a nobis litteras
18 exspecta; ast plures etiam ipse mittito.   Velim ad me
scribas cuiusmodi sit 'Αμαλθεῖον tuum, quo ornatu,
qua τοποθεσίᾳ; et quae poëmata quasque historias de
'Αμαλθείᾳ habes, ad me mittas.   Libet mihi facere in

15. **Amaltheo:** the villa of Atticus near Buthrotum, in Epirus,
was so called from the nymph
Amalthea. The library of this
villa was adorned with the busts
of noted Romans. Cicero's was
among the rest. Beneath the busts
(Nepos, *Att.* 18. 5) were com-
memorative inscriptions. Cicero
is pleased to receive this recognition, especially as the contemporary poets at Rome, Thyillus and
Archias, are neglecting him. Archias is well known because of
Cicero's oration in his behalf. He
had begun a poem upon Cicero's
consulship (*pro Ar.* 28). — **Caecilianam fabulam:** we know from
Cicero's oration in support of Archias of the friendship existing
between the latter and the Caecilii
Metelli. The work here mentioned
would seem to have been a dramatic composition founded upon
the achievements of the Caecilian
family. One of the earlier writers

of comedy was Caecilius Statius,
whom Cicero calls (*Att.* 7. 3. 10)
malus auctor Latinitatis, and **Caecilianam fabulam** may therefore
have a double meaning, 'a play in
the manner of Caecilius (Statius)
upon the Caecilians.'
   16. **Antonio:** C. Antonius, Cicero's colleague in the consulship,
and now governor of Macedonia,
a province which he had received
in return for not supporting the
Catilinarians. Cicero had asked
Antonius to grant Atticus some
favor (*Fam.* 5. 5). — **Mallio:** perhaps T. Manlius, a *negotiator* of
Thespiae in whose interest *Fam.*
13. 22 was written. — **quo darem,** *where to send it.* — **valde
te venditavi,** *I have heartily
praised you, i.e.* to Antonius.
   17. **Cincius:** cf. Ep. I. 1 n.
   18. **facere:** *i.e.* an Amaltheum.
— **nihil erat absoluti,** *I have
nothing finished.* For the tense,
cf. Intr. 84 *c.*

Arpinati. Ego tibi aliquod de meis scriptis mittam. Nihil erat absoluti.

VI. (*Att.* 1. 17.)

CICERO ATTICO SAL.

Magna mihi varietas voluntatis et dissimilitudo opi- 1 nionis ac iudici Q. fratris mei demonstrata est ex litteris tuis, in quibus ad me epistularum illius exempla misisti: qua ex re et molestia sum tanta adfectus, quantam mihi meus amor summus erga utrumque vestrum adferre debuit, et admiratione, quidnam accidisset, quod adferret Q. fratri meo aut offensionem tam gravem aut commutationem tantam voluntatis. Atque illud a me iam ante intellegebatur, quod te quoque ipsum discedentem a nobis suspicari videbam, subesse nescio quid opinionis incommodae, sauciumque esse

VI. Rome, Dec. 5, 61 B.C. At this time there had been a disagreement of long standing between Quintus Cicero and his wife Pomponia, who was the sister of Atticus. On leaving Rome to assume the propraetorship of Asia in 61 B.C., Quintus had invited Atticus to accompany him as *legatus*, and Atticus had declined the invitation (cf. Ep. V. 14). This refusal and the suspicion of Quintus that Pomponia was abetted in her opposition by her brother (cf. *odiosas suspiciones*, 1), had led to such a serious breach between the two men that Quintus, as current rumor said, had expressed himself very unfavorably in regard to his brother-in-law at Rome, and had actually left the city without writing to him (cf. 4). Atticus naturally felt ag-grieved, and in his letter to Marcus Cicero took occasion to remind his friend of the services which he had rendered him in the past (cf. 5). To avoid a misunderstanding with Atticus, and to put his brother's conduct in a more favorable light, without aggravating the quarrel between Quintus and Pomponia, and without putting Atticus in the wrong, constitute the delicate task which Cicero essays. With this letter cf. Ep. XXX. 3, 4.

1. **epistularum . . . exempla**: the letters which Quintus addressed to Atticus from Thessalonica (cf. 4), which would seem to have been very bitter in their tone. Cf. *offensionem tam gravem*, below.— **discedentem**: *sc.* for Epirus at the close of 62 or in the early part of 61 B.C.(cf. *Att.* 1. 13. 1).

eius animum et insedisse quasdam odiosas suspiciones, quibus ego mederi cum cuperem antea saepe et vehementius etiam post sortitionem provinciae, nec tantum intellegebam ei esse offensionis quantum litterae tuae declararunt, nec tantum proficiebam quantum volebam. 2 Sed tamen hoc me ipse consolabar, quod non dubitabam quin te ille aut Dyrrachi aut in istis locis uspiam visurus esset; quod cum accidisset, confidebam ac mihi persuaseram fore ut omnia placarentur inter vos, non modo sermone ac disputatione, sed conspectu ipso congressuque vestro. Nam quanta sit in Quinto fratre meo comitas, quanta iucunditas, quam mollis animus et ad accipiendam et ad deponendam offensionem, nihil attinet me ad te, qui ea nosti, scribere. Sed accidit perincommode, quod eum nusquam vidisti. Valuit enim plus quod erat illi nonnullorum artificiis inculcatum quam aut officium aut necessitudo aut amor vester ille 3 pristinus, qui plurimum valere debuit. Atque huius incommodi culpa ubi resideat, facilius possum existimare quam scribere; vereor enim ne, dum defendam meos, non parcam tuis. Nam sic intellego, ut nihil a domesticis vulneris factum sit, illud quidem quod erat eos certe sanare potuisse. Sed huiusce rei totius vi-

---

—insedisse: *sc. in animo.*— antea saepe: it is evident that the ill-feeling of Quintus antedated the refusal of Atticus to serve as *legatus.*

2. in istis locis: *i.e.* in Epirus, where Atticus now was. Cf. Ep. V. 15 n. — nihil attinet: cf. *de quo quid sentiam, nihil attinet dicere, Fam.* 4. 7. 3. — perincommode: cf. Intr. 77.—nonnullorum artificiis: the anger of Quintus had evidently been inflamed by some of the enemies of Atticus.

3. facilius . . . scribere: Cicero touches upon one of the fundamental and unknown causes of the enmity of Quintus, which, however, he does not dare state in a letter. — meos . . . tuis: the plural used politely for the singular (cf. *ego autem*, Ep. VII. 1), as Cicero can be thinking only of Quintus and Pomponia respectively. — ut nihil, *granting that no,* etc. — domesticis: *i.e.* Pomponia.

tium, quod aliquanto etiam latius patet quam videtur, praesenti tibi commodius exponam. De iis litteris quas ₄ ad te Thessalonica misit, et de sermonibus quos ab illo et Romae apud amicos tuos et in itinere habitos putas, ecquid tantum causae sit ignoro; sed omnis in tua posita est humanitate mihi spes huius levandae molestiae. Nam, si ita statueris, et irritabiles animos esse optimorum saepe hominum et eosdem placabiles, et esse hanc agilitatem, ut ita dicam, mollitiamque naturae plerumque bonitatis, et, id quod caput est, nobis inter nos nostra sive incommoda sive vitia sive iniurias esse tolerandas, facile haec, quemadmodum spero, mitigabuntur. Quod ego ut facias te oro; nam ad me, qui te unice diligo, maxime pertinet neminem esse meorum, qui aut te non amet aut abs te non ametur. Illa pars ₅ epistulae tuae minime fuit necessaria, in qua exponis quas facultates aut provincialium aut urbanorum commodorum et aliis temporibus et me ipso consule praetermiseris. Mihi enim perspecta est ingenuitas et magnitudo animi tui, neque ego inter me atque te quicquam interesse umquam duxi praeter voluntatem institutae vitae, quod me ambitio quaedam ad honorum stu-

---

4. **de iis litteris**: cf. Intr. 91.—
de sermonibus: cf. introd. note, and *Att.* I. 19. 11 (written in March, 60 B.C.) *Quintus frater purgat se mihi per litteras et affirmat nihil a se cuiquam de te secus esse dictum.* — **causae**: *sc.* for his conduct. — **irritabiles**: cf. *Q. fr.* I. I. 37 *omnes enim, qui istinc veniunt, ita de tua virtute integritate humanitate commemorant, ut in tuis summis laudibus excipiant unam iracundiam.*

5. **provincialium** probably refers not to political positions but to business opportunities in the provinces which Atticus had neglected in serving the interests of Cicero, notably during the latter's candidacy for the consulship and incumbency of that office. Most of the business ventures of Atticus, who was a money-lender, were carried on in the provinces. — **voluntatem institutae vitae**: Cicero was interested in politics while Atticus held aloof from them; cf. Intr. 58. — **honorum**: public distinctions, especially political offices. — **cum . . . dis-**

dium, te autem alia minime reprehendenda ratio ad
honestum otium duxit.   Vera quidem laude probitatis
diligentiae religionis neque me tibi neque quemquam
antepono, amoris vero erga me, cum a fraterno amore
6 domesticoque discessi, tibi primas defero.   Vidi enim,
vidi penitusque perspexi in meis variis temporibus et
sollicitudines et laetitias tuas.   Fuit mihi saepe et lau-
dis nostrae gratulatio tua iucunda et timoris consolatio
grata.   Quin mihi nunc te absente non solum consilium
quo tu excellis, sed etiam sermonis communicatio, quae
mihi suavissima tecum solet esse, maxime deest — quid
dicam ?   in publicane re, quo in genere mihi neglegenti
esse non licet, an in forensi labore, quem antea propter
ambitionem sustinebam, nunc ut dignitatem tueri gratia possim, an in ipsis domesticis negotiis, in quibus
ego cum antea tum vero post discessum fratris te ser-
monesque nostros desidero ?   Postremo non labor meus,
non requies, non negotium, non otium, non forenses
res, non domesticae, non publicae, non privatae carere
diutius tuo suavissimo atque amantissimo consilio ac
7 sermone possunt.   Atque harum rerum commemora-
tionem verecundia saepe impedivit utriusque nostrum;
nunc autem ea fuit necessaria propter eam partem
epistulae tuae, per quam te ac mores tuos mihi purgatos ac probatos esse voluisti.   Atque in ista incommo-
ditate alienati illius animi et offensi illud inest tamen
commodi, quod et mihi et ceteris amicis tuis nota fuit

---

cessi, *if I except the love of my*
brother and of my family. Cf.
Fam. 6. 12. 2 *Caesaris familiares*
. . . cum ab illo discesserint, me
habeant proximum. — primas: *sc.*
partes.

6. sustinebam, nunc: *sc. sus-*
tineo.

7. purgatos ac probatos: cf.
Intr. 93. — nota . . . testificata:
Atticus had informed Cicero sev-
eral months before of his intention

et abs te aliquanto ante testificata tua voluntas omit-
tendae provinciae, ut quod una non estis non dissensione ac discidio vestro, sed voluntate ac iudicio tuo factum esse videatur.   Quare et illa quae violata expia-
buntur et haec nostra quae sunt sanctissime conservata
suam religionem obtinebunt.   Nos hic in re publica 8
infirma misera commutabilique versamur.   Credo enim
te audisse nostros equites paene a senatu esse diiunc-
tos; qui primum illud valde graviter tulerunt, promul-
gatum ex senatus consulto fuisse ut de eis qui ob iudicandum accepissent quaereretur.   Qua in re decer-
nenda cum ego casu non adfuissem sensissemque id
equestrem ordinem ferre moleste neque aperte dicere,
obiurgavi senatum, ut mihi visus sum, summa cum auctoritate et in causa non verecunda admodum gravis et

not to go to Asia, and had probably based his refusal upon his
well-known policy of keeping out
of politics (cf. Ep. V. 14).   These
facts would absolve Atticus from
the charge of cherishing any ill-
will toward Quintus. — **et illa . . .
et haec nostra:** the letter up to
this point consists of two distinct
parts; in the first part (1–4) the
relations existing between Atticus
and Quintus are discussed, in the
second part (5–7) the relations
between Atticus and Marcus Cicero. A third division of the letter,
devoted to politics, begins with 8.

8. ob iudicandum: this senatorial investigation was directed
particularly against the jury in the
Clodian trial, the majority of
which was supposed to have been
bribed (cf. Ep. V. 5). Cato, who
proposed the investigation (cf. *Att.*
2. 1. 8), was acting simply in the
interests of justice; but, as many
of the suspected jurors were *equi-*

tes, the equestrian order regarded
the investigation as a covert attack
upon themselves, which at the
same time they could not oppose
(**neque aperte dicere**) without
appearing to defend crime.   The
incident offers an excellent opportunity to contrast the methods of
Cato and of the political group to
which he belonged, with those of
Cicero and his school. Cato wishes
to punish the offenders regardless
of the political consequences, or,
as Cicero puts it (*Att.* 2. 1. 8), *dicit
. . . tamquam in Platonis* πολιτείᾳ,
*non tamquam in Romuli faece sen-
tentiam.*   Cicero abhors the deed,
but does not wish to punish the
evil-doers, for fear of alienating
the class to which they belonged,
and thus weakening the opposition
to the democracy. Cf. *Att.* 2. 1. 8
(end). Cato prevailed. — **accepissent:** used absolutely, as in *Att.* 5.
21. 5 and 11. 22. 2. Ordinarily *pecuniam* is expressed. Cf. Crit. Append.

9 copiosus fui. Ecce aliae deliciae equitum vix ferendae! quas ego non solum tuli, sed etiam ornavi. Asiam qui de censoribus conduxerant, questi sunt in senatu se cupiditate prolapsos nimium magno conduxisse; ut induceretur locatio postulaverunt. Ego princeps in adiutoribus, atque adeo secundus ; nam ut illi auderent hoc postulare Crassus eos impulit. Invidiosa res, turpis postulatio et confessio temeritatis. Summum erat periculum ne, si nihil impetrassent, plane alienarentur a senatu. Huic quoque rei subventum est maxime a nobis, perfectumque ut frequentissimo senatu et liberalissimo uterentur, multaque a me de ordinum dignitate et concordia dicta sunt Kal. Decembr. et postridie. Neque adhuc res confecta est, sed voluntas senatus perspecta. Vnus enim contra dixerat Metellus consul designatus, unusque erat dicturus, ad quem propter diei brevitatem perventum non est, heros ille noster

10 Cato. Sic ego conservans rationem institutionemque nostram tueor, ut possum, illam a me conglutinatam

9. **ecce aliae** takes the place of a correlative to *primum*, 8.— **aliae deliciae,** *another charming scheme.* — **Asiam**: the privilege of collecting the taxes in the provinces for a period of five years was assigned to the highest bidders by the censors (cf. Marquardt's *Staatsverwaltung* II.² 248 ff.). Those who had contracted for the taxes in Asia, finding that they had offered too much, demanded that their contracts should be cancelled (**ut induceretur locatio**). — **atque adeo** : to introduce a correction; equivalent to *vel potius.* Cf. Cic. *in Caec.* 68 and Dziatzko on Ter. *Phorm.* 389. — **secundus**: Cicero was their second champion in point of time and of prominence. Cras-

sus was probably heavily interested in a pecuniary way in the matter. Perhaps he also wished to widen the breach between the senate and the knights in order to further his own political plans. — **summum . . . periculum**: see Crit. Append. — **frequentissimo senatu**: at a *frequens senatus* mentioned in *Att.* I. 14. 5 there were 415 members present, while a *frequens senatus* in the December holiday season contained 200 members (cf. *Q. fr.* 2. 1. 1, and Willems, *Le Sénat de la Répubĺ. Rom.* II. 165–170). — **Metellus**: *i.e.* Q. Metellus Celer; cf. *Att.* 2. 1. 4; *pro Cael.* 59. — **heros ille** : because regardless of the political consequences. Cf. note to *ob iudicandum,* above.

concordiam; sed tamen, quoniam ista sunt tam infirma, munitur quaedam nobis ad retinendas opes nostras tuta, ut spero, via quam tibi litteris satis explicare non possum, significatione parva ostendam tamen: utor Pompeio familiarissime. Video quid dicas. Cavebo quae sunt cavenda, ac scribam alias ad te de meis consiliis capessendae rei publicae plura. Lucceium scito con- 11 sulatum habere in animo statim petere; duo enim soli dicuntur petituri: Caesar — cum eo coire per Arrium cogitat — et Bibulus — cum hoc se putat per C. Pisonem posse coniungi. Rides? Non sunt haec ridicula, mihi crede. Quid aliud scribam ad te, quid? Multa sunt, sed in aliud tempus. Si exspectare velis, cures ut sciam. Iam illud modeste rogo quod maxime cupio, ut quam primum venias. Nonis Decembribus.

10. **concordiam**: cf. *coniunctione*, Ep. V. 6 n. — **quaedam . . . tuta . . . via**: in response to a warning from Atticus, Cicero explains his political plans in *Att.* 2. 1. 6, as follows: *non ut ego de optimati illa mea ratione decederem, sed ut ille (Pompeius) esset melior et aliquid de populari levitate deponeret.* He has hopes even of Caesar: *quid si etiam Caesarem . . . reddo meliorem.*

11. **Lucceium**: cf. intr. note to Ep. XVIII. Cicero is writing of the elections which would take place in midsummer of 60 B.C. Caesar allied himself with Lucceius, but the Optimates partially frustrated the combination by the election of Bibulus as Caesar's colleague. — **cum eo**: *i.e.* Caesar. — **Arri-** um: a man of neither ability nor distinguished antecedents, but put forward by Crassus to support Caesar. — **cogitat, putat**: *sc.* Lucceius. — **cum hoc**: *i.e.* Bibulus; cf. Ep. VII. 2 n. — **C. Pisonem**: C. Calpurnius Piso, who had been consul in 67 B.C. and later governor of Gallia Narbonensis, was an extreme member of the party of the Optimates, and a bitter enemy of Caesar, who had brought a legal action against him a few years before. He could therefore be relied upon to use his best efforts to further the cause of Bibulus, upon whom the Optimates centered their efforts in their struggle against Caesar. — **mihi crede**: cf. *mihi crede*, Ep. XXVII. 1 n.

VII. (*Att.* 2. 19.)

CICERO ATTICO SAL.

1 Multa me sollicitant et ex rei publicae tanto motu et ex iis periculis quae mihi ipsi intenduntur et sescenta sunt; sed mihi nihil est molestius quam Statium manu missum:

Nec meum imperium, — ac mitto imperium: non simultatem meam Revereri saltem!

Nec quid faciam scio neque tantum est in re quantus est sermo. Ego autem irasci ne possum quidem iis quos valde amo. Tantum doleo, ac mirifice quidem. Cetera in magnis rebus. Minae Clodi contentionesque, quae mihi proponuntur, modice me tangunt. Etenim vel subire eas videor mihi summa cum dignitate vel declinare nulla cum molestia posse. Dices fortasse: 'Digni-

VII. Rome, July, 59 B.C. In accordance with the compact made in 60 B.C. between Caesar, Pompey, and Crassus, who formed what is commonly called the First Triumvirate, Caesar had been elected consul for 59 B.C., and the radical measures whose passage he had secured or was securing with the help of Pompey (cf. *Att.* 2. 16. 2) opened Cicero's eyes to the character of Pompey, and to the danger which threatened the state. The letter presents a lively picture of the political turmoil in Rome, throws light upon the attitude of the populace toward Caesar and Pompey, as viewed from an aristocratic standpoint, and discloses Cicero's realization for a moment of the danger with which the designs of Clodius threaten him.

1. sescenta: cf. *miliens*, Ep. V. 4 n.— Statium manu missum (*esse*): Quintus Cicero had lately set his slave Statius free, and this action had given color to the rumor that Statius exerted too great an influence over Quintus. Cf. *Q. fr.* 1. 2. 3 *quod autem me maxime movere solebat, cum audiebam illum plus apud te posse quam gravitas istius aetatis imperi prudentiae postularet*, etc. — nec meum imperium, etc.: from Ter. *Phorm.* 232. — mitto, *I waive.* — revereri: an exclamatory infinitive expressing indignation. — ego autem, etc.: perhaps a general statement, or Cicero may refer to his brother alone, as on grounds of politeness or discretion he often employs the plural when thinking of a single person. — cetera, etc.: pointing back to multa me sollicitant;

tatis ἅλις, tamquam δρυός : saluti, si me amas, consule.'
Me miserum! cur non ades ? Nihil profecto te praeteriret; ego fortasse τυφλώττω et nimium τῷ καλῷ προσπέπονθα. Scito nihil umquam fuisse tam infame, tam 2
turpe, tam peraeque omnibus generibus ordinibus
aetatibus offensum quam hunc statum qui nunc est;
magis mehercule quam vellem, non modo quam putaram. Populares isti iam etiam modestos homines sibi-
lare docuerunt. Bibulus in caelo est, nec quare scio,
sed ita laudatur quasi

> Vnus homo nobis cunctando restituit rem.

Pompeius, nostri amores, quod mihi summo dolori est,
ipse se adflixit. Neminem tenent voluntate; ne metu
necesse sit iis uti vereor. Ego autem neque pugno
cum illa causa propter illam amicitiam, neque approbo,
ne omnia improbem quae antea gessi; utor via. Populi 3

'my other troubles concern important matters.'—dignitatis ἅλις,
tamquam δρυός, *quite enough of
dignity, as men said of the oak.*
The proverbial expression, ἅλις
δρυός, refers to the time when men
gave up a diet of acorns for one of
bread. In general language, 'times
are changed, and what suited the
past is ill adapted to the present.'
Jeans aptly cites the same proverb
from Voltaire : ' *Le siècle du gland
est passé, vous donnerez du pain
aux hommes.*' Cf. also Intr.
102.— τυφλώττω and τῷ καλῷ
προσπέπονθα (*am passionately attached*) are very likely naturalized
Greek phrases. Cf. Intr. 97.
2. generibus, ordinibus, *to
all parties, classes.*—non modo
quam putaram: 'to say nothing
of what I had anticipated.'—
populares : the triumvirs, who
found their supporters in the
democratic party.— Bibulus: Caesar's colleague in the consulship;
cf. *Lucceium*, Ep. VI. 11 n. He
opposed Caesar's plans to the
best of his ability, but his opposition was rather obstinate than
effective. Cf. Mommsen, *Rom.
Hist.* IV. 245. Subsequently he
was commander of Pompey's fleet
in the Civil War. — in caelo est,
is extolled to the skies. — unus
homo, etc.: the celebrated line
from the *Annals* of Ennius descriptive of Fabius Maximus Cunctator, ironically applied to the passive resistance of Bibulus. — ipse
se adflixit: *i.e.* by allying himself
with Caesar. — tenent: *sc.* the triumvirs. — illa causa: the cause of
the triumvirs. — illam amicitiam:
Cicero's well-known friendship for
Pompey. — utor via: *i.e.* the *via
media*, turning off neither to the
one side nor to the other.

sensus maxime theatro et spectaculis perspectus est.
Nam gladiatoribus qua dominus qua advocati sibilis
conscissi; ludis Apollinaribus Diphilus tragoedus in
nostrum Pompeium petulanter invectus est;

Nostra miseria tu es magnus . . .

miliens coactus est dicere;

Eandem virtutem istam veniet tempus cum graviter gemes

totius theatri clamore dixit, itemque cetera — nam et
eiusmodi sunt ii versus ut in tempus ab inimico Pompei scripti esse videantur — ;

Si neque leges te neque mores [cogunt] . . .

et cetera magno cum fremitu et clamore sunt dicta.
Caesar cum venisset, mortuo plausu Curio filius est
insecutus. Huic ita plausum est ut salva re publica
Pompeio plaudi solebat. Tulit Caesar graviter. Litte-

3. **theatro et spectaculis**: abl.
of time. Cf. *gladiatoribus*, Ep.
V. 11 n. and Intr. 83 *d.* Upon
political demonstrations on such
occasions, Böckel cites *pro Sestio*,
115–126. — **qua . . . qua** = *et . . .
et:* a usage not occurring in Cicero outside the letters, but found
in comedy; cf. Plaut. *Men.* 666. —
dominus : this seems from the
connection to refer to Pompey.
As Tyrrell remarks, to the Roman
at this time the figure in the foreground was Pompey, not Caesar.
Pompey attended the gladiatorial
show which was given by Gabinius
(*Att.* 2. 24. 3). — ludis **Apollinaribus**: given July 6–13, under the
direction of the *praetor urbanus.*
— **istam**: difficult to understand
as referring to the subject of **gemes ;** but perhaps we may understand, 'the time shall come when
you (Pompey) shall bitterly repent

of this very prowess of yours,' *i.e.*
in carrying everything through
with a high hand. — **mortuo plausu,** *as the applause* (for Caesar)
died away. The contrast revealed
Caesar's unpopularity. Allowance should be made for the fact
that Cicero was sitting among the
senators and knights, who favored
Curio, and at a distance from
the lower classes, who were in the
rear of the theatre, and could not
well compare the applause from
the two sections, even if he were
impartial. — **Curio filius :** the
younger Curio continued to be
Caesar's most active and dangerous opponent until 50 B.C., when
Caesar purchased his support by
the payment of a large sum of
money. Cf. *Fam.* 2. 1 ; 2. 7 ; 8. 10.
3 ; 16. 11. 2, and Vell. Paterc. 2.
48. 3.—**litterae . . . erat susceptum:** the tenses in this paragraph

rae Capuam ad Pompeium volare dicebantur.   Inimici
erant equitibus qui Curioni stantes plauserant, hostes
omnibus.   Rosciae legi, etiam frumentariae minita-
bantur.   Sane res erat perturbata.   Equidem malueram
quod erat susceptum ab illis silentio transiri, sed vereor
ne non liceat.   Non ferunt homines quod videtur esse
tamen ferendum; sed est iam una vox omnium, magis
odio firmata quam praesidio.   Noster autem Publius 4
mihi minitatur, inimicus est; impendet negotium, ad
quod tu scilicet advolabis.   Videor mihi nostrum illum
consularem exercitum bonorum omnium, etiam satis
bonorum habere firmissimum.   Pompeius significat studium erga me non mediocre; idem adfirmat verbum de
me illum non esse facturum, in quo non me ille fallit,
sed ipse fallitur.   Cosconio mortuo sum in eius locum
invitatus.   Id erat vocari in locum mortui.   Nihil mihi

are probably epistolary. Cf. Intr. 84 *c.* — **equitibus qui**, etc. : the hostility of the *equites* toward Caesar is hard to understand, as his legislation to relieve the *publicani* who had bid too high for the privilege of collecting the taxes (*Att.* 1. 17. 9 ; 2. 16. 2) was calculated to win their favor. — **Capuam**: Pompey was at Capua as a member of the commission appointed under Caesar's agrarian laws. —**Rosciae legi**: the *lex Roscia,* proposed by L. Roscius Otho in 67 B.C., set apart 14 rows of seats for the knights immediately behind the orchestra, where the senators sat.   This law had been threatened in Cicero's consulship also; cf. *Att.* 2. 1. 3 and Mommsen, *St. R.* III. 520. — **frumentariae**: the *lex Terentia et Cassia* passed in 73 B.C. fixed a low price for corn. Cf. Cic. *Verr.* ii. 3. 163, 174.

The repeal of this law would be aimed at the poor people, as the repeal of the Roscian law would injure the *equites.* — **quam praesidio**: *i.e.* than by power of resistance.

4. **noster** : the possessive is often thus used ironically in the letters of one whom the writer dislikes or despises. Cf. Intr. 88 *b.* — **impendet negotium**: Clodius wished to take vengeance upon Cicero for the latter's evidence on the trial for sacrilege, and for the discomfiture which he had suffered at his hands in the debate in the senate (cf. Ep. V. 2 n). Cf. Intr. 14. — **consularem exercitum**:*i.e.* the backing which Cicero's consulship won him. — **illum (facturum)**: *i.e.* Clodius. — **in locum mortui**: Cosconius had been a member of Caesar's land commission.   Cicero is offended that, in-

turpius apud homines fuisset, neque vero ad istam ipsam ἀσφάλειαν quicquam alienius; sunt enim illi apud
bonos invidiosi, ego apud improbos meam retinuissem
5 invidiam, alienam adsumpsissem.   Caesar me sibi vult
esse legatum.   Honestior declinatio haec periculi; sed
ego hoc non repudio.   Quid ergo est ?   Pugnare malo;
nihil tamen certi.   Iterum dico: utinam adesses! sed
tamen, si erit necesse, arcessemus.   Quid aliud? quid?
Hoc opinor: certi sumus perisse omnia.   Quid enim
ἀκκιζόμεθα tamdiu ?   Sed haec scripsi properans et
mehercule timide.   Posthac ad te aut, si perfidelem
habebo cui dem, scribam plane omnia, aut, si obscure
scribam, tu tamen intelleges.   In iis epistulis me Laelium, te Furium faciam; cetera erunt ἐν αἰνιγμοῖς.   Hic
Caecilium colimus et observamus diligenter.   Edicta
Bibuli audio ad te missa.   Iis ardet dolore et ira noster
Pompeius.

stead of making him an original
member of the commission, the
triumvirs should wait until a member died, and should then offer
him the chance of stepping into
a dead man's shoes, so to speak.
The phrase implies also that one
holding a place on the commission
would be dead politically. — istam: Atticus had evidently recommended a conciliatory course; see
above, '*saluti, si me amas, consule.*'
— apud bonos invidiosi : the division of the public lands was
always bitterly opposed by the
Boni.

5. legatum: as Caesar's legate during his proconsulship,
Cicero might hope for protection
against the attacks of Clodius.
Cf. *Att.* 2. 18. 3. Cicero's agitation shows itself in the abruptness
of the style (Billerbeck). — perfi-

delem: cf. Intr. 77. — Laelium:
Cicero elsewhere (Ep. III. 3) compares himself to Laelius.   In his
next letter to Atticus (*Att.* 2. 20.
5) he announces his intention of
calling himself Laelius in the letters and leaving the name of
Atticus unchanged.   The plan
suggested here does not seem to
have been carried out.   Furius, consul 136 B.C., was a friend of the
younger Laelius. — cetera erunt
ἐν αἰνιγμοῖς: numerous illustrations of this fact may be found in
the care with which Cicero often
avoids referring to people by their
names.   He alludes also to delicate personal and political matters
in a covert way.   Cf. Intr. 104. —
Caecilium: cf. Ep. I. 3. — edicta
Bibuli : Bibulus, Caesar's colleague in the consulship, after in-
effectual efforts to oppose Caesar's

VIII. (*Att. 2. 22.*)

CICERO ATTICO SAL.

Quam vellem Romae! Mansisses profecto si haec 1
fore putassemus; nam Pulchellum nostrum facillime
teneremus aut certe quid esset facturus scire possemus. Nunc se res sic habet: volitat, furit; nihil habet
certi, multis denuntiat; quod fors obtulerit, id facturus
videtur. Cum videt quo sit in odio status hic rerum,
in eos qui haec egerunt impetum facturus videtur; cum
autem rursus opes eorum et exercitus recordatur, con-
vertit se in bonos. Nobis autem ipsis tum vim, tum
iudicium minatur. Cum hoc Pompeius egit et, ut ad 2
me ipse referebat, — alium enim habeo neminem testem — vehementer egit, cum diceret in summa se per-
fidiae et sceleris infamia fore, si mihi periculum crea-
retur ab eo quem ipse armasset, cum plebeium fieri

action, shut himself up in his own
house and issued proclamations
declaring Caesar's acts illegal. Cf.
Mommsen, *Rom. Hist.* IV. 247. —
noster: cf. 4 n.

VIII. Rome, Aug. or Sept., 59
B.C. The excited tone and the
abrupt style of the letter betray
the writer's appreciation of the
imminence of the danger threatening him.

1. **quam vellem Romae :** if
the text is correct, either to be
connected with the greeting (cf.
Fam. I. 10), or an extreme case
of ellipsis, with *te esse* understood. Cf. *Att.* 13. 21. 6 *de
Caesaris adventu scripsit ad me
Balbus non ante Kal.;* 13. 2. 1
*Pisonem sicubi (poteris, conveni,
ut) de auro (conficias),* and Intr.
95. — **Pulchellum :** cf. Ep. V.
10 n.— **nunc:** in the existing state

of affairs, in contrast to what
would have been true had Atticus
remained. — **denuntiat** (*sc. vim*):
the absolute use of *denuntio* is remarkable. See Crit. Append.—**eos:**
i.e. the triumvirs. — **exercitus:**
the force awaiting Caesar in Gaul.

2. **cum hoc:** *i.e. Clodio.* — **alium
... testem:** this suggests a doubt
of the truth of Pompey's statement.
There can in fact be little doubt
that Caesar and Pompey understood the designs of Clodius, and
tacitly approved of his election to
the tribuneship. It was part of
their plan to break down the prestige of the senate, and that could
be accomplished in no better way
than by degrading one of its leaders and discrediting its somewhat
autocratic treatment of the Catilinarian conspiracy. — **cum . . .
passus esset :** Pompey actually

passus esset; fidem recepisse sibi et ipsum et Appium
de me; hanc si ille non servaret, ita laturum ut omnes
intellegerent nihil sibi antiquius amicitia nostra fuisse.
Haec et in eam sententiam cum multa dixisset, aiebat
illum primo sane diu multa contra, ad extremum autem
manus dedisse et adfirmasse nihil se contra eius voluntatem esse facturum. Sed postea tamen ille non desti-
tit de nobis asperrime loqui; quod si non faceret, tamen
ei nihil crederemus atque omnia, sicut facimus, para-
3 remus. Nunc ita nos gerimus ut in dies singulos et
studia in nos hominum et opes nostrae augeantur.
Rem publicam nulla ex parte attingimus; in causis
atque in illa opera nostra forensi summa industria versamur, quod egregie non modo iis qui utuntur opera
nostra, sed etiam in vulgus gratum esse sentimus. Domus celebratur, occurritur; renovatur memoria consulatus, studia significantur; in eam spem adducimur, ut
nobis ea contentio quae impendet interdum non fugi-
4 enda videatur. Nunc mihi et consiliis opus est tuis et
amore et fide; quare advola. Expedita mihi erunt

took some part in the proceedings
of the *comitia curiata* when Clodius was adopted; cf. *Att.* 2. 12. 1.
— **fidem recepisse**, etc.: 'both
Clodius and Appius have given
him (Pompey) a promise not to
attack me.' *Recipio* in this sense
is colloquial. The full expression
is *in me recipio.* — **Appium**: Appius Claudius Pulcher, the brother
of Clodius, had been Cicero's friend
until the quarrel with Clodius occurred. He was in 52 B.C. Cicero's
predecessor as governor of Cilicia.
The 13 letters of Bk. 3, *ad Fam.*,
are addressed to him. — **multa
contra** (*sc. dixisse*) : cf. Intr. 95.
The verb of saying is most fre-

quently omitted, as here, in re-
porting the words of another.

3. in causis: in this year Cicero
delivered orations in behalf of
C. Antonius, of A. Thermus, and
of L. Flaccus. Of these a portion
of the oration for Flaccus is preserved. — **occurritur** : men run
to meet me when I appear upon
the street.

4. **expedita**, etc.: Cicero in later
years did not consider the advice
of Atticus, who came to Rome
to help him, so judicious as he
had hoped it would be; cf. Ep.
XV. 1 (written in 57 B.C.) *cognoram . . . te in consiliis mihi dandis
nec fortiorem nec prudentiorem*

omnia, si te habebo.   Multa per Varronem nostrum agi possunt, quae te urgente erunt firmiora, multa ab ipso Publio elici, multa cognosci, quae tibi occulta esse non poterunt, multa etiam — sed absurdum est singula explicare, cum ego requiram te ad omnia.   Vnum illud 5 tibi persuadeas velim, omnia mihi fore explicata, si te videro; sed totum est in eo, si ante quam ille ineat magistratum.   Puto Pompeium Crasso urgente, si tu aderis, qui per Βοῶπιν ex ipso intellegere possis qua fide ab illis agatur, nos aut sine molestia aut certe sine errore futuros.   Precibus nostris et cohortatione non indiges.   Quid mea voluntas, quid tempus, quid rei

quam me ipsum. — **Varronem:** cf. intr. to Ep. LX. Varro was an intimate friend of Pompey, and could therefore be of service to Cicero.

5. **si te videro**: protases of the future form often stand in the *oratio obliqua* in the indicative to indicate the time relation solely (Böckel). Cf. also Intr. 84 *a.* — **si ante:** *sc. te videro*; cf. *quam vellem*, 1 n. — **ille ineat magistratum**: Clodius would become tribune in December. — **puto Pompeium**, etc.: 'I think that if you are here, while Crassus is urging Pompey on, you, who can find out from the prime mover himself through her of the ox-eyes, with how much sincerity the triumvirs are acting, I think, I say, that we shall be either free from annoyance or at least from misconceptions.' — **Crasso urgente:** the dislike which Crassus felt for Cicero seems to date from 66 B.C., when Cicero, in his speech for the Manilian law, by exaggerating the part which Pompey had played in certain matters, had belittled the

achievements of Crassus. An apparent, not a real, reconciliation took place in the senate in 61 B.C. (cf. Ep. V. 5 n; XIII. 2). Another open quarrel between the two men occurred in 54 B.C.; cf. *Fam.* I. 9. 20. — **Βοῶπιν:** Clodia, the sister of Clodius. This epithet of Hera as applied to her has a double meaning. On the one hand, as with Hera, the brilliancy of Clodia's eyes was one of her claims to beauty. Cicero speaks of her *flagrantia oculorum, pro Cael.* 49. On the other hand, her will was imperious, and her fondness to control men and things as well marked as was that of Hera. She was the Lesbia of the poet Catullus, and the mistress of the young orator Caelius, by whom the letters of Bk. 8, *ad Fam.* were written. For a sketch of her life, cf. Boissier, *Cicéron et ses Amis*, 174–186. Cf. also Merrill's *Catullus*, Intr. 18 ff. She hated Cicero, and knew and sympathized with her brother's plans against him. Apparently Atticus was one of her friends.

6 magnitudo postulet intellegis.   De re publica nihil
habeo ad te scribere, nisi summum odium omnium
hominum in eos qui tenent omnia.   Mutationis tamen
spes nulla; sed, quod facile sentias, taedet ipsum Pompeium vehementerque paenitet.   Non provideo satis
quem exitum futurum putem, sed certe videntur haec
7 aliquo eruptura.   Libros Alexandri, neglegentis hominis et non boni poëtae, sed tamen non inutilis, tibi
remisi.   Numerium Numestium libenter accepi in amicitiam; et hominem gravem et prudentem et dignum
tua commendatione cognovi.

IX. (*Att.* 2. 23.)

CICERO ATTICO SAL.

1   Numquam ante arbitror te epistulam meam legisse,
nisi mea manu scriptam.   Ex eo colligere poteris
quanta occupatione distinear; nam, cum vacui temporis nihil haberem et cum recreandae voculae causa

6. de re publica: cf. Intr. 91.
— nihil habeo ad te scribere, *I
have nothing to write you.* Cf. Cic.
pro Balb. 33 *quid habes igitur
dicere de Gaditano foedere.* — qui
tenent omnia: *i.e.* the triumvirs.
— non provideo satis, etc.: colloquial for *non provideo satis qui
exitus futurus sit.*   Such peri-
phrases occur most frequently
after *dicere, arbitrari, credere,* and
praedicare.   They are very frequent in Latin comedy, as *sed finem
fore quem dicam nescio,* Plaut.
Trin. 2; *sed dic tamen unde onu-
stam celocem agere te praedicem,*
Plaut. *Pseud.* 1306; *inimiciorem
nunc utrum credam magis soda-
lemne esse an Bacchidem, incertum
admodumst,* Plaut. *Bacch.* 500 f.

7. libros Alexandri: in 59 B.C.
Cicero was at work on his *Cho-
rographia,* a treatise upon geography (cf. *Att.* 2. 4. 3; 2. 6. 1;
2. 7. 1), and Atticus had sent to
him a poem upon the same subject, written by Alexander of Ephesus (*Att.* 2. 20. 6). — Numerium
Numestium : recommended to
Cicero by Atticus; cf. *Att.* 2. 20. 1.
IX. Rome, Aug. or Sept., 59
B.C.
1. nisi mea manu scriptam:
cf. Intr. 64. — quanta occupatione distinear : his attention
was given to professional matters
rather than to politics; cf. 3. —
voculae: cf. *pulchellus,* Ep. V.
10 n, and *voculas,* Ep. LI. 2 n. —
ambulare: Quintilian, 11. 3. 19,

necesse esset mihi ambulare, haec dictavi ambulans. Primum igitur illud te scire volo, Sampsiceramum no- 2 strum amicum vehementer sui status paenitere restitui- que in eum locum cupere ex quo decidit, doloremque suum impertire nobis et medicinam interdum aperte quaerere, quam ego posse inveniri nullam puto; deinde omnes illius partis auctores ac socios nullo adversario consenescere, consensionem universorum nec voluntatis nec sermonis maiorem umquam fuisse. Nos autem — 3 nam id te scire cupere certo scio — publicis consiliis nullis intersumus, totosque nos ad forensem operam laboremque contulimus, ex quo, quod facile intellegi possit, in multa commemoratione earum rerum quas gessimus desiderioque versamur. Sed Βοώπιδος no-

recommends walking, among other things, as good for the voice. — **dictavi**: Tiro, Cicero's principal secretary, was an expert shorthand writer and the author of a system of stenography. Cf. Intr. 57. — **haec dictavi ambulans**: no better proof could be required that Cicero did not intend his letters for publication than the fact that many of them were composed while on a journey, or just as the vessel is weighing anchor, between the courses at dinner, or while the messenger is impatiently standing behind him with cloak and hat on. Cf. Ep. LXX. 1. To his brother, who had complained of the illegibility of his letters, he writes: *sed hoc facio semper, ut quicumque calamus in manus meas venerit, eo sic utar tamquam bono, Q. fr.* 2. 14. 1. Cf. also *ante lucem*, Ep. XVI. 7 and Intr. 64.

2. **Sampsiceramum**: a nick- name several times applied to Pompey (cf. *Att.* 2. 17. 1). Samp- siceramus was the petty ruler of Emesa, which Pompey had con- quered. Elsewhere (*Att.* 2. 17. 3) Pompey is alluded to as *Arabar- ches*, the despot of eastern Egypt, or *Hierosolymarius*, 'the Jerusa- lemite' (*Att.* 2. 9. 1) from his cap- ture of Jerusalem. The applica- tion of these nicknames to Pom- pey suggests that after his return from the East, he assumed an arro- gant and autocratic manner more befitting a petty eastern despot than a Roman citizen. The very sound of his nicknames would also suggest his pompous manner. — **ex quo decidit**: cf. *quia de- ciderat ex astris, Att.* 2. 21. 4. — **medicinam . . . quaerere**: a favorite metaphor, not only with Cicero but with other Roman writers; developed at great length, for instance, by Servius Sulpicius in Ep. LXXV. 5. Cf. also Intr. 99.

3. **desiderio versamur**: *i.e.* I am haunted by a painful remem- brance of my past achievements. — **Βοώπιδος**: cf. Ep. VIII. 5 n. —

strae consanguineus non mediocres terrores iacit atque
denuntiat, et Sampsiceramo negat, ceteris prae se fert
et ostentat. Quamobrem, si me amas tantum quantum
profecto amas, si dormis, expergiscere, si stas, ingre-
dere, si ingrederis, curre, si curris, advola. Credibile
non est quantum ego in consiliis et prudentia tua, quodque maximum est, quantum in amore et fide ponam.
Magnitudo rei longam orationem fortasse desiderat,
coniunctio vero nostrorum animorum brevitate con-
tenta est. Permagni nostra interest te, si comitiis non
potueris, at declarato illo esse Romae. Cura ut valeas.

X. (*Att.* 3. 4.)

CICERO ATTICO SAL.

Miseriae nostrae potius velim quam inconstantiae
tribuas, quod a Vibone quo te arcessebamus subito

nostrae: cf. *noster*, Ep. VII. 4 n.
Clodia had at one time hoped to
attract Cicero by her charms, and
her hatred of him was partly due
to the failure of her efforts.— si
comitiis (*esse Romae*) non potueris: the elections were to take place
Oct. 18 (cf. *Att.* 2. 20. 6), but the
tribunes did not enter on the duties
of their office until December 10.

Cicero's urgent requests for the
presence of Atticus would seem
to have been successful, as there
is a break in the correspondence
between the two men from November, 59, to March, 58, during
which time Atticus was doubtless
in Rome.

The correspondence of the year
59 B.C. reveals the utter helplessness of the senatorial party to cope
with the triumvirs. The former
were without a 'platform' and with-

out leaders. The petulant opposition of Bibulus and the tact-
less obstinacy of Cato excited only
ridicule and anger. These letters
as a whole disclose also Cicero's
lack of political insight in failing
utterly to appreciate the strength
of the Triumvirate, and in failing
to see up to the last moment the
danger of his own position (cf.
also Intr. 14). In striking contrast
to the letters of this year are those
written six months later.

X. Vibo, about April 12, 58 B.C.
The letters of this third book,
ad Att., written in exile, expose
perhaps more than any other portion of his correspondence, the
weak side of Cicero's character.
He is unmanly, selfish, and un-
grateful. In contrast the letters
of 44 and 43 B.C. breathe a spirit
of unfailing courage and unselfish

discessimus; adlata est enim nobis rogatio de pernicie mea, in qua quod correctum esse audieramus erat eiusmodi, ut mihi ultra quadringenta milia liceret esse, illo pervenire non liceret. Statim iter Brundisium versus contuli ante diem rogationis, ne et Sica, apud quem eram, periret et quod Melitae esse non licebat. Nunc tu propera ut nos consequare, si modo recipiemur. Adhuc invitamur benigne, sed quod superest timemus. Me, mi Pomponi, valde paenitet vivere, qua in re apud

patriotism. It is only when two such epochs in Cicero's life are placed side by side that the reader can discover the true key to his character, which is to be found in the fact that he was peculiarly sensitive to his surroundings, and was exalted or depressed by circumstances which would have had no abiding influence upon a more phlegmatic nature (cf. Intr. 50).

Without waiting to see what action would be taken upon the bill of Clodius, which did not mention him by name (*qui civem Romanum indemnatum interemisset, ei aqua et igni interdiceretur*, Vell. Paterc. 2. 45), Cicero left Rome about March 20, 58 B.C., and went to his friend Sica, near Vibo. Here news reached him of the amended bill directed against him personally. He therefore hastily left Vibo for Tarentum and Brundisium. See Intr. 15 f.

quo te arcessebamus: in *Att.* 3. 3. — rogatio: cf. Ep. V. 2 n. The *rogatio* in this case read as follows: *velitis iubeatis ut M. Tullio aqua et igni interdictum sit;* cf. Cic. *de Domo*, 47.— correctum: the amended bill forbade Cicero to remain at any point within 400 miles of Italy. After a bill had been brought forward an interval of 17 days, a *trinundinum* (cf.

Herzog, I. 1092, n. 2; see, however, Momm. *St. R.* III. 376, n. 1) was allowed to elapse before a vote was taken upon it, during which time it could be modified. — illo: to Sicily or Malta. — rogationis : *sc. ferendae.* — ne et: carelessly used for *et ne*, as the force of **ne** does not extend to the second of the two correlative clauses. — ne . . . periret: those who should harbor an exile within the prescribed limits made themselves liable to a severe penalty. — Melitae: Malta was within the 400-mile limit. — mi Pomponi: Cicero rarely addresses his correspondent by name in a letter. In the 397 letters to Atticus, Atticus is addressed by name only 28 times : *mi Attice* nineteen times, *mi Tite* once, and *mi T. Pomponi* once, otherwise as in this letter. The omission of the praenomen, as Tyrrell remarks, indicated intimacy; cf. *quod sine praenomine familiariter, ut debebas, ad me epistulam misisti*, etc., *Fam.* 7. 32. 1. The polite order was *mi Pomponi*, and Cicero deviates from this order but once, when in a jesting letter he addresses a friend, *Testa mi*. Cf. also *Cicero mi*, Curius, *Fam.* 7. 29. 1. In general, the possessive pronoun indicates informality. — paenitet vivere, qua

me tu plurimum valuisti.   Sed haec coram.   Fac modo
ut venias.

XI. (*Fam.* 14. 4.)

TVLLIVS S. D. TERENTIAE ET TVLLIAE ET
CICERONI SVIS.

1   Ego minus saepe do ad vos litteras quam possum
propterea quod cum omnia mihi tempora sunt misera,
tum vero cum aut scribo ad vos aut vestras lego, con-
ficior lacrimis sic ut ferre non possim.   Quod utinam
minus vitae cupidi fuissemus!   certe nihil aut non multum in vita mali vidissemus.   Quod si nos ad aliquam
alicuius commodi aliquando reciperandi spem fortuna
reservavit, minus est erratum a nobis; si haec mala
fixa sunt, ego vero te quam primum, mea vita, cupio
videre et in tuo complexu emori, quoniam neque dii,
quos tu castissime coluisti, neque homines, quibus ego
2 semper servivi, nobis gratiam rettulerunt.   Nos Brun-

---

in re ... valuisti: Cicero seems to
have contemplated suicide. Cf. *Att.*
3. 7. 2, first sentence, and *Att.* 3. 3
*utinam illum diem videam, cum
tibi agam gratias quod me vivere
coëgisti ! adhuc quidem valde me
paenitet.*— **coram:** cf. Intr. 95.

XI. Brundisium, April 29, 58
B.C. On **suis,** cf. *suis,* Ep. XIII.
superscription, n.

1. **litteras:** *litterae* probably indicates here, as in several other
passages, more than one letter;
cf. *litteris,* Ep. XCIX. 1 n. — **vitae cupidi:** Cicero may be regret-
ting either his mistake in not having met death while making an
armed resistance to Clodius, as
some of his friends advised, or his
failure to commit suicide; cf. *paenitet vivere,* Ep. X. n. — **aliquam**

alicuius . . . aliquando: these
words indicate sufficiently Cicero's
despair. — **dii ... servivi:** a statement suggestive of the respective
attitudes of the two sexes in Cicero's time in religious matters. —
neque homines . . . rettulerunt:
Cicero's friends did, however,
stand by him, and many of those
outside Rome, like Flaccus at
Brundisium (2) and Plancius at
Thessalonica (*Att.* 3. 14. 2), assisted him at the peril of their
lives and fortunes, while his friends
at Rome and the people throughout Italy worked steadily for his
recall. For the risk which Flaccus
ran, cf. *pro Planc.* 97 *in hortos me
M. Laeni Flacci contuli, cui cum
omnis metus publicatio bonorum
exsilium mors proponeretur haec*

disi apud M. Laenium Flaccum dies XIII fuimus, virum
optimum, qui periculum fortunarum et capitis sui prae
mea salute neglexit, neque legis improbissimae poena
deductus est quo minus hospiti et amicitiae ius offici-
umque praestaret.   Huic utinam aliquando gratiam
referre possimus! Habebimus quidem semper.   Brun- 3
disio profecti sumus a. d. II K. Mai.; per Macedoniam
Cyzicum petebamus.   O me perditum! O adflictum!
Quid nunc rogem te ut venias, mulierem aegram et
corpore et animo confectam ? Non rogem ?   Sine te
igitur sim ?   Opinor, sic agam: si est spes nostri reditus, eam confirmes et rem adiuves; sin, ut ego metuo,
transactum est, quoquo modo potes ad me fac venias.
Vnum hoc scito: si te habebo, non mihi videbor plane
perisse. Sed quid Tulliola mea fiet ? Iam id vos videte;
mihi deest consilium.   Sed certe, quoquo modo se res
habebit, illius misellae et matrimonio et famae servi-

*perpeti, si acciderent, maluit quam
custodiam mei capitis dimittere.*

2. **capitis** : citizenship in its
broadest sense. — **poena** : cf. *ne
periret,* Ep. X. n.

3. **profecti sumus**: a regular
use of the epistolary perfect for
the present. Cicero is on the
point of sailing. — **a. d. II K. Mai.**:
an unusual expression for *pridie
K. Mai.*, but for the same formula,
cf. *C. I. L.* I. 902, 979. — **petebamus**: a regular epistolary im-
perfect, indicating what would be
going on at the time the letter
was received. Cf. Intr. 84 *c.* —
aegram . . . corpore: Terentia's
health would seem to have been
delicate at the best, if we may
judge from Cicero's earnest words
in several letters, *e.g.* Ep. LVIII.
and *Fam.* 14. 22. Cf. also Ep. LVI.

— **sic agam:** a colloquial phrase,
meaning little more than 'this is
the best plan.' Its stereotyped
character is shown by the fact that
Cicero proceeds to state a plan of
action, not for himself but for
Terentia. — **confirmes . . . adiuves**: on the mood and tense, cf.
Intr. 84 *b.* — **transactum est,** *it's
all over ;* a colloquialism. *Actum
est* is more common; cf. *e.g. Att.*
5. 15. 1; 9. 12. 4, and Plaut. *Trin.*
308; Ter. *And.* 465. Both phrases
convey the idea of an unfortunate
conclusion. In Ter. *Heaut.* 564
that idea is more fully expressed
by the addition of *perii.* — **quid
Tulliola mea fiet:** cf. *Att.* 6. 1.
14 *quid illo fiet? quid me ?* On
the diminutives **Tulliola** and **misellae** (below), cf. Intr. 76 and
pulchellus, Ep. V. 10 n. — **matri-**

endum est. Quid? Cicero meus quid aget? Iste
vero sit in sinu semper et complexu meo. Non queo
plura iam scribere; impedit maeror. Tu quid egeris
nescio; utrum aliquid teneas an, quod metuo, plane sis
4 spoliata. Pisonem, ut scribis, spero fore semper nostrum. De familia liberata nihil est quod te moveat.
Primum tuis ita promissum est, te facturam esse ut
quisque esset meritus; est autem in officio adhuc Or-
pheus, praeterea magnopere nemo; ceterorum servorum
ea causa est ut, si res a nobis abisset, liberti nostri
essent, si obtinere potuissent; sin ad nos pertinerent,
servirent praeterquam oppido pauci. Sed haec minora
5 sunt. Tu quod me hortaris ut animo sim magno et
spem habeam reciperandae salutis, id velim sit eiusmodi ut recte sperare possimus. Nunc miser quando
tuas iam litteras accipiam? Quis ad me perferet? Quas
ego exspectassem Brundisi, si esset licitum per nautas,
qui tempestatem praetermittere noluerunt. Quod reliquum est, sustenta te, mea Terentia, ut potes hone-
stissime. Viximus, floruimus; non vitium nostrum, sed
virtus nostra nos adflixit; peccatum est nullum, nisi
quod non una animam cum ornamentis amisimus. Sed
si hoc fuit liberis nostris gratius, nos vivere, cetera,

---

monio: Tullia's marriage to her
first husband Piso; cf. *Pisonem
nostrum*, Ep. XIII. 2 n. Cicero is
thinking of the payment of the
dowry. — Cicero meus: Marcus
Cicero, the orator's son.

4. de familia liberata: Cicero's
disposition of his own slaves before leaving Rome is fully explained in the sentence, *ceterorum
servorum . . . oppido pauci.* Terentia evidently fears the loss of *her*
slaves. Cicero quiets her anxiety

by assuring her that the control of
her slaves rests in her own hands
(te facturam esse, etc.).— in officio, *faithful.*— si obtinere potuissent, *if they could maintain*
(their claim to freedom against
my enemies). — oppido: a colloquial word; cf. Dziatzko on Ter.
Phorm. 317 and Wölfflin, *Lat. u.
rom. Comparation*, 21.

5. esset licitum : cf. *licitum est*,
Ep. LXXV. 3 n. — ornamentis:
i.e. position and dignity.

quamquam ferenda non sunt, feramus. Atque ego, qui
te confirmo, ipse me non possum. Clodium Philhetae- 6
rum quod valetudine oculorum impediebatur, hominem
fidelem, remisi. Sallustius officio vincit omnes. Pescennius est perbenevolus nobis, quem semper spero
tui fore observantem. Sica dixerat se mecum fore, sed
Brundisio discessit. Cura, quod potes, ut valeas et sic
existimes, me vehementius tua miseria quam mea commoveri. Mea Terentia, fidissima atque optima uxor,
et mea carissima filiola et spes reliqua nostra, Cicero,
valete. Pr. K. Mai. Brundisio.

XII. (*Att.* 3. 12.)

CICERO ATTICO SAL.

Tu quidem sedulo argumentaris quid sit sperandum, 1
et maxime per senatum, idemque caput rogationis proponi scribis, quare in senatu dici nihil liceat; itaque
siletur. Hic tu me accusas quod me adflictem, cum ita

6. **Clodium Philhetaerum,
Sallustius, Pescennius**: freedmen. — **Sica**: cf. Ep. X. — **perbenevolus**: cf. Intr. 77. — **quod
potes**: with *posse* the restrictive
relative *quod* and *quod eius* are
often found with the indic. in Cicero and in Terence (Böckel). Cf.
Att. 10. 2. 2 *tu tamen, quod poteris,
ut adhuc fecisti, nos consiliis iuva-
bis.* In this letter, one of the most
familiar and unreserved in the
correspondence, there is a pronounced colloquial tone, *e.g. sic
agam, transactum est* (3), *oppido* (4),
and *esset licitum* (5). — **Brundisio**:
cf. Intr. 62.

XII. Thessalonica, July 17, 58
B.C. Cicero stayed at Thessalonica
from May to November, 58 B.C.,

under the protection of the quaestor Plancius.

1. **sedulo**: probably from the
conversational vocabulary, if we
may judge from its frequency in
comedy and in the Letters, and its
infrequency (*e.g.* Cic. *de Fin.* 3. 16;
Livy, 34. 14. 3) elsewhere. Cf. Ter.
Ad. 251, 413; *Eun.* 362; *Heaut.*
126; Cic. *Att.* 9. 15. 6; *Fam.* 5.
10 A. 2. It is found oftenest with
facio. — **caput . . . scribis**: cf.
Att. 3. 15. 6 *at tute scripsisti ad
me quoddam caput legis Clodium
in curiae poste fixisse* NE REFERRI
NEVE DICI LICERET ('that no motion should be brought forward
and no speech made'). — **hic**:
this word may express surprise
here as elsewhere in the Letters:

sim adflictus ut nemo umquam, quod tute intellegis?
Spem ostendis secundum comitia. Quae ista est eodem
2 tribuno pl. et inimico consule designato? Percussisti
autem me etiam de oratione prolata. Cui vulneri, ut
scribis, medere, si quid potes. Scripsi equidem olim
ei iratus quod ille prior scripserat, sed ita compresseram
ut numquam emanaturam putarem. Quomodo exciderit
nescio; sed quia numquam accidit ut cum eo verbo uno
concertarem, et quia scripta mihi videtur neglegentius
quam ceterae, puto posse probari non esse meam. Id,
si putas me posse sanari, cures velim; sin plane perii,
3 minus laboro. Ego etiam nunc eodem in loco iaceo,
sine sermone ullo, sine cogitatione ulla. Licet tibi, ut
scribis, significarim ut ad me venires; dudum tamen
intellego te istic prodesse, hic ne verbo quidem levare
me posse. Non queo plura scribere, nec est quod scribam: vestra magis exspecto. Data XVI Kal. Sextiles
Thessalonicae.

'do you blame me, *then?*' Cf. Ep.
LXXIX. 4 *hic tu me abesse urbe
miraris, in qua domus nihil delectare possit*, etc.? or it may mean,
'at this point in your letter,' after
writing of the action of Clodius.
— **secundum comitia**: Pompey
expressed later the same hope of
favorable action 'after the comitia'; cf. *Att.* 3. 18. 1.— **eodem . . .
designato**: *i.e.* with Clodius as
tribune and Metellus Nepos as
consul designatus. Metellus Nepos
proved to be friendly. See Cicero's
letter of thanks for the support
of Metellus Nepos, *Fam.* 5. 4; cf.
also *pro Sest.* 130.
   2. **de oratione prolata**: Cicero
had written a speech against Curio
the elder, which unfortunately was
published. Cf. also *Att.* 3. 15. 3
in senatu rem probe scribis actam;

*sed quid Curio? an illam orationem
non legit? quae unde sit prolata
nescio.* This must be a different
oration from the one of which we
have extracts in Ep. V. 9. — **quod
ille prior scripserat**: probably
just before or after the trial of
Clodius, as Curio was the champion of Clodius in the senate; cf.
Att. 1. 14. 5. — **quomodo exciderit**, *how it got out.* — **puto . . .
meam**: Cicero's intention to dis-
avow the authorship of this speech
finds some extenuation in the des-
perate nature of his position. For
other questionable acts, cf. Intr. 47.
   3. **ut ad me venires**, etc.: see
Crit. Append. — **istic**, *there, where
you are, i.e.* in Rome. — **vestra**:
(not *tua*) to include letters from
other friends also. — **data** (*sc. est
epistula*) XVI **Kal.**: in the letters

XIII. (*Fam.* 14. 2.)

TVLLIVS S. D. TERENTIAE SVAE ET TVLLIOLAE ET CICERONI SVIS.

Noli putare me ad quemquam longiores epistulas 1 scribere, nisi si quis ad me plura scripsit cui puto rescribi oportere; nec enim habeo quid scribam, nec hoc tempore quicquam difficilius facio. Ad te vero et ad nostram Tulliolam non queo sine plurimis lacrimis scribere; vos enim video esse miserrimas quas ego beatissimas semper esse volui, idque praestare debui et, nisi tam timidi fuissemus, praestitissem. Pisonem no- 2

of the third book to Atticus, the date is regularly given without *a.d.* The same statement is not true of the letters to others during this period. — **Thessalonicae**: cf. Intr. 62.

XIII. Thessalonica, Oct. 5, 58 B.C. **suis** in the superscription is plural because it belongs to both the children. For variations of this salutation, cf. *Fam.* 14. 1, 3, and 6. The possessive pronoun indicates familiarity, and Cicero uses it in addressing the members of his family only. It is used in all the 24 letters to his wife, in Bk. 14, *ad Fam.*, with one exception: in the fifteenth letter, Ep. LVIII., which is cold and formal, he writes, *Tullius s. d. Terentiae.* Upon the significance of the possessive in this use, cf. *Fam.* 16. 18. 1. In a previous letter to his freedman Cicero had written, *Tullius Tironi sal.*, omitting Tiro's praenomen. The latter evidently remarked upon the salutation as too familiar for a letter from patron to freedman. Upon which Cicero put at the head of his next letter the same

salutation, and added in the body of the letter, *Quid igitur ? non sic oportet ? equidem censeo sic; addendum etiam* SVO.

1. **nisi si**: apparently a favorite pleonasm for *nisi* in the language of everyday life; see Intr. 101, and cf. Reisig-Schmalz, *Lat. Syn.* note 612 d ; Schmalz, *Jahresb.* Mannheim, 1881, p. 44. Schmalz says that it has crowded the classical *nisi* out of use in the Latin of the Christian fathers. — **nec . . . scribam**: note the difference in meaning between *non habeo quod scribam, non habeo quid scribam,* and *non habeo scribere.* Cf. Ep. VIII. 6 n. — **Tulliolam**: see Intr. 53. On the diminutive, cf. *pulchellus,* Ep. V. 10 n. — **tam timidi**: Lucullus had advised (Plut. *Cic.* 31) the use of force in opposing Clodius. Atticus and others had apparently counselled moderation. Cf. *Fam.* 1. 9. 13; *Att.* 3. 15. 7. The change to the plural is probably made to include these two friends and others who had advised a moderate course.

2. **Pisonem nostrum**: cf. Intr.

strum merito eius amo plurimum.   Eum, ut potui, per
litteras cohortatus sum gratiasque egi, ut debui.   In
novis tr. pl. intellego spem te habere.   Id erit firmum,
si Pompei voluntas erit; sed Crassum tamen metuo.
A te quidem omnia fieri fortissime et amantissime
video, nec miror, sed maereo casum eiusmodi ut tantis
tuis miseriis meae miseriae subleventur.   Nam ad me
P. Valerius homo officiosus scripsit, id quod ego maximo
cum fletu legi, quemadmodum a Vestae ad tabulam
Valeriam ducta esses.   Hem, mea lux, meum desiderium, unde omnes opem petere solebant!   Te nunc, mea
Terentia, sic vexari, sic iacere in lacrimis et sordibus,

53. He worked devotedly to prevent Cicero's exile, and afterwards
to secure his recall; cf. *Fam.* 14. 1.
4; 14. 3. 3.— **in novis tr. pl.**:
the new tribunes would come into
office Dec. 10, and had all promised to help Cicero. One of the
number was Milo, leader of the
'physical force' section of the senatorial party. — **voluntas erit**: *sc.
firma.* — **Crassum**: cf. Ep. VIII.
5 n. — **P. Valerius**: mentioned
several times in the Letters, but
little is known of him. — **a** (*sc.
templo*) **Vestae**: cf. the English
expression 'from St. Paul's.' This
ellipsis of *templum* or *aedes* between the preposition and the
genitive of the name of a divinity,
according to C. F. W. Müller, appears first in Ter. *Ad.* 582. ' It
belongs, therefore, to the colloquial language of the Scipionic
circle, and must be considered
rather familiar than vulgar or
archaic.' Cf. *ad Opis, Att.* 14. 14.
5; *ad Apollinis*, Ep. XVI. 3; *ad
Vestae*, Hor. *Sat.* 1. 9. 35. Somewhat similar is *ad L. Tondei* (*domum*) *vorsu, C. I. L.* I. 1143. See
also Intr. 95 and *Arch. f. lat. Lex.*

II. 368. Terentia's half-sister Fabia
was a Vestal virgin, and Terentia
had probably taken refuge with
her. — **ad tabulam Valeriam**:
Pliny, *N. H.* 35. 22, quoted by Hofmann, tells us that there was a
painting upon the side wall of the
Curia Hostilia, executed by the
order of M.' Valerius Maximus to
celebrate his victories. Near this
painting (the *Tabula Valeria*) there
was probably a banker's stall, to
which Terentia was forced to come
to make an affidavit with reference
to her property, or possibly to secure a loan. — **hem**: a colloquial
word, to be distinguished from the
demonstrative particle *em*. It expresses joy, astonishment, or, as
here, grief. It is frequent in comedy; cf. Ter. *And.* 383, 420, 462.
and see Intr. 92. — **mea lux,
meum desiderium**: cf. *Fam.* 14.
5. 1 *si tu et Tullia, lux nostra,
valetis ;* Ep. XI. 6 *mea Terentia,
fidissima atque optima uxor ; Fam.*
14. 5. 2 *vos, mea suavissima et optatissima Terentia.* Cf. Intr. 49,
52. — **unde . . . solebant**: as they
hoped to win Cicero's legal or
political support through her in-

idque fieri mea culpa, qui ceteros servavi ut nos peri-
remus! Quod de domo scribis, hoc est de area, ego 3
vero tum denique mihi videbor restitutus, si illa nobis
erit restituta. Verum haec non sunt in nostra manu.
Illud doleo, quae impensa faciendast, in eius partem te
miseram et despoliatam venire. Quod si conficitur
negotium, omnia consequemur; sin eadem nos fortuna
premet, etiamne reliquias tuas misera proicies? Obsecro te, mea vita, quod ad sumptum attinet, sine alios
qui possunt, si modo volunt, sustinere, et valetudinem
istam infirmam, si me amas, noli vexare; nam mihi
ante oculos dies noctesque versaris; omnis labores te
excipere video; timeo ut sustineas. Sed video in te
esse omnia. Quare, ut id quod speras et quod agis
consequamur, servi valetudini. Ego ad quos scribam 4

tercession. — **iacere**, etc.: cf. Ep.
XII. 3 *eodem in loco iaceo*, etc. The
infinitives **vexari**, etc., are exclamatory. — **qui ceteros**, etc.: the execution of Lentulus and his fellow-
conspirators, by which Cicero had
saved Roman citizens from murder and arson, was the pretext for
his banishment.

3. **de domo**: cf. Intr. 16. —
illud doleo, etc.: a common Latin
idiom; cf. *Att.* 2. 24. 1 *quas Nu-
mestio litteras dedi, sic te iis evoca-
bam.* — **negotium**: *i.e.* Cicero's
recall. *Negotium* with the force of
res is colloquial, and frequent in all
periods. Cf. the slang expression,
'Tell me the whole business.' —
mea vita: cf. note upon *mea lux*
above. — **sine alios . . . sustinere**: Terentia proposed to sell
her own property in order to raise
money for the expenses attendant
upon her husband's recall. Cicero
opposes this plan still more ur-
gently in *Fam.* 14. 1. 5 *quod ad me,*

*mea Terentia, scribis te vicum ven-
dituram, quid, obsecro te, — me miserum ! — quid futurum est ? et, si
nos premet eadem fortuna, quid
puero misero fiet ?* Cf. also Ep.
XI. 3. — **si me amas**: this expression and *amabo te, sis (si vis)*
and *sodes (si audes)* are set phrases
in colloquial Latin which are
joined to words of command for
the sake of politeness and emphasis, *e.g. da mihi hoc, mel meum, si
me amas, si audes,* Plaut. *Trin.* 244;
*amabo te, si quid quod opus fuerit
Appio facies, ponito me in gratia,*
Fam. 8. 6. 5. Cf. also Intr. 100,
and *Arch. f. lat. Lex.* IX. 485–
491. — **mihi ante oculos dies
noctesque versaris**: a colloquial
pleonasm which occurs also in
Fam. 14. 3. 2, and would not perhaps have been employed, had the
writer been in a calmer frame of
mind. See note to *nisi si*, 1. Cf.,
however, *mihi soli versatur ante
oculos, Lael.* 102.

nescio, nisi ad eos qui ad me scribunt, aut ad eos de quibus ad me vos aliquid scribitis. Longius, quoniam ita vobis placet, non discedam; sed velim quam saepissime litteras mittatis, praesertim si quid est firmius quod speremus. Valete, mea desideria, valete. D. a. d. III Non. Oct. Thessalonica.

XIV. (*Att.* 3. 22.)

CICERO ATTICO SAL.

1 Etsi diligenter ad me Q. frater et Piso quae essent acta scripserant, tamen vellem tua te occupatio non impedisset quo minus, ut consuesti, ad me quid ageretur et quid intellegeres perscriberes. Me adhuc Plancius liberalitate sua retinet, iam aliquotiens conatum ire in Epirum. Spes homini est iniecta, non eadem quae mihi, posse nos una decedere; quam rem sibi magno honori sperat fore. Sed iam, cum adventare milites dicentur, faciendum nobis erit ut ab eo discedamus; quod cum faciemus, ad te statim mittemus, ut 2 scias ubi simus. Lentulus suo in nos officio, quod et re et promissis et litteris declarat, spem nobis nonnullam adfert Pompei voluntatis; saepe enim tu ad me scripsisti eum totum esse in illius potestate. De Me-

---

4. **mea desideria**: the plural includes wife, daughter, and son.

XIV. Thessalonica, with a postscript from Dyrrachium, Nov. 25, 58 B.C.

1. **Piso**: cf. Ep. XIII. 2 n. — **consuesti**: cf. Intr. 82. — **Plancius**: quaestor of Macedonia and Cicero's host at Thessalonica. In return for his kindness Cicero defended him in 54 B.C., in the *Or. pro Plancio*. Cf. also *Fam.* 14. 1.

3. — **milites**, etc.: the province of Macedonia had been assigned to the consul L. Calpurnius Piso for 57 B.C., and Cicero feared the coming of his soldiers.

2. **Lentulus**: elected to the consulship for 57 B.C. Cicero based great hopes upon this man's friendship for him and influence with Pompey. — **de Metello**: Q. Caecilius Metellus Nepos was to be the colleague of Lentulus. He had, as tribune, prevented Cicero, at the close of his consulship (*Fam.*

tello scripsit ad me frater quantum sperasset pro-
fectum esse per te. Mi Pomponi, pugna ut tecum et 3
cum meis mihi liceat vivere, et scribe ad me omnia.
Premor luctu, desiderio omnium meorum, qui mihi me
cariores semper fuerunt. Cura, ut valeas.

Ego quod, per Thessaliam si irem in Epirum, per- 4
diu nihil eram auditurus et quod mei studiosos habeo
Dyrrachinos, ad eos perrexi, cum illa superiora Thessalonicae scripsissem. Inde cum ad te me convertam,
faciam ut scias, tuque ad me velim omnia quam diligentissime, cuicuimodi sunt, scribas. Ego iam aut
rem aut ne spem quidem exspecto. Data vi Kal. Decembr. Dyrrachi.

XV. (*Att.* 4. 1.)

CICERO ATTICO SAL.

Cum primum Romam veni fuitque cui recte ad te 1
litteras darem, nihil prius faciendum mihi putavi quam

5. 2. 7), from making the customary speech to the people. Atticus
had subsequently brought about a
reconciliation. Cf. also Ep. XII. 1 n.

3. **mi Pomponi**: cf. Ep. X. n.
— **scribe ad me omnia**: a request
to be found in almost every letter
of this period. Cicero puts more
confidence in the letters of Atticus
than in those of his brother Quintus; cf. *Att.* 3. 18. 2 *Q. frater,
homo mirus, qui me tam valde
amat, omnia mittit spei plena, metuens, credo, defectionem animi mei;
tuae autem litterae sunt variae, neque enim me desperare vis nec
temere sperare.*

4. **cuicuimodi**: a very rare genitive form for *cuiuscuiusmodi.* Cf.
also *Fam.* 4. 7. 4, *pro Sext. Rosc.* 95,
and *Verr.* ii. 5. 107. It is perhaps

found in Plaut. *Bacch.* 400. See
Krebs, *Antibarbarus*, Neue, *For-
menlehre*, II.[2] 246; and Wilkins,
Cic. *de Or.* 3. 94. — **Dyrrachi**: cf.
Thessalonicae, Ep. XII. 3 n.

XV. Rome, Sept., 57 B.C. Cicero landed at Brundisium Aug. 5,
57 B.C., after an absence of 16
months (Plut. *Cic.* 33). He entered Rome Sept. 4, delivered the
Oratio post Reditum in the senate
Sept. 5, and directly afterwards
addressed the people (cf. 5 of this
letter); Sept. 7 he proposed a bill
in the senate putting Pompey in
charge of the corn commission,
and after the adjournment of the
senate advocated the bill before
the people (6). It became a law
Sept. 8 (7).

1. **recte**, *with safety.* — **tibi**

ut tibi absenti de reditu nostro gratularer; cognoram
enim — ut vere scribam — te in consiliis mihi dandis
nec fortiorem nec prudentiorem quam me ipsum, nec
etiam pro praeterita mea in te observantia nimium in
custodia salutis meae diligentem, eundemque te, qui
primis temporibus erroris nostri aut potius furoris
particeps et falsi timoris socius fuisses, acerbissime
discidium nostrum tulisse plurimumque operae, studi,
diligentiae, laboris ad conficiendum reditum meum con-
2 tulisse.   Itaque hoc tibi vere adfirmo, in maxima laetitia et exoptatissima gratulatione unum ad cumu-
landum gaudium conspectum aut potius complexum
mihi tuum defuisse; quem semel nactus numquam dimisero ac, nisi etiam praetermissos fructus tuae suavi-

---

absenti: Atticus was in Epirus.
— **cognoram enim**: the reason
for the congratulation, which is
the main thought, is contained in
the second infinitive clause, **eundem te . . . contulisse**; the
first infinitive clause, **te . . . diligentem**, which is concessive, and
therefore logically subordinate, is
in a free way made coördinate
with the other. — **nec fortiorem**,
etc.: in *Att.* 3. 15. 4 also Cicero
reproaches Atticus for a lack of
wisdom and bravery: *sed tu tantum
lacrimas praebuisti dolori meo.* Cf.
tam timidi, Ep. XIII. 1 n. — **nec
. . . nimium diligentem**: this
means in formal Latin, 'not too
active,' but here it means, 'not
very active,' without any idea of
excess, or, as we say, 'none too
active.'   This use of *nimium*,
nimio, and *nimis* is frequent in
colloquial Latin. Cf. *homo nimium lepidus*, 'a very charming man'
(not 'too charming a man'), Plaut.
Mil. 998; *locos nimium mirabilis*,
'exceedingly strange places,' *Trin.*

931; *illud non nimium probo*, 'I
don't particularly approve of it,'
Cic. *Fam.* 12. 30. 7. Cf. also Intr.
90. — **erroris nostri**: in assuming
that the first bill of Clodius, which
did not mention Cicero by name,
was directed against him, and in
confessing thereby its applicability
to him. Cf. Ep. X., introd. note.
— **plurimum operae**, etc.: during
Cicero's exile Atticus not only
made the best use of his wide
acquaintance with politicians of
all factions to secure Cicero's recall (cf., *e.g.*, *Metello*, Ep. XIV.
2 n), but also aided Cicero's family, which was in financial straits
(Ep. XIII.).

2. **quem**: antecedent in **tuum**.
— **dimisero**: in early Latin the
fut. perf. did not involve the idea
of completion before the occurrence of another event (cf. F. Cra-
mer, *Arch. f. lat. Lex.* IV. 594–
598), so that Plautus writes, *huc
aliquantum abscessero, Trin.* 625;
immo alium potius misero, Capt.
341.   In the later period the dis-

tatis praeteriti temporis omnes exegero, profecto hac restitutione fortunae me ipse non satis dignum iudicabo. Nos adhuc in nostro statu quod difficillime re- 3 ciperari posse arbitrati sumus, splendorem nostrum illum forensem et in senatu auctoritatem et apud viros bonos gratiam magis quam optamus, consecuti sumus; in re autem familiari, quae quemadmodum fracta, dissipata, direpta sit non ignoras, valde laboramus, tuarumque non tam facultatum, quas ego nostras esse iudico, quam consiliorum ad colligendas et constituendas reliquias nostras indigemus. Nunc, etsi omnia aut scripta 4 esse a tuis arbitror aut etiam nuntiis ac rumore perlata, tamen ea ipse scribam brevi, quae te puto potissimum ex meis litteris velle cognoscere. Pr. Nonas Sextiles Dyrrachio sum profectus, ipso illo die, quo lex est lata de nobis. Brundisium veni Nonis Sextilibus. Ibi mihi Tulliola mea fuit praesto natali suo ipso die, qui casu idem natalis erat et Brundisinae coloniae et tuae vicinae Salutis; quae res animadversa a multitudine summa Brundisinorum gratulatione celebrata est. Ante diem VI Idus Sextiles cognovi litteris Quinti mirifico studio omnium aetatum atque ordinum, incredibili con-

---

tinction between the fut. and fut. perf. was introduced into formal Latin, but was not always observed in colloquial Latin; cf. Cic. *Att.* 3. 19. 1 *nusquam facilius hanc miserrimam vitam vel sustentabo vel, quod multo est melius, abiecero.*

3. **forensem:** *i.e.* as a lawyer. — **optamus:** he fears his position may excite envy. — **in re autem familiari** : Cicero's house upon the Palatine had been destroyed, his villas plundered, and the rest of his property had been so badly managed by Terentia and her dis-

honest steward Philotimus that he found himself nearly bankrupt on his return. He was even forced to put up his Tusculan villa for sale; cf. *Att.* 4. 2. 7. — **fracta**, etc.: for the metaphor, cf. *contraxi vela*, Ep. V. 2 n.

4. **Tulliola:** cf. *pulchellus*, Ep. V. 10 n. — **coloniae** : its establishment as a *colonia* dated from 245 B.C. Cf. Müller's *Handbuch*, III. 475. — **Salutis** : for the erection and decoration of the temple of Salus, see Livy, 10. 1, Pliny, *N. H.* 35. 19, and Val. Max. 8. 14.

cursu Italiae legem comitiis centuriatis esse perlatam.
Inde a Brundisinis honestissimis ornatus iter ita feci
ut undique ad me cum gratulatione legati convenerint.
5 Ad urbem ita veni ut nemo ullius ordinis homo nomenclatori notus fuerit qui mihi obviam non venerit, praeter
eos inimicos quibus id ipsum, se inimicos esse, non
liceret aut dissimulare aut negare.   Cum venissem ad
portam Capenam, gradus templorum ab infimo plebe
completi erant, a qua plausu maximo cum esset mihi
gratulatio significata, similis et frequentia et plausus
me usque ad Capitolium celebravit, in foroque et in
ipso Capitolio miranda multitudo fuit.   Postridie in
senatu, qui fuit dies Nonarum Septembr., senatui gra-
6 tias egimus.   Eo biduo cum esset annonae summa
caritas et homines ad theatrum primo, deinde ad senatum concurrissent, impulsu Clodi mea opera frumenti

6.— concursu Italiae: Cicero was
more popular with the people of
Italy than with the populace at
Rome, and by a decree of the senate the former were urged to come
to Rome to uphold his cause. —
ornatus: used absolutely without
the abl. of the thing, as in *Fam.*
I. I. 3. — legati: delegates representing the towns on the *Via
Appia.*

5. nomenclatori : the *nomen-
clator* stood at his master's elbow,
and whispered in his ear the name
and the calling of those whom his
master met, and any fact of importance concerning them.   For
the valuable services which he
rendered a candidate, cf. Hor.
Ep. I. 6. 49–54. — ad portam
Capenam: the *Via Appia* entered
the city through the *porta Capena*,
at the right of which was the temple of Honos and Virtus. — ab

infimo, *from top to bottom*. — plebe : as Böckel remarks, Cicero
wishes to emphasize the enthusiasm which the lower classes
showed.— usque ad Capitolium:
i.e. between the Palatine and Cae-
lian, thence through the Forum,
and up the *Clivus* to the Capitol.
— senatui gratias egimus : in
the *Oratio post Reditum*, though
the authenticity of the extant oration bearing that title is sometimes
questioned.

6. ad theatrum: to the tem-
porary theatre where the *ludi
Romani* were being held. — impulsu Clodi : Böckel shows by
a quotation from Asconius that
there had been scarcity at Rome
for three months.   Perhaps, however, the populace had been led
by Cicero's friends to expect a
return of prosperity upon his recall, and as they found that this

inopiam esse clamarent, cum per eos dies senatus de annona haberetur et ad eius procurationem sermone non solum plebis, verum etiam bonorum Pompeius vocaretur, idque ipse cuperet multitudoque a me nominatim ut id decernerem postularet, feci et accurate sententiam dixi, cum abessent consulares, quod tuto se negarent posse sententiam dicere, praeter Messallam

result did not follow, there was a popular reaction against him, led by Clodius. — id ipse (*sc. Pompeius*) cuperet: in the latter part of 58 B.C. Pompey and Clodius had a violent quarrel, and were still at enmity with each other. Atticus might therefore have supposed that the position, which was to be offered to Pompey, since it was the result of the agitation led by Clodius, was distasteful to Pompey. — ut id decernerem, *that I should advocate that course.* — quod ... dicere: Cicero comments bitterly upon the cowardice of the Optimates in an oration delivered a short time after this: *at enim non nulli propter timorem, quod se in senatu tuto non esse arbitrabantur, discesserunt. Non reprehendo, nec quaero fueritne aliquid pertimescendum ; puto suo quemque arbitratu timere oportere, de Domo,* 8. The entire sentence beginning with eo biduo, with its rapid succession of temporal clauses, the rapidity of whose effect is heightened by the use of asyndeton, with its graphic description of the movements of the populace, is calculated to present the urgency of the popular demand in a forcible manner. Cicero seems to feel that his action in coming forward as the champion of a measure which would give Pompey extraordinary power, and thereby offend the Optimates,

may appear unwise, and therefore calls for justification. Its unwisdom would consist in its tendency to estrange the Optimates at the moment when Cicero needed their help in getting indemnification for the loss of his house on the Palatine. It would also seem inconsistent with Cicero's political principles to advocate increasing the power of one of the triumvirs. Cicero strives to meet these two objections by presenting the urgency of the case and the fact, if we may accept it as a fact, that Pompey's appointment was favored by the *Boni* (verum etiam bonorum). Böckel acutely remarks that it may have been the purpose of Clodius to force Cicero to propose the grant of extraordinary powers, in order to compromise him in the eyes of the aristocracy and the *pontifices.* He certainly succeeded in putting him in a dilemma: to oppose the bill would have been to brave the wrath of the people and the enmity of Pompey, who had labored to secure his recall from exile; to favor the measure was to antagonize the aristocracy. — quod ... negarent: on the subj., cf. *diceret,* Ep. I. 3 n. — Messallam: M. Valerius Messalla Niger, consul in 61 B.C. He is highly praised by Cicero, in *Att.* I. 14. 6, for his integrity. Messalla and Afranius were supporters of Pompey. On Afra-

et Afranium. Factum est senatus consultum in meam
sententiam, ut cum Pompeio ageretur ut eam rem sus-
ciperet lexque ferretur; quo senatus consulto recitato,
continuo, cum more hoc insulso et novo plausum meo
nomine recitando dedissent, habui contionem; omnes
magistratus praesentes praeter unum praetorem et duos
7 tribunos pl. dederunt. Postridie senatus frequens, et
omnes consulares nihil Pompeio postulanti negarunt.
Ille legatos quindecim cum postularet, me principem
nominavit et ad omnia me alterum se fore dixit. Legem
consules conscripserunt, qua Pompeio per quinquennium
omnis potestas rei frumentariae toto orbe terrarum da-
retur; alteram Messius, qui omnis pecuniae dat potesta-

---

nius, cf. *Auli filius*, Ep. V. 12 n. —
eam rem: *i.e.* the procuring of corn.
— **meo nomine**: Cicero had been
a leading advocate of the bill, so
that his name probably appeared
in the list of those who put it
into legal form; cf. note on *legem
. . . conscripserunt* below. — **recitando**: here, as frequently in Livy
(*e.g.* 25. 30. 6) and occasionally in
Tacitus, the ablative of the ge-
rundive takes the place of the miss-
ing pres. part. pass. — **praetorem**:
the praetor was Appius Claudius
Pulcher, the brother of Clodius.
Cf. Ep. VIII. 2. The two tribunes, Sex. Atilius Serranus and
Q. Numerius Rufus, had already
opposed Cicero in other matters.
Cf. Cic. *pro Sest.* 72, 94. — **dederunt** (*sc. contionem*): a *contio* was
either an assembly of the people
held to consider a question but
not to vote upon it, or a speech
delivered before such an assembly.
Only a magistrate could give a
private citizen the right of speaking in a *contio*, and the technical
phrase for such permission was

contionem dare or *in contionem
producere.*
7. **senatus frequens** (*sc. fuit*):
cf. *frequentissimo senatu*, Ep.
VI. 9 n. — **alterum se** : cf. *vide
quam mihi persuaserim te me esse
alterum*, Ep. XXI. 1, and *verus
amicus est tanquam alter idem*,
Lael. 80. — **legem . . . conscripserunt**: the senate voted upon a
general proposition or upon a number of propositions laid before it.
If a motion was adopted, it was
written out in legal form, after its
passage, by a committee containing
the leading representatives of the
party which had supported it. It
contained, when thus drawn up, the
title, the year, the day, the place
of meeting, the name of the pro-
poser and of those who witnessed
the drawing up of the bill, and
then the enacting clause or clauses,
with sometimes an indication of
the number present. For a *senatus consultum* in legal form, cf.
Allen, *Remnants of Early Latin*,
Nos. 82, 105; Cic. *Fam.* 8. 8. 5. Cf.
also Willems, II. 206–216. — **Mes-**

tem et adiungit classem et exercitum et maius imperium in provinciis quam sit eorum qui eas obtineant.   Illa nostra lex consularis nunc modesta videtur, haec Messi non ferenda.   Pompeius illam velle se dicit, familiares hanc.   Consulares duce Favonio fremunt; nos tacemus et eo magis, quod de domo nostra nihil adhuc pontifices responderunt.   Qui si sustulerint religionem, aream praeclaram habebimus, superficiem consules ex senatus consulto aestimabunt; sin aliter, demolientur, suo nomine locabunt, rem totam aestimabunt.   Ita sunt res 8 nostrae, 'ut in secundis fluxae, ut in adversis bonae.' In re familiari valde sumus, ut scis, perturbati.   Praeterea sunt quaedam domestica, quae litteris non com-

---

sius: a tribune and a follower of Pompey; cf. *Att.* 8. 11 D. 2. — **maius imperium in provinciis**, etc.: the bill of Messius would have subordinated Caesar to Pompey. — **consularis**: because action was proposed by a consul, not by a tribune, as in the case of the other law. — **Pompeius . . . hanc**: a good illustration of Pompey's political methods. — **Favonio**: a man of more energy than tact; an admirer and imitator of Cato. Although only a quaestor, the boldness with which he advocated the cause of the Optimates brought even the *consulares* to accept him as their leader. He was praetor when the Civil War opened, took Pompey's side, and was pardoned by Caesar after the battle of Pharsalus. He fought on the side of the *liberatores* in the battle of Philippi, and was put to death after the battle by the order of Octavius. — **de domo nostra**: cf. Ep. XIII. 3 n. Either the pontifices may decide that the consecration by Clodius was void (**si sustulerint religio-**

nem), return the site to Cicero, and reimburse him for the loss of his house; or they may consider the consecration legal (**sin aliter**) and indemnify him for the loss of both house and grounds.

8. **ut in secundis . . . bonae:** probably an iambic verse from an old poet. The quotation occurs, *Att.* 4. 2. 1, *Ep. ad Brut.* 1. 10. 2. Cf. Ribbeck, *Trag. Rom. Frag.* p. 274. — **in re familiari**: cf. note on 3 above. — **quaedam domestica** : the first reference in Cicero's letters to the trouble between himself and Terentia, which led eleven years later to a divorce. Cf. *Att.* 4. 2. 7 (written a month later) *cetera, quae me sollicitant, μυστικώτερα sunt : amamur a fratre et a filia.* The omission of Terentia's name here is very significant. The reference to domestic troubles immediately after a statement concerning the unsatisfactory condition of his property lends color to the hypothesis that the reckless management of Cicero's property by Terentia and her

mitto. Q. fratrem insigni pietate, virtute, fide praedi-
tum sic amo ut debeo. Te exspecto et oro ut matures
venire, eoque animo venias ut me tuo consilio egere
non sinas. Alterius vitae quoddam initium ordimur.
Iam quidam, qui nos absentes defenderunt, incipiunt
praesentibus occulte irasci, aperte invidere; vehementer
te requirimus.

XVI. (Q. fr. 2. 3.)

MARCVS QVINTO FRATRI SALVTEM.

1   Scripsi ad te antea superiora; nunc cognosce postea
quae sint acta. A Kal. Febr. legationes in Idus Febr.
reiciebantur. Eo die res confecta non est. A. d. IIII
Non. Febr. Milo adfuit. Ei Pompeius advocatus venit;

steward was one of the causes of
the misunderstanding. Cf. Intr.
52. — **quidam**: the Optimates,
whose sympathy, shown while he
was in misfortune, had now given
way to the same jealousy which
they had evinced towards him in
former years. Cf. *voluntates nobi-*
lium, Ep. I. 2 n. They disap-
proved also of his political course
after his return; cf. *quod dicere*,
6 n.

XVI. Rome, written Feb. 12,
sent Feb. 15, 56 B.C. This letter
presents in a graphic manner the
disordered state of affairs in
Rome in 56 B.C. and the isolation
of Pompey. The latter fact led
Pompey to meet Caesar at Luca
in April and renew the Triumvirate, notwithstanding his manifest
jealousy of Caesar and his open enmity towards Crassus; cf. Momm.
Rom. Hist. IV. 354–370.

1. **antea**: in his last letter, *Q.*
fr. 2. 2, written Jan. 17. — **lega-**
tiones: *i.e.* audiences given to foreign embassies. — **reiciebantur**,

were postponed. The reception of
foreign embassies was the regular
order of business for February. —
eo die: *i.e.* the Ides. — **res**: Ptolemy Auletes, the king of Egypt,
being unable to maintain his position at home, had fled to Rome for
help, and in his absence the Alex-
andrians had placed his daughter
Berenice on the throne. The senate, at the suggestion of the consul
Lentulus Spinther, voted that the
consul who should receive Cilicia
as his province should restore
Ptolemy. Cilicia fell to Lentulus,
but the friends of Pompey con-
tended that the restoration of
Ptolemy should be placed in his
hands. For the dispute which
followed, cf. *Fam.* I. I. Cicero
espoused the cause of Lentulus.
He uses simply **res** in referring to
the matter here, as he had written
in detail upon the subject in his
last letter to Quintus (*Q. fr.* 2. 2.
3). — **adfuit** (*sc. comitiis tributis*):
Milo was accused of riotous proceedings by Clodius. For the

dixit Marcellus a me rogatus; honeste discessimus; prodicta dies est in VIII Idus Febr. Interim reiectis legationibus in Idus referebatur de provinciis quaestorum et de ornandis praetoribus; sed res multis querelis de re publica interponendis nulla transacta est. C. Cato legem promulgavit de imperio Lentulo abrogando. Vestitum filius mutavit. A. d. VIII Id. Febr. Milo 2 adfuit. Dixit Pompeius, sive voluit; nam ut surrexit, operae Clodianae clamorem sustulerunt, idque ei perpetua oratione contigit, non modo ut acclamatione, sed ut convicio et maledictis impediretur. Qui ut peroravit — nam in eo sane fortis fuit: non est deterritus; dixit omnia, atque interdum etiam silentio, cum auctoritate peregerat — sed ut peroravit, surrexit Clodius. Ei tantus clamor a nostris (placuerat enim referre gratiam) ut neque mente nec lingua neque ore consisteret. Ea

method of procedure before the *comitia tributa*, cf. Momm. *St. R.* III. 354–357. — **advocatus**: the *advocatus* appeared to give advice and to lend the defendant the benefit of his moral support; M. Marcellus was the *patronus*, or legal adviser and advocate.— **honeste discessimus**, *we came out of it with flying colors*. — **prodicta dies**: a trial before the *comitia tributa* ran through four meetings of that assembly. In this case the days of the trial were Feb. 2, Feb. 6, Feb. 17 (2, end), and May 7 (cf. *Q. fr.* 2. 5. 4).— **de ornandis praetoribus**: *i.e.* supplying the praetors with the troops necessary for their provinces.— **querelis . . . interponendis**: abl. cause; cf. *recitando*, Ep. XV. 6 n. — **C. Cato**: a tribune and enemy of Pompey (*Fam.* I. 5 B. I); not to be confused with M. Cato.— **de abro-**

gando: so as to checkmate the plans of Lentulus with reference to Egypt. — **vestitum filius mutavit**: the son put on mourning in order to excite sympathy for his father and prevent the passage of the bill, as did Cicero's friends in 58 B.C., when the law threatening him with banishment was proposed; cf. *Att.* 3. 15. 5.

2. sive: like *sive potius* to correct a statement. — **sane**: with adjectives and adverbs, a common colloquialism in Cicero's letters for the more formal *valde ;* cf. *sane plenum*, *Att.* 7. 4. 1; *sane commode*, *Att.* 7. 14. 2, etc. Cf. also Intr. 90. — **peregerat**: the change of tense is strange. The text is probably corrupt. — **a nostris**: especially the '*operae*' of Milo.— **referre gratiam**, *to return the compliment* (Tyrrell). — **ut . . . consisteret**, *so that he lost his*

res acta est, cum hora sexta vix Pompeius perorasset, usque ad horam VIII, cum omnia maledicta, versus denique obscenissimi in Clodium et Clodiam dicerentur. Ille furens et exsanguis interrogabat suos in clamore ipso quis esset qui plebem fame necaret. Respondebant operae: 'Pompeius.' Quis Alexandream ire cuperet. Respondebant: 'Pompeius.' Quem ire vellent. Respondebant: 'Crassum.' Is aderat tum Miloni animo non amico. Hora fere nona quasi signo dato Clodiani nostros consputare coeperunt. Exarsit dolor. Vrgere illi ut loco nos moverent. Factus est a nostris impetus; fuga operarum; eiectus de rostris Clodius, ac nos quoque tum fugimus, ne quid in turba. Senatus vocatus in curiam. Pompeius domum. Neque ego tamen in senatum, ne aut de tantis rebus tacerem aut in Pompeio defendendo (nam is carpebatur a Bibulo, Curione, Favonio, Servilio filio) animos bonorum virorum

self-possession, his tongue, and control of his countenance. — **ea res . . . ad horam VIII**, *this scene, although it was nearly noon when Pompey had finished speaking, continued clear up to 2 o'clock.* — **versus . . . dicerentur**: serious charges were freely made concerning the relations existing between Clodius and his sister. On Clodia, cf. Ep. VIII. 5 n. — **qui plebem fame necaret**: by failing in his duties as corn commissioner. Cf. Ep. XV. 6 f. — **Alexandream**: cf. *res*, 1 n. — **consputare**: see Intr. 79. — **fuga operarum**: *sc. facta est.* — **de rostris**: the trial of Milo took place in the Forum, where the *comitia tributa* commonly met. — **ne quid in turba** (*sc. accideret nobis*): the frequent ellipses, the historical infinitive **urgere**, the condensed expres-

sions, and the rapid transition from one idea to another in this whole passage give a panoramic effect to the description, and illustrate Cicero's skill in narrative. — **in curiam**: the *Curia Hostilia*, or original senate-house, faced the *comitium*, an open space at the north corner of the Forum. — **Bibulo**: cf. Ep. VII. 2, 5 nn. — **Curione**: cf. Ep. V. 1 n. — **Favonio**: cf. Ep. XV. 7 n. — **Servilio filio**: P. Servilius Vatia Isauricus was, like Favonius, an admirer and imitator of Cato. These four men with M. Cato were leaders of the ultra-conservative element of the aristocratic party. — **bonorum virorum**: here evidently used strictly as the name of a political party, opposed to *mali* or *improbi*. — **in posterum**: *sc. diem.* — **Quirinalia**: this festival was held Feb. 17.

offenderem. Res in posterum dilata est. Clodius in
Quirinalia prodixit diem. A. d. VII Id. Febr. senatus 3
ad Apollinis fuit, ut Pompeius adesset. Acta res est
graviter a Pompeio. Eo die nihil perfectum est. A. d.
VI Id. Febr. ad Apollinis senatus consultum factum est:
EA QVAE FACTA ESSENT ·A. D. VIII ID. FEBR. CONTRA
REM PVBLICAM ESSE FACTA. Eo die Cato vehementer
est in Pompeium invectus et eum oratione perpetua
tamquam reum accusavit, de me multa me invito cum
mea summa laude dixit; cum illius in me perfidiam
increparet auditus est magno silentio malevolorum.
Respondit ei vehementer Pompeius, Crassumque descripsit, dixitque aperte se munitiorem ad custodiendam
vitam suam fore quam Africanus fuisset, quem C. Carbo
interemisset. Itaque magnae mihi res iam moveri vide- 4
bantur; nam Pompeius haec intellegit nobiscumque
communicat, insidias vitae suae fieri, C. Catonem a
Crasso sustentari, Clodio pecuniam suppeditari, utrumque et ab eo et a Curione, Bibulo ceterisque suis ob-
trectatoribus confirmari, vehementer esse providendum
ne opprimatur, contionario illo populo a se prope alie-

3. **ad Apollinis:** cf. *a Vestae*,
Ep. XIII. 2 n. — **ut Pompeius
adesset :** since Pompey's house
was probably near the *Circus Fla-
minius*, this arrangement enabled
him to avoid the danger of coming
through the city to the *Curia*. —
Cato: the tribune; cf. 1 n. — **me
invito:** Cicero did not wish to be
drawn into the dispute. — **illius
in me perfidiam :** in allowing
Cicero to be banished. — **magno
silentio malevolorum:** a speech
in which Pompey was censured
and Cicero praised would tend
to make them enemies, and would

therefore please the democrats.
— **Crassum descripsit:** *i.e.* without mentioning his name. — **quem
C. Carbo interemisset :** Scipio
Africanus Minor was found dead
in his bed, and probably died a
natural death ; but the statement
of Pompey was the explanation of
his decease which the aristocrats
gave for party purposes. In this
case Pompey is the Africanus, and
C. Cato, secretly supported by
Crassus, the Carbo.

4. **contionario illo populo:** cf.
contionalis hirudo aerari, Ep. V.
11 n. — **populo . . . alienato**, etc.:

nato, nobilitate inimica, non aequo senatu, iuventute
improba. Itaque se comparat, homines ex agris arces-
sit; operas autem suas Clodius confirmat; manus ad
Quirinalia paratur. In eo multo sumus superiores ipsius copiis; et magna manus ex Piceno et Gallia exspec-
tatur, ut etiam Catonis rogationibus de Milone et
5 Lentulo resistamus. A. d. IIII Idus Febr. Sestius ab
indice Cn. Nerio Pupinia de ambitu est postulatus et
eodem die a quodam M. Tullio de vi. Is erat aeger.
Domum, ut debuimus, ad eum statim venimus eique
nos totos tradidimus, idque fecimus praeter hominum
opinionem, qui nos ei iure suscensere putabant, ut
humanissimi gratissimique et ipsi et omnibus videre-
mur, itaque faciemus. Sed idem Nerius index edidit
ad adligatos Cn. Lentulum Vatiam et C. Cornelium
Bestiam. Eodem die senatus consultum factum est,
VT SODALITATES DECVRIATIQVE DISCEDERENT LEXQVE

a striking commentary upon Pompey's weakness as a political leader
and upon his present isolation.
The populace was controlled by
Clodius, who had quarreled with
Pompey; the aristocracy and senate regarded Pompey as the leading member of the Triumvirate,
which threatened their supremacy;
the coming generation of young
politicians (iuventute) were extreme democrats.— improba: with
a political rather than a moral significance. Cf. note on *bonorum
virorum* above. — in eo, *in this
respect.* — ipsius: *i.e.* Pompey. —
ex Piceno: which was filled with
Pompey's followers; cf. Vell. Pat.
2. 29. — Gallia : Gallic recruits
would be furnished by Caesar. —
Lentulo: cf. note above on *de
abrogando.*
    5. Sestius: as tribune in 58–57

B.C., he had worked earnestly for
Cicero's recall. — Pupinia: *sc. tri-
bu.*— nos ei iure suscensere: Cicero may have well been offended
at Sestius's method of advocating
his cause, which showed more zeal
than judgment and was likely to
injure his prospects. Of the bill
which Sestius offered in his interest Cicero writes (*Att.* 3. 20. 3):
*rogatio Sesti neque dignitatis satis
habet nec cautionis.* — sed idem
Nerius, etc., *in addition to the
others implicated, Nerius has lodged
information against Vatia and Bestia also.* The charge made was
evidently that of bribery; cf. *ambitus* above. — sodalitates decuri-
atique: the former were originally
social, religious, or semi-religious
societies; cf. Cic. *de Sen.* 45. It
was soon found convenient, however, to use such organizations for

DE IIS FERRETVR VT QVI NON DISCESSISSENT EA POENA
QVAE EST DE VI TENERENTVR.   A. d. III Idus Febr. 6
dixi pro Bestia de ambitu apud praetorem Cn. Domitium in foro medio maximo conventu, incidique in eum
locum in dicendo, cum Sestius multis in templo Casto-
ris vulneribus acceptis subsidio Bestiae servatus esset.
Hic προῳκονομησάμην quiddam εὐκαίρως de his, quae
in Sestium apparabantur crimina, et eum ornavi veris
laudibus magno adsensu omnium.   Res homini fuit

political purposes; cf. *de Pet. Cons.*
19 *nam hoc biennio quattuor sodalitates hominum ad ambitionem
gratiosissimorum tibi obligasti . . .
qua re hoc tibi faciendum est, hoc
tempore ut ab iis quod debent exigas
saepe commonendo rogando con-
firmando curando ut intellegant
nullum se umquam aliud tempus
habituros referendae gratiae.* Clodius saw the advantage to be
derived from such bodies, and reorganized them in 58 B.C. Under
his control they played a part in
politics not unlike that of the political clubs in France before the
Revolution. The **decuriati** were
men organized into *decuriae* or
groups, in this case for political
purposes ; cf. *pro Sest.* 34. — **que**
is explanatory ; 'political clubs,
i.e. definite organizations.' — **discederent,** *should disband.* — **lex
. . . ferretur:** *i.e.* in the *comitia.*
Cf. Ep. V. 2 n. Such organizations were not effectually controlled until under Julius Caesar's
constitution the permission of the
senate was required before permanent societies with fixed times of
meeting and standing deposits
could be organized.

6. **pro Bestia:** L. Calpurnius
Piso Bestia, the tribune who in 63
B.C. by a speech against Cicero was
to give the signal to the conspira-

tors for active operations (Sall. *Cat.*
43. 1). The oration for Bestia has
not been preserved. — **Cn. Domitium** (*Calvinum*): he supported in
later years the cause of Caesar in
the Civil War. The last reference
to him is in connection with an un-
successful campaign against Phar-
naces in 47 B.C. (*Bell. Alex.* 65).
— **cum Sestius,** etc.: in Jan., 57
B.C., after many delays a proposition to recall Cicero from exile
was laid before the people; but as
Clodius had already filled the
comitium and the *curia* with armed
men, a riot followed, in which
Sestius was seriously wounded.
The forces of Cicero's friends had
taken up their position at the temple of Castor, on the south side
of the Forum ; cf. *pro Sest.* 75 f.
— **προῳκονομησάμην,** *brought out
in advance.* By eulogistic references to Sestius, Cicero wished to
pave the way for the oration in
his behalf, which was delivered a
month later and brought about
his acquittal (*Q. fr.* 2. 4. 1). —
homini: here, as elsewhere in the
Letters, almost equivalent to a pronoun. This use may be colloquial,
as it is unusually frequent in comedy, *e.g.* Ter. *Ad.* 536 SY. *Facio
te apud illum deum? virtutes narro.*
CT. *Meas?* SY. *Tuas; homini
ilico lacrumae cadunt.*

vehementer grata. Quae tibi eo scribo quod me de
7 retinenda Sesti gratia litteris saepe monuisti. Pridie
Idus Febr. haec scripsi ante lucem. Eo die apud
Pomponium in eius nuptiis eram cenaturus. Cetera
sunt in rebus nostris huiusmodi ut tu mihi fere diffi-
denti praedicabas, plena dignitatis et gratiae; quae
quidem tua, mi frater, patientia virtute pietate suavitate etiam tibi mihique sunt restituta. Domus tibi
ad lucum Pisonis Luciniana conducta est; sed, ut spero,
paucis mensibus post K. Quinctilis in tuam commigrabis. Tuam in Carinis mundi habitatores Lamiae
conduxerunt. A te post illam Olbiensem epistulam
nullas litteras accepi. Quid agas et ut te oblectes
scire cupio, maximeque te ipsum videre quam primum.
Cura, mi frater, ut valeas et, quamquam est hiems,
tamen Sardiniam istam esse cogites. xv K. Martias.

7. **pridie Idus Febr.**: this remark fixes the date of the letter
proper. What follows is a postscript written, as we see from the
last sentence, Feb. 15.— **ante lucem**: cf. *haec dictavi ambulans*,
Ep. IX. 1 n. See also *Q. fr.* 2. 5.
4.— **in eius nuptiis** : *sc.* with
Pilia. A daughter was born to
them, Caecilia, who married M.
Agrippa, and their daughter Vip-
sania Agrippa was the first wife of
Tiberius. — **patientia** : Quintus
could scarcely lay claim to *patientia* or *suavitas ;* cf., *e.g.*, *Q. fr.*
1. 1. 37.— **domus . . . conducta
est,** *the house which belonged to
Lucinius near Piso's park has been
hired for you.* Tyrrell would
change **lucum** to *lacum,* as *lucus*
is elsewhere regularly applied to
a grove sacred to a god.— **K.
Quinctilis**: July 1 was 'moving
day' in Rome (Böckel); see Suet.
Tib. 35.— **in tuam commigrabis**:
the house of Quintus on the Palatine adjoining his brother's was
being rebuilt under the direction
of the celebrated architect Cyrus;
cf. *Q. fr.* 2. 2. 2.— **in Carinis**:
between the Forum and the Esqui-
line. — **mundi habitatores Lamiae,** *respectable tenants, the Lamiae.* — **Olbiensem,** *from Olbia,*
in the northeastern part of Sardinia. — **tamen Sardiniam,** etc.:
the climate of Sardinia where
Quintus was stationed (cf. Intr.
55) was dangerous, even in the winter; see also Pomp. Mela, 2. 123.

XVII. (*Att.* 4. 4 B.)

CICERO ATTICO SAL.

Perbelle feceris si ad nos veneris.   Offendes dis- 1
signationem Tyrannionis mirificam librorum meorum,
quorum reliquiae multo meliores sunt quam putaram.
Etiam velim mihi mittas de tuis librariolis duos aliquos,
quibus Tyrannio utatur glutinatoribus, ad cetera admi-
nistris, iisque imperes ut sumant membranulam ex qua
indices fiant, quos vos Graeci, ut opinor, σιλλύβους
appellatis.   Sed haec, si tibi erit commodum.   Ipse 2
vero utique fac venias, si potes in his locis adhaerescere

XVII. Antium, June, 56 B.C.
1. perbelle: upon *per* in compounds, cf. Intr. 77. *Bellefacis,bene
facis,* etc., are colloquial phrases to
express gratitude.   Cf. *bene benig-
neque arbitror te facere,* Plaut.
Most. 816 ; *bene hercle factum et
habeo vobis gratiam, Rud.* 835.—
Tyrannionis: a grammarian and
teacher who was brought to Rome
as a prisoner by L. Lucullus.   He
was at one time tutor of the young
Cicero.   His services in arranging
Cicero's books are mentioned in
Att. 4. 8 A; *Q. fr.* 3. 4. 5, and Ep.
XXIII. 6 also.   The place in which
this letter was written is determined by comparing it with *Att.*
4. 8 A.— tuis librariolis: cf. Intr.
58.   Some of Cicero's works were
probably published by Atticus; cf.
Att. 2. 1. 2 *tu, si tibi placuerit liber,
curabis ut et Athenis sit et in ceteris oppidis Graeciae.*— duos aliquos: an indefinite small number ;
cf. Cic. *de Fin.* 2. 62 *tres aliqui
aut quattuor.* — glutinatoribus:
strips of papyrus from 8 to 14
inches long and 3 to 12 inches

wide were pasted together (*gluti-
nare*) at the sides in the proper
order after they had been written
upon.   A stick was fastened to
the last sheet, and on this the book
was rolled into a *volumen.*   The
ends of the stick were furnished
with knobs (*cornua*); to the upper
one was attached a strip of parchment containing the title (*index*).
Cf. Birt, *Das antike Buchwesen,*
242.— glutinatoribus . . . ad-
ministris : for the asyndeton, cf.
Intr. 94, and Draeg. *Hist. Syn.* II.
193 f.
2. si potes, etc.: for the quiet
and isolation of Antium, cf. *Att.* 2.
6 *sic enim sum complexus otium, ut
ab eo divelli non queam.   Itaque
aut libris me delecto, quorum habeo
Anti festivam copiam, aut fluctus
numero, nam ad lacertas captandas
tempestates non sunt idoneae; . . .
mihi quaevis satis iusta causa ces-
sandi est, qui etiam dubitem an hic
Anti considam et hoc tempus omne
consumam, ubi quidem ego mallem
duum virum quam Romae me fuisse.
. . . Esse* [to think that there is]

et Piliam adducere; ita enim et aequum est et cupit
Tullia.   Medius fidius ne tu emisti ludum praeclarum;
gladiatores audio pugnare mirifice.   Si locare voluisses,
duobus his muneribus liberasses.   Sed haec posterius.
Tu fac venias et de librariis, si me amas, diligenter.

XVIII. (*Fam.* 5. 12.)

M. CICERO S. D. L. LVCCEIO Q. F.

1   Coram me tecum eadem haec agere saepe conantem
deterruit pudor quidam paene subrusticus, quae nunc

*locum tam prope Romam ubi multi
sint qui Vatinium numquam vide-
rint! ubi nemo sit praeter me qui
quemquam ex vigintiviris vivum et
salvum velit.* Cf., however, Intr.
50. — Piliam: cf. *in eius nuptiis,*
Ep. XVI. 7 n.— medius fidius :
for *ita me deus fidius adiuvet.* —
ne : the emphatic particle. — tu
emisti ludum praeclarum, *you
have bought a splendid band* (of
gladiators).   Atticus would seem
to have bought a troop of gladiators, whom he was at present having trained, that he might let them
out (locare) to the aediles for the
public games.— pugnare: of practice contests. — duobus his muneribus liberasses: if we accept
this reading, the meaning perhaps
is: 'from the results of the two
spectacles this year you might have
set (them) free.'   For distinguished
bravery and skill gladiators at the
request of the people were sometimes presented with a *rudis*, or
wooden sword, and allowed to re-
tire from service.   Cicero writes to
Atticus a few days later: *tu scribas
ad me velim de gladiatoribus, sed
ita, bene si rem gerunt; non quaero,
male si se gesserunt, Att.* 4. 8 A. 2.
Boot believes that the gladiators

have turned out badly, and that
the passage is ironical : ' if you
had been willing to let them out,
you might have set them free
(from slavery, for they would have
been killed by their opponents).'
— diligenter: *sc. cura* or *facias.*
   XVIII. Arpinum, June, 56 B.C.
A thorough analysis of this letter
to Lucceius, as Böckel points out,
will reveal the fact that it is as carefully constructed as any of Cicero's
orations: 1, *prooemium;* 2, 3, *hortatio ;* 4–8, *probatio ;* 9, 10, *conclusio.*
Yet, while the earnestness of his
purpose is apparent throughout, by
the light conversational tone which
he gives the letter Cicero glosses
over the 'impudence' of his request, puts the seriousness of the
offense against historical truth in
the background, and strives to
secure the consent of Lucceius on
the score of friendship.   For Cicero's own judgment of the epistle,
cf. *Att.* 4. 6. 4 *epistulam, Lucceio
nunc quam misi, qua meas res ut
scribat rogo, fac ut ab eo sumas —
valde bella est.*   L. Lucceius was an
orator and a man of some literary
note.   In politics and military
affairs he was less successful; he
was a candidate with Caesar for

expromam absens audacius; epistula enim non erube-
scit. Ardeo cupiditate incredibili neque, ut ego arbitror,
reprehendenda, nomen ut nostrum scriptis inlustretur
et celebretur tuis. Quod etsi mihi saepe ostendis te
esse facturum, tamen ignoscas velim huic festinationi
meae. Genus enim scriptorum tuorum etsi erat semper
a me vehementer exspectatum, tamen vicit opinionem
meam, meque ita vel cepit vel incendit, ut cuperem quam
celerrime res nostras monumentis commendari tuis.
Neque enim me solum commemoratio posteritatis ad
spem quandam immortalitatis rapit, sed etiam illa cupiditas, ut vel auctoritate testimoni tui vel indicio bene-
volentiae vel suavitate ingeni vivi perfruamur. Neque 2
tamen, haec cum scribebam, eram nescius quantis
oneribus premerere susceptarum rerum et iam institu-
tarum; sed quia videbam Italici belli et civilis historiam
iam a te paene esse perfectam, dixeras autem mihi te
reliquas res ordiri, deesse mihi nolui quin te admonerem
ut cogitares, coniunctene malles cum reliquis rebus
nostra contexere an, ut multi Graeci fecerunt, Callisthenes Phocicum bellum, Timaeus Pyrrhi, Polybius Nu-

the consulship in 60 B.C. (cf. Ep.
VI. 11 n), but was defeated, and in
the Civil War was one of the intem-
perate leaders in Pompey's camp.

1. **subrusticus**: cf. Intr. 77. The
opposite idea to *pudor subrusticus*
is conveyed by *frons urbana*
(Hor. *Ep.* 1. 9. 11). — **ardeo . . .
commendari tuis** : Böckel notes
that the orator and the historian
adopt the periodic form of construction with the verb at the end
of the clause, as the one best fitted
to impart dignity and force to
what they say, while often in letters, as in this passage, a writer
affects an apparent carelessness

upon this point in order to convey
the impression of spontaneity and
sincerity.— **genus scriptorum tuorum** : we know very little more
of the historical work of Lucceius
than this letter tells us. Cf. Asconius, pp. 91–93, ed. Orelli.

2. **Italici belli et civilis**: the
Social War and the struggle between Sulla and the Marian party.
— **Callisthenes**, etc.: subjects of
some verb like *scripserunt* suggested by **fecerunt**. Callisthenes
wrote not only a general history of
Greece (Ἑλληνικά), but a special
treatise on the Phocian War. Timaeus published a history of his

mantinum, qui omnes a perpetuis suis historiis ea quae
dixi bella separaverunt, tu quoque item civilem coniu-
rationem ab hostilibus externisque bellis seiungeres.
Equidem ad nostram laudem non multum video interesse, sed ad properationem meam quiddam interest, non
te exspectare dum ad locum venias, ac statim causam
illam totam et tempus arripere, et simul, si uno in
argumento unaque in persona mens tua tota versabitur,
cerno iam animo quanto omnia uberiora atque ornatiora
futura sint.   Neque tamen ignoro quam impudenter
faciam, qui primum tibi tantum oneris imponam —
potest enim mihi denegare occupatio tua — deinde
etiam ut ornes me postulem.   Quid si illa tibi non
3 tanto opere videntur ornanda ?   Sed tamen, qui semel
verecundiae finis transierit, eum bene et naviter oportet
esse impudentem.   Itaque te plane etiam atque etiam
rogo ut et ornes ea vehementius etiam quam fortasse
sentis, et in eo leges historiae neglegas, gratiamque

native land, Sicily, and also a sketch
of the campaigns of Pyrrhus. Polybius wrote, besides his universal
history, an account of the war of
Numantia.   The last illustration
is especially in point, for as Polybius was led to write a separate
history of the Numantine War by
his friendship for its hero Scipio,
Cicero hopes that Lucceius may
be induced by a similar sentiment
to compose a special treatise. —
primum ... deinde: Cicero makes
two requests of Lucceius: (1) that
he shall write a separate treatise,
(2) that he shall emphasize his
achievements.

3. bene et naviter: archaic and
colloquial.   The use of *bene* with
the force of *valde* to intensify

adjectives and adverbs came into
vogue in Cicero's time.   Only two
instances of this use occur in
Latin comedy, but having once
found a foothold in the language,
it became quickly a favorite colloquialism.   Cf. Ital. *bene* and Fr.
bien.   Cf. also *sane*, Ep. XVI. 2 n.,
and see Intr. 90. — te plane etiam
atque etiam rogo: cf. *hoc te vehementer etiam atque etiam rogo*, Cic.
Fam. 13. 5. 3. — leges historiae
neglegas : cf. Cic. *de Or.* 2. 62
*nam quis nescit primam esse histo-
riae legem, ne quid falsi dicere
audeat ? deinde ne quid veri non
audeat ? ne quae suspicio gratiae
sit in scribendo ? ne quae simul-
tates ? haec scilicet fundamenta nota
sunt omnibus.*   See also Pliny, *Ep.*

illam de qua suavissime quodam in prooemio scripsisti,
a qua te flecti non magis potuisse demonstras quam
Herculem Xenophontium illum a Voluptate, eam, si
me tibi vehementius commendabit, ne aspernere, amo-
rique nostro plusculum etiam quam concedet veritas
largiare.   Quod si te adducemus ut hoc suspicias, erit,
ut mihi persuadeo, materies digna facultate et copia
tua.   A principio enim coniurationis usque ad reditum 4
nostrum videtur mihi modicum quoddam corpus confici
posse, in quo et illa poteris uti civilium commutationum
scientia vel in explicandis causis rerum novarum vel in
remediis incommodorum, cum et reprehendes ea quae
vituperanda duces, et quae placebunt exponendis rationibus comprobabis, et si liberius, ut consuesti, agendum
putabis, multorum in nos perfidiam insidias proditio-
nem notabis.   Multam etiam casus nostri varietatem
tibi in scribendo suppeditabunt plenam cuiusdam voluptatis, quae vehementer animos hominum in legendo, te
scriptore, tenere possit; nihil est enim aptius ad delectationem lectoris quam temporum varietates fortunae-
que vicissitudines.   Quae etsi nobis optabiles in experi-
endo non fuerunt, in legendo tamen erunt iucundae;
habet enim praeteriti doloris secura recordatio delectationem.   Ceteris vero nulla perfunctis propria molestia, 5

7. 33. 10 *nam nec historia debet
egredi veritatem et honeste factis
veritas sufficit.* But the prevail-
ing ancient conception of history
was a low one; see Quint. 10. 1.
31 ; Sen. *N. Q.* 7. 16. 1, 2. Both
Atticus and Cicero wrote an account of Cicero's consulship in
Greek ; cf. *Att.* 2. 1. 1, 2. — **a
qua** : the use of the preposition
shows that *gratia* is personified.

— **Herculem Xenophontium** :
cf. Xen. *Mem.* 2. 1. 21. — **plusculum**: cf. *pulchellus*, Ep. V. 10 n.

4. **modicum quoddam corpus**:
corpus is an entire 'work'; *liber*
a part complete in itself. — **habet
. . . delectationem** : this recalls
Verg. *Aen.* 1. 203 *forsan et haec
olim meminisse iuvabit.*

5. **ceteris . . . iucunda**: for
the sentiment, cf. Lucr. 2. 1–4. —

casus autem alienos sine ullo dolore intuentibus etiam
ipsa misericordia est iucunda. Quem enim nostrum ille
moriens apud Mantineam Epaminondas non cum quadam miseratione delectat ? Qui tum denique sibi evelli
iubet spiculum, postea quam ei percontanti dictum est
clipeum esse salvum, ut etiam in vulneris dolore aequo
animo cum laude moreretur. Cuius studium in legendo
non erectum Themistocli fuga exituque retinetur?
Etenim ordo ipse annalium mediocriter nos retinet,
quasi enumeratione fastorum; at viri saepe excellentis
ancipites variique casus habent admirationem exspectationem, laetitiam molestiam, spem timorem; si vero
exitu notabili concluduntur, expletur animus iucundis-
6 sima lectionis voluptate. Quo mihi acciderit optatius, si
in hac sententia fueris, ut a continentibus tuis scriptis,
in quibus perpetuam rerum gestarum historiam complec-
teris, secernas hanc quasi fabulam rerum eventorum-
que nostrorum — habet enim varios actus multasque
actiones et consiliorum et temporum. Ac non vereor
ne adsentatiuncula quadam aucupari tuam gratiam
videar, cum hoc demonstrem, me a te potissimum
ornari celebrarique velle. Neque enim tu is es qui

Epaminondas: cf. *de Fin.* 2. 97;
Tusc. Disp. 2. 59. The career of
Epaminondas was a favorite theme
in the schools of the rhetoricians
(*de Fin.* 2. 67). Cicero confesses
to a similar feeling (*Tusc. Disp.* 1.
96) on reading the account of
Theramenes's death. — fuga exituque: the MSS. read *fuga redituque*, but Themistocles died in exile, so that some change is necessary. See Crit. Append.
   6. fabulam: the technical word
for a drama. The comparison sug-

gested by it is only partially carried out in the following clause.
— actus : the main divisions in
the play; actiones : the subdi-
visions of the *actus.* Cf. Krebs,
Antibarbarus, on *actus* and *scaena.*
— adsentatiuncula quadam, *by
a bit of flattery, as it were ;* cf.
pulchellus, Ep. V. 10 n. — neque
enim tu is es, etc., *for neither
are you the man not to know
what you are, and not to think
that the people are envious who
do not admire you rather than that*

quid sis nescias et qui non eos magis, qui te non admirentur, invidos quam eos, qui laudent, adsentatores arbitrere; neque autem ego sum ita demens ut me sempiternae gloriae per eum commendari velim, qui non ipse quoque in me commendando propriam ingeni gloriam consequatur.   Neque enim Alexander ille gra- 7 tiae causa ab Apelle potissimum pingi et a Lysippo fingi volebat, sed quod illorum artem cum ipsis, tum etiam sibi gloriae fore putabat.   Atque illi artifices corporis simulacra ignotis nota faciebant; quae vel si nulla sint, nihilo sint tamen obscuriores clari viri.   Nec minus est superstes Agesilaus ille perhibendus, qui neque pictam neque fictam imaginem suam passus est esse, quam qui in eo genere laborarunt; unus enim Xenophontis libellus in eo rege laudando facile omnes imagines omnium statuasque superavit.   Atque hoc praestantius mihi fuerit et ad laetitiam animi et ad memoriae dignitatem, si in tua scripta pervenero quam si in ceterorum, quod non ingenium mihi solum suppeditatum fuerit tuum, sicut Timoleonti a Timaeo aut ab Herodoto Themistocli, sed etiam auctoritas clarissimi et spectatissimi viri et in rei publicae maximis gravissimisque causis cogniti atque in primis probati, ut mihi non solum praeconium,

---

those persons are sycophants who praise you.

7. **Alexander**, etc.: cf. Pliny, *N. H.* 7. 125 *idem hic imperator edixit nequis ipsum alius quam Apelles pingeret, quam Pyrgoteles scalperet, quam Lysippus ex aere duceret.* Cf. also Hor. *Ep.* 2. 1. 239. — **vel si nulla**, etc.: cf. Tac. *Agr.* 46. — **qui neque**, etc. : cf. Nep. *Ages.* 8. — **qui . . . laborarunt**, *who have exerted themselves*

along that line, i.e. of commemorating their names by having likenesses of themselves made by painters or sculptors. — **Xenophontis libellus** : the *Agesilaus.* — **Timaeo**: as historian of Sicily, he recorded with praise the distinguished services which Timoleon of Corinth rendered the Sicilians in their struggles for independence. — **ab Herodoto**: in his account of the Persian wars. —

quod, cum in Sigeum venisset, Alexander ab Homero
Achilli tributum esse dixit, sed etiam grave testimonium
impertitum clari hominis magnique videatur.   Placet
enim Hector ille mihi Naevianus qui non tantum 'lau-
8 dari' se laetatur, sed addit etiam 'a laudato viro.' Quod
si a te non impetro, hoc est, si quae te res impedierit
— neque enim fas esse arbitror quicquam me rogantem
abs te non impetrare, — cogar fortasse facere quod
nonnulli saepe reprehendunt: scribam ipse de me, multorum tamen exemplo et clarorum virorum.   Sed, quod
te non fugit, haec sunt in hoc genere vitia: et vere-
cundius ipsi de sese scribant necesse est, si quid est
laudandum, et praetereant, si quid reprehendendum est.
Accedit etiam ut minor sit fides, minor auctoritas, multi
denique reprehendant et dicant verecundiores esse praecones ludorum gymnicorum, qui cum ceteris coronas
imposuerint victoribus eorumque nomina magna voce
pronuntiarint, cum ipsi ante ludorum missionem corona
donentur, alium praeconem adhibeant, ne sua voce se
9 ipsi victores esse praedicent.   Haec nos vitare cupimus
et, si recipis causam nostram, vitabimus, idque ut facias
rogamus.   Ac ne forte mirere cur, cum mihi saepe
ostenderis te accuratissime nostrorum temporum consilia atque eventus litteris mandaturum, a te id nunc

---

cum in Sigeum venisset: cf. Cic.
pro Arch. 24. — **Hector Naevi-**
anus : *i.e.* Hector in the tragedy
(*Hector proficiscens*) of Naevius.
Writing to his literary friend Lucceius, Cicero cites the exact authority (*Hector Naevianus*) without
hesitation.   In a letter to Cato
(Ep. XXXVIII.), making the same
quotation, he adds, *inquit Hector,*
OPINOR *apud Naevium.*

8. **scribam ipse de me:** Cicero
had already written a ' Memoir ' of
his consulship in Greek (*Att.* 2. 1.
1; 1. 20. 6), and two years later he
composed a poem in three books
upon the same subject (*Fam.* 1. 9.
23). — **multorum** : *e.g.* Sulla and
M. Scaurus. — **praecones :** after
the other contests the heralds con-
tended with one another, and the
victor received a wreath.

tanto opere et tam multis verbis petamus, illa nos
cupiditas incendit, de qua initio scripsi, festinationis,
quod alacres animo sumus ut et ceteri viventibus nobis
ex libris tuis nos cognoscant et nosmet ipsi vivi gloriola
nostra perfruamur.   His de rebus quid acturus sis, si 10
tibi non est molestum, rescribas mihi velim.   Si enim
suscipis causam, conficiam commentarios rerum omnium;
sin autem differs me in tempus aliud, coram tecum
loquar.   Tu interea non cessabis et ea quae habes instituta perpolies nosque diliges.

XIX.   (*Fam.* 7. 1.)

M. CICERO S. D. M. MARIO.

Si te dolor aliqui corporis aut infirmitas valetudinis 1
tuae tenuit quo minus ad ludos venires, fortunae magis

9. **gloriola:** cf. note on *adsentatiuncula* above.

10. **si . . . molestum:** a polite
colloquial formula; cf. Catull. 55.
1 *si forte non molestum est;* Martial 1. 96. 1 *si non molestum est
teque non piget ;* Plaut. *Rud.* 120
*sed nisi molestumst, paucis percon-
tarier volo ego ex te ;* Ter. *Ad.* 806
*ausculta paucis, nisi molestumst,
Demea ;* Cic. *Cluent.* 168. Cf. also
Intr. 100. — **rescribas:** no reply is
preserved or mentioned elsewhere.
It is quite possible, however, that
Lucceius complied with Cicero's
request; cf. *Att.* 4. 11. 2. — **commentarios:** perhaps Cicero refers
to these notes when he writes to
Atticus a year later: *tu Lucceio nostrum librum dabis, Att.* 4. 11. 2. —
cessabis : for the tense, cf. Intr.
84 *b*. — **nos diliges :** most of Cicero's letters end abruptly, but when
a polite formula is used, it is commonly, (1) an admonition concern-

ing the health of the recipient, as in
most of the letters to Atticus, *e.g.*
cura ut valeas; (2) an expression of
esteem: *te valde amamus nosque a
te amari cum volumus, tum etiam
confidimus* (*Fam.* 7. 14); (3) both
(1) and (2) *cura ut valeas et me, ut
amas, ama* (*Fam.* 7. 5); *bene vale et
me dilige ;* or (4) a reference to the
family of the recipient: *Piliae et puellae Caeciliae bellissimae salutem
dices* (*Att.* 6. 4).   Cf. also Intr. 62.

XIX. Rome, Oct., 55 B.C. Cicero's friend, M. Marius, to whom
Fam. 7. 1–4 are addressed, was
confined to his villa at Stabiae
by an attack of the gout (*Fam.*
7. 4), and was therefore unable
to witness the games at Rome
which Pompey gave in honor of
the dedication of his theatre and
the temple of Venus Victrix. This
theatre, which was erected on the
Campus Martius, and would accommodate 40,000 people (Plin.

tribuo quam sapientiae tuae; sin haec, quae ceteri mirantur, contemnenda duxisti et, cum per valetudinem
posses, venire tamen ṇoluisti, utrumque laetor, et sine
dolore corporis te fuisse et animo valuisse, cum ea quae
sine causa mirantur alii neglexeris, modo ut tibi con-
stiterit fructus oti tui, quo quidem tibi perfrui mirifice
licuit, cum esses in ista amoenitate paene solus relictus.
Neque tamen dubito quin tu in illo cubiculo tuo, ex quo
tibi Stabianum perforasti et patefecisti sinum, per eos
dies matutina tempora lectiunculis consumpseris, cum
illi interea, qui te istic reliquerunt, spectarent communis
mimc̣s semisomni.   Reliquas vero partis diei tu consu-

N. H. 36. 115), was the first permanent theatre constructed in
Rome, and its opening was celebrated by gorgeous pageants and
by combats between men and wild
beasts, in which, according to
Pliny, 20 elephants and 500 lions
were killed.   The distaste which
Cicero shows for the vulgar display, and the pity which the slaugh-
ter of the unfortunate beasts excited in him, honorably distinguish
him ·from his contemporaries.
These particular *venationes* were so
bloodthirsty that even the Roman
populace was moved to pity when
the elephants, seeing their escape
cut off, seemed to beg for mercy:
*amissa fugae spe, misericordiam
vulgi inenarrabili habitu quaeren-
tes supplicavere, quadam sese la-
mentatione complorantes, tanto populi dolore ut oblitus imperatoris
ac munificentiae honori suo exquisitae flens universus consurgeret
dirasque Pompeio poenas impreca-
retur*, Plin. N. H. 8. 21.

1. **Stabianum . . . sinum**: the
Italians of the present day who
have villas on the lakes or sea-
shore, often cut down the trees

in front of their houses, that they
may obtain an unobstructed view
across the water; so Marius would
seem to have cut the trees down
in a line through his Stabian estate (lit. 'he bored through') to
the shore, and thus brought the
bay into view. — **lectiunculis**, *by
reading a bit here and a bit there.*
mimos: the *mimus*, which was
introduced into Rome from Tarentum in the third century B.C., was
at the outset a character presentation by dancers, but, in the second century probably, dialogue
and songs were introduced. Facial
expression always played an important part in it, so that the performers did not wear masks.   In
Cicero's time *mimi* were put on
the stage only as afterpieces (cf.
Ep. LXI. 7).   The degraded taste
of imperial times, however, preferred them to the drama proper,
so that they practically drove the
latter from the stage. Cf. also
Ribbeck, *Römische Dichtung*, I.
217, 218. — **semisomni**: at this
period dramatic performances began early in the day, and those
for whom seats were not reserved

mebas iis delectationibus, quas tibi ipsi ad arbitrium tuum compararas, nobis autem erant ea perpetienda quae Sp. Maecius probavisset. Omnino, si quaeris, ludi 2 apparatissimi, sed non tui stomachi; coniecturam enim facio de meo. Nam primum honoris causa in scaenam redierant ii quos ego honoris causa de scaena decesse arbitrabar; deliciae vero tuae noster Aesopus eiusmodi fuit ut ei desinere per omnis homines liceret. Is iurare cum coepisset, vox eum defecit in illo loco: 'Si sciens fallo.' Quid tibi ego alia narrem? Nosti enim reliquos ludos, qui ne id quidem leporis habuerunt quod solent mediocres ludi; apparatus enim spectatio tollebat omnem hilaritatem, quo quidem apparatu non dubito quin animo aequissimo carueris. Quid enim delectationis habent sescenti muli in Clytaemestra, aut in Equo Troiano creterrarum tria milia, aut armatura varia peditatus et

found it necessary to be in their places several hours before the performance began. Physical fatigue, therefore, and the stupidity of the performances made the audience listless. — **Sp. Maecius** (*Tarpa*): he had charge of the plays. In Hor. *Sat.* 1. 10. 38 and *A. P.* 387 he is mentioned as an authorized critic.

2. **honoris causa ... honoris causa,** *to honor the occasion ... to save their reputation* (Tyrrell). Cf. Intr. 103. — **decesse:** for *decessisse.* A rare case of syncopation, like *successe* (?) for *successisse* (Ep. XC. 2). Similar syncopated forms occur elsewhere in colloquial Latin, *e.g. detraxe,* Plaut. *Trin.* 743; *despexe, M. G.* 553; *iusse,* Ter. *Heaut.* 1001; *divisse,* Hor. *Sat.* 2. 3. 169. See also Intr. 82. — **deliciae tuae :** cf. *nostri amores,* Ep. VII. 2, and

mea lux, Ep. XIII. 2 n. — **Aesopus:** elsewhere praised highly as an actor by Cicero; cf. *pro Sest.* 120, *de Div.* 1. 80, etc., but in his old age his voice has failed. Cf. also Ribbeck, *Römische Tragödie,* 674–676.— **si sciens fallo:** the first words of an oath. Cf. Liv. 1. 24. Ribbeck (*Röm. Trag.* p. 49) suggests that perhaps Aesopus played the part of Sinon in the *Equus Troianus* of Naevius (or of Andronicus) and that this oath was introduced in some such speech as that put into the mouth of Sinon by Vergil in *Aen.* 2. 154. — **sescenti :** for an indefinitely large number; cf. *miliens,* Ep. V. 4. — **Clytaemestra :** one of the plays of L. Accius.— **creterrarum tria milia :** supposed to refer to the spoils of Troy (*crateresque auro solidi,* Verg. *Aen.* 2. 765), which were represented in a realistic way upon the

equitatus in aliqua pugna ? Quae popularem admirationem habuerunt, delectationem tibi nullam attulissent.
3 Quod si tu per eos dies operam dedisti Protogeni tuo,
dummodo is tibi quidvis potius quam orationes meas
legerit, ne tu haud paulo plus quam quisquam nostrum
delectationis habuisti; non enim te puto Graecos aut
Oscos ludos desiderasse, praesertim cum Oscos vel in
senatu vestro spectare possis, Graecos ita non ames ut
ne ad villam quidem tuam via Graeca ire soleas. Nam
quid ego te athletas putem desiderare, qui gladiatores
contempseris ? In quibus ipse Pompeius confitetur se
et operam et oleum perdidisse. Reliquae sunt vena-

stage. Compare with this whole passage the trenchant criticism which Horace passes upon the taste for realism and vulgar display upon the stage in his day (Ep. 2. 1. 189–207).

3. **Protogeni :** the slave who read aloud to Marius. — **ne tu:** cf. *ne*, Ep. XVII. 2 n. — **Graecos aut Oscos ludos :** comedy and tragedy were essentially of Greek origin, and Cicero speaks of them therefore as *ludi Graeci* in distinction from the *fabulae Atellanae* (*ludi Osci*), which were indigenous to Italian soil. These Atellan farces were comic representations of life with fixed characters. They were cast in dialogue form, varied by occasional songs. The action was lively, and the language the vulgar Latin. After the conquest of Campania, in 211 B.C., these farces were introduced into Rome, given in course of time a more distinctly dramatic form, and used as after-pieces on the stage. Cf. Ep. LXI. 7; also Ribbeck, *Röm. Dichtung*, I. 207–217. — **in senatu vestro:** Marius would seem to have been a *decurio*, or member of the town

council, probably in Pompeii, and in the deliberations of his Oscan colleagues upon petty matters of town government, he could find all the elements of an ' Oscan burlesque' without taking the trouble to come to Rome for them. — **via Graeca:** perhaps a road leading to his villa which Marius did not use; but the point of the jest is obscure to us. — **athletas:** a term applied properly to those who took part in the five contests — running, wrestling, boxing, the *pentathlum* (made up of five distinct games), the *pancratium* (boxing *and* wrestling). As we may infer from the text, in quibus, etc., the Roman people showed little enthusiasm for these Greek games, and this continued to be the case until they gained an artificial stimulus by receiving the approval of certain emperors. Nero in particular was very fond of them (Tac. *Ann.* 14. 20). — **gladiatores :** on Cicero's own distaste for gladiatorial contests, cf. *Att.* 2. 1. 1 *Kal. Iuniis eunti mihi Antium et gladiatores M. Metelli cupide relinquenti*, etc. — **operam et oleum perdidisse:**

tiones binae per dies quinque, magnificae — nemo negat,
— sed quae potest homini esse polito delectatio, cum
aut homo imbecillus a valentissima bestia laniatur aut
praeclara bestia venabulo transverberatur ? Quae tamen, si videnda sunt, saepe vidisti; neque nos qui haec
spectamus quicquam novi vidimus. Extremus elephan-
torum dies fuit. In quo admiratio magna vulgi atque
turbae, delectatio nulla exstitit; quin etiam misericordia
quaedam consecutast atque opinio eiusmodi, esse quandam illi beluae cum genere humano societatem. His 4
ego tamen diebus, ludis scaenicis, ne forte videar tibi
non modo beatus, sed liber omnino fuisse, dirupi me
paene in iudicio Galli Canini familiaris tui. Quod si
tam facilem populum haberem quam Aesopus habuit,
libenter mercule artem desinerem tecumque et cum
similibus nostri viverem. Nam me cum antea taede-
bat, cum et aetas et ambitio me hortabatur et licebat

a proverbial expression probably
applied originally to an article
spoiled in cooking; cf. *tum pol ego
et oleum et operam perdidi*, Plaut.
Poen. 332. The use of alliteration
in such everyday expressions in all
languages is well known. Cf. Intr.
93, 102. — **venationes**: from the
introduction of the *venatio* at
Rome in 186 B.C., it was a favorite form of amusement with the
people, and was carried to an
almost incredible pitch of extravagance and barbarism by the later
emperors. — **venabulo** : the elephants were attacked with javelins
by the Gaetulians (Plin. *N.H.*8.20).
— **misericordia**: cf. introd. note.

4. **Galli Canini**: L. Caninius
Gallus, as tribune in 56 B.C., pro-
posed that the restoration of King
Ptolemy should be entrusted to
Pompey (*Q. fr.* 2. 2. 3). In the

year following his tribuneship
(55 B.C.) he was attacked on some
political charge by the enemies
of Pompey, and Cicero defended
him, doubtless at Pompey's request. With some two or three
exceptions (*e.g.* Cic. *de Or.* 2. 253)
the *cognomen* is never placed before the *nomen* in formal Latin in
the Ciceronian period, but this
order is common enough in colloquial Latin, *e.g. Bassus Caecilius*,
Ep. LXXXVI. 4; *Pollio Asinius*,
Ep. XCVII. 1; *Cimber autem Tillius*, *Fam.* 6. 12. 2; *Balbi quoque
Corneli*, *Fam.* 8. 11. 2; in Horace
we read *Fuscus Aristius*, *Musa
Antonius*, etc.; in Livy, *Geminus
Servilius*, *Antias Valerius*, etc.
In the writers of the Silver Age
this innovation, like many others,
was accepted without question. —
ambitio: *e.g.* in his purpose to

denique quem nolebam non defendere, tum vero hoc
tempore vita nullast.   Neque enim fructum ullum laboris exspecto, et cogor nonnumquam homines non optime
de me meritos, rogatu eorum qui bene meriti sunt, de-
5 fendere. Itaque quaero causas omnis aliquando vivendi
arbitratu meo, teque et istam rationem oti tui et laudo
vehementer et probo, quodque nos minus intervisis, hoc
fero animo aequiore, quod, si Romae esses, tamen neque nos lepore tuo neque te — si qui est in me — meo
frui liceret propter molestissimas occupationes meas.
Quibus si me relaxaro — nam ut plane exsolvam non
postulo, — te ipsum, qui multos annos nihil aliud com-
mentaris, docebo profecto quid sit humaniter vivere.
Tu modo istam imbecillitatem valetudinis tuae sustenta
et tuere, ut facis, ut nostras villas obire et mecum simul
6 lecticula concursare possis.   Haec ad te pluribus verbis
scripsi quam soleo, non oti abundantia, sed amoris erga
te, quod me quadam epistula subinvitaras, si memoria
tenes, ut ad te aliquid eiusmodi scriberem quo minus
te praetermisse ludos paeniteret.   Quod si adsecutus
sum, gaudeo; sin minus, hoc me tamen consolor, quod

defend Catiline in 65 B.C.; cf. Ep.
II. 1. — **rogatu eorum**: as when
he defended Vatinius in 54 B.C. at
the request of Caesar (*Fam.* 1.9.19),
although he had bitterly attacked
him in an oration delivered only
two years before.

5. **humaniter**: adverbs in -*iter*
from adjectives in -*us* are peculiar
in this period to colloquial Latin.
In Cicero of these formations we
find only *naviter* (Ep. XVIII. 3),
firmiter, *humaniter* and its compounds ; and these forms occur
only in the Letters and in those
writings to which Cicero intention-

ally gives an archaic coloring, *i.e.*
the *de Re Publica* and the *Oeco-
nomicus*. This ending became so
common in ecclesiastical Latin as
to crowd out -*e*.

6. **haec . . . scripsi**: apologies
at the end of a letter for its length
are so common as to indicate that
the etiquette of letter-writing approved of them, regardless of the
length of the epistle. Cf. close of
Ep. XXXVII. — **subinvitaras**,
you had hinted. Cf. subrusticus,
Ep. XVIII. 1 n. — **ut . . . scriberem**, etc.: Cicero may therefore
have exaggerated his distaste for

posthac ad ludos venies nosque vises neque in epistulis relinques meis spem aliquam delectationis tuae.

XX. (*Q. fr.* 2. 9 [11].)

MARCVS QVINTO FRATRI SALVTEM.

Epistulam hanc convicio efflagitarunt codicilli tui. 1 Nam res quidem ipsa et is dies quo tu es profectus nihil mihi ad scribendum argumenti sane dabat. Sed quemadmodum, coram cum sumus, sermo nobis deesse non solet, sic epistulae nostrae debent interdum alucinari. Tenediorum igitur libertas securi Tenedia prae- 2 cisa est, cum eos praeter me et Bibulum et Calidium et Favonium nemo defenderet. De te a Magnetibus ab 3 Sipylo mentio est honorifica facta, cum te unum dicerent postulationi L. Sesti Pansae restitisse. Reliquis diebus si quid erit quod te scire opus sit, aut etiam si nihil erit, tamen scribam cotidie aliquid. Pridie Idus neque tibi neque Pomponio deero. Lucreti poëmata,

the games. — **praetermisse** : for *praetermisisse.* Cf. *decesse*, 2 n.

XX. Rome, Feb., 54 B.C.

1. **codicilli**: cf. Intr. 59. Quintus had apparently sent his brother a message written upon waxen tablets, expecting him to erase the writing and send back an answer upon the same tablets.— **res ipsa**: perhaps the fact that certain foreign affairs in which Quintus was interested (cf. 3) had not then been discussed.

2. **Tenediorum**: the people of Tenedos petitioned the senate for home rule, but were refused. — **securi Tenedia** : tradition states that Tenes, the first king of Tenedos, among other severe regulations, established one punishing adultery with immediate death by the ax, so that *securis Tenedia* was a proverbial expression for an immediate and severe sentence. In this case of course the phrase effects a word-play with **Tenediorum**. — **Bibulum**: cf. Ep. VII.

2. — **Calidium** : M. Calidius as praetor in 57 B.C. had worked for Cicero's recall. — **Favonium**: cf. Ep. XV. 7 n.

3. **postulationi** : evidently Q. Cicero, when propraetor in Asia, had opposed some exorbitant demand made on the Magnetes by Pansa. Magnesia in Lydia was called *Magnesia ab Sipylo* to distinguish it from the city of the same name in Caria (*Magnesia ad Maeandrum*). — **Pomponio** : *i.e.*

ut scribis, ita sunt: multis luminibus ingeni, multae
tamen artis.   Sed cum veneris ∗ . Virum te putabo, si
Sallusti Empedoclea legeris, hominem non putabo.

XXI.   (*Fam.* 7. 5.)

CICERO CAESARI IMP. S. D.

1   Vide quam mihi persuaserim te me esse alterum, non
modo in iis rebus quae ad me ipsum, sed etiam in iis

Atticus, Quintus's brother-in-law;
the business in question was evidently some family matter. — **Lucreti poëmata**: St. Jerome in his
Chronicle says: *T. Lucretius poeta
. . . cum aliquot libros per inter-
valla insaniae conscripsisset, quos
postea Cicero emendavit*, etc. This
statement that Cicero edited the
poem *de Rerum Natura* has given
rise to a deal of discussion. It is
certainly true that Cicero and Lucretius exerted an influence upon
each other.   Lucretius borrowed
freely from Cicero's *Aratea*, while
several passages in the philosophical writings of Cicero closely
resemble verses of Lucretius (cf.
Martha, *Le Poëme de Lucrèce*, 351,
Munro on Lucr. 5.619, and Merrill
in *Class. Rev.* for 1896, 19). —
ita: cf. *sic*, Ep. V. 3 n. — **multis
. . . artis**: Lucretius probably died
in 55 B.C., so that this criticism
was written within a few months
of his death.   It is commonly
supposed that in **ingeni** Cicero
sums up the main characteristics
of the earlier school of Latin poetry, while **artis** represents the tendencies of the νεώτεροι; '(a poem)
with many indications of brilliant
genius and yet with much of artistic excellence.'   With this estimate of Lucretius, cf. Aul. Gell.
1. 21 *poeta ingenio et facundia prae-*

cellens. — **virum te putabo . . .
hominem non putabo**, *if you go
through the Empedoclea of Sallust,
I shall regard you as a man of
mettle, not as an ordinary mortal.*
See Crit. Append. — **Sallusti Empedoclea** : evidently a book upon
the philosophy of Empedocles.
    XXI. Rome, April, 54 B.C. C.
Trebatius Testa, the date of whose
birth is uncertain, came as a boy
to Rome to study law. He became attached to Cicero, and
pleased the latter by both his wit
and good-fellowship, and also assisted him by his knowledge of
jurisprudence.   Being anxious,
however, to see something of the
world, to win his spurs, and to
make a fortune, perhaps, in the
provinces, Trebatius set out for
the Roman camp in Gaul, carrying
with him this letter of recommendation.   Cicero's relations with
Trebatius were of a most intimate
nature, as his seventeen letters to
him (*Fam.* 7. 6–22) prove. Like
most of the young men who served
upon Caesar's staff in Gaul, Trebatius became his devoted admirer,
and followed his fortunes in the
Civil War. He was one of the few
members of that coterie of young
men about Caesar who survived
the Civil War and lived to see
Rome at peace under Augus-

quae ad meos pertinent. C. Trebatium cogitaram, quocumque exirem, mecum ducere, ut eum meis omnibus
studiis beneficiis quam ornatissimum domum reducerem;
sed postea quam et Pompei commoratio diuturnior erat
quam putaram, et mea quaedam tibi non ignota dubitatio aut impedire profectionem meam videbatur aut
certe tardare, (vide quid mihi sumpserim!) coepi velle
ea Trebatium exspectare a te quae sperasset a me,
neque mercule minus ei prolixe de tua voluntate promisi quam eram solitus de mea polliceri. Casus vero 2
mirificus quidam intervenit, quasi vel testis opinionis
meae vel sponsor humanitatis tuae. Nam cum de hoc
ipso Trebatio cum Balbo nostro loquerer accuratius

tus. Horace introduces him as
a speaker in *Sat.* 2. 1.

1. **me alterum**: cf. Ep. XV. 7 n.
— **quocumque exirem** : Pompey
had named Cicero as one of his
15 *legati* on the corn commission
in 57 B.C. (Ep. XV. 7), and Cicero
would naturally have gone to some
province in connection with that
matter, but as he preferred to stay
at Rome, his place was taken by
Quintus, who went to Sardinia
(Ep. XVI. 7); or perhaps reference is made to the fact that the
province of Spain was assigned to
Pompey at the close of his consulship in 55 B.C., and Cicero may
have been invited to accompany
him as his *legatus*, but, as we
know, Pompey remained at Rome.
— **dubitatio:** Cicero's hesitation
to leave Rome was due perhaps
partly to a fear that Clodius might
attack him during his absence, and
partly to a fondness for Rome. Cf.
si potes, etc., Ep. XVII. 2 n. — **exspectare . . . sperasset:** in the
contrast between these two words
lies a delicate compliment to Cae-

sar. The favor of the successful
governor of the Gauls would in-
sure to Trebatius what the friendship of a *legatus* to Spain could
only make probable. — **prolixe:**
not infrequently in the Letters with
verbs of hoping, thinking, and
promising, adverbs are used instead of the neut. acc. plur. of the
adj. used substantively, *e.g. ut ipse
facile animadverterem male* (for
mala) *eum de me cogitare, Fam.* 8,
12. 1; *non licuit diutius bene de eo
sperare, Fam.* 10. 21. 1; *si humaniter et sapienter et amabiliter in
me cogitare vis, Att.* 14. 13 A. 2.
This is a colloquial usage. — **promisi :** used of a formal agreement, while **polliceri** implies a
voluntary promise.

2. **Balbo:** L. Cornelius Balbus,
a native of Gades, who had received Roman citizenship for his
services against Sertorius ; cf. Cic.
pro Balbo, 5 f. He attached himself closely to Caesar, and was
often Caesar's confidential agent
in Rome. We have three of his
letters to Cicero, *Att.* 9. 7 A, 7 B,

domi meae, litterae mihi dantur a te, quibus in extremis scriptum erat: 'M. Iteium, quem mihi commendas,
vel regem Galliae faciam, vel hunc Leptae delega, si
vis.   Tu ad me alium mitte quem ornem.'   Sustulimus
manus et ego et Balbus.   Tanta fuit opportunitas, ut
illud nescio quid non fortuitum sed divinum videretur.
Mitto igitur ad te Trebatium, atque ita mitto ut initio
mea sponte, post autem invitatu tuo mittendum duxe-
3 rim.   Hunc, mi Caesar, sic velim omni tua comitate
complectare ut omnia, quae per me possis adduci ut
in meos conferre velis, in unum hunc conferas.   De
quo tibi homine haec spondeo, non illo vetere verbo
meo, quod, cum ad te de Milone scripsissem, iure lu-
sisti, sed more Romano, quomodo homines non inepti
loquuntur, probiorem hominem, meliorem virum, pu-
dentiorem esse neminem; accedit etiam quod familiam
ducit in iure civili singulari memoria, summa scientia.
Huic ego neque tribunatum neque praefecturam neque

and 13 A. — **M. Iteium** : nothing
is known of him. See Crit. Append. — **Leptae:** Q. Lepta held
some minor position under Caesar
at this time. *Fam.* 6. 18 and 19
are addressed to him. — **sustulimus manus:** a gesture of surprise.
— **invitatu:** apparently used nowhere else.   Parallel forms, however, as Tyrrell remarks, are *invo-
latus* (Ep. LXV. 7), *reflatus* (*Att.*
12. 2. 1), *itus* (*Att.* 15. 5. 3).

   3. mi Caesar: cf. *mi Pomponi*,
Ep. X. n.— **non illo . . . Romano,**
*not with that overworked phrase of
mine,* . . . *but in the* (hearty) *Roman
fashion.*   What the 'overworked
phrase' was, or for what purpose
Cicero wrote to Caesar concerning Milo, is unknown.   Milo
wished to be a candidate for the

consulship for 52 B.C., and Cicero may have tried to secure for
him Caesar's support, or at least
his neutrality.   For more **Romano,** cf. *ego te Balbo, cum ad
vos proficiscetur, more Romano
commendabo,* Ep. XXVI. 3.   See
also Ep. XXIV. 3. — **familiam
ducit,** *he leads the profession, sc.*
as concerns memory and knowledge of jurisprudence.   Trebatius
was a special legal adviser of Augustus; cf. Justin. *Inst.* 2. 25. — **tribunatum :** it was the fashion for
young men of good family at
Rome to go out to the provinces
with the title of *tribunus militum.*
Such men often had neither a
taste for a military career nor the
intention of adopting it, but desired the political and social pres-

ullius benefici certum nomen peto, benevolentiam tuam et liberalitatem peto, neque impedio quo minus, si tibi ita placuerit, etiam hisce eum ornes gloriolae insignibus. Totum denique hominem tibi ita trado, ' de manu,' ut aiunt, ' in manum ' tuam istam et victoria et fide praestantem. Simus enim putidiusculi, quamquam per te vix licet; verum, ut video, licebit. Cura ut valeas et me, ut amas, ama.

XXII. (*Q. fr.* 2. 15 [16].)

MARCVS QVINTO FRATRI SALVTEM.

Cum a me litteras librari manu acceperis, ne paulum 1 quidem me oti habuisse iudicato, cum autem mea, pau-

tige which such an experience would give them on their return to Rome (cf. Tac. *Agr.* 5). Caesar has these military tyros in mind when he says: *hic (timor) primum ortus est a tribunis militum praefectis reliquisque, qui ex urbe amicitiae causa Caesarem secuti non magnum in re militari usum habebant, B. G.* I. 39. 2. Trebatius received the position of tribune from Caesar. — **gloriolae** : such positions, being purely honorary, indicated little with regard to a man's real merits, but carried a certain distinction along with them. Hence **gloriola**, not *gloria*. — **de manu . . . in manum**: a characteristic of colloquial language is its fondness for concrete phrases in expressing a thought which formal language conveys in abstract phrases. In such phrases *manus* is of frequent occurrence. Thus, in the language of everyday life 'generously' is often *manu plena (Att.* 2. 25. 1), 'to be present' *prae manu esse, i.e.* to be 'on hand' (Plaut.

Bacch. 623), 'to assist' *manum dare, i.e.* 'to lend a hand,' etc. Cf. also Otto, *Sprichwörter der Römer*, p. 210. 6, Landgraf, 329, Krebs, *Antibarbarus* under *manus.* — **putidiusculi,** *something of a bore ;* cf. *pulchellus*, Ep. V. 10 n. — **quamquam . . . licebit:** *i.e.* although it is scarcely pardonable to take advantage of one who is so generous, by laying upon him such a task as I do in turning Trebatius over completely to your care, yet I feel you will pardon the liberty. — **cura . . . ama :** cf. Ep. XVIII. (end) n. The generous spirit in which Caesar responded to the request of Cicero is indicated by his reply, the substance of which Cicero quotes in a letter to Quintus (2. 13. 3) : *Trebatium quod ad se (i.e. Caesarem) miserim, persalse et humaniter etiam gratias mihi agit; negat enim in tanta multitudine eorum qui una essent quemquam fuisse, qui vadimonium concipere posset.*

XXII. Rome, August, 54 B.C.

lum.   Sic enim habeto, numquam me a causis et
iudiciis districtiorem fuisse, atque id anni tempore gravissimo et caloribus maximis.   Sed haec, quoniam tu
ita praescribis, ferenda sunt, neque committendum ut
aut spei aut cogitationi vestrae ego videar defuisse,
praesertim cum, si id difficilius fuerit, tamen ex hoc
labore magnam gratiam magnamque dignitatem sim
conlecturus.   Itaque, ut tibi placet, damus operam ne
cuius animum offendamus atque ut etiam ab iis ipsis
qui nos cum Caesare tam coniunctos dolent diligamur,
ab aequis vero aut etiam propensis in hanc partem
2 vehementer et colamur et amemur.   De ambitu cum
atrocissime ageretur in senatu multos dies, quod ita
erant progressi candidati consulares ut non esset ferendum, in senatu non fui.   Statui ad nullam medici-
3 nam rei publicae sine magno praesidio accedere.   Quo
die haec scripsi, Drusus erat de praevaricatione a tribunis aerariis absolutus, in summa quattuor sententiis,

1. **sic habeto**: cf. *sic habeto*,
Ep. XXVI. 1 n. — **anni tempore**:
August, the weather being hot
even for that month; cf. *Q. fr.* 3.
1. 1. — **vestrae**: *sc.* of you and
Caesar. — **ex hoc labore** : Cicero
is probably referring to his support
of the Triumvirate.   During the
year 54, he delivered orations in
behalf of Gabinius (cf. *pro Rabi-
rio Post.* 32), Vatinius, and Messius (cf. *Att.* 4. 15. 9), all of whom
were tools of the triumvirs, and
the first two had been former enemies of Cicero.   Cf. note to *Vatinium* below. — **ab iis ipsis qui
. . . dolent** : the oration which
Cicero delivered in the same year
in defense of M. Aemilius Scaurus
(cf. *Att.* 4. 15. 9), son of the Scaurus
who so earnestly championed the

cause of the aristocracy, would
naturally please the Optimates. —
aequis, *fairminded*, *i.e.* toward
Caesar. — **propensis**, etc. : Caesar's supporters.

2. **de ambitu**: cf. *Q. fr.* 3. 2. 3
(written two months later) *de ambitu postulati sunt omnes qui consulatum petunt: a Memmio Domitius, a Q. Acutio, bono et erudito
adulescente, Memmius, a Q. Pompeio Messalla, a Triario Scaurus.*
Cf. also *Att.* 4. 17. 2.

3. **Drusus** : probably Livius
Drusus Claudianus, grandfather of
the emperor Tiberius. — **absolutus**, etc.: each of the three *decuriae*,
composed respectively of senators,
knights, and *tribuni aerarii*. voted
separately (cf. Madvig, *Verf. u.
Verw.* II. 328).   In this case a ma-

cum senatores et equites damnassent. Ego eodem die
post meridiem Vatinium eram defensurus. Ea res
facilis est. Comitia in mensem Septembrem reiecta
sunt. Scauri iudicium statim exercebitur, cui nos non
deerimus. Συνδείπνους Σοφοκλέους, quamquam a te
factam fabellam video esse festive, nullo modo probavi. Venio nunc ad id quod nescio an primum esse 4
debuerit. O iucundas mihi tuas de Britannia litteras!
Timebam Oceanum, timebam litus insulae; reliqua non
equidem contemno, sed plus habent tamen spei quam
timoris, magisque sum sollicitus exspectatione ea quam

jority of the senators and a majority of the knights voted for
conviction, a majority of the *tribuni aerarii* for acquittal. The
guilt or innocence of the accused
party was, however, decided by a
majority of *all* the *iudices*, and in
this instance there was a majority
of four for acquittal. The number of jurors sitting in a trial was
determined by the statute under
which the charge was brought; the
lowest number mentioned is 32, the
highest 75 (cf. Madvig, *Verf. u.
Verw.* II. 308). — **Vatinium** : P.
Vatinius had made himself notorious during his tribuneship as
Caesar's agent, but escaped punishment for his misdeeds. In 57 B.C.
he failed as a candidate for the
aedileship. In 56 he appeared as
a witness against Sestius, whom
Cicero was defending, and Cicero
attacked him mercilessly. (Cf.
e.g. pro Sest. 132 ff.; *in Vat. Interr.;
Fam.* 1. 9. 7; *Q.fr.* 2. 4. 1.) The trial
here referred to was on an accusa-
tion *de sodaliciis* in 54 B.C. Cicero
undertook the defense at Caesar's
request. For Cicero's explanation
of his conduct, cf. *Fam.* 1. 9. 19.
It is a significant fact that in his

letters to Atticus he nowhere mentions the matter. *Fam.* 5. 9, 10 A
and 10 B are letters written to Cicero in 45–44 B.C. by Vatinius. —
comitia . . . reiecta sunt : the
bribery scandals and the disturb-
ances in Rome actually caused the
postponement of the consular elections until July, 53. Cf. Dio Cassius, 40. 17. — **Scauri iudicium** :
the charge of misgovernment in
Sardinia had been brought against
Scaurus in July, but the trial had
been postponed for 30 days. —
Συνδείπνους Σοφοκλέους : perhaps
a translation of the Σύνδειπνοι of
Sophocles; cf. Ribbeck, *Röm. Tragödie*, 620. During the summer
and autumn of 54 B.C. Quintus
devoted some time to the translation and adaptation of various
Greek plays, especially those of
Sophocles; cf. *Q. fr.* 3. 1. 13 and
Ep. XXIII. 7.

4. **o iucundas . . . litteras:**
Cicero had written in July (*Att.*
4. 15. 10) : *ex Q. fratris litteris suspicor iam eum esse in Britannia :
suspenso animo exspecto quid agat.*
Caesar was at this time making
his second expedition to Britain.
Quintus had transferred his ser-

metu. Te vero ὑπόθεσιν scribendi egregiam habere
video. Quos tu situs, quas naturas rerum et locorum,
quos mores, quas gentes, quas pugnas, quem vero ipsum
imperatorem habes! Ego te libenter, ut rogas, quibus
rebus vis adiuvabo, et tibi versus quos rogas, hoc est
5 'Athenas noctuam,' mittam. Sed heus tu! celari videor
a te. Quomodonam, mi frater, de nostris versibus Caesar? Nam primum librum se legisse scripsit ad me
ante, et prima sic ut neget se ne Graeca quidem meli-
ora legisse; reliqua ad quendam locum ῥᾳθυμότερα
— hoc enim utimur verbo. Dic mihi verum : num
aut res eum aut χαρακτὴρ non delectat? Nihil est
quod vereare; ego enim ne pilo quidem minus me
amabo. Hac de re φιλαληθῶς et, ut soles scribere,
fraterne.

XXIII. (*Q. fr.* 3. 5, 6.)

MARCVS QVINTO FRATRI SALVTEM.

1   Quod quaeris quid de illis libris egerim quos, cum
essem in Cumano, scribere institui, non cessavi neque

vices from Pompey to Caesar at
the beginning of the year.—**versus
... rogas**: Quintus is evidently
writing a poem on Caesar's achievements in Britain, and requests some
verses from his brother. The poem
is not extant. — **Athenas noctuam**: the proverb, 'coals to New-
castle,' as we say, appears in its
Greek form, γλαῦκ' εἰς 'Αθήνας,
Fam. 9. 3. 2; 6. 3. 4.

5. **heus tu**: cf. Ep. XXXV. 25 n.
— **celari**, *to be kept in the dark.*
— **de nostris versibus**: Cicero's
poem, *de Temporibus Meis.* Cf.
also *Fam.* 1. 9. 23; *Q. fr.* 3. 1. 24.
— ῥᾳθυμότερα, *a trifle careless.* —

hoc . . . verbo: the word ῥᾳθυμότερα had not been used by Caesar, but Cicero believes that it
expresses Caesar's opinion of the
latter part of the poem. — **ne pilo
quidem minus**, *not a whit the less.*
Cf. the similar proverbial expressions, *nec . . . flocci facio, Att.* 13.
50. 3; *non nauci facio,* Plaut.
Bacch. 1102.

XXIII. Tusculum, Oct., 54 B.C.
1. **de illis libris**: the books
of the *de Re Publica.* — **novendialibus iis feriis**: cf. Cic. *de Re
Pub.* 1. 14 *nam cum P. Africanus
hic, Pauli filius, feriis Latinis Tuditano et Aquilio cos. constituisset*

cesso, sed saepe iam scribendi totum consilium rationemque mutavi. Nam iam duobus factis libris, in quibus novendialibus iis feriis, quae fuerunt Tuditano et
Aquilio consulibus, sermo est a me institutus Africani
(paulo ante mortem) et Laeli, Phili, Manili, P. Rutili,
Q. Tuberonis, et Laeli generorum, Fanni et Scaevolae,
sermo autem in novem et dies et libros distributus de
optimo statu civitatis et de optimo cive (sane texeba-
tur opus luculente, hominumque dignitas aliquantum
orationi ponderis adferebat), ii libri cum in Tusculano
mihi legerentur audiente Sallustio, admonitus sum ab
illo multo maiore auctoritate illis de rebus dici posse,
si ipse loquerer de re publica, praesertim cum essem
non Heraclides Ponticus, sed consularis, et is qui in
maximis versatus in re publica rebus essem; quae tam
antiquis hominibus attribuerem, ea visum iri ficta esse;
oratorum sermonem in illis nostris libris qui essent de
ratione dicendi belle a me removisse, ad eos tamen
rettulisse, quos ipse vidissem; Aristotelem denique,
quae de re publica et praestanti viro scribat, ipsum
loqui. Commovit me, et eo magis quod maximos mo- 2
tus nostrae civitatis attingere non poteram, quod erant
inferiores quam illorum aetas qui loquebantur. Ego
autem id ipsum tum eram secutus, ne in nostra tem-

---

in hortis esse. — **Tuditano et
Aquilio consulibus:** *i.e.* 129 B.C.
— **sermo est,** etc.: cf. *Att.* 4. 16.
2 (written in July of this year) — **in
novem . . . libros :** the finished
work actually contained but six
books (cf. *de Div.* 2. 3). About
one-third of it is extant. — **hominum:** *i.e.* Africanus, Laelius, and
the others. — **Sallustio :** probably
the man to whom *Fam.* 2. 17 is

addressed, and who relates Cicero's dream in *de Div.* I. 59. —
consularis: and therefore a man
of much experience in managing
the affairs of a great commonwealth, and not a mere publicist
like Heraclides. — **de ratione dicendi:** the *de Oratore,* which pur-
ports to be a discussion that took
place in Cicero's youth (B.C. 91).

2. **inferiores,** *more recent.* —

pora incurrens offenderem quempiam. Nunc et id
vitabo et loquar ipse tecum, et tamen illa quae institu-
eram ad te, si Romam venero, mittam. Puto enim te
existimaturum a me illos libros non sine aliquo meo
3 stomacho esse relictos. Caesaris amore, quem ad me
perscripsti, unice delector; promissis iis quae ostendit
non valde pendeo. Nec sitio honores nec desidero
gloriam, magisque eius voluntatis perpetuitatem quam
promissorum exitum exspecto; vivo tamen in ea ambi-
tione et labore, tamquam id quod non postulo exspec-
4 tem. Quod me de versibus faciendis rogas, incredibile
est, mi frater, quam egeam tempore, nec sane satis
commoveor animo ad ea quae vis canenda. Διατυπώσεις vero ad ea quae ipse ego ne cogitando quidem
consequor, tu, qui omnes isto eloquendi et exprimendi
genere superasti, a me petis ? Facerem tamen ut possem, sed, quod te minime fugit, opus est ad poëma
quadam animi alacritate, quam plane mihi tempora
eripiunt. Abduco me equidem ab omni rei publicae
cura dedoque litteris, sed tamen indicabo tibi quod
mehercule in primis te celatum volebam. Angor, mi
suavissime frater, angor nullam esse rem publicam,
nulla iudicia, nostrumque hoc tempus aetatis, quod

loquar ipse tecum: this purpose
Cicero abandoned, returning to his
original plan. His letters of this
period contain many references
to the *de Re Pub.*, *e.g. Q. fr.* 2. 12
(14). 1 ; *Att.* 4. 16. 2; *Att.* 6. 1. 8.—
relictos : see Crit. Append. Tyrrell
suggests *refictos* ('remodeled').

4. versibus : cf. *versus rogas*,
Ep. XXII. 4 n. Cf. also *Q. fr.*
3. 4. 4. Cicero apparently yielded
at last to his brother's request;
cf. *Q. fr.* 3. 9. 6 *habeo absolu-*

tum suave, mihi quidem uti vide-
tur, ἔπος *ad Caesarem.* — διατυπώσεις: perhaps with reference to
the descriptive portions of the
poem; cf. *quos tu situs,* etc., Ep.
XXII. 4. — superasti: cf. *Q. fr.* 3.
4. 4 *tibi istius generis in scribendo*
priores partes tribuo quam mihi. —
quod (mehercule) : for the acc.,
cf. Ter. *Hec.* 645 *nosne hoc celatos*
tamdiu ! Elsewhere Cicero uses
de (or *in*) with the abl. of the
thing, *e.g. debes existimare te maxi-*

in illa auctoritate senatoria florere debebat, aut forensi
labore iactari aut domesticis litteris sustentari, illud
vero, quod a puero adamaram,

> πολλὸν ἀριστεύειν καὶ ὑπείροχος ἔμμεναι ἄλλων,

totum occidisse, inimicos a me partim non oppugnatos,
partim etiam esse defensos, meum non modo animum,
sed ne odium quidem esse liberum, unumque ex omnibus Caesarem esse inventum qui me tantum quantum
ego vellem amaret, aut etiam, sicut alii putant, hunc
unum esse qui vellet.   Quorum tamen nihil est eiusmodi ut ego me non multa consolatione cotidie leniam;
sed illa erit consolatio maxima, si una erimus.   Nunc
ad illa vel gravissimum accedit desiderium tui.   Gabi- 5
nium si, ut Pansa putat oportuisse, defendissem, conci-
dissem.   Qui illum oderunt — ii sunt toti ordines —,
propter quem oderunt, me ipsum odisse coepissent.
Tenui me, ut puto, egregie, tantum ut facerem quantum omnes viderunt; et in omni summa, ut mones,
valde me ad otium pacemque converto.   De libris 6

mis de rebus a fratre esse celatum,
Fam. 5. 2. 9. — πολλὸν . . . ἄλλων:
Hom. *Il.* 6. 208. — defensos: cf.
ex hoc labore, Ep. XXII. 1 n, and
Vatinium, Ep. XXII. 3 n.

5. Gabinium si . . . defendissem : Gabinius was accused *de*
maiestate, de repetundis, and *de*
ambitu (cf. *Q. fr.* 3. 1. 15; 3. 3. 2).
On the first charge he was acquitted (*Q. fr.* 3. 4. 1) through
the efforts of Pompey, his political
master. Cicero was induced by
Pompey and Caesar to defend him
when he came up for trial under
the second charge, but he was convicted (*pro Rabir. Post.* 20, 32 f.).
Gabinius had assisted Clodius in

securing Cicero's exile, for which
action Cicero attacked him fiercely;
cf. *pro Sest.* 17 ff. In the text Cicero is speaking of the first trial.
— Pansa : C. Vibius Pansa, a
supporter of Caesar, and picked
out by him for the consulship for
43. With his colleague Hirtius he
was killed in the *bellum Mutinense*
in the spring of that year. Pansa
had probably urged Cicero in Caesar's name to undertake the defense of Gabinius. — tantum ut
facerem : Cicero appeared as a
witness against Gabinius in the
first trial; cf. *Q. fr.* 3. 4. 3.

6. de libris: cf. *Q. fr.* 3. 4. 5 *de*
bibliotheca tua Graeca supplenda,

Tyrannio est cessator. Chrysippo dicam; sed res ope-
rosa est et hominis perdiligentis. Sentio ipse, qui in
summo studio nihil adsequor. De Latinis vero quo
me vertam nescio; ita mendose exscribuntur et vene-
unt, sed tamen quod fieri poterit non neglegam. C.
Rebilus, ut ante ad te scripsi, Romae est, et qui omnia
adiurat, debere tibi valde renuntiant. De aerario puto
confectum esse, dum absum.

7   Quattuor tragoedias sedecim diebus absolvisse cum
scribas, tu quicquam ab alio mutuaris? et πάθος quaeris, cum Electram et Aëropam scripseris? Cessator
esse noli et illud γνῶθι σεαυτὸν noli putare ad adro-
gantiam minuendam solum esse dictum, verum etiam
ut bona nostra norimus. Sed et istas et Erigonam
mihi velim mittas. Habes ad duas epistulas proximas.

XXIV. (*Fam.* 7. 16.)

1   In Equo Troiano scis esse in extremo: 'sero sapiunt.' Tu tamen, mi vetule, non sero. Primas illas

libris commutandis, Latinis com-
parandis, valde velim ista confici
. . ., sed ego mihi ipsi ista per quem
agam non habeo. — **Tyrannio,**
Chrysippo: expert *librarii;* cf.
Ep. XVII. 1.— **ita mendose ex-**
scribuntur: an interesting bit of
information in regard to the un-
trustworthiness of copyists. Cf.
also Birt, *Das antike Buchwesen*,
222. — **C. Rebilus**: probably a
centurion in Quintus's legion on
furlough in Rome (Tyrrell). — **qui**
omnia, etc.: see Crit. Append. —
de aerario: the reference is unknown. Cf. *Q. fr.* 3. 4. 5.
    7. **Electram et Aëropam**: the

Electra and *Erigona* were probably
translations of plays of the same
name by Sophocles. The original
of the *Aëropa* is not known with
certainty. Cf. Ribbeck, *Röm. Trag.*
pp. 619–621, and Bücheler, *Quinti*
Ciceronis Reliquiae, 18. — γνῶθι
σεαυτὸν: the inscription over the
entrance to the temple of Apollo
at Delphi. — **Erigonam**: Cicero
first refers to this work in Sept.
(cf. *Q. fr.* 3. 1. 13). It had not
reached him, however, in Dec. (cf.
Q. fr. 3. 9. 6), and he fears that it
has been lost on the way.— **habes**:
sc. responsum.
    XXIV. Rome, Nov., 54 B.C.

rabiosulas sat fatuas dedisti; deinde quod τῶν Βρεττανῶν minus φιλοθέωρον te praebuisti, plane non reprehendo. Nunc vero in hibernis iniectus mihi videris,
itaque te commovere non curas.

Vsquequaque sapere oportet; id erit telum acerrimum.

Ego si foris cenitarem, Cn. Octavio familiari tuo non 2
defuissem; cui tamen dixi, cum me aliquotiens invi-

1. **Equo Troiano**: cf. Ep. XIX.
2 n. — **sero sapiunt**: Cicero
quotes here, as he did in Ep. XIX.
2 (*si sciens fallo*), the first words
of a familiar passage, which had
passed into a proverb. The expression is thus explained by Festus, I. 510, de Pon.: '*sero sapiunt
Phryges' proverbium est natum a
Troianis qui decimo denique anno
velle coeperunt Helenam quaeque
cum ea erant rapta reddere.* Cf. also
Ribbeck, *Röm. Trag.* 49. — **non sero**: Trebatius had gone to Caesar
with such rose-colored ideas of a
soldier's life and of the immediate
wealth and distinction to be won
in it, that the inevitable hardships
and monotony made him discon-
tented and homesick, so that Cicero had written him reprovingly:
*primorum mensum litteris tuis ve-
hementer commovebar, quod mihi
interdum — pace tua dixerim —
levis in urbis urbanitatisque desiderio, interdum piger, interdum
timidus in labore militari, saepe
autem etiam, quod a te alienissi-
mum est, subimpudens videbare;
tamquam enim syngrapham ad
imperatorem, non epistulam attu-
lisses*, etc., *Fam.* 7. 17. 1. This
letter evidently had the effect intended, for Cicero's words, **non
sero**, as well as **mi vetule**, indicate that Trebatius had repented
of his discontent. — **primas illas**:
sc. tuas epistulas. — **rabiosulas**,

a trifle crazy. Cf. *pulchellus*, Ep.
V. 10 n. The phrase, **rabiosulas
sat fatuas**, is probably quoted
from some comic poet. Cf., however, Ribbeck, *Com. Rom. Frag.*
p. xliv. — **τῶν Βρεττανῶν** minus
φιλοθέωρον, *not very fond of seeing the sights in Britain.* In the
summer of 55 B.C. Caesar made
his first expedition to Britain, in
which Trebatius did not care to
join. — **in hibernis iniectus**: Cicero is writing toward the end of
November. — **te commovere**, *to
stir ;* as of one crawling out from
under a blanket in cold weather. —
usquequaque, etc.: probably the
words of Ulysses in the same play
from which the quotation **sero
sapiunt** was taken. Cf. Ribbeck,
Röm. Trag. p. 49, and *Trag. Rom.
Frag.* p. 246. — **sapere**: perhaps
with a double meaning, *to be wise*
and *to be learned in the law.* Cf.
Ep. XXV. 1 n. — **id erit telum
acerrimum**: Mezger quotes Fal-
staff's words, 'Discretion is the
better part of valor.'

2. **cenitarem**: this frequentative
is not found in Cicero outside of
the Letters. — **Cn. Octavio**: evidently a pushing fellow, who
wanted the distinction of enter-
taining Cicero. Cf. *Fam.* 7. 9. 3
*Cn. Octavius est an Cn. Cornelius
quidam, tuus familiaris, summo
genere natus, terrae filius. Is me,
quia scit tuum familiarem esse,*

taret: 'Oro te, quis tu es?' Sed mercules, extra
iocum, homo bellus est; vellem eum tecum abduxisses.
3 Quid agatis et ecquid in Italiam venturi sitis hac hieme
fac plane sciam. Balbus mihi confirmavit te divitem
futurum. Id utrum Romano more locutus sit, bene
nummatum te futurum, an quomodo Stoici dicunt,
omnes esse divites qui caelo et terra frui possint,
postea videbo. Qui istinc veniunt superbiam tuam
accusant, quod negent te percontantibus respondere.
Sed tamen est quod gaudeas; constat enim inter omnis
neminem te uno Samarobrivae iuris peritiorem esse.

XXV. (*Fam.* 7. 10.)

M. CICERO S. D. TREBATIO.

1   Legi tuas litteras, ex quibus intellexi te Caesari
nostro valde iure consultum videri. Est quod gaudeas
te in ista loca venisse ubi aliquid sapere viderere.
Quod si in Britanniam quoque profectus esses, profecto

crebro ad cenam invitat. — **mercules:** cf. *mercule,* Ep. XXV. 3 n. — **homo bellus,** *a good fellow.* See Martial, 3. 63. *Bellus,* the diminutive of *bonus,* is used familiarly in the Letters with the peculiar force which colloquial Latin often gave to the diminutive (cf. *pulchellus,* Ep. V. 10 n), *e.g. puellae Caeciliae bellissimae salutem dices, Att.* 6. 4. 3; *illum pueris locum esse bellissimum duximus, Att.* 5. 17. 3; so *belle se habere* ('to be in first-rate health'), *Att.* 12. 37. 1.

3. **in Italiam:** *i.e.* to Luca. — **Romano more:** cf. *more Romano,* Ep. XXI. 3 n, and *more maiorum,* Ep. I. 1 n. — **bene nummatum:** a colloquial expression which Horace adopts for comic effect

(*Epp.* 1. 6. 38) perhaps from this passage. Cf. also Cic. *de leg. Agr.* 2. 59. — **quod negent:** cf. *diceret,* Ep. I. 3 n. — **respondere:** here with a double meaning, viz., *to reply to* and *to give legal advice to.* Cf. *cautior,* Ep. XXV. 2 n. — **constat . . . peritiorem esse:** Trebatius could at least congratulate himself upon discovering a place where he was the most learned lawyer — because he was the only one. Cf. quotation, Ep. XXI. (end).

XXV. Rome, December, 54 B.C.

1. **te Caesari . . . videri:** cf. quotation, Ep. XXI. (end). — **sapere:** with special reference to technical legal knowledge. — **in**

nemo in illa tanta insula peritior te fuisset. Verum
tamen — rideamus licet ; sum enim a te invitatus —
subinvideo tibi, ultro etiam accersitum ab eo ad quem
ceteri non propter superbiam eius sed propter occupa-
tionem adspirare non possunt.   Sed tu in ista epistula 2
nihil mihi scripsisti de tuis rebus, quae mercule mihi
non minori curae sunt quam meae.   Valde metuo ne
frigeas in hibernis.   Quamobrem camino luculento
utendum censeo (idem Mucio et Manilio placebat),
praesertim qui sagis non abundares.   Quamquam vos
nunc istic satis calere audio; quo quidem nuntio valde
mercule de te timueram.   Sed tu in re militari multo es

Britanniam: cf. τῶν Βρεττανῶν,
Ep. XXIV. 1 n. — in . . . insula
peritior: where all were savages.
A similar jest at end of Ep. XXIV.
—sum . . . invitatus: the letters of
Trebatius were apparently written
in a personal and humorous vein.
— subinvideo tibi, *I envy you a
trifle.* Cf. Intr. 77. — accersitum:
sc. to give advice.

2. minori curae : colloquial
Latin showed a fondness for the
predicate dative after *esse ;* and
curae, often with an adjective,
magnae, minori, summae, etc., is
very frequently found in this construction. — valde metuo, etc.,
*I am very much afraid that you
are suffering from cold in your
winter quarters ; so I advise you
to keep a bright fire going on the
hearth (Mucius and Manilius hold
the same opinion), especially as you
are not well supplied with clothing
for a campaign, and yet I understand that you find it hot enough
over there just at present.* The
humor of the passage consists in
the rapid transition from the literal to the metaphorical meaning
of certain words, and in the cita-

tion of learned authorities in support of self-evident conclusions.
frigeas in hibernis is perhaps
best taken literally, sagis non
abundares with a double meaning, and calere figuratively. —
Mucio: Q. Mucius Scaevola, pon-
tifex maximus, consul in 95 B.C.,
an eminent jurist and Cicero's pre-
ceptor ; cf. *Lael.* 1. — Manilio :
M'. Manilius, consul in 149 B.C. ; an
authority upon civil law often mentioned with Scaevola. — placebat:
like censeo a technical legal word.
— sagis non abundares : inasmuch as Trebatius is not well supplied with heavy garments, and the
weather is cold, his only protection
lies in keeping a good fire ; but the
sagum was the typical garment of
a soldier, as the *toga* was the main
article in the dress of a civilian
(thus *sagati,* Non. II. 202, Müll., is
opposed to *togati*), and to say that
Trebatius was not well supplied
with *saga* implied that he avoided
the dangers of the campaign. —
calere: used metaphorically of the
'warm work' which the insurrec-
tion of the Gauls under Ambiorix
(Caes. *B. G.* 5. 23–53) gave the

cautior quam in advocationibus, qui neque in Oceano
natare volueris, studiosissimus homo natandi, neque
spectare essedarios, quem antea ne andabata quidem
defraudare poteramus.   Sed iam satis iocati sumus.
3 Ego de te ad Caesarem quam diligenter scripserim, tute
scis, quam saepe, ego; sed mercule iam intermiseram,
ne viderer liberalissimi hominis meique amantissimi
voluntati erga me diffidere.   Sed tamen iis litteris quas
proxime dedi putavi esse hominem commonendum.   Id
feci; quid profecerim facias me velim certiorem, et simul
de toto statu tuo consiliisque omnibus; scire enim
cupio quid agas, quid exspectes, quam longum istum

Romans. See Intr. 99. — **cautior,**
more discreet.   Cavere as a legal
term means, ' to provide for a person,' as his counsel.   Cicero suggests that Trebatius showed more
discretion as a soldier, in keeping
out of range, than he did as a lawyer.   The same pun occurs in another letter to Trebatius (*Fam.* 7. 6.
2) *tu, qui ceteris cavere didicisti, in
Britannia ne ab essedariis decipiaris caveto.*   One of the main sources
of humor in Cicero's letters to
Trebatius lies in the double meaning which he gives to judicial
terms,— a form of wit which would
appeal forcibly to the legal mind
of Trebatius ; cf. *placebat* and
censeo above and *respondere* in
the foregoing letter.   Cf. also Cic.
Philipp. 2. 7 *quam multa ioca solent esse in epistulis quae, prolata
si sint, inepta videantur!*— **qui . . .
volueris:** a humorous way of saying that Trebatius avoided the
dangers and hardships of the British campaign by staying in Gaul.
See *in Britanniam,* 1 n. — **studiosissimus homo natandi :** Trebatius's fondness for swimming

Horace wittily uses for his own
purposes in *Sat.* 2. 1. 8. — **spectare :** cf. τῶν Βρεττανῶν, Ep.
XXIV. 1 n. — **andabata:** Trebatius had been so fond of combats
in Rome that his friends had not
been able to keep him away, even
from the shows where blindfolded
warriors fought on horseback.   It
is strange, therefore, that he feels
so little interest in seeing similar
contests in Britain.   The *essedarii*
were especially dreaded by the
Roman soldiers. — **defraudare:** a
colloquial word, which, though
common enough in Plautus and
Terence, Cicero uses elsewhere
perhaps only in a proverbial expression, *Or.* 221.

3. **mercule:** this oath is found
in Cicero's correspondence in the
forms, *hercules, mehercules* (or
mercules), and *mehercule* (or *mercule*).   Cicero himself writes (*Or.*
157) *mehercule libentius dixerim
quam mehercules,* and the more
polished letter-writers of this period seem to have agreed with
him. — **hominem:** cf. *homini,* Ep.
XVI. 6 n.

tuum discessum a nobis futurum putes. Sic enim tibi ₄
persuadeas velim, unum mihi esse solacium quare facilius
possim pati te esse sine nobis, si tibi esse id emolumento
sciam; sin autem id non est, nihil duobus nobis est
stultius, me qui te non Romam attraham, te qui non
huc advoles. Vna mercule nostra vel severa vel iocosa
congressio pluris erit quam non modo hostes, sed etiam
fratres nostri Aedui. Quare omnibus de rebus fac ut
quam primum sciam:

> Aut consolando aut consilio aut re iuero.

XXVI.   (*Fam.* 7. 18.)

CICERO TREBATIO S.

Accepi a te aliquot epistulas uno tempore, quas tu ₁
diversis temporibus dederas. In quibus me cetera
delectarunt; significabant enim te istam militiam iam
firmo animo ferre et esse fortem virum et constantem;
quae ego paulisper in te ita desideravi, non imbecilli-
tate animi tui, sed magis ut desiderio nostri te aestuare
putarem. Quare perge, ut coepisti; forti animo istam
tolera militiam. Multa, mihi crede, adsequere; ego
enim renovabo commendationem, sed tempore. Sic

---

4. **nihil**: stronger than *nemo.* —
advoles: Lorenz, on Plaut. *Pseud.*
535, says: The Roman *sermo cotidianus* had a host of substitutes for
ire and *abire, e.g. ambulare, se agere,
se penetrare, se adferre, se dare, se
immergere, se ducere, se abripere,*
etc. Such substitutes as *advolare*
and *convolare* are especial favorites, because of their exaggerative
character. Cf. *Att.* I. 14. 5; Ep.
LXIX. I.— **fratres nostri Aedui**:
a thrust at the absurdity of bestow-

ing such complimentary titles
upon remote barbarians, whose
'brotherhood' did not keep them
from frequent treachery and insub-
ordination. The grant of the title
is mentioned in Caes. *B. G.* I. 33.
With the sentiment, cf. *Fam.* 7. 11.
2 *una mercule conlocutio nostra
pluris erit quam omnes Samarobrivae.* — **aut**, etc.: Ter. *Heaut.* 86.
   XXVI.   A villa near Ulubrae,
April 8, 53 B.C.
   1. **sic habeto**: like *scito* (cf. Intr.

habeto, non tibi maiori esse curae ut iste tuus a me
discessus quam fructuosissimus tibi sit quam mihi.
Itaque, quoniam vestrae cautiones infirmae sunt, Graeculam tibi misi cautionem chirographi mei.   Tu me
velim de ratione Gallici belli certiorem facias; ego enim
2 ignavissimo cuique maximam fidem habeo.   Sed ut ad
epistulas tuas redeam, cetera belle; illud miror: quis
solet eodem exemplo plures dare qui sua manu scribit?
Nam quod in palimpsesto, laudo equidem parsimoniam;
sed miror quid in illa chartula fuerit quod delere malu-
eris quam haec in nova scribere, nisi forte tuas formu-

89), a lively colloquial expression
which is used frequently in the
Letters. *Sic* takes the place of an
object. Cf. *Fam.* I. 7. 4; 16. 4. 4;
Ep. LXI. 2.   The construction is
indicated in *Fam.* 2. 6. 5 *unum hoc
sic habeto*, etc.   *Habere* with the
force of *scire* or *audivisse*, though
found most frequently in the imperative, is not confined to that
mode. Cf. *habes omnia, Att.* 5. 20.
7; *habes consilia nostra, nunc cognosce de Bruto, Att.* 5. 21. 10.   Cf.
the English colloquial expression,
'you have it,' *i.e.* you have the idea.
— maiori curae: cf. Ep. XXV. 2 n.
— vestrae cautiones ... chirographi mei: 'the guaranty-bonds
drawn up by you lawyers for your
clients are so poor that I am afraid
your position will not be a stable
one if you depend upon your own
support. This letter, therefore, is
a guaranty, with a Greek coloring
to it, to be sure, of my support.'
Graeculam is very obscure, but
in the diminutive force the key to
the explanation seems to lie. Cf.
Tusc. Disp. 1. 86, where Cicero
characterizes the extravagant congratulations which the Neapoli-
tans offered to Pompey on his
recovery after a dangerous illness

as *ineptum sane negotium et Grae-
culum;* and *pro Flacc.* 23 *motus quidam temerarius Graeculae contio-
nis.*   The assembly showed the
instability so characteristic of the
Greeks.   The congratulations for
Pompey were marked by that
extravagance or lack of dignity
which one is accustomed to look
for in the Greeks. With this explanation of **Graeculam** the meaning is : 'I send you therefore in
this letter, lacking as it may seem
in seriousness, because of its light
tone of raillery, a promise of my
support.' — ignavissimo cuique:
Cicero cannot mean, as many suppose, that he would like the evidence of a spectator concerning the
Gallic war, *because Caesar's Commentaries were thought to put matters in too rose-colored a light.*   The
Commentaries were published two
years later.
  2. cetera belle: *sc. fuerunt.*
Cf. *sic,* Ep. V. 3 n, and *bellus,*
Ep. XXIV. 2 n. — eodem exemplo, *with identical contents.* — sed
miror, etc.: the matter must have
been very poor which Trebatius
erased to make room for such a
letter as the one was which took
its place. — tuas formulas : at-

las; non enim puto te meas epistulas delere ut reponas tuas. An hoc significas, nihil fieri, frigere te, ne chartam quidem tibi suppeditare ? Iam ista tua culpa est, qui verecundiam tecum extuleris et non hic nobiscum reliqueris. Ego te Balbo, cum ad vos proficiscetur, 3 more Romano commendabo. Tu, si intervallum longius erit mearum litterarum, ne sis admiratus; eram enim afuturus mense Aprili. Has litteras scripsi in Pomptino, cum ad villam M. Aemili Philemonis devertissem, ex qua iam audieram fremitum clientium meorum, quos quidem tu mihi conciliasti; nam Vlubris honoris mei causa vim maximam ranunculorum se commosse constabat. Cura ut valeas. vi Idus April. de Pomptino.

Epistulam tuam, quam accepi ab L. Arruntio, con- 4 scidi innocentem; nihil enim habebat quod non vel in contione recte legi posset. Sed et Arruntius ita te mandasse aiebat et tu adscripseras. Verum illud esto. Nihil te ad me postea scripsisse demiror, praesertim tam novis rebus.

tracted by **haec** into the acc. — **non enim puto**, etc., *you are not scratching out my letters, are you, to make room for yours?* — **frigere te** : cf. Intr. 99. — **chartam** : cf. Intr. 59. — **verecundiam**: in Ep. XXI. 3 Cicero recommends Trebatius to Caesar on the score of modesty.

3. **Balbo**: cf. Ep. XXI. 2 n. — **more Romano**: cf. Ep. XXI. 3 n. — **eram afuturus**: cf. Intr. 84 *c.* — **M. Aemili Philemonis**: freedman of M. Lepidus. — **devertissem,** *had put up at.* — **fremitum clientium meorum** : Trebatius was the patron of Ulubrae, a little town near the Pomptine marshes, and on leaving Rome for Caesar's camp had entrusted the interests

of the town to Cicero. The latter, upon passing through the district, is saluted by Trebatius's clients the frogs, for the marshes were full of them, as we know also from Hor. *Sat.* i. 5. 14.

4. **legi**: cf. Ep. V. 8 n. — **ita** : referring back to **conscidi**. — **demiror** (for *miror*): a tendency to exaggerate has already been noticed as a characteristic of colloquial language (Intr. 96). Like the frequentative (cf. Intr. 79), the verb compounded with a prep. takes the place of the simple verb, because it is stronger; but from frequent use it ultimately loses its characteristic meaning, and does not differ in sense from the simple verb. Cf. also Intr. 76, 78.

XXVII. (*Fam.* 16. 16.)

QVINTVS MARCO FRATRI S.

1 De Tirone, mi Marce, ita te meumque Ciceronem et
meam Tulliolam tuumque filium videam, ut mihi gratissimum fecisti, cum eum indignum illa fortuna iudicasti ac nobis amicum quam servum esse maluisti.
Mihi crede, tuis et illius litteris perlectis exsilui gaudio
2 et tibi et ago gratias et gratulor. Si enim mihi Stati
fidelitas est tantae voluptati, quanti esse in isto haec
eadem bona debent additis litteris, sermonibus, humanitate, quae sunt his ipsis commodis potiora! Amo te omnibus equidem de maximis causis, verum etiam propter
hanc, vel quod mihi sic ut debuisti nuntiasti. Te totum in
litteris vidi. Sabini pueris et promisi omnia et faciam.

XXVIII. (*Fam.* 7. 15.)

CICERO TREBATIO.

1 Quam sint morosi qui amant vel ex hoc intellegi
potest: moleste ferebam antea te invitum istic esse;
pungit me rursus quod scribis esse te istic libenter.

XXVII. Transalpine Gaul, May,
53 B.C.
　　1. mi **Marce**: cf. *mi Pomponi*,
Ep. X. n. — **meam**: (not *tuam*)
to indicate his affection for Tullia.
— **Tulliolam**: cf. *pulchellus*, Ep.
V. 10 n. and Intr. 76. — **amicum**
. . . **maluisti**: with reference to
Tiro's manumission. Cicero seems
to refer to the same event in
nostra . . . fient, *Fam.* 16. 10. 2,
and *dies promissorum adest, quem
etiam repraesentabo, si adveneris,
Fam.* 16. 14. 2. — **mihi crede**: this

phrase and *crede mihi* are common
in the correspondence. The latter
seems to be the colloquial, and
mihi crede the more formal order.
— **exsilui gaudio**: in harmony
with the familiar tone of the letter.
　　2. **Stati**: cf. Ep. VII. 1 n. —
sic . . . nuntiasti: for the absolute use of *nuntio*, cf. Ter. *Hec.*
642, *bene, ita me di ament, nuntias.*
— **Sabini**: unknown.
　　XXVIII. Rome, June, 53 B.C.
　　1. **quam sint morosi qui
amant**: Böckel considers this a

Neque enim mea commendatione te non delectari facile
patiebar et nunc angor quicquam tibi sine me esse
iucundum. Sed hoc tamen malo ferre nos desiderium
quam te non ea quae spero consequi. Quod vero in C. 2
Mati, suavissimi doctissimique hominis, familiaritatem
venisti, non dici potest quam valde gaudeam. Qui fac ut
te quam maxime diligat. Mihi crede, nihil ex ista provincia potes quod iucundius sit deportare. Cura ut valeas.

XXIX. (*Fam.* 3. 2.)

M. CICERO PROCOS. S. D. APPIO PVLCHRO IMP.

Cum et contra voluntatem meam et praeter opinio- 1
nem accidisset ut mihi cum imperio in provinciam

quotation from some poet, and
compares for the sentiment Plaut.
Trin. 668 : *Itast amor, ballista ut
iacitur, nil sic celerest neque vo-
lat :* | *Atque is mores hominum
moros et morosos efficit.*

2. **C. Mati:** cf. Ep. XCI., introd.
note, and XCII. — **suavissimi:**
Ep. XCII. affords excellent proof
of the correctness of this characterization. — **doctissimi:** Matius not
only wrote a book upon gastronomy, but Cicero found the
impulse to some of his best
philosophical work in the lively
sympathy of Matius. Cf. φιλοσοφούμενα, Ep. XCI. 5 n. — **familiaritatem:** the friendship formed between Matius and Trebatius in
Gaul continued unshaken through
all the vicissitudes of the Civil War.
Cf. Ep. XCI. 1, *Att.* 9. 15 A. —
mihi crede : cf. Ep. XXVII. 1 n.

XXIX. After leaving Rome,
about Mar., 51 B.C. Cicero's request, embodied in this letter, that
Appius Claudius Pulcher, his

predecessor in the proconsulship
of Cilicia, should turn over the
province to him in as satisfactory
a condition as possible, was far
from being fulfilled; and Cicero
found himself under the necessity
of changing many of the corrupt
and tyrannous practices of the
late governor, — a course which
brought upon him the enmity of
Appius. Upon his return to Rome,
Appius was charged with misgovernment by Dolabella, Cicero's son-
in-law, but escaped punishment with
the help of Pompey. For the limits
of Cicero's province, cf. Intr. 23.

The possession of the title *proconsul* (procos.), carrying along
with it the *imperium*, indicates
that Cicero wrote this letter at
some point outside of Rome. Appius received the title of *imperator*
(imp.) from his troops, because of
a successful campaign against the
mountaineers of his province.

1. **contra voluntatem . . . et
praeter opinionem:** Cicero had

proficisci necesse esset, in multis et variis molestiis
cogitationibusque meis haec una consolatio occurrebat,
quod neque tibi amicior quam ego sum quisquam
posset succedere, neque ego ab ullo provinciam accipere qui mallet eam quam maxime mihi aptam expli-
catamque tradere. Quod si tu quoque eandem de mea
voluntate erga te spem habes, ea te profecto numquam
fallet. At te maximo opere pro nostra summa coniunctione tuaque singulari humanitate etiam atque etiam
quaeso et peto ut, quibuscumque rebus poteris — poteris autem plurimis, — prospicias et consulas rationibus
2 meis. Vides ex senatus consulto provinciam esse
habendam. Si eam, quod eius facere potueris, quam
expeditissimam mihi tradideris, facilior erit mihi quasi
decursus mei temporis. Quid in eo genere efficere
possis, tui consili est; ego te quod tibi veniet in mentem mea interesse valde rogo. Pluribus verbis ad te
scriberem, si aut tua humanitas longiorem orationem
exspectaret aut id fieri nostra amicitia pateretur aut res
verba desideraret ac non pro se ipsa loqueretur. Hoc

declined a province both at the
close of his praetorship and of his
consulship. The words **contra
voluntatem** indicate that in declining Macedonia in favor of C.
Antonius in 63 B.C. he did not show
so much self-abnegation as he
would lead us elsewhere to infer.
Cf. Ep. XXXIV. 13 *si quisquam*,
etc. His assignment to a province
in this case was one of the results
of a law passed rather unexpectedly; cf. Intr. 22. — **amicior**: cf.
Appium, Ep. VIII. 2 n. — **summa
coniunctione** : both were augurs.
See also *amicior* above. — **quaeso**:
here (with **peto**) followed by an
object clause, — a rare use. In

classical prose *quaeso* is used parenthetically either alone or with a
single word for an object, especially *deos* or a personal pronoun
(cf. *Phil.* 7. 8). — **consulas,** etc. :
instead of complying with this request, Appius proposed a decrease
in the scanty military force in the
province (cf. *Fam.* 3. 2), and
treated Cicero with marked disre-
spect (cf. *Fam.* 3. 8. 6). The letters
of the two men are full of mutual
recriminations and explanations ;
cf. *Fam.* 3. 7. 2 ; 3. 9. 1 ; 3. 11. 5.
2. **eius** : neuter, partitive genitive ; cf. *Fam.* 5. 8. 5; *Att.* 11. 12.
4. — **si . . . intellexero**: cf. *si . . .
videro*, Ep. VIII. 5 n.

velim tibi persuadeas, si rationibus meis provisum a te
esse intellexero, magnam te ex eo et perpetuam voluptatem esse capturum.   Vale.

XXX. (*Att.* 5. 1.)

CICERO ATTICO SAL.

Ego vero et tuum in discessu vidi animum et meo 1
sum ipse testis; quo magis erit tibi videndum ne quid
novi decernatur, ut hoc nostrum desiderium ne plus sit
annuum.   De Annio Saturnino curasti probe.   De sa- 2
tisdando vero te rogo, quoad eris Romae, tu ut satisdes,
et sunt aliquot satisdationes secundum mancipium,

XXX. Minturnae, about May 7,
51 B.C. Cicero apparently left Rome
May 1, spent a day at his Tusculan villa with Philotimus, his business agent, and Atticus (3), and
went thence to Minturnae by the
way of Arpinum and Aquinum (3).
He reached his destination, Laodicea in Phrygia, July 31 (*Att.* 5.
15. 1).   With 3–5 of this letter,
cf. Ep. VI.

1. **ego vero:** these words imply
that Cicero has in mind a remark
in the letter of Atticus. Cf. *Fam.*
16. 10. 1. — **ut . . . ne:** *ut ne* is
frequent in Latin comedy in clauses
both of result and of purpose, and
the explanation would seem to be
that originally *ne* had purely a negative force in the combination, *e.g.*
faciemus ut, quod viderit, ne viderit,
Plaut. *M. G.* 149; *merito ut ne
dicant, id est (mi in manu),* Plaut.
Trin. 105.   Colloquial language,
being conservative of old usages,
retained this archaism and others
after they had disappeared from
general use in formal language.
The separation of *ut* and *ne* is

remarkable, but finds parallels,
especially in Latin comedy : cf. *ut
quom opus sit ne in mora nobis
siet,* Ter. *Ad.* 354, and Plaut.
M. G. 149 (above); in fact, the
use of *ut ne* instead of *ne* makes
it possible to put *ne* in the middle
or near the end of the sentence,
and thus secure the desired emphasis upon the negation.   According to Seyffert-Müller (on
Laelius, 305), *ut ne* frequently
appears in the language of the laws
where we should expect *ne.*   This
coincidence between the legal and
colloquial style is due to the con-
servatism of each form of speech,
and is especially noticeable in the
letter from the jurist Sulpicius
(Ep. LXXV.).

2. **Annio Saturnino:** probably
a freedman of T. Annius Milo.
— **aliquot satisdationes secundum mancipium,** *some satisfactory evidence with reference to
ownership.*   Cicero was apparently
about to sell some property, and
advises Atticus to give such proof
of the validity of his title as was

veluti Mennianorum praediorum vel Atilianorum.   De
Oppio factum est ut volui, et maxime quod DCCC aperuisti; quae quidem ego utique vel versura facta solvi
volo, ne extrema exactio nostrorum nominum exspecte-
3 tur.   Nunc venio ad transversum illum extremae epistulae tuae versiculum, in quo me admones de sorore.
Quae res se sic habet.   Vt veni in Arpinas, cum ad
me frater venisset, in primis nobis sermo, isque multus,
de te fuit, ex quo ego veni ad ea quae fueramus ego et
tu inter nos de sorore in Tusculano locuti.   Nihil tam
vidi mite, nihil tam placatum quam tum meus frater
erat in sororem tuam, ut etiam si qua fuerat ex ratione
sumptus offensio, non appareret.   Illo sic die; postridie
ex Arpinati profecti sumus.   Vt in Arcano Quintus
maneret dies fecit, ego Aquini, sed prandimus in Arcano.   Nosti hunc fundum.   Quo ut venimus, humanissime Quintus 'Pomponia' inquit, 'tu invita mulieres,

given in the case of the Mennian
estate — *or the Atilian* (*as I had
better call it*). — de Oppio : C.
Oppius, Caesar's agent in Rome,
belonged to that little group of
young men who followed Caesar's
cause faithfully. His biography of
Caesar probably formed the basis
of Plutarch's sketch.— quod DCCC
(*sc. sestertia*) aperuisti, *because you
have expressed a readiness to pay
the 800,000 sesterces*. The meaning
of aperuisti is, however, doubtful.
This debt to Caesar, which was
still outstanding in Dec., 50 B.C.
(*Att.* 7. 3. 11), was evidently expected to block Cicero's opposition to the triumvirs. The plan
accomplished its object ; cf. *Att.*
7. 3. 11 'But you know how much
is still due him. Do you think,
pray, that I have reason to fear
lest some Pompeian may twit me

with it, if my opposition to Caesar
is rather half-hearted, or lest Caesar may call in the loan, if I oppose
him somewhat vigorously ? I fancy
that, if I ever speak boldly in the
senate in behalf of the commonwealth, I fancy, I say, that your
Tarshish friend Balbus will meet
me at the door and say, " Pray let
me have a cheque for that money."'
— vel versura facta, *even if a
(new) loan has to be made*.

3. transversum . . . versiculum: the line written lengthwise
along the margin. — sorore: Pomponia, the wife of Quintus. —
Arpinas: *sc. praedium.*— in Tusculano: see intr. to letter.— mite:
cf. *patientia*, Ep. XVI. 7 n. —
nihil : cf. Ep. XXV. 4 n. — dies
fecit : the day being a holiday, it
was incumbent upon Quintus to
spend it upon his estate with his

ego accivero pueros.' Nihil potuit, mihi quidem ut
visum est, dulcius, idque cum verbis tum etiam animo
ac vultu. At illa audientibus nobis: 'Ego sum,' inquit,
'hic hospita' — id autem ex eo, ut opinor, quod ante-
cesserat Statius ut prandium nobis videret. Tum
Quintus 'En,' inquit mihi, 'haec ego patior cotidie.'
Dices: 'Quid, quaeso, istuc erat?' Magnum; itaque me 4
ipsum commoverat: sic absurde et aspere verbis vultu-
que responderat. Dissimulavi dolens. Discubuimus
omnes praeter illam, cui tamen Quintus de mensa
misit; illa reiecit. Quid multa? nihil meo fratre lenius,
nihil asperius tua sorore mihi visum est, et multa praetereo quae tum mihi maiori stomacho quam ipsi Quinto
fuerunt. Ego inde Aquinum; Quintus in Arcano re-
mansit et Aquinum ad me postridie mane venit mihique
narravit nec secum illam dormire voluisse et, cum dis-
cessura esset, fuisse eiusmodi qualem ego vidissem.
Quid quaeris? vel ipsi hoc dicas licet, humanitatem ei
meo iudicio illo die defuisse. Haec ad te scripsi fortasse pluribus quam necesse fuit, ut videres tuas quoque
esse partes instituendi et monendi. Reliquum est, ut 5

tenants and slaves. — **accivero** :
the fut. perf. indicates sometimes
what will happen while something
else takes place. Cf. *dimisero*, Ep.
XV. 2 n. — **pueros** : probably
young Marcus and young Quintus,
who accompanied the orator to
Cilicia. — **ego . . . hospita**, *I am a
stranger here.* — **Statius** : Pomponia was annoyed at what she
regarded as the officiousness of
Statius. Cf. Ep. VII. 1 n. — **ut
. . . videret**, *to see to :* a colloquial
use of *videre.* Cf. *talaria videamus,
Att.* 14. 21. 4 and Ter. *Heaut.* 459.
— **en**, *see that ;* a common inter-

jection in lively conversation, as
Latin comedy abundantly proves.
Cf. Brix, Plaut. *Trin.* 3.
4. **sic absurde** : this use of *sic*
to express intensity with verbs and
adjectives is found chiefly in Cicero and the comic writers (Tyrrell).
Similar cases, perhaps, are Hor.
Sat. 1. 5. 69; 2. 3. 1. — **stomacho,**
annoyance ; common in this sense
only in the Letters. — **quid quaeris** : cf. Ep. V. 4 n. — **tuas . . .
monendi** : Atticus is requested to
reprove his sister, just as he had
apparently asked Cicero to reprove Quintus; cf. 3. Quintus and

antequam proficiscare mandata nostra exhaurias, scribas
ad me omnia, Pomptinum extrudas, cum profectus eris,
cures ut sciam, sic habeas, nihil mehercule te mihi nec
carius esse nec suavius.   A. Torquatum amantissime
dimisi Minturnis, optimum virum, cui me ad te scripsisse aliquid in sermone significes velim.

XXXI. (*Fam*. 8. 1.)

CAELIVS CICERONI S.

1   Quod tibi discedens pollicitus sum me omnes res
urbanas diligentissime tibi perscripturum, data opera

Pomponia were divorced about
seven years later.

5. Pomptinum: C. Pomptinus,
who was praetor in 63 B.C., was
Cicero's able assistant in the sup-
pression of the Catilinarian conspiracy; cf. *in Cat*. 3. 5. He was
a man of military experience, and
Cicero, appreciating his own igno-
rance in military affairs, and the
danger which threatened his province from the Parthians, had made
him one of his four *legati*. — **sic
habeas**: cf. *sic habeto*, Ep. XXVI.
1 n. — **cui . . . velim**: 'I wish that
you would tell him that I have
written to you about him.' The
reference is to the complimentary
remarks just made.

XXXI. Rome, about May 24,
51 B.C. M. Caelius Rufus was born
about 85 B.C., and came to Rome
when fifteen or sixteen years of
age to study law and politics.
He sympathized with Catiline, but
took no active part in the conspiracy. In 52 B.C. as tribune he
vigorously supported the aristocratic cause, but in later life he

went over to Caesar. In 51 B.C.,
when his letters to Cicero begin,
Caelius was a candidate for the
curule aedileship. In January, 49,
he opposed the senate, and fled
with Curio to Caesar's camp. Disappointed with the 'spoils' which
fell to his share, he joined Milo in
an uprising in southern Italy, and
was put to death by Caesar's
troops in 48. In the social world his
intimacy with Clodia (Ep. VIII. 5)
gave him great notoriety.   The
wit and beauty of Caelius attracted
this 'Palatine Medea,' and the ban-
quets and revels at Rome and
Baiae, in which Caelius and Clodia
were the central figures, were the
talk of Rome.   At last they quar-
relled, and many of the difficulties
in which Caelius was subsequently
involved could be traced directly
to her, in one of which, a charge
of murder, Cicero delivered in his
defense the *Or. pro Caelio*.

It was natural that Cicero, when
setting out for a distant province
at so critical a moment, should
choose in preference to all others

paravi qui sic omnia persequeretur, ut verear ne tibi nimium arguta haec sedulitas videatur; tametsi tu scio quam sis curiosus et quam omnibus peregrinantibus gratum sit minimarum quoque rerum, quae domi gerantur, fieri certiores. Tamen in hoc te deprecor ne meum hoc officium adrogantiae condemnes, quod hunc laborem alteri delegavi, non quin mihi suavissimum sit et occupato et ad litteras scribendas, ut tu nosti, pigerrimo tuae memoriae dare operam, sed ipsum volumen quod tibi misi facile, ut ego arbitror, me excusat. Nescio quoius oti esset non modo perscribere haec, sed omnino animadvertere; omnia enim sunt ibi s. c. edicta fabulae rumores. Quod exemplum si forte minus te delectarit, ne molestiam tibi cum impensa mea exhibeam fac me certiorem. Si quid in re p. maius actum erit quod 2

a man so familiar with the ins and outs of politics and society, to keep him informed of the course of events at Rome. The letters of Bk. 8, *ad Fam.* are not only of great interest on account of their intrinsic literary and historical value, but they offer sufficient material upon which to base a comparison between the epistolary style of Cicero and that of one of his contemporaries.

1. **discedens**: Caelius accompanied Cicero part of the way from Rome to Brundisium. See *Cumarum tenus*, 2 n. — **diligentissime perscripturum**: cf. Intr. 77. — **paravi qui . . . persequeretur**: Caelius had evidently employed a reporter to collect news, probably a certain Chrestus. Cf. Ep. XXXIII. 1. — **peregrinantibus gratum**: so eager for news were the Romans in the provinces that certain persons in Rome drove a thriving trade by sending them reports of the news of the day. In 59 B.C. their task was lightened by the law of Caesar requiring the doings in the senate and the courts and in the field, together with some events of a private character, to be published officially in the *Acta diurna*, which were copied and sent in great numbers to the provinces. Cf. *Fam.* 12. 23. 2 *rerum urbanarum acta tibi mitti certo scio.* Cf. also *Att.* 3. 15. 6; 6. 2. 6; Mommsen, *St. R.* III. 1017 f. — **meum hoc officium**, *this method of keeping my promise.* — **volumen**: the document of Chrestus apparently took the form of a diary of political happenings. Cf. *senatus consulta edicta*, etc., below. In 8. 11. 4 Caelius calls it a *commentarium rerum urbanarum.* — **edicta**: *sc consulum et praetorum* (Manutius). — **delectarit**: cf. Intr. 82.

isti operarii minus commode persequi possint, et quemadmodum actum sit et quae existimatio secuta quaeque
de eo spes sit diligenter tibi perscribemus. Vt nunc
est, nulla magnopere exspectatio est. Nam et illi
rumores de comitiis Transpadanorum Cumarum tenus
caluerunt ; Romam cum venissem, ne tenuissimam quidem auditionem de ea re accepi; praeterea Marcellus,
quod adhuc nihil rettulit de successione provinciarum
Galliarum et in K. Iun., ut mihi ipse dixit, eam distulit
relationem, sane quam eos sermones expressit qui de
3 eo tum fuerant, cum Romae nos essemus. Tu si Pompeium, ut volebas, offendisti, qui tibi visus sit et quam
orationem habuerit tecum quamque ostenderit voluntatem — solet enim aliud sentire et loqui, neque tantum
valere ingenio, ut non appareat quid cupiat —, fac

2. **existimatio**: in this one paragraph there are five substantives in
-io. Cf. Intr. 75. — **ut nunc est:**
a colloquial expression. Cf. *Fam.*
8. 4. 2 and Hor. *Sat.* 1. 9. 5. —
nulla magnopere exspectatio,
*there is nothing in particular ex-
pected.* *Magnopere* with an adj.
(here **nulla**) is rare in classical
usage. Cf. *magnopere nemo,* Ep.
XI. 4. — **de comitiis Transpadanorum**: it was said that Caesar
had ordered the Transpadanes to
elect *quattuorviri (Att.* 5. 2. 3).
By such action their towns would
become *municipia.* The rumor
anticipated Caesar's action by a
year and a half. Cf. Marq. *Röm.
Staatsverwaltung,* I. 62, n. 3. — **Cumarum tenus**: Caelius found the
rumor common until he passed
Cumae on his return, but on reaching Rome the report was heard
nowhere. — **caluerunt :** on the
metaphor, cf. Intr. 99. — **de successione . . . Galliarum**: M. Mar-

cellus, the consul, proposed to
bring in a bill appointing a successor to Caesar. — **sane quam :**
this expression occurs five times
in the 17 letters of Caelius, and but
four times in the other 853 letters
of Cicero's correspondence. Brix,
in his note upon *nimis quam cupio*
(Plaut. *Capt.* 102), says : ' *nimis
quam cupio,* the fusion of two expressions, *nimis cupio* and *quam
cupio.*' In a similar way *sane quam,
valde quam* and *perquam* are to be
explained. — **eos sermones expressit,** *he has revived that gossip ;*
reference is made to the dilatory
course of Marcellus. If we read
*eos sermones repressit, he has put
an end to the stories,* as some pre-
fer, the reference is to the proposal
to displace Caesar; but cf. *nuntii
varios sermones excitarunt, Fam.*
8. 10. 2.

3. **Pompeium :** Cicero met
Pompey near Tarentum. Cf. *Att.*
5. 7.

mihi perscribas. Quod ad Caesarem, crebri et non ₄
belli de eo rumores, sed susurratores dumtaxat veniunt.   Alius equitem perdidisse, quod, opinor, certe
factum est; alius septimam legionem vapulasse, ipsum
apud Beluacos circumsederi interclusum ab reliquo exercitu. Neque adhuc certi quicquam est, neque haec
incerta tamen vulgo iactantur, sed inter paucos quos
tu nosti palam secreto narrantur; at Domitius, cum
manus ad os apposuit. Te a. d. ix K. Iun. subrostrani (quod illorum capiti sit !) dissiparant perisse;
urbe ac foro toto maximus rumor fuit te a Q. Pompeio
in itinere occisum. Ego, qui scirem Q. Pompeium

4. **quod ad Caesarem**: *sc. atti-net;* a favorite phrase with Cae-lius, who uses it five times in his letters, while *de* with abl. (cf. Intr. 91) occurs four times. — **belli**: cf. Ep. XXIV. 2 n. — **susurratores**: probably coined by Caelius. It is apparently found elsewhere only in the Vulgate translation of the Bible. Cf. also Intr. 74. — **equi-tem** : for *equites.* — **opinor**: this unusual parenthetical use of *opi-nor*, like that of *puto* (*e.g. in thea-trum Curionis Hortensius introiit, puto, ut suum gaudium gaudere-mus, Fam.* 8. 2. 1), belongs to the language of conversation. Cf. Intr. 86. — **septimam . . . vapulasse** : this rumor was apparently without foundation; cf. *B. G.* 8. 8. — **vapu-lasse,** *has been whipped.* For a simi-lar metaphorical use, cf. Ep. XCIII. 1 *verberavi te,* etc. *Vapulare* and *verberare* are frequent in comedy, both in a literal and in a meta-phorical sense. Cf. Plaut. *Stich.* 751; *Pseud.* 15. In a literal sense they are used of the flogging of slaves. Their use in other con-nections, therefore, carries with it, as here, a comic force. — **apud**

Beluacos: Caesar in 51 B.C. en-gaged in a war with these people; cf. *B. G.* 8. 6 ff. His position was in point of fact at this time a perilous one; cf. *B. G.* 8. 11 f. — **quos tu nosti**: *sc.* Caesar's enemies. — **pa-lam secreto** : cf. Intr. 94. — **Do-mitius**: *sc. haec narrat.* On Domi-tius, cf. Ep. I. 3 n.—**cum manus ad os apposuit**: probably a proverbial expression signifying, 'with the greatest air of mystery'; or does it mean that he uses his hands for a trumpet — 'from the house-tops,' as we say ? — **subrostrani** : the loungers about the *rostra.* The word occurs only here. Plau-tus calls the same class of people *subbasilicani, Capt.* 815. — **quod illorum capiti sit,** *may it be the death of the rascals themselves.* Per-haps **capiti** is the locative or dative of the end; cf. Draeg. *Hist. Syn.* I.² 427. So Ter. *Phor.* 491 *metuo lenonem nequid . . .* (Ge.) *suo suat capiti ?* See also Cic. *Att.* 8. 5. 1. For the phrase, cf. Otto, *Die Sprichwörter der Römer,* p. 75. — **dissiparant** : *sc. sermones.* — **Q. Pompeio** : a friend of Clodius and enemy of Cicero, living now

Baulis embaeneticam facere et usque eo, ut ego mise-
rerer eius, esurire, non sum commotus, et hoc menda-
cio, si qua pericula tibi impenderent, ut defungeremur
optavi.   Plancus quidem tuus Ravennaest, et magno
congiario donatus a Caesare nec beatus nec bene
instructus est.   Tui politici libri omnibus vigent.

XXXII. *(Fam.* 13. 1.)

M. CICERO S. D. C. MEMMIO.

1   Etsi non satis mihi constiterat cum aliquane animi
mei molestia an potius libenter te Athenis visurus

in exile. — **embaeneticam** : the
word which Caelius used is hopelessly lost.   The meaning is that
Q. Pompeius has been reduced to
such a degree that he has been
obliged to take up with some mean
employment. See Crit. Append. —
defungeremur : *sc. iis periculis.*
— **Plancus tuus,** *your friend
Plancus.* Cf. *noster,* Ep. VII. 4 n.
T. Munatius Plancus, an enemy of
Cicero, also living in banishment.
— **Ravennaest:** the MSS. of Cicero's Letters offer several un-
doubted instances of crasis, *e.g.
Ravennaest* (= *Ravennae est*) here,
neglegentiast (*Fam.* 8. 3. 1), *com-
mentariost* (*Fam.* 8. 11. 4), *stoma-
chost* (*Fam.* 8. 13. 2).   All the instances cited here are in the letters
of Caelius, and harmonize perfectly
with the Plautine tone of his correspondence. Cf. also *benest* (Balbus, *Att.* 9. 7 B. 1 and *Fam.* 14.
15 = Ep. LVIII.). — **tui politici libri omnibus vigent,** *your
work on civil government is well
received on all sides.*   The *de Re
Publica* is meant. Cf. Ep. XXIII.
    XXXII. Athens, between June
25 and July 6, 51 B.C.   Gaius

Memmius was praetor in 58 B.C.,
and in 57 went out as governor of
Bithynia, where the poets Catullus
and Helvius Cinna were members
of his staff (cf. Cat. *cc.* 10 and
28, and for a sketch of Memmius
as an orator, Cic. *Brut.* 247.)   He
belonged at that time to the party
of the Optimates, but later he
became a democrat, and in 54 was
supported by Caesar for the consulship, but having made a dis-
graceful political bargain with the
consuls of that year (*Att.* 4. 15. 7),
was banished.   At this time he
was living in Athens, and having
become the owner of the garden
and of the ruins of the house which
had belonged to Epicurus, he proposed to pull the house down in
order to put up a dwelling of his
own.   The Epicureans, greatly distressed, applied to Cicero through
Atticus to intercede with Memmius
in their behalf.   Cicero, although
not on the best of terms with Memmius, acceded to their request.
Nothing is known of the result of
his intercession.
    As an example of Cicero's skill
in handling a delicate subject, this

essem, quod iniuria quam accepisti dolore me adfi-
ceret, sapientia tua qua fers iniuriam laetitia, tamen
vidisse te mallem. Nam quod est molestiae, non sane
multo levius est, cum te non video, quod esse potuit
voluptatis certe, si vidissem te, plus fuisset. Itaque
non dubitabo dare operam ut te videam, cum id satis
commode facere potero. Interea quod per litteras et
agi tecum et, ut arbitror, confici potest, agam. Nunc 2
a te illud primum rogabo ne quid invitus mea causa
facias, sed id quod mea intelleges multum, tua nullam
in partem interesse, ita mihi des, si tibi, ut id libenter
facias, ante persuaseris. Cum Patrone Epicurio mihi
omnia sunt, nisi quod in philosophia vehementer ab eo
dissentio. Sed et initio Romae, cum te quoque et tuos
omnes observabat, me coluit in primis et nuper, cum

letter may be compared with the
one to Lucceius (Ep. XVIII.). The
case was beset with difficulties.
Memmius had been banished, unjustly as he thought, at the moment when he was suing for the
consulship. He was now passing
a disappointed life in exile, and
was so far estranged from Cicero
that he had gone to Mytilene to
avoid him. He had been annoyed
by the importunity of the Epicureans, for whom at the best he had
apparently great contempt, in spite
of the fact that Lucretius had dedicated to him the *de Rerum Natura*,
and his selfish nature brooked no
interference with his plans. Finally,
Patro, the leader of the Epicurean
school, was personally distasteful
to him.

Cicero's itinerary from Minturnae
to Athens was as follows : Cumae,
Beneventum, May 11; Venusia,
May 14; Tarentum, May 18; Brundisium, May 22; Actium, June 14;

Athens, June 25. The longest
stop on the way was a halt of three
weeks at Brundisium.

1. **non satis**, etc.: before Cicero
reached Athens. — **te . . . visurus
essem**: Memmius had withdrawn
to Mitylene, to avoid meeting Cicero (*Att.* 5. 11. 6), because the
latter had been unwilling to defend him against the charge of
ambitus. — iniuria : although the
banishment of Memmius was de-
served, technically it was *iniuria*,
because, as Memmius had turned
state's evidence, and had brought
a charge of *ambitus* against Cn.
Domitius Calvinus (*Q. fr.* 3. 2. 3),
he might have reasonably expected
exemption from punishment.

2. **cum Patrone . . . sunt,**
*Patro and I are quite devoted to
one another*. Patro was at the
head of the Epicurean school in
Athens. Cicero was an adherent
of the Academy, and had little in
common with the Epicureans. —

ea quae voluit de suis commodis et praemiis consecutus est, meme habuit suorum defensorum et amicorum fere principem, et iam a Phaedro, qui nobis, cum pueri esse-mus, ante quam Philonem cognovimus, valde ut phi-losophus, postea tamen ut vir bonus et suavis et officiosus probabatur, traditus mihi commendatusque

3 est. Is igitur Patro cum ad me Romam litteras misis-set, uti te sibi placarem peteremque ut nescio quid illud Epicuri parietinarum sibi concederes, nihil scripsi ad te ob eam rem, quod aedificationis tuae consilium commendatione mea nolebam impediri; idem, ut veni Athenas, cum idem ad te scriberem rogasset, ob eam causam impetravit, quod te abiecisse illam aedificatio-

4 nem constabat inter omnes amicos tuos. Quod si ita est et si iam tua plane nihil interest, velim, si qua offensiuncula facta est animi tui perversitate aliquorum — novi enim gentem illam —, des te ad lenitatem, vel propter summam humanitatem, vel etiam honoris mei causa. Equidem, si quid ipse sentiam quaeris, nec cur ille tantopere contendat video nec cur tu repugnes, nisi

de suis commodis et praemiis: possibly fees due him from his students, which Cicero helped him to collect. — **meme**: the colloquial double form for the acc. ; cf. Intr. 87 *b* and the double form *tete*, Plaut. *Epid.* 82, Ter. *Ad.* 33.— **Phaedro**: the Epicurean Phaedrus was one of Cicero's first teachers in philosophy. — **Philonem**: until he came to Rome as a fugitive in 88 B.C., Philo had been the leader of the New Academy at Athens. His teachings made a deep im-pression upon Cicero, and deter-mined his philosophical attitude.

3. **uti te sibi placarem**: Mem-mius and Patro had not been on

good terms for some unknown reason ; cf. *Att.* 5. 11. 6. — **illud ... parietinarum** : with a minimiz-ing force ; cf. *hoc litterarum*, Ep. XXXIII. 3 n. — **aedificationem**: for *aedificandi consilium* (Manu-tius).

4. **offensiuncula**: cf. *pulchellus*, Ep. V. 10 n. — **nisi**: Brix, on Plaut. *Trin.* 233, says: '*nisi* has after negative sentences (*i.e.* in old Latin) the force of a weak adver-sative particle, *however*, *but.*' This archaic force is retained in the passage before us ; cf. *nihil mihi gratius facere potes, nisi tamen id erit mihi gratissimum, si quae tibi mandavi confeceris, Att.* 5. 14. 3.

tamen multo minus tibi concedi potest quam illi laborare sine causa.   Quamquam Patronis et orationem et
causam tibi cognitam esse certo scio: honorem officium, testamentorum ius, Epicuri auctoritatem, Phaedri
obtestationem, sedem domicilium vestigia summorum
hominum sibi tuenda esse dicit.   Totam hominis vitam
rationemque quam sequitur in philosophia derideamus
licet, si hanc eius contentionem volumus reprehendere; sed mehercules, quoniam illi ceterisque quos
illa delectant non valde inimici sumus, nescio an ignoscendum sit huic, si tantopere laborat; in quo etiamsi
peccat, magis ineptiis quam improbitate peccat.   Sed ₅
ne plura — dicendum enim aliquando est —, Pomponium
Atticum sic amo ut alterum fratrem.   Nihil est illo
mihi nec carius nec iucundius.   Is (non quo sit ex istis;
est enim omni liberali doctrina politissimus, sed valde
diligit Patronem, valde Phaedrum amavit) sic a me hoc
contendit, homo minime ambitiosus, minime in rogando
molestus, ut nihil umquam magis, nec dubitat quin ego
a te nutu hoc consequi possem, etiamsi aedificaturus
esses.   Nunc vero si audierit te aedificationem depo-
suisse neque tamen me a te impetrasse, non te in me
inliberalem, sed me in se neglegentem putabit.   Quamobrem peto a te ut scribas ad tuos posse tua voluntate decretum illud Areopagitarum, quem ὑπομνηματισ-

— honorem officium : his reputation and his duty as leader of
the Epicurean sect.—testamentorum ius: Epicurus had bequeathed
his garden and house to his disci-
ples. — Phaedri obtestationem:
Phaedrus had probably enjoined
upon his successor Patro the necessity of recovering the property.
   5. nihil: cf. Ep. XXV. 4 n. —

nec . . . nec introduce distinct
phases of the general thought, and
so do not destroy the negation. —
non quo sit ex istis: Atticus was
an Epicurean. — diligit . . . amavit: Tyrrell cites Cic. *Ep. ad Brut.*
I. I. I *Clodius trib. pleb. designatus
valde me diligit, vel ut ἐμφατικώτε-
ρον dicam, valde me amat.* — decretum illud : the right of Mem-

6 μὸν illi vocant, tolli.   Sed redeo ad prima : prius velim
tibi persuadeas ut hoc mea causa libenter facias quam
ut facias ; sic tamen habeto, si feceris quod rogo, fore
mihi gratissimum.   Vale.

XXXIII. (*Fam.* 2. 8.)

M. CICERO PROCOS. S. D. M. CAELIO.

1   Quid? tu me hoc tibi mandasse existimas, ut mihi
gladiatorum   compositiones,   ut vadimonia   dilata,   ut
Chresti compilationem mitteres et ea quae nobis, cum
Romae sumus, narrare nemo audeat?   Vide quantum
tibi meo iudicio tribuam — nec mercule iniuria ; πολιτικώτερον enim te adhuc neminem cognovi — : ne illa
quidem curo mihi scribas quae maximis in rebus rei
publicae geruntur cotidie, nisi quid ad me ipsum per-
tinebit.   Scribent alii, multi nuntiabunt, perferet multa

mius to remove the ruins of the
house of Epicurus rested upon a
decree of the Areopagus.
   6. sic habeto: cf. Ep. XXVI.
1 n.
   XXXIII. Athens, July 6, 51 B.C.
This is Cicero's reply to the chronicle of events at Rome, which the
agent of Caelius had prepared
with such care (Ep. XXXI. 1).
   1. gladiatorum compositiones : as we might say 'circus
posters.'   Public announcement
was made upon the walls of the
number of combatants, the date
of the contests, etc.   Such an
announcement found upon the
walls of Pompeii runs as follows:
[C]N ·ALLEI · NIGIDI·MAI · QVINQ[VEN-
NALIS]·GL[ADIATORVM] · PAR[IA]·XXX·
ET·EOR[VM]·SVPP[OSITICII]· PVGN[A-

BVNT]·POMPEIIS·VIII· VII · VI· K· DEC.
. . . VEN[ATIO] · ERIT· (*C. I. L.* IV.
1179).— Chresti compilationem,
the pilfering of Chrestus, i.e. the
'hotch potch' which Chrestus,
the agent of Caelius, has taken
indiscriminately from the journals
of the senate, the records of the
courts, and the placards of the
games.   Perhaps, however, Chrestus was a thief whose exploits
formed one of the items in the
diary.   Cicero really desires to
know, *cum formam rei publicae
viderit, quale aedificium futurum
sit.* — narrare nemo audeat: for
Cicero's distaste for gladiatorial
contests, cf. Ep. XIX. introd. note.
— πολιτικώτερον . . . cognovi :
cf. Ep. XXXI. introd. note. — abs
te: cf. Ep. I. 4 n.

etiam ipse rumor. Quare ego nec praeterita nec praesentia abs te, sed, ut ab homine longe in posterum
prospiciente, futura exspecto, ut ex tuis litteris cum
formam rei publicae viderim, quale aedificium futurum
sit scire possim. Neque tamen adhuc habeo quod te 2
accusem; neque enim fuit quod tu plus providere posses
quam quivis nostrum, in primisque ego, qui cum Pompeio complures dies nullis in aliis nisi de re publica
sermonibus versatus sum; quae nec possunt scribi nec
scribenda sunt. Tantum habeto, civem egregium esse
Pompeium et ad omnia, quae providenda sunt in re
publica, et animo et consilio paratum. Quare da te
homini; complectetur, mihi crede. Iam idem illi et
boni et mali cives videntur qui nobis videri solent.
Ego cum Athenis decem ipsos dies fuissem multum- 3
que mecum Gallus noster Caninius, proficiscebar inde
pridie Nonas Quinctiles, cum hoc ad te litterarum dedi.
Tibi cum omnia mea commendatissima esse cupio, tum
nihil magis quam ne tempus nobis provinciae proroge-
tur; in eo mihi sunt omnia. Quod quando et quomodo
et per quos agendum sit tu optime constitues.

2. **cum Pompeio** : cf. Ep.
XXXI. 3 n.—**tantum habeto**: cf.
Ep. XXVI. 1 n. — **quare . . .
crede** : these words form a hex-
ameter verse, which may be acci-
dental, as Böckel thinks, but it has
the appearance of being a quotation, and is ascribed by L. Müller
(p. 160) to Lucilius. For similar
expressions, cf. *Att.* 7. 12. 3; *da te
hodie mihi*, Ter. *Ad.* 838. — **mihi
crede**: cf. Ep. XXVII. 1 n.—**illi**:
i.e. Pompeio.

3. **ipsos**, *exactly;* as often with
numerals. Cf. *Att.* 3. 21; 6. 8. 4.
—**fuissem, proficiscebar, dedi**:
all the events mentioned here
would belong to the past when the
letter reached Caelius; cf. Intr.
84 *c.* — **Gallus Caninius** : cf. Ep.
XIX. 4 n. — **hoc litterarum**, *this
apology for a letter.* Reference is
apparently made not so much to
the brevity of the letter as to its
trivial character. Cf. *ipsum volumen*, Ep. XXXI. 1.

XXXIV. (*Fam.* 15. 4.)

M. CICERO IMP. S. D. M. CATONI.

1   Summa tua auctoritas fecit meumque perpetuum de tua singulari virtute iudicium, ut magni mea interesse putarem et res eas quas gessissem tibi notas esse, et non ignorari a te qua aequitate et continentia tuerer socios provinciamque administrarem.   Iis enim a te cognitis arbitrabar facilius me tibi quae vellem proba-

2 turum.   Cum in provinciam pr. K. Sext. venissem et propter anni tempus ad exercitum mihi confestim esse eundum viderem, biduum Laodiceae fui, deinde Apameae quadriduum, triduum Synnadis, totidem dies Philomeli.   Quibus in oppidis cum magni conventus fuissent, multas civitates acerbissimis tributis et gravissimis

XXXIV.   Cilicia, close of 51 or early part of 50 B.C.   Cicero, having completed a successful campaign against the independent mountaineers of his province, wrote this letter to secure Cato's support to his request for a *supplicatio*.   Understanding the blunt and frank nature of his correspondent, he affects a similar style, and presents the facts without comment, but with much skill in bringing his best achievements into the foreground, and in making it appear that the retreat of the Parthians was due to their dread of his prowess.   The letter presents a side of Cicero's life which is brought out nowhere else. It has also many points of resemblance to Caesar's Commentaries on the Gallic War.   The first part of it is essentially a military report without embellishment, addressed, it is true, to Cato, but to all intents and purposes an 'open let-

ter.'   So Caesar's Commentaries are a soldier's diary, intended for the eye of the Roman people.   In these two documents, therefore, a comparison may fairly be made between the styles of the two men. Cicero's campaign is also described at some length in *Att.* 5. 20; *Fam.* 2. 10 ; and in two letters to the senate, *Fam.* 15. 1 and 2.

For Cato's reply to this letter, cf. Ep. XXXVII.

2. **Laodiceae**: for Cicero's itinerary to Athens, cf. Epp. XXX, XXXII., introd. notes. He set out from the Piraeus July 6, reached Ceos July 8, Gyarus July 9, Syrus July 10, Delos July 11, Ephesus July 22, and, after a halt of 4 days in that city, Tralles July 27, and Laodicea July 31.   Cf. *Att.* 5. 12. 1; 5. 13. 1; *Fam.* 3. 5. 1; *Att.* 5. 15. 1. — **acerbissimis tributis** : Cicero's letters from Cilicia show the nature of these demands ; *e.g.* the towns in Cilicia, already hope-

usuris et falso aere alieno liberavi.   Cumque **ante**
adventum meum seditione quadam exercitus esset dis-
sipatus, quinque cohortes sine legato, sine tribuno
militum, denique etiam sine centurione ullo, apud Philo-
melium consedissent, reliquus exercitus esset in Lycaonia, M. Anneio legato imperavi ut eas quinque cohortes
ad reliquum exercitum duceret, coactoque in unum
locum exercitu castra in Lycaonia apud Iconium faceret.   Quod cum ab illo diligenter esset actum, ego in 3
castra a. d. VII K. Sept. veni, cum interea superioribus
diebus ex s. c. et evocatorum firmam manum et equitatum sane idoneum et populorum liberorum regumque
sociorum auxilia voluntaria comparavissem.   Interim
cum exercitu lustrato iter in Ciliciam facere coepissem

lessly in debt, were required at
great expense to send envoys to
Rome to thank the senate for the
beneficent government of the mon-
ster Appius (*Fam.* 3. 8. 2 f). Caelius had the hardihood to ask
Cicero to levy a tax upon the provincials to pay for the games which
he was to give at Rome as a candidate for the aedileship (Ep.
XXXV. 21). — **gravissimis usuris** : cf. Intr. 23. — **falso aere
alieno**, *from a debt fraudulently
charged against them.* Cicero relates in *Att.* 5. 21. 12 a flagrant
instance of the kind, where a
money-lender, Scaptius by name,
a financial agent of M. Brutus
(*Att.* 5. 21. 10), tried to extort
200 talents from the people of
Salamis in Cyprus, who owed him
only 106. — **M. Anneio legato** :
cf. 8 n. — **apud Iconium** : *apud*
with the acc. for the locative or *in*
with the abl. is archaic ; cf. *e.g.*
apud aedem Duelonai in the *senatus consultum de Bacchanalibus.*
The expression is here used as a

set form of speech for a military
report ; cf. *apud Issum, Fam.* 2.
10. 3. It is also preserved with
certain words in colloquial Latin.
In this case, as in many others,
colloquial Latin and official Latin
preserved forms of expression after
they had disappeared elsewhere, as
colloquial and official (especially
legal) English preserve certain
otherwise obsolete phrases. Silver
Latin, straining after novelties,
brought this, as well as many
other archaisms, into use again;
cf. Nipperdey on Tac. *Ann.* 1.
5 ; Rönsch, *Itala u. Vulgata*,
391. See also *ut ne*, Ep. XXX.
1 n.

3. **a. d. VII K. Sept.**: Aug 24.
Under the pre-Julian calendar
August had 29 days. — **evocatorum** : veterans who had served
their time, but might be called
upon for volunteer service, enjoying therein certain privileges. —
auxilia: usually light-armed troops.
— **exercitu lustrato** : Cicero had
14,000 men ; cf. *Att.* 5. 18. 2 ; 6.

K. Sept., legati a rege Commageno ad me missi pertumultuose, neque tamen non vere, Parthos in Syriam
4 transisse nuntiaverunt.   Quo audito vehementer sum
commotus cum de Syria, tum de mea provincia, de
reliqua denique Asia.   Itaque exercitum mihi ducen-
dum per Cappadociae regionem eam, quae Ciliciam
attingeret, putavi.   Nam si me in Ciliciam demisissem,
Ciliciam quidem ipsam propter montis Amani naturam
facile tenuissem; duo sunt enim aditus in Ciliciam ex
Syria, quorum uterque parvis praesidiis propter angu-
stias intercludi potest, nec est quicquam Cilicia contra
Syriam munitius.   Sed me Cappadocia movebat, quae
patet a Syria regesque habet finitimos, qui etiamsi
sunt clam amici nobis, tamen aperte Parthis inimici
esse non audent.   Itaque in Cappadocia extrema non
longe a Tauro apud oppidum Cybistra castra feci, ut et
Ciliciam tuerer et Cappadociam tenens nova finitimo-
5 rum consilia impedirem.   Interea in hoc tanto motu
tantaque exspectatione maximi belli rex Deiotarus, cui
non sine causa plurimum semper et meo et tuo et
senatus iudicio tributum est, vir cum benevolentia et
fide erga populum R. singulari, tum praesentia magni-

1. 14. — rege Commageno: Antiochus, king of Commagene, a district on the northern border of
Syria.—pertumultuose: although
the regular superlative form *tu-
multuosissime* is used in his orations, *e.g. in Verr.* ii. 2. 37, here
Cicero prefers the colloquial form
with *per-*. Similarly in the Letters
Cicero uses the intensive forms
peracer, peramans, and *perlubens,*
while in his other writings only the
regular superlative forms are used
to indicate the possession of a
quality in a very high degree. Cf.

also Intr. 77. — neque non vere,
and not without justification.
4. nec . . . quicquam: cf. similar
use of *nihil* for *nemo,* Ep. XXV.
4. — apud oppidum : cf. *apud
Iconium,* 2 n. — nova finitimorum
consilia : the intentions of Arta-
vasdes, the king of Armenia, were
a matter of doubt; cf. *Fam.* 15.
2. 2.
5. rex Deiotarus : Cicero defended him in 45 B.C. against the
charge of planning to murder
Caesar. — fide, etc.: cf. Cic. *Phil.*
11. 34 *quid de Cn. Pompeio lo-*

tudine et animi et consili, legatos ad me misit, se cum omnibus suis copiis in mea castra esse venturum. Cuius ego studio officioque commotus egi ei per litteras gratias, idque ut maturaret hortatus sum.   Cum autem 6 ad Cybistra propter rationem belli quinque dies essem moratus, regem Ariobarzanem, cuius salutem a senatu te auctore commendatam habebam, praesentibus insidiis necopinantem liberavi, neque solum ei saluti fui, sed etiam curavi ut cum auctoritate regnaret.   Metram et eum quem tu mihi diligenter commendaras, Athenaeum, importunitate Athenaidis exsilio multatos, in maxima apud regem auctoritate gratiaque constitui, cumque magnum bellum in Cappadocia concitaretur, si sacerdos armis se, quod facturus putabatur, defenderet, adule-scens et equitatu et peditatu et pecunia paratus et totus iis qui novari aliquid volebant, perfeci ut e regno ille discederet rexque sine tumultu ac sine armis omni auctoritate aulae communita regnum cum dig-nitate obtineret.   Interea cognovi multorum litteris 7

quar? qui unum Deiotarum in toto orbe terrarum ex animo ami-cum vereque benevolum, unum fide-lem populo Romano iudicavit. — se . . . venturum: upon the omis-sion of the verb of saying, cf. Intr. 95.

6. cuius salutem, etc.: the dis-closure in this letter of the rela-tions which existed between Rome and Ariobarzanes, throws a side-light upon the attitude which the Roman Republic assumed toward her provinces. Ariobarzanes, being harassed by plots within and wars without his kingdom, sought pro-tection from Rome, and became thereby deeply involved in debt to Pompey and M. Brutus (cf. *Att.* 6. 1. 3). Knowing that the de-position of Ariobarzanes would mean the loss of their money, Pompey and Brutus secured a decree of the senate through the influence of Cato, the uncle of Brutus (te auctore), to the effect that Cicero should maintain him upon his throne. — praesentibus insidiis: Athenais, the mother of Ariobarzanes, had plotted with Archelaus, the priest of the tem-ple of Bellona at Comana, to de-pose her son. In pursuance of their plans, Metras and Athenaeus, the ministers of the king, had been banished; cf. also *Fam.* 15. 2. 4, 8. — adulescens: in apposi-tion with sacerdos. — et totus iis: cf. *tota tibi est puella*, Tib. 4. 6. 3.

atque nuntiis magnas Parthorum copias et Arabum ad
oppidum Antiocheam accessisse magnumque eorum
equitatum, qui in Ciliciam transisset, ab equitum meorum turmis et a cohorte praetoria, quae erat Epiphaneae
praesidi causa, occidione occisum. Quare, cum viderem
a Cappadocia Parthorum copias aversas non longe a
finibus esse Ciliciae, quam potui maximis itineribus
ad Amanum exercitum duxi. Quo ut veni, hostem
ab Antiochea recessisse, Bibulum Antiocheae esse
cognovi. Deiotarum confestim iam ad me venientem
cum magno et firmo equitatu et peditatu et cum omnibus suis copiis certiorem feci non videri esse causam cur
abesset a regno, meque ad eum, si quid novi forte acci-
8 disset, statim litteras nuntiosque missurum esse. Cumque eo animo venissem ut utrique provinciae, si ita
tempus ferret, subvenirem, tum id quod iam ante statu-
eram vehementer interesse utriusque provinciae, pacare

7. **occidione occisum**: the *figu-ra etymologica*, *i.e.* the bringing together of two words from the same stem, which are closely connected logically and grammatically, was a favorite device in colloquial Latin. Cf. *e.g.* from Plaut. *Pseud.: misere miser*, 13; *ludo ludere*, 24; *cursim currere*, 358; *condimentis condire*, 820. The same figure is common in the Letters, *e.g. solacio consolamur*, *Att.* 4. 6. 1; *facile facies*, *Fam.* 3. 9. 1; *amavi amorem tuum*, Ep. LXI. 1; *ut suum gaudium gauderemus*, Cael., *Fam.* 8. 2. 1. See also *copias occidione occiderit*, *Phil.* 14. 36. — **quo . . . recessisse** : the writer skilfully conveys the impression that the retreat of the Parthians was the result of his own action. Cf. also the first part of this section. A

perusal of the letter, indeed, fails to reveal the fact that any one else than Cicero was acting against the Parthians. In reality the scene of the struggle lay entirely outside of Cicero's province. The Parthians, emboldened by the defeat of Crassus, began just before this time to threaten Syria. The proquaestor C. Cassius checked their advance upon Antioch, defeated them in a pitched battle, and forced them to retreat in disorder. In a similar vein Cicero writes to Atticus: *rumore adventus nostri et Cassio, qui Antiochia tenebatur, animus accessit et Parthis timor iniectus est. Itaque eos cedentes ab oppido Cassius insecutus rem bene gessit*, *Att.* 5. 20. 3. — **Bibulum**: Bibulus, who had been consul in 59 B.C., was proconsul of Syria.

Amanum et perpetuum hostem ex eo monte tollere, agere perrexi. Cumque me discedere ab eo monte simulassem et alias partis Ciliciae petere, abessemque ab Amano iter unius diei et castra apud Epiphaneam fecissem, a. d. IIII Id. Oct., cum advesperasceret, expedito exercitu ita noctu iter feci ut a. d. III Id. Oct., cum lucisceret, in Amanum ascenderem, distributisque cohortibus et auxiliis, cum aliis Quintus frater legatus mecum simul, aliis C. Pomptinus legatus, reliquis M. Anneius et L. Tullius legati praeessent, plerosque necopinantis oppressimus, qui occisi captique sunt, interclusi fuga. Eranam autem, quae fuit non vici instar, sed urbis, quod erat Amani caput, itemque Sepyram et Commorim, acriter et diu repugnantibus Pomptino illam partem Amani tenenti, ex antelucano tempore usque ad horam diei x, magna multitudine hostium occisa cepimus, castellaque vi capta complura incendimus. His rebus ita gestis castra in radicibus 9 Amani habuimus apud Aras Alexandri quadriduum, et in reliquiis Amani delendis agrisque vastandis, quae pars eius montis meae provinciae est, id tempus omne consumpsimus. Confectis his rebus ad oppidum Eleu- 10 therocilicum Pindenissum exercitum adduxi, quod cum esset altissimo et munitissimo loco, ab iisque incoleretur qui ne regibus quidem umquam paruissent, cum et fugitivos reciperent et Parthorum adventum acerrime exspectarent, ad existimationem imperi pertinere arbi-

8. apud Epiphaneam: cf. *apud Iconium*, 2 n. — Quintus . . . legati: usually there was one *legatus* to a legion, but Cicero had four for his two legions. — repugnantibus: *sc. iis.* The omission of the subject is so remarkable that

Baiter and Wesenberg would read *repugnantes* or insert *hostibus*.

9. Aras Alexandri : the place took its name from the three altars which Alexander had consecrated to Jupiter, Hercules, and Minerva; cf. Q. Curt. 3. 33.

tratus sum comprimere eorum audaciam, quo facilius
etiam ceterorum animi, qui alieni essent ab imperio
nostro, frangerentur. Vallo et fossa circumdedi; sex
castellis castrisque maximis saepsi; aggere viniis turri-
bus oppugnavi, ususque tormentis multis, multis sagit-
tariis magno labore meo, sine ulla molestia sumptuve
sociorum septimo quinquagensimo die rem confeci, ut
omnibus partibus urbis disturbatis aut incensis com-
pulsi in potestatem meam pervenirent. His erant
finitimi pari scelere et audacia Tebarani; ab iis Pindenisso capto obsides accepi ; exercitum in hiberna
dimisi; Quintum fratrem negotio praeposui ut in vicis
aut captis aut male pacatis exercitus conlocaretur.
11 Nunc velim sic tibi persuadeas, si de iis rebus ad
senatum relatum sit, me existimaturum summam mihi
laudem tributam, si tu honorem meum sententia tua
comprobaris, idque, etsi talibus de rebus gravissimos
homines et rogare solere et rogari scio, tamen admo-
nendum potius te a me quam rogandum puto. Tu es
enim is qui me tuis sententiis saepissime ornasti, qui
oratione, qui praedicatione, qui summis laudibus in
senatu, in contionibus ad caelum extulisti, cuius ego
semper tanta esse verborum pondera putavi ut uno
verbo tuo cum mea laude coniuncto omnia adsequi me

---

10. **viniis**: a parallel form for
vineis. — **quinquagensimo** : cf.
quadragensimum, Ep. XC. 1 n. —
pari scelere : their crime would
seem to have been their independence. No other charge is made
against them. — **Pindenisso capto**: Cicero understands how his
metropolitan friends will take the
news of his victory over these
petty mountaineers, whose name,
even, was not known to the average

Roman; cf. *Att.* 5. 20. 1 *Saturnalibus mane se mihi Pindenissitae
dediderunt septimo et quinquage-
simo die postquam oppugnare eos
coepimus.* '*Qui, malum ! isti Pindenissitae, qui sunt ?*' *inquies,*
'*nomen audivi numquam.*' *Quid
ego faciam ? num potui Ciliciam
Aetoliam aut Macedoniam reddere?*

11. **a me** : for *mihi*, to secure
the contrast with **te**. — **ad caelum
extulisti** : it was Cato who be-

arbitrarer; te denique memini, cum cuidam clarissimo
atque optimo viro supplicationem non decerneres, dicere
te decreturum, si referretur ob eas res quas is consul
in urbe gessisset; tu idem mihi supplicationem decre-
visti togato, non, ut multis, re p. bene gesta, sed, ut
nemini, re p. conservata.　Mitto quod invidiam, quod 12
pericula, quod omnis meas tempestates et subieris et
multo etiam magis, si per me licuisset, subire para-
tissimus fueris, quod denique inimicum meum tuum
inimicum putaris, cuius etiam interitum, cum facile
intellegerem mihi quantum tribueres, Milonis causa in
senatu defendenda adprobaris.　A me autem haec sunt
profecta quae non ego in benefici loco pono, sed in
veri testimoni atque iudici, ut praestantissimas tuas
virtutes non tacitus admirarer — quis enim id non facit?
— sed in omnibus orationibus, sententiis dicendis, causis agendis, omnibus scriptis, Graecis Latinis, omni
denique varietate litterarum mearum te non modo iis
quos vidissemus, sed iis de quibus audissemus, omnibus
anteferrem.　Quaeres fortasse quid sit quod ego hoc 13

---

stowed upon Cicero the title '*pater
patriae*' in 63 B.C. — **cuidam clarissimo**: P. Cornelius Lentulus
Spinther, one of Cicero's predecessors in Cilicia. He had secured
a triumph in 51 B.C.; cf. *Att.* 5. 21.
4. — **decerneres**: a shorter expression for *decernendam censeres.* —
ob eas res: his efforts to secure
Cicero's recall from banishment in
57 B.C. — **non ut multis**, etc.: cf.
in Cat. 4. 20.

　12. **inimicum meum**: with
special reference to Clodius. —
Milonis causa, etc. : cf. Ascon.
in Mil. p. 53 *fuerunt qui crederent
M. Catonis sententia eum esse abso-*

*lutum, nam . . . et studebat in peti-
tione consulatus Miloni et reo
adfuerat.* — **orationibus** : *e.g. pro
Mur.* 54 *M. Cato, homo in omni
virtute excellens ; pro Sest.* 12 *M.
Cato, fortissimus atque optimus
civis ; pro Mur.* 61 *in M. Catone,
iudices, haec bona quae videmus
divina et egregia, ipsius scitote esse
propria.*　While respecting the
uprightness of Cato, Cicero considered him lacking in tact and
judgment; cf. *e.g. Att.* 1. 18. 7
curat (*rem publicam*) *constantia
magis et integritate . . . quam consilio aut ingenio Cato.* — **Graecis
Latinis**: cf. Intr. 94.

nescio quid gratulationis et honoris a senatu tanti aesti-
mem.   Agam iam tecum familiariter, ut est et studiis
et officiis nostris mutuis et summa amicitia dignum et
necessitudine etiam paterna.   Si quisquam fuit umquam
remotus et natura et magis etiam, ut mihi quidem sentire videor, ratione atque doctrina ab inani laude et
sermonibus vulgi, ego profecto is sum.   Testis est
consulatus meus, in quo, sicut in reliqua vita, fateor ea
me studiose secutum ex quibus vera gloria nasci posset,
ipsam quidem gloriam per se numquam putavi expeten-
dam.   Itaque et provinciam ornatam et spem non
dubiam triumphi neglexi, sacerdotium denique, cum,
quemadmodum te existimare arbitror, non difficillime
consequi possem, non appetivi; idem post iniuriam
acceptam quam tu rei p. calamitatem semper appellas,
meam non modo non calamitatem, sed etiam gloriam,
studui quam ornatissima senatus populique R. de me
iudicia intercedere.   Itaque et augur postea fieri volui
quod antea neglexeram, et eum honorem qui a senatu
tribui rebus bellicis solet, neglectum a me olim, nunc
14 mihi expetendum puto.   Huic meae voluntati, in qua

13. honoris a senatu: the connection of two substantives by a
preposition is especially frequent
in the case of *a* ; cf. *Antibarbarus*,
I. p. 38.   For the construction in
general, see Reisig-Schmalz, *Lat.
Syn.* note 512. — provinciam ornatam: cf. *de ornandis praetoribus*,
Ep. XVI. 1 n.   Macedonia fell to
Cicero by lot, and Cisalpine Gaul
to C. Antonius.   To secure the
support of Antonius, Cicero exchanged provinces with him, and
afterward declined Cisalpine Gaul.
For another statement of his feelings with reference to a province,

cf. *contra voluntatem*, Ep. XXIX.
1 n.— sacerdotium: the augurate.
But Cicero writes to Atticus, 59
B.C.: *de istis rebus exspecto tuas
litteras . . . cuinam auguratus deferatur, quo quidem uno ego ab
istis capi possum, Att.* 2. 5. 2.   He
was elected a member of the college of augurs in 53 B.C. — iniuriam : one of Cicero's euphemisms
for *exsilium.* — meam calamitatem: *sc.* his exile.— eum honorem
qui . . . solet : the nearest approach to a definite statement of
his wish for a *supplicatio.* Such a
statement he purposely avoids.

inest aliqua vis desideri ad sanandum vulnus iniuriae,
ut faveas adiutorque sis, quod paulo ante me negaram
rogaturum, vehementer te rogo, sed ita, si non ieiunum
hoc nescio quid quod ego gessi et contemnendum videbitur, sed tale atque tantum ut multi nequaquam paribus rebus honores summos a senatu consecuti sint.
Equidem etiam illud mihi animum advertisse videor —
scis enim quam attente te audire soleam — te non tam
res gestas quam mores, instituta, atque vitam impera-
torum spectare solere in habendis aut non habendis
honoribus.   Quod si in mea causa considerabis, reperies me exercitu imbecillo contra metum maximi belli
firmissimum praesidium habuisse aequitatem et conti-
nentiam.   His ego subsidiis ea sum consecutus quae
nullis legionibus consequi potuissem, ut ex alienissimis
sociis amicissimos, ex infidelissimis firmissimos redde-
rem, animosque novarum rerum exspectatione sus-
pensos ad veteris imperi benevolentiam traducerem.
Sed nimis haec multa de me, praesertim ad te, a quo 15
uno omnium sociorum querelae audiuntur.   Cognosces
ex iis qui meis institutis se recreatos putant.   Cumque
omnes uno prope consensu de me apud te ea quae mihi
optatissima sunt praedicabunt, tum duae maximae cli-
entelae tuae, Cyprus insula et Cappadociae regnum,
tecum de me loquentur ; puto etiam regem Deiotarum

14. **paulo ante** : in 11.— **hoc
nescio quid**: a phrase of modesty;
cf. 13. — **mores, instituta, atque
vitam** : when in Cicero three or
more substantives follow one another, no connective is used, or a
connective is used with each pair
of substantives, or the members
of the last pair only are connected,
in which case *que* is commonly
employed.

15. **Cyprus insula**: Cyprus had
been taken from the Ptolemies
by Cato in 58 B.C., and henceforth
he was its *patronus*. It was part
of Cicero's province.— **Cappadociae regnum** : cf. *cuius salutem*,
etc., 6.   For Cicero's services to

qui uni tibi est maxime necessarius. Quae si etiam
maiora sunt, et in omnibus saeculis pauciores viri
reperti sunt qui suas cupiditates quam qui hostium
copias vincerent, est profecto tuum, cum ad res belli-
cas haec quae rariora et difficiliora sunt genera virtutis
adiunxeris, ipsas etiam illas res gestas iustiores esse et
16 maiores putare. Extremum illud est, ut quasi diffidens
rogationi meae philosophiam ad te adlegem, qua nec
mihi carior ulla unquam res in vita fuit nec hominum
generi maius a diis munus ullum est datum. Haec
igitur quae mihi tecum communis est societas studiorum atque artium nostrarum, quibus a pueritia dediti
ac devincti soli propemodum nos philosophiam veram
illam et antiquam, quae quibusdam oti esse ac desidiae
videtur, in forum atque in rem p. atque in ipsam aciem
paene deduximus, tecum agit de mea laude, cui negari
a Catone fas esse non puto. Quamobrem tibi sic persuadeas velim: si mihi tua sententia tributus honos ex
meis litteris fuerit, me sic existimaturum, cum auctoritate tua, tum benevolentia erga me mihi, quod maxime
cupierim, contigisse.

Ariobarzanes, cf. 6; for his services
to Cyprus, cf. *falso*, 2 n.

16. **philosophiam veram**: Cicero, in so far as ethics was concerned, was, like Cato, a Stoic.—
quae . . . videtur: the innate
prejudice of the Romans against
what Cicero elsewhere (*Att.* 2. 16.
3) calls ὁ θεωρητικὸς βίος was very
strong.—**a Catone**: for a similar

effective use of the proper noun for
the pronoun, cf. *Fam.* 2. 4. 1 *quid
est quod possit graviter a Cicerone
scribi ad Curionem* (instead of *a
me scribi ad te*)? — **ex meis litteris**: *i.e.* on the basis of the facts
stated in this letter and in *Fam.*
15. 1 and 2, addressed to the senate. For *litterae* of more than
one letter, cf. Ep. XCIX. 1 n.

XXXV. (*Att.* 6. 1. 17–26.)

De statua Africani — ὦ πραγμάτων ἀσυγκλώστων! 17
sed me id ipsum delectavit in tuis litteris —, ain tu?
Scipio hic Metellus proavum suum nescit censorem
non fuisse? Atqui nihil habuit aliud inscriptum nisi
CENS. ea statua, quae ad Opis per te posita in excelso
est; in illa autem, quae est ad Πολυκλέους Herculem,
inscriptum est COS., quam esse eiusdem status amictus
anulus imago ipsa declarat. At mehercule ego, cum
in turma inauratarum equestrium quas hic Metellus in

XXXV. Laodicea, Feb. 20,
50 B.C. (The first 16 sections of
this letter, dealing with provincial
affairs, are omitted.)
17. **de statua Africani . . .
Metelli**: in his *de Re Pub.* Cicero
had made Laelius lament the fact
that no statue had been erected
to the memory of Scipio Nasica
Serapion (cf. Macr. *Comment.* 1.
4). Q. Caecilius Metellus Scipio,
a descendant of Nasica, called the
attention of Atticus to what he
considered Cicero's error, as he
himself had set up a gilded equestrian statue in honor of his ances-
tor (cf. **quas . . . posuit**), to say
nothing of the ancient statue of
Serapion already standing near the
temple of Ops. But the statue
standing near the temple of Ops
has CENSOR inscribed upon it, and
cannot therefore represent Serapion, who never held that office.
Furthermore, the two ancient
statues, standing **ad Opis** and
ad Πολυκλέους Herculem, represent the same person, as a comparison of the two shows. Now
the statue **ad . . . Herculem** is a
likeness of Africanus. Therefore
the other ancient statue (**ad Opis**)
must represent the same person,

and consequently the reproduction
which Metellus has had made,
and upon whose base he has put
the name of Serapion, is in reality
a reproduction of an ancient likeness of Africanus. — ὦ πραγμάτων
ἀσυγκλώστων, *confusion worse con-
founded;* a reference to the lack
of arrangement in the letter of
Atticus; cf. 11 *sed* οἰκονομία *mea*
(*i.e. my arrangement*) *si perturba-
tior est, tibi assignato; te enim
sequor* σχεδιάζοντα (*i.e. who wrote
whatever came into your head*).
— **ain tu**, *is it possible? Ain tu,
ain tandem,* and *ain vero* are frequently used in colloquial Latin
to express surprise; cf. Ter. *And.*
875; Plaut. *Trin.* 987; Cic. *Fam.* 9.
21. 1. — **ad Opis**: *sc. templum;* cf.
a Vestae, Ep. XIII. 2 n. — **per te**:
Atticus was an enthusiastic student of Roman history, of antiquities, and of genealogy, and his
interest in these subjects led him
to erect the statue. Cf. Nep.
Att. 18. 1. — **turma,** etc.: among
the statues on the Capitol were
those of the kings, of Brutus,
Tiberius Gracchus, and Fabius
Maximus; cf. Pliny, *N. H.* 34. 23;
33. 10; Cic. *in Cat.* 3. 19. At the
time of Augustus the number had

Capitolio posuit animadvertissem in Serapionis sub-
scriptione Africani imaginem, erratum fabrile putavi,
18 nunc video Metelli. Ο ἀνιστορησίαν turpem! Nam
illud de Flavio et fastis, si secus est, commune erratum est, et tu belle ἠπόρησας, et nos publicam prope
opinionem secuti sumus, ut multa apud Graecos. Quis
enim non dixit Εὔπολιν, τὸν τῆς ἀρχαίας, ab Alcibiade
navigante in Siciliam deiectum esse in mare? Redarguit Eratosthenes ; adfert enim quas ille post id
tempus fabulas docuerit. Num idcirco Duris Samius,
homo in historia diligens, quod cum multis erravit,
irridetur? Quis Zaleucum leges Locris scripsisse non
dixit? Num igitur iacet Theophrastus, si id a Timaeo
tuo familiari reprehensum est? Sed nescire proavum
suum censorem non fuisse turpe est, praesertim cum
post eum consulem nemo Cornelius illo vivo censor

grown so great that many were
removed to the Campus Martius,
and Caligula forbade any one to
erect a statue to a living man
without his permission ; cf. Suet.
Calig. 34.   The *rostra* was similarly adorned with statues ; cf. Cic.
Phil. 9. 16.

18. illud de Flavio et fastis:
in the *de Re Pub.* Atticus thought
(cf. 8) that Cicero meant to put
Cn. Flavius, who published the calendar for the benefit of the people
(cf. Livy, 9. 46. 5; Cic. *pro Mur.*
25), before the time of the decem-
virs. — tu belle ἠπόρησας, *you
made a good point.* — ut multa
(*errata*) apud Graecos : Cicero
wishes to show that his country-
men are no more inaccurate with
reference to their history than the
Greeks are in their history. Cicero
prided himself also upon his knowledge of nice points in Greek his-

tory and literature, which the discussion gives him an opportunity
to air. — Εὔπολιν, τὸν τῆς ἀρχαίας
(κωμῳδίας) ; Eupolis, of the fifth
century B.C., was a writer of the
old comedy. The story ran that
Alcibiades put him to death for
ridiculing him in a comedy. —
redarguit Eratosthenes : *sc.* in
his book περὶ Κωμῳδίας. — Zaleucum : as we learn from *de Leg.* 2.
15, Theophrastus mentions Zaleu-
cus as the law-giver of the Lo-
crians, while Timaeus maintained
that no such man ever lived. —
num . . . Theophrastus, *is Theophrastus then not read?* Theophrastus was a disciple of Plato,
and afterwards of Aristotle. —
Timaeo: cf. Ep. XVIII. 7 n. —
nemo Cornelius : Cicero commonly uses *nemo* in preference
to *nullus* with nouns indicating
persons.

fuerit.   Quod de Philotimo et de solutione HS. xx DC 19
scribis, Philotimum circiter Kal. Ianuarias in Cherso-
nesum audio venisse.   At mihi ab eo nihil adhuc.   Reliqua mea Camillus scribit se accepisse: ea quae sint
nescio et aveo scire.   Verum haec posterius et coram
fortasse commodius.   Illud me, mi Attice, in extrema 20
fere parte epistulae commovit.   Scribis enim sic, τί
λοιπόν; deinde me obsecras amantissime ne obliviscar
vigilare et ut animadvertam quae fiant.   Num quid de
quo inaudisti ?   Etsi nihil eiusmodi est — πολλοῦ γε
καὶ δεῖ — nec enim me fefellisset nec fallet ; sed ista
admonitio tua tam accurata nescio quid mihi signifi-
care visa est.   De M. Octavio iterum iam tibi rescribo 21
te illi probe respondisse; paulo vellem fidentius.   Nam
Caelius libertum ad me misit et litteras accurate
scriptas et de pantheris et a civitatibus.   Rescripsi

19. **de Philotimo** : in *Att.* 6. 4.
3; 6. 5. 2, and 6. 7. 1 Cicero gives
Atticus to understand in an indirect manner that Philotimus, Terentia's freedman, has appropri-
ated some of the money coming
from the sale of Milo's effects; cf.
also *Fam.* 8. 3. 2.   In the management of his own property Cicero,
upon returning from exile, questioned the honesty of the same
man. — **HS. XX DC** : 20,600 sesterces ; cf. Ep. V. 13 n. — **Camillus:** a friend of Cicero skilled
in real-estate law and interested in
the Milo affair. — **haec** : *sc. con-
feremus.*

20. **mi Attice:** cf. *mi Pomponi,*
Ep. X n. — τί λοιπόν: cf. *novi tibi
quidnam scribam ? quid ? etiam,*
etc., *Att.* 1. 13. 6; *aliud quid ?
etiam ; quando,* etc., *Att.* 2. 6. 2. —
quae fiant: *sc.* by members of
Cicero's retinue. — **etsi,** *and yet ;*

by way of correction, as often in
Cicero ; cf., *e.g., Att.* 14. 14. 1 ;
Phil. 2. 75. — πολλοῦ, etc., *far
from it ;* a phrase used frequently
by Demosthenes. — **admonitio :**
cf. Intr. 75.

21. **de M. Octavio :** Caelius,
who was running for the aedileship, had urged Cicero, *e.g. Fam.* 8.
9. 3, to send him some panthers to
exhibit in the games.   Octavius, a
candidate for the same office (cf.
Fam. 8. 2. 2), hearing of this, in-
quired of Atticus if Cicero could
not be prevailed upon to do the
same thing for him.   Atticus feared
it would be impossible (*Att.* 5. 21.
5). — **litteras . . . a civitatibus:**
Caelius probably wrote with reference to the panthers, and sent also
by his freedmen certain letters,
which purported to come from the
states in Cicero's province, offering to contribute money to defray

alterum me moleste ferre, si ego in tenebris laterem,
nec audiretur Romae nullum in mea provincia nummum
nisi in aes alienum erogari, docuique nec mihi concili-
are pecuniam licere nec illi capere, monuique eum
quem plane diligo ut, cum alios accusasset, cautius
viveret; illud autem alterum alienum esse existimatione mea, Cibyratas imperio meo publice venari.
22 Lepta tua epistula gaudio exsultat ; etenim scripta
belle est meque apud eum magna in gratia posuit.
Filiola tua gratum mihi fecit quod tibi diligenter
mandavit ut mihi salutem adscriberes ; gratum etiam
Pilia, sed illa officiosius quod mihi, quem numquam
vidit.   Igitur tu quoque salutem utrique adscribito.
Litterarum datarum dies, pr. Kal. Ianuar., suavem
habuit recordationem clarissimi iuris iurandi, quod ego
non eram oblitus.   Magnus enim praetextatus illo die

the expense of the games which
he wished to give.   These letters
he desired to have the proper officials in the various states sign.
Such a compulsory free-will offering would be no more remarkable
than the embassy which was forced
to go to Rome to thank the senate for sending them Appius as
their governor (cf. *Fam.* 3. 8. 2).
— alterum ... alterum, *the second
matter . . . the first ;* the first **alterum** refers to the levying of taxes
for such a purpose ; the second
to the proposition concerning the
panthers. — **nec . . . licere** : Cicero had approved of the course of
his brother Quintus, who, as propraetor of Asia, had issued an
edict directing that money should
not be raised in the provinces to
pay for games which the aediles
gave in Rome ; cf. *Q. fr.* 1. 1. 26.
The levying of taxes or contribu-

tions in the provinces was probably governed by general or special
laws, perhaps by the *lex Cornelia*
of 85 B. C.; cf. *Fam.* 3. 10. 6; Tac.
Ann. 3. 62. — **cum alios accusasset**: referring to Caelius's prosecution of C. Antonius for misgovernment in Macedonia.

22. **Lepta** : Cicero's *praefectus
fabrum ;* cf. *Fam.* 3. 7. 4. — **illa**:
i.e. filiola. — **quod mihi**: *sc. salutem adscripsit.* — **pr. Kal. Ianuar.**:
in apposition with **dies**. — **iuris
iurandi** : on laying down the consulship, Cicero swore that he had
saved the republic : *cum ille (i.e.*
Metellus Nepos, the tribune) *mihi
nihil nisi ut iurarem permitteret,
magna voce iuravi verissimum pul-
cherrimumque ius iurandum quod
populus idem magna voce me vere
iurasse iuravit, Fam.* 5. 2. 7.   Cf.
Intr. 8. — **Magnus praetextatus**, *a Pompey in praetexta.*

fui.   Habes ad omnia, non, ut postulasti, χρύσεα χαλκείων, sed paria paribus respondimus.   Ecce autem 23 alia pusilla epistula, quam non relinquam ἀναντιφώνητον. Bene mehercule proposuit Lucceius Tusculanum, nisi forte dolet ei quod suo tibicine egebit.   Velim scire qui sit status eius.   Lentulum quidem nostrum omnia praeter Tusculanum proscripsisse audio.   Cupio hos expeditos videre, cupio etiam Sestium, adde sis Caelium, in quibus omnibus est

Αἴδεσθεν μὲν ἀνήνασθαι, δεῖσαν δ' ὑποδέχθαι.

For a similar comparison of his peaceful achievements with the military successes of Pompey and others, cf. Ep. III. 3; *in Cat.* 4. 21 f. — χρύσεα χαλκείων and **paria paribus** (*respondere*) are proverbial expressions; cf. *e.g. Il.* 6. 236; Plato, *Symp.* 2. 9; Ter. *Phorm.* 212. For the alliteration, cf. Intr. 93. The Latin expression occurs in a fuller form in Plaut. *Pers.* 223 *par pari respondes dicto.* This substantival use of a neuter adj. in the dat. is very unusual in Latin. The nearest parallel in Cicero is *parva magnis conferuntur, Orat.* 14. Cf. also a quotation from a letter written by Atticus (*Att.* 16. 7. 6) *unde par pari respondeatur.*

23. **ecce**: used in colloquial language to introduce a new subject, and oftentimes one which causes surprise, *e.g. ecce Apollo mi ex oraclo imperat*, Plaut. *Men.* 841 ; *ecce postridie Cassio litterae Capua a Lucretio, Att.* 7. 24. It is therefore often accompanied by *subito, repente, de improviso,* and the ethical dative; cf. Intr. 83 *c.* This use of *ecce* is in harmony with its use in comedy to announce an unexpected appearance, *e.g. ecce autem video rure redeuntem senem*, Ter. *Eun.* 967. For the phrases

used to indicate a transition where no surprise is expressed, cf. Intr. 91. — ἀναντιφώνητον, *without an answer*. There are more than 70 Greek words in the Letters containing *a* privative. Their frequency in colloquial language is due to the fact that they enabled a writer to avoid a long Latin expression; cf. Intr. 95.— **proposuit**, *has offered for sale.* — **Lucceius**: not the historian. This Lucceius was so heavily in debt (*Att.* 5. 21. 13) that he proposed to sell his Tusculan villa. — **nisi forte**, etc.: see Crit. Append. — **tibicine**, *rooftree* (lit. *pillar supporting roof*); cf. Festus, I. 558, ed. de Ponor ; Juv. 3. 193. — **Lentulum**: his indebtedness is mentioned by Caesar *B. C.* 1. 4. He was consul in 49 B.C., accompanied Pompey to Greece, and after the battle of Pharsalus was put to death by King Ptolemy in Egypt; cf. Caes. *B. C.* 3. 104. 3.— **cupio etiam Sestium** : *sc. expeditum videre.* — **Sestium**: see Ep. XVI. 5 f. — **sis**: for *si vis*, as frequently in Latin comedy and satire. Cf. *sultis* for *si vultis.* — αἴδεσθεν, etc. : from *Il.* 7. 93. As the leaders of the Greeks were afraid to accept and ashamed to decline the challenge

De Memmio restituendo ut Curio cogitet te audisse
puto. De Egnati Sidicini nomine nec nulla nec magna
spe sumus. Pinarium, quem mihi commendas, diligentissime Deiotarus curat graviter aegrum. Respondi
24 etiam minori. Tu velim, dum ero Laodiceae, id est ad
Idus Maias, quam saepissime mecum per litteras collo-
quare et, cum Athenas veneris — iam enim sciemus de
rebus urbanis, de provinciis, quae omnia in mensem
Martium sunt collata — utique ad me tabellarios mittas.
25 Et heus tu, iamne vos a Caesare per Herodem talenta
Attica L extorsistis ? In quo, ut audio, magnum odium
Pompei suscepistis; putat enim suos nummos vos come-
disse, Caesarem in Nemore aedificando diligentiorem
fore. Haec ego ex P. Vedio, magno nebulone, sed

of Hector, so the leading Optimates were afraid to accept but
loath to decline Caesar's offers of
financial aid. In the one case they
would be under obligation to
Caesar ; in the other they would
miss a chance of paying long outstanding debts. Lentulus was one
of the men whom in the following
year Caesar sought to win over by
the means indicated; cf. *Att.* 8. 11.
5. — **Memmio** : cf. Ep. XXXII.
introd. note. — **Curio** : *i.e.* C. Scri-
bonius Curio ; cf. Ep. VII. 3 n.
— **nomine** : Egnatius apparently
owed money to Cicero. — **Pinarium**: a financial agent. — **minori**:
sc. epistulae.

24. **sunt collata,** *have been set
down for.* February was the usual
month for the consideration of
foreign affairs. Cf. *Q. fr.* 2. 13.
3 ; *Fam.* 1. 4. 1.

25. **heus**: confined to conversational Latin, and commonly followed or preceded by a pronoun
or the name of the person addressed, with a question or a com-

mand. — **Herodem** : an Athenian
friend of Atticus and Cicero, and
afterwards in a certain sense the
guardian of young Cicero while the
latter was studying at Athens; cf.
Att. 14. 16. 3; 14. 18. 4. — **suos
nummos**: Pompey, for some unknown reason, thought that this
money should have come to him
rather than to Atticus. — **Nemore** : the grove of Diana, not
far from Aricia, near which Caesar
was building a villa (cf. Suet. *Iul.*
46). Why Caesar was expected
to be more active in building after
losing part of his capital it is difficult to understand. As for Pompey's feeling in the matter, perhaps
Caesar owed him money, and the
expenditure of a large sum upon
the villa near Aricia would lessen
the chances of payment. He
would in that case look with dis-
favor upon Caesar's building plans.
Possibly, however, we should read
with Boot *nec Caesarem . . . diligentiorem* (economical). — **P. Vedio** : Vedius Pollio is said to have

Pompei tamen familiari, audivi. Hic Vedius venit mihi
obviam cum duobus essedis et raeda equis iuncta et
lectica et familia magna, pro qua, si Curio legem pertu-
lerit, HS. centenos pendat necesse est. Erat praeterea
cynocephalus in essedo nec deerant onagri. Numquam
vidi hominem nequiorem. Sed extremum audi. De-
versatus est Laodiceae apud Pompeium Vindullum; ibi
sua deposuit, cum ad me profectus est. Moritur interim Vindullus. Quod res ad Magnum Pompeium
pertinere putabatur, C. Vennonius domum Vindulli
venit ; cum omnia obsignaret, in Vedianas res incidit. In his inventae sunt quinque imagunculae ma-
tronarum, in quibus una sororis amici tui, hominis
' bruti,' qui hoc utatur, et uxoris illius ' lepidi,' qui

caused slaves who had offended
him to be thrown to the lampreys
in his fish-pond. His name became, like that of Lucullus, a
synonym for extravagance ; cf.
Tac. *Ann.* 1. 10. — nebulone : a
word of contempt for a worthless
fellow. In general in colloquial
Latin personal nouns in *o* carry
with them a contemptuous force,
and indicate one who is proficient
in a questionable accomplishment;
thus *erro* (*a tramp*), Hor. *Sat.* 2.
7. 113; *popino* (*a glutton*), *Sat.* 2.
7. 39, etc.; and in the Letters,
combibo (*a crony*), *Fam.* 9. 25. 2;
salaco (*a braggart*), Ep. LXXXI.
2; *verbero* (*a rascal*), *Att.* 14. 6. 1;
baro (*a blockhead*), 5. 11.6. Cf. also
R. Fisch, in *Arch. f. lat. Lex.* V.
56–89, and W. Meyer, *ibid.* 223–234.
— cum duobus essedis: the use
of the *essedum* by people in private life was a mark of extreme
affectation. Even in the case of
an official it was very repugnant
to Roman taste. Cf. Cicero's account of Antony's official prog-

ress: *vehebatur in essedo tribunus
plebis; lictores laureati antecedebant,*
etc., *Phil.* 2. 58. — raeda: a light
four-wheeled travelling wagon, such
as Horace used during one stage
of his journey to Brundisium ;
cf. *Sat.* 1. 5. 86. — legem : reference is made to some sumptuary
law, the provisions of which we
do not know, imposing a tax either
upon *familiae* or the equipages
of travellers. The cynocephalus
and onagri had no other value
than that they were rare and therefore expensive. — ad Magnum
Pompeium: the cognomen, which
is the distinguishing part of this
name, when compared with Pompeium Vindullum, is put first
for the sake of emphasis. Vindullus had died intestate and without an heir, so that his property
seemed likely to come to his patron
Pompey. — in his, etc.: as Vedius
was a noted rake, the incident oc-
casioned much gossip, but, strange
to say, Brutus kept up his friendly
relations with Vedius (qui hoc

haec tam neglegenter ferat. Haec te volui παριστο-
26 ρῆσαι, sumus enim ambo belle curiosi. Vnum etiam
velim cogites. Audio Appium πρόπυλον Eleusine
facere. Num inepti fuerimus, si nos quoque Academiae fecerimus ? ' Puto,' inquies. Ergo id ipsum
scribes ad me. Equidem valde ipsas Athenas amo.
Volo esse aliquod monumentum; odi falsas inscripti-
ones statuarum alienarum. Sed ut tibi placebit, faci-
esque me in quem diem Romana incidant mysteria
certiorem et quomodo hiemaris. Cura ut valeas. Post
Leuctricam pugnam die septingentesimo sexagesimo
quinto.

utatur), and Lepidus treated the affair with indifference. — **sumus . . . belle curiosi,** *we are both awfully fond of gossip.* The statement is emphasized by the position of **sumus.** On **belle,** cf. Ep. XXIV. 2 n.

26. **πρόπυλον :** an inscription found at Eleusis in 1860, and quoted by Boot, throws light upon this passage: AP · CLAVDIVS · AP · F· PVLCHER · PROPYLVM · CERERI · ET · PROSERPINAE · COS · VOVIT · IMPE-RATOR · COEPIT · PVLCHER · CLAV-DIVS · ET · REX · MARCIVS·FECERVNT (*C.I.L.* I.¹ 619). — **num,** etc.: Cicero asks Atticus the same question in *Att.* 6. 6. 2. — **Academiae :** *sc.* πρόπυλον. — **Athenas:** cf. *valde me Athenae delectarunt, Att.* 5. 10. 5. — **monumentum :** *i.e.* something to commemorate himself in connection with Athens, although he cannot endure the thought of having his name attached to some one of the famous statues of other men in Athens, a practice which

some Romans had followed. — **mysteria :** the festival of the *Bona Dea,* which occurred in May. The mention of *Bona Dea* brings up to Cicero's mind the celebrated sacrilege of Clodius (cf. Ep. V.), with its long train of disasters for him, and leads him to date his letter from the day of Clodius's murder by Milo. To this event Cicero jestingly gives the name of *pugna Leuctrica,* for, as Greece had been freed from the tyranny of the Spartans by the battle of Leuctra, so Rome was relieved of the domination of its tyrant Clodius by the street-fight in which he fell. Cf. *Att.* 5. 13. 1 *Ephesum venimus a. d. XI Kal. Sext. sexagesimo et quingentesimo post pugnam Bovillanam* (Clodius was killed at Bovillae). Clodius was murdered Jan. 18, 52 B.C., so that the date of this letter would be Feb. 20, 50 B.C. (cf. Schmidt, *Briefw.* p. 76).

XXXVI. (*Fam.* 2. 11.)

M. CICERO IMP. S. D. M. CAELIO AEDILI CVRVLI.

Putaresne umquam accidere posse ut mihi verba 1
deessent, neque solum ista vestra oratoria, sed haec
etiam levia nostratia? Desunt autem propter hanc
causam, quod mirifice sum sollicitus quidnam de provinciis decernatur. Mirum me desiderium tenet urbis,
incredibile meorum atque in primis tui, satietas autem
provinciae, vel quia videmur eam famam consecuti ut
non tam accessio quaerenda quam fortuna metuenda
sit, vel quia totum negotium non est dignum viribus
nostris, qui maiora onera in re publica sustinere et
possim et soleam, vel quia belli magni timor impendet,
quod videmur effugere si ad constitutam diem decede-
mus. De pantheris, per eos qui venari solent agitur 2

XXXVI. Cilicia, Apr. 4, 50 B.C.
Since Ep. XXXIII. was written
Caelius has been elected curule
aedile (cf. **aedili curuli**), and has
entered on the duties of the office.
1. **ut mihi**, etc. : cf. *Fam.* 4. 4.
1 *quem* (*i.e. me*) *tu divitias orationis
habere dicis, me non esse verborum
admodum inopem agnosco.*— ista
vestra oratoria, *of you orators
there in Rome.* Caelius's strength
as a lawyer lay in his skill in prosecution ; cf. Quint. 6. 3. 69 *idem*
(Cicero) *per allegoriam M. Caelium, melius obicientem crimina
quam defendentem, bonam dex-
tram, malam sinistram habere dicebat.* — **levia nostratia** : used of
the discussion of familiar topics
in familiar language, and especially
of the *sermo cotidianus.* Thus
Cicero, while recognizing the value
of Greek culture, adds, *ego autem
— existimes licet quidlibet — miri-*

*fice capior facetiis, maxime nostra-
tibus*, Ep. LXVII. 2 ; in *Tusc. Disp.*
5. 90, speaking of Roman philosophers as opposed to Greek, he
calls the former *nostrates philoso-
phi.* The passage is important,
as indicating that Cicero recognized the existence of a colloquial
Latin by the side of a more formal language. Cf. also Intr. 71.
— **decernatur** : Cicero fears that
his term of office may be pro-
longed. — **desiderium urbis** : cf.
si potes, etc., Ep. XVII. 2 n. —
fortuna: *i.e.* a change of fortune.
— **belli**: *sc.* with the Parthians.

2. **pantheris**, etc.: Cicero's reply
to the urgent and repeated requests
of Caelius, gravely couched in
official language, as if the capture
of these panthers had been the
most serious object of his provincial administration. Cf. also *Octavio*, Ep. XXXV. 21 n. — **agitur**

mandatu meo diligenter; sed mira paucitas est et eas
quae sunt valde aiunt queri, quod nihil cuiquam insidiarum in mea provincia nisi sibi fiat; itaque constituisse
dicuntur in Cariam ex nostra provincia decedere.   Sed
tamen sedulo fit, et in primis a Patisco.   Quicquid erit,
tibi erit, sed quid esset plane nesciebamus.   Mihi
mercule magnae curae est aedilitas tua ; ipse dies me
admonebat, scripsi enim haec ipsis Megalensibus.   Tu
velim ad me de omni rei publicae statu quam diligentissime perscribas ; ea enim certissima putabo quae ex
te cognoro.

XXXVII. (*Fam.* 15. 5.)

M. CATO S. D. M. CICERONI IMP.

1   Quod et res p. me et nostra amicitia hortatur, libenter facio, ut tuam virtutem innocentiam diligentiam,

mandatu meo: such a phrase
as an official might use in a report
to his government, while **ex . . .
decedere** suggests the dignified
retirement of those who felt ag-
grieved. — **insidiarum** : with reference on the one hand to traps
for panthers, and on the other to
the lying in ambush of highway-
men, or the snares laid for the
provincials by the money-lenders,
whose iniquitous proceedings Cicero claimed to have suppressed. —
sedulo: cf. Ep. XII. 1 n. — **Patisco** : an official engaged in securing panthers; cf. *Fam.* 8. 9. 3. —
nesciebamus: epistolary imperf.;
cf. Intr. 84 *c.* — **ipsis Megalensibus**: the Megalensian games, last-
ing from Apr. 4 to 10, were managed by the curule aediles.

   XXXVII. Rome, the end of
April or the early part of May,
50 B.C. This is Cato's reply to

Ep. XXXIV. It is interesting
as the only thing we have from
his pen. The blunt manner, the
brevity of the letter, and the rigid-
ity of its style not only seem characteristic of the writer, but make
the letter an excellent foil to the
epistle of Cicero, which is re-
markably guarded in referring to
the matter at issue, is circumstan-
tial in its statements, and varied
in its style. The *supplicatio* was de-
creed by the senate, but Cato voted
against it. For Cicero's opinion
of Cato's course, cf. *Att.* 7. 2. 7
*qui (i.e. Cato) quidem in me turpi-
ter fuit malevolus: dedit integri-
tatis iustitiae clementiae fidei mihi
testimonium, quod non quaerebam;
quod postulabam, id negavit.*

   1. **quod . . . me . . . hortatur:**
the use of two accusatives is very
common in archaic Latin after
verbs of *seeking, warning,* etc.,

cognitam in maximis rebus domi togati, armati foris
pari industria administrari gaudeam. Itaque, quod pro
meo iudicio facere potui, ut innocentia consilioque tuo
defensam provinciam, servatum Ariobarzanis cum ipso
rege regnum, sociorum revocatam ad studium imperi
nostri voluntatem sententia mea et decreto laudarem,
feci. Supplicationem decretam, si tu, qua in re nihil 2
fortuito, sed summa tua ratione et continentia rei p.
provisum est, dis immortalibus gratulari nos quam tibi
referre acceptum mavis, gaudeo; quod si triumphi praerogativam putas supplicationem et idcirco casum potius
quam te laudari mavis, neque supplicationem sequitur
semper triumphus et triumpho multo clarius est sena-

especially when one of the accusatives is a neuter pronoun (cf. *e.g.*
Ter. *And.* 918; *Heaut.* 353); and
this construction, which is perhaps a colloquial survival in the
prose of the Ciceronian period (cf.
Reisig-Schmalz, *Lat. Syn.* note
562), is frequent in the Letters;
cf. *multa deos venerati sunt, Fam.*
6. 7. 2 ; *illud te peto*, Ep. LII. 2.
— virtutem . . . administrari :
this would be a very harsh expression for Cicero, but is perhaps not
to be changed in a letter from Cato.
— togati: in agreement with the
genitive implied in tuam. — ut
innocentia, etc.: in his summary
of Cicero's achievements, Cato
bluntly disregards his claim that
he has barred the progress of
the Parthians and driven them
back (cf. Ep. XXXIV. 7), and in
fact practically ignores his military
exploits in general. innocentia
refers to abstinence from corrupt
use of power for personal gain.
—Ariobarzanis : cf. Ep. XXXIV.
6.— decreto : cf. *Fam.* 8. 11. 2
tantum Catoni (Hirrus) adsensus

*est, qui (i.e. Cato) de te locutus
honorifice non decrerat supplica-
tiones.*
  2. nihil fortuito: *sc. factum est*
from provisum est.— sed (*nihil*)
. . . provisum est : used carelessly for *sed omnia provisa sunt.*
— referre acceptum : a business
expression, meaning, 'to set down
to one's credit.'— praerogativam:
the vote of the first century in the
comitia, the *centuria praerogativa*,
was a pretty sure indication of the
result of the entire election, so
that *praerogativa* means often, as
here, 'sure indication.' — potius
. . . mavis : such pleonasm is not
uncommon in colloquial Latin ;
cf. *mihi magis lubet cum probis
potius quam cum improbis vivere
vanidicis*, Plaut. *Trin.* 274 ; *magis
decorumst libertum potius quam
patronum onus in via portare,
Asin.* 689 ; *arbitror malle te quietam senectutem et honorificam potius agere quam sollicitam, Att.* 14.
13 A. 3 (from Antony). Cf. also
'I *preferred* to go *rather* than to
stay.'

tum iudicare potius mansuetudine et innocentia imperatoris provinciam quam vi militum aut benignitate
deorum retentam atque conservatam esse, quod ego
3 mea sententia censebam. Atque haec ego idcirco ad
te contra consuetudinem meam pluribus scripsi ut,
quod maxime volo, existimes me laborare ut tibi per-
suadeam me et voluisse de tua maiestate quod amplissimum sim arbitratus, et quod tu maluisti factum esse
gaudere. Vale et nos dilige et instituto itinere severitatem diligentiamque sociis et rei p. praesta.

XXXVIII. (*Fam.* 15. 6.)

M. CICERO S. D. M. CATONI.

1   'Laetus sum laudari me,' inquit Hector, opinor apud
Naevium, 'aps te, pater, a laudato viro'; ea est enim
profecto iucunda laus quae ab iis proficiscitur qui ipsi
in laude vixerunt. Ego vero vel gratulatione litterarum
tuarum vel testimoniis sententiae dictae nihil est quod
me non adsecutum putem, idque mihi cum amplissimum, tum gratissimum est, te libenter amicitiae dedisse quod liquido veritati dares. Et si non modo
omnes, verum etiam multi Catones essent in civitate
nostra, in qua unum exstitisse mirabile est, quem ego
currum aut quam lauream cum tua laudatione con-

3. **contra consuetudinem meam** : contrary to his habit as an
individual, and to the teaching
of his fellow - philosophers the
Stoics.

XXXVIII. Tarsus, July, 50 B.C.
Cicero's reply to Ep. XXXVII.

1. **laetus sum**: for Cicero's real
opinion of Cato's course, cf. Ep.

XXXVII. introd. note. — **Hector,
opinor**, etc.: cf. Ep. XVIII. 7 n. —
aps te: archaic for *abs te* (=*a te*).—
sententiae dictae : *sc.* in the senate. — **te . . . dedisse**: Cicero was
gratified that Cato's statement of
the case in the senate was the free-
will offering of a friend. — **currum,
lauream** : these were among the

ferrem? Nam ad meum sensum et ad ´illud sincerum
ac subtile iudicium nihil potest esse laudabilius quam
ea tua oratio, quae est ad me perscripta a meis necessariis. Sed causam meae voluntatis — non enim dicam 2
cupiditatis — exposui tibi superioribus litteris, quae
etiamsi parum iusta tibi visa est, hanc tamen habet
rationem, non ut nimis concupiscendus honos, sed
tamen, si deferatur a senatu, minime aspernandus esse
videatur. Spero autem illum ordinem pro meis ob rem
p. susceptis laboribus me non indignum honore, usitato
praesertim, existimaturum. Quod si ita erit, tantum
ex te peto, quod amicissime scribis, ut, cum tuo iudicio
quod amplissimum esse arbitraris mihi tribueris, si id
quod maluero acciderit, gaudeas. Sic enim fecisse
te et sensisse et scripsisse video, resque ipsa declarat
tibi illum honorem nostrum supplicationis iucundum
fuisse, quod scribendo adfuisti; haec enim senatus consulta non ignoro ab amicissimis eius, cuius de honore

insignia of a triumph. — **ad meum
sensum**, etc., *as far as my feelings
go and resting one's opinion upon
a really honest and keen judgment.*

2. **superioribus litteris**: cf.
idem post iniuriam, etc., Ep.
XXXIV. 13 (end). — **honos**: not
the *supplicatio*, but the *triumphus.*
— **usitato praesertim**: possibly
a thrust at Cato himself, who secured a thanksgiving of twenty
days for his son-in-law Bibulus
(*Att.* 7. 2. 7), although Cicero
says of him, *Att.* 6. 8. 5: *ego, ntsi
Bibulus qui, dum unus hostis in
Syria fuit, pedem porta non plus
extulit quam domo sua* (when during his consulship with Caesar he
shut himself up in his own house),
adniteretur de triumpho, aequo

animo essem. — **ex te**: the Letters
have not only the regular construction *aliquid abs te peto,* but
also *aliquid ex te peto* and *aliquid
te peto.* Cf. Ep. XXXVII. 1 n.;
LII. 2 n. — **quod amicissime
scribis**: cf. *existimes . . . quod . . .
gaudere,* Ep. XXXVII. 3. — **id
quod maluero**: *i.e.* a triumph.
The expression contains a thrust
at Cato for his presumption in try-
ing to secure for Cicero a resolution complimenting him upon the
uprightness of his administration
(cf. Ep. XXXVII. 1) for which he
had not asked, instead of a thanksgiving and a possible future triumph, which he did desire. —
scribendo adfuisti: *i.e.* when the
bill was drawn up in legal form;
cf. *legem conscripserunt,* Ep. XV.

agitur, scribi solere.   Ego, ut spero, te propediem videbo, atque utinam re p. meliore quam timeo!

XXXIX. (*Fam.* 16. 4.)

TVLLIVS TIRONI SVO S. P. D. ET CICERO ET Q.
FRATER ET Q. F.

1   Varie sum adfectus tuis litteris, valde priore pagina
perturbatus, paulum altera recreatus.   Quare nunc
quidem non dubito quin, quoad plane valeas, te neque
navigationi neque viae committas.   Satis te mature
videro, si plane confirmatum videro.   De medico et
tu bene existimari scribis et ego sic audio ; sed plane
curationes eius non probo; ius enim dandum tibi non
fuit, cum κακοστόμαχος esses; sed tamen et ad illum
2 scripsi accurate et ad Lysonem.   Ad Curium vero,
suavissimum hominem et summi offici summaeque
humanitatis, multa scripsi, in iis etiam, ut, si tibi vide-

---

7 n. — re publica meliore : the
violent discussions in the senate
concerning a successor to Caesar
were at their height.

XXXIX. Leucas, Nov. 7, 50 B.C.
Cicero apparently left Tarsus July
30 (cf. *Fam.* 2. 17. 1), and, after a
delay of several weeks in Rhodes
and Ephesus, reached the Piraeus
Oct. 14.   Toward the end of the
month he set out by land for
Rome.   Tiro, who was with him,
was taken ill on the way, and was
left behind at Patrae, while Cicero
continued his journey through
Alyzia and Leucas.

1. existimari : probably imper-
sonal, although after *de* introducing a transition we find such
loose constructions that it would
be possible to consider existimari

personal with an omitted *eum* for
its subject.   Cf. *de Quinto fratre,
scito eum non mediocriter laborare,*
etc., *Att.* 10. 15. 4. — ius, *soup.* —
κακοστόμαχος : as the physicians
were usually Greeks, technical medical expressions were in Greek. Cf.
the prescription which Cicero urges
upon Tiro (*Fam.* 16. 18. 1): *ea*
(*i.e. valetudo*) *quid postulet, non
ignoras ;* πέψιν, ἀκοπίαν, περίπατον
σύμμετρον, τρῖψιν, εὐλυσίαν κοιλίας.
— Lysonem : Tiro was staying at
Lyso's house.

2. Curium : M.' Curius, a Roman knight carrying on a banking
business in Patrae.   The one letter
which we have from him, *Fam.* 7.
29, full as it is of commercial
terms, would of itself betray his
calling.   *Fam.* 7. 28, 30, and 31

retur, te ad se transferret; Lyso enim noster vereor
ne neglegentior sit, primum, quia omnes Graeci, deinde
quod, cum a me litteras accepisset, mihi nullas remisit.
Sed eum tu laudas; tu igitur quid faciendum sit iudi-
cabis. Illud, mi Tiro, te rogo, sumptu ne parcas ulla
in re, quod ad valetudinem opus sit. Scripsi ad Curium,
quod dixisses daret. Medico ipsi puto aliquid dandum
esse, quo sit studiosior. Innumerabilia tua sunt in me 3
officia, domestica forensia, urbana provincialia, in re
privata in publica, in studiis in litteris nostris; omnia
viceris, si, ut spero, te validum videro. Ego puto te
bellissime, si recte erit, cum quaestore Mescinio decursurum. Non inhumanus est teque, ut mihi visus est,
diligit. Et cum valetudini tuae diligentissime con-
sulueris, tum, mi Tiro, consulito navigationi. Nulla
in re iam te festinare volo; nihil laboro nisi ut salvus
sis. Sic habeto, mi Tiro, neminem esse qui me amet 4

are addressed to him. — **ad se,** *to
his house.* — **omnes Graeci** : cf.
Q. fr. 1. 2. 4 *Graecorum ingenia
ad fallendum parata; . . . per-
taesum est* (*eorum*) *levitatis adsen-
tationis, animorum non officiis, sed
temporibus servientium.* — **sumptu** : the contracted form for the
dative in the fourth decl. seems
to occur most frequently in poetry and in post-Augustan prose,
although it is found occasionally
in the prose of both Caesar and
Cicero; cf. Neue, *Formenlehre,* I.[2]
356–358.

3. **domestica forensia,** etc. :
cf. Intr. 94. — **litteris** : cf. Gell.
6. 3. 8 *Tiro Tullius, M. Ciceronis
libertus, sane quidem fuit ingenio
homo eleganti et hautquaquam rerum litterarumque veterum indoc-
tus, eoque ab ineunte aetate liberali-
ter instituto adminiculatore et quasi*

*administro in studiis litterarum
Cicero usus est; Fam.* 16. 10. 2
*litterulae meae sive nostrae tui de-
siderio oblanguerunt.* See also Intr.
57. — **bellissime** : cf. *bellus,* Ep.
XXIV. 2 n.; XLI. 1. — **recte erit:**
cf. Intr. 85 *a.* — **Mescinio:** the
poor opinion which Cicero had of
his quaestor L. Mescinius Rufus
(*Att.* 6. 4. 1 *nihil minus probari
poterat quam quaestor Mescinius*)
is not out of harmony with the
lukewarm expression **non inhumanus est.** In *Fam.* 13. 26,
written four years later, Cicero
recommends him to Servius Sulpicius, but in terms which are cold
in comparison with those found in
his other letters of introduction.
Fam. 5. 19 and 20 are to him. —
decursurum: as we say, 'make the
run,' *i.e.* from Patrae to Leucas.

4. **sic habeto:** cf. Ep. XXVI. 1 n.

quin idem te amet, et cum tua et mea maxime interest
te valere, tum multis est curae. Adhuc, dum mihi
nullo loco deesse vis, numquam te confirmare potuisti;
nunc te nihil impedit ; omnia depone, corpori servi.
Quantam diligentiam in valetudinem tuam contuleris,
tanti me fieri a te iudicabo. Vale, mi Tiro, vale, vale
et salve. Lepta tibi salutem dicit et omnes. Vale.
VII Id. Nov. Leucade.

XL. (*Fam.* 16. 6.)

TVLLIVS ET CICERO ET QQ. TIRONI S. P. D.

1 Tertiam ad te hanc epistulam scripsi eodem die,
magis instituti mei tenendi causa, quia nactus eram
cui darem, quam quo haberem quid scriberem. Igitur
illa: quantum me diligis, tantum adhibe in te diligentiae; ad tua innumerabilia in me officia adde hoc, quod
mihi erit gratissimum omnium. Cum valetudinis ratio-
2 nem, ut spero, habueris, habeto etiam navigationis. In
Italiam euntibus omnibus ad me litteras dabis, ut ego
euntem Patras neminem praetermitto. Cura, cura te, mi
Tiro. Quoniam non contigit ut simul navigares, nihil
est quod festines, nec quicquam cures nisi ut valeas.
Etiam atque etiam vale. VII Idus Nov. Actio vesperi.

—**nullo loco**: for *nulla in re.*
Cf. *omnibus locis*, Ep. XLII. 1.—
Lepta: cf. Ep. XXXV. 22.

XL. Actium, Nov. 7, 50 B.C. —
QQ. (=*Quinti duo*): *i.e.* the brother
and nephew of Cicero. Cf. the
salutations in Ep. XXXIX. and
XLII.

1. **tertiam** : the other two were
Ep. XXXIX. and *Fam.* 16. 5. —
cui darem : for the lack of a
postal system among the Romans,
see Intr. 64.

2. **dabis**: cf. Intr. 84 *b.* — **simul**:
sc. nobiscum ; cf. Ep. XLI. 2.—**etiam
atque etiam vale**: cf. Intr. 62.

XLI. (*Fam.* 16. 9.)

TVLLIVS ET CICERO TIRONI SVO S. P. D.

Nos a te, ut scis, discessimus a. d. IIII Non. Nov. 1
Leucadem venimus a. d. VIII Id. Nov., a. d. VII Actium.
Ibi propter tempestatem a. d. VI Idus morati sumus.
Inde a. d. V Id. Corcyram bellissime navigavimus.
Corcyrae fuimus usque ad a. d. XVI K. Dec., tempesta-
tibus retenti.   A. d. XV K. in portum Corcyraeorum
ad Cassiopen stadia CXX processimus.   Ibi retenti
ventis sumus usque ad a. d. VIIII K.   Interea qui
cupide profecti sunt multi naufragia fecerunt.   Nos 2
eo die cenati solvimus; inde austro lenissimo, caelo
sereno nocte illa et die postero in Italiam ad Hydruntem
ludibundi pervenimus, eodemque vento postridie (id
erat a. d. VII K. Dec.) hora IIII Brundisium venimus,
eodemque tempore simul nobiscum in oppidum introiit
Terentia, quae te facit plurimi.   A. d. V K. Dec. servus
Cn. Planci Brundisi tandem aliquando mihi a te ex-
spectatissimas litteras reddidit, datas Idibus Nov., quae
me molestia valde levarunt; utinam omnino liberassent!
Sed tamen Asclapo medicus plane confirmat propediem
te valentem fore.   Nunc quid ego te horter ut omnem 3

XLI. Brundisium, Nov. 26, 50 B.C. Cicero's affection for Tiro is shown, not only by the anxiety which he feels for his health, but also by the care with which he suggests and provides all those little things which may increase his comfort.   Cf. Intr. 49 (end).

1. **a te discessimus** : *i.e.* at Patrae. — **a. d. XVI K. Dec.**: used substantively and governed by the preposition **ad**; cf. **a. d. VII K. Dec.**, below.

2. **id erat**, etc.: for the more common expression *qui dies erat*, etc., cf. Ep. XV. 5. — **eodem tempore simul nobiscum**: note the pleonasm; cf. **tandem aliquando,** below. — **Terentia** : she came to Brundisium at Cicero's request ; cf. *Fam.* 14. 5. 1.   Two years later, when Cicero returned to Italy after the battle of Pharsalus, he discountenanced Terentia's proposal to meet him at Brundisium ; cf. Ep. LIII.

diligentiam adhibeas ad convalescendum? Tuam prudentiam temperantiam amorem erga me novi; scio te
omnia facturum ut nobiscum quam primum sis; sed
tamen ita velim, ut ne quid properes. Symphoniam
Lysonis vellem vitasses, ne in quartam hebdomada
incideres; sed quoniam pudori tuo maluisti obsequi
quam valetudini, reliqua cura. Curio misi ut medico
honos haberetur et tibi daret quod opus esset; me cui
iussisset curaturum. Equum et mulum Brundisi tibi
reliqui. Romae vereor ne ex K. Ian. magni tumultus
4 sint. Nos agemus omnia modice. Reliquum est ut te
hoc rogem et a te petam, ne temere naviges. Solent
nautae festinare quaestus sui causa. Cautus sis, mi
Tiro; mare magnum et difficile tibi restat. Si poteris, cum Mescinio — caute is solet navigare; si minus,
cum honesto aliquo homine cuius auctoritate navicu-
larius moveatur. In hoc omnem diligentiam si adhibu-
eris teque nobis incolumem steteris, omnia a te habebo.
Etiam atque etiam, noster Tiro, vale. Medico, Curio,
Lysoni de te scripsi diligentissime. Vale salve.

3. **symphoniam**: the singing of a chorus of slaves (*symphoniaci*) was a favorite entertainment with the Romans at dinner; cf. Macrob. *Sat.* 2. 4. 28. In earlier times the music was of a simpler sort. Cf. Quint. I. 10. 20 *sed veterum quoque Romanorum epulis fides ac tibias adhibere moris fuit.* For musical entertainments on similar occasions, cf. Juv. 11. 180; Plin. *Ep.* 1. 15. 2; Gellius, 19. 9. 4. — **in quartam hebdomada**: every seventh day was regarded as a critical period in an illness. Tiro had suffered from three of these hebdomadal attacks. — **honos**, *his fee.* — **me . . . curaturum**: Curius as

a banker would have correspondents in Rome, and Cicero proposed to pay one of these correspondents the sum which Curius might pay out in settling the bill for medical attendance. — **reliqui**: epistolary perfect. — **ex K. Ian.**: the consuls for 49 B.C. were inclined to take vigorous measures against Caesar.

4. **cautus sis**: cf. Intr. 84 *b*. — **mi Tiro**: cf. *mi Pomponi*, Ep. X. n. — **cum Mescinio**: *sc. naviga.* — **noster Tiro**: the other members of Cicero's family often join in the valedictory address to him. — **vale salve**: cf. Ep. XXXIX. 4 (end).

XLII. (*Fam.* 16. 11.)

TVLLIVS ET CICERO TERENTIA TVLLIA QQ. TIRONI
S. P. D.

Etsi opportunitatem operae tuae omnibus locis desi- 1
dero, tamen non tam mea quam tua causa doleo te non
valere ; sed quoniam in quartanam conversa vis est
morbi (sic enim scribit Curius), spero te diligentia
adhibita iam firmiorem fore ; modo fac, id quod est
humanitatis tuae, ne quid aliud cures hoc tempore
nisi ut quam commodissime convalescas. Non ignoro
quantum ex desiderio labores ; sed erunt omnia facilia,
si valebis. Festinare te nolo ne nauseae molestiam

XLII. Near Rome, Jan. 12, 49 B.C. Cicero reached Rome, after his absence in Cilicia, Jan. 4, 49 B.C. (cf. 2), but, being anxious to obtain a triumph, remained without the city. This enabled him to avoid participating in the exciting debates which took place in the senate Jan. 1–2 and 5–6, and left him free to negotiate for peace between Caesar and Pompey. On Jan. 1 Curio, Caesar's representative, laid before the senate a proposition to the effect that Caesar should be allowed to sue for the consulship while absent from the city, in accordance with the special law passed in 52 B.C. granting him that privilege (cf. Intr. 26), or if it should be considered necessary for him to give up his army and provinces, that Pompey should be required to do the same. Although this document was read in the senate, the consuls refused to allow a vote upon it, and after fiery speeches by Lentulus, Scipio, and others,

it was voted *uti ante certam diem* (July 1, 49) *Caesar exercitum dimittat ; si non faciat, eum adversus rem publicam facturum videri* (Caes. *B. C.* 1. 2). After consultations with Pompey, whose *imperium*, as he was still governor of Spain, did not allow him to enter the city, on Jan. 7 the senate passed the *senatus consultum ultimum : dent operam consules praetores tribuni plebis quique pro consulibus sint ad urbem, ne quid res publica detrimenti capiat* (Caes. *B. C.* 1. 5). — **QQ.**: cf. Ep. XL. introd. note.

1. **doleo . . . valere:** that while the course of political events was of such absorbing interest at Rome, Cicero's thoughts are first directed towards Tiro and Tiro's illness, affords a striking proof of his affection for his faithful freedman. — **quartanam :** the appearance of the *febris quartana* indicated convalescence. Cf. Juv. 4. 57 *quartanam sperantibus aegris.* — **Curius:** cf. Ep. XXXIX. 2 n.

2 suscipias aeger et periculose hieme naviges. Ego ad urbem accessi pr. Non. Ian. Obviam mihi sic est proditum ut nihil possit fieri ornatius; sed incidi in ipsam flammam civilis discordiae vel potius belli, cui cum cuperem mederi et, ut arbitror, possem, cupiditates certorum hominum (nam ex utraque parte sunt qui pugnare cupiant) impedimento mihi fuerunt. Omnino et ipse Caesar, amicus noster, minacis ad senatum et acerbas litteras miserat et erat adhuc impudens, qui exercitum et provinciam invito senatu teneret, et Curio meus illum incitabat; Antonius quidem noster et Q. Cassius nulla vi expulsi ad Caesarem cum Curione pro-

2. **obviam mihi** : cf. Cicero's account of his reception on returning from exile in Ep. XV. 5. — **mederi** : Cicero's absence from Italy while civil war was brewing, his absence from the senate during the stormy debates of the first week in January, as well as his well-known opportunism in politics, and his friendly relations with both Caesar and Pompey, seemed to make him the natural mediator between the opposing factions. That he hoped to effect a compromise is clear from many remarks in the Letters (cf., *e.g.*, Ep. LXV. 5). What many condemn as cowardice in his course during the Civil War finds at least partial justification in his desire to keep a neutral attitude, which would enable him to negotiate a peace. — **ex utraque parte** : among others Cicero is thinking of the Pompeians Scipio and Lentulus, and the Caesarians Antony and Cassius; cf. Caes. *B. C.* I. 1–4, and see Ep. LXV. 6 *victa est*, etc. — **minacis . . . litteras** : the letter read by Curio in the senate Jan. 1 (see introd. note). Caesar (*B. C.* I.

5) characterizes the propositions contained in his letter as *lenissima postulata*. Cicero's characterization of the letter would seem to be justified, however, by Caesar's own statement of his purpose in *B. C.* I. 22 *ut se et populum Romanum factione paucorum oppressum in libertatem vindicaret*. See also Dio Cass. 41.1. — **provinciam:** Caesar was proconsul of Gallia Cisalpina, Illyricum, and Gallia Narbonensis. — **Curio meus** : cf. Ep. VII. 3 n. He advised Caesar to advance upon Rome at once, without waiting to offer a compromise. — **nulla vi expulsi** : Antonius and Q. Cassius, two of the tribunes, vetoed the *senatus consultum ultimum* (cf. introd. note), and although such action was strictly within the limits of their power, serious threats were made against them in the senate. Cf. Caes. *B. C.* I. 2 *refertur confestim de intercessione tribunorum. Dicuntur sententiae graves : ut quisque acerbissime crudelissimeque dixit, ita maxime ab inimicis Caesaris collaudatur*, and according to Dio Cassius 41. 3 the consul Lentulus went so

fecti erant, postea quam senatus consulibus, pr., tr. pl.,
et nobis qui pro cos. sumus, negotium dederat, ut cura-
remus ne quid res p. detrimenti caperet.   Numquam 3
maiore in periculo civitas fuit, numquam improbi cives
habuerunt paratiorem ducem.   Omnino ex hac quoque
parte diligentissime comparatur.   Id fit auctoritate et
studio Pompei nostri qui Caesarem sero coepit timere.
Nobis inter has turbas senatus tamen frequens flagita-
vit triumphum; sed Lentulus consul, quo maius suum
beneficium faceret, simul atque expedisset quae essent
necessaria de re p., dixit se relaturum.   Nos agimus
nihil cupide, eoque est nostra pluris auctoritas.   Italiae
regiones discriptae sunt, quam quisque partem tuere-
tur.   Nos Capuam sumpsimus.   Haec te scire volui.

far as to summon them ὑπεξελθεῖν,
πρὶν τὰς ψήφους διενεχθῆναι. The
principle that the tribune could
not be held responsible for his
official acts seems to have been
first called into question in the
year 98, in the case of C. Furius,
who had been tribune in the preceding year, and similar prosecu-
tions occurred in the years 94, 86,
74, 66, and 65 B.C. (cf. *Herzog*, I.
1167 ff.; *Madvig*, *Verf. u. Verw.*
I. 467). The case before us would
seem to have been the first instance when an attempt was made
to hold a tribune accountable during his term of office.   As Caesar puts it, *de sua salute septimo
die* (of the calendar year) *cogitare
coguntur*, *B. C.* I. 5. Cf. also
Appian, *Bell. Civ.* 2. 33. Cicero's
words, therefore, **nulla vi expulsi,**
while technically true, misrepre-
sent the real state of the case. It
was this infringement of the rights
of the tribune which Caesar urged
in justification of his advance

upon Rome. — **ad Caesarem**:
Caesar was at Ravenna. — **senatus,** etc.: cf. Caes. *B. C.* 1. 5.

3. **ex hac . . . parte**: *i.e.* on the
side of the Optimates. — **qui . . .
timere**: this thought recurs frequently in the letters of the next six
months; cf., *e.g.*, *Att.* 8. 8. 1 (*Pompeius) eundem (i.e. Caesarem) repente
timere coeperat, condicionem pacis
nullam probarat, nihil ad bellum
pararat.* — **senatus . . . triumphum**: the right of introducing
a subject rested with the presiding
officer. — **maius suum beneficium**: a greater favor on his part,
since he could arrange a triumph
more worthy of Cicero after the
disposal of Caesar's case. — **nos
Capuam sumpsimus**: Cicero's
principal duty was to protect Campania and raise levies there. Cf.
Att. 7. 14. 2 *me Pompeius Capuam
venire voluit et adiuvare dilectum,
in quo parum prolixe respondent
Campani coloni;* see also Intr.
29.

Tu etiam atque etiam cura ut valeas, litterasque ad me
mittas quotienscumque habebis cui des. Etiam atque
etiam vale. D. pr. Idus Ian.

XLIII. (*Fam.* 14. 14.)

TVLLIVS TERENTIAE ET PATER TVLLIAE, DVABVS
ANIMIS SVIS, ET CICERO MATRI OPTIMAE,
SVAVISSIMAE SORORI S. P. D.

1   Si vos valetis, nos valemus.   Vestrum iam consilium
est, non solum meum, quid sit vobis faciendum.   Si
ille Romam modeste venturus est, recte in praesentia
domi esse potestis; sin homo amens diripiendam urbem
daturus est, vereor ut Dolabella ipse satis nobis prodesse possit.   Etiam illud metuo, ne iam intercludamur,
ut, cum velitis exire, non liceat.   Reliquum est, quod
ipsae optime considerabitis, vestri similes feminae sint-
ne Romae; si enim non sunt, videndum est ut honeste
vos esse possitis.   Quomodo quidem nunc se res habet,
modo ut haec nobis loca tenere liceat, bellissime vel
mecum vel in nostris praediis esse poteritis.   Etiam
illud verendum est, ne brevi tempore fames in urbe sit.

2   His de rebus velim cum Pomponio, cum Camillo, cum
quibus vobis videbitur consideretis, ad summam animo
forti sitis.   Labienus rem meliorem fecit ; adiuvat

XLIII.   Minturnae, Jan. 23,
49 B.C.
   1. ille: *i.e.* Caesar. — ut Dolabella . . . possit: Dolabella, Tullia's husband, had joined Caesar's
party, and could therefore protect
Terentia and Tullia from Caesar's
followers. — vestri similes : *i.e.* of
your rank. — praediis : see Intr.
45.

2. Camillo: C. Furius Camillus,
a legal friend of Cicero.— ad summam, *in short ;* a frequent colloquial phrase. Cf. *Fam.* 8. 14. 4 ; *Att.*
14. 1. 1; Petron. 2, 37, 45, etc.—
Labienus, etc. : cf. *Fam.* 16. 12. 4
(*Caesar*) *maximam autem plagam
accepit, quod is qui summam auctoritatem in illius exercitu habebat, T.
Labienus, socius sceleris esse noluit;*

etiam Piso, quod ab urbe discedit et sceleris condem-
nat generum suum. Vos, meae carissimae animae,
quam saepissime ad me scribite et vos quid agatis et
quid istic agatur.   Quintus pater et filius et Rufus
vobis s. d.   Valete.   VIII K. Minturnis.

XLIV.   (*Att.* 8. 12 D.)

CN. MAGNVS PROCOS. S. D. L. DOMITIO PROCOS.

Litterae mihi a te redditae sunt a. d. XIII Kal. 1
Martias, in quibus scribis Caesarem apud Corfinium
castra posuisse.   Quod putavi et praemonui fit, ut nec
in praesentia committere tecum proelium velit et omnibus copiis conductis te implicet, ne ad me iter tibi

reliquit illum et nobiscum est, mul-
tique idem facturi esse dicuntur;
cf. also *Att.* 7. 13. 1 and Caes. *B. G.*
8. 52; *B. C.* 3. 13. — **Piso**: L. Calpurnius Piso Caesoninus, whose
daughter Calpurnia was the wife
of Caesar.   Piso was consul in
58 B.C., and joined Cicero's enemies in helping to banish him.
Cicero retaliated in the *Or. in
Pison.* — **Rufus**: probably Mescinius Rufus; cf. Ep. XXXIX. 3 n.

XLIV. Luceria, Feb. 17, 49 B.C.
Caesar crossed the boundary of
his province Jan. 10, 49 B.C. (Nov.
22, 50 B.C., according to the Julian
calendar), with a force of five
cohorts, which had increased to
40,000 men by Feb. 14, when he
arrived before Corfinium. In this
town and its vicinity there were
thirty-one cohorts (cf. *Att.* 8. 12 A.
1), mainly under the command of
L. Domitius Ahenobarbus (cf. Ep.
I. 3 n.), designated as Caesar's
successor in Transalpine Gaul.
Confidently expecting the arrival
of Pompey, to whom he had sent

letters describing his imminent
danger, Domitius had neglected
all preparations for defense. This
letter from Pompey, declining to
come to his relief, decided the
fate of the town, which was delivered over to Caesar after a
siege of seven days. Thus the
last obstacle in the way of Caesar's
advance into southern Italy was
removed.   The intense interest
with which the Pompeians watched
the course of events at Corfinium indicates the supreme importance which they attached to
that struggle, and makes this letter one of the most important
documents relating to the Civil
War.   *Di immortales, qui me hor-*
ror perfudit! quam sum sollicitus
quidnam futurum sit, writes Cicero (*Att.* 8. 6. 3), upon hearing
that Corfinium was besieged by
Caesar.   For the details of the
siege, cf. Caes. *B. C.* 1. 19 ff.

1. **implicet**: the letters of Pompey contain, as we might expect,
many technical military words and

expeditum sit atque istas copias coniungere optimorum
civium possis cum his legionibus, de quarum voluntate
dubitamus; quo etiam magis tuis litteris sum commotus. Neque enim eorum militum quos mecum habeo
voluntate satis confido ut de omnibus fortunis rei
publicae dimicem, neque etiam, qui ex dilectibus con-
2 scripti sunt consulibus, convenerunt. Quare da operam, si ulla ratione etiam nunc efficere potes, ut te
explices, huc quam primum venias, antequam omnes
copiae ad adversarium conveniant. Neque enim celeriter ex dilectibus huc homines convenire possunt et, si
convenirent, quantum iis committendum sit qui inter
se ne noti quidem sunt contra veteranas legiones non
te praeterit.

expressions. To this class *impli-
care* and *explicare*, which occur
five times in his six letters, would
seem to belong. — **optimorum
civium**: the troops at Corfinium
were made up of recruits from the
Alban, Marsian, and Paelignian
territory, and represented the most
reliable force in Pompey's Italian
army. — **his legionibus**: in 50 B.C.
the senate required Pompey and
Caesar to furnish one legion each
for use in the Parthian war. Caesar obeyed, and Pompey complied
by demanding of Caesar a legion
which he had previously lent him.
Both legions were drawn, therefore, from Caesar's army. They
were not used in the Parthian war,
but were stationed in Italy. Before their departure from Caesar's

camp they had received the gifts
of money which soldiers received
in case of a triumph. This fact,
coupled with their admiration for
their former commander, made
their devotion to the Pompeian
cause doubtful. — **consulibus**:
dat. of advantage.

2. **etiam nunc**: although the
siege has begun. — **explices**: cf.
implicet, 1 n. — **ad adversarium**:
the MSS. do not contain **ad**, but we
must either insert it or regard its
omission as not unnatural in a letter from Pompey, written in haste.
See Crit. Append. Pompey always
speaks of Caesar as an *adversarius*
(cf., *e.g.*, *Att.* 8. 12 B. 1 (*bis*); 8. 12
C. 1).   Probably the senate had
not technically declared him an
hostis (cf. Schmidt, *Briefw.* 112).

XLV. (*Att.* 8. 3.)

CICERO ATTICO SAL.

Maximis et miserrimis rebus perturbatus, cum coram 1
tecum mihi potestas deliberandi non esset, uti tamen
tuo consilio volui.   Deliberatio autem omnis haec est:
si Pompeius Italia cedat, quod eum facturum esse
suspicor, quid mihi agendum putes ; et quo facilius
consilium dare possis, quid in utramque partem mihi
in mentem veniat explicabo brevi.   Cum merita Pom- 2
pei summa erga salutem meam familiaritasque quae
mihi cum eo est, tum ipsa rei publicae causa me addu-
cit, ut mihi vel consilium meum cum illius consilio vel
fortuna mea cum illius fortuna coniungenda esse videatur.   Accedit illud: si maneo et illum comitatum
optimorum et clarissimorum civium desero, cadendum
est in unius potestatem, qui etsi multis rebus significat
se nobis esse amicum — et ut esset a me est, tute scis,
propter suspicionem huius impendentis tempestatis
multo ante provisum, — tamen utrumque consideran-
dum est, et quanta fides ei sit habenda et, si maxime
exploratum sit eum nobis amicum fore, sitne viri fortis

XLV. Cales, Feb. 18, 49 B.C.
Cicero had received a letter from
Pompey (*Att.* 8. 11 A) directing
him to proceed to Luceria at once
and join the other Pompeians.
He accordingly left Formiae on
Feb. 17 (cf. *Att.* 8. 11 D. 1) and
advanced to Cales, from which
place this letter was written, apparently in the night of Feb. 18.
Finding his way blocked by Caesar's troops, he turned back (cf. 7)
and was in Formiae again Feb. 21.

2. **erga salutem meam**: *sc.* in
helping to secure his recall from exile. — **unius** : *i.e. Caesaris.* — **provisum** : in 56 B.C. Cicero had pla-
cated Caesar by withdrawing his
opposition to certain of Caesar's
agrarian laws (*Q. fr.* 2. 6 [8]. 2),
by speaking in favor of a grant of
money to Caesar's troops (*de Prov.
Cons.* 28), by extolling Caesar's
success in Gaul, and by opposing
the withdrawal of a province from
him (*ibid.* 17–35), and in 54 B.C.

et boni civis esse in ea urbe, in qua cum summis honoribus imperiisque usus sit, res maximas gesserit, sacerdotio sit amplissimo praeditus, non futurus sit qui
fuerit, subeundumque periculum sit cum aliquo fore
dedecore, si quando Pompeius rem publicam recipe-
3 rarit.   In hac parte haec sunt ; vide nunc quae sint
in altera.   Nihil actum est a Pompeio nostro sapienter,
nihil fortiter; addo etiam, nihil nisi contra consilium
auctoritatemque meam.   Omitto illa vetera, quod istum
in rem publicam ille aluit, auxit, armavit, ille legibus
per vim et contra auspicia ferendis auctor, ille Galliae
ulterioris adiunctor, ille gener, ille in adoptando P. Clodio augur, ille restituendi mei quam retinendi studio-

by defending some of Caesar's
friends. — summis honoribus
imperiisque : *i.e.* as praetor and
consul. The connection precludes
any reference to the military *imperium* which he had just held as
proconsul. — sacerdotio : cf. Ep.
XXXIV. 13 n. The most plausible conjecture for the emendation
of this passage is to insert sit qui
fuerit with Lehmann. The meaning then is : 'whether it is proper
for a brave man and a good citizen to remain in a city in which,
after enjoying the most exalted
positions of honor and power,
. . . he will not be the man he
was, and must undergo the risk
of bringing some shame upon
himself, etc.'   See Crit. Append.
— fore : in apposition to and explanatory of periculum. *Ne* with
the subj. would be a more natural
construction, but cf. *de Or.* 2. 334
*cum subest ille timor, ea (utilitate)
neglecta ne dignitatem quidem posse
retineri.*   The statement of one
side of the question, which began
with 2, comes to an end with this
sentence.

3. istum : *i.e. Caesarem.* — ille :
i.e. Pompeius. — legibus . . . ferendis : *i.e.* the laws whose passage Caesar effected in his consulship in 59 B.C. For Pompey's
attitude toward these laws, cf. *Att.*
2. 16. 2.   When Caesar's agrarian
law, assigning lands to Pompey's
veterans, came before the people,
Bibulus and Cato, the leaders of
the opposition, were treated with
great roughness ; cf. Plut. *Cat.
Min.* 32 ; Suet. *Iul.* 20. — contra
auspicia : to the many attempts
which the Optimates made to
postpone the *comitia* on religious
grounds (cf. Dio Cass. 38. 6)
Caesar paid little heed. — Galliae
. . . adiunctor : Caesar's third
province (cf. Intr. 13) was volun-
tarily added by the senate, probably through the influence of Pompey. — gener : *sc.* by his marriage
to Caesar's daughter Julia. — ille
. . . augur : Pompey was present
at the meeting of the *comitia curiata* when Clodius was adopted,
and, as augur, could have prevented the adoption. Cf. *Att.* 2.
12. 1. — restituendi mei, etc.: the

sior, ille provinciae propagator, ille absentis in omnibus
adiutor, idem etiam tertio consulatu, postquam esse
defensor rei publicae coepit, contendit ut decem tribuni
pl. ferrent, ut absentis ratio haberetur, quod idem ipse
sanxit lege quadam sua, Marcoque Marcello consuli
finienti provincias Gallias Kalendarum Martiarum die
restitit. Sed ut haec omittam, quid foedius, quid per-
turbatius hoc ab urbe discessu sive potius turpissima
fuga ? Quae condicio non accipienda fuit potius quam
relinquenda patria ? Malae condiciones erant, fateor,
sed num quid hoc peius ? ʻAt reciperabit rem publi- 4
cam.' Quando ? aut quid ad eam spem est parati ?
Non ager Picenus amissus ? Non patefactum iter ad
urbem ? Non pecunia omnis et publica et privata
adversario tradita ? Denique nulla causa, nullae vires,

reference is to Cicero's exile.
Although Pompey exerted himself
personally to secure Cicero's recall,
he had not interfered to prevent
his banishment; cf. *Att.* 10. 4. 3
*qui se nihil contra huius (i.e.
Caesaris) voluntatem aiebat facere
posse.* — **ille . . . propagator** :
through the *lex Pompeia Licinia*
(cf. Intr. 26), passed in Pompey's
consulship, and perhaps proposed
by him. Upon substantives in
-tor, cf. Intr. 75. See also **auctor,
adiunctor, adiutor,** and **defensor** in this passage. — **ut . . .
haberetur**: *i.e.* that Caesar might
be accepted as a candidate without coming to Rome. Cf. Ep.
XLII. introd. note, and Intr. 26.
— **Marco Marcello**: one of the
consuls in 51 B.C. — **finienti**: by
a bill looking to the displacement
of Caesar Mar. 1, 50 B.C.; cf. *Fam.*
8. 8. 9.— **provincias**: cf. *Galliae
adiunctor,* above. — **condiciones**:
apparently the last proposals for

peace were those submitted to the
Pompeians at Teanum Sidicinum,
Jan. 25, to the effect that Caesar
should disband his army, hand
over the provinces to his successors, and sue for the consulship in
the regular way, while Pompey
was to depart for Spain, and Italy
to disarm; cf. *Fam.* 16. 12. 3;
Caes. *B. C.* 1. 8–11. — **hoc**, etc.:
the desertion of Rome, the flight
of Pompey, and the prospective
abandonment of Italy.

4. **pecunia omnis**: cf. Caes.
B. C. 1. 14 *quibus rebus Romam
nuntiatis tantus repente terror in-
vasit ut, cum Lentulus consul ad
aperiendum aerarium venisset ad
pecuniam Pompeio ex senatus consulto proferendam, protinus aperto
sanctiore aerario ex urbe profuge-
ret.* — **nulla causa**: Cicero recognized now the fact that the
plans of Pompey were as selfish as
those of Caesar; cf. *Att.* 8. 11. 2
dominatio quaesita ab utroque est,

nulla sedes quo concurrant qui rem publicam defensam
velint. Apulia delecta est, inanissima pars Italiae et
ab impetu huius belli remotissima; fuga et maritima
opportunitas visa quaeri desperatione. Invite cepi
Capuam, non quo munus illud defugerem, sed pacis
causa, in qua nullus esset ordinum, nullus apertus pri-
vatorum dolor, bonorum autem esset aliquis, sed hebes,
ut solet. Sed ut ipse sensi quam esset multitudo et
infimus quisque propensus in alteram partem, quam
multi mutationis rerum cupidi, dixi ipsi me nihil sus-
5 cepturum sine praesidio et sine pecunia. Itaque habui
nihil omnino negoti, quod ab initio vidi nihil quaeri
praeter fugam. Eam si nunc sequor, quonam? Cum
illo non; ad quem cum essem profectus, cognovi in iis
locis esse Caesarem ut tuto Luceriam venire non
possem. Infero mari nobis incerto cursu, hieme

non id actum, beata et honesta civitas ut esset. . . . Sed neutri σκοπὸs
est ille ut nos beati simus ; uterque
regnare vult. — defensam (sc.
esse): cf. Cic. Cat. 2. 27 monitos
etiam atque etiam volo. The perfect infinitive passive, usually as
here without esse, after verbs of
wishing (especially after volo) is
commoner in Cicero, in whose
writings it occurs at least 26 times
(cf. Ziemer, Junggrammat. Streifzüge, pp. 76 ff.), than in any other
author. It indicates the impa-
tience with which the realization
of a wish is awaited. — Apulia:
Pompey's headquarters were at
Luceria; cf. Ep. XLIV. and Intr.
29. — cepi, sensi, dixi, habui,
and vidi are preterites. Cicero
had already resigned his position
at Capua. Cf. Intr. 29. — dolor,
sympathy. — multitudo et infimus quisque: cf. Mommsen, Rom.

Hist. IV. 453 : 'In fact Caesar's
antecedents were anything but reassuring, and still less reassuring
was the aspect of the retinue that
now surrounded him. Individuals
of the most broken reputation,
notorious personages like Quintus
Hortensius, Gaius Curio, Marcus
Antonius — the latter the stepson
of the Catilinarian Lentulus, who
was executed by the orders of
Cicero — were the most prominent
actors in it ; the highest posts of
trust were bestowed on men who
had long ceased even to reckon
up their debts.' Cf. also Att. 9.
19. 1. — ipsi : i.e. Pompeio.

5. nihil . . . fugam : cf. Att.
7. 23. 3 quod quaeris hic quid agatur, tota Capua et omnis hic dilectus iacet, desperata res est, in
fuga omnes sunt. — essem profectus : see introd. note. — hieme maxima, in mid-winter; cf.

maxima navigandum est. Age iam, cum fratre an sine eo cum filio? an quomodo? In utraque enim re summa difficultas erit, summus animi dolor. Qui autem impetus illius erit in nos absentes fortunasque nostras? acrior quam in ceterorum, quod putabit fortasse in nobis violandis aliquid se habere populare. Age iam, has compedes, fasces, inquam, hos laureatos efferre ex Italia quam molestum est! Qui autem locus erit nobis tutus, ut iam placatis utamur fluctibus, antequam ad illum venerimus? qua autem aut quo, nihil sciemus. At si restitero et fuerit nobis in hac parte locus, idem 6 fecero quod in Cinnae dominatione L. Philippus, quod

---

multa nocte. — **age iam** : *age* with or without the adverbs *iam, ergo, igitur*, etc., or duplicated (*age, age*), is common in colloquial Latin to give force to a question, concession, or command ; cf. *age, age ut lubet,* Ter. *And.* 310; *age, da veniam filio,* Ter. *Ad.* 937. — **cum fratre** : Quintus had been Caesar's legate, and his espousal of Pompey's cause would seem an act of ingratitude, and bring down the wrath of Caesar upon both Quintus and his brother. — **illius** : *i.e. Caesaris.* — **populare** : Cicero, although respected by the Italian peasantry, was thoroughly unpopular with the democracy of Rome. Cf. *Att.* 8. 11 D. 7 *ut mea persona semper ad improborum civium impetus aliquid videretur habere populare.* — **fasces . . . laureatos** : in hopes of a triumph for his military successes in Cilicia, he still retained the insignia of an imperator, although the retention of them exposed him to ridicule. Cf. *Att.* 7. 10. 1 *subito consilium cepi, ut ante quam luceret exirem, ne qui conspectus fieret aut sermo, lictori-*

bus praesertim laureatis. This picture of Cicero lends a touch of comedy to the tragedy of the Civil War. — **ut . . . utamur** : a hortatory clause with a concessive force. — **illum** : *i.e. Pompeium.* — **qua** : *sc. via.*

6. **in hac parte** : *i.e.* in Italy. Cicero's reference to a retreat from Italy on the part of the Pompeians is in the nature of a prophecy. In so far as official information had been given out, a stand was to be made at Luceria. Strangely enough, however, only the day before this letter was written Pompey had ordered his forces to collect at Brundisium with a view to crossing to Dyrrachium (cf. *Att.* 8. 12 A. 3), but Cicero did not know this. — **in Cinnae dominatione** : when Marius and Cinna in 87 B.C. approached Rome, many of the Optimates fled, as the same class of men did on the approach of Caesar, but **Philippus, Flaccus,** and **Mucius** remained in the city, and **Mucius** (Q. Mucius Scaevola) was murdered a few years

L. Flaccus, quod Q. Mucius, quoquo modo ea res huic quidem cecidit; qui tamen ita dicere solebat, se id fore videre quod factum est, sed malle quam armatum ad patriae moenia accedere. Aliter Thrasybulus, et fortasse melius; sed est certa quaedam illa Muci ratio atque sententia, est illa etiam, et, cum sit necesse, servire tempori et non amittere tempus, cum sit datum. Sed in hoc ipso habent tamen iidem fasces molestiam. Sit enim nobis amicus, quod incertum est, sed sit, deferet triumphum: non accipere ne periculosum sit, accipere invidiosum ad bonos. 'O rem,' inquis, 'difficilem et inexplicabilem!' Atqui explicanda est; qui autem fieri potest? Ac ne me existimaris ad manendum esse propensiorem, quod plura in eam partem verba fecerim, potest fieri, quod fit in multis quaestionibus, ut res verbosior haec fuerit, illa verior. Quamobrem ut maxima de re aequo animo deliberanti, ita mihi des consilium velim. Navis et in Caieta est parata

7 nobis et Brundisi. Sed ecce nuntii scribente me haec ipsa noctu in Caleno, ecce litterae, Caesarem ad Corfinium, Domitium Corfini cum firmo exercitu et pugnare cupiente. Non puto etiam hoc Gnaeum nostrum commissurum ut Domitium relinquat, etsi Brundisium Sci-

---

later. — **quoquo modo**, etc., *however that decision turned out in* HIS *case.* — **malle**: *sc. perire.* — **Thrasybulus** (*sc. fecit*): he left Athens when the Thirty Tyrants came into power, but returned to drive them out; cf. Xen. *Hell.* 2. 3. 42; 2. 4. — **sit** (enim): *sc. Caesar.* — **non** accipere, (*I am afraid) that not to accept (a triumph) may be a perilous thing (as far as Caesar is concerned), that to accept it may be shameful in the eyes of good citi-*

zens. Something like *vereor* is understood before **ne**, as in *de Fin.* 5. 8 *sed ne, dum huic obsequor, vobis molestus sim.* Cf. also Tac. *Hist.* 3. 46. — **res . . . haec**: *i.e.* the advisability of staying in Italy. — **Caieta**: Cicero had an estate here.

7. **ecce**: cf. Ep. XXXV. 23 n. — **Corfinium**: see introd. to Ep. XLIV. — **ut . . . relinquat**: Pompey's refusal to relieve Corfinium, which Ep. XLIV. contains, was

pionem cum cohortibus duabus praemiserat, legionem
Fausto conscriptam in Siciliam sibi placere a consule
duci scripserat ad consules.   Sed turpe Domitium
deseri implorantem eius auxilium.   Est quaedam spes,
mihi quidem non magna, sed in his locis firma, Afranium in Pyrenaeo cum Trebonio pugnasse, pulsum
Trebonium, etiam Fabium tuum transisse cum cohortibus, summa autem, Afranium cum magnis copiis adventare.   Id si est, in Italia fortasse manebitur.   Ego
autem, cum esset incertum iter Caesaris, quod vel ad
Capuam vel ad Luceriam iturus putabatur, Leptam
ad Pompeium misi et litteras; ipse ne quo inciderem

not yet known to Cicero. Cf. *in
hac parte*, 6 n. — **Scipionem** : cf.
Ep. I. 3 n. — **Fausto** : Faustus,
the son of L. Cornelius Sulla,
was the son-in-law of Pompey.
The dat. **Fausto** for *a Fausto*
comes under the principle stated
by Madvig on *de Fin.* I. 11 'that
the dative, when thus used, contains some idea of advantage, so
that the thing is thought of as
having been done not only *by* some
one but *for* some one, as with the
verb *quaero*.' — **Afranium** : cf.
Auli filium, Ep. V. 12 n. — in **Pyrenaeo**: the hopes of the Pompeians were fixed upon relief from
Spain ; cf. *dilectus enim magnos
habebamus putabamusque illum me-
tuere, si ad urbem ire coepisset, ne
Gallias amitteret, quas ambas habet
inimicissimas praeter Transpadanos, ex Hispaniaque sex legiones et
magna auxilia Afranio et Petreio
ducibus habet a tergo, Fam.* 16. 12. 4.
— **Trebonio** : C. Trebonius was
rewarded for the services which he
rendered to Caesar during his tri-
bunate by being appointed as Caesar's legate in Gaul, where he was

still in command.   Later he became *praetor urbanus*, and through
Caesar's influence propraetor of
Spain. He, however, joined the
conspirators against Caesar's life
in 44 B.C.   He was murdered in
Syria in the same year by Dolabella, being thus the first one of
the *liberatores* to suffer for his
connection with that plot. — **Fabium**: another of Caesar's legates
in Gaul. The reports that he had
deserted, and that Trebonius had
been defeated, were without foundation ; cf. Caes. *B. C.* 1. 40. —
transisse, *has come over to our
side.* The desertion of Labienus,
the most trusted and skilful of
Caesar's lieutenants, gave the
Pompeians great hopes of further
defections from Caesar's forces,
and the air was full of rumors of
such desertions. — **magnis copiis**:
Afranius, Petreius, and Varro had
seven legions and a large number
of auxiliary troops in Spain ; cf.
Caes. *B. C.* 1. 38. — **Leptam**: see
Ep. XXXV. 22 n. — **litteras**: the
letter has not been preserved. — **ne
quo inciderem** : cf. *cognovi*, etc., 5.

reverti Formias. Haec te scire volui scripsique seda-
tiore animo quam proxime scripseram, nullum meum
iudicium interponens, sed exquirens tuum.

XLVI. (*Att.* 8. 13.)

CICERO ATTICO SAL.

1   Lippitudinis meae signum tibi sit librari manus et
eadem causa brevitatis, etsi nunc quidem quod scriberem nihil erat.   Omnis exspectatio nostra erat in
nuntiis Brundisinis. Si nactus hic esset Gnaeum
nostrum, spes dubia pacis, sin ille ante tramisisset,
exitiosi belli metus.   Sed videsne in quem hominem
inciderit res publica ? quam acutum, quam vigilantem,
quam paratum ? Si mehercule neminem occiderit nec
cuiquam quicquam ademerit, ab iis qui eum maxime
2 timuerant maxime diligetur.   Multum mecum munici-
pales homines loquuntur, multum rusticani.   Nihil
prorsus aliud curant nisi agros, nisi villulas, nisi num-
mulos suos.   Et vide quam conversa res est : illum
quo antea confidebant metuunt, hunc amant quem

XLVI. Formiae, March 1, 49 B.C.
1. librari manus : cf. Intr. 64.
— hic : *i.e.* Caesar. — ille : *i.e.*
Pompey. — tramisisset : *sc.* the
Adriatic. — quam acutum, etc.:
of course descriptive of Caesar.

2. villulas, nummolos: cf. Intr.
76. — quam conversa res est :
in Plautus the indicative was frequently used in what seem to be
indir. questions, especially after
certain imperatives and imperative questions (cf. Morris's *Pseu-
dolus*, v. 262, and E. Becker, *De
Syntaxi Interrogationum Obliqua-
rum*, etc.). In this passage we
have a survival of that usage after

vide. Cf. *hoc sis* (= *si vis*) *vide,
ut alias res agunt,* Plaut. *Pseud.*
152. See also Intr. 84 *a* and *quam
sollicitus sum,* Ep. XLVIII. 1 n.
— hunc: *i.e. Caesarem.* The petty
landed proprietors had dreaded
Caesar because of his supposed
revolutionary principles, his previous extravagance and bankruptcy
in Rome, his former political associates, and his present followers.
Cf. *multitudo,* Ep. XLV. 4 n. The
dread of these people had been
turned into affection by the generosity with which Caesar had
treated the inhabitants of the captured towns (cf. Caes. *B. C.* I. 21-

timebant. Id quantis nostris peccatis vitiisque evenerit non possum sine molestia cogitare; quae autem
impendere putarem, scripseram ad te et iam tuas
litteras exspectabam.

XLVII. (*Att.* 9. 6 A.)

CAESAR IMP. S. D. CICERONI IMP.

Cum Furnium nostrum tantum vidissem, neque loqui
neque audire meo commodo potuissem, properarem
atque essem in itinere praemissis iam legionibus, praeterire tamen non potui quin et scriberem ad te et
illum mitterem gratiasque agerem, etsi hoc et feci
saepe et saepius mihi facturus videor: ita de me mere-
ris. Imprimis a te peto, quoniam confido me celeriter
ad urbem venturum, ut te ibi videam, ut tuo consilio
gratia dignitate ope omnium rerum uti possim. Ad

23), by the vigor with which he protected their own lives and property, and by his policy of not confiscating the estates even of his enemies. This letter may be well compared with Ep. XLVIII. 1.

XLVII. March 2–5, 49 B.C. The phrase **essem in itinere** indicates that this letter was written while Caesar was hastening to Brundisium to intercept Pompey if possible, before he should escape from Italy. Caesar reached Brundisium Mar. 9 (*Att.* 9. 13 A. 1). Cicero sent this letter to Atticus with one of his own (cf. *Att.* 9. 6.6).

Furnium: an ex-tribune, and a friend of Caesar and Cicero, to whom *Fam.* 10. 25 and 26 are addressed. — **praeterire**: Cicero was still at Formiae. — **tuo consilio . . . ope**: Caesar made strenuous efforts to induce Cicero to return

to Rome and lend him the benefit of his influence, and Cicero kept up a correspondence with him in the hope of terminating the Civil War. Three weeks later a conference took place between them (cf. Intr. 29 f.) which led Cicero to give up all hope of a peaceful settlement of the difficulty. Cf. *consilio*, Ep. XLIX. 1 n. The proposal which Caesar made in this letter was left unanswered, since Cicero was at this moment waiting for some decisive news from Brundisium (cf. *Att.* 9. 7. 5), and also distrusted Caesar's purposes; cf. *Att.* 9. 7. 5 *noli enim putare tolerabiles horum insanias nec unius modi fore. . . . Legibus iudiciis senatu sublato, libidines audacias sumptus egestates tot egentissimorum hominum nec privatas posse res nec rem publicam sustinere.*

propositum revertar : festinationi meae brevitatique litterarum ignosces ; reliqua ex Furnio cognosces.

XLVIII. (*Fam.* 8. 15.)

CAELIVS CICERONI S.

1   Ecquando tu hominem ineptiorem quam tuum Cn. Pompeium vidisti, qui tantas turbas, qui tam nugax esset, commorit ? Ecquem autem Caesare nostro acriorem in rebus gerendis, eodem in victoria temperatiorem aut legisti aut audisti ? Quid est ? Nunc tibi nostri milites, qui durissimis et frigidissimis locis, taeterrima hieme bellum ambulando confecerunt, malis orbiculatis esse pasti videntur ? ' Quid iam ? ' inquis. Gloriose omnia.   Si scias quam sollicitus sum, tum

XLVIII. Place of writing unknown; about March 9, 49 B.C.

1. **tuum** : opposed to **nostro** below. — **nugax** : adjectives in *ax* are found relatively much more frequently in colloquial Latin ; cf., *e.g.*, Plaut. *Pers.* 410, 421 ; *Capt.* 959; Petron. 43 ; 132. Cicero in his own letters uses only one such adjective, *tagax* (*Att.* 6. 3. 1). In the letters to Cicero we find *minax* (*Fam.* 11. 3. 1) ; *pugnax* (*Fam.* 8. 13. 1 and 10. 31. 5) ; *efficax* (*Fam.* 8. 10. 3) ; *sagax* (*Fam.* 10. 23. 4), and *nugax* here. — **commorit:** for syncopation in the Letters, cf. Intr. 82. The loss of *v* in the perfect tenses of *moveo* and its compounds is peculiar, since the lost letter is not the sign of the perfect system but belongs to the stem. Cf. Priscian, 10. 3. 16 (Keil, II. 508), upon this point. — **temperatiorem**: cf. *hunc*, Ep. XLVI. 2 n. — **quid est ?** nunc tibi, etc., *well ! do our soldiers, who in the roughest*

and coldest sort of a country, in the most abominable winter weather, have promenaded through the war, seem to you to have dined on truffles ?   Caesar crossed the Rubicon Jan. 10, 49 B.C., of the old calendar, but as the time of year was really late autumn, the season was not in itself unfavorable to military operations; but his troops had been obliged to make a difficult passage over the Apennines. In this campaign of two months Caesar had invested northern Italy, and made 30,000 men prisoners of war without a serious engagement. Upon **quid est**, cf. Intr. 98. — **ambulando confecerunt** and **malis orbiculatis esse pasti** look like proverbial expressions.   The *malum orbiculatum*, a fine fruit so named from its shape, was regarded as a great delicacy. — **gloriose omnia** : *sc. facta sunt.* — **quam sollicitus sum** : this MSS. reading need

hanc meam gloriam, quae ad me nihil pertinet, derideas; quae tibi exponere nisi coram non possum, idque
celeriter fore spero; nam me, cum expulisset ex Italia
Pompeium, constituit ad urbem vocare ; id quod iam
existimo confectum, nisi si maluit Pompeius Brundisi
circumsederi.　Peream si minima causa est properandi 2
isto mihi, quod te videre et omnia intima conferre discupio; habeo autem quam multa.　Hui vereor, quod
solet fieri, ne, cum te videro, omnia obliviscar.　Sed
tamen quod ob scelus iter mihi necessarium retro ad
Alpis versus incidit ?　Adeo, quod Intimeli in armis
sunt, neque de magna causa.　Bellienus, verna Deme-
tri, qui ibi cum praesidio erat, Domitium quendam,
nobilem illi, Caesaris hospitem, a contraria factione

---

not excite surprise in so colloquial
a letter ; cf. *quam conversa*, etc.,
Ep. XLVI. 2 n. See also Ter.
And. 650, and Spengel on Ter.
And. 45. — quae . . . pertinet :
the failure of Caelius to share in
Caesar's glory is explained by
nam me, etc. — quae (tibi): with
reference to the general statements of the preceding sentence,
especially the anxiety of Caelius.
— expulisset : *sc. Caesar.* — id
quod : with reference to the ex-
pulsion of Pompey from Italy. —
nisi si: cf. *nisi si,* Ep. XIII.
1 n.

2. peream si : cf. *ne vivam,*
Ep. IV. 4 n. — isto: archaic form;
cf. Servius on Verg. *Aen.* 8. 423
pro huc HOC *veteres dicere solebant,
sicut pro illuc* ILLO *dicimus.* See
also Intr. 81.　In isto the demonstrative particle -*c*(*e*) is lacking, as
it is in *illi* below. — discupio, etc.,
I am dying to see you, etc. Verbs
intensified by the addition of *dis-*
belong exclusively to colloquial

Latin, and are similar in meaning
to those compounded with *per* (cf.
Intr. 77). Cicero allows such compounds, when not applied to physical matters, only in his more informal writings (cf. *discrucio, Att.* 14. 6.
1 ; *dilaudo, Att.* 4. 17. 5), but in Latin
comedy a considerable list of them
is found, — *discaveo, discrucio, discupio, disperdo, dispereo, dispudet,
distaedet.* — quam : not to be regarded as exclamatory (' how
many ! '), but as intensive ; cf. *reiecit se in eum flens quam familiariter,* Ter. *And.* 136. We should
then consider the phrase elliptical
(*tam*) *multa quam* (*habere possum*).
— hui : like *hem* (Ep. XIII. 2)
confined to colloquial Latin ; cf.,
e.g., Plaut. *Truc.* 29 ; *Rud.* 154.
See also Intr. 92. — ad Alpis versus : the combination *ad . . . versus* occurs in Caesar, Sallust, and
Livy, but not in Cicero.　*Versus*
is to be taken adverbially with
the preposition.　It emphasizes
the direction. — illi : for *illic ;* see

nummis acceptis comprendit et strangulavit; civitas ad
arma iit; eo nunc cum VIII cohortibus mihi per nives
eundum est. 'Vsque quaque,' inquis, 'se Domitii male
dant.' Vellem quidem Venere prognatus tantum animi
habuisset in vestro Domitio, quantum Psacade natus in
hoc habuit. Ciceroni f. s. d.

XLIX. (*Att.* 9. 11 A.)

CICERO IMP. S. D. CAESARI IMP.

1   Vt legi tuas litteras, quas a Furnio nostro acceperam, quibus mecum agebas ut ad urbem essem, te velle

note on *isto* above. — se . . . dant,
*the Domitii are everywhere going
wrong.* One Domitius surrendered
Corfinium, and another has now
let himself be killed, so that Caelius is obliged to make a long
march to the Alps in the middle
of winter. On *se dare*, see *advoles,* Ep. XXV. 4 n. — Venere
prognatus : *i.e.* Caesar, who
claimed to be descended from
Venus. — Psacade natus : *i.e.*
Bellienus. *Psacas* (Ψακάς) means
a 'crumb,' 'morsel,' or anything
insignificant.   Psacade natus
would therefore mean 'the son of
a nobody,' and is coined by Caelius to offset Venere prognatus.
He wishes that Caesar had shown
as much sternness in putting Domitius Ahenobarbus to death after
the capture of Corfinium as Bellienus had shown in the case of the
other Domitius. — f. s. d.: for *filio
salutem dices ;* cf. *nos diliges,* Ep.
XVIII. (end) n. and Intr. 62. The
admiration which Caelius felt for
Caesar, and his enthusiasm for
the latter's brilliant campaign, give
to the letter an extravagant and
unconventional tone, which nat-

urally finds expression in the use
of colloquial and archaic words
and phrases. Cf. the notes on
*nugax, commorit, ambulando con-
fecerunt, malis orbiculatis,* etc.,
*quam sollicitus sum, nisi si, peream
si, isto, illi, discupio, quam multa,
hui,* and *se . . . dant.* The style
of the letter confirms the judgment of Tacitus in regard to Caelius (*Dial.* 21) : *Sordes autem illae
verborum et hians compositio et
inconditi sensus redolent antiqui-
tatem, nec quemquam adeo anti-
quarium puto ut Caelium ex ea
parte laudet qua antiquus est.*

    XLIX. Formiae, March 19 (or
20), 49 B.C. Cicero's reply to Ep.
XLVII. A copy of it was for-
warded to Atticus with *Att.* 9. 11
(cf. *Att.* 9. 11, end). Cicero still
cherishes the hope that he may be
able to effect a reconciliation between Caesar and Pompey, and
with that object in view, and perhaps also to present himself in a
favorable light before Caesar, he
emphasizes the neutrality of his
course thus far, and condemns the
radical steps taken by the Pompeians. Caesar's definite request

uti consilio et dignitate mea minus sum admiratus; de
gratia et de ope quid significares, mecum ipse quaerebam, spe tamen deducebar ad eam cogitationem, ut te
pro tua admirabili ac singulari sapientia de otio, de
pace, de concordia civium agi velle arbitrarer, et ad
eam rationem existimabam satis aptam esse et naturam
et personam meam. Quod si ita est et si qua de Pom- 2
peio nostro tuendo et tibi ac rei publicae reconciliando
cura te attingit, magis idoneum quam ego sum ad eam
causam profecto reperies neminem, qui et illi semper
et senatui, cum primum potui, pacis auctor fui, nec
sumptis armis belli ullam partem attigi, iudicavique eo
bello te violari, contra cuius honorem populi Romani
beneficio concessum inimici atque invidi niterentur.

that Cicero should come to Rome
and assist him in restoring public
order is not answered categori-
cally. This letter was published,
and called forth some unfavorable
criticism. For Cicero's own interpretation of certain parts of it, cf.
Att. 8. 9. 1 f.

1. **consilio**: in the letter to
Atticus accompanying this epistle
Cicero writes: *huic* (*i.e. Matio*)
*ego in multo sermone epistulam ad
me Caesaris ostendi, eam, cuius exemplum ad te antea misi, rogavique
ut interpretaretur quid esset quod
ille scriberet, ' consilio meo se uti
velle gratia dignitate ope rerum
omnium.' Respondit se non dubitare quin et opem et gratiam meam
ille ad pacificationem quaereret,
Att.* 9. 11. 2 ; cf. also *Att.* 9. 16. 1.
— **admirabili**: for Cicero's explanation of his use of this adj., cf.
Att. 8. 9. 1. — **de pace**: Caesar,
after his return to Rome from
Brundisium, proposed to negotiate
with Pompey, and the senate ap-

proved the plan, but no one was
willing to act as envoy (cf. Caes.
B. C. I. 32, 33). — **naturam**: *sc.*
as a man of peace, and not inclined to extremes in politics.

2. **magis idoneum**: see introd.
note to Ep. XLII. and *mederi*,
Ep. XLII. 2 n. — **cum primum
potui**: *sc.* after Jan. 4, on his arrival from Cilicia. Cf. *Fam.* 4. 1. 1;
16. 12. 2 ; 4. 14. 2 ; Vell. Paterc.
2. 48. 5. — **belli**: Cicero is thinking of the fact that he had not
accompanied the Pompeians in
their flight. Furthermore, he had
done practically nothing to levy
recruits for the Pompeians in Campania. Cf. *nihil fugam*, Ep. XLV.
5 n. While Cicero's statement in
the text seems to be true, it does
not harmonize with the impression
which he sought to convey to
Pompey a month earlier ; cf. *Att.*
8. 11 B. 2. See also *Att.* 7. 14. 2.
— **beneficio**: with reference to
the law passed in 52 B.C. giving
Caesar the right to sue for the

Sed, ut eo tempore non modo ipse fautor dignitatis tuae fui, verum etiam ceteris auctor ad te adiuvandum, sic me nunc Pompei dignitas vehementer movet; aliquot enim sunt anni cum vos duo delegi quos praecipue colerem et quibus essem, sicut sum, amicissimus.

3 Quamobrem a te peto vel potius omnibus te precibus oro et obtestor ut in tuis maximis curis aliquid impertias temporis huic quoque cogitationi, ut tuo beneficio bonus vir, gratus, pius denique esse in maximi benefici memoria possim. Quae si tantum ad me ipsum pertinerent, sperarem me a te tamen impetraturum, sed, ut arbitror, et ad tuam fidem et ad rem publicam pertinet me, et pacis et utriusque vestrum amicum, ad vestram et ad civium concordiam per te quam accommodatissimum conservari. Ego, cum antea tibi de Lentulo gratias egissem, cum ei saluti, qui mihi fuerat, fuisses, tum lectis eius litteris quas ad me gratissimo animo de tua liberalitate beneficioque misit, eandem me salutem a te accepisse putavi quam ille; in quem si me intellegis esse gratum, cura, obsecro, ut etiam in Pompeium esse possim.

consulship while absent from the city. Cf. Ep. XLII. introd. note, and Intr. 26.

3. aliquid impertias temporis: for Cicero's comments on this phrase, see *Att.* 8. 9. 1. — tuo beneficio : *sc.* in not forcing him to give up his neutrality, and thus losing a chance to help Pompey. — pius : *sc.* in remembering the duty he owed to his old friend Pompey. — ad tuam fidem : Caesar steadily maintained that he desired peace. — per te . . . conservari : *i.e.* that I be not constrained to appear at Rome and thus lose my neutral position, and with it my ability to secure a peaceful solution of the present difficulty. — de Lentulo: Cicero had thanked Caesar in a previous letter for his generosity in allowing Lentulus Spinther, who had been captured at Corfinium, to go free. For Caesar's reply, cf. *Att.* 9. 16. At this time Lentulus was at Puteoli; cf. *Att.* 9. 11. 1. — qui ... fuerat : in 57 B.C. Lentulus as consul had worked for Cicero's recall from exile. Cf. also Ep. XIV. 2.

L. (*Fam.* 8. 16.)

CAELIVS CICERONI S.

Exanimatus tuis litteris, quibus te nihil nisi triste 1
cogitare ostendisti, neque id quid esset perscripsti,
neque non tamen quale esset quod cogitares aperuisti,
has ad te ilico litteras scripsi. Per fortunas tuas,
Cicero, per liberos oro obsecro ne quid gravius de
salute et incolumitate tua consulas; nam deos homines-
que amicitiamque nostram testificor me tibi praedixe
neque temere monuisse, sed postquam Caesarem con-
venerim sententiamque eius, qualis futura esset parta
victoria, cognorim, te certiorem fecisse. Si existimas

L. Intimelium, April 16, 49 B.C.
This letter also appears in the collection of letters to Atticus, *Att.*
10. 9 A.

1. **tuis litteris** : in this letter,
which has not been preserved, Cicero must have conveyed the impression that he intended to join the
Pompeians. — **nihil nisi triste** :
attributive acc. Cf. Intr. 83 *a* ;
see also Stinner, 58, n. 2 ; Becher,
31. — **perscripsti** : for *perscrip-
sisti ;* cf. *praedixe* for *praedixisse*,
below. Cf. Intr. 82. — **Cicero**: the
earnestness of Caelius is shown
by his use of the vocative *Cicero*
twice in this letter. It occurs but
once elsewhere in his letters. —
oro obsecro : the use of such
double expressions is especially
common in colloquial language.
The writer or speaker seeks to
bring the idea home by coupling
words or phrases which have
essentially the same meaning. Cf.,
e.g., in this letter, *salute et incolumitate*, 1 ; *atrox et saevum*, 1 ;
sciens prudensque, 5 ; *insolentiam*

et iactationem, 5. — **testificor**: for
the fondness of colloquial Latin
for *facere* in various phrases, see
Intr. 89. As for words compounded
with *facio*, in early Latin their number was limited, but in the Vulgate
there is a host of such verbs as
beatificare, castificare, damnificare,
and this formation gave rise in
turn to *certifier, notifier*, etc., in the
Romance languages, so that the
formation supports the view that
the Romance languages were derived not from literary but from
colloquial Latin. Cf. also *civitatem*, Ep. LII. 3 n. ; *quicquid in
buccam*, Ep. LXIX. 2 n. — **sententiam**: a kind of prolepsis especially frequent in comedy ; see
Draeger, *Hist. Syn.* II. 498, and cf.
Plaut. *Trin.* 373 *scin tu illum quo
genere gnatus sit ?* Plaut. *Men.* 247
*ego illum scio quam carus sit cordi
meo*, etc. Caelius himself writes
similarly (*Fam.* 8. 10. 3): *nosti Marcellum quam tardus sit.* In general, cf. Reisig-Schmalz, *Lat. Syn.*
n. 554 and Ziemer's *Junggramma-*

eandem rationem fore Caesaris in dimittendis adversa-
riis et condicionibus ferendis, erras.   Nihil nisi atrox
et saevum cogitat atque etiam loquitur.   Iratus senatui
exiit, his intercessionibus plane incitatus est; non me-
2 hercules erit deprecationi locus.   Quare, si tibi tu, si
filius unicus, si domus, si spes tuae reliquae tibi carae
sunt, si aliquid apud te nos, si vir optimus, gener tuus,
valemus, quorum fortunam non debes velle conturbare,
ut eam causam, in quoius victoria salus nostra est,
odisse aut relinquere cogamur aut impiam cupiditatem
contra salutem tuam habeamus — denique illud cogita,
quod offensae fuerit in ista cunctatione, te subisse;
nunc te contra victorem Caesarem facere, quem dubiis
rebus laedere noluisti, et ad eos fugatos accedere quos
resistentis sequi nolueris, summae stultitiae est.   Vide
ne, dum pudet te parum optimatem esse, parum dili-
3 genter quid optimum sit eligas.   Quod si totum tibi

---

tische Streifzüge, 60 ff. — **eandem
rationem** : *i.e.* as in the case of
Domitius at Corfinium. — **nihil
cogitat** : see note on *nihil nisi
triste*, above. — **exiit**: *sc. ex urbe;*
for the reason of Caesar's anger,
see Caes. *B. C.* 1. 33. — **intercessionibus** : the tribune L. Metellus forbade Caesar's removal
of the treasure from the temple of
Saturn, and opposed all his plans
in the senate. — **mehercules** : cf.
mercule, Ep. XXV. 3 n.

2. **domus** : Cicero's family were,
however, urging him to join the
Pompeians. Cf. *Att.* 9. 6. 4 *praesertim cum ii ipsi, quorum ego causa
timidius me fortunae committebam,
uxor filia Cicerones pueri me illud
(i.e.* the cause of Pompey) *sequi mal-
lent, hoc turpe et me indignum putarent; nam Quintus quidem frater*,

*quicquid mihi placeret, id rectum
se putare aiebat, id animo aequissimo sequebatur.* — **gener tuus** :
P. Cornelius Dolabella, who was
a pronounced Caesarian. — **illud
cogita** : see note on *nihil*, 1. —
offensae : on *offensa*, Meyer (*De
Ciceronis in epistolis ad Atticum
sermone*, 17) says : ' used only in
conversation.' Cicero himself does
not use the word even in his letters, employing *offensio* in its stead.
The more colloquial writers of a
later period, however (*e.g.* Plin.,
Suet., and Petron.), use it frequently. — **optimatem . . . optimum** : the singular form **optimatem**, which is very rare in Latin,
is used here for the sake of the
pun with **optimum**. ' Don't be
so good a *nobleman* as to shut
your eyes to what is *noble*.'

persuadere non possum, saltem dum quid de Hispaniis
agamus scitur exspecta; quas tibi nuntio adventu Caesaris fore nostras.   Quam isti spem habeant amissis
Hispaniis nescio; quod porro tuum consilium sit ad
desperatos accedere, non medius fidius reperio.   Hoc, 4
quod tu non dicendo mihi significasti, Caesar audierat
ac simulatque ' Have ' mihi dixit, statim quid de te
audisset exposuit.   Negavi me scire, sed tamen ab eo
petii ut ad te litteras mitteret quibus maxime ad rema-
nendum commoveri posses.   Me secum in Hispaniam
ducit; nam, nisi ita faceret, ego prius quam ad urbem
accederem, ubicumque esses, ad te percurrissem et hoc
a te praesens contendissem atque omni vi te retinuissem.   Etiam atque etiam, Cicero, cogita ne te tuos- 5
que omnis funditus evertas, ne te sciens prudensque
eo demittas unde exitum vides nullum esse.   Quod
si te aut voces optimatium commovent aut nonnullorum hominum insolentiam et iactationem ferre non
potes, eligas censeo aliquod oppidum vacuum a bello,
dum haec decernuntur quae iam erunt confecta.   Id si
feceris, et ego te sapienter fecisse iudicabo et Caesarem
non offendes.

3. **de Hispaniis** : Caesar had
set out for Spain in the early part
of April. — **isti** : *i.e.* the Pompeians. — **accedere**: in apposition
to **tuum consilium**. A more regular construction would be *acce-
dendi.* — **medius fidius** : cf. Ep.
XVII. 2 n.

4. **dicendo** : the abl. of the
gerund indicating manner is rare
before Livy's time. Cf., however,
bellum ambulando confecerunt, Ep.
XLVIII. 1, also from Caelius.

— **litteras** : probably *Att.* 10. 8 B.
— **contendissem**: here transitive.
Cf. Intr. 83 *a*.

5. **sciens prudensque** : ' the
proverbial expression *sciens prudensque*, or *prudens et sciens*, was
used of one who takes an ill-
advised course with his eyes open '
(Landgraf,318).— **aut voces**, etc.:
i.e. the reproaches of the Optimates
on the one hand, or the insolent
demeanor of the Caesarians on
the other.

LI. (*Fam.* 2. 16.)

M. CICERO IMP. S. D. M. CAELIO.

1   Magno dolore me adfecissent tuae litterae nisi iam
et ratio ipsa depulisset omnes molestias et diuturna
desperatione rerum obduruisset animus ad dolorem
novum.   Sed tamen quare acciderit ut ex meis superioribus litteris id suspicarere quod scribis nescio; quid
enim in illis fuit praeter querelam temporum, quae non
meum animum magis sollicitum habent quam tuum?
Nam non eam cognovi aciem ingeni tui, quod ipse
videam, te id ut non putem videre.   Illud miror, adduci
potuisse te, qui me penitus nosse deberes, ut existima-
res aut me tam improvidum qui ab excitata fortuna ad
inclinatam et prope iacentem descilderem, aut tam in-
constantem ut collectam gratiam florentissimi hominis
effunderem a meque ipse deficerem et, quod initio
2 semperque fugi, civili bello interessem.   Quod est igitur meum 'triste consilium'?   Vt discederem fortasse
in aliquas solitudines.   Nosti enim non modo stomachi

LI. Cumae, May 4, 49 B.C. This
is Cicero's reply to Ep. L. A
month after he wrote this letter,
in which he disclaims any intention of joining the Pompeians, he
set out for the East. This seems
to be a frank statement, however,
of Cicero's intentions at the time.

  1. **meis superioribus litteris** :
cf. *tuis litteris*, Ep. L. 1 n. — **sollicitum habent** : the analytical
method of forming the perfect
tenses, as illustrated by *habeo dictum* for *dixi*, which came into
vogue in late Latin and in the
Romance languages, developed
out of such combinations as this ;

cf. Thielmann in *Arch. f. Lat. Lex.*
II. 372 ff. See also Intr. 84 *d*. —
nam non eam, etc., *for I have
appreciated your penetration too
well to suppose that you do not see
what I see.* Cicero's high appreciation of the political judgment
and foresight of Caelius was shown
by his selection of him as his special correspondent in 51–50 B.C. —
hominis : *i.e. Caesaris*.

  2. **triste consilium** : with reference probably to *te . . . ostendisti*,
Ep. L. 1, and to *tuum consilium*,
etc., L. 3. — **solitudines** : Dolabella, a few weeks later, in Ep.
LII. 3, suggests a similar plan. —

mei, cuius tu similem quondam habebas, sed etiam oculorum in hominum insolentium indignitate fastidium.
Accedit etiam molesta haec pompa lictorum meorum
nomenque imperi quo appellor. Eo si onere carerem,
quamvis parvis Italiae latebris contentus essem; sed
incurrit haec nostra laurus non solum in oculos, sed
iam etiam in voculas malevolorum. Quod cum ita
esset, nil tamen umquam de profectione nisi vobis
approbantibus cogitavi. Sed mea praediola tibi nota
sunt; in his mihi necesse est esse ne amicis molestus
sim. Quod autem in maritimis facillime sum, moveo
nonnullis suspicionem velle me navigare, quod tamen
fortasse non nollem, si possem ad otium; nam ad bellum
quidem qui convenit? praesertim contra eum cui spero
me satis fecisse, ab eo cui iam satis fieri nullo modo
potest. Deinde sententiam meam tu facillime perspi- 3
cere potuisti iam ab illo tempore, cum in Cumanum
mihi obviam venisti. Non enim te celavi sermonem
T. Ampi; vidisti quam abhorrerem ab urbe relinquenda,

---

quondam : Caelius had formerly
belonged to the senatorial party.
— **hominum insolentium** : cf.
insolentiam, Ep. L. 5. — **nostra
laurus** : cf. *fasces laureatos*, Ep.
XLV. 5 n. — **voculas** : the diminutive expresses contempt. The same
word, as used in Ep. IX. 1 (*recreandae voculae causa*), has its natural diminutive force, 'my weak
voice.' — **praediola** : used for
modesty's sake, while *specula* (5)
implies not that the hope is a
faint one, but that the personal
gain to Dolabella is a small advantage in comparison with the loss
which the state suffers. — **maritimis** : *sc. praediolis.* Cicero was
at Cumae. — **facillime** : cf. Intr.

85.— **ad otium** : depending loosely
upon **navigare**, as does **ad bellum** below. — **qui (convenit)** : the
archaic ablative ; cf. Intr. 81. —
contra eum : *i.e. Caesarem.* — **ab
eo**, *on his side ; sc.* the side of
Pompey.

3. **obviam venisti** : *sc.* when
Cicero returned from Cilicia. —
T. Ampi (*Balbi*) : one of Cicero's
predecessors as governor of Cilicia (cf. *Fam.* 1. 3. 2), and during
the Civil War an extreme Pompeian (cf. Vell. Paterc. 2. 40 ; Cic.
Fam. 6. 12. 3). — **ab urbe relinquenda** : for Cicero's first im-
pressions of the wisdom of the
Pompeians in abandoning Rome,
cf. *Att.* 7. 10. See also Ep. XLV.

cum audissem.   Nonne tibi adfirmavi quidvis me potius
perpessurum quam ex Italia ad bellum civile exiturum?
Quid ergo accidit cur consilium mutarem?   Nonne
omnia potius, ut in sententia permanerem?   Credas hoc
mihi velim, quod puto te existimare, me ex his miseriis
nihil aliud quaerere, nisi ut homines aliquando intellegant me nihil maluisse quam pacem, ea desperata nihil
tam fugisse quam arma civilia.   Huius me constantiae
puto fore ut numquam paeniteat.   Etenim memini in
hoc genere gloriari solitum esse familiarem nostrum
Q. Hortensium, quod numquam bello civili interfuisset;
hoc nostra laus erit inlustrior, quod illi tribuebatur
ignaviae, de nobis id existimari posse non arbitror.
4 Nec me ista terrent quae mihi a te ad timorem fidissime
atque amantissime proponuntur.   Nulla est enim acer-
bitas quae non omnibus hac orbis terrarum perturbatione impendere videatur;   quam quidem ego a re
publica meis privatis et domesticis incommodis libentissime vel istis ipsis, quae tu me mones ut caveam,
5 redemissem.   Filio meo, quem tibi carum esse gaudeo,
si erit ulla res publica, satis amplum patrimonium
relinquam in memoria nominis mei; sin autem nulla
erit, nihil accidet ei separatim a reliquis civibus.   Nam
quod rogas ut respiciam generum meum, adulescentem

---

3. — **exiturum** : after *potius quam*
in indirect discourse the infin. is
the regular construction; cf. Krebs,
Antibarbarus, II. 310. — **me nihil
maluisse**, etc.: upon Cicero's sin-
cere desire for peace, cf. *cum primum potui*, Ep. XLIX. 2 n. — **Q.
Hortensium**: the orator, who had
died in 50 B.C.

4. **quae . . . proponuntur**: with
reference to certain statements in
Caelius's letter, *e.g. si existimas,*

etc., Ep. L. 1. — **incommodis vel
istis ipsis** : *i.e.* those very misfortunes which you mention in your
letter, *e.g.* Ep. L. 5 *etiam atque
etiam, Cicero, cogita ne te tuosque
omnis funditus evertas.*

5. **memoria** : Hofmann quotes
de Domo, 146 *liberis nostris satis
amplum patrimonium paterni nominis ac memoriae nostrae relin-
quemus*, and *de Off.* 1. 121 *optima
hereditas a patribus traditur liberis*

optimum mihique carissimum, an dubitas, cum scias
quanti cum illum tum vero Tulliam meam faciam, quin
ea me cura vehementissime sollicitet, et eo magis quod
in communibus miseriis hac tamen oblectabar specula,
Dolabellam meum vel potius nostrum fore ab iis molestiis, quas liberalitate sua contraxerat, liberum? Velim
quaeras quos ille dies sustinuerit, in urbe dum fuit,
quam acerbos sibi, quam mihimet ipsi socero non
honestos. Itaque neque ego hunc Hispaniensem casum 6
exspecto, de quo mihi exploratum est ita esse ut tu
scribis, neque quicquam astute cogito. Si quando erit
civitas, erit profecto nobis locus; sin autem non erit, in
easdem solitudines tu ipse, ut arbitror, venies, in quibus nos consedisse audies. Sed ego fortasse vaticinor
et haec omnia meliores habebunt exitus; recordor enim
desperationes eorum qui senes erant adulescente me.
Eos ego fortasse nunc imitor et utor aetatis vitio. Velim
ita sit; sed tamen — . Togam praetextam texi Oppio 7

omnique patrimonio praestantior
gloria virtutis rerumque gestarum.
— **an dubitas** : when an answer
to a difficulty is thrown into the
form of a question, it is commonly
introduced by *an;* cf. *Tusc. Disp.*
1. 14 *quasi non necesse sit, quicquid*
isto modo pronunties, id aut esse
aut non esse. An tu dialecticis ne
imbutus quidem es. See also *Phi-*
lipp. 2. 38. — **liberum**: Dolabella,
when he was in power at Rome a
few years later, actually proposed
novae tabulae; cf. *Att.* 11. 23. 3.
— **quos ille dies**, etc.: *sc.* when
pressed by his creditors for payment.
    6. **Hispaniensem casum** : cf.
de Hispaniis, Ep. L. 3 n. — **astute**
cogito : for *astutum cogito;* cf.
prolixe, Ep. XXI. 1 n. — **fortasse**

vaticinor, *perhaps I am a false*
prophet. **fortasse** appears to be
cynical. Its use is quite in harmony with the markedly calm tone
which Cicero affects throughout
in replying to the impulsive letter
of Caelius. — **sed tamen** : such
an aposiopesis is especially common in the Letters when the suppressed possibility is an unpleasant
one. Böckel quotes *Att.* 7. 23.
2 *manebo igitur, etsi vivere — ;*
Fam. 14. 3. 5 *si perficitis quod agi-*
tis, me ad vos venire oportet; sin
autem — .
    7. **Oppio** : upon Oppius, see
Ep. XXX. 2. Cicero humorously
expresses in **togam praetextam**
texi the hope which Oppius cherished of securing public office
through the influence of his friend

puto te audisse; nam Curtius noster dibaphum cogitat, sed eum infector moratur. Hoc adspersi ut scires me tamen in stomacho solere ridere. De re Dolabellae quod scripsi, suadeo videas, tamquam si tua res agatur. Extremum illud erit: nos nihil turbulenter, nihil temere faciemus; te tamen oramus, quibuscumque erimus in terris, ut nos liberosque nostros ita tueare ut amicitia nostra et tua fides postulabit.

LII.   (*Fam.* 9. 9.)

DOLABELLA S. D. CICERONI.

1   S. v. g. V. et Tullia nostra recte v. Terentia minus belle habuit, sed certum scio iam convaluisse eam;

Caesar. — **Curtius** : M. Curtius Postumus, like Oppius, one of Caesar's enthusiastic admirers and followers ; cf. *Att.* 9. 2 A. 3. — **dibaphum cogitat**, *has his eye on the purple robe.* The death of Hortensius (cf. 3) had caused a vacancy in the college of augurs, and Curtius hoped to secure the position. The official robe of the augur is spoken of as **dibaphum**, either because it was of two colors, or because in obtaining one of its colors, purple, two processes were necessary. Cf. *Att.* 2. 9. 2. — **infector**, *the dyer, i.e.* Caesar. — **de re ... scripsi** : *i.e.* in 5.

LII. Caesar's camp near Dyrrachium, June, 48 B.C. For Dolabella, see Intr. 56. For Cicero's movements after writing Ep. LI., cf. Intr. 31. Dolabella was in Caesar's camp, and Cicero was probably in Pompey's.

1. **s. v. g. v.** : for *si vales, gaudeo. Valeo.* Literary Latin failed to perpetuate *gaudeo* in its archaic sense, which crops out here and

there in colloquial Latin. In Plautus it is regularly used in welcoming a friend on his return from foreign parts ; cf., *e.g.*, *Trin.* 1097 *et salve et salvom te advenisse gaudeo.* It is quite natural that Dolabella in his free and easy style should write **s. v. g.** instead of the common formula *s. v. b. e.* Cf. also Intr. 62. — **recte** : regularly used in inquiries and answers concerning one's health. Cf., *e.g.*, *satine recte* (*valetis*) ? Ter. *And.* 804 ; *nempe recte valet?* Plaut. *Bacch.* 188 ; DEM. *quid agitur?* SY. *recte* (*agitur*), Ter. *Adel.* 884. — **minus belle** (*sc. se*) **habuit** : on **belle**, see *bellus*, Ep. XXIV. 2 n. The omission of *se* in this phrase and in similar ones is colloquial ; cf. Ter. *Adel.* 365 *omnem rem modo seni quo pacto haberet enarramus ordine ; Phorm.* 429 *bene habent tibi principia.* While in Cicero the pronoun is ordinarily expressed in this phrase (cf., *e.g.*, *ea res sic se habet, Fam.* 3. 5. 3), in one or two passages it is omitted. Cf. *Fam.*

praeterea rectissime sunt apud te omnia. Etsi nullo tempore in suspicionem tibi debui venire, partium causa potius quam tua tibi suadere ut te aut cum Caesare nobiscumque coniungeres aut certe in otium referres, praecipue nunc iam inclinata victoria ne possum quidem in ullam aliam incidere opinionem nisi in eam, qua scilicet tibi suadere videar quod pie tacere non possim. Tu autem, mi Cicero, sic haec accipies ut, sive probabuntur tibi sive non probabuntur, ab optimo certe animo ac deditissimo tibi et cogitata et scripta esse iudices. Animadvertis Cn. Pompeium nec nomi- 2 nis sui nec rerum gestarum gloria neque etiam regum ac nationum clientelis quas ostentare crebro solebat esse tutum, et hoc etiam, quod infimo cuique contigit, illi non posse contingere, ut honeste effugere possit, pulso Italia, amissis Hispaniis, capto exercitu veterano, circumvallato nunc denique, quod nescio an nulli um-

16. 15. 1 *is etsi mihi nuntiavit te plane febri carere et belle habere; pro Mur.* 14 *bene habet.* A similar ellipsis occurs in colloquial Latin with *facere, agere, capessere, probare, recipere,* etc. — **certum scio** : that *certum* in the common phrases *certum scio* and *certum nescio* is an adverb is evident from Cic. *pro Scauro,* 34 *qui sive patricius sive plebeius esset, nondum enim certum constituerat;* Hor. *Sat.* 2. 6. 27 *postmodo, quod mi obsit, clare certumque locuto;* 2. 5. 100 *certum vigilans* (Hofmann). — **rectissime sunt** : cf. Intr. 85. — **suadere** : in apposition to **suspicionem**; cf. *accedere,* Ep. L. 3 n. — **inclinata victoria,** *since victory has already turned* (from the Pompeians). — **mi Cicero** : cf. *mi Pomponi,* Ep. X. n. — **ab animo** : most editors strike out **ab,** but the style

of Dolabella is very colloquial, and the Latin of everyday life was fond not only of personification in general, but of the representation of the individual by this word *animus;* cf. *anime mi (e.g.* Plaut. *Curc.* 165 ; *Men.* 182) as a term of endearment; cf. also Ep. LXXVII. 1 *praesertim vel animo defetigato tuo qui nunc requiem quaerat ex magnis occupationibus;* Ep. LXI. 8 *volo enim videre animum qui mihi audeat ista . . . apponere.*

2. **ostentare crebro solebat** : cf. Intr. 79. — **Italia**: for *ex Italia.* Cicero never omits *ex* with names of countries, and, with the exception of one passage in Caesar (*B. C.* 3. 58), perhaps the construction does not occur in prose again until we reach Silver Latin. — **circumvallato** : a dative. Pompey was surrounded by Caesar's forces ;

quam nostro acciderit imperatori. Quamobrem, quid
aut ille sperare possit aut tu, animum adverte pro tua
prudentia; sic enim facillime quod tibi utilissimum erit
consili capies.   Illud autem te peto ut, si iam ille evi-
taverit hoc periculum et se abdiderit in classem, tu tuis
rebus consulas et aliquando tibi potius quam cuivis sis
amicus.   Satis factum est iam a te vel officio vel
familiaritati, satis factum etiam partibus et ei rei p.
3 quam tu probabas.   Reliquum est, ubi nunc est res p.,
ibi simus potius quam, dum illam veterem sequamur,
simus in nulla.   Quare velim, mi iucundissime Cicero,
si forte Pompeius pulsus his quoque locis rusus alias
regiones petere cogatur, ut tu te vel Athenas vel in
quamvis quietam recipias civitatem.   Quod si eris
facturus, velim mihi scribas, ut ego, si ullo modo potero,
ad te advolem.   Quaecumque de tua dignitate ab impe-

cf. Caes. *B. C.* 3. 42 ff. — **animum
adverte** : for *animadverte*, a Plautine usage. — **illud te peto** : cf.
quod . . . hortatur, Ep. XXXVII.
1 n. and Intr. 83 *a*.

3. **reliquum est,** etc.: the omission of *ut* is archaic. — **mi iucundissime Cicero** : adjectives as
well as pronouns are sometimes
joined with proper names in colloquial Latin. Such adjectives usually express affection, admiration,
or sympathy, and are used both
with the names of persons addressed or with those of persons
spoken of. This usage is very
rare in formal Latin, and is employed only under certain well-
defined circumstances ; cf. Naegelsbach, *Stilistik*,[7] 251 ff. — **his
quoque locis** : the use of **his**
shows that Dolabella was in the
immediate vicinity of Pompey's
headquarters, *i.e.* that he was in

Caesar's camp before Dyrrachium,
and not at Rome. Had he been
writing from Rome, he would have
said *illis* or *istis*. Cf. also *circumvallato*, above. — **rusus** : an archaic form for *rursus ;* cf. Intr.
81. — **tu** : the pleonastic use of
pronouns is characteristic of the
more informal letters. In this letter, for instance, *tu* is used five
times, and in three of these cases
quite unnecessarily. Cf. *tibi tu*, Ep.
L. 2. — **civitatem** : a colloquial
substitute for *urbs* or *oppidum*.
This is its first appearance in this
sense in prose. In late Latin and
in general in the Romance languages it completely usurped the
functions of the two words mentioned above. The history of this
word offers another illustration of
the connection existing between
colloquial Latin and the Romance
languages ; cf. *testificor*, Ep. L.

ratore erunt impetranda, qua est humanitate Caesar, facillimum erit ab eo tibi ipsi impetrare, et meas tamen preces apud eum non minimum auctoritatis habituras puto.   Erit tuae quoque fidei et humanitatis curare, ut is tabellarius quem ad te misi reverti possit ad me et a te mihi litteras referat.

LIII. (*Fam.* 14. 12.)

TVLLIVS TERENTIAE SVAE S. D.

Quod nos in Italiam salvos venisse gaudes, perpetuo gaudeas velim; sed perturbati dolore animi magnisque iniuriis metuo ne id consili ceperimus quod non facile explicare possimus.   Quare quantum potes adiuva; quid autem possis mihi in mentem non venit.   In viam quod te des hoc tempore, nihil est.   Et longum est iter et non tutum et non video quid prodesse possis, si veneris.   Vale.   D. pr. Non. Nov. Brundisio.

1 n. — **advolem** : cf. *advoles*, Ep. XXV. 4 n. — **non minimum**: *non mediocre*, *non pessimum*, and other similar expressions are common in the Letters.

LIII. Brundisium, Nov. 4, 48 B.C. With reference to the battle of Pharsalus and Cicero's subsequent movements, cf. Intr. 31 f.

iniuriis : *sc.* at the hands of the Pompeians, who were angry at his refusal to take charge of their forces after the defeat at Pharsalus. — **metuo** : on the one hand, Caesar had forbidden the Pompeians to return to Italy, so that the ultimate triumph of the Caesarians would be fraught with danger to Cicero ; on the other hand, in view of their anger at him, the success of the Pompeians would be equally dangerous. — **in viam . . . nihil est** : Terentia had expressed a wish to join him at Brundisium, and the coolness with which Cicero receives the proposal is another indication of the estrangement between husband and wife. — **d. pr.** : cf. Intr. 62 (end).

LIV. (*Fam.* 14. 19.)

TVLLIVS TERENTIAE SVAE S. D.

In maximis meis doloribus excruciat me valetudo Tulliae nostrae, de qua nihil est quod ad te plura scribam; tibi enim aeque magnae curae esse certo scio. Quod me propius vultis accedere, video ita esse faciendum; etiam ante fecissem, sed me multa impediverunt, quae ne nunc quidem expedita sunt. Sed a Pomponio exspecto litteras, quas ad me quam primum perferendas cures velim. Da operam ut valeas.

LV. (*Fam.* 14. 17.)

TVLLIVS TERENTIAE SVAE S. D.

S. v. b. e. V. Si quid haberem quod ad te scriberem, facerem id et pluribus verbis et saepius. Nunc quae sint negotia vides; ego autem quomodo sim adfectus ex Lepta et Trebatio poteris cognoscere. Tu fac ut tuam et Tulliae valetudinem cures. Vale.

LIV. Brundisium, Nov. 27, 48 B.C.

in maximis . . . doloribus: cf. Intr. 32. — quod . . . accedere: Atticus had given the same advice (*Att.* 11. 5. 2), but Cicero had hesitated to adopt it, for fear of injury at the hands of the Caesarians. — multa, etc.: *e.g.* his lictors; see *Att.* 11. 6. 2. — Pomponio: cf. Intr. 58.

LV. Brundisium, Dec. 18, 48 B.C.

s. v. b. e. v.: cf. Intr. 62 and Ep. LVI. n. — Lepta: cf. Ep. XXXV. 22. — Trebatio: see Ep. XXI. introd. note. Lepta and Trebatius had met Cicero at Brundisium. Cicero's state of mind is more fully indicated in a letter written to Atticus (*Att.* 11. 8) at this time.

LVI. (*Fam.* 14. 8.)

TVLLIVS TERENTIAE SVAE S.

Si vales, bene est.   Ego valeo.   Valetudinem tuam velim cures diligentissime; nam mihi et scriptum et nuntiatum est te in febrim subito incidisse.   Quod celeriter me fecisti de Caesaris litteris certiorem, fecisti mihi gratum.   Item posthac, si quid opus erit, si quid acciderit novi, facies ut sciam.   Cura ut valeas. Vale.   D. IIII Non. Iun.

LVII. (*Fam.* 14. 11.)

TVLLIVS S. D. TERENTIAE SVAE.

S. v. b. E. v.   Tullia nostra venit ad me pr. Idus Iun.; cuius summa virtute et singulari humanitate graviore etiam sum dolore adfectus nostra factum esse neglegentia, ut longe alia in fortuna esset atque eius pietas ac dignitas postulabat.   Nobis erat in animo Ciceronem ad Caesarem mittere, et cum eo Cn.

LVI. Brundisium, June 2, 47 B.C.

si vales, bene est. ego valeo: Cicero never uses this formula in writing to Quintus, Atticus, or Tiro, nor in his early letters to Terentia, viz. *Fam.* 14. 2 (Ep. XIII.), 3 and 4 (Ep. XI), and in general he employs it only in formal letters. Its use here is therefore an indication of the coolness which had sprung up between him and his wife; cf. Intr. 52.— **facies:** cf. Intr. 84 *b*.

LVII. Brundisium, June 14, 47 B.C.

s. v. b. e. v.: *si vales, benest.*

Ego valeo; or *si vales, bene est. Valeo.* Cf. Intr. 62 and Ep. LVI., LVIII. nn. — **ad me:** *i.e.* to Brundisium ; cf. Intr. 32. — **neglegentia** : Cicero refers probably to Tullia's unpleasant position as the wife of Dolabella, a financial and moral bankrupt, who showed little affection for her, and whose agitation at this very moment for an abolition of debts was bringing further disgrace upon Tullia and her family.   But Tullia's betrothal and marriage to Dolabella took place against her father's judgment during his absence in Cilicia.   Cf. Intr. 56. — **Ciceronem:** the same

Sallustium.   Si profectus erit, faciam te certiorem.
Valetudinem tuam cura diligenter.   Vale.   xvii K.
Quinctilis.

LVIII.   *(Fam.* 14. 15.)

TVLLIVS S. D. TERENTIAE.

Si vales, benest.   Constitueramus, ut ad te antea
scripseram, obviam Ciceronem Caesari mittere, sed
mutavimus consilium, quia de illius adventu nihil audi-
ebamus.   De ceteris rebus, etsi nihil erat novi, tamen
quid velimus et quid hoc tempore putemus opus esse
ex Sica poteris cognoscere.   Tulliam adhuc mecum
teneo.   Valetudinem tuam cura diligenter.   Vale.   xii
K. Quinctilis.

LIX.   *(Fam.* 14. 20.)

TVLLIVS S. D. TERENTIAE SVAE.

In Tusculanum nos venturos putamus aut Nonis aut
postridie.   Ibi ut sint omnia parata.   Plures enim

plan is mentioned in a letter to
Atticus (*Att.* 11. 17. 1). Cf. also
si . . . conduceret, Ep. LXXIV. 2 n.
    LVIII. Brundisium, June 19,
47 B.C.
    si vales, benest : this form of
greeting is indicated by the abbreviation (*s. v. b.*) in *Fam.* 7. 29. Cf.
also *Ravennaest*, Ep. XXXI. 4 n.
— **ut . . . scripseram** : *sc.* Ep.
LVII. — **mutavimus consili-
um** : young Marcus apparently
remained in Rome until the following year, when he set out for
Athens to pursue his studies there;
cf. Intr. 54 and *Att.* 11. 18. 1. —
de illius adventu: Caesar arrived
at Tarentum from the East Sept.
24. — **Sica** : cf. Ep. X.

LIX. Venusia, Oct. 1, 47 B.C.
Cicero went to meet Caesar on
his arrival at Tarentum, Sept. 24,
and received permission to remain
in Italy. He accordingly set out
two days later for his Tusculan
villa, and wrote this letter on his
way thither. It is the last one
extant to Terentia and makes an
appropriate climax to the series of
cold, formal letters which Cicero
wrote to her during the course of
this year. At the moment of meeting his wife after an absence of
more than two years, he merely
gives certain instructions in regard
to the arrangement of the house,
in a tone almost brutal, and quite
at variance with the extreme

fortasse nobiscum erunt et, ut arbitror, diutius ibi
commorabimur.   Labrum si in balineo non est, ut
sit ; item cetera quae sunt ad victum et ad valetudinem
necessaria.   Vale.   K. Oct. de Venusino.

LX. (*Fam.* 9. 1.)

CICERO M. VARRONI S.

Ex iis litteris quas Atticus a te missas mihi legit, 1
quid ageres et ubi esses cognovi ; quando autem te
visuri essemus, nihil sane ex isdem litteris potui suspicari.   In spem tamen venio appropinquare tuum adventum; qui mihi utinam solacio sit! Etsi tot tantisque
rebus urgemur, ut nullam adlevationem quisquam non
stultissimus sperare debeat ; sed tamen aut tu potes
me aut ego te fortasse aliqua re iuvare.   Scito enim 2
me, postea quam in urbem venerim, redisse cum vete-

politeness shown everywhere else,
even in writing to his enemies.
They were divorced a few months
later.

LX. Rome, close of 47 B.C. or
early part of 46.   M. Terentius
Varro is a fine type of the old
Roman character, and one of the
most picturesque figures in the
later years of the republic. While
better known to us for his literary
work, he was by no means without ability in politics and the art
of war. He espoused the cause
of the senate in the Civil War,
and was sent to Spain as Pompey's legate. After the defeat of
Afranius and Petreius he was compelled to leave Spain, but Caesar
pardoned him, and chose him to
take charge of the library which
he intended to found.   Having

incurred the enmity of Antony, he
was put on the list of the proscribed, but rescued by a friend.
He died in 27 B.C., in his 90th
year.   He was a most fruitful
writer of both prose and poetry,
leaving behind him 74 works, containing some 620 books, dealing
with almost all the departments
of human knowledge, — with literature, history, jurisprudence,
grammar, philosophy, geography,
and agriculture. Cf. Quint. 10. 1.
95. Of his works we possess only
books 5–10 *de Lingua Latina*, and
3 books *Rerum Rusticarum*, with
fragments of his *Saturae Menip-
peae*.

1. **legit**: cf. *aliis legi*, Ep. V.
8 n.

2. **in urbem** : probably in Oct.,
47, on his return from Brundisium;

ribus amicis, id est cum libris nostris, in gratiam; etsi
non idcirco eorum usum dimiseram, quod iis suscense-
rem, sed quod eorum me suppudebat.   Videbam nimirum me in res turbulentissimas infidelissimis sociis
demissum praeceptis illorum non satis paruisse.   Igno-
scunt mihi, revocant in consuetudinem pristinam teque,
quod in eo permanseris, sapientiorem quam me dicunt
fuisse.   Quamobrem, quoniam placatis iis utor, videor
sperare debere, si te viderim, et ea quae premant et ea
quae impendeant me facile transiturum.   Quamobrem,
sive in Tusculano sive in Cumano ad te placebit sive,
quod minime velim, Romae, dummodo simul simus, per-
ficiam profecto ut id utrique nostrum commodissimum
esse diiudicetur.

LXI.   (*Fam*. 9. 16.)

CICERO [PAPIRIO] PAETO S.

1   Delectarunt me tuae litterae, in quibus primum
amavi amorem tuum, qui te ad scribendum incitavit,

cf. Ep. LIX. introd. note. — **libris
nostris** : one of the products of
his literary work was the *Brutus*,
which Cicero began in the autumn
of 47 B.C. and completed the following spring. — **eorum usum
dimiseram** : for a period of six
years, 52–47 B.C., Cicero wrote
nothing and apparently did little
literary work of any sort. — **suppudebat** : for the force of *sub*, cf.
Intr. 77. — **praeceptis illorum** :
i.e. especially the precepts of the
philosophers.   Cicero's favorite
philosopher Theophrastus advised
an absolute abstention from poli-
tics (cf. *Att.* 2. 16. 3). — **ad** (=*apud*)
te placebit : *sc. nos simul esse.*

LXI. Tusculum, July, 46 B.C.
L. Papirius Paetus, to whom are
addressed *Fam*. 9. 15–26, was a
friend of long standing.   We first
hear of him through a collection
of books which he presented to
Cicero in 60 B.C. (*Att.* 1. 20. 7; 2.
1. 12).   Like Atticus, he was an
Epicurean and held himself aloof
from politics.   The large fortune
which he had inherited made it
unnecessary for him to engage in
business, and he was able to give
himself up to the pleasures of a
literary and social life.   Cicero's
letters to him testify to their intimate relations, and offer the best
commentary upon his character

verentem ne Silius suo nuntio aliquid mihi sollicitudinis attulisset; de quo et tu mihi antea scripseras —
bis quidem eodem exemplo, facile ut intellegerem te
esse commotum — et ego tibi accurate rescripseram ut,
quomodo in tali re atque tempore, aut liberarem te ista
cura aut certe levarem.   Sed quoniam proximis quo- 2
que litteris ostendis quantae tibi curae sit ea res, sic, mi
Paete, habeto: quicquid arte fieri potuerit — non enim
iam satis est consilio pugnare ; artificium quoddam
excogitandum est, — sed tamen quicquid elaborari
aut effici potuerit ad istorum benevolentiam conciliandam et conligendam, summo studio me consecutum
esse, nec frustra, ut arbitror; sic enim color, sic observor ab omnibus iis qui a Caesare diliguntur, ut ab
iis me amari putem.   Nam etsi non facile diiudicatur
amor verus et fictus, nisi aliquod incidit eiusmodi
tempus ut, quasi aurum igni, sic benevolentia fidelis
periculo aliquo perspici possit — cetera sunt signa
communia, — sed ego uno utor argumento, quamobrem
me ex animo vereque arbitrer diligi, quia et nostra
fortuna ea est et illorum ut simulandi causa non sit.
De illo autem, quem penes est omnis potestas, nihil 3

and tastes.   No better specimens
of the *sermo urbanus* and no better
proof of Cicero's wit and brilliancy as a letter-writer can be
found than in the letters to Paetus.

1. amavi amorem : cf. *occidione occisum*, Ep. XXXIV. 7 n., and
*cura ut valeas meque ames amore
illo tuo singulari*, *Fam.* 15. 20. 3.
— Silius: probably P. Silius Nerva,
to whom, when he was propraetor
of Bithynia in 51 and 50 B.C., several letters of recommendation
(*Fam.* 13. 47, 61–65) are addressed.

— bis : for fear that one might be
lost. — eodem exemplo, *to the
same effect ;* as in *Q. fr.* 2. 10 (12).
5. *Exemplum* without *idem*, when
applied to letters, means ' a copy,'
*e.g. Caesaris litterarum exemplum
tibi misi, Att.* 7. 23. 3. — quomodo :
equivalent to *quoquomodo*, as in
Fam. 14. 14. 1 *quomodo quidem
nunc se res habet, . . . bellissime
mecum esse poteritis.*

2. sic . . . habeto : cf. Ep.
XXVI. 1 n. and Intr. 89. — istorum : *i.e.* Caesar and his friends.

video quod timeam, nisi quod omnia sunt incerta, cum
a iure discessum est, nec praestari quicquam potest,
quale futurum sit quod positum est in alterius voluntate, ne dicam libidine. Sed tamen eius ipsius nulla
re a me offensus est animus; est enim adhibita in ea
re ipsa summa a nobis moderatio. Vt enim olim arbitrabar esse meum libere loqui, cuius opera esset in
civitate libertas, sic ea nunc amissa nihil loqui quod
offendat aut illius aut eorum qui ab illo diliguntur
voluntatem. Effugere autem si velim nonnullorum
acute aut facete dictorum opinionem, fama ingeni mihi
4 est abicienda, quod, si possem, non recusarem. Sed
tamen ipse Caesar habet peracre iudicium, et, ut Servius, frater tuus, quem litteratissimum fuisse iudico,
facile diceret ' Hic versus Plauti non est, hic est,'
quod tritas auris haberet notandis generibus poetarum
et consuetudine legendi, sic audio Caesarem, cum volu-
mina iam confecerit ἀποφθεγμάτων, si quod adferatur
ad eum pro meo, quod meum non sit, reicere solere;

3. **cuius opera** : *sc.* in the sup-
pression of the Catilinarian conspiracy.

4. **Servius** : Ser. Claudius, son-
in-law of the Roman grammarian
L. Aelius Stilo (cf. Suet. *de Gram.*
3), and a well-known editor of
Plautus (cf. Aul. Gell. 3. 3. 1). He
was the cousin or half-brother of
Paetus (cf. *Att.* 1. 20. 7 ; 2. 1. 12).
— **notandis generibus poeta-
rum** : *i.e.* by noticing the characteristics of the different poets. —
ἀποφθεγμάτων : that Caesar in
his youth made a collection of
witticisms we know from Suet.
Iul. 56 *feruntur et a puero et ab
adulescentulo quaedam scripta, ut*
Laudes Herculis, *tragoedia* Oedi-

pus, *item* Dicta Collectanea; *quos
omnes libellos vetuit Augustus pub-
licari in epistula, quam brevem
admodum ac simplicem ad Pompeium Macrum, cui ordinandas
bibliothecas delegaverat, misit.* —
quod meum non sit : cf. *pro
Planc.* 35 *quod quisque dixit, me id
dixisse dicunt . . . stomachor, cum
aliorum non me digna in me conferuntur ; Fam.* 7. 32. 1 *ais enim,
ut ego discesserim* (to Cilicia), *omnia omnium dicta . . . in me con-
ferri. Quid ? tu id pateris ? non
me defendis ? non resistis ? equidem
sperabam ita notata me reliquisse
genera dictorum meorum ut cognosci sua sponte possent.* Of the
ioci Ciceronis in their published

quod eo nunc magis facit, quia vivunt mecum fere cotidie illius familiares; incidunt autem in sermone vario
multa quae fortasse illis, cum dixi, nec inlitterata nec
insulsa esse videantur; haec ad illum cum reliquis actis
perferuntur; ita enim ipse mandavit. Sic fit ut, si quid
praeterea de me audiat, non audiendum putet. Quamobrem Oenomao tuo nihil utor; etsi posuisti loco versus
Accianos. Sed quae est 'invidia' aut quid mihi nunc 5
invideri potest? Verum fac esse omnia; sic video
philosophis placuisse, iis qui mihi soli videntur vim
virtutis tenere, nihil esse sapientis praestare nisi culpam, qua mihi videor dupliciter carere, et quod ea
senserim quae rectissima fuerunt, et quod, cum viderem praesidi non satis esse ad ea obtinenda, viribus
certandum cum valentioribus non putarim; ergo in
officio boni civis certe non sum reprehendendus. Reliquum est, ne quid stulte, ne quid temere dicam aut
faciam contra potentis. Id quoque puto esse sapientis.
Cetera vero, quid quisque me dixisse dicat aut quomodo
ille accipiat aut qua fide mecum vivant ii qui me assi-

form Quintilian, however, expresses (6. 3. 5) a rather unfavorable opinion. — **cum reliquis actis**, *with the rest of the day's doings.*
— **Oenomao tuo**: Paetus, with a
flattering application to Cicero,
had quoted the words of King
Oenomaus from the *Oenomaus* of
Accius: the king speaks of his
position made difficult by the envy
of men, and compares himself to
a rock, on which the waves of
envy beat. *Saxum id facit angusti-
tatem, et sub eo saxo exuberans |
Scatebra fluviae radit rupem.* Cf.
Ribbeck, *Trag. Rom. Frag.* p. 201,
and *Röm. Trag.* p. 437. — **loco**,
appositely enough.

5. **sic** : limiting **placuisse** and
explained by **nihil . . . culpam.**
Cf. *sic habeto,* 2 n. — **praestare,**
to be responsible for; commonly
used with a thing to be desired,
e.g. felicitatem, but here employed,
as is now and then the English
phrase by which it is translated, of
a thing to be guarded against ; cf.
T. D. 3. 34 *videt culpam nullam esse
cum id, quod ab homine non potuerit praestari, evenerit.* — in **officio,**
in so far as it concerns the duty.
Cf. *liberalis in populo, Att.* 4. 17.
3 ; *quo me animo in servis esse
censes, Q. fr.* 1. 1. 17, and often in
the Letters. — **ille** : *i.e.* Caesar.

6 due colunt et observant, praestare non possum.   Ita fit
ut et consiliorum superiorum conscientia et praesentis
temporis moderatione me consoler, et illam Acci similitudinem non iam ad 'invidiam,' sed ad fortunam trans-
feram, quam existimo levem et imbecillam ab animo
firmo et gravi 'tamquam fluctum a saxo frangi' oportere.   Etenim cum plena sint monumenta Graecorum
quemadmodum sapientissimi viri regna tulerint vel
Athenis vel Syracusis, cum servientibus suis civitatibus fuerint ipsi quodammodo liberi, ego me non putem
tueri meum statum sic posse ut neque offendam ani-
7 mum cuiusquam nec frangam dignitatem meam ?   Nunc
venio ad iocationes tuas, quoniam tu secundum Oenomaum Acci, non, ut olim solebat, Atellanam, sed, ut
nunc fit, mimum introduxisti.   Quem tu mihi popellum,
quem cantharum narras ?   quam tyrotarichi patinam ?
Facilitate mea ista ferebantur antea; nunc mutata res
est.   Hirtium ego et Dolabellam dicendi discipulos

6. ad fortunam : while I am
not exposed to envy, the passage
which you quote from Accius may
well be used to describe the position of the brave man, exposed to
the assaults of fortune, as I have
been. — sapientissimi viri : *e.g.*
Socrates in Athens and Plato in
Syracuse.

7. iocationes : not found in
Cicero's orations or philosophical
works; cf. Intr. 75. — secundum
Oenomaum: the first part of your
letter was serious in its tone, the
last part humorous. 'You have
brought out, as they do at the
theatre, first a tragedy, and then
not a farce, as was done in olden
times, but a mime.' — solebat : *sc.*
fieri. — Atellanam : cf. *Oscos lu-*
dos, Ep. XIX. 3 n. — mimum :

cf. *mimos*, Ep. XIX. 1 n. — popellum : see Crit. Append. —
cantharum : see Crit. Append.
The MS. reading *denarium* can
hardly be correct, as the name of
some cheap dish is expected. —
narras : colloquial for *nominas* or
dicis. Cf. Plaut. *Men.* 402 ; Ter.
And. 367, 434, 466 ; *Heaut.* 520 ;
Ep. LXVII. 3; *Att.* 2. 7. 2 ; 11. 1 ;
13. 51. 2. — tyrotarichi patinam :
a plebeian dish of cheese and salt
fish, which, as Cicero elsewhere
also intimates in jest, Paetus was
in the habit of offering to his
guests : *ipse autem eo die in Paeti*
nostri tyrotarichum imminebam,
Att. 14. 16. 1. — Hirtium : best
known as the author of Bk. VIII.
of the *Gallic War* (cf. Suet. *Iul.*
56).   He was also the author,

habeo, cenandi magistros ; puto enim te audisse, si forte ad vos omnia perferuntur, illos apud me declamitare, me apud illos cenitare. Tu autem quod mihi bonam copiam eiures, nihil est; tum enim, cum rem habebas, quaesticulis te faciebat attentiorem, nunc, cum tam aequo animo bona perdas, non est quod non eo sis consilio ut, cum me hospitio recipias, aestimationem te aliquam putes accipere ; etiam haec levior est plaga ab amico quam a debitore. Nec tamen eas 8 cenas quaero, ut magnae reliquiae fiant ; quod erit, magnificum sit et lautum. Memini te mihi Phameae

apparently, of the celebrated 'open letter' to Cicero, which was intended to counteract the political effect of Cato's suicide and of Cicero's eulogy upon him (cf. Intr. 33, 42). — **Dolabellam** : see Intr. 56. Cassius and Pansa were also pupils of Cicero ; cf. *Fam.* 7. 33. 2. Cicero's object in giving his time to these aspirants for oratorical honors seems to have been largely a desire to secure through them the friendship of Caesar, for he writes to Atticus two years later : *haud amo vel hos designatos (i.e.* Hirtius and Pansa) *qui etiam declamare me coëgerunt, ut ne apud aquas quidem acquiescere liceret ; sed hoc meae nimiae facilitatis ; nam id erat quondam quasi necesse, Att.* 14. 12. 2.— **declamitare, cenitare:** see Intr. 79. Hirtius was fond of dining well ; cf. *Att.* 12. 2. 2 *ibi Hirtius et isti omnes ; et quidem ludi dies VIII.: quae cenae! quae deliciae!* Cf. also Ep. LXIII. 2. — **tu . . . eiures,** etc., *the fact that you take oath before me to your insolvency goes for nothing ;* cf. *eiurare militiam,* 'to swear oneself unfit for service.' Paetus is legally estopped from pleading poverty as

an excuse for not serving a fine dinner.— **quaesticulis :** cf. Intr. 76. The subject of **faciebat** is *res* understood. — **bona perdas :** as a partial relief to the debtor class, Caesar appointed arbitrators to estimate the value which certain property had before the Civil War began, and this property creditors were obliged to take at its estimated value ; cf. Caes. *B. C.* 3. 1. 2 *per eos (i.e. arbitros) fierent aestimationes possessionum et rerum, quanti quaeque earum ante bellum fuisset, atque hae creditoribus traderentur.* Many creditors, of whom Paetus seems to have been one, had suffered seriously from being obliged to accept this depreciated property.— **aestimationem . . . accipere,** *there is no reason why you should n't take the attitude of thinking that when you receive me generously, you are accepting one of the many 'cuts' in your property to which you have submitted. Aestimatio* is used concretely for the depreciated property.

8. **Phameae :** a rich and vulgar freedman like the host whom Petronius satirizes in his *Cena Tri-*

cenam narrare. Temperius fiat, cetera eodem modo.
Quod si perseveras me ad matris tuae cenam revocare,
feram id quoque; volo enim videre animum qui mihi
audeat ista quae scribis apponere, aut etiam polypum
miniani Iovis similem. Mihi crede, non audebis. Ante
meum adventum fama ad te de mea nova lautitia veniet.
Eam extimesces. Neque est quod in promulside spei
ponas aliquid, quam totam sustuli; solebam enim antea
9 debilitari oleis et lucanicis tuis. Sed quid haec loqui-
mur? Liceat modo isto venire. Tu vero — volo enim
abstergere animi tui metum — ad tyrotarichum anti-
quum redi. Ego tibi unum sumptum adferam, quod
balneum calfacias oportebit; cetera more nostro. Su-
10 periora illa lusimus. De villa Seliciana et curasti
diligenter et scripsisti facetissime; itaque puto me prae-
termissurum; salis enim satis est, sannionum parum.

malchionis; cf. also Ep. LXXXI.
2. He was grandfather of the
well-known musician Tigellius (cf.
Ep. LXXXI. 1).—temperius fiat:
the approved time for the *cena* in
Cicero's day was the ninth hour;
cf. *Fam.* 9. 26. 1 *accubueram hora
nona.* To begin the dinner too
early or to prolong it beyond a
reasonable hour was in bad form.
— ad matris tuae cenam: Manutius explains: *ut accipias me fru-
gali cena, qualem dare solebat mater
tua.* — animum: cf. *ab animo*, Ep.
LII. 1 n. — polypum . . . similem: the polypus, which is still a
favorite article of food with the
poorer people in Italy, was probably served in a red broth. This
fact suggests the comparison with
the statue of Jove, which on festal
days in olden times was streaked
with vermilion; cf. Pliny, *N. H.*
33. 111 *enumerat auctores Verrius
quibus credere necesse sit Iovis*

*ipsius simulacri faciem diebus festis
minio illini solitam*, etc., and he
adds (35. 157) *fictilem eum fuisse
et ideo miniari solitum.* See also
Crit. Append. — mihi crede: cf.
Ep. XXVII. 1 n. — promulside:
the *cena* proper in Cicero's day
was preceded by the *gustus, gusta-
tio,* or *promulsis,* as it was sometimes called from the *mulsum* or
mead which was commonly drunk
with this course. The *promulsis*
consisted of light articles of food,
such as eggs, sausage, salads,
olives, artichokes, asparagus, etc.
9. isto: cf. Ep. XLVIII. 2 n.
10. de villa Seliciana: a villa
near Naples, belonging to Q. Selicius. Cf. also Ep. LXVII. 3. —
salis . . . parum: perhaps Paetus had referred to salt works
upon the estate of Selicius, and
Cicero is commenting upon the
statement, giving a double meaning to salis. *Sannio* was one of

LXII. (*Fam.* 9. 18.)

CICERO S. D. [L. PAPIRIO] PAETO.

Cum essem otiosus in Tusculano, propterea quod 1
discipulos obviam miseram ut eadem me quam maxime
conciliarent familiari suo, accepi tuas litteras plenissi-
mas suavitatis, ex quibus intellexi probari tibi meum
consilium, quod, ut Dionysius tyrannus, cum Syracusis
pulsus esset, Corinthi dicitur ludum aperuisse, sic ego
sublatis iudiciis amisso regno forensi ludum quasi
habere coeperim. Quid quaeris? me quoque delectat 2
consilium ; multa enim consequor. Primum, id quod
maxime nunc opus est, munio me ad haec tempora.
Id cuiusmodi sit nescio ; tantum video, nullius adhuc
consilium me huic anteponere; nisi forte mori melius
fuit. In lectulo, fateor. Sed non accidit; in acie non

the regular characters in the Atel
lan farces (cf. *Oscos ludos*, Ep.
XIX. 3 n.). The sentence would
then mean: ' there is *sal* (*i.e.* ' salt '
and ' material for jests ') enough
already, but few who are in the
mood of jesting.' With *sanorum*
or *saniorum* (both gen. plur. neut.),
which some editors read, the meaning would be nearly the same. If
salis is used in a metaphorical
sense, and without a double meaning, Cicero must have in mind the
statements made in 3 f. See Crit.
Append.

LXII. Tusculum, about July
20, 46 B.C.

1. **discipulos :** *i.e.* Hirtius and
Dolabella. Cf. Ep. LXI. 7 n. —
obviam (*sc. Caesari*) : the battle
of Thapsus took place in April,
46, and Caesar was on his way
back to Rome. He reached the

city July 25. — **eadem** (*sc. opera*):
this omission is common in Plautus with *eadem* and *una*. Cf. *M. G.*
303, and Brix on *Trin.* 581. —
Dionysius : *sc.* the younger. —
sublatis iudiciis : the orderly administration of justice, with which
politics had interfered for many
years, had been almost suspended
during the Civil War ; cf. *pro
Marc.* 23 (delivered in this very
year) *omnia sunt excitanda tibi, C.
Caesar, uni, quae iacere sentis, belli
ipsius impetu, quod necesse fuit,
perculsa atque prostrata : constitu-
enda iudicia,* etc. — **regno forensi:**
cf. *regnum iudiciale*, Ep. I. 1.

2. **quid quaeris:** cf. Ep. V. 4 n.
and Intr. 98. — **id . . . nescio :** *i.e.*
' I do not know of what value
this protection is which the friendship of such men as Hirtius and
Dolabella gives me.' — **in acie non**

fui. Ceteri quidem, Pompeius, Lentulus tuus, Scipio,
Afranius foede perierunt. 'At Cato praeclare.' Iam
istuc quidem, cum volemus, licebit; demus modo operam ne tam necesse nobis sit quam illi fuit, — id quod
3 agimus. Ergo hoc primum. Sequitur illud: ipse melior
fio, primum valetudine, quam intermissis exercitationi-
bus amiseram; deinde ipsa illa, si qua fuit in me, facul-
tas orationis, nisi me ad has exercitationes rettulissem,
exaruisset. Extremum illud est, quod tu nescio an
primum putes : pluris iam pavones confeci quam tu
pullos columbinos. Tu istic te Hateriano iure delectas,
ego me hic Hirtiano. Veni igitur, si vir es, et disce a
me προλεγομένας quas quaeris ; etsi sus Minervam.
4 Si, quomodo video, aestimationes tuas vendere non

fui : see Intr. 31 (end). — **Pompeius** : see Intr. 31. — **Lentulus** :
on his death, cf. Ep. XXXV. 23 n.
— **Scipio** : Metellus Scipio, while
attempting to escape after the
battle of Thapsus, fell into the
hands of the Caesarians, and was
put to death or took his own life
(cf. *Bell. Afr.* 96). — **Afranius** :
after escaping from the battle of
Thapsus, he was captured by a
detachment of Caesar's troops,
and was murdered during an uprising of the soldiers (cf. *Bell.
Afr.* 95). See also Intr. 33. For
an account of Cato's death, see
Bell. Afr. 88. — **hoc primum** :
pointing back to *munio . . .
tempora*, above.

3. **pavones** : Hortensius is said
to have been the first to introduce the peacock as a table delicacy, at the dinner which he gave
on being elected augur (cf. Varr.
R. R. 3. 6. 6). Cf. also Hor. *Sat.*
2. 2. 23–28. In Ep. LXIII. 2 Cicero jestingly remarks upon his

boldness in giving a dinner to
Hirtius without a peacock. —
istic : *sc.* in Naples. — **iure** : with
a double meaning, 'legal proce-
dure' and 'sauce.' Cf. *ius Verri-
num, in Verr.* ii. 1. 121. Haterius
was a jurist, staying probably with
Paetus, at Naples. — **προλεγομένας** (or προηγμένα, as Mendelssohn prefers) : with a double
reference, to the 'principles' of
law and to 'receipts' in cooking.
— **sus Minervam** (*sc. docebo*) : a
favorite proverb in both Greek
and Latin for 'teaching one's bet-
ters.' Cf. *Acad.* 1. 18 *nam etsi non
sus Minervam, ut aiunt, tamen
inepte quisquis Minervam docet.*
Cf. Intr. 102.

4. **si, quomodo video, aestimationes** , *if, as I fancy, you cannot*, etc. See Crit. Append. —
aestimationes tuas : concretely
used for the land which, after its
value had been estimated, had
been turned over to him as credi-
tor. Cf. *bona perdas* and *aestima-*

potes neque ollam denariorum implere, Romam tibi
remigrandum est; satius est hic cruditate quam istic
fame.   Video te bona perdidisse ; spero idem istuc
familiaris tuos.   Actum igitur de te est, nisi provides.
Potes mulo isto quem tibi reliquum dicis esse, quoniam
cantherium comedisti, Romam pervehi.   Sella tibi erit
in ludo tamquam hypodidascalo proxima; eam pulvinus
sequetur.

LXIII.   (*Fam.* 9. 20.)

CICERO PAETO.

Dupliciter delectatus sum tuis litteris, et quod ipse 1
risi et quod te intellexi iam posse ridere ; me autem a
te, ut scurram velitem, malis oneratum esse, non mo-

tionem accipere, Ep. LXI. 7. —
ollam denariorum implere : this
phrase has a proverbial ring to it,
and calls up the picture of the
miser with his pot of gold, as he
is represented in the *Aulularia*, for
instance.   In this case, however,
the pot of Paetus contained not
gold but only silver *denarii*.   The
Greek genitive after *complere* and
implere, which is frequent in Plautus (cf., *e.g.*, *Amph.* 471 ; *Aul.* 552,
and Brix on *Men.* 901), is found
several times in Cicero. — **satius
est** : *sc. mori.* — **spero idem istuc** :
sc. passos esse.   In that case, they
could not give Paetus dinners to
keep him from going to Rome. —
actum igitur de te est, *it is all
up with you.*   Cf. *transactum est,*
Ep. XI. 3 n. — **in ludo** : *i.e.* in
Cicero's school of oratory. — **proxima** : *sc. meae sellae.*

LXIII. Rome, early part of
Aug., 46 B.C.

1. **scurram velitem** : the *scurra*
was the professional wit and diner-
out, whose object in life was to
secure a good dinner, and whose
stock in trade was flattery, wit, and
buffoonery, — the character which
has been immortalized by Terence
in the person of Phormio, and by
Plautus in Peniculus.   The *veles*
was a skirmisher.   Therefore a
scurra veles would be a wit who
carried on a guerilla warfare, taking a shot at every one and everything about him.   The comparison is made more apt by the fact
that in these very letters (*e.g.* Ep.
LXI. 7) Cicero has been threatening to dine with Paetus whether
he wishes him or not.   The opportunity of the *scurra* at a dinner
came with the *secunda mensa,*
when the company gave itself up
to conversation and jest, but the
mala (apples), which were brought
on at this point, lent themselves
as ready missiles to be used against
the jester.   In a similar way, to
the volley of wit which Cicero had
aimed at Paetus in his letters Pae-

leste tuli; illud doleo, in ista loca venire me, ut con-
stitueram, non potuisse; habuisses enim non hospitem,
sed contubernalem. At quem virum! Non eum quem
tu es solitus promulside conficere; integram famem ad
ovum adfero, itaque usque ad assum vitulinum opera
perducitur. Illa mea quae solebas antea laudare, ' O
hominem facilem! O hospitem non gravem!' abierunt;
nam omnem nostram de re p. curam, cogitationem de
dicenda in senatu sententia, commentationem causarum
abiecimus, in Epicuri nos, adversari nostri, castra conie-
cimus, nec tamen ad hanc insolentiam, sed ad illam
tuam lautitiam, veterem dico, cum in sumptum habe-
2 bas, etsi numquam plura praedia habuisti. Proinde te
para; cum homine et edaci tibi res est et qui iam aliquid intellegat; ὀψιμαθεῖς autem homines scis quam
insolentes sint. Dediscendae tibi sunt sportellae et
artolagani tui. Nos iam ex arte ista tantum habemus
ut Verrium tuum et Camillum — qua munditia homines, qua elegantia! — vocare saepius audeamus. Sed
vide audaciam; etiam Hirtio cenam dedi, sine pavone

tus replies with *mala* (raillery).
Upon the military metaphor, cf.
quas ego, etc., Ep. V. 1 n. — in ista
loca : to Paetus's villa near Naples. — promulside : cf. Ep. LXI.
8 n. — ad ovum : eggs were commonly included in the *promulsis*,
or first course at dinner. — assum
vitulinum : a favorite article of
food in the second course, or *cena*
proper, where the substantial
dishes were served. — ad hanc
insolentiam (*sc. venimus*), *to the
extravagance in vogue at present*
(or *here*). — habebas, *had money;*
the verb is used absolutely.—plura
praedia, *although you have never*

had more estates. Cf. Ep. LXI.
7 n.

2. ὀψιμαθεῖς : Horace's *seri studiorum* (*Sat.* 1. 10. 21), whose
late and superficial acquisition of
knowledge upon a subject only
increased their insolent conceit.
Cf. Aul. Gell. 11. 7. Cicero's
newly acquired knowledge had
come from Hirtius and Dolabella.
Cf. Ep. LXI. 7. — Verrium, Camillum : men noted as connois-
seurs in dinner-giving. Camillus
was a prominent real-estate lawyer;
cf. *Fam.* 5. 20. 3. — etiam Hirtio:
cf. *cenitare*, Ep. LXI. 7 n. — sine
pavone : cf. Ep. LXII. 3 n. —

tamen.   In ea cena cocus meus praeter ius fervens
nihil non potuit imitari.   Haec igitur est nunc vita 3
nostra : Mane salutamus domi et bonos viros multos,
sed tristis, et hos laetos victores qui me quidem perofficiose et peramanter observant.   Vbi salutatio defluxit,
litteris me involvo; aut scribo aut lego.   Veniunt etiam
qui me audiunt quasi doctum hominem, quia paulo sum
quam ipsi doctior.   Inde corpori omne tempus datur.
Patriam eluxi iam et gravius et diutius quam ulla mater
unicum filium.   Sed cura, si me amas, ut valeas, ne
ego te iacente bona tua comedim ; statui enim tibi ne
aegroto quidem parcere.

LXIV.   (*Fam.* 9. 17.)

CICERO [L. PAPIRIO] PAETO.

Non tu homo ridiculus es, qui, cum Balbus noster 1
apud te fuerit, ex me quaeras quid de istis municipiis

tamen : the position is colloquial.
Cf. Plaut. *Capt.* 393 *istuc ne
praecipias, facile memoria memini
tamen.*   Cf. also *ibid.* 187, 404 ;
Rud. 569, etc.

3. **bonos viros** : the Optimates.
See *bonorum virorum*, Ep. XVI.
2 n. — **perofficiose et peramanter** : cf. Intr. 77. — **salutatio** : a
good illustration of the colloquial
use of a noun in *-tio*.   Cf. Intr.
75.   In this day's programme no
mention is made of law practice
or public business, although in
earlier days Cicero has told us
that he was compelled by press
of business to forego even the
siesta which all Romans were supposed to take at midday.   The
ordinary life of a prominent Roman included the *ientaculum*, the

salutatio, the day's business, the
prandium at midday, the siesta,
the daily exercise, the bath about
3 P.M. (to the last two Cicero
refers in **inde corpori**, etc.), and
the *cena*. — **si me amas** : cf. Ep.
XIII. 3 n. and Intr. 100. — **comedim** : this archaic form leads
Böckel to regard **bona tua comedim** as a quotation from some old
poet.   Perhaps, however, the form
survived in popular speech, and
was used here to heighten the
humorous effect.

LXIV.   Rome, Aug. or Sept.,
46 B.C.

1. **Balbus** : see Ep. XXI. 2 n.
For the visit, cf. *Fam.* 9. 19. — **de
. . . agris** : there was a possibility
that land in Campania would be
assigned to Caesar's veterans, and,

et agris futurum putem? quasi aut ego quicquam sciam
quod iste nesciat, aut, si quid aliquando scio, non ex
isto soleam scire.   Immo vero, si me amas, tu fac ut
sciam quid de nobis futurum sit ; habuisti enim in tua
potestate ex quo vel ex sobrio vel certe ex ebrio scire
posses.   Sed ego ista, mi Paete, non quaero, primum
quia de lucro prope iam quadriennium vivimus, si aut
hoc lucrum est aut haec vita, superstitem rei p. vivere;
deinde quod scire quoque mihi videor quid futurum sit.
Fiet enim quodcumque volent qui valebunt, valebunt
autem semper arma.   Satis igitur nobis esse debet,
quicquid conceditur.   Hoc si qui pati non potuit, mori
2 debuit.   Veientem quidem agrum et Capenatem meti-
untur ; hoc non longe abest a Tusculano ; nihil tamen
timeo.   Fruor dum licet, opto ut semper liceat ; si id
minus contigerit, tamen, quoniam ego vir fortis idemque philosophus vivere pulcherrimum duxi, non possum
eum non diligere, cuius beneficio id consecutus sum.
Qui si cupiat esse rem p., qualem fortasse et ille vult
et omnes optare debemus, quid faciat tamen non habet;
3 ita se cum multis conligavit.   Sed longius progredior ;
scribo enim ad te.   Hoc tamen scito, non modo me
qui consiliis non intersum, sed ne ipsum quidem principem scire quid futurum sit; nos enim illi servimus,

if this were done, the estates of
Paetus would go with the rest. —
immo vero : commonly used to
make an emphatic correction; cf.,
e.g., Ter. *Phorm.* 936 ; *And.* 854.
In combination with *si, immo
vero* and *immo* are very common
in colloquial Latin ; cf., *e.g.*, Ter.
Eun. 355 ; Cic. *Fam.* 8. 8. 2 ; 8.
9. 1. — **de nobis** : in contrast to
de municipiis, above. — **primum**

. . . **vivimus** : *i.e.* the mere chance
to live was an unexpected boon.
— **de lucro** : a mercantile expression ; cf. Liv. 40. 8 ; Ter. *Phorm.*
251 *quicquid praeter spem eveniet,
omne id deputabo esse in lucro.*
For a similar use of *de*, cf. Cic. *in
Verr.* ii. 3. 105 *de publico convivari.*
   2. **ille** : *i.e.* Caesar. — **quid . . .
habet,** *he does n't know what to
do.*

ipse temporibus. Ita nec ille quid tempora postulatura sint nec nos quid ille cogitet scire possumus. Haec tibi antea non rescripsi, non quo cessator esse solerem, praesertim in litteris, sed, cum explorati nihil haberem, nec tibi sollicitudinem ex dubitatione mea nec spem ex adfirmatione adferre volui. Illud tamen adscribam, quod est verissimum, me his temporibus adhuc de isto periculo nihil audisse. Tu tamen pro tua sapientia debebis optare optima, cogitare difficillima, ferre quaecumque erunt.

LXV. (*Fam.* 6. 6.)

M. CICERO S. D. A. CAECINAE.

Vereor ne desideres officium meum — quod tibi pro 1 nostra et meritorum multorum et studiorum parium coniunctione deesse non debet, — sed tamen vereor ne litterarum a me officium requiras, quas tibi et iam pridem et saepe misissem, nisi cotidie melius exspectans gratulationem quam confirmationem animi tui

---

3. **cessator**: cf. Intr. 75. — **de isto periculo**: cf. *de istis municipiis*, 1.

LXV. Rome, Sept. or Oct., 46 B.C. A. Caecina, descended from an old Etruscan family, was a man of considerable ability, both as a writer and as an orator. Cf. Sen. *Nat. Quaest.* 2. 56. 1 *hoc apud Caecinam invenio, facundum virum et qui habuisset aliquando in eloquentia nomen, nisi illum Ciceronis umbra pressisset.* In fact it was his course as a political pamphleteer, rather than as a soldier, which led Caesar to banish him (cf. Suet. *Iul.* 75). He was at this time in Sicily. It was in his father's behalf that Cicero deliv-

ered the oration *pro Caecina* in 69 B.C. Cicero wrote two other letters to the younger Caecina (viz. *Fam.* 6. 5 and 8), one in his behalf (*Fam.* 13. 66), and received one from him (*Fam.* 6. 7).

1. **studiorum parium**: Caecina was an authority upon the Etruscan method of interpreting omens, and had written a book, *de Etrusca Disciplina*, while Cicero, after his elevation to the augurate, had interested himself in the same class of subjects, and had written a treatise called *de Auguriis*. Cf. also *Fam.* 6. 9. 1. — **litterarum**: used as a plural; cf. *litteris*, Ep. XCIX. 1 n. — **melius**: cf. *prolixe*, Ep. XXI. 1 n.

complecti litteris maluissem.   Nunc, ut spero, brevi
gratulabimur; itaque in aliud tempus id argumentum
2 epistulae differo.   His autem litteris animum tuum,
quem minime imbecillum esse et audio et spero, etsi
non sapientissimi, at amicissimi hominis auctoritate
confirmandum etiam atque etiam puto, nec iis quidem
verbis quibus te consoler ut adflictum et iam omni spe
salutis orbatum, sed ut eum de cuius incolumitate non
plus dubitem quam te memini dubitare de mea.   Nam
cum me ex re p. expulissent ii qui illam cadere posse
stante me non putarent, memini me ex multis hospiti-
bus qui ad me ex Asia, in qua tu eras, venerant, audire
3 te de glorioso et celeri reditu meo confirmare.   Si te
ratio quaedam Etruscae disciplinae, quam a patre, nobilissimo atque optimo viro, acceperas, non fefellit, ne
nos quidem nostra divinatio fallet ; quam cum sapi-
entissimorum virorum monumentis atque praeceptis
plurimoque, ut tu scis, doctrinae studio, tum magno
etiam usu tractandae rei p. magnaque nostrorum tem-
4 porum varietate consecuti sumus.   Cui quidem divina-
tioni hoc plus confidimus, quod ea nos nihil in his tam
obscuris rebus tamque perturbatis umquam omnino
fefellit.   Dicerem quae ante futura dixissem, ni vererer

2. ii qui ... putarent : Cicero
probably has Caesar and Pompey
in mind as well as Clodius. — in
qua tu eras : engaged in business
transactions probably ; cf. *Fam.* 6.
8. 2.

3. Etruscae disciplinae : cf.
studiorum parium, I. — quam ...
consecuti sumus : Cicero's forecast of the future rests upon : (1)
the teachings of wise men (monumentis atque praeceptis) and
his own study of philosophy (doc-

trinae studio); (2) his long and
varied experience in public affairs.
— plurimo : the attributive use of
the singular *plurimus* is rare in
classical prose, and is scarcely
found outside the formula *plurimam salutem dicere* (Böckel).

4. quod ea ... fefellit : cf. Cicero's own words in *Att.* 3. 15. 5 *hic
mihi primum meum consilium non
solum defuit, sed etiam obfuit.
Caeci, caeci, inquam, fuimus in ves-
titu mutando* (in putting on mourn-

ne ex eventis fingere viderer.   Sed tamen plurimi sunt
testes me et initio, ne coniungeret se cum Caesare,
monuisse Pompeium et postea, ne seiungeret; coniunctione frangi senatus opes, diiunctione civile bellum
excitari videbam.   Atque utebar familiarissime Caesare,
Pompeium faciebam plurimi, sed erat meum consilium
cum fidele Pompeio, tum salutare utrique.   Quae prae- 5
terea providerim praetereo ; nolo enim hunc de me
optime meritum existimare ea me suasisse Pompeio,
quibus ille si paruisset, esset hic quidem clarus in toga
et princeps, sed tantas opes, quantas nunc habet, non
haberet.   Eundum in Hispaniam censui.   Quod si
fecisset, civile bellum nullum omnino fuisset.   Rationem haberi absentis non tam pugnavi ut liceret quam
ut, quoniam ipso consule pugnante populus iusserat,
haberetur.   Causa orta belli est.   Quid ego praeter-
misi aut monitorum aut querelarum, cum vel iniquissi-
mam pacem iustissimo bello anteferrem ?   Victa est 6
auctoritas mea, non tam a Pompeio (nam is moveba-

ing), etc. — ne . . . seiungeret :
cf. *mederi*, Ep. XLII. 2 n., and
Philipp. 2. 24 *mea illa vox est nota
multis :* ' *Vtinam, Pompei, cum
Caesare societatem aut numquam
coisses aut numquam diremisses.*'
— Pompeium . . . plurimi : cf.
Att. 8. 2. 4 (written in 49 B.C.) *ego
pro Pompeio libenter emori possum ; facio pluris omnium hominum neminem.*
   5. hunc : *i.e.* Caesar. — ille :
i.e. Pompey. — eundum in Hispaniam censui : the province of
Spain, which Pompey had received
at the close of his second consulship, in 55 B.C., for a period of
five years, was granted to him for
five years longer at the close of
his third consulship, in 52 B.C.

While retaining the province, Pompey stayed, however, in Italy, — a
course of action the illegality of
which laid him open to the attacks
of the Caesarians ; and Cicero, in
advising that Pompey should go
to Spain, would have been acting
in the interests of harmony.   Cicero probably gave the advice indicated during the meeting of Pompeians at Capua, on Jan. 25, 49
B.C.; cf. *Fam*. 16. 12. 3 with *Att.*
7. 15. 2 ; cf. also *Att.* 7. 14. 1. —
rationem absentis : the right of
suing for the consulship while
absent from the city.   See Ep.
XLII. introd. note; also *ut absentis
ratio haberetur*, Ep. XLV. 3 n., and
Intr. 21. — ipso consule pugnante : *sc.* Pompey.

tur) quam ab iis qui duce Pompeio freti peropportunam et rebus domesticis et cupiditatibus suis illius belli victoriam fore putabant. Susceptum bellum est quiescente me, depulsum ex Italia manente me, quoad potui, sed valuit apud me plus pudor meus quam timor; veritus sum deesse Pompei saluti, cum ille aliquando non defuisset meae. Itaque vel officio vel fama bonorum vel pudore victus, ut in fabulis Amphiaraus, sic ego 'prudens et sciens ad pestem ante oculos positam' sum profectus ; quo in bello nihil adversi accidit non praedicente me. Quare quoniam, ut augures et astrologi solent, ego quoque augur publicus ex meis superioribus praedictis constitui apud te auctoritatem auguri et divinationis meae, debebit habere fidem nostra praedictio. Non igitur ex alitis involatu nec e cantu sinistro oscinis, ut in nostra disciplina est, nec ex tripudiis

7

6. **rebus**, etc.: both Cicero and Caesar believed that many Pompeians urged on the Civil War in the hope of relieving themselves from their heavy indebtedness. Cf. *Att.* 11. 6. 2 ; *Fam.* 7. 3. 2 ; and Caes. *B. C.* 3. 32 *erat plena lictorum et imperiorum provincia, differta praefectis atque exactoribus, qui praeter imperatas pecunias suo etiam privato compendio serviebant; dictitabant enim se domo patriaque expulsos omnibus necessariis egere rebus, ut honesta praescriptione rem turpissimam tegerent.* — **pudor meus** : cf. *Fam.* 7. 3. 1 *pudori tamen malui famaeque cedere quam salutis meae rationem ducere ; Att.* 9. 19. 2 *pergamus igitur, . . . nec mehercule hoc facio rei publicae causa, quam funditus deletam puto, sed ne quis me putet ingratum in eum qui me levavit iis incommodis quibus idem affecerat.* — **ali-**

quando : Pompey, who had allowed Cicero to be exiled without protest, exerted himself at last to secure his recall. — **ut in fabulis Amphiaraus** : Amphiaraus, the seer, foresaw that he should be ruined in the struggle of the Seven against Thebes (cf. Ribbeck, *Röm. Trag.* 487). Cicero probably has in mind some tragedy, perhaps the Eriphyle of Accius (cf. *ibid.* 487–497), founded upon his fate. — **prudens et sciens** : cf. Ep. L. 5 n. The phrase **prudens . . . positam** probably forms part of two iambic verses quoted from some tragic poet. Cf. Ribbeck, *Trag. Rom. Frag.* p. 256.

7. **non . . . involatu nec . . . oscinis** : birds were divided into two classes, *alites* (or *praepetes*) and *oscines ;* the latter gave omens by singing, the former by their flight and the motion of their wings; cf.

sollistimis aut soniviis tibi auguror, sed habeo alia signa
quae observem; quae etsi non sunt certiora illis, minus
tamen habent vel obscuritatis vel erroris.   Notantur 8
autem mihi ad divinandum signa duplici quadam via,
quarum alteram duco e Caesare ipso, alteram e temporum civilium natura atque ratione.   In Caesare haec
sunt : mitis clemensque natura, qualis exprimitur prae-
claro illo libro ' Querelarum ' tuarum.   Accedit quod
mirifice ingeniis excellentibus, quale est tuum, delecta-
tur.   Praeterea cedit multorum iustis et officio incensis, non inanibus aut ambitiosis voluntatibus, in quo
vehementer eum consentiens Etruria movebit.   Cur 9
haec igitur adhuc parum profecerunt ?   Quia non putat
se sustinere causas posse multorum, si tibi, cui iustius
videtur irasci posse, concesserit.   ' Quae est igitur,'
inquies, ' spes ab irato ? '   Eodem fonte se hausturum
intelleget laudes suas e quo sit leviter adspersus.
Postremo homo valde est acutus et multum providens:
intellegit te, hominem in parte Italiae minime contemnenda facile omnium nobilissimum et in communi
re p. cuivis summorum tuae aetatis vel ingenio vel

Serv. on Verg. *Aen.* 3. 361. In
taking the auspices, the augur
faced south, and the east, from
which favorable omens came,
would be to his left (*sinistra*). —
involatu : cf. *invitatu*, Ep. XXI. 2
n. — in **nostra disciplina** : Cicero
became an augur in 53 B.C. — **nec
. . . soniviis**: if the sacred chickens
ate the pulse so rapidly that a
part of it fell to the ground, the
auspices were favorable.

8. **Querelarum**: Caecina's *Liber
Querelarum* was evidently a book
complimentary to Caesar, which
Caecina wrote while in exile.

Billerbeck surmises that it was
similar to Ovid's *Tristia*. On
Caesar's clemency, cf. Suet. *Iul.*
75 and Caesar's own words to
Cicero (*Att.* 9. 16. 2) : *recte augu-
raris de me — bene enim tibi cognitus sum — nihil a me abesse longius
crudelitate.* — **consentiens Etruria** : Etruria, as Caecina's native
province, would favor his recall.

9. **leviter adspersus**: in Caecina's first political pamphlet. Cf.
introd. note. To encourage Caecina, Cicero minimizes the viru-
lence of his attack on Caesar.
Suetonius (*Iul.* 75), however, char-

gratia vel fama populi R. parem, non posse prohiberi
re publica diutius.   Nolet hoc temporis potius esse
10 aliquando beneficium quam iam suum.   Dixi de Caesare ; nunc dicam de temporum rerumque natura.
Nemo est tam inimicus ei causae quam Pompeius
animatus melius quam paratus susceperat, qui nos
malos civis dicere aut homines improbos audeat.   In
quo admirari soleo gravitatem et iustitiam et sapi-
entiam Caesaris :   numquam nisi honorificentissime
Pompeium appellat.   ' At in eius persona multa fecit
asperius.'   Armorum ista et victoriae sunt facta, non
Caesaris.   At nos quemadmodum est complexus!   Cassium sibi legavit, Brutum Galliae praefecit, Sulpicium
Graeciae, Marcellum cui maxime suscensebat cum
11 summa illius dignitate restituit.   Quo igitur haec spec-
tant ?   Rerum hoc natura et civilium temporum non

acterizes his pamphlet as a *crimi-
nosissimus liber*. — **beneficium:** a
tardy forgiveness would do little
credit to Caesar's generosity.

   10. **nos :** *i.e.* the Pompeians. —
in eius persona : with this use of
in Böckel compares Cic. *Philipp.*
14. 9 (*animus*) *dicere reformidat
quae L. Antonius in Parmensium
liberis et coniugibus effecerit ;* and
on *persona* he cites appositely
Seyffert-Müller on *Lael.* p. 21:
'*persona*, a term taken from the
masks used upon the stage, does
not mean the "person " in the
sense of the "individual ' (*homo*),
but refers always to the rôle which
one takes, or to the external relations which position, rank, and
office suggest, to that which one
is, represents, or wishes to represent.'   So here the reference is to
Pompey as the political leader. —
Cassium : in the Civil War C.
Cassius had commanded a part of

the Pompeian fleet (cf. Caes. *B. C.*
3. 101), but submitted to Caesar
soon after the battle of Pharsalus. — **Brutum :** Caesar entrusted
M. Brutus with the province of
Cisalpine Gaul in 47 B.C. — **Sulpicium :** cf. Ep. LXXV. introd.
note.   At the outbreak of the
Civil War, Servius Sulpicius Rufus, like Cicero, maintained a neutral attitude, and after the battle
of Pharsalus withdrew even from
the scene of the struggle.   At this
time he was governor of Achaia,
on Caesar's appointment. — **Marcellum :** M. Claudius Marcellus,
consul in 51 B.C., had been a bold
and consistent champion of the
senatorial party, had served under
Pompey in the Civil War until the
battle of Pharsalus was fought,
and had then gone into voluntary
banishment to Mytilene.   He was
pardoned by Caesar ; cf. *Fam.* 4.
7 and 4. 9.

patietur, nec manens nec mutata ratio feret, primum
ut non in causa pari eadem sit et condicio et fortuna
omnium, deinde ut in eam civitatem boni viri et
boni cives nulla ignominia notati non revertantur, in
quam tot nefariorum scelerum condemnati reverterunt.
Habes augurium meum ; quo, si quid addubitarem, non 12
potius uterer quam illa consolatione, qua facile fortem
virum sustentarem : te, si explorata victoria arma
sumpsisses pro re p. — ita enim tum putabas, — non
nimis esse laudandum; sin propter incertos exitus even-
tusque bellorum posse accidere ut vinceremur putas-
ses, non debere te ad secundam fortunam bene paratum
fuisse, adversam ferre nullo modo posse. Disputa-
rem etiam quanto solacio tibi conscientia tui facti,
quantae delectationi in rebus adversis litterae esse
deberent. Commemorarem non solum veterum, sed
horum etiam recentium vel ducum vel comitum tuorum
gravissimos casus, etiam externos multos claros viros
nominarem ; levat enim dolorem communis quasi legis
et humanae condicionis recordatio. Exponerem etiam 13
quemadmodum hic et quanta in turba quantaque in

---

11. **tot . . . condemnati** : cf.
Caes. *B. C.* 3. 1 *nonnullos ambitus
Pompeia lege* (of 52 B.C.) *damnatos
illis temporibus, quibus in urbe
praesidia legionum Pompeius habu-
erat . . . in integrum restituit.* Cf.
also Cic. *Att.* 10. 4. 8 ; *Fam.* 15.
19. 3 ; Suet. *Iul.* 41.

12. **illa** : explained by the following *oratio obliqua.* — **te, si explorata victoria**, etc., *if you had
taken up arms, when you thought
victory assured.* — **adversam . . .
posse**: opposed in thought to the
clause with **paratum fuisse.**
Both **paratum fuisse** and **posse**

depend on **debere.** — **quantae
delectationi** : cf. *Fam.* 6. 12. 5
*sed est unum perfugium doctrina
ac litterae . . . quae secundis rebus
delectationem modo habere videbantur, nunc vero etiam salutem.*
— **ducum vel comitum tuorum**:
cf. Ep. LXII. 2 nn. — **multos claros viros** : not *multos et claros
viros*, because **claros viros** constitutes a single idea. Cicero may
be thinking, for instance, of Alcibiades and Themistocles, who died
in banishment.

13. **quanta . . . viveremus** :
Cicero suggests the same consola-

confusione rerum omnium viveremus; necesse est enim minore desiderio perdita re p. carere quam bona. Sed hoc genere nihil opus est. Incolumem te cito, ut spero, vel potius, ut perspicio, videbimus. Interea tibi absenti et huic, qui adest, imagini animi et corporis tui, constantissimo atque optimo filio tuo, studium officium operam laborem meum iampridem et pollicitus sum et detuli, nunc hoc amplius, quod me amicissime cotidie magis Caesar amplectitur, familiares quidem eius sicuti neminem. Apud quem quicquid valebo vel auctoritate vel gratia, valebo tibi. Tu cura ut cum firmitudine te animi tum etiam spe optima sustentes.

LXVI. (*Fam.* 6. 14.)

CICERO LIGARIO.

1 Me scito omnem meum laborem, omnem operam curam studium in tua salute consumere; nam cum te

tory thought to another exile, Torquatus : *nos qui Romae sumus miserrimos esse duco, Fam.* 6. 4. 3. — hoc genere: *sc. consolationis.* — me . . . Càesar amplectitur : cf. Ep. LXI. 2. — familiares eius : *i.e.* Hirtius, Balbus, Dolabella, Matius, etc.; cf. *Fam.* 6. 12. 2. With Cicero's utterances in 4–6, *Fam.* 4. 1. 1; 6. 21. 1, and 4. 14. 2 may be profitably compared.

LXVI. Rome, Nov. 26 (Sept. 23 of the Julian calendar), 46 B.C. Q. Ligarius was in 50 B.C. legate in charge of the province of Africa. When in 49 B.C. the Pompeian P. Attius Varus, who had formerly been propraetor of Africa, appeared in the province, Ligarius delivered it over to him, and assisted him later in maintaining his position against L. Aelius Tu-

bero, who had been sent out by the senate as governor. After the battle of Thapsus, in which Ligarius took part against Caesar, he was captured by the Caesarians, and in 46 B.C. was living in exile. The combined efforts of Cicero and the relatives of Ligarius had thus far failed to secure his recall. To prevent the success of the movement in his behalf, Q. Tubero, son of Aelius Tubero, brought a charge *de vi* against him. In his defense Cicero delivered an oration (still extant), which made so deep an impression upon Caesar, who presided at the trial (cf. *pro Lig.* 37), that Ligarius was ultimately recalled. He joined later the conspiracy against Caesar, and was probably put to death under the Second Triumvirate.

semper maxime dilexi, tum fratrum tuorum, quos aeque
atque te summa benevolentia sum complexus, singularis pietas amorque fraternus nullum me patitur offici
erga te studique munus aut tempus praetermittere.
Sed quae faciam fecerimque pro te, ex illorum te litteris quam ex meis malo cognoscere; quid autem sperem
aut confidam et exploratum habeam de salute tua, id
tibi a me declarari volo.   Nam si quisquam est timidus
in magnis periculosisque rebus semperque magis ad-
versos rerum exitus metuens quam sperans secundos,
is ego sum et, si hoc vitiumst, eo me non carere con-
fiteor.   Ego idem tamen, cum a. d. v K. intercalares 2
priores rogatu fratrum tuorum venissem mane ad
Caesarem atque omnem adeundi et conveniendi illius
indignitatem et molestiam pertulissem, cum fratres et
propinqui tui iacerent ad pedes et ego essem locutus,
quae causa, quae tuum tempus postulabat, non solum
ex oratione Caesaris, quae sane mollis et liberalis fuit,

1. **exploratum habeam** : cf.
sollicitum habent, Ep. LI. 1 n. and
Intr. 84 *d.*

2. **a. d. v. K.,** etc.: *i.e.* Nov.
26 under the old calendar, or
Sept. 23 under the new.   The
Roman calendar was so far from
correct at this time, that Jan. 1,
46 B.C., came in the middle of
the autumn.   This state of
things Caesar remedied by the in-
sertion of 90 extra days into the
year 46 B.C.   The year 46 contained, therefore, 445 days.   After
the *Terminalia* (Feb. 23), an intercalary month of 23 days was inserted, and between November and
December two intercalary months
were inserted containing together
67 days.   These months were distinguished as *mensis intercalaris*

prior and *mensis intercalaris poste-
rior.*   Cf. *Zeitrechnung d. Griechen
u. Römer* by von Unger in Müller's
Handbuch, I. 816 f. — **mane ad
Caesarem** : cf. *Att.* 14. 1. 2 *cum
Sesti rogatu apud eum fuissem ex-
spectaremque sedens quoad vocarer,
dixisse eum : 'Ego dubitem quin
summo in odio sim, cum M. Cicero
sedeat nec suo commodo me convenire possit ?'*   These two passages
indicate a most significant change
in the old Roman *salutatio.*   There
is now one *patronus par excellence,*
viz. Caesar, and all Romans are
his *clientes,* who, whether plebeian
or aristocrat, must wait their turn
in his antechamber (*exspectarem
sedens*), and seek favors at his
hands by the most abject signs of
submission (**iacerent ad pedes**).

sed etiam ex oculis et vultu, ex multis praeterea si-
gnis, quae facilius perspicere potui quam scribere, hac
opinione discessi, ut mihi tua salus dubia non esset.
3 Quamobrem fac animo magno fortique sis et, si tur-
bidissima sapienter ferebas, tranquilliora laete feras.
Ego tamen tuis rebus sic adero, ut difficillimis, neque
Caesari solum, sed etiam amicis eius omnibus, quos
mihi amicissimos esse cognovi, pro te, sicut adhuc
feci, libentissime supplicabo.   Vale.

LXVII. (*Fam.* 9. 15.)

CICERO PAETO S.

1   Duabus tuis epistulis respondebo, uni quam quadri-
duo ante acceperam a Zetho, alteri quam attulerat Phi-
leros tabellarius.   Ex prioribus tuis litteris intellexi pergratam tibi esse curam meam valetudinis tuae, quam tibi
perspectam esse gaudeo; sed, mihi crede, non perinde
ut est reapse ex litteris perspicere potuisti.   Nam cum
a satis multis (non enim possum aliter dicere) et coli
me videam et diligi, nemo est illorum omnium mihi te

LXVII. Rome, first intercalary
month after Nov., 46 B.C. (Oct.
of the Julian calendar) ; see Ep.
LXVI. introd. note.   For Paetus,
see Ep. LXI. introd. note.
    1. Zetho : probably a freed-
man. — pergratam : cf. Intr. 77.
— mihi crede : see Ep. XXVII.
1 n. — perinde ut : the comparative phrases *perinde ut, proinde
ac* (cf. *Fam.* 10. 31. 2; Ep. XCII.
2), *proinde ut* (cf. *Fam.* 10. 4. 4),
and *pro eo ac* (Ep. LXXV. 1)
seem to be either legal or archaic.
Cf. Palmer's note on Plaut. *Amph.*
685. — reapse : for *re eapse = re*

ipsa. In Plautus such forms as
eumpse, eampse, and *eapse* are not
uncommon (cf. *Trin.* 974 ; *Poen.*
272, etc.).   *Reapse* occurs in some
five or six other passages in Cicero, but apparently in every case
Cicero is affecting an archaic or
colloquial tone. — satis : Wölfflin
(*Lat. u. rom. Comparation*, 23) has
shown that *satis* in Plautus and in
late Latin sometimes has the force
of *valde*, and that would seem to
be its meaning here.   Cf., for this
meaning, Plaut. *M. G.* 918 ; Ter.
And. 475 ; Cic. *Fam.* 11. 10. 3 ; 8.
11. 3 ; 10. 21 A.

iucundior. Nam quod me amas, quod id et iam pridem
et constanter facis, est id quidem magnum atque haud
scio an maximum, sed tibi commune cum multis ; quod
tu ipse tam amandus es tamque dulcis tamque in omni
genere iucundus, id est proprie tuum. Accedunt non 2
Attici, sed salsiores quam illi Atticorum, Romani veteres atque urbani sales. Ego autem — existimes licet
quidlibet — mirifice capior facetiis, maxime nostratibus, praesertim cum eas videam primum oblitas Latio
tum cum in urbem nostram est infusa peregrinitas,
nunc vero etiam bracatis et transalpinis nationibus, ut
nullum veteris leporis vestigium appareat. Itaque te
cum video, omnis mihi Granios, omnis Lucilios, vere
ut dicam, Crassos quoque et Laelios videre videor.

2. **Attici** (*sales*): the Athenians
were noted for their wit. Cf., *e.g.*,
Cic. *de Off.* I. 104 *duplex omnino
est iocandi genus : unum inliberale
petulans flagitiosum obscenum, alterum elegans urbanum ingeniosum
facetum. Quo genere non modo
Plautus noster et Atticorum anti-
qua comoedia, sed etiam philoso-
phorum Socraticorum libri referti
sunt.* The whole passage may be
read to advantage in connection
with the letter before us. — **capior
facetiis :** Cicero himself was a
noted wit, and collections of his
witticisms were made both by his
freedman Tiro, and by his friend
Trebonius. Cf. *quod meum*, etc.,
Ep. LXI. 4 n. and *Fam.* 15. 21. 2.
— **nostratibus:** cf. Ep. XXXVI.
1 n. — **oblitas Latio :** *i.e.* adulter-
ated or tinctured by the admixture
of Latin elements. — **tum :** *i.e.*
about 90 B.C., when the Italians
received the right of Roman
citizenship. — **bracatis et transalpinis nationibus :** Suetonius
(*Iul.* 80) gives the following satiri-
cal couplet as one sung in the
streets after Caesar gave the Gauls
the right of citizenship : *Gallos
Caesar in triumphum ducit, idem
in curiam.* | *Galli bracas deposue-
runt, latum clavum sumpserunt.*
— **veteris leporis :** the contests
in wit between the representatives
of different Italian towns had been
from time immemorial the favorite entertainment of the people at
their public gatherings, until they
gave way to more conventional
dramatic performances of a more
or less un-Roman character. Cf.
Fam. 7. 31. 2. — **Granios :** the
generalizing plural. Granius, a
herald noted for his wit, was a
contemporary of the orator L.
Crassus. Cicero mentions him
frequently, saying of him (*de Or.*
2. 244): *Granio quidem nemo dica-
cior.* Cf. also *Brut.* 172 ; *pro
Planc.* 33. — **omnis Lucilios :** *i.e.*
Lucilius and men like him. Cicero
refers to C. Lucilius, the satirist
(180–103 B.C.). Cf. Horace's estimate of the wit of Lucilius in *Sat.*

Moriar si praeter te quemquam reliquum habeo in quo possim imaginem antiquae et vernaculae festivitatis agnoscere. Ad hos lepores cum amor erga me tantus accedat, miraris me tanta perturbatione valetu-
3 dinis tuae tam graviter exanimatum fuisse ? Quod autem altera epistula purgas te non dissuasorem mihi emptionis Neapolitanae fuisse, sed auctorem moderationis, urbane, neque ego aliter accepi; intellexi tamen idem quod his intellego litteris, non existimasse te mihi licere id quod ego arbitrabar, res has non omnino quidem sed magnam partem relinquere. Catulum mihi narras et illa tempora. Quid simile ? ne mi quidem ipsi tunc placebat diutius abesse ab rei p. custodia; sedebamus enim in puppi et clavum tenebamus; nunc
4 autem vix est in sentina locus. An minus multa s. c. futura putas, si ego sim Neapoli ? Romae cum sum

---

1. 4 and 10. — **Crassos** : L. Licinius Crassus, the orator. Cf. Cic. *Brut.* 143 *erat summa gravitas, erat cum gravitate iunctus facetiarum et urbanitatis oratorius, non scurrilis lepos.* — **Laelios**: C. Laelius (Sapiens), the chief interlocutor in the *de Amicitia*, and introduced as a speaker into the *de Re Publica* and the *de Senectute*. Cicero says of him (*de Off.* 1. 108): *in C. Laelio multa hilaritas.* Cf. also Hor. *Sat.* 2. 1. 71 ff. It is strange, as Manutius observes, that Cicero does not in this connection mention C. Julius Caesar Strabo Vopiscus, of whom he remarks (*de Off.* 1. 133): *sale vero et facetiis Caesar, Catuli patris frater, vicit omnes.* — **moriar si**: see *ne vivam*, Ep. IV. 4 n. — **vernaculae**, *native;* opposed to *peregrinus.*

3. **emptionis Neapolitanae** : with reference to Cicero's pur-

chase of the villa of Selicius ; cf. Ep. LXI. 10. — **auctorem moderationis** : Paetus had deprecated Cicero's apparent purpose of retiring entirely from public life. — **urbane** : *sc. fecisti.* — **magnam partem** : an attributive accusative, and not the object of **relinquere** ; the attributive accusatives *magnam partem, maiorem partem,* and *maximam partem* have acquired in colloquial Latin the force of adverbs, and we find them frequently used as such in Plautus (*e.g. M. G.* 94, *Poen.* 413, etc.) and in the Letters (*e.g. Fam.* 8. 9. 3). — **Catulum**: Q. Lutatius Catulus, consul in 78 B.C. and one of the leaders of the aristocracy just after Sulla's legislation had put that party in power. — **narras,** *you talk to me of ;* cf. Ep. LXI. 7 n. — mi: cf. *mi*, Ep. XCIII. 2 n. — in puppi: cf. *contraxi vela*, Ep. V. 2 n.

et urgeo forum, s. c. scribuntur apud amatorem tuum,
familiarem meum; et quidem, cum in mentem venit,
ponor ad scribendum et ante audio s. c. in Armeniam
et Syriam esse perlatum, quod in meam sententiam factum esse dicatur, quam omnino mentionem ullam de
ea re esse factam.   Atque hoc nolim me iocari putes;
nam mihi scito iam a regibus ultimis adlatas esse litteras, quibus mihi gratias agant quod se mea sententia
reges appellaverim, quos ego non modo reges appellatos,
sed omnino natos nesciebam.   ' Quid ergo est?' Tamen, 5
quamdiu hic erit noster hic praefectus moribus, parebo
auctoritati tuae; cum vero aberit, ad fungos me tuos
conferam.   Domum si habebo, in denos dies singulos
sumptuariae legis dies conferam; sin autem minus in-
venero quod placeat, decrevi habitare apud te, scio
enim me nihil tibi gratius facere posse.   Domum Sul-
lanam desperabam iam, ut tibi proxime scripsi, sed
tamen non abieci.   Tu velim, ut scribis, cum fabris

4. **urgeo forum** : this use of
urgeo is perhaps found nowhere
else. Cf., however, *altum urgere*,
Hor. *Od.* 2. 10. 2. — **amatorem
tuum** : *i.e. Caesarem.* — **ponor ad
scribendum** : cf. *legem conscripserunt*, Ep. XV. 7 n. Those who
had witnessed and signed a bill
were said *scribendo adfuisse.* —
scito : see Ep. II. 1 n.

5. **quid ergo est**: cf. *quid quaeris*, Ep. V. 4 n. and Intr. 98. —
praefectus: in 46 B.C. Caesar was
invested with the functions of the
censorship under the new title of
praefectus morum ; cf. Dio Cass.
43. 14 ; Suet. *Iul.* 76. — **parebo
auctoritati tuae** : *i.e.* in advising
me to remain at Rome. Cicero
speaks as if he were the youth
and Paetus the man of wisdom and

experience, while the humorous
effect is heightened by the unexpected form in which the second
alternative is put, **ad fungos me
tuos conferam.** — **fungos**: highly esteemed by the Romans. Horace's Epicurean friend Catius includes them in his list of delicacies
(*Sat.* 2. 4. 20); cf. also *Fam.* 7. 26.
2 ; 9. 10. 2. Paetus would seem to
have been an experienced dinner-
giver. — **domum** : *sc.* at Naples;
cf. 3. — **sumptuariae legis** : the
expenditure which the sumptuary
laws allowed for one day, should
in Cicero's case suffice for ten.
Cicero is probably thinking of the
lex Iulia sumptuaria (cf. Lange,
Röm. Alt. 3. 450), passed in the
autumn of 46 B.C.; cf. also *Fam.*
9. 26. 4 ; 7. 26.

eam perspicias; si enim nihil est in parietibus aut in
tecto viti, cetera mihi probabuntur.

LXVIII. (*Att.* 12. 11.)

CICERO ATTICO SAL.

Male de Seio; sed omnia humana tolerabilia ducenda.
Ipsi enim quid sumus aut quamdiu haec curaturi sumus?
Ea videamus quae ad nos magis pertinent, nec tamen
multo: quid agamus de senatu. Et, ut ne quid prae-
termittam, Caesonius ad me litteras misit, Postumiam
Sulpici domum ad se venisse. De Pompei Magni filia
tibi rescripsi nihil me hoc tempore cogitare. Alteram
vero illam quam tu scribis, puto, nosti: nihil vidi foedius. Sed adsum; coram igitur.

LXVIII. Tusculum, second in-
tercalary month after Nov., 46
B.C. (old calendar); about Nov. 24
(Julian calendar).

male de Seio: *male* and *factum
male* were formulae used of a friend
recently deceased. Cf. *Att.* 15. 1 A.
1 *O factum male de Alexione; Att.*
12. 10 *male mehercule de Atha-
mante.* Cf. also Catullus, *Carm.*
3. 16 *O factum male, O miselle pas-
ser;* Ter. *Phorm.* 751 *male factum.*
Of a joyous event *factum bene* was
used; cf. Ter. *And.* 975. M. Seius,
a Roman knight, was a common
friend of Cicero and Atticus. On
him, cf. Cic. *de Off.* 2. 58; Plin.
N.H. 15. 1. — **Caesonius**: Cf. Ep.
I. 1 n. — **Postumiam Sulpici** (*sc.
uxorem*) : the omission of words of
relationship, *uxor*, *filius*, *filia* (and
servus), is very rare in Latin prose,
and Cicero allows it perhaps only
in his earlier speeches and in the

Letters. Cf., for the Letters, *Att.*
12. 20. 2 *Serviliae Claudi* (*sc. uxoris*) *pater; Att.* 12. 21. 4 *Oviae* (*sc.
uxoris*) *C. Lolli.* In Latin poetry
the omission is common. Cf.
Verg. *Aen.* 3. 319 *Hectoris* (*uxor*)
Andromache; Ovid, *Met.* 12. 622
Oileos (*filios*) *Aiax.* See also
Tac. *Ann.* 4. 11 ; Plin. *Ep.* 2. 20.
2, etc. — **domum ad se venisse** :
Cicero's divorce from Terentia
must have occurred some months
before this letter was written (cf.
Intr. 52), and Postumia was interested in Cicero's second marriage.
— **Pompei Magni filia** : over-
tures were evidently being made
for a marriage between Cicero
and Pompey's daughter. Who
the other lady was (**alteram
illam**) we do not know. — **obsignata epistula** : *signare*, *consignare*,
and *obsignare* are technical terms
for affixing the seal to a letter.

Obsignata epistula accepi tuas.   Atticae hilaritatem libenter audio; commotiunculis συμπάσχω.

LXIX. (*Att.* 12. 1.)

CICERO ATTICO SAL.

Vndecimo die postquam a te discesseram hoc lit- 1 terularum exaravi egrediens e villa ante lucem, atque eo die cogitabam in Anagnino, postero autem in Tusculano; ibi unum diem.   V Kalend. igitur ad constitutum.   Atque utinam continuo ad complexum meae Tulliae, ad osculum Atticae possim currere !   Quod quidem ipsum scribe quaeso ad me, ut, dum consisto in Tusculano, sciam quid garriat, sin rusticatur, quid

— **commotiunculis**: Attica was suffering from a *febricula ;* cf. Ep. LXIX. 2.

LXIX. Near Arpinum, second intercalary month after Nov., 46 B.C. (old calendar) ; Nov. 24 (Julian calendar).

1. **a te**: Atticus was probably in Rome. — **hoc litterularum,** *these few lines ;* a still stronger expression than *hoc litterarum,* which Cicero uses elsewhere. Cf. also *ne patiamur intermitti litterulas, Att.* 14. 4. 2· *nescio quid ab eo litterularum, Att.* 15. 4. 1. — **exaravi**: for *scripsi. Exarare* is properly used of writing with a *stilus* upon waxen tablets. It is almost certain, however, that Cicero's letters were written with pen and ink upon papyrus (cf. Intr. 59), and that *exarare* was loosely applied to the new method of writing, just as we carelessly speak of 'sealing a letter.' *Exarare* was also used of something written in haste ; cf. *ante lucem cum scriberem contra Epicureos, de eodem oleo et opera*

exaravi nescio quid ad te et ante lucem dedi, Att. 13. 38. 1 ; *certior a Pilia factus mitti ad te Idibus tabellarios, statim hoc nescio quid exaravi, Att.* 14. 22. 1 ; *plura* (*sc.* *scribam*) *otiosus ; haec, cum essem in senatu, exaravi, Fam.* 12. 20. Cf. the English expression 'to scratch off a few lines.' In the following passage, however, the reference would certainly seem to be to waxen tablets : *accubueram hora nona, cum ad te harum exemplum in codicillis exaravi, Fam.* 9. 26. 1 ; and it is possible that the letter before us, being brief, and being sent only from Arpinum to Rome, was written on waxen tablets. — **e villa**: *i.e.* from his villa at Arpinum. — **inAnagnino** : *sc. esse.* Cf. Ep. LX. 2 (end). — **ad** **constitutum** : *i.e. in locum* (or *loco*), *ubi tecum constitui* (Boot). — **Atticae** : Attica, the daughter of Atticus, must have been at this time less than eight years old. Cf. also *in eius nuptiis,* Ep. XVI. 7 n — **quod ipsum** : referring loosely to

scribat ad te; eique interea aut scribes salutem aut
nuntiabis, itemque Piliae. Et tamen, etsi continuo
congressuri sumus, scribes ad me si quid habebis.

2　　Cum complicarem hanc epistulam, noctuabundus ad
me venit cum epistula tua tabellarius, qua lecta de
Atticae febricula scilicet valde dolui. Reliqua quae
exspectabam ex tuis litteris cognovi omnia. Sed quod
scribis 'igniculum matutinum γεροντικόν,' γεροντικώτε-
ρον est memoriola vacillare. Ego enim iiii Kal. Axio
dederam, tibi iii, Quinto, quo die venissem, id est
prid. Kal. Hoc igitur habebis. Novi nihil. Quid ergo
opus erat epistula? quid, cum coram sumus et garri-
mus quicquid in buccam? Est profecto quiddam λέσχῃ,

osculum. — scribes . . . nuntiabis : Cicero is uncertain whether
Pilia and Attica are in the country
or with Atticus in Rome. — scribes: cf. Intr. 84 b.

2. complicarem : the technical
word for fastening a letter. —
noctuabundus, *after travelling all
night long ;* found nowhere else in
Latin, nor is there a verb *noctuare*
known. Adjectives in *-bundus* belong exclusively to archaic or vulgar Latin. Gellius (*N. A.* 11. 15)
indicates correctly the force of the
ending. — febricula, *slight attack
of fever.* — sed quod scribis,
etc., *but as for your writing that
'a bit of fire in the morning is a
sign of old age,' it is a surer sign
when one's memory is weak and
tottering.* Cicero was about to
visit Atticus, and had asked him
to have a little fire for him in the
morning. This request Atticus
makes the basis of a sally at his
expense, upon which Cicero re-
torts ; for, as he goes on to say,
he had written to Atticus that
he should spend with him the

third day before the Kalends, but
Atticus had forgotten the day, and
thought Cicero was to be with
him on the fifth day before the
Kalends. — memoriola : the large
number of diminutives for so short
a letter, *litterularum, igniculum,*
and memoriola, is worthy of note.
All three of these words are rare,
and have not only a diminutive
force but express other shades of
meaning, *e.g.* memoriola expresses
commiseration and sympathy. —
dederam : the object is iiii Kal.,
i.e. quartum Kal. — quo dic venissem : *sc. Romam.* — hoc igitur habebis, *take that then ;* a
phrase from the arena, of one who
has received a telling thrust or
blow. hoc refers to γεροντικώ-
τερον . . . vacillare. On habebis,
cf. *habes,* Ep. XC. 7 n. — garri-
mus : a colloquial word properly applied to the chattering of
children, as in 1. — quicquid in
buccam (*venerit*) : the vulgar expression for *quicquid in mentem
venerit.* The same phrase is found
in *Att.* 1. 12. 4 ; 7. 10 ; 14. 7. 2. In

quae habet, etiamsi nihil subest, collocutione ipsa
suavitatem.

LXX. (*Fam.* 15. 17.)

M. CICERO C. CASSIO S.

Praeposteros habes tabellarios, etsi me quidem non 1
offendunt. Sed tamen, cum a me discedunt, flagitant
litteras; cum ad me veniunt, nullas adferunt. Atque
id ipsum facerent commodius, si mihi aliquid spati ad
scribendum darent, sed petasati veniunt, comites ad
portam exspectare dicunt. Ergo ignosces; alteras
habebis has brevis, sed exspecta πάντα περὶ πάντων.
Etsi quid ego me tibi purgo, cum tui ad me inanes
veniant, ad te cum epistulis revertantur? Nos hic, ut 2
tamen ad te scribam aliquid, P. Sullam patrem mortuum habebamus: alii a latronibus, alii cruditate dice-
bant. Populus non curabat, combustum enim esse

all these cases the letters, as is this
one, are of a very colloquial character. The vulgar *bucca* has been
preserved in the Romance languages (Fr. *bouche*, Ital. *bocca*),
while its literary equivalent *os* has
been lost, just as in *cheval* and
cavallo, caballus has survived at the
expense of *equus*. Cf. *testificor*,
Ep. L. 1 n., and *civitatem*, Ep. LII.
3 n. — **est profecto quiddam**
λέσχη, *mere talk is really worth
something*.

LXX. Rome, about the close
of Dec., 46 B.C. On Cassius, cf.
Ep. LXXXVI. introd. note.

1. **praeposteros,** *unreasonable.*
—**petasati**: on journeys, especially
in hot countries, the Romans wore
broad-brimmed hats (*petasi* or *cau-
siae*). Thus of the Sycophanta in
the *Trinummus,* who is supposed

to have just arrived from Seleucia,
Charmides says (*Trin.* 851): *pol
hic quidem fungino genere st : capite
se totum tegit.* Harpax, who is to
impersonate a messenger from
abroad, is provided with a *chla-
mys,* a *machaera,* and a *petasus*
(*Pseud.* 735). Perhaps, however,
Cicero means that Cassius's messengers are always on the move,
like Mercury, who wore the *petasus.* — **ignosces**: cf. Intr. 84 *b.*
— **alteras,** etc., *this second letter
from me will be short.*

2. **P. Sullam patrem**: P. Cornelius Sulla, in whose defense
against the charge of having
taken part in the Catilinarian conspiracy Cicero delivered the oration *pro Sulla* in 62 B.C. — **habebamus**: cf. *sic habeto,* Ep. XXVI.
1 n. —**populus,** etc.: *i.e.* 'the peo-

constabat.   Hoc tu pro tua sapientia feres aequo animo; quamquam πρόσωπον πόλεως amisimus.   Caesarem putabant moleste laturum, verentem ne hasta refrixisset; Mindius macellarius et Attius pigmen-
3 tarius valde gaudebant se adversarium perdidisse.   De Hispania novi nihil, sed exspectatio valde magna; rumores tristiores, sed ἀδέσποτοι.   Pansa noster paludatus a. d. III K. Ian. profectus est, ut quivis intellegere posset, id quod tu nuper dubitare coepisti, τὸ καλὸν δι᾽ αὑτὸ αἱρετὸν esse; nam quod multos miseriis levavit et quod se in his malis hominem praebuit, mirabilis eum virorum bonorum benevolentia prose-

ple do not care (to know how he died), as long as they know he is dead.' There is probably, as Reid suggests, a double meaning in **combustum**. *Comburere* is used literally of burning **a** man's body upon a funeral pyre, as in *Att.* 14. 10. 1, and figuratively of 'roasting' a man in the courts, as our slang phrase has it. Cf. *Q. fr.* 1. 2. 6 *deinde rogas Fabium ut et patrem et filium vivos comburat, si possit; si minus, ad te mittat uti iudicio comburantur.* — **hoc tu,** etc. : Cassius replied (*Fam.* 15. 19. 3) *cuius (i.e. Sullae) ego mortem forti mercules animo tuli.* — **πρόσωπον πόλεως,** *a familiar face in the city.* — **ne hasta refrixisset :** a *hasta* stuck in the ground was the sign of an auction. Sulla gained possession at such sales of many estates confiscated by Caesar ; cf. *Fam.* 15. 19. 3 *Sulla . . . omnia bona coëmit.* This fact caused his unpopularity. Cicero speaks of his death in the same way in writing to Dolabella (*Fam.* 9. 10. 3) : *ego ceteroqui animo aequo fero ; unum vereor ne hasta Caesaris refrixerit.* Upon **refrixisset,** cf.

Intr. 99. — **Mindius . . . perdidisse :** the butcher Mindius and the perfumer Attius have now no competitor at auction sales.

3. **de Hispania :** upon **de,** cf. Intr. 91. Caesar went to Spain (cf. *Bell. Hisp.* 2) in Nov., 46 B.C., and the battle of Munda took place Mar. 17, 45, *i.e.* only a few months after this letter was written. The difficulties in which Caesar was involved, and the imminence of the decisive contest, were doubtless known at Rome. — **Pansa :** C. Vibius Pansa, the colleague of Hirtius in the consulship in 43. He had set out to join Caesar in Spain; cf. Schmidt, *Briefw.* 272. — **paludatus :** of a soldier, as *togatus* is used of a civilian. The *paludamentum* was the cloak of a commander, the *sagum* the cloak of a common soldier. — **nuper :** Cassius had lately become an Epicurean ; cf. *Fam.* 15. 16. 1. — **τὸ καλὸν δι᾽ αὑτὸ αἱρετὸν :** a Stoic doctrine which the Epicureans rejected. Cassius's analysis of Pansa's conduct is : *Pansa, qui ἡδονὴν sequitur, virtutem retinet, Fam.* 15. 19. 3.

cuta est. Tu quod adhuc Brundisi moratus es, valde 4
probo et gaudeo, et mercule puto te sapienter facturum, si ἀκενόσπουδος fueris ; nobis quidem, qui te
amamus erit gratum. Et, amabo te, cum dabis posthac aliquid domum litterarum, mei memineris. Ego
numquam quemquam ad te, cum sciam, sine meis
litteris ire patiar. Vale.

LXXI. (*Fam.* 13. 72.)

M. CICERO P. SERVILIO COLLEGAE S.

Caerelliae, necessariae meae, rem nomina possessi- 1
ones Asiaticas commendavi tibi praesens in hortis tuis
quam potui diligentissime, tuque mihi pro tua consuetudine proque tuis in me perpetuis maximisque officiis
omnia te facturum liberalissime recepisti. Meminisse

4. **si ἀκενόσπουδος fueris :** the
Epicureans discouraged an active
participation in politics, and Cicero, perhaps ironically, approves
of the consistency with which
Cassius puts into practice his new
faith by remaining at Brundisium,
remote from dangers and annoy-
ances, while Pansa had unwisely
stayed in Rome, the center of political action, and given himself
annoyance by relieving the distress
of the unfortunate Pompeians.

LXXI. Rome (?), 46 B.C. P. Servilius Vatia Isauricus (the younger
man of that name), to whom Cicero addressed *Fam.* 13. 66–72, was
in 46 B.C. proconsul of Asia. He
had been praetor in 54 B.C., and
consul in 48, and was an active
and influential member of the
party of the Optimates. He apparently belonged to the extreme
wing of that party, as he is classed

by Cicero with Bibulus, Curio, and
Favonius (Ep. XVI. 2). He was
Cicero's colleague in the college
of augurs.

1. **Caerelliae :** a woman, probably about Cicero's own age, of
whom we hear little up to the last
few years of Cicero's life, when an
intimate friendship sprung up between them. In *Att.* 13. 21. 5
Cicero calls the attention of Atticus to the fact that Caerellia succeeded in getting a copy of the *de
Finibus* from the copyists of Atticus before the book was published.
She attempted as a common friend
to bring about a reconciliation between Cicero and Publilia (cf. *Att.*
14. 19. 4 ; 15. 1. 4). Of Cicero's
letters to her only this fragment
is preserved : *haec* (*sc. Caesaris
tempora*) *aut animo Catonis ferenda
sunt aut Ciceronis stomacho* (*Quint*
6. 3. 112). — **nomina**, *debts.*

te id spero; scio enim solere. Sed tamen Caerelliae
procuratores scripserunt te propter magnitudinem provinciae multitudinemque negotiorum etiam atque etiam
2 esse commonefaciendum. Peto igitur ut memineris te
omnia quae tua fides pateretur mihi cumulate recepisse.
Equidem existimo habere te magnam facultatem — sed
hoc tui est consili et iudici — ex eo s. c. quod in here-
des C. Vennoni factum est, Caerelliae commodandi. Id
senatus consultum tu interpretabere pro tua sapientia;
scio enim eius ordinis auctoritatem semper apud te
magni fuisse. Quod reliquum est, sic velim existimes,
quibuscumque rebus Caerelliae benigne feceris, mihi te
gratissimum esse facturum.

LXXII. (*Att.* 12. 16.)

CICERO ATTICO SAL.

Te tuis negotiis relictis nolo ad me venire. Ego
potius accedam, si diutius impediere; etsi ne disces-
sissem quidem e conspectu tuo, nisi me plane nihil
ulla res adiuvaret. Quod si esset aliquod levamen, id
esset in te uno, et cum primum ab aliquo poterit esse,
a te erit. Nunc tamen ipsum sine te esse non possum.

2. **recepisse**: cf. Ep. VIII. 2 n.
— **C. Vennoni**: probably the man
mentioned in Ep. XXXV. 25.

LXXII. Astura, Mar. 10, 45
B.C. The death of his only daughter, Tullia, in the latter part of
Feb., 45, robbed Cicero of the one
person to whom he was deeply
attached, and left him inconsola-
ble. He betook himself at once
to a house belonging to Atticus,
near Rome, and then in a short
time to his solitary villa upon the
island of Astura, where he remained alone, writing daily letters
to Atticus (*Att.* 12. 9-44), and receiving letters of condolence from
Sulpicius, Dolabella, and others.
Cf. also Intr. 51, 53.

nunc ipsum, *at this very moment*. With this meaning, 'pre-
cisely' or 'just,' *ipsum* is now and
then found with adverbs of time;
cf. *nunc ipsum non dubitabo rem
tantam abicere, Att.* 7. 3. 2 ; *ne tum
ipsum accideret*, etc., *de Or.* I.

Sed nec tuae domi probabatur nec meae poteram, nec, si propius essem uspiam, tecum tamen essem ; idem enim te impediret quo minus mecum esses quod nunc etiam impedit.   Mihi adhuc nihil prius fuit hac solitudine, quam vereor ne Philippus tollat; heri enim vesperi venerat.   Me scriptio et litterae non leniunt, sed obturbant.

LXXIII. (*Fam.* 9. 11.)

CICERO DOLABELLAE S.

Vel meo ipsius interitu mallem litteras meas deside- 1
rares quam eo casu quo sum gravissime adflictus; quem ferrem certe moderatius, si te haberem ; nam et oratio tua prudens et amor erga me singularis multum leva-ret.   Sed quoniam brevi tempore, ut opinio nostra est, te sum visurus, ita me adfectum offendes ut multum a te possim iuvari, non quo ita sim fractus ut aut homi-nem me esse oblitus sim aut fortunae succumbendum

123. — **tuae domi** : where he re-mained for a short time after Tul-lia's death. — **poteram** : *sc. esse.* — **Philippus** : L. Marcius Philip-pus, the stepfather of Augustus, had a villa in the neighborhood ; cf. *Att.* 12. 18. 1. — **scriptio et litterae** : not letter-writing, but literary work.   Cf. Intr. 51. — **obturbant** : a colloquial substi-tute for *turbare ;* cf. Intr. 78.   In his letters only, according to Stin-ner, Cicero admits the following compounds of *ob: obduro, oblan-guesco, obtendo,* and *occalesco.*

LXXIII. The villa of Atticus, at Ficulea, soon after April 20, 45 B.C.   Upon Dolabella, cf. Intr. 56.   This letter is written in reply to a letter of condolence which Dolabella had sent to Cicero on hearing of Tullia's death.   Dola-bella was at this time in Spain, acting as Caesar's legate.

1. **opinio nostra** : on the ex-pectation of a decisive battle in Spain, cf. *de Hispania,* Ep. LXX. 3 n. — **ut . . . iuvari** : Cicero does not reveal, either in this letter or in his letters to Atticus, the bitter-ness which we should expect him to feel on account of the heartless and mercenary treatment which Tullia had suffered at Dolabella's hands ; cf. Ep. LVII n. — **fortu-nae . . . putem** : in a letter of sym-pathy to Titius (*Fam.* 5. 16. 2) Cic-ero writes : *est autem consolatio per-vulgata quidem illa maxime, quam semper in ore atque in animo ha-bere debemus, homines nos ut esse meminerimus ea lege natos ut om-*

putem, sed tamen hilaritas illa nostra et suavitas quae
te praeter ceteros delectabat erepta mihi omnis est ;
firmitatem tamen et constantiam, si modo fuit aliquando in nobis, eandem cognosces quam reliquisti.
2 Quod scribis proelia te mea causa sustinere, non tam
id laboro ut, si qui mihi obtrectent, a te refutentur,
quam intellegi cupio, quod certe intellegitur, me a te
amari.   Quod ut facias te etiam atque etiam rogo
ignoscasque brevitati litterarum mearum; nam et celeriter una futuros nos arbitror et nondum satis sum con-
firmatus ad scribendum.

LXXIV. (*Att.* 12. 32.)

CICERO ATTICO SAL.

1   Haec ad te mea manu.   Vide, quaeso, quid agendum
sit.   Publilia ad me scripsit matrem suam — ut cum
Publilio loquerer — ad me cum illo venturam et se una,
si ego paterer.   Orat multis et supplicibus verbis ut
liceat et ut sibi rescribam.   Res quam molesta sit
vides.   Rescripsi mihi etiam gravius esse quam tum

nibus telis fortunae proposita sit
vita nostra. Cf. also *Fam.* 5. 17.
3 *te ut hortarer rogaremque ut et*
hominem te et virum esse memi-
nisses, id est, ut et communem in-
certumque casum, quem neque vi-
tare quisquam nostrum nec prae-
stare ullo pacto potest, sapienter
ferres et dolori fortiter ac fortunae
resisteres. — hilaritas illa nostra:
the gaiety which Cicero showed in
his letters to Fadius Gallus (Ep.
IV.), to Trebatius (Ep. XXIV.–
XXVI., XXVIII.), or to Paetus
(Ep. LXI.–LXIV., LXVII.).   Cf.
also *Att.* 12. 40. 3 *hilaritatem illam*

qua hanc tristitiam temporum con-
diebamus in perpetuum amisi.
    2. proelia te sustinere : Quin-
tus, Cicero's nephew, who was
with Caesar in Spain, was speaking ill of his uncle to Caesar.
    LXXIV. Astura, Mar. 28, 45 B.C.
    1. mea manu : cf. Intr. 64. —
Publilia : cf. Intr. 52.— Publilio :
the brother of Publilia. — tum :
Publilia seems to have felt some
jealousy of the devotion which
Cicero showed for his daughter,
and the failure on Publilia's part
to show a proper feeling at Tullia's
death led him to separate from her.

cum illi dixissem me solum esse velle; qua re nolle me hoc tempore eam ad me venire.   Putabam, si nihil rescripsissem, illam cum matre venturam, nunc non puto ; apparebat enim illas litteras non illius esse. Illud autem quod fore video ipsum volo vitare, ne illae ad me veniant.   Et una est vitatio, ut alio : nollem, sed necesse est.   Te hoc nunc rogo ut explores ad quam diem hic ita possim esse ut ne opprimar.   Ages, ut scribis, temperate.   Ciceroni velim hoc proponas, ita 2 tamen, si tibi non iniquum videbitur, ut sumptus huius peregrinationis, quibus, si Romae esset domumque conduceret, quod facere cogitabat, facile contentus futurus erat, accommodet ad mercedes Argileti et Aventini et, cum ei proposueris, ipse velim reliqua moderere, quemadmodum ex iis mercedibus suppeditemus ei quod opus sit.   Praestabo nec Bibulum nec Acidinum nec Messallam, quos Athenis futuros audio, maiores sumptus

— **illas litteras non esse illius** : *sc.* but dictated by her mother. — **alio** : *sc. discedam.* — **nollem,** *I am sorry.* — **ut scribis** : *i.e. quemadmodum scribere soles* (Boot).

2. **ita . . . si,** *only in case that.* Words which denote degree obtain often from the context the idea of limitation. Cf. Ep. XXXII. 2 *a te rogabo,* . . . *ita mihi des, si tibi ut id libenter facias ante persuaseris ; in Cat.* 3. 16 *tam diu* ('only so long'); *pro Flac.* 34 *dixit tantum : nihil ostendit, nihil protulit.* — **peregrinationis** : young Cicero had just gone to Athens to prosecute his studies there, and as Cicero himself would be absent from Rome, he requested Atticus to pay the young man's expenses from the rental of certain houses. — **quibus** : referring forward to **mercedes.** — **si . . . conduceret,**

quod . . . cogitabat : only a few weeks before this time, Cicero's son, growing restive under the paternal roof, perhaps because of the treatment which his mother had received, and because of his father's marriage to Publilia, had laid before his father two alternatives, either that he should be allowed to join Caesar in Spain, or that he should have a house of his own at Rome ; (*filium*) *velle Hispaniam, requirere liberalitatem, Att.* 12. 7. 1. — **Argileti** : the Argiletum entered the Forum from the north, passing between the Curia and the Basilica Aemilia. Cicero evidently had houses (*insulae*) which he rented in the Argiletum and on the Aventine. — **Bibulum, Acidinum, Messallam** : rich young aristocrats, who were likewise to pursue their

facturos quam quod ex iis mercedibus recipietur. Itaque velim videas, primum, conductores qui sint et
quanti, deinde, ut sint qui ad diem solvant, et quid via-
tici, quid instrumenti satis sit. Iumento certe Athenis
nihil opus erit ; quibus autem in via utatur, domi sunt
plura quam opus erit, quod etiam tu animadvertis.

LXXV. (*Fam.* 4. 5.)

SERVIVS CICERONI S.

1　　Postea quam mihi renuntiatum est de obitu Tulliae
filiae tuae, sane quam pro eo ac debui graviter molesteque tuli, communemque eam calamitatem existimavi,

studies in Athens. — **quanti**: gen.
of price. — **ut sint qui ... solvant**:
the tenants failed to pay as
promptly as Cicero wished; cf.
Att. 15. 17. 1 *quod scribis tibi deesse H S C, quae Ciceroni curata
sint, velim ab Erote quaeras ubi
sit merces iusularum.* — **iumento**:
i.e. equis.

LXXV. Athens, March, 45 B.C.
Servius Sulpicius Rufus, who was
of about the same age as Cicero,
was for a time his rival in oratory,
but, soon recognizing his friend's
matchless oratorical powers, he
turned his attention to the study
of jurisprudence, and was for
many generations a leading authority in that subject. His opinions are frequently quoted in the
Digest. In politics he was, like
Cicero, a conservative and a lover
of peace, and, as such, strove during his consulship in 51 to avert
the impending struggle between
Caesar and Pompey. When the
other Pompeians left Rome at the
outbreak of the Civil War, Sulpicius was prevented by illness from

accompanying them, and, like Cicero, he hesitated long whether to
maintain a neutral position or to
join them. A lively correspondence upon this point passed between the two in 49 (cf. *Fam.* 4. 1,
2). In 46 he was made governor
of Achaia by Caesar (cf. Ep. LXV.
10). After the death of Caesar,
in the struggle between Antony
and D. Brutus, his sympathies
were again upon the side of peace
and compromise, and he was sent
by the senate, in 43 B.C., upon a
peace embassy to Antony, who
was laying siege to Mutina. While
on his way thither he died. Cicero's ninth Philippic is a eulogy on
him. This epistle, like the letters
from Caesar, Lucceius, and Dolabella (Intr. 53), was called forth
by the death of Tullia, and is perhaps the most widely known of
all the letters in the correspondence of Cicero.

1. **sane quam**: cf. Ep. XXXI.
2 n. — **(pro eo) ac**: for *ut ;* cf. *perinde ut,* Ep. LXVII. 1 n. — **graviter molesteque**: cf. *oro obsecro,*

qui, si istic adfuissem, neque tibi defuissem coramque meum dolorem tibi declarassem. Etsi genus hoc consolationis miserum atque acerbum est, propterea quia, per quos ea confieri debet propinquos ac familiaris, ii ipsi pari molestia adficiuntur neque sine lacrimis multis id conari possunt, uti magis ipsi videantur aliorum consolatione indigere quam aliis posse suum officium praestare, tamen, quae in praesentia in mentem mihi venerunt decrevi brevi ad te perscribere, non quo ea te fugere existimem, sed quod forsitan dolore impeditus minus ea perspicias. Quid est quod tanto opere 2 te commoveat tuus dolor intestinus? Cogita quemadmodum adhuc fortuna nobiscum egerit : ea nobis erepta esse quae hominibus non minus quam liberi cara esse debent, patriam honestatem dignitatem honores omnis. Hoc uno incommodo addito quid ad dolorem adiungi potuit? Aut qui non in illis rebus exercitatus animus callere iam debet atque omnia minoris existimare? An illius vicem, credo, doles? Quo- 3

Ep. L. 1 n. — **istic adfuissem**: pleonastic for *adfuissem*. — **istic** : *i.e.* in Italy. Servius was in Athens. — **miserum atque acerbum**: see *graviter molesteque*, above. — **confieri**: colloquial from two points of view: (1) it is used for the simple verb *fieri*. Lorenz, Introd. to *Pseud.* n. 36, says: 'In general compounds with *con* are popular throughout the old comic poetry, and must have been extremely common in the Roman vulgar language of that day. The loss of force which the preposition suffers in almost every case bears witness to this fact'; (2) *facio*, when compounded with a preposition, has *-fici* for its passive form. Such

forms as *confieri* and *defieri* for *confici* and *defici* are found only in colloquial and archaic Latin. Cf., *e.g.*, Plaut. *Trin.* 408; *M. G.* 1261; and Thielmann, *De sermonis proprietatibus in primis Ciceronis libris*, 52. — **propinquos ac familiaris** : cf. *graviter molesteque*, above. The words quoted are thrown in loosely, as an appositive to **quos**. — **perspicias** : the mood is determined by **forsitan**.

2. **qui** : cf. Intr. 81. — **minoris existimare**: *existimare* (for *aestimare*) with the genitive is colloquial. Cf. Plaut. *Capt.* 682 *dum ne ob malefacta peream, parvi existumo*; Suet. *Aug.* 40 *magni existimans*. Cf. also Intr. 78.

tiens in eam cogitationem necesse est et tu veneris et
nos saepe incidimus, hisce temporibus non pessime cum
iis esse actum quibus sine dolore licitum est mortem
cum vita commutare! Quid autem fuit quod illam hoc
tempore ad vivendum magno opere invitare posset?
Quae res? Quae spes? Quod animi solacium? Vt cum
aliquo adulescente primario coniuncta aetatem gereret?
Licitum est tibi, credo, pro tua dignitate ex hac iuventute generum diligere, cuius fidei liberos tuos te tuto
committere putares! An ut ea liberos ex sese pareret, quos cum florentis videret laetaretur, qui rem a
parente traditam per se tenere possent, honores ordinatim petituri essent, in re publica, in amicorum nego-

3. **tu veneris . . . nos incidimus:** there is an implied compliment in the application of **veneris** to Cicero and **incidimus** to
himself. — **cum iis esse actum :**
cf. *nobiscum egerit,* 2. — **licitum
est :** *licitum est* and *placitum est,*
for *licuit* and *placuit,* belong to the
sermo cotidianus. Cf. *Fam.* 8. 4. 4 ;
Ep. XI. 5; and see Krebs, *Antibarbarus,* II. 22. These passive forms
are frequent in comedy. Cf. Plaut.
Men. 589 ; Ter. *And.* 443, and
Donatus, note. See also *placitum est,* Ep. LXXXVI. 2 n. —
quae res? **quae spes?** a case of
assonance. — **adulescente :** Tullia's last husband, Dolabella, must
have been about 18 years old at
the time of their marriage ; cf.
Appian, *B. C.* 2. 129. — **primario :**
adjectives in *-arius* are very rare
in Cicero, but common in colloquial Latin. Cf. *manufestarius,*
Plaut. *Aul.* 469 ; *praesentarius,*
Trin. 1081 ; *quasillarius, Petron.*
132, etc. Cf. also Lorenz to Plaut.
Pseud. 952. In late Latin the ending is especially common, *e.g. bar-*

*baricarius, scandularius, muliercu-
larius,* etc. — **ut . . . gereret :**
ironical. Tullia's first husband,
Piso, died prematurely, and from
Crassipes and Dolabella she was
divorced after an unhappy wedded
life (cf. Intr. 53). — **licitum est :**
cf. *licitum est,* above. Schmalz
thinks that **licitum est . . . putares** may be an adaptation of Ter.
Hec. 212: *qui illum decrerunt dignum, suos quoi liberos committerent.*
— **ex hac iuventute :** the degen-
erate youth of to-day, as they
seemed to be to the old man of 60,
although Sulpicius has in mind
Tuliia's unhappy married life in
particular. — **honores ordinatim :**
i.e. the offices of quaestor, aedile,
praetor, and consul. — **ordinatim:**
for classical *ordine.* Adverbs in
-im are found frequently in early
and late Latin, but in the Ciceronian period, with a few exceptions, their use is confined to colloquial Latin. Neue, *Formenlehre,*
II. 662, says : ' Adverbs in *-im*
are especially common in archaic
Latin, and in late writers who

tiis libertate sua usuri ? Quid horum fuit quod non
prius quam datum est, ademptum sit ? ' At vero malum
est liberos amittere.'   Malum : nisi hoc peius sit, haec
sufferre et perpeti.   Quae res mihi non mediocrem 4
consolationem attulit, volo tibi commemorare, si forte
eadem res tibi dolorem minuere possit.   Ex Asia redi-
ens cum ab Aegina Megaram versus navigarem, coepi
regiones circumcirca prospicere.   Post me erat Aegina,
ante me Megara, dextra Piraeus, sinistra Corinthus,

affected an archaic style '; and of
ecclesiastical Latin, Rönsch writes
(*It. u. Vulg.* 473): ' In the formation of adverbs the substitution
of the endings *-im* and *-iter* for *-e*
is especially common.' In Cicero's
letters to Atticus we find *affatim*,
summatim, and *syllabatim*.   No
one of these forms occurs, however, in the orations. — **malum
. . . perpeti**: ' it is a misfortune
to lose one's children, unless it
may be regarded as so much
greater a misfortune to witness
the ruin of one's country and the
loss of one's liberty that all other
afflictions become insignificant.'

4. **volo tibi commemorare** :
used politely for *tibi commemo-
rabo*. — **si forte** : the use of these
particles with the subjunctive is
Plautine (Schmalz). — **ex Asia** :
i.e. from Samos, whither he had
gone after the battle of Pharsalus.
— **ab Aegina** : *ab* and *ex* to denote motion from, and *in* to denote
position in and motion towards,
with names of towns and islands
are archaic. Cf. *ex Epheso*, Plaut.
Bacch. 236 ; *in Epheso*, *M. G.*
778 ; *in Ephesum*, *Bacch.* 171.
Spengel (to Ter. *And.* 70). — **circumcirca** : to be joined with **regiones**.   The use of an adverb
for an attributive adj. is of colloquial origin.   It becomes espe-

cially common in Livy ; cf., *e.g.*,
Liv. 3. 26. 3 *nulla magnopere clade
accepta* ; 6. 39. 6 *nullo publice emolumento*.   In the Letters we find
(*Fam.* 12. 14. 3) *ullae privatim
iniuriae* ; (*Att.* 11. 12. 1) *profecti-
onis meae tum* ; (Ep. XCI. 2) *tuus
deinde discessus.* Cf. Intr. 85 *b* ;
Brenous, *Les Hellénismes dans la
Syn. Lat.* pp. 394 ff. ; Nägelsbach,
Stil. pp. 229 f.   Such compounds
as *circumcirca, praeterpropter*, and
exadversum are colloquial. — **post
me erat . . . esse natum**: Schmalz
(*Z. f. Gymn.* 1881, p. 90) calls
attention to an interesting imitation of this passage in one of St.
Ambrose's letters (*Ep.* 39. 3) :
*nempe de Bononiensi veniens urbe,
a tergo Claternam, ipsam Bononiam, Mutinam, Rhegium derelin-
quebas, in dextera erat Brixillum,*
etc. *Tot igitur semirutarum urbium cadavera terrarumque sub eodem conspectu exposita funera non
te admonent*, etc.   Byron's stanzas
in Childe Harold (IV. 44) are also
inspired by it. — **Aegina**: its decline probably dated from its submission to Athens, in 457 or 456 B.C.
— **Megara**: destroyed in 307 B.C.
by Demetrius Poliorcetes. — **Piraeus** : taken by Sulla in 86 B.C.
— **Corinthus** : utterly destroyed
by Mummius in 146 B.C. Cf. Cic.
de Leg. Agr. 2. 87 *Corinthi vesti-*

quae oppida quodam tempore florentissima fuerunt,
nunc prostrata et diruta ante oculos iacent. Coepi
egomet mecum sic cogitare : ' Hem! nos homunculi
indignamur, si quis nostrum interiit aut occisus est,
quorum vita brevior esse debet, cum uno loco tot oppidum cadavera proiecta iacent ? Visne tu te, Servi,
cohibere et meminisse hominem te esse natum ? '
Crede mihi, cogitatione ea non mediocriter sum con-
firmatus. Hoc, idem si tibi videtur, fac ante oculos
tibi proponas. Modo uno tempore tot viri clarissimi
interierunt, de imperio p. R. tanta deminutio facta est,
omnes provinciae conquassatae sunt ; in unius mulierculae animula si iactura facta est, tanto opere commo-
veris ? Quae si hoc tempore non diem suum obisset,
paucis post annis tamen ei moriendum fuit, quoniam
5 homo nata fuerat. Etiam tu ab hisce rebus animum

gium vix relictum est. — **quodam
tempore**: for *quondam ;* cf. Intr.
101. — **prostrata et diruta** : cf.
graviter molesteque, 1. — **mecum
. . . cogitare**: a pleonasm common
in the older poets; cf., *e.g.*, Ter. *Ad.*
30, 500 ; *Eun.* 629; *Heaut.* 385. —
hem : cf. Intr. 92. — **homunculi** :
the diminutive expresses contempt.
— **nos homunculi . . . iacent** :
Böckel quotes from Rutilius Na-
matianus, 1. 413 :

*Non indignemur mortalia corpora
solvi :
Cernimus exemplis oppida posse
mori.*

— **oppidum** : the shorter form
of the genitive plural of the second
declension is especially common in
early Latin. — **visne te cohibere**:
imperative ; see Intr. 84 *b*, and
cf. Petron. 111 *vis tu reviviscere ?
vis discusso muliebri errore, quam*

diu licuerit, lucis commodis frui?
— **si tibi videtur**: a colloquial
expression, while *si videtur* is the
more formal and elegant phrase.
The former is therefore the common expression in the Letters.
Cicero himself uses *si videtur*
in the Letters but once, while
si tibi videtur occurs 18 times
or more. Cf. *Att.* 8. 6. 2, etc. —
ante oculos tibi: cf. *mihi ante
oculos*, Ep. XIII. 3 n. — **tot viri
clarissimi** : cf. Ep. LXII. 2 nn.
— **deminutio** : the struggle between Caesar and Pompey had
lessened the majesty of Rome,
and weakened the sense of alle-
giance on the part of peoples dependent on her. — **mulierculae,
animula** : the diminutives convey
an idea of pity and depreciation. —
mulierculae, *a delicate woman.* —
hoc tempore : for *nunc ;* cf. *quodam tempore*, above.

ac cogitationem tuam avoca atque ea potius reminiscere
quae digna tua persona sunt : illam quamdiu ei opus
fuerit vixisse, una cum re publica fuisse, te patrem
suum praetorem consulem augurem vidisse, adulescentibus primariis nuptam fuisse, omnibus bonis prope
perfunctam esse ; cum res publica occideret, vita ex-
cessisse. Quid est quod tu aut illa cum fortuna hoc
nomine queri possitis? Denique noli te oblivisci Ciceronem esse et eum qui aliis consueris praecipere et
dare consilium, neque imitari malos medicos qui in
alienis morbis profitentur tenere se medicinae scien-
tiam, ipsi se curare non possunt, sed potius, quae aliis
tute praecipere soles, ea tute tibi subice atque apud
animum propone. Nullus dolor est quem non longin- 6
quitas temporis minuat ac molliat. Hoc te exspectare
tempus tibi turpe est ac non ei rei sapientia tua te
occurrere. Quod si qui etiam inferis sensus est, qui
illius in te amor fuit pietasque in omnis suos, hoc certe
illa te facere non vult. Da hoc illi mortuae, da ceteris
amicis ac familiaribus qui tuo dolore maerent, da
patriae, ut, si qua in re opus sit, opera et consilio tuo
uti possit. Denique, quoniam in eam fortunam de-
venimus ut etiam huic rei nobis serviendum sit, noli

---

5. persona : cf. *persona*, Ep.
LXV. 10 n.—adulescentibus primariis: cf. *adulescente primario*, 3.
— praecipere et dare consilium:
cf. *graviter molesteque*, 1.—neque :
the negative idea of the preceding
noli has turned the conjunction
into a negative; cf. Hor. *Od.* 2. 12. 2.
— malos medicos, tute tibi:
cf. Intr. 93. Servius uses the
strengthened forms *tute* and *egomet*, 4.

6. minuat ac molliat, tem-

pus tibi turpe : alliterative. —
hoc . . . est : the use of tibi and
te in the same clause is unclas-
sical. In his use of the same
phrase, *Fam.* 4. 6. 1, Cicero omits
the dative. — illi mortuae : a fair
instance of the use of the demonstrative as equivalent to the Greek
article. Cf. *Tusc. Disp.* 5. 78 *quae
est victrix, ea laeta prosequentibus
suis una cum viro in rogum impo-
nitur, illa victa maesta discedit*
(Watson).—denique, etc.: added

committere ut quisquam te putet non tam filiam quam
rei publicae tempora et aliorum victoriam lugere. Plura
me ad te de hac re scribere pudet ne videar prudentiae
tuae diffidere. Quare, si hoc unum proposuero, finem
faciam scribendi : vidimus aliquotiens secundam pul-
cherrime te ferre fortunam magnamque ex ea re te
laudem apisci ; fac aliquando intellegamus adversam
quoque te aeque ferre posse neque id maius quam
debeat tibi onus videri, ne ex omnibus virtutibus haec
una tibi videatur deesse. Quod ad me attinet, cum te
tranquilliorem animo esse cognoro, de iis rebus quae
hic geruntur, quemadmodumque se provincia habeat,
certiorem faciam. Vale.

LXXVI. (*Fam.* 4. 6.)

M. CICERO S. D. SER. SVLPICIO.

1   Ego vero, Servi, vellem, ut scribis, in meo gravissimo
casu adfuisses; quantum enim praesens me adiuvare
potueris et consolando et prope aeque dolendo facile
ex eo intellego quod litteris lectis aliquantum adquievi ;

as an afterthought. — **finem faciam**: alliterative. Cf. **ferre fortunam**, below. — **apisci**: Cicero
uses *apisci* only twice, *Att.* 8. 14.
3 and *de Leg.* 1. 52. Cf., however, Plaut. *Trin.* 367 ; Ter.
Heaut. 693 ; *Phorm.* 406. — **quod
. . . attinet** : cf. Intr. 91. — **provincia** : *i.e.* Achaia.

While the letter reveals the real
sorrow of Sulpicius at Cicero's
loss, he seeks to comfort his
friend, not so much by assuring
him of his sympathy, as by setting before him certain philosophical considerations. The training

of Sulpicius as a lawyer and a
jurist goes far to explain the peculiarities in his style and Latinity.
The epistle will illustrate how
closely allied legal, archaic, and
colloquial Latin are; in fact, the
expressions which have been noted
as common in colloquial speech,
are really legal archaisms as used
by Sulpicius.

LXXVI. From the villa of
Atticus, at Ficulea, Apr., 45 B.C.
Cicero's reply to Ep. LXXV.

1. **ego vero**: cf. Ep. XXX. 1 n.
— **adfuisses** : without *hic;* cf.
Ep. LXXV. 1 n. — **Servius tuus:**

nam et ea scripsisti quae levare luctum possent, et in
me consolando non mediocrem ipse animi dolorem ad-
hibuisti. Servius tamen tuus omnibus officiis, quae illi
tempori tribui potuerunt, declaravit et quanti ipse me
faceret et quam suum talem erga me animum tibi
gratum putaret fore. Cuius officia iucundiora scilicet
saepe mihi fuerunt, numquam tamen gratiora. Me
autem non oratio tua solum et societas paene aegritu-
dinis, sed etiam auctoritas consolatur; turpe enim esse
existimo me non ita ferre casum meum ut tu, tali
sapientia praeditus, ferendum putas. Sed opprimor
interdum et vix resisto dolori, quod ea me solacia defi-
ciunt quae ceteris, quorum mihi exempla propono,
simili in fortuna non defuerunt. Nam et Q. Maximus,
qui filium consularem, clarum virum et magnis rebus
gestis, amisit, et L. Paullus, qui duo septem diebus, et
vester Galus, et M. Cato, qui summo ingenio, summa
virtute filium perdidit, iis temporibus fuerunt ut eorum
luctum ipsorum dignitas consolaretur ea quam ex re
publica consequebantur. Mihi autem amissis orna- 2
mentis iis quae ipse commemoras quaeque eram maxi-

the son of Sulpicius. — **iucundiora,** *more productive of pleasure.*
— **gratiora,** *more worthy of gratitude;* cf. *Att.* 3. 24. 2 *ista veritas,
etiam si iucunda non est, mihi tamen
grata est.* — **societas:** cf. Servius's
expression of personal sorrow in
Ep. LXXV. 1. — **mihi exempla
propono:** cf. *fac*, etc., Ep. LXXV.
4 n. — **Q. Maximus:** Q. Fabius
Maximus, who won the epithet of
Cunctator in the war with Hanni-
bal. — **magnis rebus gestis:** parallel with **clarum.** — **L. Paullus:** L. Aemilius Paullus, the
conqueror of Perseus in 168 B.C.
— **vester Galus:** C. Sulpicius

Galus conquered the Ligurians in
166 B.C. He belonged to the Sul-
pician *gens,* hence **vester. — M.
Cato:** M. Porcius Cato, the censor. On these instances, cf. *Tusc.
Disp.* 3. 70 *quid, qui non putant
lugendum viris? qualis fuit Q.
Maximus efferens filium consularem, qualis L. Paullus duobus
paucis diebus amissis filiis, qualis
M. Cato praetore designato mortuo
filio, quales reliqui, quos in Consolatione collegimus. Quid hos
aliud placavit nisi quod luctum et
maerorem esse non putabant viri?*

2. **quae ipse commemoras:**
cf. Ep. LXXV. 5. — **unum illud**

mis laboribus adeptus, unum manebat illud solacium,
quod ereptum est. Non amicorum negotiis, non rei
publicae procuratione impediebantur cogitationes meae,
nihil in foro agere libebat, adspicere curiam non poteram, existimabam, id quod erat, omnis me et industriae
meae fructus et fortunae perdidisse. Sed cum cogitarem haec mihi tecum et cum quibusdam esse communia,
et cum frangerem iam ipse me cogeremque illa ferre
toleranter, habebam quo confugerem, ubi conquiesce-
rem, cuius in sermone et suavitate omnis curas dolo-
resque deponerem. Nunc autem hoc tam gravi vulnere
etiam illa quae consanuisse videbantur recrudescunt ;
non enim, ut tum me a re publica maestum domus
excipiebat quae levaret, sic nunc domo maerens ad
rem publicam confugere possum ut in eius bonis adqui-
escam. Itaque et domo absum et foro, quod nec eum
dolorem, quem de re publica capio, domus iam consolari
3 potest nec domesticum res publica. Quo magis te
exspecto teque videre quam primum cupio : maius
mihi solacium adferre ratio nulla potest quam coniunctio consuetudinis sermonumque nostrorum ; quamquam sperabam tuum adventum — sic enim audiebam
— appropinquare. Ego autem cum multis de causis te
exopto quam primum videre, tum etiam ut ante com-
mentemur inter nos qua ratione nobis traducendum sit
hoc tempus, quod est totum ad unius voluntatem
accommodandum et prudentis et liberalis et, ut per-

solacium: *i.e.* the companionship
and sympathy of Tullia. — amicorum negotiis: as an advocate ;
cf. *sublatis iudiciis*, Ep. LXII. 1 n.
— curiam: the ascendancy of Caesar had taken away the dignity
and influence of the senate. Cf.

Ep. LXVII. 4. — consanuisse :
found only here in Cicero.
    3. sperabam : an epistolary
tense ; cf. Intr. 84 *c*. — ante : before Caesar's return from Spain,
which took place in Sept., 45 B.C.
— unius : *i.e. Caesaris*. — ami-

spexisse videor, nec a me alieni et tibi amicissimi. Quod cum ita sit, magnae tamen est deliberationis quae ratio sit ineunda nobis non agendi aliquid, sed illius concessu et beneficio quiescendi. Vale.

LXXVII. (*Fam.* 5. 14.)

L. LVCCEIVS Q. F. S. D. M. TVLLIO M. F.

S. v. b. E. v. sicut soleo, paululo tamen etiam dete- 1
rius quam soleo. Te requisivi saepius ut viderem;
Romae quia postea non fuisti quam discesseram, miratus sum; quod item nunc miror. Non habeo certum quae te res hinc maxime retrahat. Si solitudine
delectare, cum scribas et aliquid agas eorum quorum
consuesti, gaudeo neque reprehendo tuum consilium.
Nam nihil isto potest esse iucundius non modo mise-
ris his temporibus et luctuosis, sed etiam tranquillis et
optatis, praesertim vel animo defetigato tuo, qui nunc
requiem quaerat ex magnis occupationibus, vel erudito,
qui semper aliquid ex se promat quod alios delectet,

cissimi : Caesar had shown his friendship for Servius by making him governor of Achaia. — vale : cf. Intr. 62.

LXXVII. Rome, May 9, 45 B.C. Lucceius urges Cicero not to give himself up entirely to grief for the loss of his daughter. On Lucceius, cf. Ep. XVIII. introd. note.

1. s. v. b. e. v.: *i.e. si vales benest. Ego valeo*, or *si vales bene est. Valeo.* Cf. Intr. 62. — habeo certum : for *scio certum ;* cf. Ep. LII. 1. See also *sic habeto*, Ep. XXVI. 1 n.— quae res : a natural substitute for *quid* from the pen of a lawyer. Cf. *quae res* for *quod*, *Fam.* 12. 14. 2. — delectare :

in the second pers. sing. Cicero uses the ending *-re* in the pres. subj., imperf. ind., and fut. ind., elsewhere the ending *-ris.* Two exceptions may be noted to the last statement : (1) in his earlier writings *-re* is also found in the imperf. subj.; (2) in verbs having no active form *-re* is also used in the pres. ind. Other cases of the use of forms in *-re*, as delectare here, are archaic or colloquial. — quorum consuesti : the case of the relative is assimilated to that of its antecedent. Cf. Hor. *Sat.* 1. 6. 15 *iudice quo nosti populo.* — animo : on the personification of *animus*, cf. Ep. LII. 1 n.

2 ipsum laudibus inlustret.   Sin autem, sicut hinc discesseras, lacrimis ac tristitiae te tradidisti, doleo quia
doles et angere, non possum te non — si concedis, quod
sentimus ut liberius dicamus — accusare.   Quid enim?
Tu solus aperta non videbis, qui propter acumen occultis-
sima perspicis? Tu non intelleges te querelis cotidianis
nihil proficere, non intelleges duplicari sollicitudines
3 quas elevare tua te prudentia postulat?   Quod si non
possimus aliquid proficere suadendo, gratia contendi-
mus et rogando, si quid nostra causa vis, ut istis te
molestiis laxes et ad convictum nostrum redeas atque
ad consuetudinem vel nostram communem vel tuam
solius ac propriam.   Cupio non obtundere te, si non
delectare nostro studio; cupio deterrere ne permaneas
in incepto.   Nunc duae res istae contrariae me con-
turbant, ex quibus aut in altera mihi velim, si potes,
obtemperes aut in altera non offendas.   Vale.

2. **sicut hinc discesseras** : as
you did when you left here. —
hinc : *i.e.* from Rome after Tullia's death. — **tristitiae te tradidisti** : alliterative. — **doleo quia:**
for *doleo quod.* Cf. Brix on Plaut.
Trin. 290, ' After verbs of emotion
(*e.g. doleo, gaudeo, suscenseo, paveo,
piget,* etc.), where later writers
employ *quod,* Plautus uses *quia,*
in conformity with colloquial
usage.'   See also Reisig-Schmalz,
Lat. Syn. note 431 *g.* — **angere:**
cf. *delectare,* 1. — **non possum** :
in a writer whose style is so condensed and careless as is that
of Lucceius (cf. *quorum consuesti, sicut hinc discesseras,* and *si*

quid nostra causa vis) such an
asyndeton is not remarkable. —
sollicitudines : probably a genuine plural.   Cf., however, Brix,
Trin. 490, and Lorenz, *Pseud.* Introd. 57. — **elevare . . . te . . .
postulat** : *postulo* followed by the
acc. and inf. is Plautine. Cf., *e.g.,
Trin.* 237 *numquam amor quemquam nisi cupidum hominem postulat se in plagas conicere.*
  3. **si quid nostra causa vis:** a
phrase from the *sermo urbanus*
(Böckel). Cf. *Fam.* 13. 71. —
obtundere, *to tire out* (by talking
or writing) ; a favorite word in
Plautus and Terence. — **delectare** : cf. *delectare,* above.

LXXVIII. (*Fam.* 4. 12.)

SERVIVS CICERONI SALVTEM PLVRIBVS VERBIS.

Etsi scio non iucundissimum me nuntium vobis 1
adlaturum, tamen, quoniam casus et natura in nobis
dominatur, visum est faciendum, quoquo modo res se
haberet, vos certiores facere.   A. d. x K. Iun., cum ab
Epidauro Piraeum navi advectus essem, ibi M. Marcellum collegam nostrum conveni eumque diem ibi
consumpsi ut cum eo essem.   Postero die ab eo digressus sum eo consilio, ut ab Athenis in Boeotiam
irem reliquamque iurisdictionem absolverem, ille, ut
aiebat, supra Maleas in Italiam versus navigaturus
erat.   Post diem tertium eius diei, cum ab Athenis 2
proficisci in animo haberem, circiter hora decima noctis P. Postumius familiaris eius ad me venit et mihi
nuntiavit M. Marcellum collegam nostrum post cenae

LXXVIII. Athens, May 31,
45 B.C. M. Claudius Marcellus,
the consul of 51 B.C., who had
been living in banishment at Mytilene since the battle of Pharsalus,
was recalled by the senate, with
the consent of Caesar, towards
the close of the year 46. The
indifference which he felt concerning his recall is shown both by the
coldness and brevity of his letter
of acknowledgment to Cicero
(*Fam.* 4. 11), and by the fact that
he did not set out for Rome until
the middle of 45 B.C. On his
way thither he was murdered at
the Piraeus, as described in this
letter, the style of which is terse
and graphic.

1. non iucundissimum : instances of litotes are common in
the Letters ; cf. *non minimum*,

non pessimum, *non mediocriter*,
etc. — visum est faciendum :
Landgraf, p. 327, notes that *facere
ut* is a colloquial expression (cf.
Fam. 10. 17. 3), while *facere* followed by the infin., as here, belongs to vulgar Latin ; cf. Petron.
51 *fecit Caesarem reporrigere*. —
navi : the regular form in early
Latin. *Nave* appears first in Cicero's time. From Livy on *nave*
is the common form. — collegam
nostrum : probably in the augurate. — ab Athenis : cf. *ab Aegina*,
Ep. LXXV. 4 n. Cf. also *ab Epidauro*, above, and *ab Athenis*, 2. —
reliquam . . . absolverem : before leaving his province he held
the circuit courts, which it was
part of a governor's duty to do. —
supra Maleas : *super* is the common preposition in this sense.

tempus a P. Magio Cilone familiare eius pugione per-
cussum esse et duo vulnera accepisse, unum in stomacho, alterum in capite secundum aurem; sperare tamen
eum vivere posse; Magium se ipsum interfecisse postea;
se a Marcello ad me missum esse qui haec nuntiaret et
rogaret uti medicos ei mitterem. Itaque medicos coegi
et e vestigio eo sum profectus prima luce. Cum non
longe a Piraeo abessem, puer Acidini obviam mihi venit
cum codicillis in quibus erat scriptum, paulo ante lucem
Marcellum diem suum obisse. Ita vir clarissimus ab
homine deterrimo acerbissima morte est adfectus, et,
cui inimici propter dignitatem pepercerant, inventus
3 est amicus qui ei mortem offerret. Ego tamen ad
tabernaculum eius perrexi. Inveni duos libertos et
pauculos servos; reliquos aiebant profugisse metu per-
territos quod dominus eorum ante tabernaculum inter-

2. **P. Magio Cilone**: certain
persons at Rome suspected that
Caesar had instigated the murder
of Marcellus ; but cf. *Att.* 13. 10. 3
*hodie Spintherem exspecto ; misit
enim Brutus ad me ; per litteras
purgat Caesarem de interitu Mar-
celli, in quem, ne si insidiis quidem
ille interfectus esset, caderet ulla
suspicio, nunc vero, cum de Magio
constet, nonne furor eius causam
omnem sustinet ? . . . Quamquam
nihil habeo quod dubitem, nisi ipsi
Magio quae fuerit causa amentiae,
pro quo quidem etiam sponsor factus erat. Nimirum id fuit ; solvendo enim non erat: credo eum
petiisse a Marcello aliquid, et illum,
ut erat, constantius respondisse.* —
secundum aurem, *directly behind
the ear.* This meaning of *secundum* is Plautine, and is found in no
other writer of the classical period.
— **ipsum**: to be joined with **Ma-**

gium. — **e vestigio,** *forthwith.*
— **eo**: *i.e.* to the Piraeus. — **codicillis**: see Intr. 59. — **diem
suum obisse**: euphemistic ; cf.
Ep. LXXV. 4. — **inimici**: Caesar
is thought of especially.

3. **ad tabernaculum eius**: the
Piraeus being in ruins (cf. Ep.
LXXV. 4), travellers were obliged
to camp in tents. — **pauculos** :
Servius shows a fondness for the
use of diminutives. Cf. *muliercula, homunculus,* and *animula,*
Ep. LXXV. — **metu** : if a citizen
was murdered by a slave, all the
slaves of the household were liable to be put to death ; cf. Tac.
Ann. 14. 42 *Pedanium Secundum
servus ipsius interfecit ; . . . ceterum
cum vetere ex more familiam omnem, quae sub eodem tecto mansi-
taverat, ad supplicium agi oporteret,*
etc. Even when the murderer was
not one of their number, the slaves

fectus esset.   Coactus sum in eadem illa lectica qua ipse delatus eram, meisque lecticariis in urbem eum referre, ibique pro ea copia quae Athenis erat, funus ei satis amplum faciendum curavi.   Ab Atheniensibus locum sepulturae intra urbem ut darent impetrare non potui, quod religione se impediri dicerent, neque tamen id antea cuiquam concesserant.   Quod proximum fuit, uti in quo vellemus gymnasio eum sepeliremus, nobis permiserunt.   Nos in nobilissimo orbi terrarum gymnasio Academiae locum delegimus ibique eum combussimus posteaque curavimus ut iidem Athenienses in eodem loco monumentum ei marmoreum faciendum locarent.   Ita, quae nostra officia fuerunt pro collegio et pro propinquitate, et vivo et mortuo omnia ei praestitimus.   Vale.   D. pr. K. Iun. Athenis.

LXXIX. (*Fam.* 5. 15.)

M. CICERO S. D. L. LVCCEIO Q. F.

Omnis amor tuus ex omnibus partibus se ostendit in 1 iis litteris quas a te proxime accepi, non ille quidem mihi ignotus, sed tamen gratus et optatus — dicerem

had good reason to fear the severity of the law. — **meis lecticariis**: abl. of means. — **pro ea copia**, *so far as the facilities* (at Athens) *allowed.* — **ut** (**darent**): the position of **ut** in the middle of the clause lays emphasis upon the words which precede. Cf. Ep. XXX. 1 n. — **quod . . . dicerent**: the subj., although not expressing a pretext but the real reason; cf. *diceret*, Ep. I. 3 n. — **neque tamen**, *and after all . . . not.* — **in quo**

vellemus gymnasio: there were three in Athens: Λύκειον, Κυνόσαργες, Ἀκαδημία. — **orbi**: locative. — **iidem Athenienses**: *i.e.* the same people who had declined to allow the ashes to be deposited within the city. — **propinquitate**: how Marcellus was related to Servius is unknown. — **d. pr. K.**, etc.: cf. Intr. 62.

LXXIX. Astura, May 10–12, 45 B.C. Cicero's answer to Ep. LXXVII.

'iucundus,' nisi id verbum in omne tempus perdidissem
— neque ob eam unam causam, quam tu suspicaris et
in qua me lenissimis et amantissimis verbis utens re
graviter accusas, sed quod illius tanti vulneris quae
2 remedia esse debebant, ea nulla sunt. Quid enim? Ad
amicosne confugiam? Quam multi sunt? Habuimus
enim fere communis, quorum alii occiderunt, alii nescio
quo pacto obduruerunt. Tecum vivere possem equidem et maxime vellem; vetustas amor consuetudo
studia paria,— quod vinclum, quaeso, deest nostrae con-
iunctionis? Possumusne igitur esse una? Nec mehercule intellego quid impediat; sed certe adhuc non
fuimus, cum essemus vicini in Tusculano, in Puteo-
lano. Nam quid dicam in urbe? in qua, cum forum
3 commune sit, vicinitas non requiritur. Sed casu nescio
quo in ea tempora nostra aetas incidit ut, cum maxime
florere nos oporteret, tum vivere etiam puderet. Quod
enim esse poterat mihi perfugium spoliato et domesticis et forensibus ornamentis atque solaciis? Litterae,
credo, quibus utor assidue; quid enim aliud facere
possum? Sed nescio quomodo ipsae illae excludere
me a portu et perfugio videntur et quasi exprobrare,

1. **iucundus**: cf. *iucundiora,
gratiora*, Ep. LXXVI. 1 n.—**ob
eam unam causam**: *sc.* the death
of Tullia. — **remedia** : *sc.* friends,
influence, freedom, civic honors,
etc. Cf. Ep. LXXVI. 2 nn.

2. **quid enim**: usually followed,
as here, by a rhetorical question
expecting a negative answer. —
occiderunt: cf. Ep. LXII. 2 nn.
—**possumusne**: ne for *nonne*.
This usage points back to the
period when *nonne* was unknown.

3. **cum ... oporteret**: Cicero
had reached an age when he might

naturally expect to reap the fruit,
in the way of influence, distinction, and friendships, of his years
of work and study. — **domesticis**:
to be joined more particularly with
solaciis. Cf. *amissis ornamentis*,
etc., Ep. LXXVI. 2. — **quibus
utor assidue**: in 45 B.C. Cicero
wrote the *Consolatio, Hortensius,
de Finibus*, and *Academica*. The
Tusculanae Disputationes and the
de Natura Deorum were partly
written in the same year.—**a portu**:
cf. *in puppi*, etc., Ep. LXVII. 3
and *contraxi vela*, Ep. V. 2 n.

quod in ea vita maneam, in qua nihil insit nisi propa-
gatio miserrimi temporis. Hic tu me abesse urbe mira- 4
ris, in qua domus nihil delectare possit, summum sit
odium temporum hominum fori curiae? Itaque sic
litteris utor, in quibus consumo omne tempus, non ut
ab iis medicinam perpetuam, sed ut exiguam oblivio-
nem doloris petam. Quod si id egissemus ego atque 5
tu — quod ne in mentem quidem nobis veniebat propter
cotidianos metus, — omne tempus una fuissemus, neque me valetudo tua offenderet neque te maeror meus.
Quod quantum fieri poterit consequamur ; quid enim
est utrique nostrum aptius ? Propediem te igitur
videbo.

LXXX. (*Fam.* 9. 8.)

CICERO VARRONI.

Etsi munus flagitare, quamvis quis ostenderit, ne 1
populus quidem solet nisi concitatus, tamen ego exspectatione promissi tui moveor ut admoneam te, non
ut flagitem. Misi autem ad te quattuor admonitores

4. **hic**: the reference is to
Romae . . . miratus sum, Ep.
LXXVII. 1. On **hic**, cf. Ep. XII.
1 n. — **domus ... possit**: because
it would remind him of Publilia's
conduct. — **ut . . . petam**: Cicero's efforts in seeking consolation
found expression especially in the
Consolatio and the *Tusculan Disputations.*

5. **si id egissemus**: *i.e.* had
lived together. The force of **si**
continues through **fuissemus.** —
omne tempus: *sc. post suum a
Thessalica pugna reditum in Italiam* (Manutius). — **valetudo tua**:
cf. Ep. LXXVII. 1.

LXXX. Tusculum, July 11 or
12, 45 B.C. On Varro, cf. Ep.
LX. introd. note.

1. **promissi tui**: Varro had
promised, as early as 47 B.C., to
dedicate one of his works to Cicero; cf. *Att.* 13. 12. 3 *Varro mihi
denuntiaverat magnam sane et gravem προσφώνησιν*; but in 45 Cicero writes impatiently (*Att.* 13. 12.
3): *biennium praeteriit, cum ille
Καλλιππίδης assiduo cursu cubitum
nullum processerit.* Ultimately
Varro's work *de Lingua Latina*
appeared, between 45 and 43 B.C.,
of which twenty books were dedicated to Cicero. — **quattuor ad-**

non nimis verecundos ; nosti enim profecto os illius adulescentioris Academiae. Ex ea igitur media excitatos misi, qui metuo ne te forte flagitent ; ego autem mandavi ut rogarent. Exspectabam omnino iamdiu meque sustinebam ne ad te prius ipse quid scriberem quam aliquid accepissem, ut possem te remunerari quam simillimo munere ; sed cum tu tardius faceres, id est, ut ego interpretor, diligentius, teneri non potui quin coniunctionem studiorum amorisque nostri quo possem litterarum genere declararem. Feci igitur sermonem inter nos habitum in Cumano, cum esset una Pomponius ; tibi dedi partis Antiochinas, quas a te probari

monitores : the four books of the *Academica*. These books, at the suggestion of Atticus, were dedicated to Varro. Cf. *Att.* 13. 19. Cicero hoped that this might stimulate Varro to the performance of his promised work. — os, *effrontery ;* a colloquial word. Cf. Plaut. *M. G.* 189 *os habet linguam perfidiam ;* Ter. *Eun.* 806 *os durum !* ('you brazenface !'). Varro was not an adherent of the New Academy. — qui ... flagitent : although these admonitores have been directed to make only a request of Varro, such is the boldness of all that comes from the *adulescentior Academia*, Cicero fears it may be a demand. — exspectabam : cf. Cic. *Acad.* I. 2 *inquit ille (i.e.* Varro) ... ' *sed habeo opus magnum in manibus idque iam pridem ; ad hunc enim ipsum ' — me autem dicebat* — ' *quaedam institui, quae et sunt magna sane et limantur a me politius.' Et ego,* ' *ista quidem,' inquam, ' Varro, iam diu exspectans non audeo tamen flagitare ; audivi enim e Libone nostro, cuius nosti studium — nihil enim eum eius*

modi celare possumus, — *non te ea intermittere, sed accuratius tractare nec de manibus umquam deponere.'* — me sustinebam : *sc.* in my desire to write to you. — coniunctionem . . . nostri : cf. Cicero's remark upon Varro in *Acad.* I. I *hominem nobiscum et studiis iisdem et vetustate amicitiae coniunctum.* — in Cumano : the dialogue is supposed to have taken place in Varro's villa at Cumae ; cf. *Acad.* I. I. — Pomponius : *i.e.* Atticus. — partis Antiochinas : Cicero composed the *Academica* at first in two books, with Q. Lutatius Catulus for the principal speaker in the first, and L. Licinius Lucullus in the second. When he learned from Atticus that Varro wished to have a work dedicated to him, he reconstructed the *Academica*, divided it into four books, and dedicated the whole work to Varro, making him a mouthpiece for the opinions of Antiochus of Ascalon. Cf. *Att.* 13. 19. 3 ; 13. 12. 3 ; 13. 25. 3. Antiochus, a pupil but not a follower of Philo, sought to harmonize Academic with Stoic and

intellexisse mihi videbar; mihi sumpsi Philonis. Puto fore ut, cum legeris, mirere nos id locutos esse inter nos quod numquam locuti sumus; sed nosti morem dialogorum. Posthac autem, mi Varro, quam plurima, 2 si videtur, et de nobis inter nos, sero fortasse; sed superiorum temporum fortuna rei p. causam sustineat, haec ipsi praestare debemus. Atque utinam quietis temporibus atque aliquo, si non bono, at saltem certo statu civitatis haec inter nos studia exercere possemus! Quamquam tum quidem vel aliae quaepiam rationes honestas nobis et curas et actiones darent; nunc autem quid est sine his cur vivere velimus? Mihi vero cum his ipsis vix, his autem detractis ne vix quidem. Sed haec coram et saepius. Migrationem et emptionem feliciter evenire volo, tuumque in ea re consilium probo. Cura ut valeas.

Peripatetic teaching. — **Philonis**: Philo, the head of the Academy, fled in 88 B.C. from Athens to Rome, where Cicero attended his lectures; cf. *Brut.* 306 *cum princeps Academiae Philo . . . Romam venisset, totum ei me tradidi admirabili quodam ad philosophiam studio concitatus, in quo hoc etiam commorabar attentius, quod etsi rerum ipsarum varietas et magnitudo summa me delectatione retinebat, tamen sublata iam esse in perpetuum ratio iudiciorum videbatur.*

2. si **videtur**: cf. *si tibi videtur*, Ep. LXXV. 4 n. — **inter nos**: *sc. loquemur.* — **superiorum temporum**, etc.: the state of public affairs might justify their literary inactivity in the past, but, since they would have no share in politics in the future, they would not be kept from the pursuit of literature. Literary work would in fact be their only feasible occupation, and failure to engage in it would be a dereliction of duty. — **haec** (*sc. tempora*) . . . **debemus**, *the responsibility for the present* (lit. *times like these*) *rests with us.* — **aliquo . . . certo statu civitatis**: a government conducted upon some fixed constitutional principles at least. — **vel** = *etiam*. — **darent**: apodosis to the condition in **tum**. — **cum his ipsis** (*studiis*) **vix**: *sc. est cur vivere velim.* — **migrationem**: *sc.* into a house lately bought. — **feliciter evenire**: a formula often used in wishing for the happy outcome of a new enterprise; cf. Cic. *pro Mur.* 1, and Plaut. *Trin.* 40 *uxor, venerare ut nobis haec habitatio bona fausta felix fortunataque evenat.* See also Ep. XC. 7 n.

LXXXI. (*Fam. 7. 24.*)

M. CICERO S. D. M. FADIO GALLO.

1   Amoris quidem tui, quoquo me verti, vestigia, vel proxime de Tigellio; sensi enim ex litteris tuis valde te laborasse. Amo igitur voluntatem. Sed pauca de re. Cipius, opinor, olim ' Non omnibus dormio.' Sic ego non omnibus, mi Galle, servio. Etsi quae est haec servitus? Olim, cum regnare existimabamur, non tam ab ullis quam hoc tempore observor a familiarissimis Caesaris omnibus praeter istum. Id ego in lucris pono, non ferre hominem pestilentiorem patria sua; eumque addictum iam tum puto esse Calvi Licini Hipponacteo

---

LXXXI.   Tusculum, a b o u t Aug. 20, 45 B.C. For Fadius, see Ep. IV. introd. note.

1. **vestigia** : *sc. sunt.* — **vel**, *for instance.* — **Tigellio** : the singer whom Horace dubs *Sardus Tigellius* (*Sat.* 1. 3. 3) from his birthplace, Sardinia, a favorite of Julius Caesar in Cicero's time, and later of Octavianus. Cf. Hor. *Sat.* 1. 2 and 3. — **Cipius . . . dormio** : Cipius, as the story goes (cf. Festus), was in the habit of feigning sleep, but when on a certain occasion a slave attempted to steal one of his master's cups, Cipius started up, saying, ' *non omnibus dormio.*' — **opinor** : probably a case of genuine uncertainty concerning the name, but cf. *Hector Naevianus*, Ep. XVIII. 7 n. — **olim**, *once upon a time.* — **sic . . . servio** : he may find it necessary to be Caesar's slave, but he will not be the slave of every one of Caesar's household. Cicero apparently uses the same story in the same connection in *Att.* 13.

49. 2 (written about the same time as this letter), where, however, the name of Cipius is omitted. — **olim** : *sc.* before Caesar's assumption of power. — **ab ullis** : *sc. observabar*, from **observor**. — **a familiarissimis** : Gallus had evidently expressed the fear that Tigellius, who was angry at Cicero, might use his influence with Caesar against him. Cicero therefore assures Gallus that there has been no change in Caesar's attitude to him. Cicero's remark here harmonizes with statements made a year before; cf. Ep. LXI. 2. — **pestilentiorem patria sua** : cf. Ep. XVI. (end) n. — **eumque . . . praeconio**, *and I think he has by this time been disposed of at the Hipponactean estimate put upon him by Calvus Licinius.* — **Calvi Licini** : Gaius Licinius Macer Calvus was known equally well as an orator (cf., *e.g.*, Cic. *Brut.* 280, 283) and as a poet (cf., *e.g.*, Sen. *Contr.* 7. 4. 7). The different tendencies in oratory which Cicero and Cal-

praeconio. At vide quid suscenseat. Phameae causam **2**
receperam, ipsius quidem causa; erat enim mihi sane
familiaris. Is ad me venit dixitque iudicem sibi operam dare constituisse eo ipso die quo de P. Sestio in
consilium iri necesse erat. Respondi nullo modo me
facere posse; quem vellet alium diem si sumpsisset,
me ei non defuturum. Ille autem, qui sciret se nepo-
tem bellum tibicinem habere et sat bonum unctorem,
discessit a me, ut mi videbatur, iratior. Habes ' Sardos venalis, alium alio nequiorem.' Cognosti meam
causam et istius salaconis iniquitatem. ' Catonem '
tuum mihi mitte; cupio enim legere. Me adhuc non
legisse turpe utrique nostrum est.

vus represented led apparently to a correspondence between them (cf. Tac. *Dial.* 18). As a poet, Calvus belonged to the νεώτεροι, (*Att.* 7. 2. 1), and was an intimate friend of Catullus, the leading representative of that school. He died about 47 B.C.; cf. *Fam.* 15. 21. 4. Calvus had assailed Tigellius in a poem, the first verse of which, preserved by Porphyrio (Hor. *Sat.* 1. 3. 4), is as follows: *Sardi Tigelli putidum caput venit* (from *veneo*). On the order **Calvi Licini,** cf. *Galli Canini,* Ep. XIX. 4 n. — **Hipponacteo** : Hipponax was a Greek writer of lampoons. — **praeconio** : the setting forth by an auctioneer of the merits of his wares; suggested by the line from Calvus.

2. **Phameae** : cf. Ep. LXI. 8 n. Tigellius was annoyed at Cicero for neglecting to act as the advocate of Phamea, his grandfather (or uncle), after having promised to do so (cf. *Att.* 13. 49. 1). — **ipsius quidem causa** : Phamea had proffered his assistance to Cicero

during the latter's canvass for the consulship (cf. *Att.* 13. 49. 1). — **P. Sestio** : Sestius was apparently charged with *ambitus;* cf. *Att.* 13. 49. 1. — **in consilium iri** : *cum iudices, de reo sententias laturi, in unum coeunt, ire in consilium dicuntur* (Manutius). Cf., however, Ep. V. introd. note. — **ille** : *i.e.* Phamea. — **sat bonum** : this archaic form of *satis* (cf. Ter. *And.* 475) seems to be found with no other adj. than *bonus* in classical prose; cf. *pro Rosc. Am.* 89; *de Or.* 3. 84; *Att.* 14. 10. 1. — **unctorem** : the reference is obscure. Manutius suggests *cantorem.* — **Sardos venalis** : the Sardinian slaves were weak and sickly because of the unhealthful climate of their native country. Hence the proverb : ' *Sardi venales ; alius alio nequior.*' Cf. Otto, *Sprichwörter der Römer*, 308. — **Catonem tuum** : probably a political biography of Cato. Cf. Intr. 33.

Att. 13. 49 may be read with profit in connection with this letter. The influence of Tigellius with

LXXXII. (*Fam.* 7. 25.)

CICERO S. D. M. FADIO GALLO.

1   Quod epistulam conscissam doles, noli laborare, salva
est ; domo petes, cum libebit. Quod autem me mones,
valde gratum est, idque ut semper facias rogo; videris
enim mihi vereri ne, si istum ludibrio habuerimus,
rideamus γέλωτα σαρδάνιον. Sed heus tu, manum de
tabula! magister adest citius quam putaramus ; vereor

Caesar and Cicero's fear of Caesar's anger prevented Cicero from
maintaining long the manly position which he assumes in this and
the following letter, for about a
month later he writes to Atticus :
*miror te nihildum cum Tigellio ;
velut hoc ipsum quantum acceperit, prorsus aveo scire nec tamen
flocci facio (Att.* 13. 50. 3); and
about the same time: *Tigellium
totum mihi* (*sc. reduc in gratiam*)
*et quidem quam primum ; nam
pendeo animi (Att.* 13. 51. 2). Cf.
Schmidt, *Briefw.* pp. 353 ff.

LXXXII. Tusculum, about
Aug. 24, 45 B.C.

1. **quod . . . salva est:** apparently Gallus had destroyed Ep.
LXXXI. after reading it, for fear
that it might fall into the hands
of Tigellius or of his friends.
Cicero seems to assure Gallus,
however, that he has preserved a
copy. — **quod,** etc. : cf. Intr. 91
and *Fam.* 7. 32, 33. — **mones** :
sc. ut cautior sim. — **istum** : *i.e.* Tigellius. — **γέλωτα σαρδάνιον** : a
bitter laugh of anger or secret
triumph. But perhaps we should
read, with Ernesti, σαρδόνιον. Σαρδόνιον was a poisonous plant of
Sardinia, which caused death when
eaten, and which so distorted the
faces of those who ate it that

they seemed to be laughing. The
jest would then be in harmony
with the sneers at the Sardinian
origin of Tigellius in the previous
letter. — **heus tu** : cf. Ep. XXXV.
25 n. — **manum de tabula :** *sc.
tolle.* The schoolmaster (Caesar)
has been away (in Spain), but suddenly returns, and those under
him (like Cicero and Gallus) had
better stop the pranks they have
been playing in his absence, or
they will suffer for it (cf. **in Catonium Catoninos**). Cicero is
probably thinking of a roomful
of schoolboys, who, instead of
giving their attention to the task
set them, have amused themselves
during the master's absence by
scribbling upon their *tabulae.* The
master suddenly appears, and the
order comes **manum de tabula**
(*tollite*). The scribbling which
Cicero and Gallus have been
guilty of during Caesar's absence,
is in writing political biographies
of Cato. Cf. *Catonem tuum*, Ep.
LXXXI. 2 n. Or the reference
may be general : 'No more indis-
cretions.' Cf. Otto, *Sprichwörter,*
210. — **citius quam putaramus** :
Caesar arrived from Spain Sept.,
45 B.C. ; (cf. Suet. *Iul.* 83). He had
been expected in the last week of
Aug. (cf. *Att.* 13. 51. 2). — **vereor**

ne in Catonium Catoninos.   Mi Galle, cave putes quic- 2
quam melius quam epistulae tuae partem ab eo loco:
' cetera labuntur.'   Secreto hoc — audi — tecum habeto.;
ne Apellae quidem, liberto tuo, dixeris.   Praeter duo
nos loquitur isto modo nemo; bene malene, videro ; sed
quicquid est, nostrum est.   Vrge igitur, nec 'transversum unguem,' quod aiunt, a stilo; is enim est dicendi
opifex.   Atque equidem aliquantum iam etiam noctis
adsumo.

. . . **Catoninos,** *I am afraid that
he will send us Catonians to the
lower world ;* or to reproduce the
pun involved in **Catonium** and
Catoninos : *I am afraid that he
will send us followers of Cato to
the world where Cato is.* The term
Catonium for the lower world was,
according to Schmidt (*Briefw.*
p. 355), a current witticism in the
last days of the Republic, origi-
nating in a mime of Laberius; cf.
Gell. 16. 7. 4.   Cf. also Hertz,
Gell. II. 281.   It has a double
meaning: as a comic derivative
from Cato, it means 'the abode
of Cato'; as a hybrid formation
from κάτω (cf. Intr. 80), it means
'the world below.'   On **Catoninos,** cf. *Archiv f. lat. Lexikog.* I.
184.

2. **ab eo loco,** *beginning with.*
Gallus's words were perhaps
quoted from Cicero's *Phaenomena.*
— **tecum habeto,** *keep it to your-
self;* for the more common construction, *tibi habeto,* cf. the formula
of divorce, *res tuas tibi habe ;* but
see *Att.* 4. 15. 6 *verum haec tu
tecum habeto,* and Plaut. *Poen.* 890
hoc tu tecum tacitum habeto. The
expression is colloquial. — **ne . . .
dixeris** : cf. Intr. 84 *b.* — **videro** :
' I am as yet undecided.' — **trans-**

versum unguem (*sc. discedas*),
the breadth of a nail ; a proverbial
expression, the meaning of which
appears from Plaut. *Aul.* 56 *si
hercle tu ex istoc loco digitum
transvorsum aut unguem latum
excesseris.*   As Manutius observes,
this letter is remarkable from the
number of popular expressions
which it contains: *rideamus* γέλωτα σαρδάνιον, *manum de tabula,*
and *transversum unguem.*   *Pro-
verbiis autem locus magis videtur
esse cum ad familiares familiariter scribimus ; nam ad spectatos
viros, in re praesertim gravi, sententiis quidem proverbiorum similibus, ut Homeri aliorumve poetarum
versibus, saepe utitur Cicero ; quae
vero proverbia vere et plane sunt,
ea non ita frequenter attingit, arbitratus fortasse Romanae gravitatis
non esse proverbia inculcare* (Manutius). — **is . . . opifex** : cf. *de
Or.* 1. 150 *stilus optimus et prae-
stantissimus dicendi effector ac
magister ;* 1. 257 *stilus ille tuus
quem tu vere dixisti perfectorem
dicendi esse ac magistrum.* — **equidem** : common in the Ciceronian
letters, while *ego quidem* is regularly used in the non-Ciceronian
letters; cf. *Fam.* 6. 7. 3; 8. 5. 1;
Ep. LXXIX. 2.

LXXXIII. (*Att.* 13. 52.)

CICERO ATTICO SAL.

1   O hospitem mihi tam gravem ἀμεταμέλητον! Fuit
enim periucunde. Sed cum secundis Saturnalibus ad
Philippum vesperi venisset, villa ita completa militibus
est ut vix triclinium ubi cenaturus ipse Caesar esset
vacaret; quippe hominum CIƆ CIƆ. Sane sum commotus quid futurum esset postridie, ac mihi Barba Cassius subvenit: custodes dedit. Castra in agro; villa
defensa est. Ille tertiis Saturnalibus apud Philippum
ad h. VII, nec quemquam admisit: rationes opinor cum
Balbo. Inde ambulavit in litore; post h. VIII in balneum; tum audivit de Mamurra; non mutavit; unctus

LXXXIII. Puteoli, Dec. 19,
45 B.C. This letter describes a
visit which Caesar, accompanied
by his bodyguard, made at Cicero's villa near Puteoli.

1. o . . . ἀμεταμέλητον, *would
you believe it, I have nothing to be
sorry for in the visit of a guest so
formidable to me!* The acc. hospitem expresses astonishment. —
tam gravem: so formidable because he had been a political
enemy. mihi tam gravem is to
be taken parenthetically, and a
contrast is intended between gravem and ἀμεταμέλητον. — fuit
enim periucunde: *sc. Caesar.*
Cf. Intr. 85. Cicero addresses
almost the same words to Caesar
(*pro Deiot.* 19): *cum in convivio
comiter et iucunde fuisses.* On the
force of per, cf. Intr. 77. — sed,
but (to my tale). Breaking off his
general comments upon the incident, he proceeds to describe it in
detail. — secundis Saturnalibus:

i.e. Dec. 18. — Philippum: cf.
Ep. LXXII. n. — quippe hominum CIƆ CIƆ: *sc. fuerunt.* — postridie: when he expected a visit
from Caesar. — Barba Cassius:
cf. *Galli Canini,* Ep. XIX. 4 n.
Cassius Barba was a friend of
Caesar; cf. *Philipp.* 13. 3.— ille: *i.e.*
Caesar. — apud Philippum: *sc.
erat.* — Balbo: Cornelius Balbus,
Caesar's financial agent. Cf. Ep.
XXI. 2 n. — in balneum: *sc. ivit.*
This was doubtless at Cicero's
villa. With these words the account of the visit proper begins,
and since no reference is made to
Caesar's arrival or to his reception by Cicero, Boot suggests with
probability that one or more lines
have fallen out after post h. VIII.
— de Mamurra: Mamurra had
been Caesar's *praefectus fabrum*
in Gaul and Britain. It is he
against whom Catullus directs his
fierce invectives, *Car.* 29 and 57.
The reference here is possibly to

est, accubuit.   'Εμετικὴν agebat ; itaque et edit et
bibit ἀδεῶς et iucunde, opipare sane et apparate, nec
id solum, sed   bene cocto
        Condito, sermone bono et, si quaeri', libenter.

Praeterea tribus tricliniis accepti οἱ περὶ αὐτὸν valde **2**
copiose ; libertis minus lautis servisque nihil defuit :
nam lautiores eleganter accepti. Quid multa? homines
visi sumus. Hospes tamen non is cui diceres : 'Amabo
te, eodem ad me, cum revertere.'   Semel satis est.

the death of Mamurra, but probably, as Manutius suggests, Cicero
has in mind his conviction under
the sumptuary laws ; cf. also Riese
on Catull. *Car.* 29. — **mutavit** :
used absolutely as in *Fam.* 16. 1.
1. — **accubuit** : Caesar followed
the regular order, viz., exercise, the
bath, dinner. — **ἐμετικὴν agebat**
(*sc.* τέχνην), *he was taking a course
of emetics.* Emetics were regularly
prescribed by physicians in order
that patients might escape the
effects resulting from eating
elaborate dinners. They were
taken in the morning, after the
bath or after the *cena.* The use of
them was, however, by no means
confined to men of a gluttonous
disposition ; cf. *pro Deiot.* 21,
where the speaker certainly has
every reason to avoid offending
Caesar : *cum . . . vomere post
cenam te velle dixisses.* See also
Marq. and Momm. *Handbuch,* VII.
330, and n. 5 and 6. For the
Greek word, cf. Intr. 97. — **opipare** : from the colloquial vocabulary. Cf. Plaut. *Bacch.* 373 ;
Caecil. Stat. 100, Ribbeck, *Com.
Rom. Frag.* It occurs also *Att.* 5.
9. 1 ; 7. 2. 3 ; and *de Off.* 3. 58 in a
quotation. — **sane** : cf. Ep. XVI.
2 n. — **apparate** : used only in
the Letters (Hofmann). — **bene**

cocto condito : *sc. cibo.* The
quotation, which is from Lucilius,
is found also *de Fin.* 2. 25 : *ex quo
illud efficitur, qui bene cenent, omnes libenter cenare, qui libenter,
non continuo bene.   Semper Laelius bene.   Quid bene ?   Dicet Lu-
cilius : 'cocto | condito' ; sed cedo
caput cenae: 'sermone bono,' quid
ex eo ? 'si quaeri', libenter.' —* **si
quaeri'** : for *si quaeris.* — **libenter** :
to be connected with some form
of *cenare* in the unquoted part of
the original.

2. **tribus tricliniis** : *in uno
liberti lautiores, in altero minus
lauti, in tertio discubuere servi*
(Manutius). — **nam,** etc. : the reason for Cicero's use of the words
minus lautis. — **quid multa,** *in
a word ;* cf. *quid quaeris,* Ep. V.
4 n. These words indicate that
what follows conveys Cicero's
general impression of the whole
affair. — **homines,** *ordinary mor-
tals* (not Caesar the dictator, and
Cicero the constitutionalist). Cf.
Ep. XX. 3 *virum te putabo, si
Sallusti Empedoclea legeris, hominem non putabo.* The dinner was
such a dinner as one gentleman
might give to another. — **amabo
te** : see Intr. 100 ; *Archiv f. lat.
Lexikog.* IX. 485 ff.; and cf. *si
me amas,* Ep. XIII. 3 n. — **ad me** :

Σπουδαῖον οὐδὲν in sermone, φιλόλογα multa. Quid quaeris? Delectatus est et libenter fuit. Puteolis se aiebat unum diem fore, alterum ad Baias. Habes hospitium sive ἐπισταθμείαν, odiosam mihi, dixi, non molestam. Ego paulisper hic, deinde in Tusculanum. Dolabellae villam cum praeteriret, omnis armatorum copia dextra sinistra ad equum nec usquam alibi. Hoc ex Nicia.

LXXXIV. (*Fam.* 13. 50.)

CICERO S. D. ACILIO.

1　Sumpsi hoc mihi pro tua in me observantia, quam penitus perspexi quamdiu Brundisi fuimus, ut ad te familiariter et quasi pro meo iure scriberem, si quae

sc. deverte. — σπουδαῖον οὐδὲν : *i.e.* no discussion of politics; see Intr. 97, and παρρησίαν, Ep. V. 8 n. Cf. also φιλόλογα and ἐπισταθμείαν, below. — quid quaeris : cf. quid multa, above. — libenter : cf. periucunde, 1. — ad Baias : *sc. fore* or *venturum esse.* — habes : cf. *sic habeto,* Ep. XXVI. 1 n. — ἐπισταθμείαν, *billeting.* — hic : *sc. ero.* — Dolabellae villam : *sc.* at Baiae. — dextra sinistra : cf. Intr. 94. — ad equum : *sc. Caesaris.* This military evolution, which consisted in parading on either side of Caesar, was intended as a compliment to Dolabella. — Nicia : a common friend of Cicero and Dolabella.

The excitement which this visit produced is reflected in the language of the letter, which in the great number of ellipses and of Greek expressions presents a fine specimen of the *sermo familiaris* (Hofmann). It is a significant fact that Caesar was assassinated

three months after the incident described in this letter. The spectacle which Caesar presented when making a progress through Italy attended by a disorderly bodyguard of 2000 men, may well have crystallized the sentiment forming against him.

LXXXIV. Rome, about Jan. 1, 44 B.C. Acilius, to whom *Fam.* 13. 30–39 also were addressed, had been twice successfully defended by Cicero (*Fam.* 7. 30. 3). He had just been sent out to Achaia to succeed Servius Sulpicius Rufus (cf. *Fam.* 7. 29. 1 ; 7. 30. 3). For M'. Curius, in whose behalf the letter was written, see Ep. XXXIX. 2. Cicero felt a debt of gratitude to him, because of the hospitality which he had shown him at Patrae, after the battle of Pharsalus (cf. *Fam.* 13. 17. 1). The letter was written in response to a request from Curius (cf. *Fam.* 7. 29. 1 ; 7. 30. 3).

1. Brundisi : from Oct., 48 B.C.,

res esset de qua valde laborarem. M'. Curius qui
Patris negotiatur ita mihi familiaris est ut nihil possit
esse coniunctius. Multa illius in me officia, multa in
illum mea, quodque maximum est, summus inter nos
amor et mutuus. Quae cum ita sint, si ullam in ami- 2
citia mea spem habes, si ea quae in me officia et studia
Brundisi contulisti vis mihi etiam gratiora efficere —
quamquam sunt gratissima, — si me a tuis omnibus
amari vides, hoc mihi da atque largire ut M'. Curium
'sartum et tectum,' ut aiunt, ab omnique incommodo
detrimento molestia sincerum integrumque conserves.
Et ipse spondeo et omnes hoc tibi tui pro me recipient,
ex mea amicitia et ex tuo in me officio maximum te
fructum summamque voluptatem esse capturum. Vale.

LXXXV. (*Fam.* 6. 15.)

CICERO BASILO S.

Tibi gratulor, mihi gaudeo ; te amo, tua tueor ; a te
amari et quid agas quidque agatur certior fieri volo.

to Sept., 47 ; cf. Intr. 32 f. —
familiaris : cf. *Fam.* 13. 17. 1.

2. **sartum et tectum** : an adaptation of the technical phrase
sarta et tecta, used by the censors
of buildings placed in the hands
of contractors to be 'put into perfect repair,' so as to be secure
against the assaults of wind and
weather. Cf. Brix on Plaut. *Trin.*
317, and Otto, *Sprichwörter,* 309.

LXXXV. Rome, probably Mar.
15, 44 B.C.   With these words
Cicero salutes L. Minucius Basilus, one of Caesar's murderers,
on the day of the assassination and after its occurrence.

Basilus had been praetor in 45 B.C.,
and actuated by chagrin at not
obtaining a province from Caesar
for the next year, joined the conspirators. For an account of his
death, see Appian, *B. C.* 3. 98.
Cicero was perhaps a witness of
Caesar's murder (cf. *Phil.* 2. 28 ;
Att. 14. 14. 4), but he had no previous knowledge of the plan (cf.
Fam. 12. 2. 1 ; 12. 4. 1).

quid agas quidque agatur :
the inquiry here indicates that this
note of congratulation was written
before Cicero's visit to the Capitol,
where the conspirators took refuge
after the assassination. Cf. Intr. 36.

LXXXVI. (*Fam.* 11. 1.)

D. BRVTVS BRVTO SVO ET CASSIO S.

1   Quo in statu simus cognoscite.   Heri vesperi apud
me Hirtius fuit ; qua mente esset Antonius demonstra-
vit, pessima scilicet et infidelissima.   Nam se neque
mihi provinciam dare posse aiebat neque arbitrari tuto

LXXXVI. Rome, Mar. 17, 44 B.C. The 17th and 18th of March were taken up with meetings of the senate (cf. *Phil.* 2. 89). Mar. 19 was a holiday (*Quinquatrus*), on which a burial could not take place, so that the burning of Caesar's body and Antony's address in the Forum cannot have taken place before Mar. 20. On the other hand, seven days seem to have been the extreme interval allowed between death and burial amongst the Romans (cf. Herodian, 4. 2. 4, with note by Marquardt, *Handbuch*, VII. 348). The burial must have taken place, therefore, on or before Mar. 22, *i.e.* Mar. 20–22 (Ruete, 16). As for the date of this letter, there is no mention in it of Caesar's burial, so that it was probably written before Mar. 20–22. In fact, the remarks in 6 make it highly probable that it was written on the morning of Mar. 17. Decimus Junius Brutus Albinus had served under Caesar with distinction in the campaigns against the Veneti in 56 B.C. (cf. *B. G.* 3. 11. 5), and against Vercingetorix in 52 (cf. *B. G.* 7. 9. 1). He followed Caesar in the Civil War (cf. Caes. *B. C.* 1. 56–58 *et passim*), and later served twice as governor of Gallia Vlterior. In spite of these favors from Caesar, he was one of the three most active and prominent leaders of the conspira-

cy (cf. Suet. *Iul.* 80; Vell. Paterc. 2. 56), and induced Caesar to go to the *curia* on the Ides of March. Caesar had designated him as one of his second heirs and as governor of Gallia Cisalpina (cf. Intr. 40). M. Junius Brutus, who is addressed (cf. **Bruto suo**), had espoused the cause of Pompey in the Civil War (cf. *Att.* 11. 4. 2), but was subsequently pardoned by Caesar and made governor of Gallia Cisalpina (cf. Ep. LXV. 10 n.). At the time of Caesar's assassination he was praetor. C. Cassius Longinus (cf. **Cassio**), as proquaestor of Syria, while Cicero was governor of Cilicia, carried on a brilliant campaign against the Parthians (cf. *quo . . . recessisse*, Ep. XXXIV. 7 n.). He supported Pompey in 49 B.C., but was subsequently pardoned by Caesar and made one of his legates (cf. Ep. LXV. 10 n.). At the time of Caesar's death he was praetor.

1. **Hirtius**: consul with Pansa in 43 B.C. Cf. Ep. LXI. 7. — **infidelissima**: this unusual superlative Cicero himself uses in Ep. LX. 2. — **provinciam**: *i.e.* Gallia Cisalpina. — **aiebat**: *sc.* Antonius. — **mediocre auxilium dignitatis**: with especial reference to **se . . . provinciam dare posse**, above. Caesar's assignment of Gallia Cisalpina to D. Brutus was, however, ratified

in urbe esse quemquam nostrum; adeo esse militum concitatos animos et plebis.   Quod utrumque esse falsum puto vos animadvertere, atque illud esse verum quod Hirtius demonstrabat, timere eum ne, si mediocre auxilium dignitatis nostrae habuissemus, nullae partes his in re p. relinquerentur.   Cum in his angustiis 2 versarer, placitum est mihi ut postularem legationem liberam mihi reliquisque nostris, ut aliqua causa proficiscendi honesta quaereretur.   Haec se impetraturum pollicitus est, nec tamen impetraturum confido; tanta est hominum insolentia et nostri insectatio.   Ac si dederint quod petimus, tamen paulo post futurum puto ut hostes iudicemur aut aqua et igni nobis interdicatur. 'Quid ergo est,' inquis, 'tui consili?'   Dandus est 3 locus fortunae: cedendum ex Italia, migrandum Rhodum aut aliquo terrarum arbitror.   Si melior casus fuerit, revertemur Romam; si mediocris, in exsilio vivemus; si pessimus, ad novissima auxilia descendemus.

---

by the senate Mar. 18. — **his**: *i.e.* Antony and his followers.

2. **placitum est**: cf. *licitum est*, Ep. LXXV. 3 n. A confusion between the active and passive forms is noticeable in early Latin and in colloquial Latin of all periods; see, *e.g.*, Guericke, *de Linguae Vulgaris Reliquiis apud Petronium*, etc., 49, and Rönsch, *It. u. Vulg.* 297 ff. See also the statement with reference to the conservative element in colloquial Latin, Intr. 70. In general, colloquial Latin is distinguished from formal Latin by a less degree of fixity in the matter of form and construction. — **legationem liberam** : cf. *legati*, Ep. I. 2 n. — **pollicitus est**: *sc.* Hirtius. — **insectatio** : apparently the first ex-

tant instance of the use of the word. Cf. Intr. 75. — **dederint** : cf. *dimisero*, Ep. XV. 2 n. — **aqua . . . interdicatur**: the technical phrase for banishment.

3. **aliquo terrarum** : cf. *quo terrarum*, Liv. 39. 54.; *ubi terrarum*, Cic. *Att.* 5. 10. 4. The limiting genitive is unusual with *aliquo*; cf. Cic. *in Cat.* 1. 17. — **ad novissima auxilia** : *i.e.* to armed resistance, as indicated by the reference to Sex. Pompeius and Bassus Caecilius below. — **novissima** : *i.e.* *extrema*, a colloquial usage noticed by Varro (*de Ling. Lat.* 6. 59), and employed by Cicero in one of his earlier orations (*pro Rosc. Com.* 30), but otherwise avoided by him (cf. Gell. 10. 21. 1 f.); cf. *novissime*

4 Succurret fortasse hoc loco alicui vestrum, cur novissimum tempus exspectemus potius quam nunc aliquid
moliamur.   Quia ubi consistamus non habemus praeter Sex. Pompeium et Bassum Caecilium, qui mihi
videntur hoc nuntio de Caesare allato firmiores futuri.
Satis tempore ad eos accedemus, ubi quid valeant sci-
erimus.   Pro Cassio et te, si quid me velitis recipere,
5 recipiam ; postulat enim hoc Hirtius ut faciam.   Rogo
vos quam primum mihi rescribatis — nam non dubito
quin de his rebus ante horam quartam Hirtius certiorem me sit facturus : quem in locum convenire
possimus, quo me velitis venire, rescribite.

6   Post novissimum Hirti sermonem placitum est mihi
postulare ut liceret nobis Romae esse publico praesidio.
Quod illos nobis concessuros non puto ; magnam enim
invidiam iis faciemus.   Nihil tamen non postulandum
putavi, quod aequum esse statuerem.

= *denique* in a letter from D.
Brutus (*Fam.* 11. 20. 1) and in one
from C. Cassius (*Fam.* 12. 13. 3).
This usage is not found in Caesar.
   4. **succurret** : for *occurret ;* a
usage not found in Cicero outside the Letters, and only three
times in them ; Ep. XC. 6 ; *Att.*
14. 1. 2. — **Sex. Pompeium** : the
son of Pompeius Magnus, who
escaped after the battle of Munda
(Caes. *fr.* p. 160, ed. Dinter), and
gathered about him in Spain
irreconcilables, freebooters, and
malcontents. — **Bassum Caecilium** : a Pompeian who, though
pardoned by Caesar after the
battle of Pharsalus, secured a
small army, entrenched himself in
Syria, and defied the power of Caesar.   On the order **Bassum Cae-**

cilium, cf. *Galli Canini*, Ep. XIX.
4 n. Brutus adopts the same order
in *Fam.* 9. 1 ; 11. 20. 1. — **de
Caesare:** euphemistic for *de morte
Caesaris.* — **pro Cassio et te:** the
letter is addressed more particularly to M. Brutus.
   6. **post . . . sermonem,** etc.:
apparently written after the conference with Hirtius referred to
above, and immediately before the
meeting of the senate on Mar. 17.
— **novissimum:** for *proximum ;*
cf. note above. — **illos:** Antony
and his followers. — **invidiam
iis faciemus:** cf. *Att.* 3. 16 *spem
facere alicui ; Fam.* 10. 18. 2 *timorem facere alicui ; Att.* 11. 8. 2
dolorem facere alicui.   It is probable that all these phrases are colloquial. Cf. Intr. 89.

LXXXVII. (*Fam.* 9. 14.)

CICERO DOLABELLAE CONSVLI SVO S.

Etsi contentus eram, mi Dolabella, tua gloria satis- 1
que ex ea magnam laetitiam voluptatemque capiebam,
tamen non possum non confiteri cumulari me maximo
gaudio, quod vulgo hominum opinio socium me adscri-
bat tuis laudibus. Neminem conveni — convenio autem
cotidie plurimos; sunt enim permulti optimi viri qui
valetudinis causa in haec loca veniant, praeterea ex
municipiis frequentes necessarii mei, — quin omnes,
cum te summis laudibus ad caelum extulerunt, mihi
continuo maximas gratias agant; negant enim se dubitare quin tu meis praeceptis et consiliis obtemperans
praestantissimum te civem et singularem consulem
praebeas.　Quibus ego quamquam verissime possum 2

LXXXVII. Pompeii, May 3,
44 B.C. One of the many dema-
gogues in Rome at this time, Herophilus or Amatius by name, who
claimed to be descended from
Gaius Marius, took advantage of
the excitement to erect an altar to
Caesar in the Forum, on the spot
where Caesar's body had been
burned. Although Herophilus was
put to death as an instigator of
riot, the altar which he had erected
remained, and a column in Caesar's honor was soon after set up.
Dolabella, Cicero's former son-in-
law, who was one of the consuls
for 44, during the absence from
Rome of his colleague Antony,
had the altar and column destroyed, and those concerned in
the movement put to death (cf.
Att. 14. 15. 1). It was this action
on Dolabella's part which called

forth this enthusiastic letter from
Cicero. The extravagant tone of
the letter has been condemned by
many, but Cicero's real purpose
was not so much to compliment
Dolabella for the vigor of his action, although he appreciated that,
as to attach him definitely to the
cause of Brutus and Cassius. This
hope of Cicero was short-lived.
Dolabella's action had been merely a bid for a bribe from the Caesarians, and when this was forth-
coming, he ceased to pose as a
republican; cf. Intr. 56.

1. **valetudinis causa**: the Bay
of Naples was and still is a favorite
health resort. Cf. *ad Baias*, Ep. V.
10 n. — **necessarii mei**: Cicero's
hold upon the *municipia* was a
strong one; cf. *concursu Italiae*,
Ep. XV. 4 n. — **ad caelum**, etc.:
cf. *Bibulus in caelo est*, Ep. VII. 2.

respondere te quae facias tuo iudicio et tua sponte facere, nec cuiusquam egere consilio, tamen neque plane adsentior ne imminuam tuam laudem, si omnis a meis consiliis profecta videatur, neque valde nego; sum enim avidior etiam quam satis est gloriae, et tamen non alienum est dignitate tua, quod ipsi Agamemnoni, regum regi, fuit honestum, habere aliquem in consiliis capiendis Nestorem, mihi vero gloriosum te iuvenem consulem florere laudibus quasi alumnum disciplinae meae.

3 L. quidem Caesar, cum ad eum aegrotum Neapolim venissem, quamquam erat oppressus totius corporis doloribus tamen, ante quam me plane salutavit, 'O mi Cicero,' inquit, 'gratulor tibi cum tantum vales apud Dolabellam, quantum si ego apud sororis filium valerem, iam salvi esse possemus; Dolabellae vero tuo et gratulor et gratias ago, quem quidem post te consulem solum possumus vere consulem dicere.' Deinde multa de facto ac de re gesta tua : nihil magnificentius, nihil praeclarius actum unquam, nihil rei p. salutarius.

4 Atque haec una vox omnium est. A te autem peto ut me hanc quasi falsam hereditatem alienae gloriae sinas cernere, meque aliqua ex parte in societatem tuarum laudum venire patiare. Quamquam, mi Dolabella — haec enim iocatus sum — libentius omnes meas, si

2. **Nestorem**: Nestor's age and experience made him the privileged counselor of his more youthful superior Agamemnon. — **iuvenem consulem**: Dolabella had been advanced to the consulship by Caesar before reaching the age required by law.

3. **L. Caesar**: cf. Ep. I. 2 n. — **cum . . . vales**: the indicative with *cum* explicative, after expressions of emotion, etc., is regular till after Cicero's time. — **sororis filium**: *i.e.* Antony; cf. Ep. I. 2 n.

4. **hereditatem . . . cernere**: a technical term used of one who wishes to accept an inheritance. — **haec iocatus sum**: *i.e. haec iocandi causa dixi;* cf. *defendam*, Ep. XCI. 7 n.; *in Verr.* ii. 1. 71 *quod interpellavit* (= *interpellandi causa dixit*) *Hortensius.*

modo sunt aliquae meae, laudes ad te transfuderim
quam aliquam partem exhauserim ex tuis. Nam cum
te semper tantum dilexerim quantum tu intellegere
potuisti, tum his tuis factis sic incensus sum ut nihil
umquam in amore fuerit ardentius; nihil est enim,
mihi crede, virtute formosius, nihil pulchrius, nihil
amabilius. Semper amavi, ut scis, M. Brutum propter 5
eius summum ingenium, suavissimos mores, singularem probitatem atque constantiam; tamen Idibus Martiis tantum accessit ad amorem ut mirarer locum fuisse
augendi in eo quod mihi iampridem cumulatum etiam
videbatur. Quis erat qui putaret ad eum amorem
quem erga te habebam posse aliquid accedere? Tantum accessit ut mihi nunc denique amare videar, antea
dilexisse. Quare quid est quod ego te horter ut digni- 6
tati et gloriae servias? Proponam tibi claros viros,
quod facere solent qui hortantur? Neminem habeo
clariorem quam te ipsum; te imitere oportet, tecum
ipse certes; ne licet quidem tibi iam tantis rebus gestis
non tui similem esse. Quod cum ita sit, hortatio non 7
est necessaria, gratulatione magis utendum est; contigit enim tibi, quod haud scio an nemini, ut summa
severitas animadversionis non modo non invidiosa, sed
etiam popularis esset et cum bonis omnibus, tum infimo

5. **singularem probitatem**:
cf., however, Intr. 23; *cuius
salutem*, Ep. XXXIV. 6 n.—
locum augendi: with this intran-
sitive use of the gerund, cf. *Att.* 7.
20. 2 *turpitudo coniungendi cum
tyranno*, and see Weissenborn *De
Gerundio et Gerundivo linguae
Latinae*, p. 138 : *neutri verborum
generi gerundia esse adscribenda*.—
amare . . . dilexisse : cf. *diligit
. . . amavit*, Ep. XXXII. 5 n.

7. **summa severitas animadversionis** : cf. Cic. *Phil.* 1. 5 *talis
animadversio fuit Dolabellae, cum
in audaces sceleratosque servos, tum
in impuros et nefarios liberos,
talisque eversio illius exsecratae
columnae ut mihi mirum videatur
tam valde reliquum tempus ab illo
uno die dissensisse.* Cf. also introd.
note. — **infimo cuique gratissima** : cf. *Att.* 14. 16. 2 *mihi
quidem videtur Brutus noster iam*

cuique gratissima. Hoc si tibi fortuna quadam conti-
gisset, gratularer felicitati tuae; sed contigit magnitudine cum animi, tum etiam ingeni atque consili. Legi
enim contionem tuam; nihil illa sapientius; ita pede-
temptim et gradatim tum accessus a te ad causam
facti, tum recessus, ut res ipsa maturitatem tibi ani-
8 madvertendi omnium concessu daret. Liberasti igitur
et urbem periculo et civitatem metu, neque solum ad
tempus maximam utilitatem attulisti, sed etiam ad exemplum. Quo facto intellegere debes in te positam
esse rem p. tibique non modo tuendos, sed etiam or-
nandos esse illos viros a quibus initium libertatis pro-
fectum est. Sed his de rebus coram plura propediem,
ut spero. Tu quoniam rem p. nosque conservas, fac
ut diligentissime te ipsum, mi Dolabella, custodias.

LXXXVIII. (*Att.* 15. 11.)

CICERO ATTICO SAL.

1 Antium veni a. d. VI Idus. Bruto iucundus noster
adventus. Deinde multis audientibus, Servilia, Ter-

*vel coronam auream per forum
ferre posse; quis enim audeat
laedere proposita cruce aut saxo,
praesertim tantis plausibus, tanta
approbatione infimorum?* — accessus . . . recessus: the figure
seems to be taken from the movements of an army in face of the
enemy. Hofmann, however, believes that Cicero is thinking of
the ebb and flow of the tide.
    8. ad tempus . . . ad exem-
plum, *you have done a very great
service, not only for the moment,
but also in the way of an example*
(for the future). — illos viros : *i.e.*

the *liberatores.* — mi Dolabella :
Cicero rarely addresses his correspondents by name (cf. Ep. X. n.).
The fact that Dolabella is addressed three times in this letter
gives to it a tone of earnestness
and of real or assumed affection.
For Dolabella's reply to this letter
cf. *Att.* 14. 21. 1 *rescripsit ad eas
(litteras) quarum exemplum tibi
miseram sane luculente.*
    LXXXVIII. Antium, June 8,
44 B.C. At a meeting of the
senate held June 5, M. Brutus and
Cassius were released from their
obligation to reside in Rome as

tulla, Porcia quaerere quid placeret. Aderat etiam
Favonius. Ego quod eram meditatus in via suadere,
ut uteretur Asiatica curatione frumenti, nihil esse iam
reliqui quod ageremus, nisi ut salvus esset; in eo etiam
ipsi rei publicae esse praesidium. Quam orationem
cum ingressus essem, Cassius intervenit. Ego eadem
illa repetivi. Hoc loco fortibus sane oculis Cassius —
Martem spirare diceres — se in Siciliam non iturum :
' Egone ut beneficium accepissem contumeliam?' 'Quid
ergo agis?' inquam. At ille in Achaiam se iturum.
' Quid tu,' inquam, ' Brute?' ' Romam,' inquit, ' si

praetors and commissioned to
supply Rome with grain. They
retired to Antium to discuss with
Cicero the best course to take in
view of the senate's action.

1. **Servilia** : sister of Cato
Vticensis and the mother of M.
Brutus, a woman of great strength
of character, political influence,
and judgment, whom Cicero calls
*prudentissima et diligentissima
femina, Ep. ad Brut.* 1. 18. 1.
After the death of her first husband, M. Junius Brutus (father of
the conspirator M. Brutus), she
married D. Junius Silanus. One
of the children of this second
marriage, Tertia or **Tertulla**,
married C. Cassius. — **Porcia** :
the daughter of Cato Vticensis
and the second wife of M. Brutus.
This little group of brilliant women,
ardent republicans and closely
bound by marriage and blood relationship to M. Brutus, C. Cassius,
and Cato, seems to have played an
important part in the politics of
this period. Cf. for instance *Servilia pollicebatur*, etc., 2, also *Att.*
13. 16. 2. — **quaerere** : *sc.* Brutus;
hist. infin. — **Favonius** : cf. Ep.
XV. 7 n. — **suadere** : hist. inf.; cf.

quaerere, above. — **Asiatica . . .
frumenti** : cf. introd. note. —
Martem spirare : cf. *Q. fr.* 3. 4.
6 Ἄρη πνέων. Cf. also Lucr. 5.
392 *tantum spirantes aequo cer-
tamine bellum ;* Hor. *Od.* 4. 13. 19
quae spirabat amores. — in **Siciliam** : no province had been assigned to Cassius or Brutus by
Caesar before his death (cf. Schelle,
*Beiträge zur Geschichte des Todes-
kampfes der römischen Republik*),
but the rumor was current that the
senate on June 5 had allotted
Sicily to Cassius, an appointment
much below his expectations. Cf.
Cicero's remarks (*Att.* 15. 9. 1) on
June 2 in anticipation of this
action : IV *Non. vesperi a Balbo
redditae mihi litterae fore Nonis
senatum, ut Brutus in Asia, Cassius
in Sicilia frumentum emendum et
ad urbem mittendum curarent. O
rem miseram! primum ullam ab
istis, dein, si aliquam, hanc legato-
riam (mercatoriam* H.) *provinciam.*
— **egone**, etc.: the question expresses his indignation at the
proposed appointment ; cf. Plaut.
Amph. 818 *tun mecum fueris ?*
Cic. *Q. fr.* 1. 3. 1 *ego tibi irascerer ?*
— ut benefi*cium, as a favor.* —

tibi videtur.' 'Mihi vero minime ; tuto enim non eris.'
'Quid si possem esse, placeretne?' 'Atque ut omnino
neque nunc neque ex praetura in provinciam ires ; sed
auctor non sum ut te urbi committas.' Dicebam ea
quae tibi profecto in mentem veniunt cur non esset
2 tuto futurus.   Multo inde sermone querebantur — atque id quidem Cassius maxime — amissas occasiones,
Decimumque graviter accusabant.   Ego negabam oportere praeterita, adsentiebar tamen.   Cumque ingressus
essem dicere quid oportuisset — nec vero quicquam
novi, sed ea quae cotidie omnes — nec tamen illum
locum attingerem, quemquam praeterea oportuisse
tangi, sed senatum vocari, populum ardentem studio
vehementius incitari, totam suscipi rem publicam, ex-
clamat tua familiaris : 'Hoc vero neminem umquam
audivi.'   Ego repressi.   Sed et Cassius mihi videbatur

---

si tibi videtur : cf. Ep. LXXV.
4 n. — **tuto eris** : cf. Intr. 85. *a*. —
atque, *yes, indeed, and ;* frequently
used in conversation in affirmative
answers ; cf. Plaut. *M. G.* 337 PA.
*Nempe tu istic ais esse erilem concu-
binam ?* SC. *Atque arguo eam me
vidisse osculantem hic intus cum
alieno viro ; ibid.* 368 PH. *Tun me
vidisti ?* SC. *Atque his quidem
hercle oculis.* — **ut . . . neque . . .
neque** : for *ne . . . aut . . . aut.* Hofmann compares *Fam.* 9. 2. 3 *ut ea
quae agebantur hic quaeque dicebantur nec viderem nec audirem ;
Att.* 15. 13. 1 *adsentior tibi ut nec
duces simus nec agmen cogamus.* —
ex praetura : *i.e.* at the close of
the year. — **auctor ut . . . committas** : for another construction,
see Ep. XLV. 3.
   2. **Decimum** : Decimus Brutus
had shown himself without plans
and without energy in the critical

days following Caesar's assassination. Cf. especially Ep. LXXXVI.
3.   The other conspirators were,
however, equally helpless.   In
his province D. Brutus had likewise been inactive. — **oportuisset** : *fieri* is omitted, as often
with *oportet, potest, solet,* etc.; cf.
Brix on Plaut. *Trin.* 705 ; Lorenz
on *M. G.* 252. — **quemquam . . .
tangi** : a covert reference to the
mistake in not killing Antony.
Cf. *Fam.* 12. 4. 1 *vellem Idibus
Martiis me ad cenam (i.e.* to the
murder of Caesar) *invitasses : reli-
quiarum nihil fuisset.   Nunc me
reliquiae vestrae exercent.*   See
also *Fam.* 10. 28. 1.   **tangi** is
euphemistic for *occidi.* — **tua familiaris** : *i.e.* Servilia. — **neminem** : *sc. dicentem.* — **ego repressi** : *sc. me,* or perhaps with Böckel
quae dicturus eram.   With such
a phrase the reference would be

iturus ; etenim Servilia pollicebatur se curaturam ut illa frumenti curatio de senatus consulto tolleretur, et noster cito deiectus est de illo inani sermone — velle Romae se dixerat. Constituit igitur ut ludi absente se fierent suo nomine ; proficisci autem mihi in Asiam videbatur ab Antio velle. Ne multa, nihil me in illo 3 itinere praeter conscientiam meam delectavit ; non enim fuit committendum ut ille ex Italia priusquam a me conventus esset discederet. Hoc dempto munere amoris atque offici sequebatur ut mecum ipse,

ἡ δεῦρ' ὁδός σοι τί δύναται [νῦν], θεοπρόπε ;

Prorsus dissolutum offendi navigium, vel potius dissipatum : nihil consilio, nihil ratione, nihil ordine. Itaque, etsi ne antea quidem dubitavi, tamen nunc eo minus evolare hinc, idque quam primum, ' ubi nec Pelopidarum facta neque famam audiam.' Sed heus tu, ne forte sis 4 nescius, Dolabella me sibi legavit a. d. IV Nonas. Id mihi heri vesperi nuntiatum est. Votiva ne tibi qui-

to quemquam . . . tangi. — iturus : *i.e.* into the province which it was thought the senate had assigned to him. — illa frumenti curatio : Servilia hoped that she could induce the senate to reconsider its assignment of the grain commission to Cassius. — noster : *sc. Brutus.* — illo inani sermone : referring to *Romam, si tibi videtur,* 1. — ludi : it was the duty of M. Brutus as *praetor urbanus* to take charge of the *ludi Apollinares.*

3. ne multa : *sc. dicam.* — hoc dempto . . . offici, *apart from this service which love and duty too required of me.* — sequebatur : subject is ut mecum (*sc. cogitarem*). — ἡ δεῦρ' ὁδός, etc.: Cicero uses the same quotation from an unknown

comic poet, of an unsatisfactory journey to Greece in *Att.* 16. 6. 2. — navigium : the state here, as often, is compared to a ship. Cf. *contraxi vela,* Ep. V. 2 n. — nihil consilio, etc.: *sc. fit.* Cf. *Decimum,* 2 n. — ubi . . . audiam : from an unknown poet (cf. Ribbeck, *Trag. Rom. Frag.* p. 252). Cicero uses the phrase in four other places. The full verse was probably *Vbi nec Pelopidarum nomen nec facta aut famam audiam.* The *Pelopidae* and their dreadful deeds typify, as in *Fam.* 7. 30. 1, the Caesarians and their course of action.

4. heus tu : cf. Ep. XXXV. 25 n. — Dolabella . . . legavit: *sc.* for his province Syria. — votiva : *sc. legatio.* The *legatio votiva* was a

dem placebat; etenim erat absurdum, quae, si stetisset
res publica, vovissem, ea me eversa illa vota dissolvere,
et habent, opinor, liberae legationes definitum tempus
lege Iulia nec facile addi potest.   Aveo genus lega-
tionis ut, cum velis, introire exire liceat, quod nunc
mihi additum est ; bella est autem huius iuris quin-
quenni licentia.   Quamquam quid de quinquennio
cogitem ?   Contrahi mihi negotium videtur ; sed βλάσφημα mittamus.

LXXXIX. *(Fam. 7. 22.)*

CICERO TREBATIO S.

Inluseras heri inter scyphos quod dixeram contro-
versiam esse possetne heres, quod furtum antea factum esset, furti recte agere.   Itaque, etsi domum bene
potus seroque redieram, tamen id caput, ubi haec con-
troversia est, notavi et descriptum tibi misi, ut scires
id quod tu neminem sensisse dicebas, Sex. Aelium,

legatio libera (cf. *legati*, Ep. I. 2 n.)
undertaken on the pretext of performing a vow. — **quae . . . vovissem,** *those vows which I had made
for the preservation of the commonwealth.* — **dissolvere :** for *sol-
vere.* — **lege Iulia :** a law proposed.
by Cicero in his consulship and
passed limited a *legatio libera* to
one year. Caesar's *lex Iulia* was
probably to the same effect ; cf.
Momm. *St. R.* II. 691. — **introire
exire liceat :** as legate of Dolabella, Cicero's term of office would
continue through Dolabella's proconsulship, *i.e.* five years, and
Cicero would be at liberty to remain in Rome or away from the
city as he pleased. On the asyndeton, cf. Intr. 94. — **exire :** *sc. ex*

urbe as in Ep. L. 1.   The ellipsis
is colloquial. — **βλάσφημα,** *ill-
omened words.*

LXXXIX. T u s c u l u m (?),
June, (?) 44 B.C.

possetne heres, etc., *whether
an heir could properly bring action
for a theft committed before* (he
became the heir). — **furti :** the
genitive to indicate the charge. —
bene potus : cf. Intr. 90. — **id
caput,** *that chapter* or *section ;* so
quoddam caput legis, Att. 3. 15. 6.
— **Sex. Aelium** *(Paetum) :* consul
in 198 B.C., an authority upon
jurisprudence and civil law, often
mentioned by Cicero, *e.g. Brut.* 78;
Tusc. Disp. I. 18. His name is
coupled with that of Manilius in *de
Or.* I. 212 also. — **M'. Manilium :**

M'. Manilium, M. Brutum sensisse.   Ego tamen Scaevolae et Testae adsentior.

XC. (*Fam.* 16. 21.)

CICERO F. TIRONI SVO DVLCISSIMO S.

Cum vehementer tabellarios exspectarem cotidie, 1
aliquando venerunt post diem quadragensimum et sextum quam a vobis discesserant.   Quorum mihi fuit
adventus exoptatissimus ; nam cum maximam cepissem
laetitiam ex humanissimi et carissimi patris epistula,
tum vero iucundissimae tuae litterae cumulum mihi
gaudi attulerunt.   Itaque me iam non paenitebat inter-

---

cf. Ep. XXV. 2 n. — **M.** (*Iunium*)
Brutum: an authority on civil law,
upon which subject he composed
three books. — **Scaevolae** : consul in 133 B.C., and frequently
quoted by Cicero as a legal authority. — **Testae** : *i.e.* Trebatius.

XC. Athens, July–Oct., 44 B.C.
On young Marcus, cf. Intr. 54.
The young man had been pursuing
his studies at Athens for about a
year and a half, but he was fonder
of the pleasures of life than of
study, and the reports which came
to the father from Leonides (cf.
Att. 14. 16. 3; 15. 16 A.), under
whose special care he had been
put, were so unfavorable that
Cicero had considered the advisability of going to Athens to investigate the matter.   In view of this
alarming possibility, the young
man wrote this letter to Cicero's
confidential secretary, Tiro.   This
and *Fam.* 16. 25 are the only
letters extant from a rather large
correspondence, known to the
ancients, of the young Marcus

with his father and with Tiro.
Most of the stylistic peculiarities
of the letter may be classified
under the following categories:
(1) extravagance of statement; (2)
the use of Greek words ; (3) a
tendency to use certain expressions otherwise rarely found outside the writings of the elder
Cicero ; (4) colloquialisms.

On dulcissimo, cf. Intr. 88 *a*.

1. post . . . sextum : the distance from Rome to Athens could
be covered in 21 days (cf. Intr. 64)
under favorable circumstances.
Possibly young Marcus had de-
layed in replying and wished to
conceal that fact.   The archaic
form **quadragensimum** is sufficiently supported by *tricensima*
(*Fam.* 10. 31. 5) and *quadra-
gensimo* (*Fam.* 10. 33. 5).   Cf. also
C.I.L. I. 198. 21 and 199. 27.
See also Crit. Append. — **exoptatissimus** : the generous use of
superlatives in the first sentence
illustrates well young Cicero's desire to please his correspondent.

capedinem scribendi fecisse, sed potius laetabar ; fructum enim magnum humanitatis tuae capiebam ex
silentio mearum litterarum.   Vehementer igitur gaudeo
te meam sine dubitatione accepisse excusationem.
2 Gratos tibi optatosque esse qui de me rumores adfe-
runtur non dubito, mi dulcissime Tiro, praestaboque
et enitar ut in dies magis magisque haec nascens de me
duplicetur opinio.   Quare, quod polliceris te bucinatorem fore existimationis meae, firmo id constantique
animo facias licet; tantum enim mihi dolorem cruciatumque attulerunt errata aetatis meae ut non solum
animus a factis, sed aures quoque a commemoratione
abhorreant.   Cuius te sollicitudinis et doloris partici-
pem fuisse notum exploratumque est mihi, nec id
mirum ; nam cum omnia mea causa velles mihi successa, tum etiam tua ; socium enim te meorum commo-

---

See also Intr. 96. — **vehementer** :
cf. Intr. 90.

   2. **gratos   optatosque** :   cf.
firmo constantique, 2 ;   *dolorem
cruciatumque*, 2 ; *sollicitudinis et
doloris*, 2 ; *frugi severaque*, 4 ;
familiaribus   et convictoribus, 5 ;
and *gratum acceptumque*, 7 ; see
also *oro obsecro*, Ep. L. 1 n.—
rumores : more favorable reports
mentioned in   Tiro's letter, to
which this epistle is an answer. —
gratos . . . esse . . . non dubito :
cf. Pollio, *Fam.* 10. 31. 5 *illud me
Cordubae pro contione dixisse nemo
vocabit in   dubium ;*   Trebonius,
Fam. 12. 16. 2 *cui nos et caritate et
amore tuum officium praestaturos
non debes dubitare.*   Cf. also Ter.
Hec. 326; Varr. *Ling. Lat.* 7. 107.
The infin. after *non dubito* is not
found in Cicero (cf., however, a
scarcely parallel passage in Cic.
de Fin. 3. 38).   In all the cases

cited the dependent verb precedes
non dubito, and the writer in using
the acc. and infin. has in mind a
verb of thinking in general, and
not the special phrase *non dubito*.
When *non dubito* precedes, *quin*
with the subj. is always used; cf.
7 of this letter. See also Schmalz,
*Ueber d. Sprachgebrauch d. Asinius
Pollio*, p. 88. — mi **dulcissime
Tiro** : cf. *mi Pomponi*, Ep. X. n.
and Intr. 88 *a*. — **in dies magis
magisque** : for the strict classical
expression *in dies magis* (cf. Cic.
pro Mil. 25). — **bucinatorem** : apparently not used in the figurative sense elsewhere. — **successa:**
Mendelssohn cites, as parallel to
this unusual participle, *custodibus
discessis* from Coelius Antipater
and *sole occaso* from Q. Claudius.
Schwabe conjectures *successe* (for
successisse) with considerable probability. Cf. *decesse*, Ep. XIX. 2 n.

dorum semper esse volui.   Quoniam igitur tum ex me 3
doluisti, nunc ut duplicetur tuum ex me gaudium praestabo.   Cratippo me scito non ut discipulum sed ut
filium esse coniunctissimum; nam cum audio illum
libenter, tum etiam propriam eius suavitatem vehementer amplector.   Sum totos dies cum eo noctisque
saepenumero partem; exoro enim ut mecum quam saepissime cenet.   Hac introducta consuetudine saepe
inscientibus nobis et cenantibus obrepit, sublataque
severitate philosophiae humanissime nobiscum iocatur.
Quare da operam ut hunc talem, tam iucundum, tam
excellentem virum videas quam primum.   Nam quid 4
ego de Bruttio dicam?   Quem nullo tempore a me
patior discedere, cuius cum frugi severaque est vita,
tum etiam iucundissima convictio; non est enim se-
iunctus iocus a philologia et cotidiana συζητήσει.   Huic
ego locum in proximo conduxi et, ut possum, ex meis
angustiis illius sustento tenuitatem.   Praeterea decla- 5
mitare Graece apud Cassium institui; Latine autem
apud Bruttium exerceri volo.   Vtor familiaribus et
cotidianis convictoribus, quos secum Mytilenis Cratip-
pus adduxit, hominibus et doctis et illi probatissimis.

3. **ut duplicetur**: for the classical acc. and infin. after *praestare*
(cf. Cic. *Tusc. Disp.* 5. 29).   The
same construction is used by Marcellus, *Fam.* 4. 11. 2.   Similarly
the negative form of the dependent
clause after *praestare* is expressed
by *ne* with the subj. in the letters
of Cicero's less careful correspondents; cf. Cael. *Fam.* 8. 10. 5; D.
Brut. Ep. XCVII. 1; C. Cass. *Fam.*
12. 13. 4. — **Cratippo**: a celebrated Peripatetic, and young Marcus's principal instructor in philosophy (cf. *de Off.* 1. 1).

4. **Bruttio**: see 5 n. — **nullo
tempore**: for *numquam;* cf. *hoc
loco* for *hic*, 7; *hoc tempore* for *iam*,
Att. 8. 12 c. 3.   Such periphrastic
expressions are common in Plautus
and Terence. — **in proximo**: for
the phrase cf. Ter. *Heaut.* 54;
Hec. 341. — **ex meis angustiis**:
a pathetic hint at an increased
allowance.   The income of young
Marcus was by no means a small
one.   Cf. Ep. LXXIV. 2 *praestabo
nec Bibulum*, etc.

5. **Cassium, Bruttium**: teachers of elocution, not mentioned else-

Multum etiam mecum est Epicrates, princeps Atheni-
ensium, et Leonides et horum ceteri similes. Τὰ μὲν
6 οὖν καθ' ἡμᾶς τάδε. De Gorgia autem quod mihi scribis, erat quidem ille in cotidiana declamatione utilis,
sed omnia postposui dummodo praeceptis patris pare-
rem ; διαρρήδην enim scripserat ut eum dimitterem
statim. Tergiversari nolui, ne mea nimia σπουδὴ
suspicionem ei aliquam importaret ; deinde illud etiam
mihi succurrebat, grave esse me de iudicio patris iudi-
7 care. Tuum tamen studium et consilium gratum
acceptumque est mihi. Excusationem angustiarum
tui temporis accipio ; scio enim quam soleas esse occupatus. Emisse te praedium vehementer gaudeo, feliciterque tibi rem istam evenire cupio. Hoc loco me
tibi gratulari noli mirari ; eodem enim fere loco tu quoque emisse te fecisti me certiorem. Habes : deponen-
dae tibi sunt urbanitates ; rusticus Romanus factus es.
Quomodo ego mihi nunc ante oculos tuum iucundissimum conspectum propono ? Videor enim videre emen-
tem te rusticas res, cum vilico loquentem, in lacinia

where. It is noticeable that both
are Romans. — **Epicrates** : otherwise unknown. — **Leonides** : cf.
introd. note. — τὰ μὲν οὖν, etc.,
*that's the way things stand with
me.* The use of Greek words and
phrases in this letter is noticeable,
but not surprising in a letter from
a student at Athens. Cf. Intr.
97.

6. **Gorgia** : an instructor whose
influence had demoralized young
Marcus, and whom the elder
Cicero had evidently ordered his
son to dismiss. — **tergiversari** :
a common word in Cicero's writings, but rare in other authors. —
σπουδὴ, *esteem* (for him). — im-

portaret : a colloquial word borrowed from commercial language ;
cf. Naegelsbach, *Stilistik*,[7] p. 346.
— **succurrebat** : for *occurrebat ;*
cf. *succurret,* Ep. LXXXVI. 4 n.

7. **feliciterque . . . cupio** : cf.
Ep. LXXX. 2 n. — **hoc loco,** *at
this point* (in my letter). Courtesy
would have naturally called for an
earlier reference to Tiro's purchase. — **habes** : used either absolutely or, as it was colloquially
employed, of a telling blow in the
arena, *i.e.* 'you are hit.' Cf. *hoc
igitur habebis,* Ep. LXIX. 2 n. See
also Verg. *Aen.* 12. 296 ; Plaut.
Most. 715 ; Ter. *And.* 83, with note
of Donatus. — **mihi . . . ante**

servantem ex mensa secunda semina.   Sed, quod ad
rem pertinet, me tum tibi defuisse aeque ac tu doleo.
Sed noli dubitare, mi Tiro, quin te sublevaturus sim, si
modo fortuna me, praesertim cum sciam communem
nobis emptum esse istum fundum.   De mandatis, quod 8
tibi curae fuit, est mihi gratum ; sed peto a te ut quam
celerrime mihi librarius mittatur, maxime quidem Grae-
cus ; multum mihi enim eripitur operae in exscribendis
hypomnematis.   Tu velim in primis cures ut valeas, ut
una συμφιλολογεῖν possimus.   Anterum tibi commendo.
Vale.

XCI. (*Fam.* 11. 27.)

M. CICERO MATIO S.

Nondum satis constitui molestiaene plus an volup- 1
tatis attulerit mihi Trebatius noster, homo cum plenus

oculos . . . **propono**: cf. *mihi ante
oculos*, Ep. XIII. 3 n. — **mensa
secunda**: when fruit was served.

8. de mandatis : cf. Intr. 91.
The stereotyped character of the
introductory phrase with *de* is
shown here by its lack of influence
upon the construction of the rest
of the sentence. — **hypomnematis** : the dative and ablative
plural of Greek nouns in *-ma* ends
sometimes in *-ibus*, sometimes in
-is, with a decided preference in
classical Latin for the heteroclite
ending *-is*, as though the noun
were a feminine noun of the first
declension or a neuter of the
second. — **Anterum** : the *tabellarius*.

The good intentions of young
Marcus stated so extravagantly
here were serious; for a month or
two before this letter was written

Trebonius, who was at Athens,
wrote to Cicero (*Fam.* 12. 16. 1),
*vidi filium tuum deditum optimis
studiis summaque modestiae fama ;
. . . noli putare, mi Cicero, me hoc
auribus tuis dare ; nihil adulescente tuo atque adeo nostro . . .
aut amabilius omnibus eis qui
Athenis sunt est aut studiosius
earum artium quas tu maxime
amas, hoc est optimarum.* It
cannot be too keenly regretted
that young Marcus makes no
mention of Horace, who was of
the same age and was pursuing his
studies in Athens at this time.

XCI. Tusculum, Aug. 23–30,
44 B.C.   C. Matius Calvena, to
whom this is written, was probably
a little younger than Cicero ; cf.
2 n. ; Ep. XCII. 5 n.   In recognition of his accomplishments
Cicero calls him *doctissimus* (Ep.

offici, tum utriusque nostrum amantissimus.   Nam,
cum in Tusculanum vesperi venissem, postridie ille ad
me, nondum satis firmo corpore cum esset, mane venit.
Quem cum obiurgarem quod parum valetudini parce-
ret, tum ille nihil sibi longius fuisse quam ut me
videret. 'Numquidnam,' inquam, 'novi?' Detulit ad
me querelam tuam, de qua prius quam respondeo pauca
2 proponam.   Quantum memoria repetere praeterita possum, nemo est mihi te amicus antiquior; sed vetustas
habet aliquid commune cum multis, amor non habet.
Dilexi te quo die cognovi, meque a te diligi iudicavi.
Tuus deinde discessus isque diuturnus, ambitio nostra
et vitae dissimilitudo non est passa voluntates nostras
consuetudine conglutinari; tuum tamen erga me animum agnovi multis annis ante bellum civile, cum Cae-

XXVIII. 2 and this letter, 8).
Later in life Matius wrote a book
upon gastronomy (Columella, 12.
4. 2). He belonged to that group
of men who attached themselves
closely to the fortunes of Caesar, but not, like many of his
comrades, with the hope of personal gain. He followed Caesar
out of pure friendship and admiration. When Caesar was killed,
therefore, he found no common
point of sympathy either with
those who rejoiced in the death of
a tyrant, as did Cicero, or with
those who used Caesar's name to
conjure with, as did Antony. His
grief at Caesar's death and his
superintendence of the public
games in his name called forth
unfriendly criticism from Cicero.
The sorrow of Matius upon hearing this fact was disclosed to
Cicero by their common friend
Trebatius (cf. Ep. XXI. introd.
note), who had made the ac-

quaintance of Matius nine years
before in Gaul (cf. Ep. XXVIII.
2), and led to the writing of this
letter.
    1. nihil sibi longius fuisse :
i.e. 'nothing was more desired by
him.' This is the meaning of the
phrase when followed by *quam ut*
or *quam dum*, but when followed
by *quam* with the infin. it means
'nothing is more tiresome.' Cf.
Antibarbarus s. v. longus. — querelam tuam : cf. introd. note.
    2. vetustas : Cicero had appar-
ently known Matius for twenty
years or more ; cf. next note. —
tuus deinde discessus: on deinde
cf. Intr. 85 *b*. The reference is to
the absence of Matius from Rome
at some time prior to Cicero's candidacy for the consulship; cf. ambitio nostra. — vitae dissimilitudo : Matius apparently never
entered public life. — conglutinari : the metaphorical use of the
word is frequent in Cicero.

sar esset in Gallia ; quod enim vementer mihi utile
esse putabas nec inutile ipsi Caesari, perfecisti ut ille
me diligeret, coleret, haberet in suis. Multa praetereo
quae temporibus illis inter nos familiarissime dicta,
scripta, communicata sunt ; graviora enim consecuta
sunt. Et initio belli civilis cum Brundisium versus 3
ires ad Caesarem, venisti ad me in Formianum.
Primum hoc ipsum quanti, praesertim temporibus illis !
Deinde oblitum me putas consili sermonis humanitatis
tuae ? Quibus rebus interesse memini Trebatium.
Nec vero sum oblitus litterarum tuarum quas ad me
misisti, cum Caesari obviam venisses in agro, ut
arbitror, Trebulano. Secutum illud tempus est cum 4
me ad Pompeium proficisci sive pudor meus coegit sive
officium sive fortuna. Quod officium tuum, quod studium vel in absentem me vel in praesentis meos defuit?
Quem porro omnes mei et mihi et sibi te amiciorem
iudicaverunt ? Veni Brundisium: oblitumne me putas
qua celeritate, ut primum audieris, ad me Tarento
advolaris, quae tua fuerit adsessio oratio confirmatio

3. **Brundisium versus**: cf. *ad
Alpis versus*, Ep. XLVIII. 2 n. —
venisti . . . in Formianum : *sc.*
Mar. 19, 49 B.C.; cf. *Att.* 9. 11. 2.
Caesar himself entered Brundisium Mar. 18. — **consili** : Matius
earnestly desired peace and without doubt encouraged Cicero in
his efforts at mediation ; cf. *Att.* 9.
11. 2. — **Trebulano** : in Campania;
but Cicero's memory is very likely
at fault, as he probably has in
mind the messages which he received from Matius from Minturnae on Mar. 20 ; cf. *Att.* 9. 12. 1.

4. **pudor meus . . . sive officium** : cf. Intr. 30 (end) and Ep.
LXV. 6.—**praesentis meos**: his

family in Rome. — **veni Brundisium** : after the battle of Pharsalus. Cf. Intr. 32. The friendly
offices of the Caesarian Matius
in this moment of helplessness and
loneliness would be especially
prized.—**adsessio,** etc.: the rapidity of movement which substantives in *-io* lend to a narrative is
nowhere better illustrated than in
this passage (cf. Intr. 75). This
rapidity of movement is further
heightened by the asyndetical
arrangement of many of the sentences and by the use of paratactical forms of expression ; for, as
Andresen remarks, in three different instances in 4 and 5 temporal

5 animi mei fracti communium miseriarum metu? Tandem aliquando Romae esse coepimus. Quid defuit
nostrae familiaritati? In maximis rebus quonam modo
gererem me adversus Caesarem usus tuo consilio sum,
in reliquis officio. Cui tu tribuisti, excepto Caesare,
praeter me ut domum ventitares horasque multas saepe
suavissimo sermone consumeres — tum cum etiam, si
meministi, ut haec φιλοσοφούμενα scriberem tu me
impulisti? Post Caesaris reditum quid tibi maiori
curae fuit quam ut essem ego illi quam familiarissi-
6 mus? Quod effeceras. Quorsum igitur haec oratio
longior quam putaram? Quia sum admiratus te, qui
haec nosse deberes, quicquam a me commissum quod
esset alienum nostra amicitia credidisse; nam praeter
haec quae commemoravi, quae testata sunt et in-
lustria, habeo multa occultiora quae vix verbis
exsequi possum. Omnia me tua delectant, sed
maxime maxima cum fides in amicitia consilium
gravitas constantia, tum lepos humanitas litterae.
7 Quapropter — redeo nunc ad querelam — ego te suffra-
gium tulisse in illa lege primum non credidi; deinde,
si credidissem, numquam id sine aliqua iusta causa
existimarem te fecisse. Dignitas tua facit ut animad-

clauses stand as independent sentences. These three cases are :
secutum illud tempus est; veni
Brundisium, and tandem . . .
coepimus.— communium miseriarum : *sc.* which would result
from the overthrow of the state.

5. tandem aliquando : in Sept.
47 B.C.; cf. Intr. 33. — φιλοσοφούμενα : probably the *Academica*,
the *de Finibus*, and the *Tusculanae
Disputationes*, although there is no

reference to Matius in any one of
these works. — post Caesaris
reditum : in Sept., 45 B.C., after
the battle of Munda. Cf. Intr. 35.
— maiori curae : cf. *minori curae*, Ep. XXV. 2 n. — quod effeceras : *sc.* before Caesar's return.

7. illa lege : probably the *lex
de permutatione provinciarum*,
whose passage Antony secured apparently in the summer of 44 B.C.
(cf. Ruete, *Die Correspondenz*

vertatur quicquid facias; malevolentia autem hominum, ut nonnulla durius quam a te facta sint proferantur. Ea tu si non audis, quid dicam nescio. Equidem, si quando audio, tam defendo quam me scio a te contra iniquos meos solere defendi. Defensio autem est duplex: alia sunt quae liquido negare soleam, ut de isto ipso suffragio; alia quae defendam a te pie fieri et humane, ut de curatione ludorum. Sed te hominem 8 doctissimum non fugit, si Caesar rex fuerit — quod mihi quidem videtur, — in utramque partem de tuo officio disputari posse, vel in eam qua ego soleo uti, laudandam esse fidem et humanitatem tuam, qui amicum etiam mortuum diligas, vel in eam qua nonnulli utuntur, libertatem patriae vitae amici anteponendam. Ex his sermonibus utinam essent delatae ad te disputationes meae! Illa vero duo quae maxima sunt laudum tuarum, quis aut libentius quam ego commemorat aut saepius? te et non suscipiendi belli civilis gravissimum auctorem fuisse et moderandae victoriae, in quo qui mihi non adsentiretur inveni neminem. Quare habeo gratiam Trebatio familiari nostro qui mihi dedit causam harum litterarum, quibus nisi credideris, me omnis offici et humanitatis expertem iudicaris; quo nec mihi gravius quicquam potest esse nec te alienius.

Ciceros, 29–30; Schmidt, *Kämpfe,* 718). See Intr. 40. — **malevolentia**: *sc. facit.* — **ea . . . audis**: with reference to **nonnulla.** — **liquido**: a word used by Cicero only in his early letters and in his letters. See also Spengel to Ter. *And.* 729. — **defendam**: for *defendendi causa dicam;* cf. *haec iocatus sum,* Ep. LXXXVII. 4 n. — **de curatione ludorum**: games

which Caesar had vowed at Pharsalus, and which were given in his name in July, 44 B.C. Cf. Ep. XCII. 6.

8. libertatem . . . anteponendam: this was probably Cicero's real view. Cf. *Att.* 15. 2. 3 *ludorum . . . apparatus et Matius ac Postumius mihi procuratores non placent.* Cf. also introd. note. — **te . . . auctorem fuisse**: cf. *consili,* 3 n.

XCII. (*Fam.* 11. 28.)

MATIVS CICERONI S.

1 Magnam voluptatem ex tuis litteris cepi, quod quam
speraram atque optaram habere te de me opinionem
cognovi. De qua etsi non dubitabam, tamen, quia
maximi aestimabam, ut incorrupta maneret laborabam.
Conscius autem mihi eram nihil a me commissum
esse quod boni cuiusquam offenderet animum. Eo
minus credebam plurimis atque optimis artibus ornato
tibi temere quicquam persuaderi potuisse, praesertim
in quem mea propensa et perpetua fuisset atque esset
benevolentia. Quod quoniam ut volui scio esse,
respondebo criminibus quibus tu pro me, ut par erat
tua singulari bonitate et amicitia nostra, saepe resti-
2 tisti. Nota enim mihi sunt quae in me post Caesaris
mortem contulerint: vitio mihi dant quod mortem
hominis necessari graviter fero atque eum quem dilexi
perisse indignor ; aiunt enim patriam amicitiae praeponendam esse, proinde ac si iam vicerint obitum eius

XCII. Rome, Aug. 23-30, 44
B.C. In the correspondence of
Cicero perhaps there is no letter
written more strongly, more skilfully constructed, and better calculated to accomplish its purpose
than Cicero's letter to Matius. It
is a work of art — but in that
very fact lies its defect, and in that
respect it is in contrast to the
reply of Matius. The latter reveals
that '*fides in amicitia*,' which the
name of Matius always suggests,
while the sincerity of his statements and the simplicity of his
style make this one of the most
admirable of the non-Ciceronian
letters. Upon Matius and this

letter cf. Schmalz in *Commenta-
tiones Wölfflinianae* (Lips. 1891),
269 ff.

1. **speraram atque optaram** :
cf. Intr. 82. — **quia aestimabam** :
quia for *quod* after **laborabam**
is probably colloquial; cf. Ep.
LXXVII. 2 n. — **par . . . bonitate**: *par*, like *aequus*, governs the
abl. occasionally, especially in
early Latin. Cf. Plaut. *Pers.* 834
et me haud par est. Böckel.

2. **nota . . . sunt quae . . .
contulerint** : for the reference cf.
Ep. XCI. 7 *ea tu si*, etc. — **patriam
. . . praeponendam esse** : cf. Ep.
XCI. 8. — **proinde ac** : cf. *perinde
ut*, Ep. LXVII. 1 n. — **vicerint** :

rei p. fuisse utilem.   Sed non agam astute : fateor
me ad istum gradum sapientiae non pervenisse; neque
enim Caesarem in dissensione civili sum secutus,
sed amicum.   Quamquam re offendebar, tamen non
deserui, neque bellum unquam civile aut etiam causam
dissensionis probavi, quam etiam nascentem exstingui
summe studui.   Itaque in victoria hominis necessari
neque honoris neque pecuniae dulcedine sum captus,
quibus praemiis reliqui, minus apud eum quam ego
cum possent, immoderate sunt abusi.   Atque etiam
res familiaris mea lege Caesaris deminuta est, cuius
beneficio plerique qui Caesaris morte laetantur remanserunt in civitate.   Civibus victis ut parceretur aeque
ac pro mea salute laboravi.   Possum igitur, qui omnis 3
voluerim incolumis, eum a quo id impetratum est
perisse non indignari, cum praesertim idem homines
illi et invidiae et exitio fuerint ?   ' Plecteris ergo,'
inquiunt, ' quoniam factum nostrum improbare audes.'
O superbiam inauditam, alios in facinore gloriari, aliis
ne dolere quidem inpunite licere!   At haec etiam

sc. dicendo ; cf. 4, below. For
the same use of *vincere*, cf. Plaut.
Most. 95 *profecto esse . . . vera vincam ;* Hor. *Sat.* 2. 3. 225 *vincet
enim stultos ratio insanire nepotes.*
— **Caesarem** : *sc.* the statesman
or general. — **summe**: as an intensive adverb *summe* is found in
Cicero's earlier writings (*e.g. Div.
in Caecil.* 57), in the *de Fin.*, and in
his correspondence (*e.g. Fam.* 4.
7. 2). — **in victoria** : *in* with the
abl. is used colloquially for a conditional or temporal clause. Here
in victoria, etc., is equivalent to
cum vicisset homo necessarius. —
lege Caesaris : the *lex Iulia de
modo credendi et possidendi intra*

Italiam, limiting the extent to
which land could be mortgaged,
etc. Cf. Lange, *Röm. Alterth.* III².
435. — **remanserunt** : their debts
would otherwise have prevented
them from doing this.

3. **idem homines** : M. Brutus
and C. Cassius were among the
former Pompeians, whose pardon
and advancement by Caesar had
probably excited the envy (**invidiae**) of those who had followed
Caesar throughout the Civil War,
and these two men joined the conspiracy to kill him (**exitio**). — **illi**:
i.e. Caesari. — **impunite** : found
only once elsewhere (Cic. *de Finibus,* 2. 59) in classical prose. —

servis semper libera fuerunt, ut timerent gauderent
dolerent suo potius quam alterius arbitrio; quae nunc,
ut quidem isti dictitant 'libertatis auctores,' metu
4 nobis extorquere conantur. Sed nihil agunt. Nullius
umquam periculi terroribus ab officio aut ab humanitate desciscam; numquam enim honestam mortem
fugiendam, saepe etiam oppetendam putavi. Sed quid
mihi suscensent si id opto, ut paeniteat eos sui facti?
Cupio enim Caesaris mortem omnibus esse acerbam.
'At debeo pro civili parte rem p. velle salvam.' Id
quidem me cupere, nisi et ante acta vita et reliqua
mea spes tacente me probat, dicendo vincere non
5 postulo. Quare maiorem in modum te rogo ut rem
potiorem oratione ducas mihique, si sentis expedire
recte fieri, credas nullam communionem cum improbis
esse posse. An quod adulescens praestiti, cum etiam
errare cum excusatione possem, id nunc aetate praecipitata commutem ac me ipse retexam? Non faciam
neque quod displiceat committam, praeterquam quod
hominis mihi coniunctissimi ac viri amplissimi doleo
gravem casum. Quod si aliter essem animatus,
numquam quod facerem negarem, ne et in peccando
improbus et in dissimulando timidus ac vanus existi-

timerent : we should expect some
verb like *sperarent* or *cuperent* before timerent. — libertatis auctores : Cicero repeatedly calls the
conspirators *liberatores, e.g. Att.*
14. 12. 2 ; *Phil.* 1. 6.

4. pro civili parte, *as a citizen.*
— reliqua mea spes, *my hope for
the future ;* corresponding to ante
acta vita. — postulo, *expect,* as
frequently in comedy. Cf. Lorenz
on Plaut. *Pseud.* 829. *Postulo* with
the simple infin. is very rare in

Cicero ; cf. Draeg. *Hist. Syn.* II².
321 f.

5. maiorem in modum, *the
more earnestly.* — si . . . fieri, *if
you think it well for the right to
prevail.* — aetate praecipitata :
this would seem to indicate that
Matius was at least fifty years old
when this letter was written. See
also Ep. XCI. 2 nn. — me ipse
retexam, *shall I undo the work of
my life ?* (Watson). — quod displiceat : *sc. cuiquam.*

marer. 'At ludos quos Caesaris victoriae Caesar 6
adulescens fecit curavi.' At id ad privatum officium,
non ad statum rei p. pertinet; quod tamen munus
et hominis amicissimi memoriae atque honoribus
praestare etiam mortui debui, et optimae spei adule-
scenti ac dignissimo Caesare petenti negare non potui.
Veni etiam consulis Antoni domum saepe salutandi 7
causa; ad quem qui me parum patriae amantem esse
existimant rogandi quidem aliquid aut auferendi causa
frequentis ventitare reperies. Sed quae haec est
adrogantia, quod Caesar numquam interpellavit quin
quibus vellem atque etiam quos ipse non diligebat
tamen iis uterer, eos qui mihi amicum eripuerunt
carpendo me efficere conari ne quos velim diligam?
Sed non vereor ne aut meae vitae modestia parum 8
valitura sit in posterum contra falsos rumores, aut ne
etiam ii qui me non amant propter meam in Caesarem
constantiam non malint mei quam sui similis amicos
habere. Mihi quidem si optata contingent, quod reliquum est vitae in otio Rhodi degam ; sin casus aliquis
interpellarit, ita ero Romae ut recte fieri semper cupiam.
Trebatio nostro magnas ago gratias, quod tuum erga me
animum simplicem atque amicum aperuit, et quod eum
quem semper libenter dilexi quo magis iure colere
atque observare deberem fecit. Bene vale et me dilige.

6. **ludos** : cf. *de curatione ludorum*, Ep. XCI. 7 n. — **Caesar
adulescens** : *sc.* Octavianus.

7. **quae** . . . **adrogantia** : explained by its appositive, the exclamatory infin. clause, **eos . . .
conari.** — **quod . . . interpellavit**:
a relative clause explained by
quin . . . uterer. The entire ex-

pression **quod . . . uterer** is parenthetical, and sets Caesar's conduct in contrast to that of the
libertatis auctores.

8. **sui similis** : for they had
killed their friend Caesar. — **bene
vale** : cf. Intr. 62. *Bene vale* is
not used by Cicero. Cf., however,
Plaut. *As.* 606 ; Curius, *Fam.* 7. 29.

XCIII.   (*Fam.* 16. 26.)

QVINTVS TIRONI SVO P. S. D.

1   Verberavi te cogitationis tacito dumtaxat convicio, quod fasciculus alter ad me iam sine tuis litteris perlatus est. Non potes effugere huius culpae poenam te patrono : Marcus est adhibendus, isque diu et multis lucubrationibus commentata oratione vide ut 2 probare possit te non peccasse. Plane te rogo: sicut olim matrem nostram facere memini, quae lagonas etiam inanis obsignabat, ne dicerentur inanes aliquae fuisse quae furtim essent exsiccatae, sic tu, etiamsi quod scribas non habebis, scribito tamen ne furtum cessationis quaesivisse videaris; valde enim mi semper et vera et dulcia tuis epistulis nuntiantur. Ama nos et vale.

XCIV.   (*Fam.* 9. 24.)

CICERO PAETO S. D.

1   Rufum istum amicum tuum, de quo iterum iam ad me scribis, adiuvarem quantum possem, etiamsi ab eo laesus

XCIII. In the country (?), autumn (?), 44 B.C. On Quintus, cf. Intr. 55; on Tiro, Intr. 57.

1. **verberavi** : in the figurative sense as in Plaut. *M. G.* 799. — **fasciculus** : a packet of letters. Cf. *Att.* 12. 53.

2. **etiamsi ... scribito tamen** : cf. *Att.* 4. 8 B. 4 *ubi nihil erit quod scribas, id ipsum scribito*, and Plin. *Ep.* 1. 11. — **mi** : for *mihi*. This form (found also in Ep. LXVII. 3) illustrates well the connection which often exists between archaism and colloquialism. In

early Latin *mi* was in good use in all forms of literature ; at the beginning of the classical period it had dropped out of use in formal literature, but had been retained in that literature which reproduced the doings and sayings of everyday life. This is the history of many forms and expressions ; cf. Intr. 70.

XCIV. Rome, before the middle of Feb., 43 B.C. On Paetus, cf. Ep. LXI, introd. note.

1. **Rufum** : we know nothing else of him with certainty except

essem, cum te tantopere viderem eius causa laborare;
cum vero et ex tuis litteris et ex illius ad me missis
intellegam et iudicem magnae curae ei salutem meam
fuisse, non possum ei non amicus esse, neque solum
tua commendatione, quae apud me, ut debet, valet
plurimum, sed etiam voluntate ac iudicio meo. Volo
enim te scire, mi Paete, initium mihi suspicionis et
cautionis et diligentiae fuisse litteras tuas, quibus litteris congruentes fuerunt aliae postea multorum. Nam
et Aquini et Fabrateriae consilia sunt inita de me
quae te video inaudisse, et, quasi divinarent quam iis
molestus essem futurus, nihil aliud egerunt nisi me ut
opprimerent ; quod ego non suspicans incautior fuissem,
nisi a te admonitus essem. Quamobrem iste tuus
amicus apud me commendatione non eget. Vtinam ea
fortuna rei p. sit ut ille me virum gratissimum possit
cognoscere! Sed haec hactenus. Te ad cenas itare 2
desisse moleste fero; magna enim te delectatione et
voluptate privasti; deinde etiam vereor — licet enim
verum dicere — ne nescio quid illud quod solebas
dediscas et obliviscare, cenulas facere. Nam, si tum
cum habebas quos imitarere non multum proficiebas,
quid nunc te facturum putem? Spurinna quidem, cum

---

what is told us in this letter. —
magnae curae ... fuisse : his
interest was shown in warning
Cicero through Paetus of the plans
forming against him. — **aliae** : *sc.*
epistulae, or *litterae* in a plural
sense; cf. *litteris,* Ep. XCIX. 1 n.
— **de me** : Cicero is apparently
referring here, as in several passages in his Philippics, to plans
made against his life by Antony
and Antony's friends. — **molestus** : he was attacking Antony

vigorously in the senate, having
already delivered eight or nine of
his Philippics, while at the same
time he was making every effort
to mass the forces of the republic
against him in the north.

2. **quos imitarere** : *e.g.* Hirtius
and Dolabella (cf. Ep. LXI. 7).
Hirtius was in northern Italy,
Dolabella in Syria. Cf. Intr. 42 f.
— **Spurinna** : the celebrated *haru-
spex* who had warned Caesar to
beware of the danger which threat-

ei rem demonstrassem et vitam tuam superiorem ex-
posuissem, magnum periculum summae rei p. demonstrabat, nisi ad superiorem consuetudinem tum cum
Favonius flaret revertisses; hoc tempore ferri posse,
3 si forte tu frigus ferre non posses. Sed mehercule,
mi Paete, extra iocum moneo te, quod pertinere ad
beate vivendum arbitror, ut cum viris bonis iucundis
amantibus tui vivas. Nihil est aptius vitae, nihil ad
beate vivendum accommodatius. Nec id ad voluptatem
refero, sed ad communitatem vitae atque victus remis-
sionemque animorum quae maxime sermone efficitur
familiari, qui est in conviviis dulcissimus, ut sapientius
nostri quam Graeci: illi συμπόσια aut σύνδειπνα, id est
compotationes aut concenationes, nos ' convivia,' quod
tum maxime simul vivitur. Vides ut te philosophando
revocare coner ad cenas. Cura ut valeas. Id foris
4 cenitando facillime consequere. Sed cave, si me amas,
existimes me quod iocosius scribam abiecisse curam
rei p. Sic tibi, mi Paete, persuade, me dies et noctes
nihil aliud agere, nihil curare, nisi ut mei cives salvi
liberique sint. Nullum locum praetermitto monendi

ened him until the Ides of March
were past. — cum Favonius flaret : this wind began to blow
during the second week in Feb.
(cf. Plin. *N. H.* 2. 122; Colum.
11. 2. 15; Ovid, *Fasti* 2. 149). The
reference helps to fix the date of
the letter (cf. Ruete, 44).

3. mehercule : cf. *mercule*, Ep.
XXV. 3 n. — mi Paete : the use
of this, for Cicero, unusual form
of address three times in this
letter shows the earnestness of
the writer, at least in the passages
where the expression occurs. Cf.
mi Pomponi, Ep. X. n. — extra

iocum : elsewhere also *remoto
ioco.*— illi, etc. : cf. *de Sen.* 45, *bene
enim maiores accubitionem epula-
rem amicorum, quia vitae coniunctionem haberet, convivium nomina-
verunt, melius quam Graeci, qui
hoc idem tum compotationem, tum
concenationem vocant.*

4. si me amas : cf. Intr. 100.
— sic . . . persuade : for *hoc . . .
persuade.* Cf. *sic*, Ep. LXI. 5 n.
— nullum locum : cf. *nec vero
ipse postea tempus ullum intermisi
de re publica non cogitandi solum,
sed etiam agendi, Fam.* 10. 28. 2
(written about Feb. 2, 43 B.C.).

agendi providendi. Hoc denique animo sum ut, si in
hac cura atque administratione vita mihi ponenda sit,
praeclare actum mecum putem. Etiam atque etiam
vale.

XCV. (*Fam.* 12. 5.)

CICERO CASSIO S.

Hiemem credo adhuc prohibuisse quo minus de te 1
certum haberemus quid ageres maximeque ubi esses;
loquebantur omnes tamen — credo, quod volebant —
in Syria te esse, habere copias. Id autem eo facilius
credebatur, quia simile veri videbatur. Brutus quidem noster egregiam laudem est consecutus; res enim
tantas gessit tamque inopinatas ut eae cum per se
gratae essent, tum ornatiores propter celeritatem.
Quod si tu ea tenes quae putamus, magnis subsidiis
fulta res p. est; a prima enim ora Graeciae usque ad
Aegyptum optimorum civium imperiis muniti erimus
et copiis. Quamquam, nisi me fallebat, res se sic 2
habebat ut totius belli omne discrimen in D. Bruto

XCV. Rome, the latter half of
Feb., 43 B.C.

1. **prohibuisse quo minus . . .
haberemus**: the infin. is the regular classical construction with
prohibere (cf. *rem geri prohibuerat*, 2), but *ne* and *quo minus* with
the subj. sometimes follow, especially when *prohibere* is in the
infinitive. — **in Syria te esse** :
Cassius probably reached Syria
at the close of the year 44 B.C.
(cf. *Fam.* 12. 4. 2), and had ultimately at least eight legions at his
disposal. — **Brutus . . . noster** :
cf. Intr. 88 *b* (3). — **a prima ora,**
from the hither shore (*i.e.* the

shore beyond the Adriatic); cf.
Philipp. 10. 10 *exterae nationes
a prima ora Graeciae usque ad
Aegyptum optimorum et fortissimo-
rum civium imperiis et praesidiis
tenentur.* Cf. also *ibid.* 10. 14
*tenet igitur res publica Macedoniam,
tenet Illyricum, tuetur Graeciam.*
For a sketch of the successes of
M. Brutus, cf. *ibid.* 10. 13–14. Cf.
also Intr. 43.

2. **fallebat** : epistolary tense, as
are the tenses of most of the verbs
in this section. — **discrimen** : Cicero expresses the same opinion
three months later in a letter to
D. Brutus himself (Ep. XCIX. 2) :

positum videretur, qui si, ut sperabamus, erupisset Mutina, nihil belli reliqui fore videbatur. Parvis omnino iam copiis obsidebatur, quod magno praesidio Bononiam tenebat Antonius ; erat autem Claternae noster Hirtius, ad Forum Cornelium Caesar, uterque cum firmo exercitu, magnasque Romae Pansa copias ex dilectu Italiae compararat. Hiems adhuc rem geri prohibuerat. Hirtius nihil nisi considerate, ut mihi crebris litteris significat, acturus videbatur. Praeter Bononiam, Regium Lepidi, Parmam, totam Galliam tenebamus studiosissimam rei p. Tuos etiam clientis Transpadanos mirifice coniunctos cum causa habebamus. Erat firmissimus senatus exceptis consularibus, 3 ex quibus unus L. Caesar firmus est et rectus. Ser. Sulpici morte magnum praesidium amisimus. Reliqui partim inertes, partim improbi. Nonnulli invident eorum laudi quos in re p. probari vident. Populi vero Romani totiusque Italiae mira consensio est. Haec erant fere quae tibi nota esse vellem. Nunc

res se sic habet: is bellum confecerit qui Antonium oppresserit. — **Claternae,** etc.: all the places mentioned were on the *via Aemilia,* and, with the exception of Regium Lepidi and Parma, lay to the southeast of Mutina, in which town D. Brutus was besieged. — **magno praesidio :** Antony had somewhat more than six legions at his disposal. Cf. *Philipp.* 8. 25. — **noster Hirtius :** cf. Intr. 42. — **Forum Cornelium :** a rare form for *Forum Corneli.* — **Caesar :** *i.e.* Octavianus. — **tuos clientis Transpadanos :** this relationship does not seem to be mentioned elsewhere. — **exceptis consularibus,** etc.: cf. *Fam.* 10. 28.

3 (written about Feb. 2, 43 B.C.) *habemus fortem senatum, consularis partim timidos, partim male sentientis ; magnum damnum factum est in Servio ; L. Caesar optime sentit, sed, quod avunculus (i.e.* of Antony) *est, non acerrimas dicit sententias.* The leader of the moderate faction was Q. Fufius Calenus. Cf. *Philipp.* 8. 11 ; 10. 3 ; 12. 3 and 18.

3. **Ser. Sulpici morte :** cf. Ep. LXXV. introd. note. The senate, on Jan. 4, 43 B.C., had appointed a commission, composed of Ser. Sulpicius Rufus, L. Piso, and L. Philippus, to lay certain demands before Antony, but Sulpicius died before reaching Antony's head-

autem opto ut ab istis Orientis partibus virtutis tuae
lumen eluceat. Vale.

XCVI.   (*Fam.* 10. 12.)

CICERO PLANCO.

Etsi rei p. causa maxime gaudere debeo tantum ei ɪ
te praesidi, tantum opis attulisse extremis paene temporibus, tamen ita te victorem complectar re p.
reciperata ut magnam partem mihi laetitiae tua
dignitas adfert, quam et esse iam et futuram am-
plissimam intellego; cave enim putes ullas umquam
litteras gratiores quam tuas in senatu esse recitatas,
idque contigit cum meritorum tuorum in rem p. eximia
quadam magnitudine, tum verborum sententiarumque
gravitate. Quod mihi quidem minime novum, qui et

quarters. — **ab istis . . . eluceat :**
Cassius is compared to the sun in
the east; cf. *Philipp.* 10. 12 *ut
quocumque venisset Brutus lux
venisse quaedam . . . videretur ;*
Hor. *Sat.* 1. 7. 24 *solem Asiae
Brutum appellat, stellasque salu-
bris appellat comites.*

XCVI. Rome, April 11, 43 B.C.
L. Munatius Plancus was in 44
B.C. made governor of northern
Gaul, with an army of four or five
legions. Immediately after Antony's attack upon Cicero in Sept.,
44 B.C., the long correspondence
(*Fam.* 10. 1–24, excepting the 8th
letter) between Cicero and Plancus begins, in which Cicero exhorts
Plancus to remain true to the
cause of the senate. His efforts
seemed to have accomplished their
purpose, as the senate had just
received a letter from Plancus
(*Fam.* 10. 8), avowing his fidelity.

The letter before us was written
upon the arrival of this document,
and in response to a letter from
Plancus (*Fam.* 10. 7), requesting
Cicero's assistance in securing a
complimentary decree from the
senate.

1. **tantum . . . praesidi :** in
response to *Fam.* 10. 7. 2 *quod
spero, si me fortuna non fefellerit,
me consecuturum, ut maximo praesidio rei publicae nos fuisse et nunc
sentiant homines et in posterum
memoria teneant.* — ita te . . .
complectar . . . ut . . . adfert :
cf. *ita te . . . videam ut . . . fecisti,*
Ep. XXVII. 1. In a similar way
after *moriar, peream, ne vivam*
the clause of condition stands in
the indicative. Cf. *Att.* 16. 13 A. 1
*ne sim salvus, si aliter scribo ac
sentio* (Böckel). — **tuas . . . in senatu . . . recitatas :** *i.e. Fam.* 10.
8 ; cf. introd. note. — **quadam,**

te nossem et tuarum litterarum ad me missarum pro-
missa meminissem et haberem a Furnio nostro tua
penitus consilia cognita; sed senatui maiora visa sunt
quam erant exspectata, non quo unquam de tua voluntate dubitasset, sed nec quantum facere posses nec
quoad progredi velles exploratum satis habebat.

2 Itaque, cum a. d. VII Idus Aprilis mane mihi tuas
litteras M. Varisidius reddidisset easque legissem, incredibili gaudio sum elatus, cumque magna multitudo
optimorum virorum et civium me de domo deduceret,
feci continuo omnis participes meae voluptatis. Interim ad me venit Munatius noster, ut consuerat. At
ego ei litteras tuas, nihildum enim sciebat; nam ad me
primum Varisidius, idque sibi a te mandatum esse
dicebat. Paulo post idem mihi Munatius eas litteras
legendas dedit quas ipsi miseras, et eas quas publice.

3 Placuit nobis ut statim ad Cornutum pr. urb. litteras
deferremus, qui, quod consules aberant, consulare
munus sustinebat more maiorum. Senatus est continuo convocatus frequensque convenit propter famam
atque exspectationem tuarum litterarum. Recitatis
litteris oblata religio Cornuto est pullariorum admonitu

---

very; strengthening the force of
the adj. — **tuarum litterarum** :
i.e. Fam. 10. 4 and 7. — **Furnio** :
the legate of Plancus. For the
statement, cf. *Fam.* 10. 6. 1 ; 10.
10. 1. — **exploratum satis habebat** : cf. Intr. 84 *d.*
   2. **M. Varisidius** : a Roman
knight, who came from the camp
of Plancus ; cf. *Fam.* 10. 7. 1. —
Munatius noster : T. Munatius
Plancus, a relative of the person
addressed. Cf. 5. — **ego ei litteras tuas** : *sc. legendas dedi.* —
nihildum : the enclitic *dum* is

appended in comedy frequently to
imperatives and interjections, and
occasionally to enumerative words
like *primum.* Cf. Brix on Plaut.
Trin. 98, and Lorenz on *Most.* 120.
In prose it is found elsewhere only
in the combinations *nondum, vix-
dum, interdum, etiamdum, agedum,*
and *agitedum.* — **eas quas publice** : the letter to the senate,
Fam. 10. 8.
   3. **quod consules aberant** : cf.
Intr. 42. — **oblata . . . est,** *a religious difficulty presented itself.* —
pullariorum : in early times the

non satis diligenter eum auspiciis operam dedisse, idque a nostro collegio comprobatum est; itaque res dilata est in posterum. Eo autem die magna mihi pro tua dignitate contentio cum Servilio, qui cum gratia effecisset ut sua sententia prima pronuntiaretur, frequens eum senatus reliquit et in alia omnia discessit, meaeque sententiae quae secunda pronuntiata erat cum frequenter adsentiretur senatus, rogatu Servili P. Titius intercessit. Res in posterum dilata. Venit 4 paratus Servilius, Iovi ipsi iniquus cuius in templo res agebatur. Hunc quemadmodum fregerim quantaque contentione Titium intercessorem abiecerim, ex aliorum te litteris malo cognoscere; unum hoc ex meis:

pullarii helped the magistrates in taking the *auspicia ex tripudiis*, but in Cicero's day this title was applied to those who assisted in taking other auspices also. Before a meeting of the senate, the presiding officer was required to sacrifice a victim and take the auspices (Willems, II. 173, n. 7). — **eum . . . dedisse**: depending on **admonitu.** — **nostro collegio**: *sc. augurum.* — **Servilio**: P. Servilius Vatia. Cf. Ep. LXXI. introd. note. — **ut sua sententia prima pronuntiaretur**: when a number of propositions had been made concerning a matter laid before the senate, the presiding officer decided upon the order in which they should be submitted to a vote, announced the first proposition to be voted on (*sententiam primam pronuntiavit*), and said to the senators, *Qui hoc censetis, illuc transite; qui alia omnia, in hanc partem* (Festus). In the division those favoring a proposition went to the side of the senate chamber on which the author of the mo-

tion sat, the opponents went to the other side. Cf. also *Fam.* I. 2. 1 *itaque, cum sententia prima Bibuli pronuntiata esset, ut tres legati regem reducerent, secunda Hortensi, ut tu sine exercitu reduceres, tertia Volcaci, ut Pompeius reduceret, postulatum est ut Bibuli sententia divideretur: . . . de tribus legatis frequentes ierunt in alia omnia* (*i.e.* voted against the proposition, as in the case before us). Cf. also *Fam.* 8. 13. 2; Plin. *Ep.* 8. 14. 19. — **P. Titius**: tribune of the people. — **res . . . dilata**: a veto in the senate affected the validity of a particular vote only. At any time after a veto a subject could be considered and submitted to a vote again, and the motion, if supported by a majority of the senators, and not again vetoed, became a *senatus consultum.* A tribune sometimes used his power therefore merely to postpone action upon a subject. Cf. *pro Sest.* 74; Willems, II. 203.

4. Iovi ipsi iniquus: a popular expression; cf. the similar phrase,

senatus gravior, constantior, amicior tuis laudibus
esse non potuit quam tum fuit, nec vero tibi senatus amicior quam cuncta civitas. Mirabiliter enim
populus R. universus et omnium generum ordi-
numque consensus ad liberandam rem p. conspiravit.
5 Perge igitur, ut agis, nomenque tuum commenda im-
mortalitati, atque haec omnia quae habent speciem
gloriae conlecta inanissimis splendoris insignibus con-
temne, brevia fucata caduca existima. Verum decus
in virtute positum est quae maxime inlustratur magnis
in rem p. meritis. Eam facultatem habes maximam,
quam quoniam complexus es, tene. Perfice ut ne
minus res p. tibi quam tu rei p. debeas. Me tuae
dignitatis non modo fautorem sed etiam amplificatorem
cognosces. Id cum rei p., quae mihi vitast mea carior,
tum nostrae necessitudini debere me iudico. Atque
in his curis quas contuli ad dignitatem tuam cepi magnam voluptatem, quod bene cognitam mihi T. Munati
prudentiam et fidem magis etiam perspexi in eius incredibili erga te benevolentia et diligentia. III Idus Apr.

XCVII.   (*Fam.* II. 9.)

D. BRVTVS S. D. M. CICERONI.

1   Pansa amisso quantum detrimenti res. p. acceperit
non te praeterit. Nunc auctoritate et prudentia tua
prospicias oportet ne inimici nostri consulibus sublatis

dis hominibusque infestus. See
also Otto, *Sprichwörter*, 179.
   XCVII. From the camp at
Regium, Apr. 29, 43 B.C. On
Brutus, cf. Ep. LXXXVI. introd.
note.
   1. consulibus sublatis: Hirtius

was killed on the field of battle,
while Pansa was mortally wounded,
and died two days later. Cf. Intr.
42. Had this catastrophe not
occurred, Antony would probably
have been crushed, and the course
of events greatly changed, as the

sperent se convalescere posse. Ego ne consistere
possit in Italia Antonius dabo operam. Sequar eum
confestim. Vtrumque me praestaturum spero ne aut
Ventidius elabatur aut Antonius in Italia moretur. In
primis rogo te ad hominem ventosissimum Lepidum
mittas, ne bellum nobis redintegrare possit Antonio
sibi coniuncto; nam de Pollione Asinio puto te perspicere quid facturus sit. Multae et bonae et firmae
sunt legiones Lepidi et Asini. Neque haec idcirco 2
tibi scribo, quod te non eadem animadvertere sciam,
sed quod mihi persuasissimumst Lepidum recte facturum numquam, si forte vobis id de hoc dubium est.
Plancum quoque confirmetis oro, quem spero pulso
Antonio rei p. non defuturum. Si se Alpes Antonius

jealousy which the senate excited
in Octavius by conferring the chief
command upon D. Brutus, led to
his withdrawal from the campaign.
— **praestaturum . . . ne** : a construction not found in Cicero (cf.,
however, *praestare ut, de Or.* 1.
44), but used by Caelius (*Fam.* 8. 10.
5), and Cassius (*Fam.* 12. 13. 4).
—**Ventidius**: P. Ventidius Bassus
with three legions joined Antony
May 3 at Vada Sabatia. — **ventosissimum** : used metaphorically
as in Cic. *Philipp.* 11. 17; Hor.
Ep. 1. 8. 12. — **Lepidum** : M.
Aemilius Lepidus, who had been
consul in 46 B.C., was now governor of Gallia Narbonensis and
Hispania Citerior. He became a
member of the Second Triumvirate
a few months later. — **mittas**: apparently Cicero complied with this
request, as about three weeks later
Lepidus wrote to him (*Fam.* 10.
34 and 34 A), describing the state
of affairs in the North, adding
*quod ad bellum hoc attinet, nec se-
natui nec rei publicae deerimus*

(*Fam.* 10. 34. 2).— **de Pollione Asinio** : C. Asinius Pollio was governor of Hispania Vlterior. True
to that tendency which in after life
kept him from an active participation in politics, he was at present
holding aloof from the struggle
about Mutina. Later he joined
Antony. In after life he is known
to us as the friend of Vergil and
Horace, and the liberal patron of
art and literature. Three of his
letters to Cicero are extant (*Fam.*
10. 31–33). His poems and historical writings are lost. On the order
of the *nomen* and *cognomen*, cf. *Galli
Canini*, Ep. XIX. 4 n. On **de**, see
Intr. 91. — **quid facturus sit** : a
suspicion of the loyalty of Pollio
to the senate is suggested.— **multae . . . legiones** : Lepidus had
seven, Pollio three, legions.

2. **persuasissimumst**: cf. Intr.
82 (end). — **id de hoc dubium
est** : a harsh expression, but the
style of D. Brutus lacks polish. —
si . . . traiecerit : cf. Plancus in
Cic. *Fam.* 10. 9. 3 *exercitum . . .*

traiecerit, constitui praesidium in Alpibus conlocare et te
de omni re facere certiorem.　III K. Mai. ex castris, Regi.

XCVIII. (*Fam.* 10. 15.)

PLANCVS CICERONI.

1　　His litteris scriptis, quae postea accidissent scire te
ad rem p. putavi pertinere.　Sedulitas mea, ut spero,
et mihi et rei p. tulit fructum.　Namque assiduis inter-
nuntiis cum Lepido egi ut omissa omni contentione re-
conciliataque voluntate nostra communi consilio rei p.
succurreret, se liberos urbemque pluris quam unum
perditum abiectumque latronem putaret, obsequioque
2 meo, si ita faceret, ad omnis res abuteretur.　Profeci.
Itaque per Laterensem internuntium fidem mihi dedit

Rhodanum traieci; so in Caesar
and frequently in Livy. Occasionally the preposition is repeated,
e.g. Liv. 21. 26. 6 *omnibus ferme
suis trans Rhodanum traiectis.*
More frequently *traicere* is followed simply by the acc. of the
thing crossed. — **Regi:** *i.e.* Regium Lepidi; cf. Ep. XCV. 2.
　XCVIII. Gallia Narbonensis,
about May 12, 43 B.C. The course
of events immediately after the
defeat of Antony near Mutina
was as follows (cf. Mendelssohn,
458, n. 3) : on April 22 Antony
retired from the vicinity of Mutina, and May 3 he and Ventidius
Bassus (Ep. XCVII. 1) formed a
junction at Vada Sabatia; on May
8 L. Antonius, with the cavalry
and a few cohorts, reached Forum
Iuli in Gallia Narbonensis, and on
the 15th M. Antonius came to the
same place.　As for D. Brutus,
April 24 he left Mutina, and came
April 25 to Regium, where he

remained up to April 29. He
reached Dertona May 5. Plancus
was at Culāro, about 350 Roman
miles from Mutina. After hearing
of Antony's defeat, and getting a
favorable reply to certain proposals
which he had made to Lepidus, he
crossed the Isara May 12, and sent
his brother forward to intercept
L. Antonius.

　1. **his litteris scriptis:** *i.e.*
Fam. 10. 11, which was sent by
the same messenger as this letter.
　— **cum Lepido egi :** cf. *cum hoc
Pompeius egit,* Ep. VIII. 2. —
abuteretur, *make full use of ;* as
in *Verr.* ii. 1. 25 *nisi omni tempore,
quod mihi lege concessum est, abu-
sus ero.*

　2. **Laterensem :** M. Juventius
Laterensis, a firm adherent of the
constitutional party, who a few
weeks later committed suicide in
consequence of his failure to keep
Lepidus loyal to the senatorial
cause (Vell. Paterc. 2. 63. 2 ;

se Antonium, si prohibere provincia sua non potuisset, bello persecuturum, me ut venirem copiasque coniungerem rogavit, eoque magis, quod et Antonius ab equitatu firmus esse dicebatur et Lepidus ne mediocrem quidem equitatum habebat; nam etiam ex paucitate eius non multis ante diebus decem qui optimi fuerant ad me transierunt. Quibus rebus ego cognitis cunctatus non sum. In cursu bonorum consiliorum Lepidum adiuvandum putavi. Adventus meus quid 3 profecturus esset vidi, vel quod equitatu meo persequi atque opprimere equitatum eius possem, vel quod exercitus Lepidi eam partem quae corrupta est et ab re p. alienata et corrigere et coercere praesentia mei exercitus possem. Itaque in Isara flumine maximo quod in finibus est Allobrogum ponte uno die facto exercitum a. d. IV Idus Mai. traduxi. Cum vero mihi nuntiatum esset L. Antonium praemissum cum equitibus et cohortibus ad Forum Iuli venisse, fratrem cum equitum quattuor milibus ut occurreret ei misi a. d. v Idus Mai. Ipse maximis itineribus cum IV legionibus expeditis et reliquo equitatu subsequar. Si nos medio- 4 cris modo fortuna rei p. adiuverit, et audaciae perditorum et nostrae sollicitudinis hic finem reperiemus; quod si latro praecognito nostro adventu rursus in Italiam se recipere coeperit, Bruti erit officium

Planc. *Fam.* 10. 23. 4). — **provincia sua** : Antony did enter Gallia Narbonensis. Cf. introd. note. — **ab equitatu firmus** : cf. *ab amicis*, Ep. I. 2 n. — **decem** : Schelle conjectures *sescenti* with probability.

3. **eius** : *i.e.* of Antony. — **eam partem** : probably the celebrated tenth legion. Cf. *Fam.* 10. 11. 2.

— **a. d. IV. Idus Mai.** : the bridge was built *a. d. v. Idus Mai.;* the cavalry under the brother of Plancus was sent across on the evening of that day, and the main army crossed the next day (**a. d. IV. Idus Mai**). Cf. Ruete, 51.

4. **in Italiam . . . coeperit** : for the forecast which D. Brutus made of the movements of Antony, cf.

occurrere ei, cui scio nec consilium nec animum
defuturum.   Ego tamen, si id acciderit, fratrem cum
equitatu mittam qui sequatur, Italiam a vastatione
defendat.   Fac valeas meque mutuo diligas.

XCIX.   (*Fam.* 11. 12.)

M. CICERO S. D. D. BRVTO IMP. COS. DES.

1   Tres uno die a te accepi epistulas : unam brevem,
quam Flacco Volumnio dederas, duas pleniores, quarum
alteram tabellarius T. Vibi attulit, alteram ad me misit
Lupus.   Ex tuis litteris et ex Graecei oratione non
modo non restinctum bellum sed etiam inflammatum
videtur.   Non dubito autem pro tua singulari prudentia quin perspicias, si aliquid firmitatis nactus sit
Antonius, omnia tua illa praeclara in rem p. merita ad

Fam. 11. 10. 4 (written May 5).
The general plan outlined in this
letter was never carried out (cf.
Fam. 10. 18).

XCIX. Rome, about May 13, 43
B.C.   For the movements of D.
Brutus after Antony's defeat near
Mutina, cf. Ep. XCVIII. introd.
note.

1. tres . . . epistulas: *sc. Fam.*
11. 9, 10, and 11, written April 29,
May 5, and May 6 respectively. —
**Flacco Volumnio, T. Vibi,
Graecei** : little more is known of
these men than we gather from
this letter. — **Lupus** : probably
P. Rutilius Lupus, who was
praetor in 49 B.C., and was probably at this time the legate of D.
Brutus, in whose letters he is frequently mentioned. — litteris : apparently in a plural sense here, as
several times in Cicero, *e.g. accipio excusationem tuam, qua usus*

*es, cur saepius ad me litteras uno
exemplo* (of the same tenor) *dedis-
ses, Fam.* 4. 4. 1; *raras tuas quidem — fortasse enim non perferuntur, — sed suaves accipio litteras,
Fam.* 2. 13. 1. Cf. also Ep. XI.
1.   In strict usage *litterae* has
always the singular meaning, unless the distributive adjective is
added to it, as *binas a te accepi
litteras, Fam.* 4. 14. 1. Cicero himself called attention to this fact; cf.
Servius ad Verg. *Aen.* 8. 168: *Cicero per epistulam culpat filium,
dicens male eum dixisse 'direxi
litteras duas,' cum litterae, quoti-
ens epistulam significant, numeri
tantum pluralis sint.* — **oratione,** *words;* cf. Epp. XXXII.
4; XCII. 5. — **inflammatum** :
cf. *Fam.* 11. 10. 3 *revertor nunc
ad Antonium, qui ex fuga cum
parvulam manum peditum haberet inermium, ergastula solvendo*

nihilum esse ventura; ita enim Romam erat nuntiatum, ita persuasum omnibus, cum paucis inermis, perterritis metu, fracto animo fugisse Antonium. Qui si ita se ² habet ut, quemadmodum audiebam de Graeceio, confligi cum eo sine periculo non possit, non ille mihi fugisse a Mutina videtur, sed locum belli gerendi mutasse. Itaque homines alii facti sunt : nonnulli etiam queruntur quod persecuti non sitis ; opprimi potuisse si celeritas adhibita esset existimant. Omnino est hoc populi maximeque nostri, in eo potissimum abuti libertate per quem eam consecutus sit. Sed tamen providendumst ne quae iusta querela esse possit. Res se sic habet: is bellum confecerit qui Antonium oppresserit. Hoc quam vim habeat te existimare malo quam me apertius scribere.

omneque genus hominum abripiendo satis magnum numerum videtur effecisse ; hoc accessit manus Ventidi; and *Fam.* II. II. I contains the news that Antony is advancing to meet Lepidus, and has sent proposals of alliance to Pollio and to Plancus. — **inermis:** from an archaic nominative *inermus.* Cicero uses both forms; cf. *e.g. inermem, Fam.* 12. 10. 3.

2. **audiebam de :** *audio ex* or *ab* is much more usual; cf. *Att.* 16. 7. 8. — **alii facti sunt :** this meaning of *alius*, which comes near that of *diversus*, belongs to colloquial Latin ; cf. Plaut. *Trin.* 160 *pro di immortales, verbis paucis quam cito | alium fecisti me : alius ad te veneram* (Böckel). — **in eo,** *in his case* or *in their treatment of him.* — **abuti:** explanatory of **hoc.** — **libertate,** *freedom of speech ;* as repeated in **eam,** however, it means

freedom in its widest sense. — **providendumst :** cf. *persuasissimumst,* Ep. XCVII. 2 n. — **res se sic habet :** a stereotyped introductory phrase, and therefore without influence upon the construction of the following sentence.— **is bellum confecerit :** the same opinion is expressed in nearly the same words in *Fam.* 10. 13. 2 ; 19. 2. — **hoc quam vim habeat:** Cicero is probably hinting at the possible disloyalty of Lepidus, Pollio, and Plancus. It is necessary to crush Antony before any one of these men goes over to Antony's side. It is noticeable that although Brutus had written to Cicero pretty plainly of his suspicions of Lepidus in particular (cf. Ep. XCVII. 1), Cicero makes no reply upon this point, although he evidently shares the distrust which was felt by Brutus.

C. (*Fam.* 10. 24.)

PLANCVS IMP. COS. DES. S. D. CICERONI.

1 Facere non possum quin in singulas res meritaque
tua tibi gratias agam, sed mehercules facio cum pudore;
neque enim tanta necessitudo, quantam tu mihi tecum
esse voluisti, desiderare videtur gratiarum actionem,
neque ego libenter pro maximis tuis beneficiis tam vili
munere defungor orationis, et malo praesens observantia indulgentia adsiduitate memorem me tibi probare.
Quod si mihi vita contigerit, omnis gratas amicitias
atque etiam pias propinquitates in tua observantia indulgentia adsiduitate vincam; amor enim tuus ac iudicium de me utrum mihi plus dignitatis in perpetuum
an voluptatis cotidie sit adlaturus, non facile dixerim.

C. In camp, July 28, 43 B.C. On
May 29, Lepidus, forced by his
soldiers, as he claimed in his letter
to the senate (*Fam.* 10. 35; cf.
also 10. 21. 4), joined his forces
with those of Antony at Pons
Argenteus, and June 30 was declared an *hostis* by the senate
(*Fam.* 12. 10. 1). Plancus had
not carried out the plan of campaign against Antony, which he
had outlined in a previous letter
(Ep. XCVIII.), but, after the
union of the forces of Antony and
Lepidus, recrossed the Isara to
wait for D. Brutus, who probably
joined him June 12 at Cularo.
Octavius, who was slighted by the
transfer of Pansa's troops to D.
Brutus, pursued a policy of inac-
tion. This is the last extant letter
in Cicero's correspondence. Cf.
Intr. 65.

1. **in singulas res:** for *ob singulas res* or *pro singulis rebus.* —

mehercules: the form preferred
by Plancus. Cf. *Fam.* 10. 11. 3;
18. 3; 23. 1; 23. 7. For Cicero's
usage, cf. *mercule*, Ep. XXV. 3 n.
— **gratiarum actionem:** cf. *quamquam gratiarum actionem a te non
desiderabam, cum te re ipsa atque
animo scirem esse gratissimum, tamen (fatendum est enim) fuit ea
mihi periucunda* (Cicero to Plancus, *Fam.* 10. 19. 1). — **amicitias
. . . propinquitates :** for *amicos
. . . propinquos.* The use of an
abstract for a concrete noun seems
to be especially common in the
case of words expressing an emotion or a state of the mind. Cf.
Draeg. *Hist. Syn.* I². 22–24. —
tua observantia : the objective
genitive *tui* would be more regular.
— **adlaturus :** agreeing in gender
with *amor*, as *iudicium de me*
merely expresses one of the means
through which the **amor** found
expression.

De militum commodis fuit tibi curae; quos ego non 2
potentiae meae causa — nihil enim me non salutariter
cogitare scio — ornari volui a senatu, sed primum quod
ita meritos iudicabam, deinde quod ad omnis casus
coniunctiores rei p. esse volebam, novissime ut ab
omni omnium sollicitatione aversos eos talis vobis praestare possem quales adhuc fuerunt. Nos adhuc hic 3
omnia integra sustinuimus; quod consilium nostrum,
etsi quanta sit aviditas hominum non sine causa capitalis victoriae scio, tamen vobis probari spero. Non
enim, si quid in his exercitibus sit offensum, magna
subsidia res p. habet expedita quibus subito impetu ac
latrocinio parricidarum resistat. Copias vero nostras
notas tibi esse arbitror. In castris meis legiones sunt
veteranae tres, tironum, vel luculentissima ex omnibus,
una; in castris Bruti una veterana legio, altera bima,
octo tironum. Ita universus exercitus numero am-

2. **de ... commodis**: a commission of ten was appointed by the senate to divide lands among the veterans of D. Brutus and Octavius (cf. *Fam.* 11. 21. 2, 5), and probably the troops of Plancus were similarly favored. Cicero apparently proposed the measure and was a member of the commission. On **de**, cf. Intr. 91 and Ep. XC. 8 n. — **novissime** : cf. *novissima*, Ep. LXXXVI. 3 n. — **omni omnium** : the so-called *figura etymologica*, of which one of the most striking cases is *optumo optume optumam operam das*, Plaut. *Amph.* 278; cf. also *occidione occisum*, Ep. XXXIV. 7 n. Combinations of various forms of *omnis* are special favorites.

3. **quanta sit ... scio**, *I know how great an eagerness people feel for a decisive victory*. See Crit.

Append. — **hominum ... victoriae** : a subjective and an objective genitive depending upon **aviditas**. — **impetu** : commonly regarded as a dative. For such contract forms, cf. Neue, *Formenlehre d. lat. Sprache* I². pp. 356–358. — **parricidarum** : used by Plancus here, as it is used in *Fam.* 10. 23. 5 of the followers of Antony. It is the epithet which Antony applied with special fondness to Caesar's assassins. Cf. Cicero's words to Cassius (*Fam.* 12. 3. 1) : *primum in statua quam posuit in rostris inscripsit* PARENTI OPTIME MERITO *ut non modo sicarii sed iam etiam parricidae iudicemini.* Cf. also Val. Max. 6. 4. 5 *M. Brutus suarum prius virtutum quam patriae parentis parricida.* The same epithet is applied by Sallust to Catiline's associates;

plissimus est, firmitate exiguus; quantum autem in
acie tironi sit committendum nimium saepe expertum
4 habemus.   Ad hoc robur nostrorum exercituum sive
Africanus exercitus, qui est veteranus, sive Caesaris
accessisset, aequo animo summam rem p. in discrimen deduceremus.   Aliquanto autem propius esse,
quod ad Caesarem attinet, videbamus.   Nihil destiti
eum litteris hortari, neque ille intermisit adfirmare
se sine mora venire, cum interim aversum illum
ab hac cogitatione ad alia consilia video se contulisse.   Ego tamen ad eum Furnium nostrum cum
mandatis litterisque misi, si quid forte proficere posset.
5 Scis tu, mi Cicero, quod ad Caesaris amorem attinet,
societatem mihi esse tecum, vel quod in familiaritate
Caesaris vivo illo iam tueri eum et diligere fuit mihi
necesse, vel quod ipse, quoad ego nosse potui, modera-
tissimi atque humanissimi fuit sensus, vel quod ex tam
insigni amicitia mea atque Caesaris hunc fili loco et

cf. Sall. *Cat.* 14. 3; 51. 25. —
nimium saepe : in the war between Caesar and Pompey, the
Pompeian forces were made up to
a great extent of recruits, while
the Caesarian troops had been
seasoned by campaigns in Gaul.
Cf. Ep. XLIV. 2; *Att.* 7. 13 A.
2, also Caes. *B. C.* 3. 4. — **expertum habemus** : for *experti sumus;* cf. Intr. 84 *d.*
    4. **Africanus exercitus** : two
legions under the command of Q.
Cornificius, governor of Africa. —
propius, etc.: *i.e.* ' that success
was easier of accomplishment (lit.,
nearer) with Caesar's support than
with that of the African army.'
The phrase **quod . . . attinet**
seems very awkward, but is perhaps not objectionable enough to

warrant a textual change in a
letter from Plancus.   See Crit.
Append. — **venire** : the present
to indicate that he will arrive in
the immediate future.   This usage
is found mainly with the first
person, and with the infin. in the
orat. obl. representing the first
person (Andresen). — **ad alia consilia** : *i.e.* his candidacy for the
consulship.   Cf. Intr. 42 (end).
— **Furnium nostrum** : cf. Ep.
XLVII. n.
    5. **mi Cicero** : cf. *mi Pomponi,*
Ep. X. n. — **in familiaritate
Caesaris** : cf. *in victoria,* Ep.
XCII. 2 n.   The reference is to Julius Caesar here, to Octavius above
(**ad Caesaris amorem**). — **quoad
. . . potui** : Plancus can scarcely
have known the nineteen-year-old

illius et vestro iudicio substitutum non proinde habere
turpe mihi videtur. Sed — quicquid tibi scribo dolen- 6
ter mehercules magis quam inimice facio — quod vivit
Antonius hodie, quod Lepidus una est, quod exercitus
non contemnendos habent, quod sperant, quod audent,
omne Caesari acceptum referre possunt. Neque ego
superiora repetam; sed ex eo tempore quo ipse mihi
professus est se venire, si venire voluisset, aut oppressum iam bellum esset aut in aversissimam illis
Hispaniam cum detrimento eorum maximo extrusum.
Quae mens eum aut quorum consilia a tanta gloria,
sibi vero etiam necessaria ac salutari, avocarit et ad
cogitationem consulatus bimestris summo cum terrore
hominum et insulsa cum efflagitatione transtulerit ex-
putare non possum. Multum in hac re mihi videntur 7
necessarii eius et rei p. et ipsius causa proficere posse,

Octavius personally. — **illius et
vestro iudicio**: Julius Caesar had
in his will made Octavius his
adopted son. **vestro** refers by
anticipation to the action of the
comitia curiata in confirming the
adoption. The confirmation had
not yet taken place.

  6. **acceptum referre,** *to set down
to the credit of.* Cf. Ep. XXXVII.
2 n. — **professus est . . . venire:**
cf. *venire,* 4 n. — **aversissimam
illis Hispaniam** : Spain, as the
former stronghold of the Pompeians, would naturally be unfriendly
to the followers of Antony. For
the reason why Octavius hesitated,
cf. Intr. 42. See also Crit. Append.
— **quorum consilia:** cf. *Ep. ad
Brut.* I. 10. 3. — **necessaria** :
Octavius and Antony were rival
representatives of the Caesarian
tradition and interests. Both had
felt the truth of that fact the year

before at Rome, so that the
destruction of Antony seemed
necessary to the full success of
Octavius. — **bimestris** : Octavius
was actually elected consul Aug.
19, but Plancus could scarcely
expect that he would be elected so
soon, and, in general, is speaking
sarcastically of the short-lived
honor. Manutius and O. E.
Schmidt would, however, read
quinquemestris. — **efflagitatione:**
the centurion Cornelius, at the
head of a deputation of the troops
of Octavius, went to Rome to
demand the consulship for their
leader; cf. Suet. *Aug.* 26. — **ex-
putare** : stronger than *putare.* Cf.
demiror, Ep. XXVI. 4 n., and see
Thielmann, *de Sermonis Proprietatibus,* etc., 39.

  7. **necessarii eius** : especially
his stepfather L. Philippus and
his brother-in-law C. Claudius

plurimum, ut puto, tu quoque, cuius ille tanta merita
habet quanta nemo praeter me; numquam enim obliviscar maxima ac plurima me tibi debere. De his
rebus ut exigeret cum eo Furnio mandavi. Quod si
quantam debeo habuero apud eum auctoritatem, pluri-
8 mum ipsum iuvero. Nos interea duriore condicione
bellum sustinemus, quod neque expeditissimam dimica-
tionem putamus neque tamen refugiendo commissuri
sumus ut maius detrimentum res p. accipere possit.
Quod si aut Caesar se respexerit aut Africanae legiones celeriter venerint, securos vos ab hac parte red-
demus. Tu, ut instituisti, me diligas rogo proprieque
tuum esse tibi persuadeas. v K. Sext. ex castris.

Marcellus. — **tu quoque** : when
Octavius came to Rome after
Julius Caesar's death, he showed
great deference for Cicero ; cf.
Att. 14. 11. 2 *modo venit Octavius,
et quidem in proximam villam
Philippi, mihi totus deditus ;* 14.
12. 2 *nobiscum hic perhonorifice et
amice Octavius,* and *Ep. ad Brut.*
1. 18. 3 (written in 43 B.C.) *cum
me pro adulescentulo ac paene puero
res publica accepisset vadem.* —
tanta merita : by his many complimentary references to Octavius
in the senate, and notably by

his action in securing a *senatus
consultum* authorizing a thanksgiving of fifty days in honor of the
victory gained by Octavius, Hirtius, and Pansa near Forum Gal-
lorum. Cf. *Philipp.* 5. 45 ; 14. 29.

8. **bellum sustinemus** : an unusual expression. Cf. *sustinere,
Antibarbarus,* and see the similar
phrase in 3, *nos adhuc,* etc. — **se
respexerit,** *shall be mindful of
his real interests.* For this phrase,
cf. Plaut. *Pseud.* 612; Ter. *Heaut.*
70; 919. — **ex castris** : at Cularo
probably.

CRITICAL APPENDIX

—••‡✇‡••—

In this Appendix many of the most important variations in the text of this edition from that of the Medicean *codices* (M. 49, 9 and 49, 18) are indicated, and the most probable conjectures for some of the doubtful passages are presented. The source of many of these conjectures has not been indicated on account of the difficulty of tracing them to their authors. Mere orthographical variations have not been noted. For the benefit of those who may wish to make a more careful study of a portion of the text, the critical notes have been made somewhat fuller for the first forty-three letters than for the rest. A complete *apparatus criticus* of the *Epistulae ad familiares* may be found in Mendelssohn's edition. The *adnotatio critica* of C. F. W. Müller contains critical notes on the *Epistulae ad Quintum fratrem*. For the *Epistulae ad Atticum* the student may be referred to the editions of Orelli, Baiter and Kayser, Wesenberg, and Tyrrell. These editions contain critical notes on the other letters of Cicero also. The other principal sources of information are C. A. Lehmann, *Quaestiones Tullianae*, and *De Ciceronis ad Atticum epistulis recensendis et emendandis*, Th. Schiche, *Zu Ciceros Briefen an Atticus*, P. Starker, *Symbolae Criticae ad M. Tullii Ciceronis epistulas*, O. Streicher, *De Ciceronis epistolis ad familiares emendandis*, and O. E. Schmidt's edition of Bks. XII and XIII of the *Epistulae ad Atticum*.

ABBREVIATIONS[1]

FOR THE *Epist. ad Fam.*

BKS. I–VIII.

M = Mediceus 49, 9 of the 9th century ⎫
G = Harleianus 2773 of the 12th century ⎬ Ω
R = Parisinus 17812 of the 12th century ⎭

[1] For a brief statement concerning these mss. cf. Intr. 68.

Mᶜ = Corrections in M of the 10th to the 12th century
Mʳ =   "   "   after 1389
P = Mediceus 49, 7 copied from M in 1389
I = Fragmentum Hamburgense
S =   "   Freierianum
T =   "   Taurinense

Bĸs. IX–XVI.

M = Mediceus 49, 9 of the 9th century   ⎫
D = Palatinus 598 of the 15th or 16th century ⎬ Ψ
H = Harleianus 2682 of the 11th century   ⎭
F = Erfurtensis now Berolinensis of the 12th or 13th century
Mᶜ = Corrections in M of the 10th to the 12th century
Mʳ =   "   "   after 1389
P = Mediceus 49, 7 copied from M in 1389
Cratander = Editio Cratandrina (1528)
Σ = late mss. and old editions

FOR THE *Epist. ad Att.* AND *ad Q. fr.*

M = Mediceus 49, 18 of the 14th century
W = Viceburgiensis of the 11th century
Cratander = Editio Cratandrina (1528)
Ien. = Editio Iensoniana (Venice, 1470)
lib. = libri i.e. the consensus of the best mss.
M¹ = Mediceus 49, 18 corrected by first hand
M² =   "   "   "   second hand
marg. = Mediceus 49, 18 corrected on the margin

Ep. I (*Att.* 1. 1)

1 opinio est *opinio se* M
  praepropera *propera* M¹
  putent. **A**quilium *potentia qui
  illum* M
  iuravit *curavit* M
  Aufidio M *Auli filio* commonly printed.
2 qui sic inopes et ab amicis
  omitted by M¹, added by M²
  ἀδύνατον ΛΛΤΝΛΤΟΠ M
  quae tum ... accuderim Ma-

nutius modified by Boot *quae
cum erit absoluta sane facile
eum libenter nunc ceteri consuli acciderim* M
3 nunc cognosce rem Madvig
  nunc cognoscere M
4 amici *animum* M
5 eius **ἀνάθημα** Schütz *eliu anaθma* M (as read by Orelli)
  eiut anaθma M (as read by
  Baiter) ἡλιον ἀνάθημα
  Cratander

Ep. II (*Att.* I. 2)

1 **te tam** *te etiam* M
   te iam Boot
   meis ad te rationibus *meis
   detractionibus* M
   a te rationibus marg.

Epist. III (*Fam.* 5. 7)

1 **quantam** Σ   *quam* Ω
2 **conciliatura** *conciliatur* MR
3 **verebare** GR   *verere* M
   ea quae nos *eaque nos* M
   maiori *maiore* M   *maiori* Σ
   maiorei Mendelssohn
   iam me Klotz   *ame* M

Epist. IV (*Fam.* 7. 23)

   Fadio *Fabio* Ω
1 **postulare** *postularent* Ω
2 **sumpsisti** *sumpsisse* Ω
   erat GR   *erant* M
3 **habebo** *habeo* Ω
   exhedria *exhadria* M   *exadria*
   GR
4 **mandaram** Ernesti *mandabam*
   M
   sorore eam *sororem eam* M
   sorore mea G *sororem meam*
   R
   faciam ut scias. Tu *faciamus
   scias tu* MG   *faciamus si es
   tu* R

Epist. V (*Att.* I. 16)

2 **pugnavitque** *pugnavique* M¹
   notum *novum* M¹
3 **a me tamen** M   *a me iam*
   Madvig
   homines nequissimos marg.
   homines quis summos M
   non . . . aerati Muretus and
   Tyrrell as modified by editor
   *non tam aerati quam ut ap-
   pellantur aerarii* M.   See
   Commentary.
   fugare *effugare* M
   maerentes *merentis* M.   See
   Commentary.

4 **impetrabat** Lambinus   *impe-
   trarat* M
   advocatorum *advocatorem* M
   iurare *iurarent* M¹
5 **praesidio** *prescio* M
   ἔσπετε ΕΣΙΤΕ M
   νῦν ΠΤΝ M
   πρῶτον . . . ἔμπεσε ΠΡΑΤΟ*n*
   ΠΕΠΤΠΕΣΕ M
   Calvum . . . illum M   *Calvum
   ἐξαπιναῖον illum laudato-
   rem meum* Boot (doubt-
   fully)
6 **delere et, quod** M²   *deleret
   quod* M¹
7 **plane** *plena* M¹
8 **in ea** *mea* M
   aliis legi M   *ab aliis legi* Madvig, but see Commentary.
9 **aut metuendo ignavissimi**
   inserted by Lambinus.
10 **quid huic** M   *quid hoc* Wesenberg and others.
   putes, inquam *putes quam* M
   mihi . . . crediderunt omitted
   M¹
11 **hirudo** *trudo* M
   iuvenes *tuens* M
12 **exspectatio** *exspectatio in* M
   deterioris M   *Doterionis* (a
   nickname of one of the two
   actors employed as agents
   by Philip) Bosius δευτερεύ-
   οντος Seyffert
   cuius domi Manutius   *cuius
   modi* M
13 **insimulatum lege Aelia** H.
   A. J. Munro   *insimul cum
   lege alia* M¹.   See Commentary.
   fabam mimum M   *Famam
   mimum* Orelli   *fabae hilum*
   Hofmann   *mimum* Wesenberg   *fabae μνοῦν* Madvig
   fabae midam Tyrrell.   See
   Commentary.
   non flocci facteon Cratander
   none loci facteon M
15 **Lucullis** Bosius   *Lucullus* M
   poëma *poetam* M¹
17 **in loco** *inlo* M

Ep. VI (*Att.* 1. 17)

1 iam ante *tam ante* M
  cum cuperem *concuperem* M[1]
  declararunt Wesenberg *declararant* M
4 ecquid Manutius *et quid* M
5 provincialium *provinciarum* M
  amore *more* M[1]
  discessi *discessu* M[1]
6 quin *qui* M
  in (before *ipsis*) omitted M
  non publicae omitted M
8 ob iudicandum accepissent M *ob iudicandum pecuniam acc.* Wesenberg *ob rem iudicandam pec. acc.* Cobet
9 summum M *sed summum* Kayser
  unusque erat Lehmann *qui erat* M
10 tam infirma *tamen firma* M
11 tempus. Si exspectare Tyrrell *tempus exspectare* M

Ep. VII (*Att.* 2. 19)

1 cetera ... Minae M *ceterum in mag. reb. minae* Kayser
2 peraeque Cratander *de reque* M[1] *denique* M[2]
  putaram *putarem* M
  amores Cratander *amore* M
  ne metu Schütz *an metu* M
3 tragoedus *tragoediis* M
  nostra ... magnus. In Val. Max. 2. 9 *miseria nostra magnus est*, and below *eandem* omitted
  transiri Manutius *transire* M
5 vult *volet* M
  non repudio M *non refugio* Wesenberg
  certi sumus *certissimus* M
  hic *hoc* M

Ep. VIII (*Att.* 2. 22)

1 Romae! Mansisses M *Romae mansisses! mansisses* Bosius
  multis denuntiat *multa denun-*
tiat or *vim multis denuntiat* Boot
  opes eorum et exercitus Orelli *opes et vim exercitus* M *opes eorum et vim exercitus* Cratander
  tum vim Ien. *cum vim* M
2 fidem Lambinus *sed fidem* M
3 opera nostra Wesenberg *opera* M
5 totum *tantum* M
  Pompeium Crasso urgente *Pompeio Crassum urgente* Schütz *Pompeium a Crasso urgeri, at si* Tyrrell
  quid tempus omitted M[1]
6 sentias *sentencias* M
  Pompeium vehementerque paenitet *Pompeiumque vehementer paenitet* M

Ep. IX (*Att.* 2. 23)

2 inveniri Lambinus *invenire* M
3 nostrae Cratander *noster* M
  si ingrederis *si non ingrederis* M[1] *si vero ingrederis* M[2]

Ep. X (*Att.* 3. 4)

  correctum Cratander *confectum* M
  illo pervenire non liceret. Statim Boot *illoc pervenirem non licere statim* M[1] *Illo cum pervenire non liceret, statim* commonly
  et quod omitted M[1]

Ep. XI (*Fam.* 14. 4)

1 fuissemus *fuisse* M
3 profecti sumus FHD *profectissimus* M
  a. d. II Rutilius *a. d. V* Ψ F deest FHD *est* M
4 abisset Lambinus *abesset* Ψ F
5 ferenda non sunt FHD *ferenda sunt* M
6 vincit omnes Pescennius Σ *vincet omnespes cennius* M

Ep. XII (*Att.* 3. 12)

1 proponi scribis *proponis. Scribis* M
3 licet . . . intellego Koch *lic. tibi ut scrib. sig. ut ad me ven. si donatam ut intellego* M *scilicet tibi, ut scribis, significaram ut ad me venires ; id omittamus ; intellego te* Madvig. See Commentary.

Ep. XIII (*Fam.* 14. 2)

2 subleventur *sublevantur* M
  mea FHD   *me* M
3 partem te FHD   *parte* M
  misera proicies *miseras proices* M
  attinet sine *attinet et sine* M
4 quoniam D   *quam* M   *quando* FH

Ep. XIV (*Att.* 3. 22)

2 adfert marg.   *asserit* M
  sperasset Wesenberg   *speraret* M
3 omnium meorum Stuerenburg   *omnium rerum* M
  fuerunt *fuerant* M
4 et quod mei *et quod et mei* M

Ep. XV (*Att.* 4. 1)

1 fuitque cui *fuit qui* M[1]   *fuit cui* M[2]
  pro . . . observantia Bosius *propter meam in te observantiam* M
  potius H Stephanus *totius* M
  timoris Pius   *rumoris* M
2 numquam M[2]   *tumquam* M[1]   *si umquam* Meutzner and commonly adopted
4 ipse scribam Lehmann *inscribam* M
  gratulatione . . . est Cratander omitted M
5 infimo Lehmann   *infima* M

6 continuo, cum more Baiter *continuo more* M[1]   *cum more* M[2]
  dedissent Baiter   *dedisset* M

Ep. XVI (*Q. fr.* 2. 3)

1 prodicta Drakenborch *producta* M
  in VIII Idus Manutius *in VII Idus* M
  Lentulo Manutius   *Lentuli* M
2 a. d. VIII Id. Manutius   *a. d. VII Id.* M
  peregerat M *perfregerat* Madvig
3 a. d. VII Id. Manutius   *a. d. VI Id.* M[2]
  a. d. VIII Id. Manutius   *a. d. VI Id.* M
4 et magna Malaspina   *sed magna* M
5 de omitted M
  adligatos Turnebus   *adlegatos* M
  Bestiam Wesenberg   *ista ei* M
7 huiusmodi ut tu *huiusmodi tu* M
  Lamiae Manutius   *Camiae* M
  Olbiensem *vibiensem* M

Ep. XVII (*Att.* 4. 4 B)

1 meorum Kayser   *meorum bibliotheca* M
  velim *vellem* M
  σιλλύβους Graevius   *sillabos* M
2 ludum Ernesti   *locum* M
  λόχον Bosius
  liberasses M   *liber esses* Pius

Ep. XVIII (*Fam.* 5. 12)

1 ad spem quandam M   *ac spes quaedam* F. Hofmann
2 cogitares *cogitare* M
  Phocicum Westermann   *troicum* Ω
  seiungeres. Equidem *seiungere se quidem* M   *se iungeres equidem* GR

ad nostram GR   *ut nostram*
M
3 **flecti** Victorius   *effecti* M   *de-flecti* G
demonstras *demonstrans* M
4 **quoddam** *quodam* M
in legendo, te scriptore (-rem
G), **tenere** GR   *in legem
dote scripto retinere* M
5 **evelli** Kayser   *avelli* Ω
Themistocli fuga exituque
Kayser   *Them. fuga redituque* M   *Them. exsilio aut
Alcibiadis fuga redituque*
Schütz   *Them. fuga, Corio-
lani fuga redituque* Tyrrell.
See Commentary.
notabili G   *votabili* MR
6 **hac** R   *haec* M
cum (or **quom**) *quam* Ω
qui quid Σ   *quid* M   *quicquid*
GR
7 **superstes** Mendelssohn   *spa-
tiates* Ω   *spartiates* Σ   *specta-
bilis* Schmalz
Sigeum *Sigetum* Ω
8 **quicquam** *quicum* Ω
si quid *si quod* Ω
9 **mirere** R   *merere* M   *meres* G

EP. XIX (*Fam.* 7. 1)

1 **in illo** Schütz   *ex illo* Ω
sinum Boot and Kiessling   *senum* M   *Misenum* others
2 **scaenam** R   *cenam* MG
qui ne G   *quid ne* MR
4 **cum et** M   *cum* GR
ambitio *abitio* M   *habitatio* GR
5 **te ipsum** *et ipsum* Ω
qui multos *quid multos* M
quod multos GR

EP. XX (*Q. fr.* 2. 9 [11])

3 a **Magnetibus** Victorius   *a
mag.* M
4 **cum veneris . . . Virum** F.
Marx. For the most impor-
tant conjectures on this passage, see Tyrrell.

EP. XXI (*Fam.* 7. 5)

1 **sperasset** R   *speras sed* MG
2 **M. Iteium** Mendelssohn (comparing Wilmann's *Exempla*
no. 2017) *M. itfiuium* M   *id-
finium* R   *id funum* G   *M.
Rufum* Schütz
quid Σ   *quod* Ω
3 **scripsissem** *scripsisse* M
singulari GR   *singularis* M
putidiusculi M   *impudentius-
culi* commonly printed
quamquam Ernesti   *quam* M

EP. XXII (*Q. fr.* 2. 15 [16])

1 **paulum quidem** Orelli   *paulum* M
propensis Wesenberg   *a propensis* M
et colamur Manutius   *ex colamur* M
3 **eram** Lambinus   *aderam* M
factam Bücheler   *actam* M
5 **utimur** M   *utitur* commonly
printed. See Commentary.

EP. XXIII (*Q. fr.* 3. 5, 6)

1 **factis** *facilis* M¹   *feci* M²
est a me *est tamen* M
P. Rutili omitted M
ea . . . esse marg.   *ea visum
mirifica esse* M¹   *ea visu mirifica esse* M²
qui essent Wesenberg   *quod
esset* M   defended by Lehmann, *Quaest. Tull.* p. 35.
2 **commovit me** *commovi me* M
relictos marg.   *redditos* M
3 **perscripsti** Buecheler   *per-
scripsit* M
tamquam Baiter   *quam* M
4 **Διατυπώσεις** Buecheler   A M—
ΠΩΕΙΣ M   *ἀμπώτεις*
Cratander
debebat Manutius   *debet* M
5 **ut puto** *ut me puto* M
viderunt Wesenberg   *viderent*
M

6 **exscribuntur** Boot *et scri-*
buntur M
C. Rebilus Orelli *Crebrius* M
et . . . adiurat M *et qui omnia*
tibi debere dixerat valde te
nunc iactat ('abuses') Boot
de aerario Boot *ab aerario* M

7 **πάθοs** Usener ΠΛΕΟΣ M
χρέοs Cratander
Aëropam Buecheler *trodam* M
verum etiam marg. *vetat iam*
(and written above *vult*
etiam) M
istas *istam* M
ad duas Orsini *duas* M

EP. XXIV (*Fam.* 7. 16)

1 **τῶν Βρεττανῶν** minus Mendelssohn *in Britannia non*
minus M *in Britannia non*
nimis commonly printed
iniectus M *intectus* A. Schottus *nive tectus* C. F. Hermann *inlectus* Teuffel

3 **ecquid in** *haec quid in* MG
videbo G *video* M *videro* Σ

EP. XXV (*Fam.* 7. 10)

1 **sapere** G *aspere* M *sperare*
R
2 **andabata** A. Schottus *anda-*
batam Ω
3 **statu tuo** GR *statuo* M
4 **possim** *possem* Ω

EP. XXVI (*Fam.* 7. 18)

1 **cautiones** *causationes* Ω
2 **quam . . . scribere** Birt *quam*
haec scribere M *quam haec*
(non) scribere Σ *quam assem*
perdere Mendelssohn
3 **villam** *villa* M
M. Aemili Manutius *metrilii*
Ω
se *sed* MG
4 **innocentem** *invocentem* GR
innocenter Mᴿ

EP. XXVII (*Fam.* 16. 16)

1 **iudicasti ac** Bücheler *ac* ΨF
retained by Mendelssohn *ac*
conditione Wesenberg *ac*
nomine Lehmann
2 **sermonibus** *et sermonibus* ΨF

EP. XXVIII (*Fam.* 7. 15)

2 **quod** Σ *quam* Ω

EP. XXIX (*Fam.* 3. 2)

2 **consili** *consuli* M¹ *consilii*
MᶜGR
magnam te M *magnam me*
C. F. W. Müller

EP. XXX (*Att.* 5. 1)

2 **quod** *quo* M
nominum Cratander *omnium*
M
3 **sumptus** Cratander *sumpta*
M
ego accivero pueros M¹ *ego*
vero ascivero pueros M² *ego*
viros ascivero Malaspina
ego viros ascivero porro Tyrrell
4 **quaeso** Manutius *quasi* M

EP. XXXI (*Fam.* 8. 1)

1 **discedens** I. F. Gronovius
decedens M *discedenti* commonly printed
et ad *ut ad* Ω
edicta *dictae* MG
exhibeam *ex ea hibea* M *ex*ᵥ
hibeat R¹ *ex ea habeat* G
2 **sit** *est* Ω
tenuissimam GR *tenuissem*
M
3 **sit** GR *sis* M
quid GR *ut quid* M
4 **eo rumores** GR *eorum mores*
M
equitem *equidem* Ω

factum M   *fictum* commonly printed

at R   *ad* G   *aut* M

manus M   *manum* Boot

sit *sint* Ω

urbe Wesenberg   *ur deurbe* M   *de urbe* GR

te a Q.*atque* M   *atque a* GR

Baulis embaeneticam M   *baulisem beneticam* R   *bauli seni beneticam* G   *Baulis* ἐμετικήν I. F. Gronovius   *Baulis iam peneticam* Klotz   *Baulis rem penaticam* O. Hirschfeld. Mendelssohn believes that reference is made to some menial occupation which Pompeius was obliged to take up, but the text has not yet been satisfactorily restored.

ut defungeremur *vide fungeremur* MR

vigent GR   *vigens* M

Ep. XXXII (*Fam.* 13. 1)

1 **an potius** HD   *andotius* M   **dolore** HD   *dolere* M

2 **nunc a te** HD   *nunc ac te* M

4 **potest** M   *potest facere nolle quod potes* Lehmann   **vitam** M   *viam* Wesenberg

Ep. XXXIII (*Fam.* 2. 8)

1 **dilata ut** GR   *dilata et* M

Ep. XXXIV (*Fam.* 15. 4)

5 **praesentia** M   *praestanti* Cratander and commonly printed. The asyndeton is unusual, but the expression is intelligible.

6 **in maxima** F. Hofmann   *maxima* M

et totus Hofmann   *et toto* M   **discederet** FHD   *disceret* M

7 **et Arabum** *Arabum* M

ab equitum *ab equitatu* M   *ab eo qui tum* HDF

8 **fuga. Eranam** *fugae ranam* M   *fugeranam* D   *fugerunt aman* F

tenenti I. F. Gronovius   *tenente* MH¹D   *tenentem* FH²

10 **iisque** Σ   *hiis quae* M

ne regibus D   *negeribus* MH   *generibus* F

Quintum *que* M omitted FHD   **pacatis** *pactis* FHD   *patis* M

11 **mihi** *tibi* ΨF

12 **cum facile** FHD   *facile* M   *ut facile* Mr

non ego FHD   *ego* M

pono FHD   *non pono* M

enim FHD   *enim te* M

non modo *modo* M

Ep. XXXV (*Att.* 6. 1. 17-26)

17 **ad Opis** Klotz   *ab Opis* M

20 πολλοῦ γε καὶ δεῖ ΠΟΛΛΕΤΤΕ M

22 **quem numquam** Manutius   *quem iam pridem numquam* M

dies pr. Kal. Wesenberg   *pr. Kal.* M

23 **proposuit** Bentivoglio   *potuit* M

nisi forte dolet ei quod suo tibicine egebit. Velim Boot   *nisi forte solet enim cum suo tibicine, et velim* M

in quibus Wesenberg   *quibus* M

25 **iamne vos** Bosius   *genuarios* M Cratander

Vindullum; ibi sua Victorius   *vidi illum ibi. Sua* M

uxoris illius Schütz   *illius* M

26 **inepti** Cratander   *in epiro* M

Ep. XXXVI (*Fam.* 2. 11)

1 **incredibile meorum** GR   *incredibile eorum* M

tam R   *iam* MG

2 **mandatu meo** Lambinus

mandatum eo M *mandato meo* GR

Ep. XXXVII (*Fam.* 15. 5)

1 hortatur F *hortatus* Ψ
2 casum *casu* MDFH

Ep. XXXVIII (*Fam.* 15. 6)

2 de honore Σ *honore* ΨF

Ep. XXXIX (*Fam.* 16. 4)

1 quoad D *quod* MFHD[1]
4 corpori servi *corpori servire corpori servi* M

Ep. XLI (*Fam.* 16. 9)

1 D (of greeting) nos *dic. nos* H *dignos* M
  Cassiopen *cassiodem* FHD *cassodem* M
  retenti . . . a. d. *retenti vens sum ususque ad a. d.* M *retenti ventis sumus usque a. d.* D
3 vellem Schütz *velim* ΨF
4 vale salve MD *vale et salve* Wesenberg

Ep. XLII (*Fam.* 16. 11)

1 iam C. F. W. Müller *etiam* ΨF
3 Capuam FHD *capiam* M

Ep. XLIII (*Fam.* 14. 14)

1 si enim FHD *sit enim* M
2 forti sitis FHD *fortis sitis* M

Ep. XLIV (*Att.* 8. 12 D)

1 praemonui fit *praemonui fore fit* marg.
  conductis te *conductis per te* M

2 ad adversarium Baiter *adversarium* M. See Commentary.

Ep. XLV (*Att.* 8. 3)

1 perturbatus cum Victorius *perturbatus sum* M[1]
  Italia cedat Victorius *Italiam accedat* M[1] *Italia excedat* M[2]
2 mea . . . fortuna omitted M added by Klotz
  non futurus . . . fuerit Lehmann *non futurus* M. See Commentary.
3 adoptando Cratander *optando* M
  propagator *prorogator* M
4 visa quaeri desperatione *vis aquari desperationem* M[1]
  pacis O. E. Schmidt *sine* M
  sed ut O. E. Schmidt *et ut* M
  sensi quam esset O. E. Schmidt *sensissem* M
  quam multi O. E. Schmidt *multi* M
5 habui Cratander *habuit* M
  an sine eo cum Hofmann *an si nec cum* M[1] *an sine et cum* M[2]
  putabit *putavit* M
  sciemus *scimus* M
6 etiam *etiam Philippi* M
  accipere invidiosum *invidiosum* M. See Commentary.
  qui autem Orelli *qui enim* M
7 deseri Orelli *deserit* M[1]

Ep. XLVII (*Att.* 9. 6 A)

meo *me* M

Ep. XLVIII (*Fam.* 8. 15)

1 quid iam ? inquis. Gloriose omnia. Si scias M with Mendelssohn's punctuation '*quid ? tam,*' inquis, '*gloriose omnia*' ? *Immo si scias* Wesenberg '*quid ? tam,*' inquis, '*gloriose*'? *Somnia ! Si scias*

C. F. Hermann. See Commentary.

sollicitus sum M *sollicitus sim* commonly printed. See Commentary.

derideas M *non derideas* Wesenberg

2 tamen quod Wesenberg *tum quam* M

qui *que* M

nunc cum VIII Mendelssohn *num* M

Venere prognatus Victorius *venerem propugnatus* M

Psacade natus Mendelssohn. *ipsa cadenatus* M *Psecade natus* Pantagathus and commonly printed. See Commentary.

Ep. XLIX (*Att.* 9. 11 A)

3 me, et pacis et utriusque M *me e paucis et ad utriusque* Bosius and commonly printed

amicum, ad vestram inserted by Lehmann.

Ep. L (*Fam.* 8. 16)

1 perscripsti, neque Becher *perscripsi* M

cogitares *cognita res* M

praedixe Mendelssohn *praedixi* M

Caesarem *Caesare* M

futura ... victoria *fuerat esset partha victa victoria* M

Caesaris *Caesar* M

exiit *exilit* M

mehercules omitted M

2 valemus *valet* M

Caesarem omitted M

quem *quam* M

quos *quod* M

optimatem *ad optatim* M

4 ac *hac* M

negavi *negavit* M

vi te retinuissem *vitae retinuissem* M

5 demittas unde *demittasum de* M

potes, eligas *potest elegas* M

quae ... feceris *quae tam erunt confeceris* M

Ep. LI (*Fam.* 2. 16)

1 habent Klotz *haberet* Ω

2 cui iam Martyni-Laguna *cui tam* M

3 existimari *existimare* M

4 domesticis R *modesticis* MG

5 cum *quin* Ω *qui* Mr

mihimet Orelli *mihi fuit* M

6 et haec *ut haec* M

de re Dolabellae O. Hirschfeld *Dolabella* (-ae Mr) M *dolo bellam* GR

Ep. LII (*Fam.* 9. 9)

1 qua Wesenberg *in qua* M

scilicet tibi H *scilicet te tibi* M

Ep. LV (*Fam.* 14. 17)

sint *sunt* ΨF

adfectus *adfictus* M

Ep. LX (*Fam.* 9. 1)

1 ut nullam *nullam* M

2 nimirum Mendelssohn *enim mihi cum* M

transiturum *turum* M with *transi* written above at later date.

Ep. LXI (*Fam.* 9. 16)

1 amavi M *animadverti* Kleyn *agnovi* Boot (doubtfully)

quomodo M *quoquomodo* commonly

2 potuerit Σ *poterit* Ψ

conciliandam et conligendam *conciliandum et conligendum* M

a Caesare H   *Caesare* MD
nam etsi M   *tam etsi* commonly
  printed
3 effugere *effungere* M
  opinionem HD   omitted M
4 praeterea de me *pratereadem*
  M
  Oenomao *denomao* MD   *de oe-*
  nomao H
5 aut faciam HD   *ut faciam* M
7 popellum Bücheler   *popillium*
  MH   *popilium* D   *pompilum*
  Rutilius   *polypum* Corradus
  cantharum Mendelssohn (cf.
  Ovid, *Hal.* 103), *thynnarium*
  Rutilius   *thynnum* Schütz
  naritam Schöll
  apud me . . . apud illos HD
  omitted M
  non est quod non eo sis con-
    silio Lehmann   *non eo sis*
    consilio M   *non est quod eo*
    sis consilio Wesenberg   *non*
    eo possis consilio uti Madvig
8 miniani M.   Mendelssohn de-
  fends the form as colloquial,
  comparing Levana, Tutanus,
  etc.   *miniati* Lambinus and
  most editors
10 sannionum D   *sannonum* M
  sanniorum H   *sanorum* F.
  Hofmann   *saniorum* Tyrrell

Ep. LXII (*Fam.* 9. 18)

1 propterea *praeterea* MD
  quibus D   *qui* M
2 consilium *consilio* MD
3 delectas D   *delectat* M
  me hic *mihi hic* MD
  disce a me Bengel   *disceam* M
  προλεγομένας M   π ρ ο η γ μ έ ν α
  Boot. Mendelssohn does not
  consider προλεγομένας good
  Greek here.
4 si, quomodo video, aestimationes Schmalz   *sed quomodo*
  video si aestimationes M and
  D (without *si*) *sed quomodo*,
  videro. Si aestimationes Bengel

idem istuc M   *item istic*
  Orelli

Ep. LXIII (*Fam.* 9. 20)

1 quae *quam* Ψ
  abierunt D *habierunt* M   *abie-*
  runt (the first letter erased)
  H
  nam D   *non* M   omitted H
  nunc or *nos* others
  castra HD   *cassatra* M
2 ex arte ista Krauss   *ex artis* M
  ex artibus Orelli   *exercitati-*
  onis Busch   *exquisitae artis*
  Wesenberg   ὀψαρτυτικῆς
  Mendelssohn   ἐξοχῆς Tyrrell
  non added by Orelli

Ep. LXIV (*Fam.* 9. 17)

1 non *ne* (affirmative particle) I.
  F. Gronovius

Ep. LXV (*Fam.* 6. 6)

1 vereor, ne desideres M   *non*
  vereor ne desideres Martyni-Laguna   a n d   commonly
  printed
  parium Victorius   *partum* Ω
  et saepe misissem *et se de-*
  misissem M   *etsi di misis-*
  sem G   *et se di misissem* R
2 putarent *putarunt* M
  celeri *ceteri* M
3 quam cum Σ   *nam cum* Ω
4 seiungeret Σ   *se iungeret* Ω
  se diiungeret Kleyn and commonly printed
7 ut in G   *aut in* MR
9 intelleget *intellegest* M   *intel-*
  lexi G   *intellexisti* R
11 mutata Σ   *muta* Ω

Ep. LXVI (*Fam.* 6. 14)

2 omnem R   *ad omnem* MG
  hac opinione Σ   *hanc opi-*
  nionem Ω

EP. LXVII (*Fam.* 9. 15)

1 curam ... tibi HD   Cratander omitted M
2 facetiis DMʳ   *facetus* H   *fac et his* M
   Latio M   *Lati* Madvig   *luto* O. Hirschfeld
3 moderationis, urbane Madvig   *moderationis urbanae* Ψ
5 parebo D   *probo* MH
   cum Σ   *quam* Ψ

EP. LXIX (*Att.* 12. 1)

1 sin rusticatur Victorius   *in rusticatu* M   *sin rusticetur* Cratander
2 γεροντικόν inserted by Lambinus
   quo die *quotidie* M
   prid. Kal. Orelli   *V Kal.* M

EP. LXX (*Fam.* 15. 17)

2 ut tamen FHD   *tamen* M
   macellarius Weiske and Madvig   *Marcellus* M
   gaudebant FD   *gaudebat* M   *gaudebunt* H
3 coepisti *cepisti* Ψ

EP. LXXI (*Fam.* 13. 72)

2 commodandi *commendandi* Ψ

EP. LXXIII (*Fam.* 9. 11)

1 eo HD   *ego* M
2 satis sum *satis* M

EP. LXXIV (*Att.* 12. 32)

1 ut cum Publilio loquerer O. E. Schmidt   *cum Publilio loqueretur* M   *cum Publilio videretur* Klotz
   mihi etiam Orelli   *me etiam* M
   alio Wesenberg   *ego* M

2 nihil opus erit Wesenberg   *nihil opus sit* M
   quam opus erit Wesenberg   *quam opus erat* M

EP. LXXV (*Fam.* 4. 5)

1 miserum Σ   *mirum* Ω
3 pareret *pararet* M
   a parente G   *apparente* MR¹
   usuri *uti* M
4 me Megara Orelli   *me megare* GR   *menegare* M
   clarissimi R   *carissimi* MG
5 imitari Mᶜ   *imitare* Ω

EP. LXXVI (*Fam.* 4. 6)

Ser. *Servilio* Ω
1 ipse *ipsi* M
   fuerunt Σ   *fuerint* Ω
   Galus M   (Mendelssohn cites Mommsen, *Römische Forschungen*, I, p. 119)   *Gallus* GR
   luctum GR   *lum* M
2 me a *mea* MR   *a* G
   de re publica GR   *ad re publica* M¹
3 maius ... nulla GR   *maior mihi vatio mihi adferre nulla* M   *maior mihi levatio* (or *maior enim levatio mihi*) *adferri* commonly printed. Mendelssohn thinks that the reading adopted results from interpolation.

EP. LXXVII (*Fam.* 5. 14)

1 discesseram GR   *discesserat* M   *discesseramus* Streicher   *decesserat* (*Tullia*) Orelli
2 hinc discesseras Σ   *hinc dicas seras* M   *indicas* GR   *inclinatus eras* Streicher
3 redeas atque ad *redeas ... ad* (space for 5 or 6 letters between *redeas* and *ad*) M   *redeas ad* G   *redeas ac* R
   nunc Martyni-Laguna *cum* M

EP. LXXVIII (*Fam.* 4. 12)

1 nobis R   *bonis* MG
   M. Marcellum Orelli   *Marcellum* M
   digressus sum Streicher   *digressus essem* M
   supra Maleas *supra maias* M   *supra kal. maias* GR   *sub Kalendas* Streicher.   See Commentary.
2 **a P. Magio Cilone** *apud magio cilone* M
   ei mitterem.   Itaque medicos omitted M
3 aiebant R   *agebant* MG
   delatus *dilatus* M
   quae *quo* MG   *quod* R

EP. LXXIX (*Fam.* 5. 15)

2 quaeso, deest Rost   *quas id est* M   *quasi est* GR
   quid (before *dicam*) GR   *quod* M
4 tu me GR   *tuae* M
   delectare *delectari* Ω

EP. LXXX (*Fam.* 9. 8)

1 ostenderit *ostenderet* Ψ
   illius HD   *eius* M
2 at saltem HD   *ad altem* M
   vel *tum vel* M

EP. LXXXI (*Fam.* 7. 24)

1 Cipius *citius* M   *cicius* G   *titius* R
2 Sestio *sentio* MR   *sextio* G
   unctorem M   *cantorem* Manutius

EP. LXXXII (*Fam.* 7. 25)

1 ne ... habuerimus Streicher   *nisi istum habuerimus* M   *ne si ist. hab.* GR   *ne, nisi istum caverimus* Victorius   *ne, nisi istum placatum habuerimus* or *ne, si istum iratum* (or

inimicum) *habuerimus* Wesenberg
   γέλωτα σαρδάνιον γελωια σαρδανιον M   γέλωτα σαρδόνιον Ernesti.   See Commentary.
   Catonium Salmasius   *Catomum* Ω.   See Commentary.
   Catoninos M   *Catonimos* G   *Catonianos* Boot
2 audi Σ   *audii* M   *audi id* GR   *audin?* Mendelssohn (doubtfully)

EP. LXXXIII (*Att.* 13. 52)

1 tam gravem **ἀμεταμέλητον** M   *gravem, tamen* ἀμεταμέλητον Boot
   non mutavit M   *non mutivit* Boot   *vultum non mutavit* commonly printed
2 eodem ad me M   *ehodum ad me* Peerlkamp.   Cf. Ter. *And.* 184

EP. LXXXIV (*Fam.* 13. 50)

   Acilio Schütz and Lallemand (cf. *Fam.* 7. 30 and 31)   *Aucto* Ψ
1 quodque HD   *quoque* M

EP. LXXXVI (*Fam.* 11. 1)

3 cedendum *caedendum* M
4 Caecilium *Caelium* Ψ

EP. LXXXVII (*Fam.* 9. 14)

1 in haec loca veniant (*conveniant* H) Ψ   *in haec loca veniant, conveniunt* Lehmann
   quin HD   *qui* M
3 et gratulor D   *ei gratulor* MH
   tua Wesenberg   *tum* MH   *cum* D
3-4 est.   A te *aestate* Ψ
4 iocatus D   *locatus* H   *locutus* M
   amore *amorem* Ψ

6 proponam *proponas* Ψ
8 quo facto *facto M*

Ep. LXXXVIII (*Att.* 15. 11)

1 placeretne? Atque M *placeretne? Placeret, atque* Wesenberg. See Commentary.
2 suscipi Orelli   *suscipere* M
   susciperem Gronovius
   velle Romae se dixerat Wesenberg   *velle esse dixerat*
   M   *velle se dixerat* Boot
   vel solum or *vel cum mortis
   periculo se Romae velle esse
   dixerat* Lehmann
3 δύναται [νῦν] Cobet. νῦν
   bracketed   f o r   metrical
   reasons.

Ep. XC (*Fam.* 16. 21)

1 quadragensimum et sextum
   M *quadragensimum sextum*
   Baiter, but cf. Neue, *Formenlehre* II² p. 163. Upon *quadragensimum* see Commentary.
   ex *et* ΨF
2 mihi successa M   *mihi successe* Schwabe omitted Lambinus. See Commentary.
3 duplicetur FHD *dupliciter* M
   nam cum audio Lambinus
   nam cum et audio MD   *nam
   cum et gaudio* F   *nam et
   cum gaudio* H   *nam et audio*
   Σ
4 iocus *locus* ΨF
5 Mytilenis Σ   *mitylenis* M
   mutilenis D *mitilenes* FH
7 Romanus M   *germanus* Ribbeck
8 de mandatis D *demandastis*
   MFH

Ep. XCI (*Fam.* 11. 27)

2 communicata sunt H   *communicata sint* MD

5 sum, in reliquis officio. Cui
   Madvig   *sum in* (*tuis* added
   by D) *reliquis officiis cui* Ψ
6 multa HD   *multo* M
7 liquido *aliquido* M   *aliquando*
   H
8 expertem *exper* M   *expers* HD

Ep. XCII (*Fam.* 11. 28)

3 fuerunt, ut timerent Baiter
   fuerunt timerent M *fuerunt
   ut sperarent* (or *ut cuperent*)
   timerent Lehmann. See Commentary.
6 at ludos H   *ad ludos* M   *ac
   ludos* D
   at id *ad id* M   *ac id* D   *at*
   omitted H
   Caesare petenti H   *Caesare
   repetenti* M   *Cesari repente* D

Ep. XCIII (*Fam.* 16. 26)

1 poenam FHD   *ponam* M
   commentata M   *commendata*
   FHD

Ep. XCIV (*Fam.* 9. 24)

1 me virum Wesenberg   *meum*
   MH   *me meum* D   *me unum*
   Baiter   *me quam* Σ   *me ami-
   cum* Starker   *meum animum*
   Klotz
3 iocum D   *locum* MH

Ep. XCV (*Fam.* 12. 5)

1 ageres *ages* M
2 reliqui M   *reliquum* commonly
   printed
   ad Forum Cornelium M   *ad
   forum Cornelii* HD
   compararat D *comparat* MH
   comparabat Ernesti

Ep. XCVI (*Fam.* 10. 12)

1 gratiores *graviores* Ψ
   exspectata *spectata* Ψ
   quoad *quod* M   *quo* HD

2 **at ego ei** M *at ego et* HD *ego ei* Wesenberg *lego ei* Boot
4 **quam tum** D *quantum* MH
5 **conlecta** M *confectam* Baiter *contecta* Gitlbauer
fucata HD *fugatia* M *fugacia* Σ
existima. Verum *existimaverim* M

Ep. XCVII (*Fam.* 11. 9)

1 **elabatur** H[2] *elaboratur* MH[1] *elaboretur* D
2 **persuasissimumst** *persuasissimum et* M *per. est* D *per. sit* H

Ep. XCVIII (*Fam.* 10. 15)

2 **decem** *sescenti* E. Schelle
optimi *optime* M
adiuvandum H *adluandum* MD
3 **quid** HD *qui* M
meo M *meo Antonium* Orelli *meo perditum hominem* (or *latronem*) Lehmann, but, as illustrating the omission of the proper name, Mendelssohn compares Cael. *Fam.* 8. 8. 4 *plane perspecta Cn. Pompei voluntate in eam partem, ut eum* (i.e. *Caesarem*) *decedere post K. Martias placeret.*

Ep. XCIX (*Fam.* 11. 12)

D. Bruto D and index to bk. XI in M *Bruto* MH

1 **et ex Graecei oratione** *et ex grecei oratione* D *ut ex grecei oratione* H *ut ex graeceio ratione* M
2 **maximeque** D[1] *maximique* MH
providendumst *providendum sit* M *providendum est* HD

Ep. C (*Fam.* 10. 24)

1 **meritaque** HD *meraque* M
indulgentia *diligentia* Lambinus *industria* Boot
in tua observantia ind. ads. omitted Gräter and Wesenberg *mea in te obs. diligentia ads.* Lambinus *mutua obs. ind. ads.* Klotz *in tui observantia* Orelli
3 **capitalis** Koch and Mendelssohn *talis* M *fatalis* Koch *consularis* Lehmann *ut ais* Andresen, omitted Wesenberg. See Commentary.
luculentissima M *locupletissima* Lehmann
4 **quod ad Caesarem attinet** M *quod Caesarem* Stroth and commonly printed, but see Commentary.
6 **aversissimam** M *adversissimam* commonly printed
illis *illi* Ψ
a tanta HD *tanta* M
bimestris M *quinquemestris* Manutius, approved by O. E. Schmidt and Mendelssohn *semestris* Lange. See Commentary.

INDEX OF PROPER NAMES [1]

(The numbers refer to pages.)

[1] The Index does not include all the less important allusions, nor the names of all insignificant or unknown persons.

INDEX TO THE NOTES

(The numbers refer to pages.)

University of Oklahoma Press

Norman